Marion Dresner

D0687491

Taking Stock of Nature

Participatory Biodiversity Assessment for Policy, Planning and Practice

In a world of increasing demands for biodiversity information, participatory biodiversity assessment and monitoring is becoming more significant. Whilst other books have focused on methods, or links to conservation or development, this book is written particularly for policy-makers and planners. Introductory chapters analyse the challenges of the approach, the global legislation context, and the significance of the Millennium Ecosystem Assessment. Specially commissioned case studies provide evidence from 17 countries, by 50 authors with expertise in both biological and social sciences. Ranging from community conservation projects in developing countries, to amateur birdwatching in the UK, they describe the context, objectives, stakeholders and processes, and reflect on the success of outcomes. Rather than advocating any particular approach, the book takes a constructively critical look at the motives, experiences and outcomes of such approaches, with cross-cutting lessons to inform planning and interpretation of future participatory projects and their contribution to policy objectives.

ANNA LAWRENCE has been working for nearly 20 years in participatory conservation and social forestry research. Following degrees from Cambridge and Oxford Universities, her early career in South America and Asia inspired a focus on interaction between local and scientific knowledge, and linking research to policy and practice. At the Environmental Change Institute, University of Oxford, she established and led the Human Ecology research group for seven years. After working in more than 20 countries she has recently moved to focus on issues closer to home, as Head of Social and Economic Research in the British Government's Forestry Commission.

Taking Stock of Nature

Participatory Biodiversity Assessment for Policy, Planning and Practice

Edited by

ANNA LAWRENCE

CAMBRIDGE UNIVERSITY PRESS

CAMBRIDGE UNIVERSITY PRESS
Cambridge, New York, Melbourne, Madrid, Cape Town, Singapore,
São Paulo, Delhi

Cambridge University Press
The Edinburgh Building, Cambridge CB2 8RU, UK

Published in the United States of America by Cambridge University Press,
New York

www.cambridge.org
Information on this title: www.cambridge.org/9780521876810

First published 2010

Printed in the United Kingdom at the University Press, Cambridge

A catalogue record for this publication is available from the British Library

ISBN 978-0-521-87681-0 hardback

Contents

v

Contributors

Amina Akida
Forestry and Beekeeping Division, Ministry of Natural Resources and Tourism, Tanzania

Tejaswini Apte
Independent Environmental Researcher/Writer, India

Christiana Bairaktari
Research Institute Wageningen University (Alterra), The Netherlands

Heidi L. Ballard
University of California, USA

Imam Basuki
CIFOR, Forestry Research, Indonesia

Sandra Bell
University of Durham, UK

Seema Bhatt
Conservation and Livelihoods, India

Tom Blomley
Senior Adviser on Participatory Forest Management, UK

Manuel Boissière
CIRAD/CIFOR, Forestry Research, Indonesia

Justin Brashares
University of California, USA

Neil Burgess
Cambridge University, UK

Doris Capistrano
Center for International Forestry Research, Indonesia

Peter Cronkleton
CIFOR, Bolivia

Robert Cunliffe
CIFOR, Indonesia

Finn Danielsen
NORDECO (Nordic Agency for Development and Ecology), Denmark

Kristen Evans
CIFOR, USA

Maria E. Fernandez-Gimenez
Colorado State University, USA

Mikkel Funder
NORDECO (Nordic Agency for Development and Ecology), Denmark

Jane Hull
Forestry Commission, UK

Arne Jensen
NORDECO (Nordic Agency for Development and Ecology), Denmark

Zhang Jinfeng
Yunnan Academy of Forestry, China

Wil de Jong
Kyoto University, Japan

David T. Jones
The Natural History Museum (BM), UK

Piia Koponen
CIFOR, Indonesia

Anna Lawrence
Forestry Commission, UK

Wang Lei
Yunnan Academy of Forestry, China

John Lewis
University of Waterloo, Canada

Nining Liswanti
CIFOR, Indonesia

Tim Lynam
CSIRO Sustainable Ecosystems, Australia

Ruth Mackenzie
University College London, UK

Mariella Marzano
Forestry Commission, UK

Marlynn Mendoza
NAPWNC Cpd., The Philippines

Alex Monro
The Natural History Museum (BM), UK

Hemant Ojha
Forest Action, Nepal

Michael Padmanaba
CIFOR, Indonesia

Krishna Prasad Paudel
Forest Action, Nepal

Dan Podjed
University of Ljubljana, Slovenia

Michael K. Poulsen
NORDECO (Nordic Agency for Development and Ecology), Denmark

Hadija Ramadhani
Ministry of Natural Resources and Tourism, Tanzania

Ciara Raudsepp-Hearne
University of Quebec, Canada

Moses K. Sam
Forestry Commission, Ghana

Marieke Sassen
CIFOR, The Netherlands

Douglas Sheil
CIFOR, Indonesia

Greg Stuart-Hill
Namibian Association of Conservancy Support Organizations and World
Wildlife Fund (WWF) Living in a Finite Environment (LIFE) Project,
Namibia

Victoria Sturtevant
Southern Oregon University, USA

Marlon ten Hoonte
Yunnan Academy of Forestry, China

Elmer Topp-Jørgensen
Greenland Home Rule, Greenland

Miriam Van Heist
CIFOR, Indonesia

Jeanette van Rijsoort
Agriterra, The Netherlands

Meilinda Wan
CIFOR, Indonesia

Acknowledgements

Although the chapters in this book are new, the idea of this book began with an internet conference in 2002. For months the UK forest policy advisory group had been discussing monitoring and reporting, in its international and high level forms. Although members were polite about my advocacy of participatory monitoring, we realized we needed evidence. So we organized an internet conference, and 300 people signed up from 55 countries. This was with the great encouragement and patience of Willemine Brinkman, at that time the coordinator of the European Tropical Forest Research Network, who offered the ETFRN website and support. The conference would never have happened without her, nor Jeannette van Rijsoort who edited the website and the proceedings. Bianca Ambrose-Oji, who co-authored the conference introduction with me, as always shared ideas creatively and generously. The papers, summaries and discussions are available at http://www.etfrn.org/etfrn/workshop/biodiversity/index.html. Acknowledgement also goes to the people who thought this was worth supporting financially. For months I had an email folder labelled 'begging letters'. Those from whom I begged successfully included John Palmer (of the Forest Research Programme, UK Department for International Development), and Tropenbos International. The internet conference also would not have taken shape without the insight of colleagues who agreed to write summaries of each day, and each theme.

That of course was not the end of it. The internet conference made us realise the important of linking experience to outcomes, and of presenting this in a way that helped policy people to decide if that was what they wanted and needed. The cases presented here are specially commissioned for this book. My biggest thanks here are to the authors, who engaged with some rather proactive editing. Dominic Lewis, Rachel Eley and Alison Evans at Cambridge University Press have also been patient and encouraging. The Environmental Change Institute (particularly the Director, Diana Liverman) took a flexible approach to funding, allowing me to use time during a research fellowship to do most of the work before I changed jobs. Sarah Gillett put in considerable support at ECI. Essential research support for this book came from Star Molteno, an infinitely patient researcher with attention to detail. Finally I thank Bianca Ambrose-Oji (again) and Chris Quine, of Forest Research, for excellent reviewing.

The book is dedicated to all the locals, community groups, amateurs, volunteers, and citizen scientists who collect information about nature, the environment, biodiversity – call it what you will – and who want their work to make a difference.

1

Introduction: learning from experiences of participatory biodiversity assessment

ANNA LAWRENCE

Introduction

A few years ago, curious to find out how individuals can bring about change in environmental policy, I arranged to meet volunteers who collect data about species distributions. My first interview was with a lively, successful group of volunteers in the south of England, who had developed a new approach for monitoring hedgerows. Ancient hedgerows are important for conservation in Britain, helping to maintain diversity of habitat, and connect up patches of otherwise isolated woodland. As a result of systematic surveys, some of them by volunteers, the British Government had changed the law and introduced incentives for farmers to replant them (in 1992), and regulations to protect them (in 1994).

Certainly the volunteers were enthusiastic about their successes and policy impact. But what they mostly wanted to talk about was the beauty of hedgerows, the pleasure they found in observing the variety in a line of trees, and the feeling that without the excuse of collecting data, they were being a little self-indulgent by spending time in nature. As one said, 'It's nice, but as long as you do it with a purpose in mind and at the end of it you feel you've done something really quite good'.

Thousands of miles away, other people were collecting data about species, but these data had a more immediate effect on their lives. They were villagers in Karnataka, in southern India, who shared management of their forests with the state Forest Department. From their point of view, some of the most useful species in the forests were medicinal plants and fruit trees, but these were gradually disappearing. The management plans for the community

Taking Stock of Nature: Participatory Biodiversity Assessment for Policy, Planning and Practice, ed. Anna Lawrence. Published by Cambridge University Press. © Cambridge University Press 2010.

forests had not taken take these 'non-timber products' into account. So, with support from an NGO and international research team, they started experimenting to find out the effect of different management approaches on these species.

I asked these people about their experiences as well. It was not so surprising to find that the project changed people's awareness of species, and their efforts to control harvesting. More surprising were the wider effects. One woman told me she had never left her village before; now, other villages wanted to hear about their experiences and she was travelling to speak at training workshops. The close partnership between the NGO and the state Forest Department drew the attention of foresters. By 2007, non-timber forest products were being included in the local management plans (or 'microplans') of community forests in Karnataka. The way one forester saw it, it was 'putting the science back into forestry'. Participatory projects were all very well, in his view, but this one included serious data, and he was paying attention.

These communities are worlds apart, but in both projects something changed as a result of data about species, gathered by people who were not trained professionals. They were motivated by something other than professional reward, whether livelihood security, self-determination, protection of nature, or emotional connection with nature. Science, or scientific data, gave their endeavours a respectability that added up to change on both the local and wider scales. In both cases, they gained new, unexpected experiences, and felt rewarded by those too.

These two cases are both examples of participatory assessment, monitoring or evaluation of biodiversity (which for convenience we can call PAMEB). All of these people are engaging with biodiversity for strong personal or political reasons, but at the same time they are seeking a tangible way to share their observations. The way that they do the assessment, the kinds of data they collect, how they interact with others collecting or using similar data, and the storage and communication of data, all affect their chances of achieving those objectives. This book focuses on such stories. Examples from more than 20 countries are examined to ask what it takes for PAMEB to be effective and to bring about desired change.

At first sight, the need for PAMEB is simple. Demand for biodiversity data is increasing sharply (Balmford *et al.*, 2005; Buckland *et al.*, 2005; Royal Society, 2003; van Jaarsveld *et al.*, 2005). Conservation 'is a vast undertaking, requiring the mobilization of existing data, huge amounts of new information, and the monitoring and management of wildlife on an unprecedented scale' (Humphries, Williams, and Vane-Wright, 1995, pp. 93–94). International environmental agreements require reports to demonstrate compliance (Mackenzie, this volume), and for planning and environmental management (Lawrence, 2006). There is a growing requirement for Environmental Impact Assessment to include biodiversity or some of its components (Convention on Biological Diversity, 2005; Slootwega and Kolhoff, 2003).

While this explosion in information demands has been going on, philosophies about natural resource management have also shifted radically, from a technocratic dependence on specialist, reductionist science, towards more pluralistic environmental management which recognizes the value and relevance of different knowledge systems (Kapoor, 2001; Plummer and Fitzgibbon, 2004; Wollenberg, Anderson and Edmunds, 2001). Over the past decade the concept of governance has also emerged, referring to new modes of decision-making that emphasize decentralization, participation, and involvement of non-government organizations (NGOs) in public policy and problem solving (Fischer, 2006; Parkins, 2006). One study concludes that 'local monitoring systems constitute an almost compulsory component of any donor-funded program/project dealing with sustainable management of natural resources' (Garcia and Lescuyer, 2008).

These two factors, the 'pull' of data demand and 'push' of pluralistic governance, are even enshrined in some policies. For example, in northern Canada it is now a requirement that 'traditional ecological knowledge' be incorporated into environmental assessment (Usher, 2000).

As a result, expectations of PAMEB can be enormous. Scientists often involve volunteers, amateurs or locals in order to provide more data, more cheaply (Boylen *et al.*, 2004; Danielsen, Burgess and Balmford, 2005; McCaffrey, 2005; Saris *et al.*, 1996; Wagner, 2005). Others hope that these approaches will enhance the relevance of data collection for practical management outcomes, and motivate participants to conserve as well as use natural resources (Danielsen *et al.*, 2005; Pilz, Ballard and Jones, 2006; Wagner, 2005). Many also hope that involvement in PAMEB will educate children and others about nature and our impact on the environment (Brossard, Lewenstein and Bonney, 2005; Pond and Rees, 2000).

How realistic are these expectations? Can participation really contribute to all of these assumed benefits? If it can, what are the factors that help that to happen? To answer these questions we need to look at real experiences, and follow through the outcomes of engaging different stakeholders in the biodiversity assessment process. We need to look at who produced the data, for what reasons, and then understand who used the data, how and why. This book is based on specially written case studies that allow us to follow through the whole PAMEB process through to outcomes, and then to compare these questions across a wide variety of contexts. In doing so, we will find that 'participation', 'biodiversity' and 'assessment' mean many things to many people. We begin by examining the meanings of these concepts.

Definitions

Biodiversity

Biodiversity is the life around us. Compared with the word 'nature', the word 'biodiversity' somehow seems scientific, objective and measurable. It hints at something within our reach, knowable, countable, and manageable. The term 'biodiversity' was first used in 1985 as a contraction of 'biological diversity'. By 1992, it was common currency as defined by the Rio Convention on Biological Diversity (CBD):

> *the variability among living organisms from all sources including, inter alia, terrestrial, marine and other aquatic ecosystems and the ecological complexes of which they are part; this includes diversity within species, between species and of ecosystems.*
>
> *(CBD, 1992)*

This definition is attractive for environmental monitoring because it appears to be structured, quantifiable and scientific. In fact the concept is recognized by many scientists as being intangible and highly debatable. The term originates in the conservation ethics of the 'north' (Gaston, 1996; Takacs, 1996; Tangwa, 1999), and conservation biologists themselves debate whether the concept is quantitative and measurable, an abstract conceptual framework, or an ideal or value judgement (Mayer, 2006; Perlman and Adelson, 1997). Some expert comments on what this means for biodiversity assessment are quoted in Box 1.1.

Perhaps in response to the confusion, the biodiversity discourse has recently moved to an emphasis on ecosystems. The Millennium Ecosystem Assessment made an explicit and global attempt to understand what this meant (Millennium Ecosystem Assessment, 2008). It adopted a highly anthropocentric approach, basically asking 'what services do ecosystems provide for humans?' Its contributors struggled with the challenge of assessment of ecosystems within different scales and conceptual frameworks, and disparities between local interests in ecosystem services and global concerns about valuing every species (Conrad, 2006; Conrad and Daoust, 2008; Faith, 2005; Hein *et al.*, 2006).

Perlman and Adelson (1997) claim that these definitions focusing on genes, species and ecosystems fail because the components are conceptually and practically impossible to measure. Furthermore the different levels cannot be

---

Box 1.1 Perspectives on the challenge of biodiversity assessment

Real-life assessments and evaluations of biodiversity are neither totally objective nor totally scientific. Once biodiversity is thought of in this way in practice, we can see it as a value-laden set of concepts that is delimited by the ideals, goals, biases, and interest of those employing the term. Moreover, we believe that once conservationists begin to recognize the diversity of human conceptions of biodiversity, they will realize that this is a real strength rather than a failing.

(Perlman and Adelson, 1997, p. 10)

Biodiversity does not exist in an absolute sense. Rather, it anchors a discourse that articulates a new relation between nature and society in global contexts of science, cultures, and economies.

(Escobar, 1998, p. 55)

Rather than calling anything and everything 'biodiversity' (and struggling to monitor a jumble of different things all under that biodiversity umbrella), we can acknowledge that sometimes we will be monitoring aspects of nature that do not have any particular biodiversity link, but do have an 'immediacy' in terms of services and human well-being.

(Faith, 2005, p. 6)

No single objective measure of biodiversity is possible, only measures relating to particular purposes or applications.

(Natural History Museum, 2001)

The only successful engagement of local people happens when they start doing the monitoring themselves.

(Hopkin, 2007, p. 403)

---

translated into each other (for example, ecosystems are more than the sum of their constituent species). Difficulties with quantifying biodiversity are bad enough. Even more disturbing to the scientific view, is the value-laden nature of human observation and measurement. A detailed and powerful study by Takacs (1996) shows that conservation biologists developed the term 'biodiversity' precisely in order to participate in policy debates, and to promote their own values.

This confusion over meanings and values is obviously heightened when the many different stakeholders and research partners brought together by pluralistic approaches are all involved in defining and measuring biodiversity. There is a widely perceived tension between local (perhaps more use-based)

Box 1.2   Terms related to monitoring

Assessment: provides a description of a state or pattern of biodiversity.

Monitoring: provides information on change in a state or pattern of biodiversity.

Evaluation: invites participants to make judgements about what is important to measure, or what is important about what has been measured.

Valuation: is a subset of evaluation which relies on economic techniques to derive apparent monetary values for biodiversity.

Indicator: is a measurable variable used to measure certain aspects of a complex variable.

---

values and global (perhaps more existence-based) values. It seems to some that the latter are favoured in PAMEB while others worry that the converse is true (Brown, 1998; Lawrence *et al.*, 2000; Lawrence *et al.*, 2006; Vermeulen and Koziell, 2002).

Nevertheless the term biodiversity has achieved widespread currency, and it may be precisely because of this fluidity of interpretation that it is so popular. By setting out contested dimensions (species, ecosystems, diversity, values), it serves as a framework for helping different stakeholders define their own meanings, and communicate more openly about differences (Lawrence *et al.*, 2000; Lawrence *et al.*, 2006).

Assessment, monitoring, evaluation and indicators

There is a great deal of discussion about the meanings of terms related to measuring biodiversity. Broadly accepted definitions are given in Box 1.2. The purpose of this book is not to set such definitions in stone, but to recognize the fluidity in approaches taken, and the need for clear communication about the purpose of the biodiversity assessment exercise. Assessment is often a one-off exercise that helps to establish the extent and condition of a resource. If it is a participatory assessment it may also include an element of evaluation, in that different stakeholders will value different parts of the resource in different ways. Monitoring is a way of tracking change in the environment or resource. It is often based on a simpler form of data collection than is assessment, and is therefore more likely to rely on indicators.

The complexity of biodiversity and its human observers has spawned a huge literature on indicators. They are valuable for communicating change in the condition or abundance of biodiversity, because they are simple. However, there is a risk that in simplification important detail is lost. As Failing and Gregory (2003) point out there is a need to 'integrate science and values to design indicators that are concise, relevant and meaningful to decision makers'.

Indicators are particularly attractive to policy-makers and planners who have to assimilate this information along with a wide range of other factors affecting their decisions (Mace and Baillie, 2007). For local stakeholders, the reductionist quantitative approach underlying choice of indicators may be an alien process, and they may prefer to rely on qualitative descriptions of change (Estrella *et al.*, 2000). A challenge for PAMEB is to find easily measured indicators that are meaningful to the participants, and inform them about the aspects of biodiversity that they value, but that *also* communicate effectively with other stakeholders.

Participation

'Participation' is another concept that is understood in many different ways. Dictionary definitions tell us it means to 'share or take part', but as a way of involving people in sharing information and decisions, it has much more radical connotations. Over the past 30 years these have sometimes become diluted and accepted into more conventional approaches, so that 'participation' is often part of a standard approach to conservation policy and management (Fischer and Young, 2007; Kapoor, 2001).

In the process the term and practice of 'participation' has come to mean many things to many people. Some favour a 'top-down' approach where those responsible for making decisions 'extract' useful information from the public or local resource users who 'participate' in the research process using a variety of methods. Others see real participation as 'bottom-up' or emancipatory and transformative. In these cases local people acquire information, experience and ultimately the power to make decisions about their social circumstances or local resources for themselves. Participation is often judged to be 'good' if it leads to (apparent) empowerment, and somehow failing if it supports the status quo (Fischer, 2006; Goodwin, 1998).

This dichotomy is, however, simplistic. Participation involves many more factors, and issues than the question of power and autonomy. There are many challenges to do with the scale of involvement (how many people to involve, in which locations, covering what area of a particular resource unit or habitat), appropriate methods, distribution of funds, implementing co-learning processes and the cultural context. Individual or group transformation can take place even within a conventionally top-down context of existing structures. For example, some volunteers who monitored mammals in a project managed by zoologists changed careers and became conservation biologists as a result of their experiences (Newman, Buesching and Macdonald, 2003). Conversely, apparently more radical efforts in data-gathering by laypersons can shore up the status quo and protect their interests (Lawrence, 2006). For example residents of Martha's Vineyard in the USA formed associations to monitor and protect their shellfish resources, in order to support their livelihoods against external change (Karney, 2000).

PAMEB is an interesting case of participation, because of the complexity of the issues involved. PAMEB engages with debates over the scientific meanings of the term 'biodiversity', the value judgements discussed above, as well as the challenge of managing social processes surrounding the production of data, knowledge and effective communication. Data are tangible, a shared (or shareable) commodity, and as such apparently objective. Scientists and the management of data may therefore have a clearer contribution to make than in other forms of participatory processes. Data production is not the only outcome of PAMEB. The process of making different values and knowledge explicit, and the possible implications for resource management, can bring emotional and cultural differences into the open. This can be daunting. While on the one had it involves 'contentious issues, tensions, and difficult political implications' (Bliss *et al.*, 2001), conflict often results from leaving those issues hidden. Involving everyone who has an interest, can lead to natural resource decisions which are 'more effective and less controversial' (Pilz, Ballard and Jones, 2006).

These variables are the fundamentals of PAMEB. The basic proposition of this book, and the case studies examined in it, is that:

> *different stakeholders can have different objectives, knowledge, information needs, cultures and power relations, as well as methods for collecting and sharing information; but these different positions and needs can be accommodated through partnerships which can provide distinct but complementary and mutually rewarding outcomes.*

This hypothesis forms the basis for the inquiry presented in this book. Before examining the case studies however, we briefly review the issues that emerge from other published literature.

Reviewing the issues in PAMEB

Who trusts whose knowledge?

Ideas about what makes knowledge reliable sit at the centre of PAMEB. Putting things simplistically, there are two broad kinds, or traditions, of knowledge that are involved, namely scientific, and non-scientific. When we scrutinize these two traditions that are often set in opposition to each other we find that each body of knowledge is in fact heterogeneous, dynamic, with 'expert' and 'lay' knowledges often overlapping and interacting constructively with the other (Agarwal, 1995). So for both traditions, knowledge creation is an evolving process that responds to the evolving context and the purposes that it serves.

Numerous studies have explored the parallels between scientific and local knowledge about biodiversity. They present a bewildering variety of findings that seem to defy generalization. For example, commenting on the knowledge of the Pokot pastoralists of Kenya, Bollig and Schulte (1999) conclude that Pokot accounts of vegetation change are factual because they include detailed descriptions of species changes that are also recognized by botanists. On the other hand they reject Pokot explanations of environmental change as based on an 'ideological and mythological frame of interpretation' (Bollig and Schulte, 1999, pp. 499–500). Other researchers find that they can rely on local knowledge to identify ecosystem services, but not individual species (Badola and Hussain, 2005; Maass *et al.*, 2005). In some cases, where scientists have trained indigenous people to collect biodiversity monitoring data, they still find that those data do not meet their requirements and they can only make qualitative interpretations, for example information about the seasonal movements and habitat preferences of hunter self-monitoring data collected by Izoceño hunters in Bolivia (Noss, Cuellar and Cuellar, 2003).

Ecologists and social scientists associated with the 'new ecology' movement have shown that such apparently 'unscientific' knowledge often underlies local management practices that improve the environment, contradicting the assumptions of scientists who reject local knowledge (Leach and Mearns, 1996; Scoones, 1999). Others have highlighted the adaptive nature of traditional knowledge in interpreting signals from the environment to guide the direction of resource management (Berkes, Colding and Folke, 2000).

These debates are not unique to developing countries. A study in Scotland found that participants could express rich mental concepts of biodiversity, including notions of balance, food chains and human–nature interactions, which were strongly related to their beliefs about how to manage biodiversity (Fischer and Young, 2007). Farmers of wetlands in the south of England were perceived by scientists as ignorant of conservation, yet farming practice contributed more effectively to conservation of the rare fen raft spider than did their own scientific management prescriptions (Burgess, Clark and Harrison, 2000).

Rather than thinking about knowledge as being either 'right' or 'wrong', a more helpful perspective is the idea of 'knowledge cultures' which are based on mutually agreed and shared rules about what counts as legitimate knowledge. Knowledge is produced through on-going social interactions within specific contexts, and the knowledge culture provides a means of relating and responding to other people (Morris, 2006; Tsouvalis, Seymour and Watkins, 2000). As the anthropologist Roy Rappaport (1979) explained, humans see nature through 'screens of belief, knowledge and purpose'. These may not be recognized by scientists, but they may encourage practices that tend to conserve resources, and consequently may be considered as more 'successful' than western scientific knowledge. Western science is one knowledge culture; Inuit traditions constitute another; and the shared practical knowledge of wetland farmers in the south of England yet another.

Members of a knowledge culture will judge the legitimacy and validity of knowledge according to whether it makes sense within a given worldview, and whether it produces useful results when applied. Whilst scientific knowledge culture provides a set of transparent rules about validity of knowledge, and is often a suitable yardstick against which to judge the usefulness of knowledge, other participants in a PAMEB process may not share or understand those rules. More quantitative, reductionist and extractive methods are favoured by the central actors in top-down and larger-scale approaches. Alternatively if a project is village-centred, actors may be seen as 'internal' (with specialist local knowledge) and 'external' (with more generalizable, and complementary, 'scientific' knowledge).

PAMEB is based on the notion of sharing data. Data are seen as objective representatives of different kinds of knowledge. Human processes of interpretation and transformation are unavoidably involved in the production of data (for example, through deceptively simple processes such as the selection of what is worth observing), collation of data into information, its transmission between different humans with different world views and experiences, and its assimilation as knowledge into the mindset of new individuals. Western scientific knowledge cultures are much more accustomed to the production, exchange and interpretation of data than are other cultures, and often the single greatest anxiety which scientists bring to PAMEB, relates to the quality of the data, i.e. its accuracy and reliability (e.g. Boudreau and Yan, 2004; Brandon *et al.*, 2003; Sharpe and Conrad, 2006; Sheil and Lawrence, 2004). These concerns also apply to other knowledge cultures, but less attention is paid to them in published accounts of PAMEB. Local and indigenous people need to know the basis for accepting the validity of data, or information presented to them. Trust among or between knowledge cultures is an important basis for the credibility of data (Baker and Bowker, 2007; Lawrence, 2009).

Effectiveness: matching objectives and outcomes

Many practitioners would claim that the purpose of biodiversity assessment is to influence and inform policy and practice (Robertson and Hull, 2003). However, it commonly fails to do so (Balmford *et al.* 2005; Moffat, Davies and Finer, 2008), and there are calls for greater involvement of a wider range of other stakeholders at all stages of the data planning and collection.

Likewise, participatory *methods* do not necessarily lead to participatory *decisions* or *actions* (Davies, 2001). PAMEB, with its focus on data collection, is even more open to separation of activities and outcomes. The academic literature does not tell us much about this; it tends to focus on either comparing local and scientific data, or discuss the implications for management. Much more rarely do authors discuss the actual outcomes of the process, and real applications of the data. The consequence of these shortcomings is that it is hard to assess whether process and data helped the participants to achieve their objectives; indeed the objectives are often not stated (Yoccoz, Nichols and Boutlinier, 2001).

A few studies do provide pointers. The sustainability of participatory efforts is a common concern. One wide-reaching review concludes, 'the handing over of monitoring systems to local communities has rarely been successful' (Garcia and Lescuyer, 2008). However, this must depend on the motivations and objectives of those involved. A follow-up survey to a project in Gabon showed that two years after government agents and local resource users were trained in ecological survey methods, only 7.7% of the officials were still using the methods, while 76.2% of locals were doing so (Thibault and Blaney, 2001).

One study that provides concrete evidence of effectiveness, analyses the number of conservation interventions planned as a result of participatory monitoring in the Philippines. Compared with scientific monitoring alone, participatory monitoring results in eight or nines times as many management interventions (Danielsen *et al.*, 2007). Although the authors acknowledge that interventions cannot be equated with conservation *per se,* and that there is no 'experimental control' (to allow us to compare what would have happened in the absence of monitoring), this is the kind of evidence that helps to indicate the value of PAMEB.

The test is whether such actions are implemented. Several authors comment on a gap between monitoring and management. For example, Pollock and Whitelaw (2005) found that in Canada, community-based monitoring needs an approach that is context-specific, iterative, and adaptive. In other words the results are specific to place and time, and need to feed in to actual management decisions.

Another study from Canada concluded that although community-based environmental stewardship groups are taking responsibility for monitoring, they do not have real access to policy and planning structures (Sharpe and Conrad, 2006), partly because their methods are not standardized and do not provide data in forms that decision-makers can understand or utilize (Conrad and Daoust, 2008). There are clearly challenges for the impact of PAMEB at different scales; it is more straightforward to feed local data into local management than into national policy, and where the larger-scale processes do happen, the sense of connection between participatory data collection, decision-making process and ultimate outcomes is more tenuous.

Finally, if participatory data are to be useful, and used, they must meet the needs of the decision-makers who influence, demand, design or use the system and its results. It is these people who are least defined in most accounts of PAMEB. Some policy studies have found that such people are making decisions about biodiversity without an understanding of the issues discussed above, or they are not very clear in describing their needs (Lazdinis, Angelstam and Lazdinis, 2007; Saris *et al.*, 1996). On the other hand there is a lot of idealism surrounding the notion of participation which concentrates on 'locals' and communities. In such circumstances the values and expectations underlying PAMEB use can lead to judgements that overlook or exclude the needs of decision-makers (Contandriopoulos, 2004).

Lessons from the case studies

In this book, we present a set of specially written case studies which link these issues, and explore the effectiveness of different approaches to PAMEB in a variety of social and ecological contexts. In doing so, we focus on the general lessons which can help the planners, designers and users of biodiversity assessments to make participation more effective.

Our case studies range from weekend birdwatching in wealthy industrialized countries where people have plenty of leisure time, to communities in economically poorer countries who are monitoring species which they manage for their own day-to-day subsistence. They extend from academic studies of one or two communities, to vast national or global exercises involving thousands of people. They provide us with a rich variety of scales, subsets of biodiversity, methods used, approaches to quantification, locus of initiative (who decided to conduct the monitoring) and directions of information flow, as well as immediate economic relevance to the actors. Nevertheless, they all involve non-experts in measuring change in the abundance, quality or distribution of biodiversity.

The next two chapters focus on global aspects of PAMEB: the international agreements that affect the demand for data, and the lessons learnt through the Millennium Ecosystem Assessment, a vast exercise of multi-scale, multi-stakeholder PAMEB.

These are then followed by the core comparative part of the book, a range of case studies, from more than twenty countries. Each author describes the ecological, social and institutional context, the objectives and approaches taken, and the experience of the stakeholders, before analysing the outcomes in terms of data and its use, decisions made, values and viewpoints of stakeholders, and the power relations among them.

Chapter 4 outlines a relatively science-led example, focusing on the decisions and political processes which underpin efforts to build local capacity to manage biodiversity in shade coffee in El Salvador. Thirteen authors combine forces in Chapter 5, to analyse success in participatory conservation monitoring in four countries selected because they 'stand out from the majority'; highlighting ways to ensure both local communities and scientists benefit. Another large team, led by scientists from the Center for International Forestry Research (CIFOR), contributes to the analysis of ten projects in Chapter 6, testing out a multi-disciplinary research-based approach across three continents, and achieves in terms of scale and credibility what many smaller but more participatory projects do not; although clearly with much less local ownership. A rare opportunity is presented in Chapter 7, where we have an exceptional analysis of a PAMEB project in China, revisited after one year and again after five years. The authors find that what seems safe to describe as a success story is very different when the project has left.

Chapter 8 examines the challenges of moving from local to national scale, in institutionalizing participatory approaches to forest inventory in Nepal. In a more academic study of different actors' values in relation to landscape in British Columbia, Canada, Chapter 9 reveals the effect on values of cultural knowledge, assumptions about management, and information available to participants at the time of valuing. Chapter 10 presents a remarkable case of the vast national planning exercise in India – with a surprising twist in the tale, as this paragon of participation was in the end rejected by the very ministry that had instigated it in the first place. A focus on the inner workings of volunteer groups provides an interesting comparison between the relatively stable context of UK birdwatching, and the highly dynamic context of post-communist Slovenia, in Chapter 11. This is complemented in Chapter 12 by a national overview of the relations between such organizations in the UK, and the cultural and political resistance that arose when attempts were made to treat their data as objective impersonal entities. Finally Chapter 13 presents a special example

of a thorough, long-term study of the efficacy of community resource monitoring in the USA, highlighting the similarities of the challenges with many
other countries. What is particularly striking in this example is the emphasis
on organizational learning, achieved not only through participatory processes
but also through the joint production of rigorous scientific data.

Trust, ownership and participation

Trust is a core issue, emphasized in almost every chapter of this book. Involving
different stakeholders in the PAMEB process itself can help to build trust, but
may block involvement where there are big value differences between them
(van Rijsoort *et al.*; Boissière *et al.*). Trust arises from the interactions of
the people involved, and the way these overcome prejudice and polarization.
These processes reduce conflict between communities, government agencies,
and environmentalists, allowing progress with resource management, in the
examples from the western United States (Ballard *et al.*). Conversely, several
chapters show that excluding stakeholders – even inadvertently, can undermine
trust (Hull *et al.*; Lawrence).

One particularly important aspect of trust is a sense of ownership of the
project or process. In Nepal the revised community forest inventory guidelines were intended to involve local people but were designed centrally and
technocratically and so failed to generate this ownership (Hull *et al.*). Political
ownership can be just as important. In the case of the Indian National Biodiversity Strategy and Action Plan, lack of political buy-in ultimately undermined a
high profile and meticulous participatory process (Bhatt and Apte).

Connected with this is the sense in which volunteers have chosen to be
involved. Voluntary involvement can strengthen commitment (e.g. Bhatt and
Apte), while conversely professionalization and commercialization can undermine volunteers' commitment, group culture and status (as in the European
case studies – Bell *et al.*; Lawrence). Sometimes voluntary or participatory
initiatives arise as a reaction to perceived government inadequacies, and this
gives them a purpose and vigour that would not exist if government were taking
the initiative (Ballard *et al.*).

All of this points to a central question about participation: is the value in
the process of participatory working or the final products and outcomes? As
pointed out above, participation can be about extraction of knowledge and
effort from a range of stakeholders, or it can be about transformation of power
and knowledge relations, resulting in an enhanced relationship with nature. Of
course the reality is not so polarized, but many of the case studies conclude
that the benefits of PAMEB include enhanced relationships between those who

previously did not understand or trust each other. In other words, trust can be an outcome as well as a precondition of PAMEB. For example, Bhatt and Apte conclude that even without adoption of the National Biodiversity Strategy and Action Plan by the Government of India, the participatory planning process generated much of value that has affected ways of working at more local government levels.

For some these relationships are the main motivation. The role of the 'deep and enduring ties', personal status within the group, international connections between groups and combinations of amateur and professional roles may be more important to participants than the dataset itself, as both case studies of natural history groups make clear (Bell *et al.*; Lawrence).

The converse of trust, distrust, can result in conflict, and participatory processes always run the risk of exposing deep lying distrust. In Nepal for example, the process of developing and implementing participatory inventory guidelines led to conflict, because it became clear that the status attached to one form of knowledge (scientific forestry) excluded the functional and effective involvement of others (communities, and NGOs) (Hull *et al.*). However, if managed with an open attitude to learning, conflict can be an informative process that helps those involved to move on to a more constructive engagement. Conflict can even be the motivation for PAMEB: in the USA, Ballard *et al.* found that it was developed as a means to help forge common understanding and experience among individuals who hold conflicting values, in the context of a highly polarized, at times violent, set of social relations with the forest ecology.

Planning and practicalities

The success of PAMEB is clearly related to good planning, and many excellent handbooks on participatory approaches already address these issues (DETR, 2000; Pilz, Ballard and Jones, 2006; Reitbergen-McCracken and Narayan, 1997). However, they are often omitted from standard handbooks on biodiversity assessment. The chapters of this book provide many illustrations of sound planning and process, including the appropriate involvement of stakeholders, definitions, goals, process, indicators, activities, analysis/learning, communication and action.

It is important that the planning itself is conducted in a participatory way involving the relevant stakeholders. Often in fact a participatory approach is planned entirely by project management staff, government or scientists, to meet their own objectives. We see this problem at large and small scale, with donors in developing countries and with national government agencies in post-industrial countries (Raudsepp-Hearne and Capistrano; Boissière *et al.*; van Rijsoort *et al.*;

Lawrence; Hull *et al.*). The planning can reflect established power structures, or it can challenge them. Ballard *et al.* describe situations in the United States where communities hire scientists to provide knowledge, rather than the more common situation where scientists draw on local knowledge. They conclude that this reversal of knowledge relations and ownership contributed to the value of the outcomes.

Ideally a PAMEB endeavour begins by identifying the appropriate stake-holders and their goals and reasons for getting involved. Sometimes this will consist simply of working with those whose enthusiasm led to the initiative. It may also help to include some who will benefit from exposure to different perspectives, to help bridge the cultural gulfs described below, or with those who give the process legitimacy (Raudsepp-Hearne and Capistrano).

However, this is not always possible. In some cases, reasons for engagement only become obvious to those involved, when things go wrong. Probably the tensions and mistrust associated with the development of the National Biodiversity Network could have been avoided with more thought and discussion at the beginning, but there can also be subconscious drives (the 'passion for birds' mentioned by Bell *et al.*, the 'need to reconnect with the land' in Ballard *et al.*) that are not immediately obvious. Sometimes a PAMEB initiative arises out of conflict and the motives are strong, but not shared or negotiated (Ballard *et al.*). What is important here is reflection by the partners, which in turn will lead to more effective projects in the future (see section on 'learning' below).

Choosing meaningful indicators is a central part of the planning. Scientists in the partnership will have their own processes and reasons for choosing indicators, but in a PAMEB process much will also depend on who is going to use the data. Many of the chapters point to the need to consider scale (e.g. ecosystems services are more subglobal than global; scientific quantitative data is needed for national reporting (Lawrence; Boissière *et al.*; Raudsepp-Hearne and Capistrano)). Where local resource users are expected to use the results, it is particularly important to identify indicators with those users, to ensure that they are meaningful to them (Boissière *et al.*; van Rijsoort *et al.*; Danielsen; Hull *et al.*).

Conversely if the local data collectors are *not* expected to use the data, or to find them immediately useful, careful consideration will have to be given to training, identification tools and remuneration (Monro and Jones; Lawrence and Hawthorne, 2006). If this is the case, the planners might well ask themselves why they are involving people who will not use the data, and check both their own expectations of the process, and the expectations of the other participants. Several of the case studies also highlight problems that can arise when activities do not lead to the expected results, whether in remote rural communities (Boissière *et al.*; van Rijsoort *et al.*) or at national level (Bhatt and Apte; Lawrence).

Some of the chapters show how poor communication can undermine otherwise promising projects. Some cases failed to establish mutual understanding on terminology, or failed to translate documents into local languages (Hull *et al.*). Finally, most of the case studies emphasize the need to consider logistics and communications, including access to sites, translation, politics, and correct social process. All of these factors are particularly important in remote places in developing countries (Boissière *et al.*). Advance planning also prompts the essential action of clarifying the costs and who will pay for what (Danielsen *et al.*).

Methods and training

Although the focus of this book is not on methods of data collection, it is important that planners are aware of PAMEB requirements in relation to methods, training and data management.

Most commonly, local and amateur data collectors will require some support in scientific principles of data collection (standardization, validation, etc). For example Hull and colleagues show how in Nepal, community forest user groups' lack of technical ability to conduct inventory undermined the implementation of a well-meaning policy initiative (Hull *et al.*). Although there have been (legitimate) criticisms of the homogenizing power of western scientific knowledge, it is also empowering for local people to be able to enter into such knowledge systems and many rural land users are keen to be trained in scientific methods (Monro and Jones).

Conversely more locally appropriate methods may be developed for people with little formal education. Local knowledge about biodiversity and ecosystem quality is not always expressed as hard facts, but through processes that help them express their knowledge. Tools can include drama, poetry, visual methods such as maps – all the classical tools of participatory rural appraisal (e.g. Raudsepp-Hearne and Capistrano; Bhatt and Apte). Scientists and local facilitators will need training in these (Danielsen *et al.*).

This links with a less widely recognized need, for training in participatory methods. As Bhatt and Apte point out, it is easy to pass too rapidly over the early planning stages, and only retrospectively to realize that the assumptions underlying participation are challenging existing norms. Time for explanation and discussion needs to be given to the rationale when first introduced, and formal training can help to ensure that this has been adopted by the partners.

Managing data

PAMEB processes may be aiming to produce a single dataset that is useful and meaningful to all concerned, for example in the UK's national biodiversity database (Lawrence). Alternatively they may be aiming to represent different people's knowledge and draw lessons from the comparisons, contrasts and complementarities between them. In either case, the people involved will need to be able to access, trust and understand the data.

There are power issues involved here. Some take the view that it is straightforward to combine different kinds of knowledge (by representing them through data), and that it is the sustainability of institutional arrangements and ownership that makes the difference in the medium to longer term (Garcia and Lescuyer, 2008). The experiences of large teams in huge and bureaucratic countries suggest, however, that even with good intentions, it is easy for those in national government, central geographic locations and scientific institutions to overlook knowledge and culture differences between themselves and those living or working at the most local level of government and in rural communities (van Rijsoort *et al.*; Bhatt and Apte).

This means that decisions need to be made about ownership of the data, and rights and responsibilities connected with access and sharing. Clear guidelines emerged in the British case, but only after a painful period of tension and misunderstanding which required careful negotiation (Lawrence).

It also means that processes are needed for establishing credibility of the data. This was a significant pressure in many of the case studies. What is rigorous and reliable to scientists is remote and abstract to local resources users; in turn their knowledge is subjective and too context specific to be respected by scientists (e.g. Raudsepp-Hearne and Capistrano). The authors of the case studies express this in different ways: the Millennium Ecosystem Assessment focused on 'relevance, credibility and legitimacy' (Raudsepp-Hearne and Capistrano); Monro and Jones refer to 'quality and inclusiveness'. Both sets of terms highlight the need for both *accuracy* (do the data represent what is really there) and *trustworthiness* (do people feel confident about using the data). Different knowledge cultures will have different approaches to establishing data accuracy and trustworthiness. For example, scientists are often uncomfortable about the use of qualitative data but researchers in the Millennium Ecosystem Assessment found that ecosystem functions cannot always be broken down into component parts and it was more useful to work with local, qualitative indicators than with no data at all (Raudsepp-Hearne and Capistrano). Other chapters show innovative ways in which data have been combined at different scales (Danielsen *et al.*, Lawrence).

Some authors point to the value of participation in the *analysis* of PAMEB data, while others deal with the data separately. In such cases it is necessary to communicate the existence of the data and the conclusions from the analysis. This is such common advice in practical handbooks of participatory research that it can sound a little threadbare, but it really is the most widely neglected (or under-funded, or squeezed out as time and funds run out) stage of participatory research. Boissière *et al.* used this as a stage of validation of data; Ballard *et al.* find that funding constrained feedback to the wider community, but that where it was possible, this was central to effectiveness. Furthermore, as Lewis' chapter shows, the way in which different people value components of biodiversity depends on their underlying knowledge; change in knowledge can lead to change in values. Feedback may then become part of an iterative process, and ultimately lead to adaptive management (as in some of the cases described by Ballard *et al.*).

Institutions and governance

Many of the issues relating to power, knowledge and values are most clearly manifested at institutional level. Institutions are the formal 'rules of the game' and PAMEB is often representative of wider governance changes. The ways in which institutions are structured to work with each other affect the ease with which they can take part in PAMEB (and other participatory processes).

For example, as Ballard *et al.* point out, the move towards community forestry in the United States is part of a wider shift from centralized regulation of natural resource use to a more community-based notion of stewardship. Sometimes donor initiatives are out of step with local institutions. For example, van Rijsoort *et al.* show how a mismatch between national, regional and local policies can undermine institutional capacity to implement a decentralized National Biodiversity Action Plan. Even in more stable institutional contexts, PAMEB can challenge organizational cultures, for example by bringing together bureaucracies and volunteers' groups (Lawrence; Bell *et al.*).

Despite these challenges, many of the case studies emphasize the importance of working with existing organizations and governance structures, rather than setting up new procedures or parallel processes. As noted above, the experiences generated by PAMEB can create new relationships of trust and cooperation within existing structures, and contribute to enhancing governance.

This of course brings its own challenges. Staff turnover is common in many of the case studies. This can mean that the initial personal commitment of particular people is lost, and participatory planning does not translate into application of results. Projects take time to plan, and political priorities and institutions may also have changed by the time methods and teams are in place (Boissière *et al.*; Bhatt and Apte). The frequency of change of policy and staff can encourage scepticism about the point of complying or getting involved (van Rijsoort *et al.*).

Governance structures have implications for the sustainability of PAMEB. The methods and lessons must become a standard part of organizational practice. If PAMEB is to be more than a one-off exercise, some real changes may be needed in governance structures. As noted earlier in this chapter, implementation on a continuous and useful basis relies in many cases on genuine devolution of management power, including responsibilities and benefits, to local stakeholders. We see this in the China case study: only those actions that could be implemented by the communities without external support, were actually carried out. In this case, institutional weakness seems to have been a significant factor in the longer-term decline of participatory monitoring (van Rijsoort *et al.*).

Impact of PAMEB

Institutional support depends on there being a visible and desired effect of the PAMEB activities, and so considerations of impact and lesson-learning are central motivations for the institutionalization of PAMEB. Where data are not seen as a management tool, and the data gatherers do not see themselves as having a role in decision-making, engagement may cease when funding runs out (e.g. van Rijsoort *et al.*).

The case studies show how difficult it is to measure impact, and how important it is to remain open to learning and adapting both the methods and the ways in which the resulting data are used. This is because participatory processes are complex, and are often working with concepts unfamiliar to some of the participants. The National Biodiversity Network has achieved an enormous database of reliable data on numbers and distribution of species in the UK, but only after resistance was overcome from key partners (Lawrence). The Millennium Ecosystem Assessment concluded with some uncertainty about the compatibility of local and scientific assessments, but has stimulated a great deal of global interest and debate about multi-stakeholder assessment of ecosystem services (Raudsepp-Hearne and Capistrano).

We cannot overemphasize the need to know more about the longer-term impacts. In some cases presented here, the projects took place and departed before impacts could be known (Boissière *et al.*; Monro and Jones). The chapter by van Rijsoort and colleagues is a rare example, showing that expectations of success and usefulness one year after the project were not fulfilled five years after the project.

Nevertheless many of the case studies in this book show clear evidence of outcomes from PAMEB projects. The most tangible approach is taken in the chapter by Danielsen *et al.*, who count all the management actions taken as a result of community wildlife monitoring in protected areas in five countries. Impact data of this kind are rare, and convincing. More qualitatively, but equally impressively, Ballard *et al.* provide a range of examples where real change in ecosystem management has resulted from community monitoring. The focus was not only on *process* but also on the production of facts, under scientific conditions, that could inform management. People are stimulated by the generation of reliable data. One described it as 'fun' to build up the knowledge that led to a change in management. Others show how findings from PAMEB processes have enabled researchers to act as advocates on behalf of communities, and promote their case with local and national government to protect resources (Boissière *et al.*).

Participation always produces results or effects that were not planned for. Planning for biological data collection may raise issues of local rights and power relations (Boissière *et al.*; Hull *et al.*); conflicts are exposed; new relationships are developed and trust enhanced. The case study from India shows how local government, and local groups, have picked up the experiences of the planning process for the National Biodiversity Strategy, and applied them in their own context (Bhatt and Apte).

All of this can be enhanced by building in opportunities for learning. PAMEB is an evolving process, and can be fine-tuned only by allowing all the participants to identify what they have learnt from their experiences. In each case they may want to ask the scientific question 'What do the data tell us about change and the causes of change?', the methodological question 'What can we learn about the methods?', and the social question 'What can we learn about different perspectives as revealed through the data?'. The answers to these questions will help to fine-tune the process, and the ways in which decisions about environmental management are taken as a result.

Although most chapters report some learning, this is rarely planned in as an explicit project objective. It was, however, planned in the examples described by Ballard *et al.* who demonstrate the value of paying attention to this aspect of PAMEB. The learning in this example led to some surprising technical lessons about resource management, as well as lessons about the values and perspectives of the different people involved. Finally this project and others consolidated the learning process by writing handbooks to record and share the experience (Pilz, Ballard and Jones, 2006).

Conclusions

Much previous work on public (or community) participation (or engagement) separates the discourses into those of the so-called developing world, with a focus on community development and local resource governance, and those of the industrialized or post-industrial world, with a focus on reconnecting people with nature and providing purposefulness for existing hobbies. These case studies do suggest a basic distinction between involving those who participate for livelihood reasons, and those who are committed for 'love-of-nature' reasons. But this distinction is not entirely geographical. Community forests are important for the livelihoods of poor communities in the USA, while communicating local appreciation of conservation value to politicians is important amongst tribal people of Indonesia.

Rather than develop separate messages for different parts of the world, it is more helpful to situate each case in its context, and draw out lessons for the ways in which PAMEB relates to these contexts. Earlier in this chapter we proposed that PAMEB results from a situation in which:

> *different stakeholders can have different objectives, knowledge, information needs, cultures and power relations, as well as methods for collecting and sharing information; these different positions and needs can be accommodated through partnerships which can provide distinct but complementary and mutually rewarding outcomes.*

This statement helps to make the principles of PAMEB universal. The case studies show that these 'complementary and mutually rewarding outcomes' are possible, but sometimes they are achieved more indirectly than at other times.

There are many more cases of participatory data collection than analysis; and more cases of analysis than use; and more cases of use than continuity and institutionalization. Here, we summarize the main lessons of relevance for those who want to make sure that policy agents, planners and other decision makers are more able to support and contribute to the process and value or make use of the results.

Ten lessons for policy-makers and planners

1. The term 'participation' includes a wide range of philosophies and objectives, ranging from combining different people's knowledge about biodiversity in order to enhance the overall knowledge base, through to empowering local stakeholders to make their own environmental management decisions. It is important to be clear what the **objectives and motivations**

are of those proposing a PAMEB approach, and those they are inviting to participate. Participatory approaches can be seen as a quick or cheap route to data acquisition, but they can end up being slower and more expensive if the different needs and objectives are not understood at the outset.

2. Ideally they also require **commitment and ownership** from all the relevant stakeholders at the outset. In practice it is highly unlikely that all the stakeholders will have a full appreciation of what they are getting involved in, and it is a feature of participatory approaches, that concepts and implications only become clear through experience. This requires **inbuilt flexibility and learning processes.** None of this exempts the organizers from making all possible efforts to ensure clarity and mutual understanding from the beginning of a PAMEB project, but it does provide the space for reorientation once projects have started.

3. Biodiversity data and management objectives cannot be separated from the human processes in which they are situated. Biodiversity **definitions and assessments are value-laden** even amongst scientific professionals, and the range of definitions and values increases only when more stakeholders are involved. While much PAMEB activity relies on increasing reliable mutually usable data, it may be an equally valid objective to approach the understanding of 'biodiversity' through PAMEB as a means to compare and communicate different perspectives and values for example between conservation planners and local people.

4. There are pre-existing **power relations** amongst and between stakeholders which will affect their willingness to be involved in participatory processes, and to trust each others' knowledge, observations and data. In the field of biodiversity assessment, these power relations are strongly affected by the status attached to scientific knowledge, and an effective process will only result when attention is paid to these issues of power as well as to technical issues. Sometimes there is an anxiety that these issues can be linked to conflict, but tension is more likely to undermine a process if it is suppressed or hidden.

5. Especially in contexts where people have leisure time and are involved for reasons other than livelihood support, PAMEB participation entails significant **social factors**. Volunteers may attach as much value to belonging to a group, and a sense of shared meaning in their activities, as to the communication of their findings to others. PAMEB processes can be seriously undermined if the emotional and cultural meanings of data collectors are overlooked.

6. Whilst individual actors can be well-meaning and integrate these lessons into their work, the challenges at institutional level are much more

formidable, because so much more cultural inertia and cumulative power is invested in them. To achieve longer-term sustainability of PAMEB, approaches will have to be included that support **organizational learning and adaptiveness**. Mechanisms that can help to achieve this include partnerships between different kinds of organizations (for example governmental and non-governmental), internal workshops and iterative planning processes.

7. PAMEB consists in the exchange of data, contributing to new knowledge. Different professions, ethnic and social groups take part in different **knowledge cultures**, which **assimilate and share data and information in different ways**. Whilst these are sometimes portrayed as distinct and mutually exclusive (for example, scientific and indigenous knowledge), in reality they are dynamic and hybridized, and there is abundant scope for creation interaction between them. In different contexts, different kinds of knowledge are revered. Sometimes by way of compensation for the universal status ascribed to scientific knowledge, local and indigenous knowledge is given primacy. However, local people's desire to learn scientific methods of data collection, and to participate in more global networks of knowledge, should not be overlooked.

8. Different knowledge cultures have different ways of establishing **credibility and accuracy of data**, and applying it to their own experience. Depending on the objectives and stakeholders involved, it may be necessary to train some stakeholders in understanding others' ways of observing, measuring and communicating biodiversity value, or to focus on establishing trust between the different groups so that they learn ways to rely on each others' observations. The choice of **indicators** will also follow from the types of people involved, and objectives, of the PAMEB exercise.

9. All of this requires appropriate **planning, logistical and financial support**, as well as expertise and training in a range of biodiversity assessment methods, and participatory and communication methods. It is important to build in a flexible process-based approach to planning and management since collaborative and participatory activities usually produce unexpected situations and outcomes that will require appropriate responses.

10. Much attention is given to the value of PAMEB for local people and scientists. On the other hand, the **role of decision-makers is often neglected**. If the results are to be applied to improved environmental governance, key people need to be included in the process, understand the power and communication issues involved, be convinced of the value of the exercise from the beginning, or at least receive the results in a format that communicates what they need to know. Such key people can include community leaders,

local politicians, ministers, conservation site managers, and others more removed from biodiversity in their daily activities but who may create the **institutional or political environment** for sharing, interpreting and using the results.

REFERENCES

Agarwal, A. (1995). Dismantling the divide between indigenous and scientific knowledge. *Development and Change* **26**, 413–439.

Badola, R. and S. A. Hussain (2005). Valuing ecosystem functions: An empirical study on the storm protection function of Bhitarkanika mangrove ecosystem, India. *Environmental Conservation* **32**, 85–92.

Baker, K. S. and G. C. Bowker (2007). Information ecology: Open system environment for data, memories, and knowing. *Journal of Intelligent Information Systems* **29**, 127–144.

Balmford, A., P. Crane, A. Dobson, R. E. Green and G. M. Mace (2005). The 2010 challenge: Data availability, information needs and extraterrestrial insights. *Philosophical Transactions of the Royal Society B – Biological Sciences* **360**, 221–228.

Berkes, F., J. Colding and C. Folke (2000). Rediscovery of traditional ecological knowledge as adaptive management. *Ecological Applications* **10**, 1251–1262.

Bliss, J., G. Aplet, C. Hartzell *et al.* (2001). Community-based ecosystem monitoring. *Journal of Sustainable Forestry* **12**, 143–167.

Bollig, M. and A. Schulte (1999). Environmental change and pastoral perceptions: degradation and indigenous knowledge in two African pastoral communities. *Human Ecology* **27**, 493–514.

Boudreau, S. A. and N. D. Yan (2004). Auditing the accuracy of a volunteer-based surveillance program for an aquatic invader bythotrephes. *Environmental Monitoring and Assessment* **91**, 17–26.

Boylen, C.-W., E.-A. Howe, J.-S. Bartkowski and L.-W. Eichler (2004). Augmentation of a long-term monitoring program for Lake George, NY by citizen volunteers. *Lake and Reservoir Management* **20**, 121–129.

Brandon, A., G. Spyreas, B. Molano Flores, C. Carroll and J. Ellis (2003). Can volunteers provide reliable data for forest vegetation surveys? *Natural Areas Journal* **23**, 254–262.

Brossard, D., B. Lewenstein and R. Bonney (2005). Scientific knowledge and attitude change: The impact of a citizen science project. *International Journal of Science Education* **27**, 1099–1121.

Brown, K. (1998). The political ecology of biodiversity, conservation and development in Nepal's Terai: confused meanings, means and ends. *Ecological Economics* **24**, 73–87.

Buckland, S. T., A. E. Magurran, R. E. Green and R. M. Fewster (2005). Monitoring change in biodiversity through composite indices. *Philosophical Transactions of the Royal Society B – Biological Sciences* **360**, 243–254.

Burgess, J., J. Clark and C. M. Harrison (2000). Knowledges in action: an actor network analysis of a wetland agri-environment scheme. *Ecological Economics* **35**, 119–132.

CBD (1992). Convention on Biological Diversity. Available at http://www.biodiv.org/convention/.

Conrad, C. (2006). Towards meaningful community-based ecological monitoring in Nova Scotia: where are we versus where we would like to be. *Environments* **34**, 25–36.

Conrad, C. T. and T. Daoust (2008). Community-based monitoring frameworks: increasing the effectiveness of environmental stewardship. *Environmental Management* **41**, 358–366.

Contandriopoulos, D. (2004). A sociological perspective on public participation in health care. *Social Science and Medicine* **58**, 321–330.

Convention on Biological Diversity (2005). Guidelines on biodiversity-inclusive Environmental 1 Impact Assessment (EIA) available at http://www.cbd.int/doc/reviews/impact/EIA-guidelines.pdf.

Danielsen, F., N. D. Burgess and A. Balmford (2005). Monitoring matters: examining the potential of locally-based approaches. *Biodiversity and Conservation* **14**, 2507–2542.

Danielsen, F., A. E. Jensen, P. A. Alviola *et al.* (2005). Does monitoring matter? A quantitative assessment of management decisions from locally-based monitoring of protected areas. *Biodiversity and Conservation* **14**, 2633–2652.

Danielsen, F., M. M. Mendoza, A. Tagtag *et al.* (2007). Increasing conservation management action by involving local poeple in natural resource monitoring. *Ambio* **36**.

Davies, A. R. (2001). Hidden or hiding? Public perceptions of participation in the planning system. *Town Planning Review* **72**, 193–216.

DETR (2000). *Public Participation in Making Local Environmental Decisions: The Aarhus Convention Newcastle Workshop. Good Practice Handbook.* London, UK: Department of the Environment, Transport and the Regions.

Escobar, A. (1998). Whose knowledge, whose nature? Biodiversity, conservation, and the political ecology of social movements. *Journal of Political Ecology* **5**, 53–82.

Estrella, M., J. Blauert, D. Campilan *et al.* (editors) (2000). *Learning from Change: Issues and Experiences in Participatory Monitoring and Evaluation. Participation in Development.* Intermediate Technology.

Failing, L. and R. Gregory (2003). Ten common mistakes in designing biodiversity indicators for forest policy. *Journal of Environmental Management* **68**, 121–132.

Faith, D. P. (2005). Global biodiversity assessment: integrating global and local values and human dimensions. *Global Environmental Change-Human and Policy Dimensions* **15**, 5–8.

Fischer, A. and J. C. Young (2007). Understanding mental constructs of biodiversity: implications for biodiversity management and conservation. *Biological Conservation* **136**, 271–282.

Fischer, F. (2006). Participatory governance as deliberative empowerment. The cultural politics of discursive space. *American Review of Public Administration* **36**, 19–40.

Garcia, C. A. and G. Lescuyer (2008). Monitoring, indicators and community based forest management in the tropics: pretexts or red herrings? *Biodiversity and Conservation* **17**, 1303–1317.

Gaston, K. J. (1996). *Biodiversity: A Biology of Numbers and Difference.* Oxford: Blackwell Science.

Goodwin, P. (1998). 'Hired hands' or 'local voice': understandings and experience of local participation in conservation. *Transactions of the Institute of British Geographers* **23**, 481–491.

Hein, L., K. van Koppen, R. S. de Groot and E. C. van Ierland (2006). Spatial scales, stakeholders and the valuation of ecosystem services. *Ecological Economics* **57**, 209–228.

Hopkin, M. (2007). Mark of respect. *Nature* **448**, 402–403.

Humphries, C. J., P. H. Williams and R. I. Vane-Wright (1995). Measuring biodiversity value for conservation. *Annual Review Ecology and Systematics* **26**, 93–111.

Kapoor, I. (2001). Toward participatory environmental management? *Journal of Environmental Management* **63**, 269–279.

Karney, R. C. (2000). Poor water quality? Not in my backyard! The effectiveness of neighborhood pond associations in the protection and improvement of shellfish growing waters on Martha's Vineyard. *Journal of Shellfish Research* **19**, 465–466.

Lawrence, A. (2006). "No Personal Motive?" Volunteers, Biodiversity and the False Dichotomies of Participation. *Ethics, Place and Environment* **9**, 279–298.

Lawrence, A. (2009). The first cuckoo in winter: phenology, recording, credibility and meaning in Britain. *Global Environmental Change* **19**, 173–179.

Lawrence, A., B. Ambrose-Oji, R. Lysinge and C. Tako (2000). Exploring local values for forest biodiversity on Mount Cameroon. *Mountain Research & Development* **20**, 112–115.

Lawrence, A. and W. Hawthorne (2006). *Plant Identification: User-friendly Field Guides for Biodiversity Management*. London: Earthscan.

Lawrence, A., K. Paudel, R. Barnes and Y. Malla (2006). Adaptive value of participatory biodiversity monitoring in community forestry. *Environmental Conservation* **33**, 325–334.

Lazdinis, M., P. Angelstam and I. Lazdinis (2007). Maintenance of forest biodiversity in a post-soviet governance model: Perceptions by local actors in Lithuania. *Environmental Management* **40**, 20–33.

Leach, M. and R. Mearns (editors) (1996). *The Lie of the Land: Challenging Received Wisdom on the African Environment*. Oxford: James Currey.

Maass, J. M., P. Balvanera, A. Castillo *et al.* (2005). Ecosystem services of tropical dry forests: Insights from long-term ecological and social research on the Pacific Coast of Mexico. *Ecology and Society* **10**.

Mace, G. M. and J. E. M. Baillie (2007). The 2010 biodiversity indicators: Challenges for science and policy. *Conservation Biology* **21**, 1406–1413.

Mayer, P. (2006). Biodiversity – the appreciation of different thought styles and values helps to clarify the term. *Restoration Ecology* **14**, 105–111.

McCaffrey, R. E. (2005). Using citizen science in urban bird studies. *Urban Habitats* **3**, 70–86 [online].

Millennium Ecosystem Assessment (2008). Millennium Ecosystem Assessment: guide to the Millennium Assessment reports, accessed 2008 available at http://www.millenniumassessment.org/en/index.aspx.

Moffat, A. J. S. Davies and L. Finer (2008). Reporting the results of forest monitoring – an evaluation of the European forest monitoring programme. *Forestry* **81**, 75–90.

Morris, C. (2006). Negotiating the boundary between state-led and farmer approaches to knowing nature: an analysis of UK agri-environment schemes. *Geoforum* **37**, 113–127.

Natural History Museum (2001). Biodiversity and worldmap: measuring biodiversity value. Accessed 2001: Natural History Museum available at http://www.nhm.ac.uk/science/projects/worldmap/diversity/index.html.

Newman, C., C. D. Buesching and D. W. Macdonald (2003). Validating mammal monitoring methods and assessing the performance of volunteers in wildlife conservation – "*Sed quis custodiet ipsos custodies?*" *Biological Conservation* **113**, 189–197.

Noss, A., E. Cuellar and R. Cuellar (2003). Hunter self-monitoring as a basis for biological research: data from the Bolivian Chaco. *Mastozoologia Neotropical/Journal of Neotropical Mammalogy* **10**, 49–67.

Parkins, J. R. (2006). De-centering environmental governance: a short history and analysis of democratic processes in the forest sector of Alberta, Canada. *Policy Sciences* **39**, 183–203.

Perlman, D. L. and G. Adelson (1997). *Biodiversity: Exploring Values and Priorities in Conservation*. Oxford: Blackwell Scientific.

Pilz, D., H. L. Ballard and E. T. Jones (2006). *Broadening Participation in Biological Monitoring: Handbook for Scientists and Managers* available at http://www.ifcae.org/projects/ncssf3/IFCAE-ParticipatoryMonitoringGuidelines-2005.pdf.

Plummer, R. and J. Fitzgibbon (2004). Co-management of natural resources: A proposed framework. *Environmental Management* **33**, 876–885.

Pollock, R. M. and G. S. Whitelaw (2005). Community-based monitoring in support of local sustainability. *Local Environment* **10**, 211–228.

Pond, K. and G. Rees (2000). Coastwatch UK: a public participation survey. *Journal of Coastal Conservation* **6**(1), 61–66.

Rappaport, R. (1979). *Ecology, Meaning & Religion*. North Atlantic Books.

Reitbergen-McCracken, J. and D. Narayan (1997). *A Resource Kit for Participation and Social Assessment*. Washington DC: The World Bank.

Robertson, D. P. and R. B. Hull (2003). Public ecology: an environmental science and policy for global society. *Environmental Science & Policy* **6**, 399–410.

Royal Society (2003). Measuring biodiversity for conservation available at http://www.royalsociety.org/displaypagedoc.asp?id=6712.

Saris, F., H. Groot, W. Hagemeijer and D. A. Van (1996). Monitoring the Dutch agricultural bird community (a choice between a data-death because of the fear of inadequate data and a practical monitoring programme). *Ekologia Bratislava* **15**, 87–96.

Scoones, I. (1999). New ecology and the social sciences: what prospects for a fruitful engagement? *Annual Review of Anthropology* **28**, 479–507.

Sharpe, A. and C. Conrad (2006). Community based ecological monitoring in Nova Scotia: challenges and opportunities. *Environmental Monitoring and Assessment* **113**, 395–409.

Sheil, D. and A. Lawrence (2004). Tropical biologists, local people and conservation: new opportunities for collaboration. *Trends in Ecology and Evolution* **19**, 634–638.

Slootwega, R. and A. Kolhoff (2003). A generic approach to integrate biodiversity considerations in screening and scoping for EIA. *Environmental Impact Assessment Review* **23**, 657–681.

Takacs, D. (1996). *The Idea of Biodiversity: Philosophies of Paradise*. Johns Hopkins University Press.

Tangwa, G. B. (1999). Globalisation or westernisation? Ethical concerns in the whole big-business. *Bioethics* **13**, 218–226.

Thibault, M. and S. Blaney (2001). Sustainable human resources in a protected area in southwestern Gabon. *Conservation Biology* **15**, 591–595.

Tsouvalis, J., S. Seymour and C. Watkins (2000). Exploring knowledge-cultures: precision farming, yield mapping, and the expert-farmer interface. *Environment and Planning A* **32**, 909–924.

Usher, P. J. (2000). Traditional ecological knoweldge in environmental assessment and management. *Arctic* **53**, 183–193.

van Jaarsveld, A. S., R. Biggs, R. J. Scholes *et al.* (2005). Measuring conditions and trends in ecosystem services at multiple scales: the Southern African Millennium Ecosystem Assessment (SAfMA) experience. *Philosophical Transactions of the Royal Society B – Biological Sciences* **360**, 425–441.

Vermeulen, S. and I. Koziell (2002). *Integrating Global and Local Values: a Review of Biodiversity Assessment*. London: IIED.

Wagner, G. A. (2005). Participatory monitoring of changes in coastal and marine biodiversity. *Indian Journal of Marine Sciences* **34**, 136–146.

Wollenberg, E., J. Anderson and D. Edmunds (2001). Pluralism and the less powerful: accommodating multiple interests in local forest management. *International Journal of Agricultural Resources, Governance and Ecology* **1**, 199–222.

Yoccoz, N. G., J. D. Nichols and T. Boutlinier (2001). Monitoring of biological diversity in space and time. *Trends in Ecology and Evolution* **16**, 446–453.

2

Monitoring and assessment of biodiversity under the Convention on Biological Diversity and other international agreements

RUTH MACKENZIE

Introduction

The central instrument in international efforts to conserve and sustainably use biodiversity is the Convention on Biological Diversity (CBD), which was opened for signature at the United Nations Conference on Environment and Development (UNCED) in Rio de Janeiro in 1992 and entered into force in December 1993. The Convention was adopted against the background of an existing web of other global biodiversity-related treaties. These include: the 1971 Ramsar Convention on Wetlands of International Importance; the 1973 Convention on Trade on Endangered Species of Wild Fauna and Flora (CITES); the 1979 Bonn Convention on Migratory Species and specific 'range state' instruments adopted under its auspices; and the 1972 World Heritage Convention. (Websites for these conventions are listed at the end of the references section of this chapter.) These are supplemented by numerous regional agreements, addressing the conservation and sustainable use of terrestrial and/or marine biological diversity.

The existence of biodiversity-related international agreements reflects a wider move towards treaty-based global environmental governance. The number of multilateral environmental agreements (MEAs) has increased significantly in the period since the 1970s as the international community has recognized the interconnectedness of global environmental threats (Sands, 2003, p. 127; Desai, 2004, p. 106). Global conferences, such as the UN Conference on the Human Environment in Stockholm in 1972 and UNCED, have often provided the impetus for the negotiation and conclusion of new MEAs. Many of the global agreements, particularly those adopted since the mid 1980s and

Taking Stock of Nature: Participatory Biodiversity Assessment for Policy, Planning and Practice, ed. Anna Lawrence. Published by Cambridge University Press. © Cambridge University Press 2010.

including the CBD, reflect similar approaches to the evolution and 'governance' of the system of rules they establish. For example, they provide for regular meetings of the parties as a mechanism for reviewing effectiveness and taking further action (see Churchill and Ulfstein, 2000); they provide for the establishment of subsidiary bodies to consider relevant scientific and technical issues; they require parties to report on measures taken to implement their obligations under the agreement; they establish mechanisms for the provision of financial assistance to developing country parties to support implementation; and they provide that protocols to the agreement may be adopted to elaborate new or more detailed obligations. Many of the more recent MEAs have attracted extremely high rates of participation. By April 2007, for example, 189 states and the European Community had become parties to the CBD. This high level of participation, the scope of coverage of the Convention's provisions, and the institutional framework it establishes for on-going cooperation makes the CBD the primary forum for international action on biodiversity issues.

The role of information, monitoring and assessment in biodiversity-related treaties

The development and implementation of biodiversity-related treaties are information-intensive endeavours. Each depends upon information relating to the conservation status of specific species, or upon threats to specific components of biodiversity (both species and habitats). Information about biodiversity, and biodiversity loss, provides the rationale for the negotiation of new instruments, and determines their form and content. Once they are adopted, the agreements require a supply of information to drive the evolution or adaptation of commitments, to determine whether and what further action is needed and how urgently. Information is also needed on the effectiveness of existing obligations and the measures taken to implement them. In regard to the latter, the CBD, in common with most other MEAs, requires parties to report regularly on measures taken to implement it (Article 26).

However, information about the status of biodiversity is often inadequate. The preamble to the CBD notes the general lack of information and knowledge concerning biological diversity, and the urgent need to develop scientific, technical and institutional capacities to provide the basic understanding upon which to plan and implement appropriate measures. The CBD has highlighted, in particular, a critical lack of the taxonomic expertise that is needed to identify components of biodiversity that may be under threat.

Information is also contested: the reliability or credibility of information from some sources may be questioned, particularly where it points to the need for drastic preventive or remedial action. The precautionary principle is, arguably, evolving into a principle of international environmental law (Sands, 2003, p. 279), so as to require that action be taken in the face of risks of serious or irreversible environmental harm even in the absence of full scientific certainty. Nonetheless, in practice insufficient or disputed information about the status of biodiversity may still be used as a reason to justify inaction.

These types of considerations suggest that a variety of sources of biodiversity information may have a role to play in contributing to the elaboration and implementation of international agreements aimed at the conservation and sustainable use of biological diversity. A wide range of potential sources of information might be considered to fall within the concept of participatory assessment and monitoring. These include the work of voluntary organizations and NGOs to gather information on the status of biodiversity, often using volunteers or amateurs to report data, for example on species sightings, as well as mechanisms to involve local communities in biodiversity management, including assessment and monitoring. It is important to bear in mind what opportunities exist to channel information derived from such sources into national and international processes addressing biodiversity, and what types of information may be useful at various levels of data-collection and decision-making. This may need to include consideration of how to manage these and other sources of information so as to provide for any appropriate calibration or validation of biodiversity data as a basis for effective decision-making.

The Convention on Biological Diversity

The objectives of the Convention on Biological Diversity are the conservation and sustainable use of biodiversity, and the fair and equitable sharing of benefits arising out of the use of genetic resources. Its provisions address a wide range of different issues related to these objectives, including the following.

- Requirements for the development of national biodiversity strategies and actions, and the integration of biodiversity considerations into other sectoral plans (Article 6).
- Identification and monitoring of components of biodiversity and threats to them (Article 7).
- In situ conservation, including the establishment and management of protected areas, and restoration of degraded habitats (Article 8).

- Ex situ conservation (Article 9).
- Sustainable use of biodiversity (Article 10).
- Public education and awareness (Article 13).
- Environmental impact assessment (Article 14).
- Provisions on access to genetic resources and the fair and equitable sharing of benefits arising out of the use of those resources (Articles 15, 16 and 19).
- Provision of financial resources for implementation of the Convention by developing country parties (Articles 20 and 21).
- National reporting requirements (Article 26).[1]

In many respects the Convention is a framework instrument (Glowka *et al.*, 1994; McGraw, 2002, pp. 19–21): it provides a guiding framework (rather than comprehensive and detailed rules) for domestic action as well as 'autonomous institutional arrangements' (Churchill and Ulfstein, 2000) that provide a mechanism for its effectiveness to be reviewed and for further development of commitments. The governing body of the Convention is the Conference of the Parties (COP), which has met regularly since the entry into force of the CBD in 1994.[2] The COP adopts decisions designed to elaborate upon and further shared understandings of the Convention's provisions and to guide implementation.[3] It is also the body that can adopt protocols to the Convention on matters deemed to require further specific and legally binding commitments.[4] The Convention

---

[1] It is beyond the scope of this chapter to go into each of these aspects in detail. For further detailed analysis of the Convention, see, for example, Glowka *et al.*, *A Guide to the Convention on Biological Diversity*, IUCN Environmental Law and Policy Paper No. 30, 1994; Gross, Johnston and Barber, *The Convention on Biological Diversity: Understanding and Influencing the Process* (United Nations University Institute of Advanced Studies, 2006); and Secretariat of the Convention on Biological Diversity, *Handbook of the Convention on Biological Diversity*, 3rd edition, 2005.

[2] The COP has held eight ordinary meetings in the period 1994–2007 and one extraordinary meeting (held over two sessions in 1999 and 2000, for the adoption of the Cartagena Protocol on Biosafety). In 1994–96, ordinary meetings of the COP were held annually, and after 1996 they have been held every two years.

[3] COP decisions are numbered according to the meeting at which they were adopted. For example, the decision on Communication, Education and Public Awareness adopted at the sixth ordinary meeting of the COP is Decision VI/19. Each COP meeting generally produces a large number of decisions (more than 30 decisions per meeting at each of the last three meetings of the COP), and a huge amount of paper in the form of official pre-session documentation, information documents and the decisions themselves, contained in the final report of the meeting. These materials can be found on the Convention's website at http://www.cbd.int. In addition, at each COP meeting, as discussed further below, a huge volume of information, publications and lobbying materials are made available by non-governmental and intergovernmental organizations.

[4] The only protocol adopted by the COP to date is the 2000 Cartagena Protocol on Biosafety. A protocol is a separate legal agreement, linked to the Convention but subject to separate signature and ratification processes. Parties to the Convention are not obliged to become parties to its protocol(s). However, only parties to the CBD may become a party to a protocol adopted under it.

also establishes a Subsidiary Body on Scientific, Technical and Technological Advice (SBSTTA), that is mandated to make recommendations to the COP on matters within its remit. SBSTTA thus plays a critical role in influencing the content of certain COP decisions. It is an 'open-ended' body, open to all parties to the CBD and to observers, rather than a small specialized expert group. In addition to these bodies, an array of ad hoc intersessional bodies has been established by the COP.[5]

The CBD represented a new approach to international co-operation in the field of conservation of species and ecosystems (Boyle, 1996, p. 33; Glowka *et al.*, 1994). It explicitly couples goals and commitments related to conservation with rights to sustainable use of biodiversity, and equitable sharing of benefits arising out of that use. In addition to commitments on conservation, it includes specific provisions addressing access to genetic resources and benefit sharing. It avoids global priority-setting and identification of species or ecosystems for special protection, leaving specific action to parties within the guiding framework and principles established by the Convention. It also goes beyond the primary focus of previous agreements on species or habitats, addressing diversity at the genetic, species and ecosystem levels. Furthermore, it explicitly recognizes the linkage between biodiversity policy and other sectoral issues, calling on parties, in Article 6(b), 'to integrate, as far as possible and as appropriate, the conservation and sustainable use of biological diversity into relevant sectoral or cross-sectoral plans, programmes and policies'. As part of the body of international environmental law emerging in the context of the UNCED process, the CBD can be regarded as a sustainable development agreement.

Nonetheless, the sheer scope of the Convention could in some ways be considered a weakness insofar as, in many respects, it does not set out detailed guidance or commitments as regards particular action that should be taken. For example, there is no globally agreed list of specially threatened species or habitats, and many of the obligations imposed on parties are qualified by phrases such as 'as far as possible and as appropriate'[6] or 'in accordance with its particular conditions and capabilities' (Article 6). Thus, much is left to the discretion of the parties to the Convention as they develop strategies and action plans for implementation, gather information about important components of biodiversity and threats to them, set priorities for action, and take

---

[5] Details of the various subsidiary bodies established by the COP can be found at http://www.cbd.int/convention/bodies.shtml.

[6] See for example, Article 4 (cooperation), Article 7 (identification and monitoring), Article 8 (in situ conservation), Article 9 (ex situ conservation), Article 10 (sustainable use of components of biological diversity), Article 11 (incentive measures) and Article 14 (impact assessment and minimizing adverse impacts).

measures to address those priorities. Thus while the Convention provides an important forum for international cooperation and can act as a catalyst, the national level is the critical locus of action if the Convention's objectives are to be achieved. However, the scope of the Convention can make it difficult, at both the national and international level, to target actions and measure their impact on the achievement of the Convention's objectives. The characteristics of the Convention make it difficult to assess a Party's compliance with its obligations under the CBD, or even, to some extent, to identify clearly the parameters of those obligations. Much attention in the COP has focused on how the implementation of the Convention can be improved, and an intersessional working group on the review of implementation has been established.

Participatory biodiversity assessment and monitoring and the CBD

The Convention does not explicitly address the subject of participatory biodiversity assessment and monitoring. Nonetheless, it contains several provisions that are relevant, or potentially relevant, to the issue, insofar as they depend upon the gathering and reporting of different types of biodiversity information. These include (i) information about the identification and monitoring of components of biodiversity under threat, and the processes and activities that may threaten them (Article 7 and Annex I); (ii) information relevant to environmental impact assessment procedures (Article 14); and (iii) information regarding the measures to implement the CBD and their effectiveness, particularly in the context of national reports (Article 6 and Article 26). These aspects of the Convention are discussed further below.

There are two issues of overarching significance to the Convention's approach that might be mentioned at the outset. First, the primary framework for action under the Convention is the ecosystem approach. This has been conceived by the COP as follows.

1. The ecosystem approach is a strategy for the integrated management of land, water and living resources that promotes conservation and sustainable use in an equitable way. Thus, the application of the ecosystem approach will help to reach a balance of the three objectives of the Convention: conservation; sustainable use; and the fair and equitable sharing of the benefits arising out of the utilization of genetic resources.
2. An ecosystem approach is based on the application of appropriate scientific methodologies focused on levels of biological organization, which encompass the essential structure, processes, functions and interactions among

organisms and their environment. It recognizes that humans, with their cultural diversity, are an integral component of many ecosystems. (Decision V/6).

Among other things, the ecosystem approach emphasizes decentralization of management to the lowest appropriate level, and the consideration of all forms of relevant information from all sources, including scientific and indigenous and local community knowledge, innovations and practices. The inclusive nature of the ecosystem approach would thus appear to support participatory approaches to assessment and monitoring of biodiversity.

Secondly, in 2002, the COP adopted the target of achieving by 2010 a significant reduction of the current rate of biodiversity loss at the global, regional and national level (Decision VI/26). The 2010 target was endorsed by the 2002 World Summit on Sustainable Development, and has become a core focus of activities under the Convention. To assess progress towards the 2010 target, the COP established a set of provisional indicators. These include assessment of status and trends of components of biodiversity, including trends in selected biomes, ecosystems and habitats, trends in abundance and distribution of selected species, and coverage of protected areas (Decision VII/30). Assessment and monitoring activities conducted by local communities or community-based organizations could have a potentially important role to play in evaluating progress towards the 2010 target. The 2010 target has provided a focal point and catalyst for non-governmental initiatives, through networks such as Countdown 2010,[7] and 'mixed' (non-governmental/intergovernmental) initiatives, such as the 2010 Biodiversity Indicators Partnership,[8] to take action on the causes of biodiversity loss and to assess progress towards the target.

The role of civil society under the CBD

As mentioned above, the CBD was adopted within the broader context of the 1992 UN Conference on Environment and Development (UNCED), in which significant attention was given to the role of civil society, or 'major groups', in efforts to achieve sustainable development. This approach is reflected in particular in Agenda 21, adopted at UNCED.

Article 13 of the CBD specifically addresses public education and awareness. It requires parties to the Convention to promote and encourage understanding of the importance of, and measures required for, the conservation of biodiversity, and to cooperate with other states and organizations in developing

---

[7] See http://www.countdown2010.net/.   [8] See http://www.twentyten.net/.

educational and public awareness programmes. In furtherance of this provision, the COP has endorsed a Global Initiative on Communication, Education and Public Awareness (CEPA) (CBD Decision VI/19). The COP has also recognized the importance of public awareness and education in the thematic work programmes it has adopted on specific ecosystems, and has urged parties to support initiatives by major groups that foster stakeholder participation in biodiversity conservation and sustainable use (CBD Decision IV/10, B). While these general goals are agreed, the specific types of stakeholder participation envisaged as a result of biodiversity education and awareness activities are not precisely articulated. It is not clear whether such efforts are intended primarily to promote awareness of the importance of biodiversity conservation and sustainable use, or also to promote and underpin more effective public participation in biodiversity-related decision-making, and other types of participation such as the collection of biodiversity data. Nonetheless, the approach under Article 13 seems, thus far at least, to be rather heavily top-down or one-way, with an emphasis on informing the public about the significance and value of biodiversity.

In some contrast to Article 13, Article 8(j) of the Convention recognizes the importance of the knowledge, innovations and practices of indigenous and local communities relevant for the conservation and sustainable use of biodiversity. It is this and related provisions, perhaps, that provide a more ready avenue for the integration of participatory biodiversity assessment and monitoring techniques into Convention processes, given that in the Article 8(j) process[9] the significance and value of existing traditional and local knowledge about biodiversity is clearly acknowledged. The CBD does not explicitly define the term 'indigenous and local communities', but there appears no reason to assume that the CBD's provisions and related work programme would exclude various forms of local knowledge and expertise that might be applied to biodiversity assessment and monitoring activities. The Convention also calls on parties to support local populations to develop and implement remedial action in degraded areas where biodiversity has been reduced (Article 10(d)).

The Convention's Strategic Plan, adopted in 2002, calls for broader engagement across society in implementation. Goals include the implementation by all parties of communication, education and public awareness strategies and the promotion of public participation; and the effective involvement of indigenous and local communities in implementation and in Convention processes at national, regional and international levels (Decision VI/26, Annex, Goal 4). The

---

[9] In 1998, the COP established a Working Group on Article 8(j), that met for the fifth time in October 2007. For further information, see http://www.cbd.int/convention/wg8j.shtml.

Strategic Plan notes that limited public participation and stakeholder involvement, lack of accessible knowledge and information, and lack of horizontal co-operation among stakeholders stand as obstacles to the implementation of the Convention. An experts' meeting in 2006 to consider implementation of the Convention beyond 2010 called for national biodiversity strategies and action plans (NBSAPs) to be prepared or updated with the participation of a broad set of people from all major groups to build ownership and commitment, and for civil society participation to be encouraged and strengthened in Convention processes (see Bhatt and Apte, this volume, for the Indian experience). The role of initiatives such as the Equator Initiative and Countdown 2010 was also recognized (Ecologic, 2006).

Non-governmental actors can play both a direct and indirect role in providing information to the Convention process in respect of the 2010 target or other specific aspects of the Convention's work programme. Non-governmental organizations (NGOs), including community-based organizations, indigenous groups, international NGOs, and scientific bodies provide information directly at sessions of the Convention's governing and advisory bodies, and also provide information to the Convention Secretariat that may be incorporated into pre-session documents. The COP and the Convention Secretariat have frequently called for the submission of information or case studies on specific aspects of the implementation of the Convention, to demonstrate different approaches to implementation and possible best practices.

NGOs may also participate actively in meetings of the COP and subsidiary bodies, including SBSTTA, through formal interventions and side events, and sometimes as members of expert advisory groups. There is thus a 'direct' role for information derived from non-governmental sources, and such information has often played a significant role in influencing the direction of action taken under the Convention. Access to the meetings of the CBD COP has tended to be relatively open, in that many different types of organization have been able to attend meetings, have had opportunities to make interventions in formal sessions of the COP plenary or committees, and have often been able to observe informal discussions in contact groups. Nonetheless, when negotiations reach a delicate stage NGOs may well be excluded entirely from observing discussions in contact groups or small drafting groups.[10] Moreover, the scale and scope of the COP meetings mean that it can be very difficult for small delegations (of governments as well as of NGOs) to follow the full range of discussions effectively: for example, because numerous meetings may take place at the same

---

[10] For an accessible explanation of how the CBD COP meetings operate, and how NGOs can participate effectively, see Gross, Johnston and Barber (2006).

time or because informal negotiations are almost invariably held in English without the provision of interpretation. In CBD meetings, as in other MEAs, NGOs frequently act in coalitions – thus burden sharing to some extent – or at least hold regular meetings to discuss the state of play.

Beyond the intergovernmental meetings, of course, a multitude of non-governmental actors are active at the domestic level, gathering data and providing information that may be used by their governments in determining national biodiversity priorities and actions, and in reporting to the CBD and other biodiversity-related international fora. Through the national reporting process, parties remain a principal route for conveying into the Convention process information that forms the 'knowledge base' upon which decisions on future action are considered and adopted, and upon which the implementation of the Convention at a global level can be assessed.

Identification and monitoring of components of biodiversity

Article 7 of the Convention requires parties to identify and monitor components of biodiversity under threat, and processes and activities which may adversely affect them. Numerous countries have identified the lack of adequate baseline data as a significant challenge to their implementation of the Convention, and in national reports under the Convention many have highlighted a lack of capacity in identification and monitoring.

One aspect specifically addressed by the COP in relation to Article 7 has been the lack of taxonomic capacity for implementation of the Convention in many countries. To address this, the Conference of the Parties took steps to establish a Global Taxonomy Initiative (GTI) in 1998. The GTI calls, in particular, for training and capacity-building in taxonomy, including parataxonomy, especially in developing countries. The GTI is intended to seek to provide the key information required for implementation of the CBD, particularly Article 7, and address the problem of insufficient knowledge of all components of biodiversity (CBD Decision VI/8). The GTI also acknowledges the potential role of traditional taxonomic knowledge.

In their third national reports, submitted in 2006 (see further below), a number of parties reported community involvement in activities related to Article 7, or more generally to in situ conservation (Article 8 of the Convention). Some, such as Canada, Estonia, Saint Lucia, Sweden, the United Kingdom and Zimbabwe reported actual or planned activities engaging public involvement in identification and monitoring initiatives. As regards Article 8 of the CBD, on in situ conservation, some parties including Ethiopia, Canada and India reported community involvement in the development and implementation of species or habitat management plans, and a number reported public participation in protected area management and monitoring.

Impact assessment

Provisions of the CBD on impact assessment provide another possible avenue for inputs from participatory biodiversity assessment and monitoring initiatives. The Convention requires parties to introduce appropriate procedures for environmental impact assessment (EIA) of proposed projects that are likely to have significant adverse effects on biodiversity and, where appropriate, to allow for public participation in such procedures (Article 14(1)). Much of the work undertaken on this issue under the Convention has focused on improving the extent to which biodiversity considerations are taken into account in EIA processes (for example, CBD Decision VII/28).

The COP has emphasized the need to ensure involvement of interested and affected stakeholders in all stages of the assessment process, including indigenous and local communities and NGOs. It has recognized that effective participation of relevant stakeholders is a precondition for successful environmental impact assessment, and that such participation can take place at different levels: informing the public (one-way flow of information); consulting the public (two-way flow of information); and 'real participation', involving shared analysis and assessment (Decision VII/28). Nonetheless the emphasis in the CBD 'biodiversity-inclusive' EIA guidelines, contained in Decision VII/28, appears to remain on the first two of these levels of participation. There is little detailed guidance to date on approaches to shared analysis and assessment. The EIA guidelines also stress that EIA does not end with the production of a report and a decision on whether a proposed project should proceed. Thus it includes the development of management plans, monitoring predicted and actual effects of a project, and compliance monitoring. Again participatory biodiversity monitoring may have a role to play here.

In 2004, the COP also adopted the Akwé: Kon Guidelines, that had been elaborated by the Working Group on Article 8(j). These voluntary guidelines address the conduct of cultural, environmental and social impact assessment regarding developments proposed to take place on, or which are likely to impact on, sacred sites and on lands and waters traditionally occupied or used by indigenous and local communities. The guidelines emphasize participation of indigenous and local communities in such procedures. Among the issues addressed by the Guidelines is the need for baseline studies as a foundation for effective environmental impact assessment of a proposed development. The Guidelines note that such studies should be conducted in consultation with affected indigenous and local communities, to ascertain those components of biodiversity of particular significance to the affected community. Among the information that should be collected as part of the baseline study are species inventories; identification of endangered species and species at risk; and identification of particularly significant habitat and of areas of particular economic significance. Baseline studies should also consider traditional knowledge innovations and practices as an important competent (Decision VII/16 F).

National biodiversity strategies and action plans and national reports

Perhaps the principal impact of the Convention lies in the fact that it provides an international framework, and a requirement, for parties to develop and implement NBSAPs (Article 6). These strategies and action plans provide the fundamental framework for domestic implementation of the Convention. But while many parties did adopt them, with financial support from the Global Environment Facility, in many instances the NBSAP has not been implemented, for reasons of lack of capacity and lack of prioritization (see e.g. Bhatt and Apte, this volume). Efforts to enhance the effectiveness of the Convention frequently address the need to mobilize efforts to implement the strategies and action plans, and to engage all relevant sectors and stakeholders.[11]

The CBD also requires parties to report regularly on measures taken to implement obligations, and their effectiveness (Article 26). The Global Environment Facility provided support for the preparation of first national reports to the CBD, and thereafter the COP has adopted simplified reporting formats in order to facilitate compliance with Article 26 and analysis of reports. National reports can be helpful in providing a broad picture of how parties are approaching implementation of the Convention, and those aspects of the Convention on which they have focused. However, the information provided can be rather 'thin' in that it does not generally include detailed analysis of effectiveness of measures. Moreover, parties often fail to submit full reports, or fail to submit them on time. No real sanctions are available under the CBD for failure to report, and parties frequently cite lack of financial and/or human resources as the reason for failing to deliver reports on time or at all. (On reporting under MEAs and international agreements generally see, for example, Chayes and Handler Chayes, 1995.) By way of example, third national reports under

---

[11] See, for example, Recommendation 2/1, Report of the Ad Hoc Working Group on Review of Implementation of the Convention on the Work of its Second Meeting, document UNEP/CBD/COP/9/4, 26 July 2007, available at: http://www.cbd.int.

Article 26 were due to be submitted by 15 May 2005. By the end of October 2005, 37 reports had been received by the Secretariat, and by the end of May 2006, 82 parties had fulfilled their reporting obligation. The Secretariat reiterated the request for submissions of reports by September 2006 and, by mid 2007, 130 national reports were available on the Convention's website (of 190 parties).

In recognition of the burden that multiple reporting obligations under different MEAs place upon parties, there has been some effort to harmonize reporting requirements among the biodiversity-related agreements. However, a fully harmonized system has not yet been put in place.

A guide for parties on the preparation of national reports under the CBD has noted the following.

> The process of developing the report is intended by the COP to be fully inclusive, involving all those bodies and institutions – governmental or non-governmental – that have an interest or a role to play in implementation of the Convention. The reporting process thus helps to disseminate information among all stakeholders about the objectives and provisions of the Convention, to identify tasks and allocate responsibilities, and to build familiarity, trust and procedures among the participants of this network that will be essential if the provisions of the Convention are to be implemented in the country as envisaged.
>
> *(Gross, 2005)*

The guidance envisages the use or establishment of a multi-stakeholder network in the preparation of the report, and the involvement of a wide range of participants in answering the questions that need to be answered in the report, noting the following.

> The nature of the biodiversity crisis and the complexity and inter-connectedness of the issues covered by the Convention demand nothing less than a committed network of stakeholders who have reason to believe that working together is the only way to see results. The text of the Convention itself and multiple decisions of the COP make it clear that implementation of this Convention, probably more than any other international agreement ... has to be a collective multi-agency, multi-sectoral, multi-stakeholder enterprise.
>
> A country that can mobilise such a network has not only made a large step towards preparing a useful and objective report, but more importantly has also taken a large step forward in implementing the objectives of the Convention.
>
> *(Gross, 2005)*

Some evidence of such multi-stakeholder involvement is evident in some of the national reports of parties to the CBD, submitted in 2006, in which parties reported on their actions to implement various provisions of the Convention and work programmes established under it. A number of parties made reference in their reports to the wide variety of non-governmental organizations and bodies that gather and contribute relevant data. For example, the UK report noted the following (and see Lawrence, Chapter 12, this volume).

At least 60 000 people routinely gather biodiversity data in the UK. The majority of them are volunteers organised into many national and local societies and recording schemes whose work is largely collected into data holdings in a variety of formats ranging from simple field notes, to card indexes to electronic databases. Much of these data are eventually published as Atlases. The National Biodiversity Network Trust (www.nbn.org.uk), was created to facilitate the development of a network to link recorders of biodiversity data in the United Kingdom to all those who wish to use this information. In so doing the network will facilitate policy development, monitoring and reporting on the UK's obligations under the Convention on Biological Diversity.

(Source: CBD Secretariat, National Reports Analyzer, available at http://www.cbd.int/reports/analyzer.aspx)

Other biodiversity-related conventions

Other biodiversity-related conventions also provide frameworks for biodiversity assessment and monitoring activities. Some of the longer-standing agreements do not contain specific or detailed provisions on public participation, but may nonetheless provide for general obligations regarding raising public awareness. Moreover, as noted previously, they do generally provide more specific, if narrower, obligations than the CBD, which might lend them more readily to compliance monitoring. Indeed, non-governmental actors have played a significant role as providers of biodiversity information, and particularly as 'watchdogs', in respect of agreements such as the Convention on International Trade in Endangered Species.

Range state agreements under the Convention on Migratory Species, such as the 1995 African-Eurasian Waterbird Agreement and the 1991 Agreement on the Conservation of Populations of European Bats, contain general public awareness provisions. The Ramsar Convention on Wetlands has established a programme on Communication, Education and Public Awareness (CEPA) for 2003–2008 (and had established an earlier outreach programme), and the Strategic Plan for that Convention recognizes the critical importance of CEPA for pursuing the Ramsar Convention's objectives. The CEPA programme notes an evolving approach within the Convention to wetland management planning that includes community participation and education, as well as evidence of rapidly growing knowledge of participatory techniques within the Convention (Ramsar Convention, Resolution VIII.31, Annex I, paragraph 49(e)).

The African Convention on the Conservation of Nature and Natural Resources, revised in 2003, contains more specific provisions requiring parties to provide procedural rights in respect of environmental information, public participation in decision-making and access to justice (Article XVI). This approach reflects more recent developments in the Rio Declaration and Aarhus Convention, discussed below, seeking to enshrine such rights in law. The African Convention also requires parties to enable active participation by local communities in the process of planning and management of natural resources upon which they depend, with a view to creating local incentives for conservation (Article XVII). Parties are also called upon to promote environmental education, training and awareness creation at all levels, and to utilize to this end the educational and training value of conservation areas and the experience of local communities (Article XX).

The significance of the provisions these agreements contain on public awareness and participation depends largely upon the extent to which they are implemented by government parties and may be relied upon by citizens at the national level. They provide at least general support, as a matter of policy, for public participation in biodiversity-related matters.

International agreements and instruments addressing public participation

Some international agreements and non-legally binding instruments address public participation in environmental matters generally.

Principle 10 of the Rio Declaration on Environment and Development provides the following.

> Environmental issues are best handled with participation of all concerned citizens, at the relevant level. At the national level, each individual shall have appropriate access to information concerning the environment that is held by public authorities, including information on hazardous materials and activities in their communities, and the opportunity to participate in decision-making processes. States shall facilitate and encourage public awareness and participation by making information widely available. Effective access to judicial and administrative proceedings, including redress and remedy, shall be provided.

While the Rio Declaration is non-binding, the language of Principle 10 provides strong support for the rights of access to information and participation in environmental decision-making. It has catalysed a range of international actions, including the Access Initiative and PP10 (the Partnership for

Principle 10)[12] established in the context of the World Summit for Sustainable Development in 2002, which monitor the development of systems at the national level for public access to information and participation and access to justice.

At the regional level, within the UN-Economic Commission for Europe, a legally binding instrument on public participation has been adopted, the 1998 Aarhus Convention on Access to Information, Public Participation in Decision-making and Access to Justice in Environmental Matters. The Aarhus Convention focuses on securing procedural rights for members of the public in relation to environmental matters, rather than on establishing substantive rules to protect the environment. It provides, subject to certain limitations, for a right of access to environmental information held by public authorities.[13] As regards public participation, it specifically requires parties: to provide for public participation in decision-making on proposed activities which may have a significant effect on the environment; to provide for public participation in the preparation of plans and programmes relating to the environment; and to promote public participation during the preparation of laws and regulations. In respect of each of these the Convention sets out more detailed procedural requirements or guidelines. For decision-making on proposed activities, these include: timely notification of the public; the provision of information about the proposed activities; procedures for public consultation; taking into account the outcome of public participation; and informing the public of the final decision taken (Article 6). While the Aarhus Convention does not directly address public participation in monitoring activities, it supports the role of the public in all levels of decision making in environmental matters and acknowledges the importance of the involvement of all stakeholders in environmental issues.

The Aarhus Convention is generally concerned with securing rights and obligations at the national level. However, the parties have also made a commitment to promote the application of the principles of the Aarhus Convention in international environmental decision-making processes and within the framework of international organizations dealing with environmental matters (Aarhus Convention, Article 3(7)). A set of guidelines has been adopted relating to this issue (Aarhus Convention, Decision II/4, 2005). These provisions support procedures and mechanisms for participation in international processes mentioned above.

---

[12] See http://www.accessinitiative.org/ and www.pp10.org, respectively.
[13] However, for a study of the effect of the Aarhus Convention on recording biodiversity data in the UK, see Lawrence, Chapter 12, this volume.

Conclusions

Effective implementation of the CBD and related agreements at the national level depends upon sound information about the status of biodiversity, as a basis for the implementation and adaptation of national biodiversity strategies and action plans. The CBD, and other biodiversity-related agreements, as well as international instruments addressing public participation in environmental matters more broadly, emphasize the importance of public awareness, stakeholder involvement and the role of local communities in the conservation and sustainable use of biodiversity, and can thus provide support for various forms of participation in biodiversity assessment and monitoring at the national level. The integration of participatory approaches to biodiversity monitoring could assist in enhancing the global-local linkages in the CBD and related instruments. At the international level, a significant opportunity for such inputs currently exists in relation to the 2010 Biodiversity Target.

Participatory approaches to biodiversity assessment and monitoring could provide, and in numerous countries are providing, important inputs to national identification and monitoring efforts, and to evaluation of the effectiveness of measures taken, by contributing detailed knowledge of specific species, habitats or ecosystems and monitoring changes over time.

Acknowledgements

The author would like to thank Tony Gross and Anna Lawrence for comments on an earlier version of this chapter. Any errors remain the responsibility of the author.

REFERENCES

Boyle, A. (1996). The Rio Convention on Biological Diversity. In *International Law and the Conservation of Biological Diversity*, eds. M. Bowman and C. Redgwell. London, The Hague, Boston: Kluwer Law International, pp. 33–49.

Chayes, A. and Handler Chayes, A. (1995). *The New Sovereignty: Compliance with International Regulatory Agreements*. Cambridge: Harvard University Press.

Churchill, R. and Ulfstein, G. (2000). Autonomous institutional arrangements in Multilateral Environmental Agreements: a little-noticed phenomenon in international law. *American Journal of International Law* **94**, 623–659.

Convention on Biological Diversity. (2007). Report of the Ad Hoc Working Group on Review of Implementation of the Convention on the Work of its Second Meeting, document UNEP/CBD/COP/9/4, 26 July 2007. Available at: http://www.cbd.int.

Desai, B. (2004). *Institutionalizing International Environmental Law*. Ardsley, NY: Transnational Publishers.

Ecologic (2006). *The Potsdam Recommendations on the Convention on Biological Diversity, Report of the Workshop on Implementation of the Convention on Biological Diversity*, Potsdam, Germany, 13–15 December 2006. Available at http://www.ecologic.de/download/projekte/950–999/998/998-potsdam-recommendations.pdf.

Glowka, L., Burhenne-Guilmin, F., Synge, H., McNeely, J. and Gundling, L. (1994). *A Guide to the Convention on Biological Diversity*. Gland, Cambridge: IUCN the World Conservation Union.

Gross, T. (2005). *A Guide for Countries Preparing Third National Reports to the Convention on Biological Diversity*. United Nations University, Institute of Advanced Studies, UNDP/GEF Unit.

Gross, T., Johnston, S. and Barber, C. (2006). *The Convention on Biological Diversity: Understanding and Influencing the Process*. United Nations University Institute of Advanced Studies.

Lawrence, A. and Turnhout, E. (2005). *Personal meaning in the public space: the bureaucratisation of biodiversity data in the UK and the Netherlands*. Available at http://www.eci.ox.ac.uk.

McGraw, D. (2002). The Story of the Biodiversity Convention: from negotiation to implementation. In *Governing Global Biodiversity: the Evolution and Implementation of the CBD*, ed. P. Le Prestre. Aldershot: Ashgate, pp. 7–38.

Sands, P. (2003). *Principles of International Environmental Law*, 2nd edition. Cambridge: Cambridge University Press.

Secretariat of the Convention on Biological Diversity. (2005). *Handbook of the Convention on Biological Diversity*, 3rd edition.

Decisions adopted by the Conference of the Parties to the CBD

CBD Decision IV/10, Measures for Implementing the Convention on Biological Diversity (1998)

CBD Decision V/6 Ecosystem Approach (2000)

CBD Decision VI/8 Global Taxonomy Initiative (2002)

CBD Decision VI/19 Communication, Education and Public Awareness (2002)

CBD Decision VI/26 Strategic Plan for the Convention on Biological Diversity (2002)

CBD Decision VII/16 Article 8(j) and Related provisions (2004)

CBD Decision VII/30 Strategic Plan – Future Evaluation of Progress (2004)

CBD Decision VIII/28 Impact Assessment: voluntary guidelines on biodiversity-inclusive impact assessment (2006)

Other MEA decisions and resolutions referred to in this chapter

Aarhus Convention on Access to Information, Public Participation in Decision-making and Access to Justice in Environmental Matters, Decision, II/4 (2005)

Ramsar Convention on Wetlands of International Importance especially as Waterfowl Habitat, Resolution VIII.31 (2002)

Websites of biodiversity-related conventions

1992 Convention on Biological Diversity www.cbd.int

1971 Ramsar Convention on Wetlands of International Importance www.ramsar.org

1973 Convention on Trade on Endangered Species of Wild Fauna and Flora (CITES) www.cites.org

1979 Bonn Convention on Migratory Species www.cms.int

1972 World Heritage Convention http://whc.unesco.org/

The 1992 Rio Declaration on Environment and Development is available at: http://www.un.org/documents/ga/conf151/aconf15126-1annex1.htm (site visited 5 December 2007).

3

The Millennium Ecosystem Assessment: a multi-scale assessment for global stakeholders

CIARA RAUDSEPP-HEARNE AND DORIS CAPISTRANO

Introduction

Government requests for information about the implications of ecosystem change for achieving social and economic goals piled up in the wake of four international environmental conventions, leading researchers and policy advisers to conduct 'one of the most ambitious ecological studies' to date, the Millennium Ecosystem Assessment (MA) between 2001 and 2005 (Tallis and Kareiva, 2006a). The aim was to assess the consequences of ecosystem change for human well-being and to establish the scientific basis for actions needed to enhance the conservation and sustainable use of ecosystems. Principle users were the international environmental conventions, such as the Convention on Biological Diversity (CBD), but the multi-disciplinary group of assessment leaders designed it to also meet the needs of the business community, the health sector, non-governmental organizations, and indigenous peoples. About 1300 participants contributed to the process as authors, and the end products included technical reports and summaries aimed at specific user groups.[1]

The MA was conceived as a multi-scale assessment, with interlinked assessments undertaken at local, watershed, national, regional, and global scales. Thus, in addition to providing global-scale information, 33 subglobal assessments aimed to meet the information needs of users[2] in the regions where they were undertaken. By conducting the assessment at multiple scales, the

---

[1] Full findings are available online at www.maweb.org.
[2] We define users as the target audiences of the assessment reports, and stakeholders as any person or group that has an interest in the assessment process or content/findings of the assessment reports.

Taking Stock of Nature: Participatory Biodiversity Assessment for Policy, Planning and Practice, ed. Anna Lawrence. Published by Cambridge University Press. © Cambridge University Press 2010.

assessment team hoped to both improve the quality of information and increase the relevance of the findings for decision-makers working at different levels of governance (Zermoglio *et al.*, 2005; Wilbanks, 2006). This approach required different processes at different scales in order to maintain the credibility, legitimacy and relevance of the information in the eyes of these different end users of the reports. These processes emphasized stakeholder participation – to focus the content of the report, improve the information in the reports, and disseminate both the approach and the findings of the assessment broadly.

As the coordinator and co-chair of the Subglobal Working Group of the MA, the authors of this chapter observed firsthand the challenges and rewards of working at multiple scales with many stakeholders. In this chapter we analyse the processes that the MA actors used to understand and respond to diverse information needs. We draw on information from working group discussions, process documents, MA reports and academic literature, as well as our own observations of the global and subglobal assessment processes. After introducing the central concepts and core principles around which the assessment processes were built, we focus particularly on how biodiversity was assessed at the global scale and then at subglobal scales within the MA.

The ecosystem service approach

The MA conceptual framework is anthropocentric by design, and focuses on the contribution of ecosystem services to human well-being (MA, 2003). The 'ecosystem services' concept was developed in order to make explicit the connections between ecosystem functions and human well-being (Ehrlich, Ehrlich and Holdren, 1977; Daily, 1997). Ecosystem services are the benefits people obtain from ecosystems, such as food, water, flood control, climate regulation, and spiritual and recreational benefits (MA, 2003). While humans have always depended on nature, we have historically taken ecosystem services for granted because they are 'free', or at least not accounted for in traditional markets (Daily, 1997; MA, 2003; Tallis and Kareiva, 2006b). Daily (1997) describes how, in the mid 1990s, some conservationists felt that they had failed to convince the general public of the importance of ecosystem contributions to social and economic goals, for example by providing basic materials for a good life, for health and security, and for good social relations (MA, 2003; Butler and Oluoch-Kosura, 2006). The use of the ecosystem service concept by the MA was intended to appeal to the public, governments and the private sector about the pragmatic need to maintain functioning ecosystems. While some conservationists have criticized the approach as 'commodifying nature'

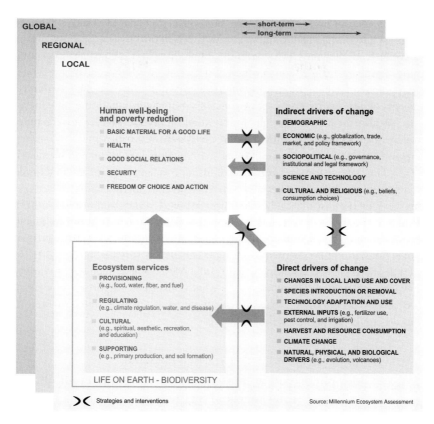

Figure 3.1. MA Conceptual Framework.

(McCauley, 2006), many have found the concept to be extremely useful for communicating the benefits of ecosystem conservation to diverse stakeholder groups (*Economist*, 2005; MA, 2005a; Reid *et al.*, 2006b).

Figure 3.1 presents the MA Conceptual Framework, that relates drivers of change to changes in biodiversity, ecosystem services and human well-being (MA, 2005b). Changes in drivers that indirectly affect ecosystems, such as population and technology, can lead to changes in drivers directly affecting ecosystems, such as the catch of fish or the application of fertilizers to increase food production. These result in changes to biodiversity and consequently to ecosystem services, thereby affecting human well-being. These interactions can take place at more than one scale and can cross scales, which is another reason for conducting a multi-scale assessment (Wilbanks, 2006). Actions can be taken either to respond to negative changes or to enhance positive changes at almost all points in this framework (MA, 2005b).

The MA adopted the CBD's definition of biodiversity: 'the variability among living organisms from all sources including terrestrial, marine and other aquatic ecosystems, and the ecological complexes of which they are part, including diversity within and among species and diversity within and among ecosystems.' Within the MA Conceptual Framework, biodiversity underpins the functioning of ecosystems and the flow of ecosystem services valued by human beings (MA, 2003; Schulze and Mooney, 1993; Loreau, Naeem and Inchausti, 2002). This human-centred application of the concept emphasizes functional diversity and redundancy as most important to the steady supply of ecosystem services (Peterson, Allen and Holling, 1998; Kremen and Ostfeld, 2005). The MA framework also recognizes non-functional aspects relating to human well-being, such as aesthetic benefits, environmental education and spiritual connections to nature (known as cultural ecosystem services in the MA). In practice, biodiversity assessment within the MA was conducted in a variety of ways, and with different views on what constituted important aspects of biodiversity, depending on the scale and location of the assessment, as well as who was involved in the assessment.

Stakeholder participation in assessments – building credibility, relevance and legitimacy

A scientific assessment is a social process to bring the findings of science to bear on the needs of decision-makers, and is particularly useful when there is uncertainty or controversy about a subject (MA, 2003). How information is gathered and contextualized is just as important as the information itself (Farrell, VanDeveer and Jager, 2001). For example, the Global Biodiversity Assessment (Heywood, 1995), tailored for the CBD, was produced without the Convention's involvement and was thus largely ignored despite its authoritative findings. Interactions with stakeholders allow assessment leaders to focus on the most relevant questions and get buy-in from assessment users.

The MA design team built the assessment process around the interacting and often synergistic principles of relevance, credibility and legitimacy, which have been established in assessment literature as key characteristics of information gathering processes (Clark and Dickson, 1999; Farrell and Jager, 2005; Mitchell *et al.*, 2006). Scientific information is relevant if it is perceived to be of value to particular groups who might use it to change management approaches, behaviour, or policy decisions (Cash *et al.*, 2003). It is credible if peers within the scientific community perceive the technical information and conclusions to be authoritative and believable (Clark and Dickson, 1999). It is legitimate if the process of assembling the information is perceived to be fair and open to input from key political constituencies, such as the private sector, governments and civil society (Farrell and Jager, 2005).

The MA global and subglobal assessments each had their own set of users and stakeholders with unique dynamics that required different approaches for achieving relevance, credibility and legitimacy. The participation of world-renowned scientists from top institutions was considered to be important in building credibility at the global scale, while the involvement of local people with intimate knowledge of their environment was important for building credibility and relevance at the community scale, for example in MA subglobal assessments in Vilcanota, Peru; Bajo Chirripo, Costa Rica; and Kristianstad Vattenrike in Sweden (Olsson, Folke and Hahn, 2004; MA, 2005a). For the global level assessment, the MA synthesized information from the scientific literature and relevant peer reviewed datasets and models. At the subglobal level, however, the general lack of data on ecosystem services sometimes made it necessary to generate data for the assessment and incorporate different types of knowledge into the analysis (MA, 2005a).

Defining biodiversity and assessment approaches at the global scale

Assessment design and stakeholder participation

An initial scoping stage began at the World Resources Institute, but the MA eventually became an independent project with an international Board of Advisors, a Science Panel and an independent Review Panel, made up of people with different expertise who were invited by the assessment initiators to participate in the design and governance of the MA. The design team and Board of Advisors were composed of representatives from the science community, the private sector, government and non-governmental organizations and indigenous communities. The design team canvassed additional decision-makers around the world to determine key questions and uncertainties related to ecosystem change and its repercussions for human well-being (Bennett, Peterson and Levitt, 2005). Those invited to participate as authors were chosen to be regionally representative and include a mix of social and physical scientists, men and women.

Conducting an environmental assessment at the global scale automatically favours some types of questions, issues and stakeholder groups simply by setting boundaries and defining what types of data and methods of analysis are suitable for that scale (Lebel, 2006). To date, subglobal decision-makers have found little use for the coarse resolution findings of the global MA (Tallis and Kareiva, 2006a). The design team was challenged to produce reports that would be useful to a very diverse stakeholder group, and they responded by focusing the subject matter of the assessment on ecosystem services and development issues that were broadly relevant across a diversity of ecosystems, geographic areas and cultures (MA, 2005c). While the priority in the MA was to develop strongly credible scientific information that would feed directly into the international environmental conventions, the design team acknowledged the importance of incorporating multiple worldviews and different types of knowledge into the analyses, and decided that a subglobal component was needed to meet wider user needs (MA, 2003). This was regarded as an experiment in dealing with spatial and temporal scales in the assessment process (Wilbanks, 2006).

The global design team's expectations for testing scientific theory on scaling were not met however, because the subglobal assessments were ultimately designed by independent subglobal teams with the needs of local stakeholders in mind. The issues that were prioritized at smaller scales did not match the interests of global stakeholders, limiting the comparability and integration of findings across scales (Lebel, 2006). In addition, global stakeholders did not consider the processes at the subglobal scales to be stringent enough to ensure the credibility of the findings. Exceptions included assessments in Southern Africa, Portugal and Sweden, which were ultimately published in peer-reviewed journals (Elmqvist *et al.*, 2004; Olsson *et al.*, 2004; Bohensky and Lynam, 2005; Pereira *et al.*, 2005a,b; van Jaarsveld *et al.*, 2005). The wider set of subglobal assessments did yield information that was valuable to global stakeholders about the assessment process and people's relationships with ecosystem services across scales (MA, 2005a; Hein *et al.*, 2006). Understanding the interests of stakeholders at different scales was considered to be crucial to identifying the most promising policy responses and actions to safeguard ecosystem services (Bohensky and Lynam, 2005; Tallis and Kareiva, 2006a).

The main user of biodiversity findings of the global assessment was the CBD, whose representatives were highly involved in the design and assessment processes. The CBD was already using ecosystem approaches to conservation, recognizing the need to understand complex feedbacks between humans and ecosystems and incorporate sustainable development into conservation plans

(Carpenter, Bennett and Peterson, 2006a; CBD, 2007). The CBD Conference of the Parties (COP) encouraged Parties to participate in the MA, and officials of the Subsidiary Body on Scientific, Technical, and Technological Advice (SBSTTA) were represented on the MA Board. Parties to the CBD provided review comments on underlying chapters of the assessment as well as the biodiversity synthesis report. SBSTTA has since prepared recommendations to the COP concerning the implications of MA findings for future CBD work (MA, 2005b). This is an example of a successful stakeholder process where the global scale of assessment was appropriate for meeting the information needs of the CBD.

How biodiversity was assessed at the global scale

The global assessment attempted to look at the implications for human well-being of changes in both the diversity of genes, species, and ecosystems in and of themselves, as well as of changes in particular components of that diversity. Species diversity is valuable because the presence of a variety of species helps to increase the resilience of an ecosystem in the face of a changing environment (Peterson *et al.*, 1998; Kremen and Ostfeld, 2005). However, a component of that diversity, such as particular medicinal plant species, may be valuable as a biological resource. Biodiversity change can impact people through losses in total biodiversity or losses in a particular component of biodiversity. Each problem requires individual attention and research, as well as its own management goals and policies (MA, 2005b).

Researchers assessed biodiversity at coarse resolutions in order to draw global conclusions, making the findings broadly applicable and scientifically credible, but not specifically relevant to particular locations or populations. The global design team chose to assess ecosystem services that are shared among many parts of the world (MA, 2005c; Lebel, 2006). Assessment teams focused on issues such as global and regional species loss and the principal drivers of biodiversity loss, and these types of broad issues were included in the global scenarios that examined trends in ecosystem services and biodiversity into the future. For example, at the request of the CBD, the MA provided an assessment of the biodiversity impacts of forest fragmentation. The global assessment succeeded in providing high-quality and relevant technical information to stakeholders interested in developing policies at global and national scales, and is considered to represent the current state of knowledge on ecosystem change and the implications of biodiversity loss for human well-being (Dooley, 2005; Tallis and Kareiva, 2006b).

The global assessment of biodiversity was constrained by a lack of knowledge about the links between biodiversity and ecosystem services. While biodiversity was considered to underpin many of the important ecosystem services assessed, the links were often presented only implicitly because most of the mechanisms linking biodiversity and aspects of biodiversity to ecosystem services have not been well-studied (Balmford and Bond, 2005; Kremen and Ostfeld, 2005; MA, 2005c). For example, recent studies establish links between biodiversity and pollination services, but the role of biodiversity in the provisioning of freshwater is less established (Kremen and Ostfeld, 2005; MA, 2005b). Another shortcoming was the lack of data on cultural and regulating services, in which biodiversity is assumed to play an important role (MA, 2005a; Clewell and Aronson, 2006; Plieninger, Hochtl and Spek, 2006; Rodriguez *et al.*, 2006). While at subglobal scales this type of information is available through anthropological, social and political studies, it is difficult to generalize about these links at the global scale (MA, 2005a; Berkes and Davidson-Hunt, 2006; Wilbanks, 2006). The assessment highlighted the need to understand the mechanisms relating biodiversity to the supply of a range of ecosystem services, and the MA may influence the biodiversity research agenda in this direction (Carpenter *et al.*, 2006b).

Defining biodiversity and assessment approaches at subglobal scales

Assessment design and stakeholder participation

The global MA found that for most ecosystem services, local loss of biodiversity (species population reduction or local extinction) is most significant for human well-being (MA, 2005b). The 33 subglobal assessments provided an opportunity to discover how biodiversity loss affects the flow of ecosystem services and the well-being of people in different parts of the world. The set of subglobal assessments was not designed to provide a representative sample of ecosystems or societies (MA, 2005a) but was developed through a combination of stakeholder interest in undertaking the assessment, interest in using the findings, and availability of resources to undertake the assessment. They ranged from community assessments (in Peru, India and South Africa), to national assessments (in Portugal and Norway), to regional assessments (southern Africa and Tropical Forest Margins).[3]

---

[3] See MA (2005a) for descriptions of all the MA subglobal assessments.

The MA global design team drew up broad guidelines for conducting subglobal assessments, and had certain expectations of how the subglobal assessments would be designed and carried out, and what kind of information would result (Lebel, 2006). The initial broad guidelines were further refined with inputs from the earliest subglobal assessment teams. Owing to the bottom-up design of the subglobal assessments, the global leaders ultimately had little influence on the design of the assessments, except in the few cases where the MA supplied large amounts of funding (for example in the southern African MA subglobal assessment, see van Jaarsveld *et al.*, 2005). Initial attempts by the global design team to specify the locations and design of the subglobal assessments were derailed due to financial and capacity constraints (Gitay *et al.*, 2005). Thus the subglobal assessments were truly designed at the community, national or regional levels to meet the needs of specific stakeholders at these scales. In the eyes of many global stakeholders, the greater local relevance and legitimacy resulted in a trade-off of less credibility and relevance at the global scale (Reid *et al.*, 2006a).

The global MA leaders specified the need for high user involvement in subglobal assessments as one of the design criteria. Most of the subglobal assessment teams ended up strongly believing that the capacity building and mutual learning from the assessment process were just as valuable as the resulting information (Gitay *et al.*, 2005). The emphasis placed on developing relevance and legitimacy in the assessment processes meant that a lot of time and resources were dedicated to interactions with stakeholders. The outcomes included high levels of knowledge sharing, dissemination of the MA approach, and learning about the science–policy interface. However, a cross-evaluation of the subglobal assessments also found that the information developed in the assessments was usually not designed to feed into specific decisions (such as a specific development plan or policy) and therefore the immediate relevance of the reports was unclear to the users.

At the subglobal level, it was often people who had had some contact with the global MA process that catalyzed an assessment. Researchers were quick to grasp the potential of assessment work, and in most cases initiated the assessment process (Gitay *et al.*, 2005). In some cases local NGOs initiated the process (for example in Peru, Costa Rica and Western Canada). The Conceptual Framework of the MA was an important tool for developing an understanding among other stakeholders of the potential benefits of an integrated ecosystem assessment, and for demonstrating the roles of biodiversity and ecosystem services in the attainment of social and economic goals (MA, 2005a). Exploratory workshops preceded the majority of the subglobal assessments and strongly shaped the processes of these assessments (MA, 2005a; Pereira *et al.*, 2005a).

For example, in Sao Paulo, Brazil, the Forestry Institute convened a large set of users in a workshop to explore environment-related uncertainties in their decision-making processes (MA, 2005a). In general, governments, non-governmental organizations, research institutions, and the private sector were canvassed and those that showed interest were invited to become involved in the assessment, usually in an advisory capacity. With a few exceptions, national governments and the private sector were not highly involved, either because the design team lacked access to leaders in these sectors, or the leaders lacked interest (Gitay *et al.*, 2005). Olsson *et al.* (2004) provide a good account of the type of networking used to establish an assessment team and stakeholder group in a community, in this case for the MA assessment in southern Sweden.

The subglobal assessments differed widely in terms of the roles stakeholders were assigned in the process (MA, 2005a). Reasons for including stakeholders included the desire to: communicate policy options to stakeholders, encourage communication among stakeholders, create buy-in to the assessment process, advocate environmental concerns, increase the diversity of perspectives in analysis, improve understanding of social processes, ensure relevance, and safeguard the rights of stakeholders (Peterson *et al.*, 2003; Olsson *et al.*, 2004; Bohensky and Lynam, 2005; Cundill, Fabricius and Marti, 2005; MA, 2005a; Pereira *et al.*, 2005a; van Jaarsveld *et al.*, 2005). The definition of users and stakeholders tended to expand or evolve in the course of an assessment, as better understanding of the dynamics of the ecosystems being assessed uncovered new or different sets of users and stakeholders (MA, 2005a).

Assessment leaders found it difficult to balance managing stakeholder communication processes with advancing on the scientific assessments (Gitay *et al.*, 2005). Stakeholder involvement was a global design requirement of the subglobal assessments, and was embraced at the subglobal level, but often by scientists with little experience in managing stakeholder processes. This sometimes resulted in either superficial stakeholder involvement accompanied by the timely publication of credible scientific reports, or in stakeholder processes that became bogged down by stakeholder interactions (Gitay *et al.*, 2005). Stakeholders sometimes influenced the content and the design of the assessments throughout the entire process, which increased the legitimacy of those assessments, but had negative impacts on the assessments' progress.

How the concept of biodiversity was applied at the subglobal scale

The subglobal assessments tackled particular components of biodiversity based on what was relevant to their respective stakeholders and/or feasible to assess based on available data. For instance, the Sinai assessment focused on the well-being of Bedouin communities and therefore on the diversity and abundance of medicinal plants. The Caribbean Sea assessment focused on the remaining cover of live coral that supports the fisheries and tourism industries (MA, 2005a).

Biodiversity in and of itself was assessed to some extent by almost all subglobal assessments, using species inventories, biodiversity indices and land cover mapping (Pereira *et al.*, 2005b; Biggs, Reyers and Scholes, 2006). Many subglobal assessments treated biodiversity as a quasi-'service' in its own right, surprisingly given the strong functional orientation of the underlying MA ecosystem service assessment approach and the limited resources available. This meant that, in addition to examining the biodiversity underpinnings of specific ecosystem services (which is how biodiversity fits into the MA Conceptual Framework), assessment teams considered general biodiversity as a service important to stakeholders. The focus on biodiversity partly reflects the fact that most subglobal assessments were led by conservation scientists (Gitay *et al.*, 2005). In addition, the lack of data at subglobal scales made it very difficult to establish credible links between ecosystem services, human well-being and biodiversity. Because biodiversity was seen as underpinning most ecosystem services, it was used as an indicator of ecosystem integrity, and future potential to generate socio-economically important ecosystem services. Components of biodiversity also served as indicators of the potential of ecosystems to continue supplying cultural services, which were difficult to assess (MA, 2005a,b). A final motivation was the role biodiversity plays in providing safety nets and resilience to populations relying on changing ecosystems, extremely relevant in contexts with high levels of poverty. Most subglobal assessments found that diversity of species, food sources, and landscapes serve as savings banks and buffers to enable people to cope with change during adverse times (Folke *et al.*, 2005).

How biodiversity was assessed at the subglobal scale

Subglobal teams assessed biodiversity in substantially different ways from those used by the global assessment. While the global assessment sought to establish the state of current knowledge on biodiversity loss using available literature on this topic, the subglobal assessments sought to provide specific information to policy-makers, and in most cases this information did not already exist. One of the most important weaknesses identified by subglobal assessments was the lack of data in the study areas with which to assess the condition and trends of ecosystem services and biodiversity (MA, 2005a). Some subglobal assessments filled these data gaps through primary data collection or expert opinions (MA, 2005a). The participation of stakeholders in the collection of primary data somewhat redefined their roles as stakeholders and 'users' of the assessment information and went against norms of independent peer review (Reid *et al.*, 2006a).

The subglobal assessments made extensive use of participatory approaches in the collection of data, with participants ranging from scientific experts at regional scales to community members at local scales (MA, 2005a). In some cases the approaches were extractive or consultative, and pulled information directly from local people about their surroundings (for example in a local assessment in South Africa and in the Salar de Atacama in Chile). In other cases, local people became core members of the assessment teams and helped to focus and guide the assessment (for example in Vilcanota, Peru, in southern Sweden, and in the Western Ghats of India). These approaches allowed for the collection of forms of data not available in the literature, for example, from traditional and indigenous knowledge at the local scale (Pereira *et al.*, 2005a). At broader scales, data gaps in the conditions and trends of various ecosystem services were sometimes filled through workshops where experts and stakeholders were asked to qualitatively assess the condition of ecosystem services (Pereira *et al.*, 2005b). The assessments used several techniques of participant involvement, including focus group workshops, semi-structured interviews with key informants, interactive theatre, participatory mapping, ranking and scoring, trend lines, problem trees, role-playing, and seasonal calendars (Cundill *et al.*, 2005; Pereira *et al.*, 2005a; Evans *et al.*, 2006). In a Southern Africa community assessment, community members were asked to rank various ecosystem services and their importance in the region and then use numbers and sizes of stones to score the water quality and quantity in various areas over the past 40 years (Shackleton and Fabricius, 2004). Despite the use of various systems of peer review such as triangulation of information between community members, between communities, or using scientific literature, some of the subglobal information was not validated (or the validation methods were not well-documented), limiting the credibility of these assessment findings to stakeholders across scales (Reid *et al.*, 2006a).

In order to develop information that was relevant to specific locations, subglobal assessments also elaborated or applied novel scientific methods, such as the Biodiversity Intactness Index in the Southern Africa regional assessment (Biggs *et al.*, 2006), irreplaceability in the Portugal assessment (Pressey and Taffs, 2001; Pereira *et al.*, 2005b), conservation status of ecosystems in Southern Africa Gariep Basin assessment (Pressey and Taffs, 2001; Reyers, 2004), the Reef Condition Index in the Papua New Guinea assessment (MA, 2005a), and the Ecological Integrity index in Coastal British Columbia assessment (Holt and Sutherland, 2004; MA, 2005a).

Information and process outcomes of the subglobal assessments

Reid *et al.* (2006a) make the point that 'conventional science based on Western paradigms and systems of knowledge is no longer adequate to deal with complexities of environmental management' and that new tools to bridge knowledge systems and scales are required in order to integrate assessment findings across scales and better inform decision-making. The use of participatory approaches, different types of knowledge and data, and local and regional expert input was one of the strengths of the subglobal assessments. Some stakeholders knew a tremendous amount about how their systems work, ecologically as well as socially (Cundill *et al.*, 2005). For example, Swedish communities in Kristianstad Vattenrike held decades of observations about flooding patterns of their fields, and also knew that local interest in preserving endangered birds and cultural traditions related to farming livelihoods would be a strong incentive for local ecosystem management (Olsson *et al.*, 2004; MA, 2005a). Local knowledge was often found to be more integrated compared to traditional academic analyses, giving insight into the complex links between ecosystem services and human well-being in ways that were often lacking in the global MA. Local knowledge is sometimes considered to be more holistic and integrated in terms of understanding linkages and feedbacks within systems because of the length of time communities have spent observing and adapting to change (Berkes and Turner, 2006) although in the MA this information was difficult to validate.

Many of the processes and patterns in ecosystem service provision identified would not otherwise be evident from coarse-grained analysis. For example, the role of biodiversity as a risk avoidance mechanism for local communities is frequently hidden until local assessments are conducted. An analysis of the local scale MA assessments found that they identified key local resources in small patches within ecosystems (even where coarser-scale assessments showed resource depletion) and provided indications of appropriate times for management interventions (Folke *et al.*, 2005). Local assessments found that environmental degradation at the local scale becomes increasingly tied to a suite of trade-offs associated with the provision of ecosystem services upon which livelihoods depend (MA, 2005a). This suggests that it is important to include an analysis of who depends on biodiversity, and what components of biodiversity are important to people's health, livelihoods and general well-being in an assessment of biodiversity and ecosystem services. The components of biodiversity that people depend upon for very basic standards of living can be considered hotspots for conflict and conservation; these especially require policy attention (MA, 2005a).

The subglobal assessments also provided insights into the intangible aspects of ecosystem services. Ecosystems provide a sense of place and identity for local people, in addition to other ecosystem services, and spiritual and cultural values of ecosystems are as important as other services for many local communities (Elmqvist *et al.*, 2004; Cundill *et al.*, 2005; MA, 2005a). The importance placed on locally defined and valued cultural services such as aesthetic appreciation, recreation, and inspiration, often leads to ingrained local management practices that conserve ecosystem functions (Elmqvist *et al.*, 2004; Colding, Lundberg and Folke, 2006). For example, the Vilcanota, Peru, assessment was unwilling to classify the Quechua culture and spiritual relationship with the environment as a cultural service, and chose instead to centre the entire assessment on culture and spirituality (Cundill *et al.*, 2005). In this case, spiritual beliefs are central to human interactions with the environment and cannot be separated from how soil or water is managed and the resulting condition and trends in these ecosystem services. Stakeholder participation in the assessment of cultural services is critical, in order to define locally relevant cultural services and also to assess their state. Because these services are not easily quantified in terms of value to human well-being, stakeholders can play an important role in qualitative assessment.

The identification of drivers of local biodiversity loss was an equally important outcome of subglobal assessments. It was possible to identify drivers affecting particular components or aspects of biodiversity most relevant to stakeholders at the subglobal scale (Peterson *et al.*, 2003; Cundill *et al.*, 2005; Pereira *et al.*, 2005a). In some cases, drivers of change were explored using participatory scenario exercises, a promising method for exploring values, uncertainties and management options related to ecosystem services and biodiversity (Peterson *et al.*, 2003; Evans *et al.*, 2006; Biggs *et al.*, 2007). Owing to resource constraints and confusion about methodology, only a few subglobal assessments attempted to build scenarios about the future; but we believe that scenario building is a very promising method for framing assessments in relation to important drivers, and more generally for bridging science and policy at subglobal scales (Peterson *et al.*, 2003; Bennett *et al.*, 2005; Bohensky, Reyers and van Jaarsveld, 2006; Biggs *et al.*, 2007; Tallis and Kareiva, 2006a).

Lessons learned across scales

The MA was an enormous undertaking, perhaps the most ambitious international science assessment to date. Lessons learned about the credibility, legitimacy and relevance of the assessment processes and findings at the global and subglobal scales will help to shape future assessment work. Currently there are no plans to repeat the global MA exercise; however, there is increasing demand for national and regional ecosystem service assessments.

Information about ecosystem services is complex and must be drawn from multiple disciplines, and preferably with the participation of diverse stakeholders. Some past assessments have focused their attention on the production of authoritative and credible technical reports. Recent research and practice have shown that underemphasizing relevance and legitimacy when gathering environmental information can lead to information that is largely ignored or underused (Farrell *et al.*, 2001; Farrell and Jager 2005; Mitchell *et al.*, 2006). Because of the rigorous assessment design of the global MA, including several rounds of peer review, the MA global reports are credible, and will impact international environmental policy, funding programmes, research agendas and public opinion on the importance of ecosystem services. It is important to continue to look at global biodiversity loss, which is relevant for future option values and for certain services such as genetic variability and bioprospecting. However, more context-relevant information and tools are needed in order to be relevant at subglobal scales, where most resource management decisions are made (Hein *et al.*, 2006; Tallis and Kareiva, 2006a). This is the principal impetus for initiating new subglobal assessments.

The ecosystem service concept, by its very nature, is more amenable to assessment at the subglobal scale. The key feature that distinguishes ecosystem services from ecosystem functions or processes is the 'explicit involvement of beneficiaries' (Chan *et al.*, 2006). With few exceptions, the beneficiaries of ecosystem services (and related elements of biodiversity) are found at the local or regional scale. It is therefore easier to develop relevance and legitimacy in stakeholder processes at these smaller scales where people can define what ecosystem services they benefit from and how (MA, 2005a; Hein *et al.*, 2006). Involving people in defining and assessing ecosystem services and biodiversity is an important communication and capacity building process and promotes the explicit exploration of the components of biodiversity that are important to specific populations. The subglobal approach supports the notion that stakeholders at different scales have different interests in ecosystem services and biodiversity (Hein *et al.*, 2006). For example, most small-scale assessments were particularly interested in components of biodiversity associated with livelihoods, medicine, food and other resources, while regional and national assessments conducted more general assessments of biodiversity. Assessments at all scales considered general biodiversity to be important as an indicator of a system's ability to continue to produce desired ecosystem services, which indicates that the concept of biodiversity is perhaps evolving from an abstract catchphrase to something more valuable in the eyes of stakeholders.

The subglobal assessments had a natural advantage over the global process in terms of maintaining relevance, but would have benefited from the more stringent design of the global process. Credibility at subglobal scales seemed to be more difficult to achieve than at the global scale, because issues of trust and communication between stakeholders and assessors created a stronger interaction between the legitimacy of the process and credibility of the findings. This interaction requires attention not only for the development of information gathering and validation rules, but also for an enhanced understanding of stakeholders' worldviews (MA, 2005a; Reid *et al.*, 2006a).

A major hurdle for ecosystem service and biodiversity assessment, at all scales, is a lack of data, and assessment approaches. This hurdle can sometimes be overcome through stakeholder participation in assessment, depending on what kind of information is needed. Both the subglobal and global assessments were more successful in the assessment of provisioning services such as food, fibre and fuel, than they were in assessing regulating and cultural services, with the exception of tourism. This gap is of concern as the condition of regulating services has direct implications for the condition of most other services (MA, 2005b). Some regulating services such as climate regulation and flood control require scientific assessment and the use of models in order to understand their dynamics. They therefore cannot usually be assessed through stakeholder knowledge alone.

The subglobal assessments found that cultural services were just as important in the lives of stakeholders as other services, but the definitions of cultural services, and the boundaries between these and other services, were unclear, leading to challenges in assessment (MA, 2005a). Apart from the uncertainty associated with the definition of various cultural services, there is a general lack of appropriate data, indicators, and tools with which to assess them (MA, 2005d). The emphasis placed on the importance of this category of services at the subglobal scale suggests that future assessments of biodiversity should not ignore the importance of the role of biodiversity in cultural practices, as this has direct policy implications.

Future subglobal assessments will need to sharply define assessment goals within their specific context, even as they build and refine new assessment tools. Most of the MA subglobal assessments were considered to be generally relevant to local stakeholders, but many did not design their processes to answer to the specific information needs of particular stakeholders (Gitay *et al.*, 2005). For example, it was not always clear whether the goal was to complete an inventory of ecosystem services important to a region, to assess the impact of changes in ecosystem services on specific development goals, or to empower and build capacity within an indigenous community to assess and manage resources autonomously. The resulting technical information was therefore not always immediately useful to decision-makers, although the group of subglobal assessments felt strongly that the level of nuanced understanding of social–ecological interactions developed through stakeholder involvement in finer scale assessments was just as important as some of the more technical findings that were sought by users (MA, 2005a).

The enormous scope of the MA required a great deal of experimentation with methods and approaches for assessing biodiversity and ecosystem services at multiple scales. The MA processes and outcomes benefited from broad participation of scientists and experts and from an openness to novel approaches and different forms of knowledge. The MA provides a useful conceptual framework for building common understanding among experts and stakeholders about the roles ecosystems play in our lives and how we might choose to manage them. The MA conceptual framework, along with comprehensive global baseline data on ecosystem services and a wealth of experience and lessons learned from the subglobal assessments, will provide a solid base on which to build future assessment processes.

Acknowledgements

We would like to offer our thanks to all who contributed to the Millenium Ecosystem Assessment Sub-Global Working Group.

REFERENCES

Balmford, A., and Bond, W. (2005). Trends in the state of nature and their implications for human well-being. *Ecology Letters* **8**, 1218–1234.

Bennett, E. M., Peterson, G. D. and Levitt, E. A. (2005). Looking to the future of ecosystem services. *Ecosystems* **8**, 125–132.

Berkes, F. and Davidson-Hunt, I. J. (2006). Biodiversity, traditional management systems, and cultural landscapes: examples from the boreal forest of Canada. *International Social Science Journal* **58**, 35–47.

Berkes, F. and. Turner, N. J. (2006). Knowledge, learning and the evolution of conservation practice for social-ecological system resilience. *Human Ecology* **34**, 479–494.

Biggs, R., Reyers, B. and Scholes, R. J. (2006). A biodiversity intactness score for South Africa. *South African Journal of Science* **102**, 277–283.

Biggs, O., Raudsepp-Hearne, C., Atkinson-Palombo, C. *et al.* (2007). Linking futures across scales: a dialog on multi-scale scenarios. *Ecology and Society* **12**(1), 17. Available at: http://www.ecologyandsociety.org/vol12/iss1/art17/

Bohensky, E. and Lynam, T. (2005). Evaluating responses in complex adaptive systems: Insights on water management from the Southern African Millennium Ecosystem Assessment (SAfMA). *Ecology and Society* **10**. Available at: http://www.ecologyandsociety.org/vol10/iss1/art11/

Bohensky, E. L., Reyers, B. and van Jaarsveld, A. S. (2006). Future ecosystem services in a Southern African river basin: a scenario planning approach to uncertainty. *Conservation Biology* **20**, 1051–1061.

Butler, C. D., and Oluoch-Kosura, W. (2006). Linking future ecosystem services and future human well-being. *Ecology and Society* **11**. Available at: http://www.ecologyandsociety.org/vol11/iss1/art30/

Carpenter, S. R., Bennett, E. M and Peterson, G. D. (2006a). Scenarios for ecosystem services: An overview. *Ecology and Society* **11**. Available at: http://www.ecologyandsociety.org/vol11/iss2/art32/

Carpenter, S. R., DeFries, R., Dietz, T. *et al.* (2006b). Millennium Ecosystem Assessment: Research needs. *Science* **314**, 257–258.

Cash, D. W., Clark, W. C., Alcock, F. *et al.* (2003). Knowledge systems for sustainable development. *Proceedings of the National Academy of Sciences of the United States of America* **100**, 8086–8091.

Convention on Biological Diversity (CBD) (2007). Available at http://biodiv.org/programmes/cross-cutting/ecosystem/background.asp

Chan, K. M. A., Shaw, M. R., Cameron, D. R., Underwood, E. C. and Daily. G. C. (2006). Conservation planning for ecosystem services. *Plos Biology* **4**, 2138–2152.

Clark, W. C. and Dickson, N. M. (1999). The global environmental assessment project: learning from efforts to link science and policy in an interdependent world. *Acclimations* **8**, 6–7.

Clewell, A. F. and Aronson, J. (2006). Motivations for the restoration of ecosystems. *Conservation Biology* **20**, 420–428.

Colding, J., Lundberg, J. and Folke, C. (2006). Incorporating green-area user groups in urban ecosystem management. *Ambio* **35**, 237–244.

Cundill, G. N. R., Fabricius, C. and Marti, N. (2005). Foghorns to the future: using knowledge and transdisciplinarity to navigate complex systems. *Ecology and Society* **10**. Available at: http://www.ecologyandsociety.org/vol10/iss2/art8/

Daily, G. C. (1997). *Nature's Services: Societal Dependence on Natural Ecosystems.* Washington D.C.: Island Press.

Dooley, E. E. (2005). Millennium Ecosystem Assessment. *Environmental Health Perspectives* **113**, A591–A591.

Economist (2005). Rescuing Environmentalism. *Economist*.

Ehrlich, P., Ehrlich, A. and Holdren, J. (1977). *Ecoscience: Population, Resources, Environment.* San Francisco: W. H. Freeman.

Elmqvist, T., Colding, J., Barthel, S. *et al.* (2004). The dynamics of social-ecological systems in urban landscapes – Stockholm and the National Urban Park, Sweden. In *Urban Biosphere and Society: Partnership of Cities*, eds. C. Alfsen-Norodom, B. Lane and M. Corry. New York: New York Academy of Sciences, pp. 308–322.

Evans, K., Velarde, S., Prieto, R. P. *et al.* (2006). *Field Guide to the Future: Four Ways for Communities to Think Ahead.* Nairobi: CIFOR, ASB, ICRAF.

Farrell, A., VanDeveer, S. D. and Jager, J. (2001). Environmental assessments: four under-appreciated elements of design. *Global Environmental Change* **11**, 311–333.

Farrell, A. E. and Jager, J. (2005). *Assessments of Regional and Global Environmental Risks: Designing Processes for the Effective Use of Science in Decisionmaking.* Washingon D.C.: RFF Press.

Folke, C., Fabricius, C., Cundill, G. and Schultz. L. (2005). Communities, ecosystems and livelihoods. In *Ecosystems and Human Well-being: Volume 4 – Multiscale Assessments.* Washington D.C.: Island Press, pp. 261–277.

Gitay, H., Raudsepp-Hearne, C., Blanco, H., Garcia, K. and Pereira, H. (2005). Assessment Process. In *Ecosystems and Human Well-being: Volume 4 – Multiscale Assessments.* Washington D.C.: Island Press, pp. 119–140.

Hein, L., van Koppen, K., de Groot, R. S. and van Ierland, E. C. (2006). Spatial scales, stakeholders and the valuation of ecosystem services. *Ecological Economics* **57**, 209–228.

Heywood, V. H. (Ed.) (1995). *Global Biodiversity Assessment. UNEP.* New York: Cambridge University Press.

Holt, R. F., and Sutherland, G. (2004). *Central Coast Coarse Filter Ecosystem Trends Risk Assessment.* Vancouver: Coast Information Team.

Kremen, C. and Ostfeld, R. S. (2005). A call to ecologists: measuring, analyzing, and managing ecosystem services. *Frontiers in Ecology and the Environment* **3**, 540–548.

Lebel, L. (2006). The politics of scale in environmental assessments. In *Bridging Scales and Knowledge Systems*, eds. W. V. Reid, F. Berkes, T. J. Wilbanks, and D. Capistrano. Washington D.C.: Island Press, pp. 37–58.

Loreau, M., Naeem, S. and Inchausti, P. (2002). *Biodiversity and Ecosystem Functioning: Sythesis and Perspectives.* Oxford: Oxford University Press.

MA (2003). *Ecosystems and Human Well-Being: A Framework for Assessment.* Washington D.C.: Island Press. Available at: http://www.millenniumassessment. org/en/Framework.aspx

MA (2005a). *Ecosystems and Human Well-being, Volume 4: Multiscale Assessments: Findings of the Sub-global Assessments Working Group.* Washington D.C.: Island Press. Available at: http://www.millenniumassessment.org/en/Multiscale.aspx

MA (2005b). *Ecosystems and Human Well-Being: Biodiversity Synthesis.* Washington D.C: World Resources Institute. Available at: http://www.millenniumassessment. org/en/Multiscale.aspx

MA (2005c). *Ecosystems and Human Well-being: Synthesis.* Washington D.C.: Island Press. Available at: http://www.millenniumassessment.org/en/Condition.aspx

MA (2005d). *Ecosystems and Human Well-being, Volume 1: Current State and Trends: Findings of the Condition and Trends Working Group.* Washington D.C.: Island Press. Available at: http://www.millenniumassessment.org/en/Condition.aspx

McCauley, D. J. (2006). Selling out on nature. *Nature* **443**, 27–28.

Mitchell, R. B., Clark, W. C., Cash, D. W. and Dickson, N. M. (2006). *Global Environmental Assessments: Information and Influence.* Cambridge: MIT Press.

Olsson, P., Folke, C. and Hahn, T. (2004). Social-ecological transformation for ecosystem management: the development of adaptive co-management of a wetland landscape in southern Sweden. *Ecology and Society* **9**. Available at: http://www.ecologyandsociety.org/vol9/iss4/art2/

Pereira, E., Queiroz, C., Pereira, H. M. and Vicente, L. (2005a). Ecosystem services and human well-being: a participatory study in a mountain community in

Portugal. *Ecology and Society* **10**. Available at: http://www.ecologyandsociety.org/vol10/iss2/art14/

Pereira, H., Reyers, B., Watanabe, M., Bohensky, E., Foale, S. and Palm, C. (2005b). Condition and trends of ecosystem services and biodiversity. In *Ecosystems and Human Well-being: Volume 4 – Multiscale Assessments*. Washington D.C.: Island Press, pp. 171–203.

Peterson, G., Allen, C. R. and Holling, C. S. (1998). Ecological resilience, biodiversity, and scale. *Ecosystems* **1**, 6–18.

Peterson, G. D., Beard, T. D., Beisner, B. E. *et al.* (2003). Assessing future ecosystem services a case study of the Northern Highlands Lake District, Wisconsin. *Conservation Ecology* **7**.

Plieninger, T., Hochtl, F. and Spek, T. (2006). Traditional land-use and nature conservation in European rural landscapes. *Environmental Science & Policy* **9**, 317–321.

Pressey, R. L. and Taffs, K. H. (2001). Scheduling conservation action in production landscapes: priority areas in western New South Wales defined by irreplaceability and vulnerability to vegetation loss. *Biological Conservation* **100**, 355–376.

Reid, W. V., Berkes, F., Wilbanks, T. J. and Capistrano, D. (2006a). *Bridging Scales and Knowledge Systems: Concepts and Applications in Ecosystem Assessment*. Washington D.C.: Island Press.

Reid, W. V., Mooney, H. A., Capistrano, D. *et al.* (2006b). Nature: the many benefits of ecosystem services. *Nature* **443**, 749.

Reyers, B. (2004). Incorporating potential land-use threats into regional biodiversity evaluation and conservation area prioritisation. *Biological Conservation* **118**, 521–531.

Rodriguez, J. P., Beard, T. D., Bennett, E. M. *et al.* (2006). Trade-offs across space, time, and ecosystem services. *Ecology and Society* **11**. Available at: http://www.ecologyandsociety.org/vol11/iss1/art28/

Schulze, E.-D. and Mooney, H. A. (editors) (1993). *Biodiversity and Ecosystem Function*. Berlin: Springer-Verlag.

Shackleton, C. M. and Fabricius, C. (2004). *Southern African Millennium Assessment: Gariep Basin Local Scale Assessments*. Grahamstown: Rhodes University.

Tallis, H. M. and Kareiva, P. (2006a). Shaping global environmental decisions using socio-ecological models. *Trends in Ecology & Evolution* **21**, 562–568.

Tallis, H. M. and Kareiva, P. (2006b). Ecosystem services. *Current Biology* **15**(17), 1–3.

van Jaarsveld, A. S., Biggs, R., Scholes, R. J. *et al.* (2005). Measuring conditions and trends in ecosystem services at multiple scales: the Southern African Millennium Ecosystem Assessment (SAfMA) experience. *Philosophical Transactions of the Royal Society B – Biological Sciences* **360**, 425–441.

Wilbanks, T. J. (2006). How scale matters: some concepts and findings. In *Bridging scales and knowledge systems*, ed. W. V. Reid, F. Berkes, T. J. Wilbanks, and D. Capistrano. Washington D.C.: Island Press, pp. 21–36.

Zermoglio, M. F., van Jaarsveld, A. S., Reid, W. V., Romm, J., Biggs, O., Yue, T. X. and Vicente, L. (2005). The multiscale approach. In *Ecosystems and Human Well-being: Volume 4 – Multiscale Assessments*, MA, editor. Washington D.C.: Island Press.

4

Conservation of biological diversity in El Salvador shade coffee: the importance of taxonomic capacity for participatory assessments

ALEX MONRO AND DAVID T. JONES

This chapter provides an overview of a project that took place in El Salvador between 1999 and 2002, entitled 'Empowering local people to manage the biodiversity of El Salvador'. The project set out to support the participation of a broad range of stakeholders in the assessment of the biological diversity associated with shade coffee farms. Led by taxonomists at the Natural History Museum (NHM) and funded by the Darwin Initiative (both UK stakeholders), it sought to demonstrate that it was feasible and practical to monitor biological diversity using direct species level measurements – without on the one hand having to compromise the quality of the data generated, or on the other hand excluding stakeholders from the process. The situation of El Salvador in general and shade coffee farms in particular presented a real demand for the data and skills that such a project could generate, both to enable shade coffee to be incorporated into the biodiversity planning process, and to aid the development of national taxonomic capacity. The chapter shows how collaborations between taxonomists and the wider users of biological diversity data can result in the generation of significant taxonomic capacity. Capacity that can be used to monitor biodiversity as part of certification schemes to leverage premiums for the crop, national biodiversity action plans or local conservation initiatives.

Background

El Salvador is the most densely populated country in Latin America, with a population of 6.9 million occupying 21 000 km² (The World Bank Group, 2007). It has been estimated that 99.5% of the land would have been forested prior to

Taking Stock of Nature: Participatory Biodiversity Assessment for Policy, Planning and Practice, ed. Anna Lawrence. Published by Cambridge University Press. © Cambridge University Press 2010.

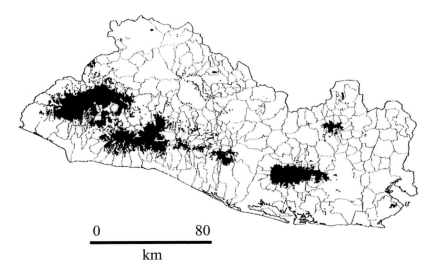

0   80

km

Figure 4.1. Distribution of shade coffee farms in El Salvador.

human occupation (Holdridge, 1975), but by 2000 the estimate of forest cover
had fallen to 5.3% with an additional 11% of shade forest used in the cultivation
of coffee (Ventura and Villacorta, 2001). Shade coffee forest therefore represents around two-thirds of El Salvador's forest cover (Figure 4.1 and Molnar,
Scherr and Khare, 2004) which, in view of the scarcity of remaining natural
forest, gives it a crucial role in El Salvador's biodiversity conservation strategy.
Its importance is not limited to the conservation of species; shade coffee also
contributes to water conservation, soil processes (maintenance of fertility and
reduction of erosion) and the provision of fuel to adjacent communities.

Between 1979 and 1992 El Salvador suffered a devastating civil war in
which 80 000 people are estimated to have died and hundreds of thousands
fled to neighbouring countries and the USA. The war had a crippling effect on
the whole of society. In particular, many academics remained in their countries of refuge after the war. The war also had a profound cultural impact,
still manifested in a lack of self-confidence in Salvadorans' own professional
skills. Post-war economic development has focused on manufacturing, and the
resulting migration from agricultural areas into the cities, has fuelled a rapid
increase in land prices and demands for water, both of which impact heavily
on the environment and biological diversity.

Coffee is produced under a variety of management systems. About 95% of
the area under coffee cultivation in El Salvador is managed as shade coffee,
defined by having some degree of forest cover, the manipulation of which is an

integral part of the coffee management. In contrast, 'sun coffee' plantations are intensive monoculture systems lacking any tree cover and of little biodiversity value. Shade coffee systems have been classified into three classes by Fuentes-Flores (1979) and Nolasco (1985). Each class contains a range of similar management systems, and is broadly related to the diversity and density of shade trees, their height and canopy cover: 'traditional polyculture' systems that are closest to natural forest in terms of their tree diversity and canopy structure; 'diverse polyculture' systems that are a mixture of remnants of the original natural forest cover and planted saplings; and 'simplified polyculture' systems where all of the shade trees have been planted.

Despite the fact that agroforest systems represent managed agricultural systems they can play an important role in the conservation of biodiversity (Schroth *et al.*, 2004) and agricultural areas represent an important component of protected areas worldwide. They are rarely, however, integral components of national conservation plans despite providing some of the last refuges for plant and animal species in many regions of the world where little natural vegetation remains. The development, consolidation and enhancement of productive but diverse sustainable agroforest systems will be necessary for a number of countries rich in biodiversity (China, for example) to meet their commitments to the Convention on Biological Diversity (CBD) and the Global Strategy for Plant Conservation.

Biodiversity value of shade coffee systems

Shade coffee farms represent a valuable habitat for many threatened bird, mammal and plant species (Márquez, Valdivia and Gómez-Pompa, 1976; Nir, 1988; Gallina, Mandujano and Gonzales-Romero, 1992; Williams-Linera, Sosa and Platas, 1995; Dietsch, 2000). Dietsch (2000) found 66 species of birds on CITES and/or IUCN threatened or endangered lists in shade coffee farms. Other studies suggest that Central American shade coffee farms represent significant wintering habitats for North American migratory birds (Greenberg *et al.*, 1997; Wunderle and Latta, 2000). For some canopy tree species in southern Mexico, shade coffee farms represent their only remaining habitat (Purata and Meave, 1993). Their value in biodiversity conservation is especially important when they are located in a highly deforested landscape (Brash, 1987; Perfecto *et al.*, 1996; Moguel and Toledo, 1999), despite the impact of increased isolation from undisturbed forest (Martínez and Peters, 1996). Conversion from traditional or diverse systems to simplifed polyculture systems has been shown to cause further significant declines in biodiversity (Borrero, 1986; Nestel and

Dickschen, 1990; Gallina *et al.*, 1992; Nestel, Dickschen and Altieri, 1993; Perfecto *et al.*, 1996).

Shade coffee production under threat: the need for economic sustainability

Shade coffee farms are currently under threat from several factors. The international coffee price between 1998 and 2003 was close to its lowest level in recorded history (The World Bank Group, 2003), making shade coffee production during this period economically unsustainable in El Salvador. For example, one shade coffee co-operative visited by this project in 2001, representing 99 families, sold 1724 quintals of coffee at $48 per quintal in the year 1999–2000, at a cost of production (excluding labour) of $41 per quintal. This represents a profit of $12 068 for the whole co-operative, i.e. $122 profit per family in the year. As a result, farmers are forced to sell their shade trees as fuel or timber or sell the land for housing or agricultural development (Ortiz, personal communication; Araujo, personal communication).

To maintain shade coffee systems, the farmers need to find a means of generating added value to their crop. There are various ways in which this value could be generated, the most obvious being: (a) premium prices in the international market for coffee certified as biodiversity or environmentally 'friendly'; (b) payments from the national government to farmers for the environmental services they provide to the nation; and (c) promotion of Salvadoran coffee as an independent 'biodiversity-friendly' brand. Any of these options will generate a need for biodiversity information in order to manage and monitor the targeted resources and services.

Shade coffee production in a national policy context

The Government of El Salvador signed the Convention on Biological Diversity (CBD) in 1992. The first National Biodiversity Strategy (NBS) (MARN, 2000) identified key priorities for the conservation of biodiversity (Box 4.1) which included a national biodiversity inventory and monitoring programme and the focusing of in situ conservation through the establishment of a network of protected areas. Complementing and integrated with this network, and in many respects a vehicle for implementing it, is the creation of the Mesoamerican Biological Corridor (CBM), through a regional project funded by the Global Environmental Fund (GEF) and GTZ, whose Salvadoran component was

Box 4.1 El Salvador's National Biodiversity Strategy (NBS)

El Salvador's first NBS is a statement on the environmental situation in the country, accompanied by a list of recommendations. The main content of the document is a summary of El Salvador's natural resources by category of use, accompanied by brief outlines as to how their use may be made sustainable and promote the development of the country and its population. It finds that El Salvador has underestimated the degradation of its natural resources and the relationship that this has with disease, poverty and violence. It concludes that in many parts of the country, basic natural resources have reduced by over 90% in the past 25 years and suggests that this reduction in resources threatens the development and stability of the nation. The NBS finds that shade coffee represents the single biggest forest resource in the country and represents the major sustainable source of fuel in rural areas. The report suggests that under effective management El Salvador's natural resources have considerable potential to support the economic development and well-being of the population as a whole. The report ends with a list of recommendations for priority actions for the sustainable use and conservation of El Salvador's biological diversity; their implementation is not however discussed in detail. The priority actions are (in order of importance): (I) a national inventory of the country's biological diversity; (II) the development of a programme of in situ and ex situ conservation measures for endangered species, which includes the establishment of a *Protected Areas Network;* (III) the training necessary to (a) lead a cultural change in society's perception of the environment and (b) support the necessary research for the sustainable use of the country's natural resources; (IV) the establishment of the political thought and agreement necessary to promote and ensure the recognition of (III) and; (V) development of operational capacity of MARN to promote and effect (I) through (IV) above.

Summarized from MARN (2000) Section Shade Policy in a National Context.

initiated in July 2000. The aim of the CBM is to create a wildlife corridor linking South America to North America by securing an interconnected network of protected areas in all seven Central American republics and the southern states of Mexico (UNDP, 1999). Five-sixths of El Salvador's contribution to the corridor is shade coffee (CBM, 2001). Despite this, there is no specific reference to shade coffee farms or the CBM in the list of priority actions in the NBS, even though the Ministry of Environment and Natural Resources (MARN) contributed to the preparation of the 1999 CBM project proposal.

The taxonomic capacity to assess and monitor biological diversity is therefore needed not only for the application of the NBS but also to help make shade coffee economically sustainable. Given existing taxonomic capacity within El Salvador (see below), available financial resources and the timescale within which assessment need to be made (both for the survival of shade coffee farms and the NBS) participatory assessment is likely to play a valuable role. Participatory assessment means that the individuals responsible for managing specific land systems play a direct role in the assessment and monitoring of biological diversity, whether they be coffee farmers, national park rangers or local community members. Logistically, this would facilitate the massive undertaking represented by a national inventory, by making available manpower and a working knowledge of survey sites. However, for participatory assessment to be possible there needs to be adequate taxonomic capacity to support it, and the development of such capacity amongst a range of stakeholders was the main aim of this project.

Taxonomic capacity in El Salvador

Taxonomic capacity is outlined by the CBD's Subsidiary Body on Scientific, Technical and Technological Advice (SBSTTA, 1996) and Monro, Jones and Araujo (2006). It represents the trained biological scientists, biological collections and nomenclatural codes required to identify, name and enumerate biological diversity at the species level. Based on this definition, the primary limitations on El Salvador's taxonomic capacity are the following.

Scarcity of baseline biodiversity data

Biodiversity data can take the form of biological collections, databases, and disseminated literature. Biological collections are essential when attempting to assess or monitor biodiversity, and can provide data for conservation planning (Australian Biological Resources Study, 1998). Existing collections serve not only as vital reference material against which specimens from the field can be compared, but also as a useful source of verifiable species data. Collections are also repositories of historical and contemporary records, and provided site collections are made using standardized methods, may offer measures of local species diversity (Jones and Eggleton, 2000).

In the chaos that accompanied the civil war, several of El Salvador's most important biological collections were lost or allowed to deteriorate (MARN, 2000). El Salvador has only 13 biological collections (Secretariat of the Convention on Biological Diversity, 2001), which with the exception of vascular plants, are all very small, have poor species coverage, and are inadequately curated. Of these collections, only one has been databased. Continued institutional impoverishment has left some of these collections facing a precarious future, with four of the cited collections placed into storage because the museum buildings are no longer safe for human occupation.

We reviewed the disseminated literature on the biological diversity of El Salvador and found 75 publications, covering 50 taxonomic groups. Only nine of these could provide taxonomic support for an inventory, to only six taxonomic groups (Monro *et al.*, 2006).

Poor access to biodiversity data

Biodiversity data in the form of biological collections, because of limited distribution and the need for interpretation, are only readily accessible to taxonomists. These data therefore do not directly support participatory biodiversity assessment. Disseminated literature can also fail to support participatory assessment if it is heavily reliant on technical language, or in a foreign language. However, if it is in a local language, with technical terms explained and illustrations, disseminated literature can be an effective means of supporting the identification of biological diversity. In the literature reviewed, of the nine field guides providing support to a taxonomic inventory, only two were accessible to non-taxonomists or Spanish speakers. The criteria used here were those products which provided the information necessary to identify, or assist in the identification of organisms to species. Information took the form of detailed descriptions, illustrations or identification keys. It did not, however, include simple lists of species names.

Lack of taxonomists and trained support staff

The NBS (MARN, 2000, p. 160) highlights the scarcity of taxonomic expertise as a national concern. A survey of taxonomists with expertise in Central American vascular plants, beetles and termites (Monro *et al.*, 2006) revealed that only 15% of the beetle experts, 3.6% of the vascular plant experts, and none of the termite experts were based in the Central American region. None was based in El Salvador. This regional problem is compounded by the isolation that accompanied years of war.

Local knowledge

Local knowledge represents an important source of biodiversity information but is rarely included in assessments of taxonomic capacity. For El Salvador, the documentation of local knowledge of biodiversity, both indigenous and non-indigenous, is largely limited to flowering plants, in particular in their capacity as medicines, food stuffs or weeds (Standley and Calderón, 1925; Choussy, 1975–1979; González, 1994; Ayala and Amador, 1999). No local knowledge of any vertebrate or invertebrate group was documented in the literature reviewed for this project (Monro *et al.*, 2006). During the civil war, hundreds of thousands of people left the countryside and moved to urban areas or overseas; and post-war economic recovery and development has resulted in continued migration to urban areas. This caused significant disruption of local knowledge of biodiversity over the past 20 years.

What we were trying to do

The aim of this project was to help develop the taxonomic capacity that would support participatory assessment and where possible, be accessible to the broad range of users or 'stakeholders' responsible for the management of biological diversity in shade coffee farms (Table 4.1). The project was led by the NHM in collaboration with MARN. The aims of the projects however resulted from a broader consultation exercise during 1997 and 1998 in which the project leaders participated in a number of formal and informal discussions with a range of stakeholders. The formal component consisted of a presentation followed by a group discussion with potential stakeholders, organized by MARN in February 1998, and NHM participation in a similar event organized by MARN and the Fundación Salvadoreña para Investigaciones del Café (PROCAFE – Salvadoran Foundation for research into coffee) to launch the World Bank funded, PRO-CAFE project 'Coffee and biodiversity'. The informal component consisted of face-to-face discussions with representatives of local NGOs (SalvaNATURA), the Botanical Garden of La Laguna (LAGU), University of El Salvador (UES) and the National Museum of Natural History of El Salvador, and coffee farmers (Miguel Araujo, Ines María Ortiz, Gilberto Barahona and David Chisholm).

From these discussions the project leaders (MARN and NHM) came to the following conclusions, which were used to determine the specific project objectives and activities.

Table 4.1. *Potential stakeholders in the participatory assessment of biological diversity in El Salvador*

Stakeholder	Knowledge (found out through the project)	Interest in biological diversity
Coffee farmers	good natural history of key groups of organisms, e.g. trees, birds, pest species	possible source of added value for crop benefits to coffee? production of key groups of organisms possible pests of coffee or principal coffee shade tree species
MARN: Sección de Patrimonio Nacional (National Heritage Section)	requirements for biological diversity data awareness of existing national biological diversity data responsible for NBS and CBM	implementation of CBM and NBS management of a number of National Parks environmental services associated with biological diversity (e.g. soil fertility)
CBM (an organization housed at MARN)	regional importance El Salvador's biological diversity mapping of El Salvador's vegetation types and coffee farms	planning El Salvador's component of CBM monitoring CBM
Local community adjacent to coffee farms	localized knowledge of uses of plant species	fuel for cooking environmental services (water and soil fertility) medicinal
Local taxonomic community (i.e. local scientists involved in the identification and enumeration of biological diversity in El Salvador; based almost exclusively at UES and LAGU)	national and regional level focused on specific groups custodians of biological collections	as research focus participation, as consultants, in NBS and CBM
NHM	taxonomic regional and global level expertise in a wide range of organisms	promote the use of biological collections promote inclusion of direct measures of

(cont.)

Table 4.1. (*cont.*)

Stakeholder	Knowledge (found out through the project)	Interest in biological diversity
	custodians of biological collections experience and knowledge of CBD	biological diversity in CBD activities develop its own collections promote its corporate profile with CBD and the Darwin Initiative
PROCAFE (an NGO established at the end of the war [1990] to provide technical advice to coffee farmers)	shade coffee production biological control of pests network of associated farms	promote premiums for shade coffee through 'Coffee and biodiversity' project as potential biological control agents
SalvaNATURA (an NGO which manages a national park and promotes conservation)	management of natural areas good natural history and taxonomic knowledge of key groups such as birds	contractors in certification of coffee farms assessment of biodiversity in El Salvador's biggest national park

- Shade coffee systems represent a natural focus for developing the capacity to monitor biological diversity, because (a) such monitoring has the potential to make such systems economically sustainable, (b) there existed very little information on the biological diversity in shade coffee farms and (c) shade farms have the potential for the implementation of the CBM, as *the* major source of forest cover in El Salvador.
- There does not exist sufficient capacity to monitor El Salvador's biological diversity, either in terms of the range of organisms for which expertise exists, or in terms of the numbers of individuals with the appropriate skills. The outputs of this project would support other components of the NBS, for example, the development of biological collections and training of taxonomists.
- There exists a strong interest amongst a broad range of stakeholders in acquiring the tools and skills to identify living organisms and therefore assess biological diversity. However, participation is limited by a lack of taxonomic support in the form of baseline information, identification tools and specialist advice.

- The project should focus on three groups of organisms for which taxonomic support was lacking and whose assessment would be of interest to as broad a range of stakeholders as possible, and does not need expensive specialist equipment.
- It should be possible to generate the taxonomic support necessary within the timescale of a Darwin Initiative project, i.e. three years.

There was broad consensus on these objectives amongst the majority of the stakeholders. There was, however, disagreement from some of the stakeholders (local taxonomic community and some parts of MARN) over the targeting of shade coffee farms rather than protected areas such as national parks. Further discussions convinced these stakeholders that shade coffee farms are amongst the most vulnerable forest habitats in El Salvador, because they do not benefit from any legal protection, and are susceptible to the national and global economy; and that therefore they urgently need study and protection.

The selection of organisms for study also provoked some discussion. The NHM, as stakeholder responsible for delivering much of the initial taxonomic support, unilaterally decided that the groups of organisms selected should have sufficient global taxonomic capacity to support their identification, and that they should represent manageable and informative levels of diversity. The project leader felt strongly that if taxonomy and taxonomists were seen to deliver taxonomic support within an agreed time-frame and cost that this would encourage MARN to increase the direct measurement of biological diversity (as opposed to reliance on remote measurements) into the NBS and national inventory strategy.

Three target groups of organisms were proposed: the trees, ferns and Pimplinae wasps, a subfamily of the Ichneumonidae. All stakeholders were in agreement over the use of trees because they define shade farms and of the majority of El Salvador's natural vegetation types. However, there was disagreement over the other two target organisms: Pimplinae wasps and ferns. Alternatives to Pimplinae wasps discussed included wasps of the subfamily Chalcidae (favoured by the entomologist at UES). Although insect parasitoids and currently in use as biological control agents, only around 15% of the species have been described (John Noyes, personal communication[1]) so identification of the collections would have taken several years. Furthermore, most species are between 0.1 and 0.2 cm in length and difficult to identify without expensive equipment and dissections, so this choice was not popular with other stakeholders. Pimplinae were selected because of their potential role in biological control (they are also all arthropod parasitoids) and their level of diversity and

---

[1] John Noyes, Researcher at NHM, Chalcidoid wasp specialist.

Table 4.2. *Project objectives*

Objective	Stakeholders
1. Collect and disseminate baseline tree, fern and wasp samples from shade coffee farms representative of the coffee growing regions of El Salvador	NHM, PROCAFE, coffee farmers, SalvaNATURA, UES
2. Provide advanced training at the NHM in London for seven Salvadoran scientists	NHM, UES, LAGU, PROCAFE, MARN
3. Provide taxonomic training through general introductory workshops held in El Salvador	NHM, UES, LAGU, MARN, PROCAFE
4. Produce and distribute identification tools in the form of field guides	NHM, UES, LAGU, coffee farmers, PROCAFE

their size range, 0.5–2.5 cm, which allows them to be identified using a hand lens.

There were similar discussions over the selection of ferns as a target organism. Both MARN, LAGU and UES would have preferred to work with orchids because of their economic importance and popularity as ornamentals within El Salvador. However, logistically this group is difficult because of CITES regulations on the shipping of herbarium material. At the initiation of the project El Salvador had no CITES designated institution and so it would not have been possible to ship duplicate herbarium collections to the UK, or elsewhere for identification. In addition the identification of orchid diversity of El Salvador is relatively well supported with the illustrated identification guides of Hamer (1974a,b, 1981) and so including this group would not have represented as significant an increase in taxonomic capacity as ferns.

Once the target organisms were selected, specific objectives were developed in collaboration with stakeholders, PROCAFE, coffee farmers and the local taxonomic community (Table 4.2). The method for meeting each objective was developed, through face-to-face discussions, with the appropriate stakeholder.

Through these objectives the project sought to generate the baseline data and local taxonomic expertise (objectives 1 and 2) that would underpin the use of the training and field guides (objectives 3 and 4). By including stakeholders in the collection of baseline data (NHM, PROCAFE, coffee farmers), the identification of the species (PROCAFE, LAGU, UES), design of the field guides (NHM, coffee farmers, UES, LAGU) and their production (NHM, UES,

LAGU) we developed the necessary contact between stakeholders to create a support network for participatory assessment that would continue after the end of the project. In terms of supporting participatory assessment, the critical objectives were the design and production of the field guides and the training courses (objective 3), which in turn built capacity to generate and access the baseline data (objective 1).

Field guides

In producing identification guides the aim was to make them accessible and able to support the identification of species by all of the stakeholders, without compromising the quality of the identifications. This requirement had a profound impact on the content as well as design of the guide layout. It often meant avoiding standard taxonomic characters with which taxonomists would be most familiar, in favour of those used by lay people in the field. Such characters were identified by asking and observing how farmers identified species in the field, and through the accumulated experience of the authors. In the case of flowering plants this meant placing greater emphasis on attributes such as the smell of the leaves when crushed, or the presence of a latex when cut. In the case of ferns, frond shape was the main attribute used by farmers. However, our field experience as taxonomists led us to place emphasis on additional characters not normally used because they are cryptic. For example, the nature of the scales present at the base of the frond or the shape of the reproductive structure found on the frond undersurface.

The gap between the farmer's and the taxonomists' classification was greatest amongst the wasps. Farmers place wasps into very broad categories, based on their size and colour, and did not view many of the smaller groups of wasps (e.g. Chalcidae) as wasps at all. The characters used by local people were of value at only a very basic level, for example, dark body colouration versus yellow and black striped body colouration. Many of the diagnostic characters necessary to identify wasps to species, such as the sculpturing of the egg-laying apparatus (ovipositor) or the shape of the compound eye lateral profile were not known to non-taxonomists. In this case there was no opportunity to adopt those characters used by lay people. Instead care was taken to explain the technical diagnostic characters in an illustrated glossary.

This approach created some challenges. Some characters that are important for lay people are very difficult to classify into the discrete states needed to aid identification and used in a field guide. For example, local people often use bark colour and texture to identify trees, but these bark attributes do not naturally fit into discrete states. This character was therefore presented in the guide at a much cruder level than local people would use it, and scientists were forced to seek out additional, more easily separated, characters such as the presence and absence of specialized leaf structures known as stipules.

To ensure that the content of the guide remained verifiable we sought to establish direct links between referenced biological collections in El Salvador and local, scientific names and illustrations. This made it possible to trace source material for a particular entry to a specific biological collection and thereby confirm or refute its identification, using contemporary literature or reference collections. The guides were thereby adapted to the needs of local taxonomists who are included amongst the stakeholders by providing a support role in inventories.

Biodiversity monitoring techniques and issues course

Two full-time two-week courses were held in San Salvador, each for around 15 individuals. The course covered El Salvador's NBS and the role of biological collections, taxonomy and shade coffee farms within it as outlined by SBSTTA (1996) and the Australian Biological Resources Study (1998). It also provided basic practical and theoretical training in inventory, monitoring and identification techniques and an overview of the taxonomic resources available within El Salvador, in the form of national collections and on the internet.

The courses brought together individuals from the many disparate parties involved in the conservation of biological diversity in El Salvador. These included park guards, environmental education workers, farm managers, members of an NGO providing technical advice to coffee farmers, members of an NGO responsible for the certification of shade coffee farms and the management of a national park and civil servants responsible for various aspects of the implementation of the NBS. A surprisingly high proportion of participants from different institutions had never made contact with each other prior to the course. For example, participants from the entomological section of PROCAFE had not met entomologists from the Facultad de Agronomía of UES, or worked with SalvaNATURA, the NGO contracted to certify shade coffee farms under the 'Coffee and Biodiversity' project. Through two open discussion sessions and team exercises, the training course was also viewed by the NHM and MARN as a means of developing and promoting contact between these parties.

What we found

This project sought to increase participation in the biodiversity assessment process by generating the necessary taxonomic capacity to support the assessment (and therefore monitoring) of biological diversity by a wider range of stakeholders than existed prior to the project. It sought to do this at a modest cost (about £175 000) and within a practical timeframe (three years). To the extent that the project developed identification tools (field guides), aimed at a wide range of users and to targeted groups of organisms within the context of enhanced specialist taxonomic capacity, it was successful. We believe that there is considerable scope to produce easy-to-use identification guides to a much broader range of organisms. We also believe that this approach could be repeated in a range of agroforestry systems across the world. For example non-intensive cacao plantations in Brazil (Faria *et al.*, 2006) and banana agroforests in Costa Rica (Harvey, Gonzalez and Somarriba, 2006) have levels of biodiversity of the same order as natural forests. China in particular, with its great diversity of agroforest systems (Huijun, Zhiling and Brookfield, 1996), pressure on natural habitats and strong indigenous taxonomic capacity would provide a natural focus for such initiatives. It will probably always be the case that the taxonomic capacity, at a regional or global level, to underpin such guides will be a major limiting factor of their production.

In this project we focused on PAMEB within the national biodiversity inventory and the coffee certification process, for reasons outlined above. PAMEB has the potential to integrate local knowledge, particularly on uses and natural history, with current scientific knowledge. This will add value to the biodiversity assessments themselves, for example, by feeding local knowledge of the natural history, ecology and uses of these organisms into the scientific community, through the use of scientific names. The production of field guides, as major tools for PAMEB, should also enable less formal and more flexible approaches to the assessment of biological diversity to be developed. Farmers may have their own interests in monitoring key aspect of biological diversity, for example, where applying a new agrochemical or farm management technique, or to anticipate the results of certification. PAMEB may also generate a more general interest in the identification of biological diversity, similar to that of amateur naturalists in the UK, amongst a new audience and so help develop El Salvador's future taxonomic capacity.

Ensuring uptake of the project results, for example use of the field guides in continued participatory assessment, is complex. No matter how much consultation takes place there will always be an element of uncertainty in the identification of stakeholders and target organisms. The project's focus on shade coffee, with both certification and a national biological diversity inventory driving a demand for biodiversity data, was one developed between the Minister and MARN and the NHM. MARN is responsible for developing the inventory strategy and a pilot certification project (Café y Biodiversidad) had been approved for funding by the World Bank. Since the initiation of the project in 1999, however, four successive Ministers have replaced the one who had planned the project, and as a result conservation priorities changed, with emphasis shifting away from the use of shade coffee farms and towards national parks. In addition, a full seven years after the publication of the NBS in 2000, there was still no detailed strategy or plan for a national biodiversity inventory, although a pilot is currently being developed in association with the Natural History Museum (Darwin Initiative Award 15/015). The World Bank certification pilot project ended in 2001 and since then an association between Rainforest Alliance and SalvaNATURA, established as part of this project, has maintained the certification process. However, certification is expensive (around $5000), and is probably only affordable to large farms and co-operatives. In addition the certification criteria developed (by Rainforest Alliance and SalvaNATURA) do not place a great emphasis on measures of biological diversity.

Despite the lack of an active biodiversity inventory process in El Salvador or an emphasis on biodiversity criteria within the coffee certification process, awareness of the project within the coffee farming community, together with the identification tools disseminated as part of the project (Monro *et al.*, 2001, 2002; Gauld, Menjivar and Monro, 2002), has generated an interest in identifying biodiversity amongst farmers. At the very least this has generated an awareness of the biodiversity value of their farms and empowered farmers with the ability to discourse with the broader Governmental and NGO community.

In summary, it is not yet clear whether this project will result in increased participation in the biodiversity assessment process in the short or medium term. The main reason is that there is little if any biodiversity assessment being undertaken in El Salvador outside the main national parks. Designing this project involved a number of predictions on environmental policy, not all of which have been implemented. The resulting training and identification tools will continue to provide taxonomic support to biodiversity assessment through the medium and long term, which should maintain the potential for participatory assessment for the future.

Acknowledgements

The authors would like to thank MARN, LAGU, the Escuela de Biología and Faculdad de Agronomía of UES, PROCAFE and SalvaNATURA for their logistical support and collaboration with the research for this article. Alex Monro would like to thank the Darwin Initiative for the Survival of Species (project

162/8/150) and the IUCN Small Grants Programme for financial assistance. David Jones would like to thank the Harold Hyam Wingate Foundation and the Embassy of Her Majesty's Government to El Salvador for their financial support. We would like to thank Jessica Sutton for help with the preparation of this manuscript.

REFERENCES

Australian Biological Resources Study. (1998). *Global Taxonomy Initiative: Shortening Distance between Discovery and Delivery*. Australian Biological Resources Study. Canberra: Environment Australia.

Ayala C. and Amador R. (1999). Estudio de las hierbas perjudiciales y benéficas más frecuentes en los cafetales de la zona occidental de El Salvador. Unpublished Ingeniero Agrónomo thesis, Universidad Técnica Latinoamericana.

Borrero, H. (1986). La substitución de cafetales de sombrío por caturales y su effecto negativo sobre la fauna de vertebrados. *Caldasia* **15**, 725–732.

Brash, A. R. (1987). The history of avian extinctions and forest conversion on Puerto Rico. *Biological Conservation* **39**, 97–111.

Choussy, F. (1975–1979). *Flora Salvadoreña*, vols. 1–4, 2nd edn. San Salvador: Editorial Universitaria.

Corredor Biológico Mesoamericano (El Salvador) (CBM) (2001). *Corredor Biológico Mesoamericano, (El Salvador), versión de trabajo, 01 de diciembre, 2001*, available at: http://www.biomeso.net

Dietsch, T. V. (2000). Assessing the conservation value of shade-grown coffee: a biological perspective using neotropical birds. *Endangered Species UPDATE* **17**, 122–124.

Faria, D., Laps, R., Baumgarten, J., and Cetra, M. C. (2006). Bat and bird assemblages from forests and shade cacao plantations in two contrasting landscapes in the Atlantic Forest of southern Bahia, Brazil. *Biodiversity and Conservation* **15**, 587–612.

Fuentes-Flores, R. (1979). Coffee production systems in Mexico. In: *Workshop on Agroforestry Systems in Latin America*, ed. F. de las Salas. CATIE, Turrialba, Costa Rica.

Gallina, S., Mandujano, S. and Gonzales-Romero, A. (1992). Importancia de los cafetales mixtos para la conservación de la biodiversidad de mamíferos. *Boletín de la Sociedad Veracruzana de Zoologia* **2**, 11–17.

Gauld, I., Menjivar, R. and Monro, A. K. (2002). *Avispas Pimpline de los Cafetales de El Salvador*. London: The Natural History Museum, 72 pp.

González, J. C. (1994). *Botánica Medicinal Popular. Etnobotánica Medicinal de El Salvador*. Antiguo Cuscatlán: Asociación Jardín Botánico La Laguna.

Greenberg, R., Bichier, P., Cruz Angon, A., and Reitsma, R. (1997). Bird populations in shade and sun coffee plantations in central Guatemala. *Conservation Biology* **11**, 448–457.

Hamer, F. (1974a). *Las Orquideas de El Salvador 1*. San Salvador: Ministerio de Educacion.

Hamer, F. (1974b). *Las Orquideas de El Salvador 2*. San Salvador: Ministerio de Educacion.

Hamer, F. (1981). *Las Orquideas de El Salvador 3*. Sarasota: The Marie Selby Botanical Gardens.

Harvey, C. A., Gonzalez, J. and Somarriba, E. (2006). Dung beetle and terrestrial mammal diversity in forests, indigenous agroforestry systems and plantain monocultures in Talamanca, Costa Rica. *Biodiversity and Conservation* 15, 555–585.

Holdridge, L. R. (1975). *Mapa ecológico de El Salvador*. MAG/FAO.

Huijun, G., Zhiling, D. and Brookfield, H. (1996). Agrodiversity and biodiversity on the ground and among the people: methodology from Yunnan. A Periodical of the United Nations University Project of Collaborative Research on People. *Land Management and Environmental Change* 6, 14–22.

Jones, D. T. and Eggleton, P. (2000). Sampling termite assemblages in tropical forests: testing a rapid biodiversity assessment protocol. *Journal of Applied Ecology* 37, 191–203.

Márquez, W., Valdivia, P. and Gómez-Pompa, A. (1976). *Resumen de los tipos de vegetación natural de las zonas cafetaleras de los estados de Veracruz, Puebla, Hidalgo y Tamaulipas*. Technical Report. Xalapa: Instituto Nacional de Investigaciones sobre recursos bióticos,

Martínez, E. and Peters G. W. (1996). La cafecultura biológica: la finca Irlanda como estudio de caso de un diseño agroecológico. In *Ecología Aplicada a la Agricultura: Temas Selectos de México*, ed. J. Trujillo, F. De Léon-González, R. Calderón and P. Torres-Lima. Universidad Nacional Autónoma de México, Mexico City, pp. 159–183.

Ministerio de Medio Ambiente y Recursos Naturales (MARN). (2000). *Estrategia Nacional de Diversidad Biológica*. San Salvador: Ministerio de Medio Ambiente y Recursos Naturales.

Moguel, P. and Toledo, V. M. (1999). Biodiversity conservation in traditional coffee systems of Mexico. *Conservation Biology* 13, 11–21.

Molnar, A., Scherr, S. J. and Khare, A. (2004). *Who Conserves the World's Forests? A New Assessment of Conservation and Investment Trends*. Washington, D.C.: Forest Trends and Ecoagriculture Partners. Available at http://www.rightsandresources.org/library/publications/global/who-conserves.pdf

Monro, A. K., Alexander, D., Reyes, J. and Ventura, N. (2001). *Arboles de los Cafetales de El Salvador*. London: The Natural History Museum, 185 pp.

Monro, A. K., Alexander, D., Monterrosa, J. and Ventura, N. (2002). *Helechos de los Cafetales de El Salvador*. London: The Natural History Museum, 72 pp.

Monro, A. K., Jones, D. T. and Araujo, P. M. (2006). Taxonomic capacity can improve environmental and economic sustainability in biodiversity-rich shade coffee farms in El Salvador. *Systematics and Biodiversity* 4, 1–8.

Nestel, D. and Dickschen, F. (1990). The foraging kinetics of ground ant communities in different Mexican coffee agroecosystems. *Oecologia* 84, 58–63.

Nestel, D., Dickschen, F. and Altieri, M. A. (1993). Diversity patterns of soil macrocoleoptera in Mexican shaded and unshaded coffee agroecosystems: an indication of habitat perturbation. *Biodiversity and Conservation* 2, 70–78.

Nir, M. A. (1988). The survivors: orchids on a Puerto Rican coffee finca. *American Orchid Society Bulletin* 57, 989–995.

Nolasco, M. (1985). *Café y Sociedad en México*. Mexico: Centro de Ecodesarrollo.

Perfecto, I., Rice, R., Greenberg, R. and Van Der Voort, M. (1996). Shade coffee: a disappearing refuge for biodiversity. *Bioscience* **46**, 596–608.

Purata, S. and Meave, J. (1993). Agroecosystems as an alternative for biodiversity conservation of forest remnants. In: *Smithsonian Migratory Bird Center, Symposium Abstracts*. Forest remnants in the tropical landscapes: benefits and policy implications, p. 9.

Schroth, G., Fonseca, G. A. B., Harvey, C. A. *et al.* (2004). *Agroforestry and Biodiversity Conservation in Tropical Landscapes*. Washington D.C.: Island Press.

Secretariat of the Convention on Biological Diversity, the Global Taxonomy Initiative, Swedish International Development Agency, Swedish Scientific Council, Instituto Nacional de Biodiversidad de Costa Rica (2001). *Assessment of Taxonomy Needs in Central America*. Preliminary Report [unpublished]. Santo Domingo de Heredia: Instituto Nacional de Biodiversidad de Costa Rica.

Standley, P. C. and Calderón, A. S. (1925). *Lista Preliminar de las Plantas de El Salvador*. San Salvador: Dutriz Hermanos.

Subsidiary Body on Scientific, Technical and Technological Advice (SBSTTA). (1996). *Practical Approaches for Capacity Building for Taxonomy* (UNEP/CBD/SBSTTA/2/5). Montreal: Subsidiary Body on Scientific, Technical and Technological Advice.

United Nations Development Programme – Global Environment Facility (UNDP). (1999). *Project Document, Establishment of a Programme for the Consolidation of the Mesoamerican Biological Corridor* (RLA/97/G31). New York: United Nations Development Programme.

Ventura, N. E. and Villacorta, R. F. (2001). *Mapeo de Vegetación Natural de Ecosistemas Terrestres y Acuáticos de El Salvador* (CD Rom). San Salvador: Ministerio de Medio Ambiente y Recursos Naturales.

Williams-Linera, G., Sosa, V. and Platas, T. (1995). The fate of epiphytic orchids after fragmentation of a Mexican cloud forest. *Selbyana* **16**, 36–40.

Wunderle, J. and Latta, S. C. (2000). Winter site fidelity of Nearctic migrants in shade coffee plantations of different sizes in the Dominican Republic. *The Auk* **117**, 596–614.

The World Bank Group (2003). *Commodity Price Data Pinksheet – May 2003*. Available at: http://www.worldbank.org/prospects/pinksheets/pink0503.htm http://go.worldbank.org/MD63QUPAF1

The World Bank Group. (2007). *El Salvador Data Profile*. Available at http://devdata.worldbank.org/external/CPProfile.asp?PTYPE=CP&CCODE=SLV

5

Taking stock of nature in species-rich but economically poor areas: an emerging discipline of locally based monitoring

FINN DANIELSEN, NEIL BURGESS, MIKKEL FUNDER,
TOM BLOMLEY, JUSTIN BRASHARES, AMINA AKIDA,
ARNE JENSEN, MARLYNN MENDOZA, GREG STUART-HILL,
MICHAEL K. POULSEN, HADIJA RAMADHANI,
MOSES K. SAM AND ELMER TOPP-JØRGENSEN

Introduction

Conventional scientist-executed forms of monitoring are expensive and rely upon highly skilled scientists or technicians (Danielsen *et al.*, 2000). As such only a small amount of this type of monitoring is undertaken in developing countries, where funding and available expertise are limited. This is unfortunate as the developing countries have the greatest importance globally in terms of their assemblages of species, including those threatened by extinction, and also have a great diversity of habitats and important ecosystem services (Millenium Ecosystem Assessment, 2005). They are also the parts of the world where habitat loss is currently proceeding at the greatest speed, and where we know least about the trends in species abundance (Balmford, Green and Jenkins, 2003; IUCN, 2007).

Recently, experiments have been made to involve less educated local people in monitoring of natural resources in developing countries. Although there are still a number of scientific questions surrounding these approaches, and many schemes are still at an early stage of development, the new approaches show a great deal of promise (Danielsen, Burgess and Balmford, 2005a; Danielsen, Burgess and Balmford, 2005c). This chapter analyses the success and challenges of four schemes that stand out from the majority, because they have been replicated and scaled-up, and are now institutionalized and adopted nationally in the respective countries. We begin by describing and explaining the

Taking Stock of Nature: Participatory Biodiversity Assessment for Policy, Planning and Practice, ed. Anna Lawrence. Published by Cambridge University Press. © Cambridge University Press 2010.

activities and outcomes for each of the four schemes, before presenting our own cross-cutting analysis of the benefits and challenges of such approaches.

Ranger-based monitoring of Ghana's savannah reserves

What we did and why

The first formal wildlife monitoring in Ghana was established by the British colonial authorities in the early 1900s. At this time, monitoring focused on several hunting reserves which were designated for use only by the colonial elite (Ghana Wildlife Division, 2000). Many West African communities, however, had their own forms of wildlife monitoring which date back hundreds or even thousands of years. For example, in many areas, local chiefs required hunters to provide a leg or other body part of every animal taken on their lands. In this way, chiefs not only received a share of the meat, but were able to monitor the rate of wildlife off-take and implement reductions of harvest if necessary.

Following independence in 1957, Ghana adopted new monitoring policies in protected areas with the stated goal of sustainably managing wildlife resources to allow bushmeat harvest and other benefits to local communities (Ghana Wildlife Division, 2000). This relied on locally based employees of the Ghana Wildlife Division (GWD, initially the Department of Game and Wildlife) to record the type and number of larger vertebrates encountered on monthly walking patrols (Brashares, Arcese and Sam, 2001) and during daily activities around camp. These counts were conducted around ranger posts within at least 11 national parks and resource reserves starting in 1968, and continue in some form in several of these reserves today (Table 5.1). The number of posts in each ranges from two to 31 so the monitoring data can illuminate both temporal and spatial patterns (Brashares and Sam, 2005).

Employees of the GWD were often drawn from local communities and received limited training in animal identification or sampling methods. Parks officials viewed the collection of count data as one means of ensuring that Division staff were active in conducting foot patrols in the field. Staff collected the data because it was part of their job and a metric by which they were evaluated, but the goal was to ensure that wildlife use was sustainable, not to prevent its use altogether (Ghana Wildlife Division, 2000).

The monitoring data were collected regularly over more than 30 years, but were used only for internal, annual wildlife estimates and seldom were fed back into the management of the protected areas from which they came. In 1999, researchers from the GWD and University of California, Berkeley, began to summarize and analyse the data using more quantitative techniques, see

Table 5.1. *Summary characteristics of the locally based natural resource monitoring schemes in Ghana, The Philippines, Tanzania and Namibia*

Country[a]	Biome[b]	Land tenure system[c]	Type of participation by community members[d]	Who compiles data[e]	What is monitored[f]	Spatial scale Total size of area monitored (ha)[g]	Interval between successive bouts of data collection (days)	Community member time spent on data collection (person-hours/ha/yr)	Payment provided to community members involved in the monitoring (USD)	Indicative recurrent costs of monitoring (USD/ha/yr)[h]	Indicative total funding for management (USD/ha/yr)
Ghana	t	PA	II(0)	R	Use/Wildl	516 500(2)	30	No community members involved[i]	No community members involved	0.06 (2003)	0.18[j]
Philippines	t(m, fw)	PA	I(350)	R/C	Use/Wildl	1 090 000 (8)	90	0.005	0 (snacks)	0.04 (2001)	1.75
Tanzania	t	PA/non-PA	I(298)	C	Use/Wildl	144 403 (4)	Varies	0.201	0–2/day	0.05 (2003)[k]	0.23
Namibia	t(fw)	C-PA	I(200)	C	Use/Wildl	7 000 000 (30)	Varies	0.005[l]	100/mth[m]	0.01 (203)[lm]	0.05–0.65[l]

[a]Source of information: Danielsen *et al.*, 2005a, pp. 2512–2513.
[b]t = terrestrial; fw = freshwater; m = marine (bracketed biomes account for a minor portion of the area under monitoring).
[c]C-PA = protected area managed by the local non-PA = outside of protected area; PA = protected area under government authority.
[d]I = Monitoring scheme intended to involve the community members in the local design of the monitoring as well as in data collection, data analysis, and monitoring-based decision-making; II = Monitoring scheme not currently intended to involve community members. The number of community members directly involved in the monitoring is indicated in brackets.
[e]C = community members; R = government rangers.
[f]Use = resource use; Wildl = wildlife species/populations and habitats.
[g]The number of areas monitored is indicated in brackets.
[h]Year in brackets; excluding depreciation of equipment.
[i]The rangers however often came from local communities.
[j]This figure includes the costs of monitoring.
[k]Funds generated locally from user fees.
[l]Many conservancies are located in large deserts.
[m]Funds generated locally from trophy hunting or tourism.

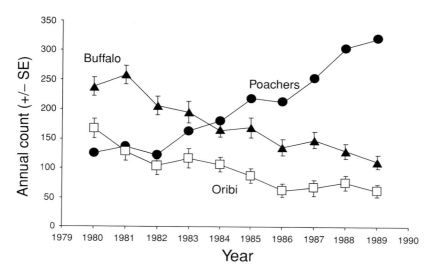

Figure 5.1. Annual counts of African buffalo (*Syncerus caffer*) (▲), oribi antelope (*Ourebia ourebi*) (□) and poachers (●) observed in Mole National Park, 1980–89, based on the locally based natural resource monitoring scheme in Ghana. Each point, except for poacher counts, represents the mean of monthly count totals ±SE. Poacher counts represent the sum of observations across months.

Figure 5.1 (Brashares and Arcese, 2002). Starting around 2001, monitoring efforts were modified and consolidated in a smaller number of defined areas within several of Ghana's parks (B. Volta-Tineh, personal communication). Field staff no longer were based at remote field camps but travelled to defined stations each month from a central park headquarters to conduct patrols and surveys. Today, wildlife data collected from field patrols are summarized in spreadsheets by park personnel and often are consulted by senior park officials when making decisions about focal areas for community outreach or allocation of patrol effort. Thus, these monitoring data are involved in the local decision-making process, and linked directly back to management at the local scale.

What was the outcome and why?

Prior to 1999, count data collected by the GWD were used only sparingly, in the formulation of annual summaries for each protected area, for example to produce species lists for a park or to ascertain whether a given species could be found in a certain region of Ghana. Surprisingly, the data were rarely used in formulating or evaluating management plans and initiatives, despite the value of the spatially explicit data.

Nor has ranger-based wildlife monitoring contributed to management decisions at a national scale. However, this is likely to change in the near future as the government of Ghana and external funding agencies look for ways to quantify the effectiveness of wildlife conservation initiatives. For example, the GWD has begun a programme to facilitate community-based management of wildlife in lands adjacent to protected areas, intended to provide communities with direct benefits from wildlife conservation while also creating habitat buffers around reserves. Measuring the effectiveness of these programmes for maintaining or enhancing wildlife in reserves requires monitoring data collected before, during and after community-based management is implemented. Thanks to its long-term wildlife monitoring efforts, Ghana has exactly those data.

Perhaps because of the more recent collaboration with an international research team, the use of GWD's monitoring data in the past five years has focused on global rather than local issues. The data were analysed to show long-term changes in wildlife abundance in relation to human demography (Brashares *et al.*, 2001). This research revealed for the first time that the density of humans around a protected area is a strong predictor of the rate of local extinction of wildlife within that area. In so doing, it suggested that understanding patterns of human demography may be a key first step in predicting future challenges for managing natural resources. Additional work using these count data showed that wildlife species differ greatly in their sensitivity to human disturbance (Brashares, 2003). Species requiring large areas of contiguous habitat were those most likely to be affected negatively by human development and activities around protected areas.

The long-term nature of the count data also provided a rare glimpse into the factors that affect human reliance on wildlife at a regional scale (Brashares *et al.*, 2004). By comparing changes in wildlife abundance and intensity of hunting across years of high and low fish supply, this research showed that rural people hunted and consumed more wildlife when alternative sources of animal protein were scarce. By identifying links between management of natural resources at such a large scale, this research emphasized the importance of considering the big picture in any conservation or management initiative. The monitoring programme in Ghana also provides a potentially powerful example for initiatives only now starting in other natural areas by illuminating the frequency and intensity of monitoring needed to accurately detect trends in animal populations (Brashares and Sam, 2005). Taken together, these more recent examinations of the monitoring data have inspired evaluation of international policies and conventions (e.g. the role of distant water fishing fleets in the decline of African fisheries), but they are yet to have a strong effect on natural resource management in Ghana.

Community-based monitoring of Philippine protected forests

What we did and why

Since 1996, protected area staff and community members have kept track of the wildlife and resource use in protected areas in the Philippines, where many people live and depend on protected area resources. Until the 1990s most protected areas in the country existed only on paper, but government was starting to question the effectiveness of the traditional top-down approach to protected area management. In 1992, the National Integrated Protected Area System Act (DENR, 1992) allowed for community participation in protected area management but was supported by little practical experience in how this could be achieved meaningfully.

In 1996–98, the Philippine Protected Areas and Wildlife Bureau (PAWB) of the Department of Environment and Natural Resources (DENR) developed a simple community- and ranger-based scheme for monitoring biodiversity and resource use in protected areas, with support from the World Bank and Danida, over three years. The process involved protected area staff, local non-governmental organizations and protected area communities. Rather than designing the 'ideal' monitoring scheme, it aimed to develop a feasible minimum starting point which could evolve over time as more resources and skilled people become available to manage and monitor biodiversity (Danielsen *et al.*, 2000). It intended to show, at the protected area level, whether or not management interventions in the area are effective in conserving biodiversity, and to enhance the participation of communities in protected area management. It focused on identifying trends in important biodiversity existence and use, to guide action in protected area management. The focus is at the field level, where most day-to-day management decisions are taken. Methods are kept simple and practical, to be easily integrated into other work activities and sustained with the locally available resources (Table 5.1).

The scheme was designed to build upon and strengthen existing community-based resource management systems. In many areas of the Philippines, traditional measures to oversee and manage natural resources still form an important part of the everyday regulation of local natural resource use. For instance, community leaders and 'ordinary' community members regularly discuss and assess the availability and quality of particular natural resources, and thereby establish a collective overview of the status and trends of these resources. If they perceive a resource to be declining or threatened, they may impose regulations to limit use.

Data were collected by government rangers and volunteer community members. By allowing rangers to participate in field assessments, the scheme encouraged them into the field and improved their capacity for management. Four field methods were used. The *focus group discussion* method involved establishment of volunteer 'Community Monitoring Groups' who collected information on resource use and biodiversity on a regular basis between quarterly discussions with protected area staff. This method was intended to indicate changes in perceived harvest volume per unit effort. The *field diary* method comprised standardized recording of routine observations and records provided by local people of biodiversity and human use of wild flora and fauna by protected area staff in a simple pocketbook during patrols. This method was intended to indicate changes in the relative abundance of species and resource use. The *fixed point photography* method comprised on-the-ground fixed-point photographing of selected hillsides in priority forest blocks at regular intervals. This method was intended to indicate changes in size of vegetation type blocks and in land-use of priority areas. The *line-transect* method comprised line-transect surveys of wildlife and resource use along permanent routes. This method was intended to indicate changes in wildlife population size, human intensity of resource use, and/or shift in range of wildlife and human resource extraction. When the monitoring scheme was designed these four methods were selected because they were field-based, possible to use in areas where 'specialist staff' are lacking, and believed to be cost-effective (Danielsen *et al.*, 2000).

In each park, the monitoring focuses on a list of 10–15 taxa and 5–10 indicators of resource use, selected by local community members together with protected area staff. Data are collected every three months. The protected area staff and community members interpret the data together, and present a small report every quarter to the Management Council of each protected area (copied to PAWB at national level).

The report is structured so as to encourage park staff to both organize, analyse and interpret the data as well as to propose specific conservation management interventions. It includes the dataset, a list of important observations of changes in species and resource use, and a list of proposed management interventions with a description of the issue identified (e.g. 'conversion of forest for farming of vegetables'), the location and the proposed action to be taken by the protected area council (Danielsen *et al.*, 2005b).

PAWB staff are supposed to regularly review the reports and provide feedback to the park staff, to keep errors at an acceptable level and assist the parks when local management interventions need back-up. It was also envisaged that the PAWB staff would extract data to prepare annual reports for the Secretary of the Environment. This work at national level, however, has suffered from under-funding and weak institutional support.

There are several reasons for the weak capacity of DENR. First, there is no programmatic approach in DENR to environment and natural resource management. Most priority setting is short term and politically or even individually driven, and shifts with the appointment of the departmental Secretaries. In recent years, the average terms of the Secretaries have been only one year. The rapidly shifting priorities have a serious impact on the follow-up and sustainability of longer-term efforts such as monitoring of natural resources. Second, the institutional structure of DENR and the roles and responsibilities of the staff are unclear and ambiguous. There is no single unit in charge of natural resource monitoring, and regularly staff supposed to be in the main responsible for the implementation of the Department's monitoring efforts are simultaneously assigned to perform a multitude of other tasks. Other key reasons include frequent re-assignments of trained staff, and lack of a results-oriented staff performance monitoring and incentive system.

What was the outcome and why?

Although direct project support ceased in 2001, the scheme continues in most sites where it was established, although efforts depend on staff availability and budgets. The government has made it mandatory for their staff to use the scheme as a management tool in protected areas (DENR, 2000) and, as a result, the scheme has spread to new sites. Some NGOs have on their own initiative begun using the scheme. There is, however, a need for further training of park staff in participatory approaches, as well as in species identification, data analysis and application of the field methods in aquatic habitats. At the national level, there is a need to build further capacity in effectively making the locally derived data available to national policy-makers.

The conservation management interventions arising from this scheme have been examined (Danielsen *et al.*, 2005b; Table 5.2). Before this monitoring scheme was established, there was little collaboration between local people and park authorities, and park monitoring was restricted to assessments of the quantity of extracted timber. As a result of two-and-a-half years of operation of the scheme by 97 rangers and 350 community volunteers, 156 interventions were undertaken in eight protected areas (Figure 5.2).

Table 5.2. *Examples of monitoring results and conservation management interventions resulting from the locally based natural resource monitoring scheme in the Philippines (Danielsen* et al.*, 2007)*

Monitoring method	Example of monitoring result	Conservation management intervention emanating from the monitoring result
Focus group discussion	A community monitoring group reported a decline in the abundance of marine fish in Basco Bay of Batanes Island (Batanes Protected Sea and Landscape).	The municipality of Basco issued an ordinance allowing fishing with hook and line but banning the use of nets and compressors in the bay. The abundance of fish in the bay reportedly increased after only seven months.
Field diary	Reports from local people of sightings of crocodile and the presence of crocodile hunters near San Mariano village (Northern Sierra Madre Natural Park).	The municipality of San Mariano issued an ordinance declaring the critically endangered Philippine crocodile *Crocodylus mindorensis* a municipal 'flagship species' and establishing penalties for violation of previous ordinances intended to protect this species.
Fixed-point photography	A new photo of a forested hill tract in the protected zone of the park showed that a swidden had been opened (Mt Kitanglad Range Natural Park).	Park staff showed the before and after photos to the head of the village. He obtained a promise from the violators not to extend the swidden without permission from the protected area management council.
Line-transect	Fewer records of giant clams (Tridacnidae) than before on the transect swim routes in the sustainable use zone (Apo Reef Natural Park).	The park staff raised awareness among local fishermen of the existing regulations on giant clam collection via the local radio and in person with fishermen when they requested permits to fish inside the park. In addition, staff requested assistance from a university on how to propagate the species and thus restock the wild population.

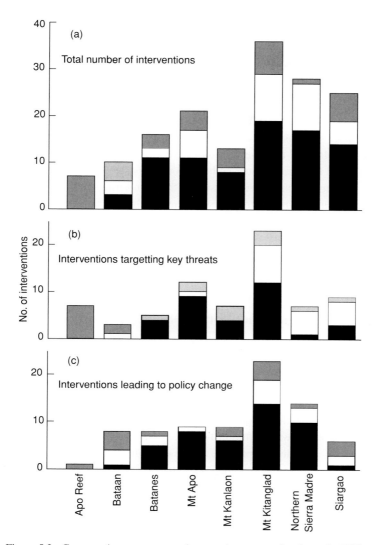

Figure 5.2. Conservation management interventions emanating from the Philippine locally based natural resource monitoring scheme and intended to improve the way local people (black), outsiders (white) and both (grey) manage resources in eight protected areas over two and a half years of operation of the scheme (a). The lower panels show the results if the analysis is restricted to those interventions that only target the three most serious threats to species populations and habitats at each site (b), and those interventions that led to policy change with a potential long-term impact on sustainable development (i.e. new resolutions or bylaws) (c).

To analyse the effectiveness of outcomes, we defined 'meaningful and justified interventions' as those with rational objectives, according to the socio-cultural, ecological and administrative contexts, and appropriate in terms of target, intensity, timing and extent (Danielsen *et al.*, 2005b). In total, 98% of these interventions were, or probably were, meaningful and justified, 47% targeted the three most serious threats to biodiversity at the site (see also Figure 5.2b), and 90% were implemented without external support, suggesting that the interventions were relevant and could be sustained over time at the local level. Many of the interventions were jointly undertaken by community members and the management authorities or consisted of local bylaws in support of park management. As a result of the monitoring, indigenous resource use regulation schemes were re-established with government recognition in several parks. The monitoring led to more diversified management responses on the part of the authorities, including a more socially acceptable and effective approach to enforcement.

Community-based monitoring of village forests in Tanzania

What we did and why

Our third example is from Tanzania, where community members record resource extraction and disturbance in village woodlands and forests. Since the early 1990s, the Tanzania forest sector has been undergoing a radical process of decentralization and devolution. A number of donor-funded projects have experimented with different forms of community-based and joint forest management, and these approaches were enshrined in revisions to the forest policy and legislation in 1998 and 2002 (Blomley and Ramadhani, 2006). Currently, mainland Tanzania has one of the most progressive community forestry jurisdictions in Africa as reflected in policy, law and practice (Wily, 2000; Blomley, 2006).

As part of this trend, the Danish government supported a pilot project in Iringa Region between 1999 and 2004 to facilitate Participatory Forest Management in 23 villages, covering 140 000 hectares of highland, evergreen forests and lowland miombo woodlands. The management agreements provide user rights to local communities including rights to collect and spend revenue from sale of natural resources extraction permits. In turn, the Village Natural Resource Committees (VNRC) are the designated forest managers and must demonstrate an ability to manage forest lands to the benefit of their constituents (the community) and in a sustainable manner (to the District Forest Officer).

The project developed a participatory monitoring scheme which does this by feeding data upwards (to district forestry staff), downwards to the wider village community and laterally (to the members of the VNRC). The scheme is built on existing village government structures, and complies with the regulations and legal duties set out in local government and forestry legislations. The aim was to be simple and cost-effective, and empower community managers to more effectively manage their woodland and forest resources (Topp-Jørgensen *et al.*, 2005; Table 5.1).

As the responsible forest managers, the VNRC maintains records of forest patrols, income, expenditure, meetings and any problems encountered. These records are compiled into a monthly summary sheet and forwarded to the district authorities for review and, where necessary, action. They are also used during routine meetings of the VNRCs to inform discussions about management strategies, harvesting volumes, patrol and enforcement and revenue collection. Since the beginning of the scheme it has been important to ensure that information gathered at village level has direct use value for the forest managers themselves – rather than just generating data for higher-level stakeholders. This created local incentives to continue the monitoring system beyond the life of the project.

The government agency responsible for supervising forestry activities in Tanzania, the Forestry and Beekeeping Division, is currently establishing a national monitoring framework as part of the National Forest Programme, that will track national indicators related to forest extent, condition, revenues, harvesting volumes and products as well as the extent of community involvement and benefits arising from participatory forest management systems (United Republic of Tanzania, 2007). Development partners supporting the forest sector in Tanzania (Danida, Ministry of Foreign Affairs of Finland and the World Bank among others) have agreed to adandon project-specific indicators and to embrace these national indicators. Similarly, rather than constructing time-bound and donor-specific monitoring systems, they have agreed to harmonize these efforts by investing in a single, long-term monitoring system which is embedded in existing government institutions (such as the VNRCs, District Councils and the Forestry and Beekeeping Division) and tracking a commonly agreed set of indicators.

The design of this new system, the National Forestry and Beekeeping Database ('NAFOBEDA'), builds strongly on the community-based models described above. Data on forests under the management of community institutions are captured, stored and compiled at the village level by VNRCs and fed through a district platform to a national database (Akida, 2007). The system, which has recently been finalized following extensive pre-testing, will soon be introduced to an initial 35 districts in the eastern and southern parts of the country through targeted training. District staff will in turn train VNRCs and other village council staff to ensure that data capture is standardized across all participating villages. Data generated at the national level will feed into policy processes such as annual ministerial budgets, annual joint donor reviews of the forestry sector, and higher-level systems tracking progress towards the goals of the Poverty Reduction Strategy (known in Tanzania as the National Strategy for Growth and Reduction of Poverty).

What was the outcome and why?

The community forestry monitoring scheme in Tanzania has operated since 2002 and continues despite the end of direct project support in 2004. Between November 2002 and June 2004, villages in the montane forest areas maintained an average rate of report returns, of 80%, while villages from lowland woodland sites maintained a slightly lower return rate (Topp-Jørgensen *et al.*, 2005). In total, 181 management interventions had been suggested as a result of monitoring and, of these, 131 had been tabled for discussions during routine meetings of the VNRCs (Figure 5.3). Of the 131 issues discussed by the VNRCs, 50% had been approved by the District Forest Officer and subsequently acted upon. Others have not yet been acted on, because they require a modification of the village forest management plan or joint forest management agreement. This process takes time and resources, and involves District staff, who have limited capacity to make changes rapidly.

Assessment of monitoring forms at Iringa District Forest Office in November 2006 showed a decrease compared with previous years (Poulsen *et al.*, 2007). Visits to nine villages, however, showed that they all continued monitoring efforts, albeit at a reduced level in some places.

Monitoring level is linked to incentives, and villages that obtain revenue to compensate local forest managers generally monitor more frequently. Although it has not been observed yet, this may have implications for long-term continuation of the scheme in montane forests where revenue is limited, as only harvest of non-timber products is permitted. Payment for other ecosystem services (e.g. water, biodiversity value, etc.) might be needed to ensure long-term monitoring in biodiversity rich areas with limited resource extraction potential.

Management interventions raised during routine monitoring at village level were analysed to assess whether they addressed 'scientifically identified threats', which in the miombo woodlands include over-harvesting of wood, and in the highland forests include fire and hunting (Figure 5.3b). Of the 23 villages, 21 had suggested management interventions that targeted the most

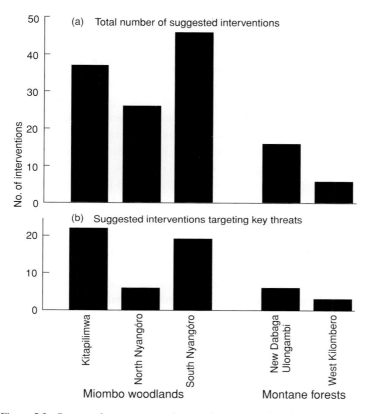

Figure 5.3. Suggested management interventions emanating from the locally based monitoring scheme in miombo woodland and montane forest areas of Tanzania after ten months of operation (a). The lower panel shows the conservation management interventions that only target the most serious threats to species populations and habitats in each area (b). The most serious threats were identified independently; they were wood extraction in the woodlands and hunting and fire in the montane forests.

important threats to their respective forests. Seventy-five percent of interventions targeting the most immediate threats had been implemented while most of the others were awaiting approval by district authorities.

A spin-off benefit from this local monitoring scheme has been its incorporation into the national forestry monitoring scheme described above. When fully operational, this will be the first time in Tanzania that data gathered, compiled and presented by village forest managers have been combined with data gathered by forestry professionals into a single national dataset.

Community-based monitoring of Namibian conservancies

What we did and why

Our final example is from Namibia, where community rangers record various aspects of their conservancy, ranging from wildlife numbers, through economic returns, to infringements of the rules. Namibian legislation provides for the establishment of 'conservancies'. Conservancies can be found in any type of habitat but often comprise large desert areas. Conservancies allow communities on communal land to benefit from wildlife in return for assuming responsibility for the sustainable management of natural resources.

One of the management tools required is a local-level monitoring scheme, to see if objectives are being reached, and to guide any corrective actions. During 2001–2003, and in response to requests for assistance from rural communities, scientists involved in Namibia's Community Based Natural Resource Management programme, with support from USAID, helped conservancies to develop a monitoring scheme known locally as the 'Event Book System'. This is designed to meet the information needs of the local community (Stuart-Hill *et al.*, 2005). Its fundamental principle is that the community decides what they want to monitor, and the technicians respond by facilitating the design (i.e. how to monitor). Conservancy employees collect and analyse the data, and are paid from funds generated locally through trophy hunting or tourism (Table 5.1).

To support the principle of local control, yet provide a rigorous methodology, the monitoring system has over time been modularized by topic, for example: problem animals, poaching, vegetation, predators, and fish. Thus conservancies adopting the system freely select what they want to monitor, and the technical support team then provides a complete kit of Event Book cards for each monitoring topic. No conservancy is ever forced to accept any module and they are free to design their own.

The Event Book is a personalized ring file maintained by each community ranger. The file contains a set of (yellow) cards, one card for each monitoring theme or topic. There is a card for poaching, a card for problem animal incidents, a card for rainfall and so on. As events occur, the ranger selects the appropriate card and records the event. At the end of the month a line is left blank, and the same card used for subsequent events in the ensuing months. At the end of the year, all of the old cards are removed, archived and a fresh set of cards inserted into the book.

It is essential that people collecting the data should also analyse and interpret them, even if the analysis is sub-optimal. This principle emerged through experience with conventional systems, where data sheets are handed over to external experts, resulting in a loss of ownership, so local people stopped collecting data. Data 'analysis' is simple. There are three types of reporting: monthly incident chart reports; annual reporting maps; and long-term trend-chart reports. On a monthly basis, all field rangers collectively complete the monthly (blue) reporting charts by colouring in boxes indicating the total number of incidents for the month (generally, one observation = one box). Incidents are recorded by hand onto the reporting map using different symbols to differentiate between types of incidents.

At the end of each year, the totals for the year are transferred onto the long-term trend (red) reporting charts. The essential difference between the 'blue' and 'red' cards is that the *x*-axis on the latter is years rather than months. Colour coding the different reporting timescales has proved to be important to avoid confusion by semi-literate community members.

The entire system is paper-based. All papers are filed in a specialized filing box, indispensable where conservancies often have no office. Such a simple, hard-copy based system is critical in remote environments where advanced computer technology is not realistically viable.

However, whilst primarily designed and managed to meet local information needs, the system also provides input to data analysis and decision-making at national level. Each year data are copied during an annual review of each conservancy and are captured within a national monitoring and evaluation database. This database belongs to the Ministry of Environment and Tourism and is used by the government and the Namibian Association of Conservancy Support Organizations to guide strategic decisions such as setting quotas, allocating technical support, and monitoring compliance.

Original raw data never leave the community. This is a key principle when data are extracted beyond the individual conservancy. The data are archived by the conservancy, and copied from paper into digital format for central storage and analysis, thereby allowing more sophisticated analysis by scientists. All data also have a spatial element and are used within a national GIS system for national map-based reporting and analysis.

What was the outcome and why?

More than 44 communal conservancies covering more than seven million hectares have adopted the Event Book System. In 2004 the Namibian Ministry of Environment and Tourism officially adopted the same approach for its national protected areas, and the scheme is also beginning to be used in neighbouring countries.

At the local level, a number of management decisions have arisen from the scheme. One of the most significant results is improved understanding and communication between community members. For example, communities have felt that lion *Panthera leo* represented the greatest threat to their livestock but the data have shown that hyaena *Hyaena* sp. and cheetah *Acinonyx jubatus* cause much more damage. This has influenced their strategies for dealing with problem animals, with the result that fewer livestock are lost to predators. Most of the conservancies use the data for setting sustainable wildlife harvesting quotas. One conservancy decided to move its crop lands away from a flood plain with the almost immediate result that crop damage incidents were reduced to a third of previous years. In a number of conservancies, declining population trends in certain species have prompted them to improve their patrolling activities.

At national level, the government and NGOs have used data from Event Books to inform decisions including:

allocation of regional wildlife harvest quotas of high value species (elephant);

design of problem animal compensation schemes;

compliance reporting of conservancies to government, e.g. showing that the annual harvest of various wildlife species is within sustainable limits;

displaying community commitment to conservation to satisfy private sector and donor investment;

allocation of technical and financial support to different communities;

contribution to a national State of Conservancies Report;

supporting Namibia and Botswana's case for limited trade in ivory at the meeting of the Convention on International Trade in Endangered Species (CITES) in 2002.

The potential for positive developments from locally based monitoring

A number of lessons have emerged from these four case studies, and other locally based monitoring schemes in developing countries. We summarize these below and offer some suggestions on what further research is required to fully evaluate the effectiveness of this strategy for monitoring natural resource values in developing countries. We base our structured overview of the key lessons on a recently proposed typology of monitoring, from conventional scientist-executed approaches through to those fully owned by local communities (Table 5.3).

Table 5.3. *Summary of different types of monitoring approaches (adapted from Danielsen et al., 2009)*

Category	Main characteristics	Primary data gatherers	Primary data users
1. Externally driven professional-researcher executed monitoring	External monitoring undertaken by professional researchers. Accuracy and precision may be high, but link to local decisions and empowerment is weak	Professional researchers	Professional researchers
2. Externally driven monitoring with local volunteers or employees	Partly external monitoring that involves either paid staff or unpaid volunteers to collect the data. Analysis undertaken away from area of data collection	Professional researchers, volunteers, paid staff	Professional researchers
3. Collaborative monitoring with external data interpretation	Local stakeholders involved with collecting the monitoring data but data are then analysed elsewhere	Local people with professional researcher advice	Local people and professional researchers
4. Collaborative monitoring with local data interpretation	Local stakeholders involved with monitoring and data analysis, but design provided by outsiders	Local people with professional researcher advice	Local people
5. Autonomous local monitoring	All steps of the monitoring and design undertaken locally	Local people	Local people

In this typology, the ranger-based monitoring scheme in Ghana can be categorised as a category-2 'employee monitoring scheme' because the primary data gatherers are paid staff and the analysis of data is undertaken by scientists away from the area of data collection. The community-based monitoring schemes in the Philippines, Namibia and Tanzania can all be categorized as category-4 'collaborative monitoring schemes with local data interpretation' because the data gatherers are local people supported by advice from scientists, and the primary users of data are local people.

There is a great difference between these categories in terms of results and effectiveness. As participation progresses from category-2 to category-5 monitoring schemes, there is less control over who collects the data, and hence who is trained by outsiders and by how much. But as participation increases there is also an increase in local interest and relevance. Therefore, while one might expect an inverted relationship between accuracy and participation, this is not *necessarily* true, although this needs further research.

Here, we examine five factors that we consider important to making a monitoring scheme relevant and useful: costs, ability to detect trends, promptness of decision-making, potential for local empowerment, and ease of feeding into national and international schemes.

Cost to local stakeholders

Locally based monitoring incurs a significant cost to local people, although resources can also be provided by external agencies. Local time input in the cases described from the Philippines, Tanzania and Namibia varied from 0.01 to 0.20 person-hours per hectare per year (Table 5.1). Available data indicates a median time input of around 0.04 person-hours per hectare per year for locally based monitoring in eight developing countries (Danielsen *et al.*, 2005a). In fully locally based monitoring (with no external involvement) the costs may be considerable, especially when measured against the overall economy of the area. Costs and benefits to local communities therefore need to be considered in the design of local monitoring to ensure a fair workload in relation to local incentives.

Careful design may reduce costs to local stakeholders in locally based monitoring with external input, e.g. by locating monitoring sites in carefully selected but easily accessible areas. There is an abundant literature on how this might be achieved (e.g. Bibby *et al.*, 2000), but as the level of engagement by scientists declines, so does the potential to influence the design of the monitoring programme and thus minimize the costs while maximizing information quality.

Another cost is that of obtaining the relevant expertise to undertake the work. Often this is provided through training by outsiders, but in other cases it is internalized. The expertise required at local level can become considerable, especially where species that are difficult to identify need to be monitored.

Cost to others

As monitoring becomes increasingly locally based then the costs to others of implementation declines. The schemes in our four examples each had recurrent costs of USD 0.01–0.06 per hectare per year to the government and NGOs (Table 5.1). In the most locally based schemes (autonomous local schemes) there are no costs to external people as no external expertise is involved.

There are a variety of different requirements for external expertise during the establishment and training phase of a monitoring programme, as compared with the requirements during implementation. In locally based monitoring the engagement in day-to-day implementation declines and necessary skills relate more to participatory approaches and empowerment. For category-4 schemes there is a need to combine both science (e.g. from foresters and biologists) with social science (sociologists and anthropologists). Careful design might reduce the level of external skill required to instigate a locally based monitoring scheme and ensure it is sustainable.

Accuracy and precision

Local stakeholders typically favour monitoring schemes that are effective, in that the minimum amount of work provides the maximum benefit in terms of taking informed decisions. Accuracy is, however, important because it is necessary for the results to be as robust and defensible as possible.

Currently there is little literature on accuracy and precision within locally based monitoring schemes. An assessment of a locally based marine scheme in the Philippines found that out of four community-collected measures (of reef-benthic cover and fish abundance), only one was correlated with the equivalent data collected by professional biologists, with local stakeholders' measures of fish abundance being far more variable than those of professionals (Uychiaoco *et al.*, 2005). This indicates an urgent need for scientific comparisons of the accuracy and precision of locally based schemes.

Through careful training and sampling design, it should be possible for locally based monitoring to yield results which are as reliable as those of conventional techniques (Yoccoz, Nichols and Boulinier, 2003), and which can shed light on aspects of biodiversity which are hard to monitor conventionally.

To ensure this, it is necessary to consider likely biases at the design stage, to plan sampling effort to minimize their impact, and to train data gatherers and data interpreters accordingly.

Promptness of decision-making

Part of the reason for monitoring natural resources is to inform policy- and decision-makers and to facilitate management interventions. We looked for prior studies on the speed of decision-making in monitoring schemes but found little information. To our knowledge, only the scheme in the example from the Philippines has examined the speed with which conservation management decisions were taken by assessing the time from data sampling to decision-making for each of 156 conservation management interventions (Danielsen *et al.*, 2005b). The mean time from sampling to decision-making in this scheme was only 97 days, probably because most (82%) of the interventions were initiated by the same people and institutions that had compiled the underlying data, sidestepping multilayered bureaucracies.

To obtain the full benefit of rapid decision-making linked to locally based monitoring also requires a supportive policy and legal environment. If local stakeholders have no ownership or control over resources, their monitoring is unlikely to lead to prompt decision-making. Features such as corruption and hidden political agendas may constrain the speed and direction of local decision-making. Careful design may improve the speed of decision-making of all categories of schemes, and in particular, each scheme needs a mechanism for feeding results from the monitoring directly into management.

Potential for local empowerment

Monitoring alone does not empower people, but locally based monitoring can be integrated with processes of local empowerment in natural resource management. This includes the application and generation of local knowledge, and greater influence on and involvement in management decisions. Locally based monitoring should be coupled to local stakeholder's rights and responsibilities, which can be set up by appropriate negotiated agreements. This also helps ensure real local interest in local monitoring.

Few quantitative data exist on the empowerment potential of monitoring schemes. In the scheme in the Philippines, one in three conservation management interventions was jointly undertaken by local community members and government authorities (F. Danielsen, unpublished data). In the Tanzanian scheme, 50% of suggested management interventions were implemented by the communities themselves (Topp-Jørgensen *et al.*, 2005). Overall, the potential for local empowerment rises with the involvement of local stakeholders in monitoring.

Ease of feeding into national and international schemes

The ability of monitoring schemes to contribute data to national and global schemes probably declines as they become more local. Data from locally based monitoring are beginning to be aggregated for national-level analysis in the examples in the Philippines, Tanzania and Namibia. These initiatives, although promising, are still in their infancy. If well done, they can bring government and communities together in a new way, improve co-ordination and decision-making, clarify roles in broader natural resource management, and raise the profile of Community Based Natural Resource Management efforts among policy-makers and scientists, as datasets are aggregated and presented in wider fora.

Analytical tools such as meta-analysis (Gurevitch, Curtis and Jones, 2001) offer substantial opportunities for analysing data from locally based sources, to provide input into tracking larger-scale trends in the status of populations and habitats (e.g. Loh *et al.*, 2005), the services they provide, and the threats they face. To do this, schemes need to use a small number of methods, each well replicated, across a large number of sites (e.g. Côté *et al.*, 2005).

Research needs

Our study shows the need for rigorous comparisons between locally based and conventional scientist-based monitoring methods. Since the conference on locally based monitoring in Denmark in 2004, a new project has been funded by the Danish Government – 'Monitoring Matters: Comparative Analysis of Innovative Approaches' (MOMA). This project is working in six countries – Ghana, Madagascar, Namibia, Nicaragua, Tanzania and the Philippines (Danielsen *et al.*, 2005c). The aim of the project is to answer some of the basic scientific questions about the importance of locally based monitoring, particularly whether locally based monitoring is able to detect changes in the abundance, distribution and utilization of resources, and whether this approach is an effective resource management tool, when compared with conventional methods.

It would, however, be a mistake to see this approach as an untested pipe dream. Locally based monitoring is already underway, and methods are being further improved. We believe the approach holds promise, but it requires rigorous testing to determine whether local people are best able to monitor changes in habitat, large animal abundances, cryptic species changes, or changes in ecosystem services. Already some important lessons have emerged from the case studies we highlight in this chapter and we expect more as the schemes mature and ways are found to embed them at the local level and within the systems of governments in developing countries.

Acknowledgements

Our thanks to Andrew Balmford, Leon Bennun, Paul Donald, Martin Enghoff, Jon Fjeldså, Hanne Hübertz, Sune Holt, Per Moestrup Jensen, Julia Jones, Anna Lawrence and Thomas Skielboe for discussion; to the Protected Area and Wildlife Bureau of the Philippine Department of Environment and Natural Resources and the Forestry and Beekeeping Division of the Ministry of Natural Resources and Tourism in Tanzania for collaborative work on locally based monitoring; and to the Research Council of the Danish Ministry of Foreign Affairs, for funding the preparation of this chapter.

REFERENCES

Akida, A. (2007). What is the National Forestry and Beekeeping Database? *The Arc Journal* **21** (September 2007), 34–35.

Balmford, A., Green, R. E. and Jenkins, M. (2003). Measuring the changing state of nature. *Trends in Ecology and Evolution* **18**, 326–330.

Bibby C. J., Burgess, N. D., Hill, D. A. and Mustoe, S. (2000). *Bird Census Techniques*: 2nd edition. London: Academic Press, 350 pp.

Blomley, T. (2006). Mainstreaming participatory forestry within the local government reform process in Tanzania. *Gatekeeper Series* **128**. London: International Institute for Environment and Development.

Blomley, T and Ramadhani, H. (2006). Going to scale with Participatory Forest Management: early lessons from Tanzania. *International Forestry Review* **8**, 93–100.

Brashares, J. S. (2003). Behavioral, ecological, and life-history correlates of mammal extinctions in West Africa. *Conservation Biology* **17**, 733–743.

Brashares, J. S. and Arcese, P. (2002). Role of forage, habitat and predation in the behavioral plasticity of a small African antelope. *Journal of Animal Ecology* **71**, 626–638.

Brashares, J. S. and Sam, M. K. (2005). How much is enough? Estimating the minimum sampling required for effective monitoring of African reserves. *Biodiversity and Conservation* **14**, 2709–2722. Available at www.monitoringmatters.org/articles/full10.pdf.

Brashares, J. S., Arcese, P. and Sam, M. K. (2001). Human demography and reserve size predict wildlife extinction in West Africa. *Proceedings Royal Society of London B* **268**, 2473–2478.

Brashares, J. S., Arcese, P., Sam, M. K. *et al.* (2004). Bushmeat hunting, wildlife declines and fish supply in West Africa. *Science* **306**, 1180–1183.

Côté, I. M., Gill, J. A., Gardner, T. A. and Watkinson, A. R. (2005). Measuring coral reef decline through meta-analysis. *Philosophical Transactions of the Royal Society of London B* **360**, 385–395.

Danielsen, F., Balete, D. S., Poulsen, M. K. *et al.* (2000). A simple system for monitoring biodiversity in protected areas of a developing country. *Biodiversity and Conservation* **9**, 1671–1705.

Danielsen, F., Burgess, N. D. and Balmford, A. (2005a). Monitoring matters: examining the potential of locally-based approaches. *Biodiversity and Conservation* **14**, 2507–2542. Available at www.monitoringmatters.org/articles/full1.pdf.

Danielsen, F., Jensen, A. E., Alviola, P. A. *et al.* (2005b). Does monitoring matter? A quantitative assessment of management decisions from locally-based monitoring of protected areas. *Biodiversity and Conservation* **14**, 2633–2652. Available at www.monitoringmatters.org/articles/full6.pdf.

Danielsen, F., Burgess, N. D. and Balmford, A. (eds.) (2005c). Monitoring matters: examining the potential of locally-based approaches. Fifteen case studies presented in *Special issue of Biodiversity and Conservation* **14**, (11), Available at http://www.monitoringmatters.org/cases.htm

Danielsen, F., Mendoza, M. M., Tagtag, A. *et al.* (2007). Increasing conservation management action by involving local stakeholders in natural resource monitoring. *Ambio* **36**, 566–570.

Danielsen, F., Burgess, N. D., Balmford, A. *et al.* (2009). Local participation in natural resource monitoring: a characterization of approaches. *Conservation Biology* **23**, 31–42. Available at http://www.monitoringmatters.org/cases.htm

Department of Environment and Natural Resources (DENR) (1992). National Integrated Protected Area System Act R. A. No. 7586 and Implementing Rules and Regulations DAO 25, Series of 1992. Manila, The Philippines: DENR, PAWB.

DENR (2000). Guidelines on the Implementation of the Biodiversity Monitoring System (BMS) in Protected Areas. Department of Environment and Natural Resources Administrative Order No. 2000–13. Quezon City, The Philippines: DENR, Diliman.

Ghana Wildlife Division (2000). *Wildlife Division Policy for Collaborative Community Based Wildlife Management.* Accra, Ghana: Ministry of Forestry, 11pp.

Gurevitch, J., Curtis, P. S. and Jones, M. H. (2001). Meta-analysis in ecology. *Advances in Ecological Research* **32**, 199–247.

IUCN (2007). *2007 IUCN Red List of Threatened Species.* Available at www.iucnredlist.org

Loh, J., Green, R. E., Ricketts, T. *et al.* (2005). The Living Planet Index: using species population time series to track trends in biodiversity. *Philosophical Transactions of the Royal Society of London B*, **360**, 289–295.

Millenium Ecosystem Assessment (2005). *Ecosystems and Human Well-Being: Synthesis Report.* Washington D.C: Island Press.

Poulsen, M. K., Massao, J., Burgess, N. and Topp-Jørgensen, E. (2007). Community based monitoring of PFM in Tanzania: initial experiences and lessons learned. *The Arc Journal* **21**, 31–33.

Stuart-Hill, G., Diggle, R., Munali, B., Tagg, J. and Ward, D. (2005). The Event Book System: a community based natural resource monitoring system from Namibia. *Biodiversity and Conservation* **14**, 2611–2631. Available at www.monitoringmatters.org/articles/full5.pdf.

Topp-Jørgensen, E., Poulsen, M. K., Lund, J. F. and Massao, J. F. (2005). Community-based monitoring of natural resource use and forest quality in montane forests and miombo woodlands in Iringa District, Tanzania. *Biodiversity and Conservation* **14**, 2653–2677. Available at www.monitoringmatters.org/articles/full7.pdf.

United Republic of Tanzania (2007). National Forest and Beekeeping Programme Monitoring Database (NAFOBEDA) Version 2.8. Monitoring Manual – Monitoring Procedures. Tanzania: Forestry and Beekeeping Division, Ministry of Natural Resources and Tourism.

Uychiaoco, A. J., Arceo, H. O., Green, S. J. *et al.* (2005). Monitoring and evaluation of reef protected areas by local fishers in the Philippines: tightening the adaptive management cycle. *Biodiversity and Conservation* **14**, 2775–2794. Available at www.monitoringmatters.org/articles/full14.pdf.

Wily, L. A. (2000). Forest law in Eastern and Southern Africa. Moving towards a community based forest future? *Unasylva* **203**, 29 pp.

Yoccoz, N. G., Nichols, J. D. and Boulinier, T. (2003). Monitoring of biological diversity – a response to Danielsen *et al. Oryx* **37**, 410.

6

Researching local perspectives on biodiversity in tropical landscapes: lessons from ten case studies

MANUEL BOISSIÈRE, MARIEKE SASSEN, DOUGLAS SHEIL,
MIRIAM VAN HEIST, WIL DE JONG, ROBERT CUNLIFFE,
MEILINDA WAN, MICHAEL PADMANABA, NINING LISWANTI,
IMAM BASUKI, KRISTEN EVANS, PETER CRONKLETON,
TIM LYNAM, PIIA KOPONEN AND CHRISTIANA BAIRAKTARI

CIFOR's Multidisciplinary Landscape Assessment approach

The Multidisciplinary Landscape Assessment (MLA) approach, initiated in 1999 by researchers at the Center for International Forestry Research (CIFOR) in collaboration with various partners, combines a technical survey of species, habitats and landscape locations with an assessment of their significance to local people. It fits the CIFOR mission to conduct research relevant to improving natural resource management and benefiting people. Its main claim to distinctiveness lies in its multi-disciplinary range of methods. The MLA landscape is defined by the people that live in it: how they define its land and vegetation types, the way they relate to it and use it: 'a holistic and spatially explicit concept that is much more than the sum of its components: terrain, soil, land cover and use, [. . .] a cultural construction' (Sheil *et al.*, 2003). The geographical scale of the landscape depends on the distances or (territories) that people cover to meet their livelihood needs. None of the studies explicitly explored local communities' concepts of 'biodiversity' and the term was never used with them. Rather the emphasis was on the environment and landscape in which people lived.

Since the first survey was conducted, others have used the approach in similar surveys. This chapter describes the basic methods; then compares the application and outcomes of the approach in ten case studies.

Taking Stock of Nature: Participatory Biodiversity Assessment for Policy, Planning and Practice, ed. Anna Lawrence. Published by Cambridge University Press. © Cambridge University Press 2010.

The basic approach

The approach and initial methods were developed during an extended two-month workshop and field trial in Malinau, East Kalimantan. Experienced local and international researchers from the social and biophysical sciences came together to discuss and evaluate procedures. With limited time and funding for field research, and a desire to cover a large area, they emphasized rapid methods. Each researcher contributed their own experiences and drew on the relevant technical literature (such as, for quantitative ethnobotany, Turner, 1988; Stoffle, Halmo and Evans, 1990; Philips, 1996; Cunningham, 2001). Methods were tested and revised through various field trials.

A full description of the methods (Sheil *et al.*, 2003) is available in English, Indonesian, French and Spanish, along with various associated publications and materials, from www.cifor.cgiar.org/mla/. Here we describe key aspects. The principles of an MLA survey are that the biophysical data are linked to their local relevance, and local perceptions inform and guide the biophysical studies. This ensures that local views are present and regarded as relevant through all stages of the study, including the collection of technical data. The survey involves six steps:

gaining acceptance and building a shared understanding with communities;
asking what occurs where (as in classical biodiversity assessments);
asking why it matters to local people;
diagnosis (evaluating implications and possible courses of action);
sharing insights and implications with stakeholders;
assessing stakeholder feedback.

The village-based activities are led by a 'village team' consisting of social scientists (i.e. socio-economist, anthropologist), while a 'field team' made up of a combination of ecologists, botanists, soil scientists and ethnobotanists carries out the biophysical components of the survey. They work together through daily reviews and planning. A minimum of four weeks is generally needed to allow for planning, community engagement, data collection, initial cross-checking and review of the data gathered.

As a first step, researchers seek local agreement and support by presenting and discussing the survey objectives in a community meeting, where they can also address community expectations and offer a daily wage to those who contribute time. Initial efforts are invested in building a shared understanding of terminology to describe landscape elements, vegetation types and resource use categories based on local perception, among and between the research team and the villagers. This guides the subsequent community exercises and fieldwork.

Both teams work with the villagers to list and map basic geographic features, landscape elements, and culturally or otherwise important sites and resources. They leave these maps with the community and ask permission to keep copies, leaving out information that the community finds sensitive.

The 'village team' solicits people's views on natural resources, land use, forest management, threats, conservation and the future. They interview household heads and key informants (leaders, healers, traders in forest products and shopkeepers) using questionnaires. Scoring exercises help to quantify the relative importance of land and forest types; of forests over time; of different sources of plants and animals (wild, cultivated, bought), and of species that the community defines in various categories of use. In these scoring exercises, respondents are divided into ethnic, gender or age groups to capture these groups' different perceptions.

The 'field team' surveys plots in each land and forest type defined by the villagers. They collect standard biophysical data, including botanical specimens and soil samples from each site, together with information from local informants (women and men) on the value of sites for different uses, the sites' histories, their use by the community, and the name and use for all plants recorded. The methods allow for one or two plots to be surveyed in a single day, depending on logistics (see Sheil *et al.*, 2003, for details on the sampling method).

Cross-checks, quality controls and team discussions are important aspects of the approach. For example, the field team cross-checks data with the village team; community meetings examine botanical specimens and discuss any contradictions, which may require additional field visits.

The surveys are led by researchers, normally without involving local people in setting objectives, or coordination. Communities give permission for the research to take place and then provide local views and guidance as described. Local guidance is particularly important in developing the local landscape maps, and identifying the locations of plants, animals, and special sites.

Overview of the ten case studies

To understand the wider relevance of this approach we describe ten case studies which applied the MLA process (Table 6.1), following a fixed format to help the reader compare experiences.

The cases range from large, long-term well-funded projects to small-scale activities with restricted budgets and short durations. Several projects covered

Table 6.1 *Overview of the MLA case studies*

Location	Scale and communities	Goals and objectives
1. Malinau (East Kalimantan, Indonesia). Largely intact tropical rainforest under concessions.	Seven villages in one watershed (2189 km²). Farmers and hunter-gatherers	Baseline study to develop, apply and evaluate methods for assessing species, habitats and locations, and their local importance. Produce good baseline information for conservation planning, based on local perspectives.
2. Gorongosa National Park (GNP) (Mozambique). Rift valley and adjacent uplands, mainly dry savanna vegetation.	Two villages, one within and one peripheral to GNP (about 400 km² around each village). Farmers and fishermen (Lake Urema).	Develop and test an alternative approach for assessing landscape importance. Develop spatial models to enable overlay of 'community values' with 'conservation values'. Inform ongoing process of management planning for Gorongosa National Park.
3. Ottotomo (Cameroon). Small forest reserve in forest mosaic landscape.	One village (10–15 km²), next to forest reserve (about 30 km²). Farmers.	Improve understanding of local perceptions and needs in order to benefit local forest management. Improve communication between communities and reserve management.
4. Palawan (Philippines). One of last remaining natural forests in Phillipines.	One village whose territory covers an important valley (about 60 km²). Farmers and hunter-gatherers.	Understand local perceptions of landscape and resources. Inform process of developing joint natural resource management.
5. Gunung Lumut (Kalimantan, Indonesia). Protection forest.	Two villages in or near protected area (about 300 km²). Farmers and hunter-gatherers.	Complement Biodiversity Assessment (GLBA) with local value information. Supply information to improve management plan for Protection Forest.

Site	Villages/area	Objectives
6. Mamberamo (Papua, Indonesia). Largely intact tropical forest, partly in swamp lowlands, remote and scarcely populated.	Three villages within Mamberamo watershed (about 5000 km^2).	Build local capacity for MLA approach to biodiversity assessment. Identify key species and sites, local conservation concerns and priorities. Build trust and collaboration between communities and CI-Papua.
7. Khe Tran (Thua Thien Hue, Vietnam). Buffer zone for planned conservation area.	One village (20 km^2). Settled (ex-swidden) farmers.	Provide information for land use planning, taking into account local perceptions. Provide baseline data for biodiversity conservation. Discuss opportunities and constraints of conservation institutions in local context.
8. Ivindo National Park (INP) (Gabon). Intact tropical forest, Ivindo river.	One village, 50 km strip along river inside INP (3000 km^2). Fishermen (Ivindo river), hunters, sand collectors. Very limited farming	Improve understanding of local perceptions and priorities regarding forest landscape. Inform and promote sustainable management of newly gazetted Ivindo National Park.
9. Uttaranchal (India). Deodar, chir and sal forest on lower Himalayan foothills.	Six villages (about 600 km^2).	Assess goods and services from forests, with special regard to local communities' perceptions. Build model for optimizing ecosystem goods and services from plantations.
10. Pando (Bolivia). Remote north Amazon, Brazil nut collection.	Two villages (80 and 40 km^2 of forest respectively).	Make MLA tools more participatory and accessible to communities. Facilitate adoption of forest monitoring techniques and findings. Document customary forest property rights.

large areas that included intact and relatively inaccessible forests (1, 6, 8, 10), while others focused on modified landscapes (3, 7, 9). Some of these areas had already been subjected to detailed biological inventories (3, 4, 7, 8) while little information on the flora, fauna or ecology existed in others (1, 6). Five cases engaged a single community (3, 4, 5, 7, 8) while two worked with more than five (1, 9). The communities depended to varying degrees on local land use; some were primarily farmers while others depended largely on wild resources. Some communities maintained access to pristine habitats (1, 6), others had been prohibited from traditional areas (3, 7) or would be as soon as conservation management became effective (8).

Government officials were sometimes involved in data collection and evaluation (1, 4, 6, 10). NGO staff, park or reserve managers, students and scientists participated in collecting data (1, 2, 3, 4, 7, 8), and capacity building (6, 8, 9, 10). In most cases a smaller team led by CIFOR or a consultant analysed the data, and reviewed results with communities whenever possible (1, 2, 3, 6, 7, 10).

Objectives included development and assessment of the methods (1, 2, 3, 7, 9, 10), and often to guide plans for a larger research programme (1, 2, 4, 8). The studies contributed to local management planning for conservation areas (2, 5, 7, 8); managing a wider landscape for conservation purposes (1, 2, 6); and mapping and zoning (1, 2, 6, 10). Training was a formal goal in only two studies, for conservation practitioners (6) and community members (10), but capacity building was important in others (3, 8, 9).

Most communities were minorities (Punan in Malinau, Batak in Palawan, Pahy in Vietnam, Pasir in Gunung Lumut). In some cases other stakeholders, including political elites, viewed local communities as backward and neglected their views in decision making processes.

Case studies

1. Malinau (Kalimantan, Indonesia)

CIFOR is committed to undertaking long-term research in Malinau, a district of East Kalimantan. Malinau's forests are threatened by logging, mining and conversion. The area had scarcely been studied previously, but scientists anticipated that such a rugged and densely forested region would possess a rich flora and fauna of global significance. Various indigenous communities depend on the forest as hunter-gatherers and swidden cultivators. CIFOR and collaborators developed the methods to survey the biodiversity and prioritize research (Sheil *et al.*, 2003).

Research focused on local communities, the Merap and Punan ethnic groups, who represent two distinct cultures. The interests of other stakeholders were already obvious (e.g. logging companies value accessible timber). Local governments did not yet exist during the initial field studies, but subsequently emerged as significant local decision makers. CIFOR worked with a Kalimantan-based NGO, Yayasan Biosfer Manusia (BIOMA), staff from Mulawarman University of Samarinda (Unmul), Bogor Institute of Agriculture (IPB), the Ministry of Forestry's Forestry Research and Development Agency (FORDA) and government scientists from the Indonesian Institute of Science (LIPI).

Results were surprising, insightful and helpful to improved forestry practices (Sheil *et al.*, 2006). For example they showed that local people value logged-over forest much less than primary forest, mainly because forest undergrowth is cleared after harvesting timber. As this practice offers no clear silvicultural benefits, researchers proposed that it be stopped. In another example, the damage often caused to local gravesites by timber harvesting equipment is a major aggravation to communities. Taboos surrounding use of these sites make them valuable for conservation, but logging companies viewed claims made against them as simply 'the communities asking for money'. Field visits verified that gravesites were damaged. The approach also clarified apparent contradictions. For example, some Punan were embarrassed to admit they depended on sago, a resource that other ethnic groups considered as indicative of backwardness. Once recognized that sago is a vital famine food, the threats caused by logging to natural sago stands, as well as to other resources, were seen in a new light.

There were significant costs after the survey, including soil analysis and botanical taxonomy; data handling, which included checking and revising in a large team; and the feedback activities with local communities; but all stages of the study were well funded.

The strength of the approach was that it allowed researchers to identify and study important components of a relatively inaccessible landscape while gaining an appreciation of their significance for local people. Ecologically and botanically the survey is the most complete in the region. The results proved rich. Though a range of related studies have been conducted as follow up (e.g. Cunliffe *et al.*, 2007) many issues have yet to be adequately pursued. The small team quickly got locked into describing the surveys, promoting and refining the methods and employing them elsewhere, rather than addressing the highlighted research topics.

Research results have been disseminated through scientific and non-scientific media (reports; books; articles in journals, newspapers and magazines; presentations; posters; cards; films). The survey results have also been used in the development of a new environmental education curriculum for the district. An impact evaluation showed that the team's poster campaign had statistically significantly improved factual knowledge of, and agreement with, concerns identified by the local communities amongst other communities, townspeople and even district government officials. It found unanimous support for conservation measures in the district (Padmanaba and Sheil, 2007).

Community members often comment that through their involvement they have learned to express what is important to them, and appreciate being better able to communicate their concerns to the local government and other stakeholders (Pye-Smith, 2005; Padmanaba and Sheil, 2007). The trust and dialogue that were built also ensured a sense of local ownership of the process. Researchers provided external perspectives and found that people were generally receptive to the global significance of local biodiversity. Elders and healers also communicated their knowledge to other members of the communities through the research activities and dissemination materials.

Impact on decision making was most evident in the case of two planned oil palm plantation projects (Basuki and Sheil, 2005), that researchers persuaded the government to move or reconsider using the survey results. In one case, NGOs used the results to persuade the central government to reconsider their plan to convert more than one million hectares of Borneo's forest area to oil palm (Kompas, 2006). The government of Indonesia has currently postponed this operation, put a moratorium on converting natural forest to plantations, and requires full impact assessments to be undertaken for all such future projects.

The research team is still promoting the results to large-scale initiatives such as national forest certification processes (involving various NGOs and national institutions). Perhaps the most significant impact is the fact that many related studies have been conducted, as reported in the rest of this chapter.

2. Gorongosa National Park (Mozambique)

The Gorongosa case study was carried out while the Gorongosa National Park (GNP) was being re-established in central Mozambique. Formerly a flagship park in terms of size, biological resources and numbers of visitors, the GNP suffered a complete breakdown of management and infrastructure during the civil war of 1982–1992, together with severe depletion of large-mammal populations and an influx of settlers into the park. By 2002 the park authorities were developing a new management plan, including new policies and procedures for working with local communities. This required a better understanding of communities within and adjacent to the park, their livelihoods, and their use of and impacts on natural resources.

While providing an opportunity for testing and extending the approach in a new ecological context (savanna), the study also yielded results relevant to rebuilding the GNP. The research was carried out as a partnership between CIFOR, the University of Zimbabwe and the GNP management authorities. The principal objective was to develop a spatial model of landscape importance to local communities, and overlay this with a map of conservation importance based on vegetation types and constituent woody plant species, so as to identify areas of greatest potential conflict between local communities and park managers.

Work was carried out in two villages, Muaredzi and Nhanchururu, differing in terms of location (central versus peripheral), ecological setting (valley floor versus escarpment slopes) and livelihood activities (family farming, supplemented by fishing in Muaredzi). Both villages were relatively small (40 and 107 households respectively). Each study area comprised a 20 km by 20 km box around the village, because residents reported that they seldom travel more than 10 km to harvest any resources.

Data were collected over about three weeks in each village. Each community selected a team (22 members in Muaredzi, 18 in Nhanchururu), comprising a balance of ages, gender and different livelihood activities. Vegetation types were defined and described using stratified vegetation sampling. The university research team subsequently overlaid community landscape values with plant biodiversity values.

From a research perspective, the study provided an extension of the original MLA approach by incorporating Bayesian modelling techniques and spatial analyses to develop spatial models of community landscape values, and by overlaying community valuations with those based on plant biodiversity results. These methodological developments stimulated further development of spatial models of importance values, notably in CIFOR's research area in East Kalimantan (Cunliffe *et al.*, 2007, Lynam *et al.*, 2007).

For local communities the study provided a good opportunity to communicate their desires to park managers. In particular, the people of Muaredzi, who were under threat of forced relocation, were able to communicate their wish to be allowed to stay (and are still in place). The approach was too complex, however, to enable the largely illiterate community members to use the results in discussions with management and, in any case, there were no structures in place for such negotiations.

Park managers had previously paid relatively little attention to local perspectives. Through continued involvement with other research projects within the GNP, in particular the Gorongosa-Marromeu component of the Southern African Millennium Ecosystem Assessment (SAfMA-GM) project, the research team was able to feed the results into park planning and management processes. For example, the project highlighted the need to develop a comprehensive vegetation and landscape map for the park, and efforts have subsequently been made to put this in place, as well as to further improve understanding of local livelihoods (Cunliffe, 2003). Similarly, the participation of senior government and NGO representatives in a user advisory group for the SAfMA-GM project and thus their exposure to project results is likely to influence understanding and policy development at the provincial and national levels.

More formal utilization of the results has been constrained by two factors. First, this was an exploratory study carried out as a discrete undertaking, rather than embedded into an ongoing research effort or within an agreed management process. Second, practical application of project results has been strongly constrained by institutional developments, particularly the much delayed process whereby the Mozambican government has developed a formal management agreement with an external private sector partner.

3. Ottotomo (Cameroon)

The MLA approach was tested in a community near the small (30 km^2) forest reserve of Ottotomo in southwest Cameroon. In this area, population pressure leads people to claim access to remaining old-growth forests such as reserves. Previous CIFOR work had examined the relationship of local communities and administration (Jum and Oyono, 2005), and the survey was intended to help managers understand local perceptions and needs. A soil study was not required.

The research took place with the Ewondo inhabitants of the village of Nkolbibanda (27 households), whose traditional territory used to extend into Ottotomo until the French colonial authorities established the forest reserve. According to community maps the territory is now about 10–15 km^2. People depend on cassava swidden agriculture and non-timber forest products (NTFPs) for income, food and medicine.

Until the time of the study, the National Forestry Development Agency (ONADEF), under the Ministry of Water and Forests (MINEF), was in charge of reserve management. Unfortunately, the reorganization process at the time of the study left reserve management responsibilities unclear. CIFOR conducted the four-week study with the local NGO Association Terre et Développement and the help of a botanist and student from the 'Université de Yaoundé'. People felt previous research and development groups had broken their promises or even stolen resources, and they were very suspicious at first. Internal conflicts also played a role. Consistently answering repeated questions and working with old and respected men in field activities, helped researchers gain people's trust and interest.

Through the different scoring patterns and explanations of older and younger groups, the study showed how attitudes towards, and knowledge of, the forested environment are changing. Growing access to information, schooling and healthcare influence people's aspirations and perceptions. Local development NGOs promote a more commercial agriculture. Whereas farming was formerly women's work, younger men now take on larger-scale cultivation of food crops such as cassava for cash, sometimes using fertilizers. Other influences, such as the promotion of NTFP harvesting and trade by NGOs and researchers seem to encourage people to see the forest and forest resources more as commodities (Sassen and Jum, 2007).

Most youths live in the village only during school holidays and this made them less interested in and knowledgeable about the forest and related traditions. Most aim to work in town after school. They nevertheless said they learned about their territory from the community map. The implications of these changes for traditional knowledge, cultural identity and for forest resource use are important yet hardly known.

The intention had been to use the results in follow-up work by CIFOR's Adaptive and Collaborative Management team on local participation in the management of the reserve, but lack of funding meant this did not happen. It is unclear what will happen to plans to involve local communities in decision-making about the forest reserve or to set up a community managed area as laid out in the reserve's management plan.

4. Palawan (Philippines)

'Levelling the Playing Field' (LPF), a four-year project based in Indonesia, Malaysia and Philippines, facilitates discussions and negotiations among stakeholders to achieve natural resource management that supports their livelihoods (Devanadera *et al.*, 2004). Palawan Island has some of the last remaining natural forest in the Philippines, where the Batak combine a hunter-gatherer livelihood with shifting cultivation. They are under threat from decreasing population (Eder, 1987), disappearing forest resources, and dependency on outsiders living on the coast. LPF was interested in using MLA methods to understand the Batak's perspectives on the landscape and resources and traditional forest management systems.

The survey was conducted with the Batak community in Kalakwasan village, and at the same time served to train LPF team members. It was organized by members of LPF-Philippines, CIFOR, two universities (Palawan State University and University of the Philippines Los Baños) and the local government's Planning and Development Office. The team included social scientists and facilitators from the district. Community members were helpful informants for village and field activities. The survey was restricted to one village of 136 inhabitants and its territory, and was carried out in 17 days (Boissière and Liswanti, 2006).

The team used all parts of the original methods except the soil analysis, which they considered both expensive and unnecessary. Philippine botanists identified the specimens, while CIFOR staff analysed the data. A crucial group of informants were the shamans, the only villagers with knowledge about non-woody plants, primarily used as medicine or for magic. Villagers' time was scarce because low rice supplies meant they needed time for gathering forest resources, but they became more willing to participate after researchers offered to pay compensation for their time.

LPF staff gained a new perspective on the Batak and their relationship with the outside world, and used the results to adapt the project activities and to involve the Batak more closely in decisions and planning. Some who did not participate in the survey were surprised by the researchers' recommendations to hold more LPF activities in the Batak village, instead of asking Batak representatives to come to the district, as was the case previously. They realized that because of very different views on resource management and unequal power relations, they would have to work with the Batak and outsiders separately, and developed a role-playing game on sustainable natural resource management with both groups independently (Campo and Villanueva, 2006). The survey also provided information on Batak priorities to donors and to Philippines institutions, including the city government in Palawan, which will give the Batak a clearer profile at local, regional and national levels.

The MLA was part of a long-term international project, which guaranteed follow-up to the survey results. Previous 'participatory' development projects in the area have seldom asked the Batak for their perspective on land management and their own priorities. Participation in the survey encouraged the team members to look at the landscape, resources and threats, from the Batak point of view. Some of the team now have new responsibilities (e.g. with the Biodiversity Research and Conservation Center based in Palawan) and their understanding of this marginalized group will influence their actions in the future.

The LPF team returned the results (such as the participatory maps) to the Batak. The main weakness of the survey was the short time in which it was conducted. Building a relationship with a community takes time and is essential for developing trust, understanding and involvement.

5. Gunung Lumut Protection Forest (Kalimantan, Indonesia)

Gunung Lumut Protection Forest (GLPF), an important area for biodiversity conservation and watershed management of Paser District, East Kalimantan, is under heavy pressure from forest encroachment and timber extraction. The Gunung Lumut Biodiversity Assessment (GLBA), co-ordinated by Tropenbos International–Indonesia (TBI-I), was initiated in order to apply for the status of World Heritage Site and to improve the GLPF management plan. TBI-I asked CIFOR to complement their biodiversity survey using the MLA approach in an area of more than 30 000 ha. The study aimed to identify species important for daily needs, and potential sites for ecotourism and other development options; and to understand local people's view on threats to forests.

The socio-economic research involved international and national research centres, and a local NGO Persatuan Masyarakat Adat Paser. The study focused on two settlements near the GLPF area, Mului and Rantau Layung. Twenty households participated in the study, including key informants (village head, hunters, teachers, healer and customary leader) with specific knowledge of local history, hunting sites, medicinal plants and rituals.

Researchers from different groups of organizations conducted the socio-economic survey and, separately, the biophysical survey. Co-ordinating 19 Indonesian and Dutch researchers and more than 30 field assistants caused frequent logistic difficulties. The approach (especially the questionnaires) was adapted to answer problems faced by the management of GLPF and to identify potential resources that would benefit both local livelihood and biodiversity conservation.

Two workshops were held to disseminate project results and recommendations to the local government and other stakeholders (Murniati *et al.*, 2006). TBI-I proposed incorporating results on local perceptions into the proposal addressed to UNESCO for the establishment of the World Heritage Site. TBI-I is also using the results to support local government plans to establish a conservation district, and to propose the Gunung Lumut area as a national park. The new management group of GLPF was formed during the workshop in Paser, combining elements of government, universities, NGOs and communities.

Villagers expressed support for the project, as long as it did not lead to plans to move them from their area and to restrict access to forest resources. However, it also raised expectations among the villagers, who believed that development programmes would be implemented.

6. Mamberamo (Papua, Indonesia)

In developing a Biodiversity Conservation Corridor in Mamberamo watershed (Papua, Indonesia), Conservation International (CI) recognizes the need to find suitable means to allow local communities to participate in decision-making processes, and to build capacity of locally based researchers and government staff to assist in planning and developing this conservation programme. CI-Papua therefore requested CIFOR to jointly develop a capacity building project for implementing an MLA in Mamberamo. The project took place in 2004 and had three phases: theoretical, field and analysis training.

CI, in collaboration with CIFOR, selected two villages for the pilot field-work: Kwerba, an 'unofficial' traditional village in the hills, and Papasena-I, a 134 households registered village in the plains. The main objectives were identification of key local sites, species and resources; local conservation concerns and priorities; possible threats to biodiversity; species importance from local perspectives; as well as training CI and government staff in the various methods (CIFOR, 2004).

CIFOR and CI organized the training and planned the survey. Trainees collected and analysed the data supervised by a botanist from LIPI and CIFOR staff. All elements of the methods were used in training, and questionnaires adjusted to fit local terminology, conditions and context. The villagers of Kwerba and Papasena-I participated as respondents and helpers during the fieldwork. CI staff; students, teaching staff and alumni from Universitas Negeri Papua and Universitas Cenderawasih; and civil servants from the Provincial Environmental Impact Monitoring Agency and the Provincial Nature Resource Conservation Agency participated in the training events.

This was the first time that CI did a biodiversity assessment from a local perspective in Indonesia, and it implemented a follow-up project to define the specific needs of each stakeholder group, adapt the methods, propose new conservation related activities, and identify new project locations in the Mamberamo area. This took place in late 2006 in Kwerba, Papasena and Kay villages, with three major activities: a socio-economic survey including a family inventory of land ownership, ground-checking activities to relate observed land use to local people's perceptions, and traditional monitoring for high economic value and critically threatened species.

The strength of this approach was its ability to build trust between villagers and the team (including CI). This is not a trivial achievement, as villagers were suspicious of outsiders interested in their natural resources. They especially appreciated the participatory maps, and youths in Papasena spent many hours preparing drawings. People quickly adopted the idea of making a map of their own territories and claimed the maps as part of their identity, so they not only helped researchers to build common understanding of the survey area, but also raised village commitment to participation in the project.

Villagers also expressed enthusiasm for a continued relationship with CI, supporting conservation activities that meet their hopes for sustainability of the forest. Local people would like to use the participatory map for discussing land conflicts and rights to resources (e.g. crocodile hunting, logging). Owing to the positive impact of this project, CI was allowed by local land owners to conduct a biodiversity survey in the Foja Mountains, highly valued and strictly protected by Papasena villagers (Yance de Fretes, 2006; Sheil and Boissière, 2006).

7. Thua Thien Hue Province (Vietnam)

Vietnam is increasing local rights to its forests (Barney, 2005), but institutions implementing decentralization and land allocation still rarely involve local people. Government strongly supports plantation and agricultural development and has forbidden the practice of traditional shifting cultivation. CIFOR aimed to (1) adapt and test the approach for the local socio-economic context, (2) provide methods and information to better take account of local perceptions in land use and conservation planning, (3) provide baseline data for biodiversity conservation and (4) discuss opportunities and constraints for conservation institutions in the local context (Boissière *et al.*, 2006).

Khe Tran village in Hue Province is situated in the buffer zone of a planned conservation area. It was chosen because of the strong presence of minority groups, and potential for a partnership with Tropenbos International Vietnam (TBI-V) and the Extension and Training Support Project (ETSP). The researchers wanted to assess people's perceptions of the importance of biological resources as well as the role they would like to play in forest management, and subsequently recommend ways to involve them in protected area management.

The key stakeholders were the villagers belonging to the Pahy minority group mixed with Kinh and Khome, and decision-makers responsible for land allocation and land use planning (local government of Phong Dien district, Phong My commune). CIFOR worked with the 20 households of Khe Tran, through groups based on gender and location (which is linked to ethnic and economic status). Socio-economists, translators and botanists from Hue and Hanoi participated in the survey, and TBI-V assisted in coordination and administration. Altogether, the team spent five weeks in the field.

The villagers were keen to participate in the activities, and one or two members represented each household during the community meetings, although they had to get formal authorization from the village head and from commune officers to work with the team every day. Researchers focused on village lands in the immediate landscape, an area of about 200 ha, and followed the main methods, except soil sampling owing to high costs.

The MLA team discussed recommendations for land use planning with the key stakeholders in a workshop at Hue, at the commune and during village meetings. They considered options for community forestry, land tenure clarification, local involvement in conservation, and economic incentives. The study was followed by a participatory planning workshop through CIFOR's Future Scenarios (FS), which brought together local people and Phong My commune officers, government planning authorities and members of Hue University of Agriculture and Forestry (HUAF) (Evans, 2006). The MLA activities encouraged the community to consider the conditions of their landscape, their hopes, and what might be done about them. They decided that improving the landscape was important and achievable. Together they agreed on actions to develop and implement a forest management plan in concert with local authorities.

The use of three languages (English, Vietnamese and Pahy) complicated inventories and discussions, and researchers found that co-ordinating data among the field and village teams (e.g. finding local species names) took a lot of effort. The area was sensitive because of the presence of minority groups, making it difficult to gain the trust of local government authorities. They demanded payments and withheld permission to conduct plot surveys farther away from the village, or for foreign researchers to stay overnight in the village. Development-oriented authorities commented that the approach was too technical and academic to be useful to conservation practitioners. The trust that nevertheless developed between villagers and team helped to obtain reliable results.

The comprehensive set of methods is sometimes impractical for local people and decision-makers; in Vietnam it has more appeal to conservation institutions and NGOs. The baseline data produced from this study may be used in planning the Phong Dien Nature Reserve in the future, if local government and conservation institutions are interested in involving local people in its management.

8. Ivindo National Park (Gabon)

Over the past few years, Gabon has committed large efforts to supporting sustainable development of its protected areas. The rehabilitation of the Ipassa research station (1962) of Makokou, north eastern Gabon, included in the newly created 300 000 ha Ivindo National Park (INP), is part of this effort. The project was implemented by the Institut de Recherche en Ecologie Tropicale (IRET) of the Centre National de Recherche Scientifique et Technologique (CENAREST) with CIFOR and local experts. One of its objectives was to support research that would inform and promote sustainable management of the INP. The research was intended to contribute to this goal by improving the understanding of local perceptions and priorities concerning the landscape, and by finding opportunities for informed negotiation between development and conservation objectives in the INP area.

The project used all parts of the methods except the soil survey because of the cost and difficulty in finding a field soil scientist in Gabon. Practical considerations (time, logistics and budget) limited the study to only one of the communities affected by the new park, Loaloa. Field work lasted four weeks and involved stays of four to six days in the forest with extensive travel downriver to (partly) account for the territory used by the villagers.

Most of Loaloa's 47 households belong to the Kota ethnic group, with some Makina and Fang. People hunt, fish and extract sand from the river bed. Agriculture is very limited and many purchase additional food from nearby Makokou, which is also a centre for the bush meat trade towards larger cities such as Libreville. Traditional hunting and fishing sites along the Ivindo are included in the new national park. The affected communities have not been involved in the plans for establishing the park or in its future management plan.

Makokou is one of the best studied sites in Africa in terms of biological and ecological research, but studies of local communities' uses and perceptions of forest resources are scarce (Sassen and Wan, 2006). This project supported three masters students to research the use and importance of specific resources, and was followed by a study on the economic valuation of goods and services provided by the park. The study provided sound scientific knowledge on the importance of the INP area to Loaloa, people's detailed knowledge of forest ecosystem functioning, their appreciation of the potential benefits of a protected area and worries about restrictions in use. Although elephants are regularly hunted for ivory and the bush meat trade is a threat, researchers believe the study supports the case for an agreement with local communities enabling them to hunt certain species sustainably while controlling commercial hunting.

The outcomes of different elements of the study appear to be consistent, so simplifications in data collection could be considered. For example, for many uses, the scores for land and forest types during village-based exercises were consistent with the numbers of useful species found in these land and forest types (Sassen and Wan, 2006).

The results were provided to scientists, donors and decision-makers, but no structure is in place to ensure direct follow-up or evaluation of impacts. To contribute to more integrated management of the Park and its surroundings, this study would have to be conducted in more communities, and provide a basis for discussion with other stakeholders such as park authorities, local government and conservation NGOs.

9. Uttaranchal (India)

'Networking Forest Plantations[1] (NETFOP) in a crowded world: optimizing ecosystem services through improved planning and management' is a research network between Wageningen University and Research (WUR) in the Netherlands, Freiburg University (FU) in Germany and the Forest Research Institute (FRI) in Dehra Dun, India. Its objective is to establish an expert network of these universities on forest planning and management, and approaches for assessing and optimising forest ecosystem goods and services.

Having incorporated elements of the MLA approach in the project document, the project sought CIFOR's advice on assessing local communities' perceptions of the benefits and services of the forests, and in training the researchers. The survey was carried out in three altitudinal zones in the lower Himalaya. The Forest Department manages state forests in the middle and upper zones, with some involvement of village committees. Since 2002 village committees have also managed community plantations. Pressure is high: most communities depend on natural resources, have small agricultural fields and collect fodder and firewood from the forest, while those close to towns and at lower altitudes also extract products commercially.

NETFOP as a whole included many stakeholders, but the MLA survey focused on local communities. Within these, women's and men's perceptions were considered separately. A two-week training and field preparation meeting was held at FRI in Dehra Dun with staff, graduates and experienced community facilitators from FRI, as well as European MSc students who were partnered

---

[1] This was the original title. It was later realized that 'plantations' was not a suitable term to use in the India context: not only planted forests, but also natural forest that are heavily harvested and managed are covered by the project.

with Indian participants, to bridge language barriers during data collection. The group was trained in participatory methods, interviewing and focus group discussions. The team developed draft questionnaires about the different ecosystem functions (based on Groot, Wilson and Boumans, 2002), in collaboration with local counterparts in India and Wageningen University. The methods and questions were practised and tested in one village and subsequently revised (Van der Meer *et al.*, 2006).

The survey took about 30 days, spread over two months in six villages. Village-based methods were adapted to the 'environmental goods and services' focus of the project. FRI staff and MSc students analysed the data, and prepared a synthesis report to EU office in New Delhi. No follow-up activities have been planned so far.

This was the first time that local communities were involved in ecosystem valuation and staff gained several lessons. The time frame set for the survey was short and did not take into account the needs for villagers to set the pace. Survey villages were small, and the same community members were often participating in many hours of interviews and exercises. Women were often not able to participate, as they had many time-consuming daily tasks. The biophysical component was carried out in isolation from the participatory value assessment in terms of teams, locations and timing, which made the MLA characteristic integration of data impossible. The intention to *quantify* environmental goods and services was only partially successful for two reasons: many of the regulatory, habitat and cultural functions are intangible and hard to quantify; and extraction of products from state forests is not allowed, so people may have been reluctant to give quantitative information about this. The team conducted an economic valuation of services including mitigation of wind erosion, primary production, nutrient cycling, soil formation and water cycling.

The project's aim is to formulate policy recommendations for improved management of forests (both natural and planted). The study showed that fodder and firewood are the two most important forest products, and recommended the use of more fodder and fuelwood species in afforestation. It also found that the Forest Department could foster more participation by working with established village government (the *Van Panchayat*), and involve communities in the design of projects, rather than only in their implementation.

10. Pando (Bolivia)

The objective of MLA adaptation and field testing in Palma Real, a community in the Bolivian Amazon, was to develop tools which were accessible to community stakeholders, and help them both conduct forest monitoring and use the findings. As the case shows, adapting the approach to a local context can increase interest, with beneficial effects on subsequent management decisions (Evans *et al.*, 2005).

Palma Real is located in Bolivia's northern department of Pando, on the Madre de Dios River. When the MLA work began CIFOR already had a collaborative arrangement with the local government[2] and had good relations with the community. As a relatively remote community that had not received much technical assistance, the Palma Real families expressed great interest when CIFOR and the municipal government approached them about participating in the field test.

The families in Palma Real collect Brazil nuts (*Bertholletia excelsa*), which provides them with a relatively high cash income by Bolivian rural standards, and forms the basis for rural livelihood in the region. The community is in the process of obtaining communal title for approximately 8000 ha of land. Families work individually to gather Brazil nuts within a customary system of property rights. While Brazil nut production has been sustained for decades, Palma Real livelihoods are threatened by loggers, ranchers and migrant colonists and the related deforestation and forest fires they bring. High Brazil nut prices in recent years have also raised competition among families and brought interlopers who violate customary gathering practices. As a result communities report increased levels of conflict and a growing sense of insecurity.

The original plan for the participatory landscape mapping had been to illustrate the principal ecosystems recognized by the community and the uses of each by the community. During initial planning, however, the community made it clear that they were interested in addressing their concerns with Brazil nut theft and conflicts that had appeared during the previous harvest. They wanted to use the mapping techniques to document their customary forest property rights. The CIFOR team decided to adapt the methods to respond to this demand.

Rather than simply drawing a rough estimation of their territory, the approach generated a geo-referenced sketch map illustrating key reference points, landmarks and boundaries. Although drawn by hand, it was to scale and accurately depicted the territory, closely approximating official maps, but including locally relevant information. The CIFOR team organized a training course that taught people to use a global positioning system (GPS) device and record

---

[2] As part of a project entitled 'Making local government more responsive to the poor: Developing indicators and tools to support sustainable livelihood development under decentralisation' funded by the German Federal Ministry for Economic Cooperation and Development.

coordinates in notebooks to later plot them manually onto scaled grid paper. With this approach participants recognized the relationship between the points they geo-referenced in the forest and the image they began to create on the sketch map. The training took one morning.

In the week after the training men and women in the community formed brigades and mapped landmarks within the territory. They plotted trails, Brazil nut storage points, key reference points like trail crossings, property datum points and the outer limits of the forest areas they traditionally used. As points were plotted onto the map, community members filled in gaps and added the names of trails and landmarks.

The resulting map showed the detailed knowledge Palma Real residents have of their territory and illustrated the relative position of traditional property claims. The sketch map indicated that the forest areas used by some families were outside the boundaries being negotiated with the state. They therefore petitioned an adjustment of their territorial boundaries.

The Palma Real residents believed that the geo-referenced sketch mapping contributed to mediating Brazil nut conflicts. They also realized that more detailed information was needed to fully document customary forest property rights. At their request, CIFOR and the municipal government have since provided additional training, and accompanied the mapping of Brazil nut groves. Community members were able to map approximately 11 000 ha of forest corresponding to the area they traditionally used, and conduct a census of Brazil nut trees, tagging 8366 trees and distributing unclaimed trees to families that controlled small groves.

Analysis of case study experience

What can we learn by comparing the ten surveys? In this section we assess lessons from these experiences. Each study adjusted the approach to the context, and we consider the effects of varying the length of the study, its scale, the communication approach and the tools used.

Lessons learned

The complementary methods that make up a typical MLA survey provide a range of benefits. Working in multi-disciplinary teams reduces the chance of major oversights or misunderstandings. Reviewing results together allows surprising or contradictory results to be queried and investigated further. This can yield unexpected insights, such as those concerning the significance of wild sago in Malinau.

Biologists gain particular benefits. The community territories in these studies were sometimes as large as 1500 km^2, poorly mapped and difficult to access. In such areas, field surveys based on local knowledge are likely to be more efficient and yield more different habitats and unique species than random sampling (Sheil *et al.*, 2006). Joint mapping and local understanding of survey methods assist this process (1, 3, 6, 8). Local people can, furthermore, shed light on landscape history, habitat variation, threats against important resources and local livelihoods, distribution of rare or restricted species, and influences on species distribution or abundance (1, 2, 3, 8).

Social researchers also find advantages. The integrated surveys can bring technical credibility to Participatory Rural Appraisal (PRA) exercises, such as taxonomic names. Although collection of soil samples and plants sometimes puzzled villagers, it also arouses their interest and curiosity, and can stimulate discussions and requests for information. For example in Malinau (1) people requested a list of all plants discussed during the survey, with local as well as scientific names.

Community research requires time to build good relations and trust, and adjust to local work schedules. In most cases research teams lived in the study villages, but logistical problems can eat into the time available. The time spent with communities varied from two days (9) to one month or more (1, 6). Some teams with short field periods (4, 9) indicated that they did not have enough time to achieve good rapport with the communities. In Uttaranchal (9) lack of time meant the village team abandoned participatory mapping and missed opportunities to build common understanding. In Pando (10), team members hoped to make the methods less costly and less demanding on villagers. They had already built local trust and rapport through previous work. Because of this, they were able to achieve real outcomes with only seven days in each community, relying on community participation and assistance to carry out focused activities, addressing specific local needs in managing conflicts.

The multi-disciplinary approach needs additional time for cross-checking and triangulation of data and concern is often expressed about the time needed for an MLA survey. Although field periods of a few weeks, such as with the MLA, would still be seen by many as too 'rapid' a method (Céfaï, 2003), we think it offers relatively rigorous methods in an adequate time frame to meet the demands of development institutions and decision-makers, beyond academic and long-term survey techniques (Boissière and Sassen, 2007). There should always be follow-up.

Botanical data, soil sampling and other technical data may not always seem necessary, and can be reduced to save time and resources. However, biophysical data enhance academic credibility, and attract influential partners. For example, the opportunity to obtain both biophysical data and local views appealed to Conservation International in Mamberamo (6), and influenced government decisions in Malinau (1).

Integrating field biophysical and socio-economic data takes time and effort. But without such integration the results are much less useful (5, 9).

Involving potentially influential stakeholders, such as civil servants, in the research requires careful consideration. They may become more open to local perspectives (1, 4, 6). However, communities are not always at ease with authorities; in their presence they are more likely to distort information that might be seen as 'illegal', 'anti-official policy' or 'primitive'. In Khe Tran (7), commune officers followed researchers' activities closely, sometimes intervening to answer questions and discouraging community members from speaking freely. In the Gorongosa survey (2), researchers recognized this possibility and excluded national park staff from the community research.

Communication is a particularly demanding aspect of this approach. Even in countries with a widespread official language, this often remains the secondary language for remote communities. Sometimes three languages were used in a single village (7). Translation takes time, reduces spontaneity and increases the risk of miscommunications. Concepts, opinions and feelings are harder to express or understand, and nuances may be lost. Older community members are often illiterate or have difficulty expressing themselves in a second language (1, 3, 8). Translators, typically educated community members, may have their own views on what information is most appropriate to transmit. These problems can be reduced through training, cross-checking between translators (8), use of drawings, and discussions in the field where subjects can be observed directly.

Data quality and interpretation

Analysis of data from the seven Malinau villages (1) suggests that scoring exercises were more consistent when conducted by villagers from richer villages with better access to education and higher literacy, numeracy and language skills. Nonetheless, even less consistent information was a basis for meaningful interpretations (Sheil and Liswanti, 2006), because villagers can often explain differences between their responses.

Quality control, data review, summary and analysis all proved significant bottlenecks, especially in the more comprehensive surveys. Researchers can create biases in the data they collect, either by their assumptions or their influence on people (Sheil and Wunder, 2002). Some challenges relate to the methods; for example, how well do informants represent common views held by most community members? Researchers typically want to work with (often older) informants who know the resources well, but others may have different views on resource dependence and use. Focus group discussions, interviews, questionnaires and community meetings can mitigate this problem.

Analyses require technical guidance and experienced practitioners. In specific, specially designed cases, local communities can perhaps learn to summarize data for themselves (10), but they would need to have an interest and adequate incentives to do so even if training were available.

Impact

Most projects fulfilled their research objectives, particularly in terms of understanding research needs and possible land use solutions. Two (1, 6) became the most extensive ecological and social surveys undertaken in their respective areas. Members of several of the case studies prepared scientific publications based on the surveys. All studies highlighted local needs and dependence on natural resources; almost all improved understanding of local conservation priorities (1, 2, 3, 7, 8, 10); some noted the inappropriateness of current or planned land uses (1) or conflicts between legal frames and local needs (1, 8, 10); one helped clarify contradictions between land reform and customary resource ownership (10); and one clarified problematic power relations between stakeholders (4).

Impact is, however, more difficult to achieve and to demonstrate. The original approach is based on the belief that follow-up activities are desirable, to clarify and build on interpretations and implications. With limited time and budgets, fewer than half the projects have done this (1, 5, 6, 10).

At the most immediate level, in some cases project practice has changed. Results from the Palawan survey (4) helped LPF improve community participation in planning exercises, and showed the need to work separately with Batak and outsiders. This has helped to overcome differences in power relations and resource management systems.

In Malinau and Mamberamo (1, 6) local awareness and pride in the outstanding biodiversity grew. Discussions about conservation, threats to the environment and sustainable use of forest resources clarified views and raised awareness on these topics among local communities.

Team members became increasingly sympathetic to local concerns. The experience of those who worked for government agencies (1, 4, 6) may change how these agencies perceive local communities. In Pando (10), where the study had full support and participation from local communities and regional organizations, the results became widely known and appreciated among development and conservation actors, and strengthened natural resource co-management (Evans *et al.*, 2005).

Other cases were successful in building links between local people and government agencies and NGOs (1, 5, 6, 10). In Gunung Lumut and Mamberamo (5, 6), local support for conservation increased. Overall, while all the cases supported local input to decision making, only one included community empowerment as a formal goal (10). Most others found that such an explicit objective would not be acceptable to local authorities, while gathering local views and inputs was less threatening.

The focus on importance to local people can have the unintended effect of raising expectations. In Khe Tran (7), for example, the community members were more used to development projects and found it hard to believe that the researchers were not planning to build or buy anything.

Achieving wider impact is a challenge. Some projects have produced policy briefs and other materials to describe the results and implications for decision makers (1, 10). In Malinau (1), CIFOR's longer-term involvement in the area allowed follow-up with additional studies and actions including communicating recommendations to communities and local decision-makers. This facilitated discussions about natural resource management, and influenced the views and knowledge of villagers, townspeople and civil servants. Significantly, it also helped convince the government to revise plans for large-scale oil palm developments.

Many impacts are hard to measure. For example, in many cases community members become more able to express their priorities to outsiders. Local people sometimes associate 'conservation' with government repression (7) or abuse by conservation NGOs (8), so building trust and engagement is valuable. The MLA approach is notable for the enthusiasm it often generates among both team and community members, who often want to apply such methods in new locations.

CIFOR maintains an overview of all these projects, and shares information about them through a website (http://www.cifor.cgiar.org/mla/).

Conclusions

When global and local conservation agendas overlap, supporting local priorities can greatly strengthen these agendas (Steinberg, 2005). Identifying local concerns and voicing them helps to ensure they are considered. This is especially true where inaccessibility, language barriers, economic marginality and prejudices limit community communication with decision-makers. It also provides a basis for recognizing win–win opportunities, options that are unlikely to gain local acceptance, or a need for trade-offs.

Because of its diagnostic character the MLA is best used at the early stages of a programme to clarify local concerns and priorities, and allow these to play a role in its design and define its focus. However, to move beyond research, and have tangible impacts, requires an ability to act on the survey findings. Several cases have not yet gone beyond data collection and scientific interest. Longer presence and commitment are needed to follow up on a survey, and results must be presented to local actors in a manner that engages their interest. Unfortunately the necessary time and resources for this are seldom planned adequately.

An MLA survey offers a bridge between community and authorities because building understanding and identifying shared concerns is a powerful means to change perceptions and build communication. In several cases local authorities would be uncomfortable with 'local empowerment' per se, but were comfortable with the 'survey oriented' goals of the studies. As a result, officials become more aware of the priorities and concerns of local people, while local people can become more aware of external concerns and how to engage with them.

It is helpful to engage the potential users of the results (e.g. local institutions, decision-makers and advocacy-NGOs) from an early stage. This can increase decision-makers' understanding of local perspectives. Working together with local people to examine, prioritize and address issues concerning biodiversity and natural resources asks for a flexible range of approaches. The ten case studies offered here show that the MLA process, though not without pitfalls, offers a powerful basis for improving how forested landscapes are perceived. The partnership and understanding developed amongst researchers and local people during these surveys is fundamental to this success.

Acknowledgements

We would like to express our gratitude to all the contributors to our work, both individuals and institutions, to the local communities that took part in our surveys, and the governments that hosted them. We would like to thank Claire Miller for editing this chapter and useful suggestions.

REFERENCES

Barney, K. (2005). *Central Plans and Global Exports: Tracking Vietnam's Forestry Commodity Chains and Export Links to China*. Forest Trend. Available at: http://www.forest-trends.org/documents/meetings/china_2005_protected/documents/other/Vietnam%20Final%20Report%206-1-05.pdf

Basuki, I. and Sheil, D. (2005). *Local Perspectives of Forest Landscapes: A Preliminary Evaluation of Land and Soils, and their Importance in Malinau, East Kalimantan, Indonesia*. Bogor: CIFOR.

Boissière, M., Basuki, I., Koponen, P., Wan, M. and Sheil, D. (2006). *Biodiversity and Local Perceptions on the Edge of a Conservation Area, Khe Tran Village, Vietnam*. Bogor: CIFOR.

Boissière, M. and N. Liswanti (2006). *Biodiversity in a Batak Village of Palawan (Philippines). A Multidisciplinary Assessment of Local Perceptions and Priorities*. Bogor: CIFOR.

Boissière, M. and Sassen, M. (2007). Mesurer l'importance de la biodiversité pour les sociétés forestières des pays du Sud. Une méthode d'investigation pluridisciplinaire. *Nature, Sciences et Sociétés* **15**(1), 23–32.

Campo P. C. and Villanueva T. R. (2006). *Multi-Agent Systems (MAS) Modelling to Improve the Management of Common Renewable Resources in Palawan, Philippines*, IASCP 2006 Conference Papers, 16 pp. Available at: http://www.iascp.org/bali/papers.html.

Céfaï, D. (2003). *L'enquête de terrain*. Paris: La Découverte MAUSS, 615 pp.

CIFOR (2004). *Building Capacity for Multidisciplinary Landscape Assessment in Papua: three phases of training and pilot assessments in the Mamberamo Basin*. Unpublished report.

Cunliffe, R. N. (2003). *Responses by the Nhanchururu Community to the two SAfMA-GM Scenarios: 'Patronage' and 'Devolution'*. Unpublished report prepared for the Gorongosa-Marromeu Transect of the Southern African Millenium Assessment, Harare: Institute of Environmental Studies, University of Zimbabwe.

Cunliffe, R. N., Lynam, T. J. P., Sheil, D. *et al.* (2007). Developing a predictive understanding of landscape importance to the Punan-Pelancau of East Kalimantan, Borneo. *Ambio* **36**(7), 593–599.

Cunningham, A. B. (2001). *Applied Ethnobotany. People, Wild Plant Use and Conservation*. People and Plants Conservation Manual Series. London: Earthscan Publications, 300pp.

Devanadera, M. E., Gamutia, A., Hartanto, H., Mallion, F. K. and Villanueva, T. (2004). *Philippines Country Report, Year 1*. LPF/03/2004, UPLB, CIRAD, CIFOR.

Eder, J. F. (1987). *On the Road of Tribal Extinction. Depopulation, Deculturation and Adaptative Well-being among the Batak of the Philippines*. Berkeley: University of California Press.

Evans, K. (2006). *Evaluating and adapting future scenarios in forest dependent communities in Hue province, Vietnam*. Unpublished report to the Swiss Agency for Development Cooperation. Bogor, Indonesia: Center for International Forestry Research (CIFOR).

Evans, K., W. de Jong, W., P. Miranda, P. and P. Cronkleton, P. (2005). *Evaluating and Adaptating Multidisciplinary Landscape Assessment in Forest-dependent Communities in the Northern Bolivian Amazon.* Bogor: CIFOR, 36 pp.

Groot, R. D. de, Wilson, M. A. and Boumans, R. M. J. (2002). A typology for the classification, description and evaluation of ecosystem functions, goods and services. *Ecological Economics* **41**, 393–408.

Jum, C. N. and Oyono, P. R. (2005). Building collaboration through action research: the case of Ottotomo Forest Reserve in Cameroon. *International Forestry Review* **7**(1), 37–43.

Kompas. (2006). Target: Tiga Juta Hektar Sawit. Swasta Perlu Insentif untuk Kembangkan Biodiesel. *Kompas* (an Indonesian National Newspaper), 26 January.

Lynam, T., Cunliffe, R., Sheil, D. *et al.* (2007). *Livelihoods, Land Types and the Importance of Ecosystem Goods and Services: Developing a Predictive Understanding of Landscape Valuation by the Punan Pelancau People of East Kalimantan.* Bogor: CIFOR.

Murniati, Padmanaba, M., Basuki, I. and Van der Ploeg, J. (2006). *Gunung Lumut Biodiversity Assessment, Socio-economic Study.* Balikpapan: Tropenbos International Indonesia.

Padmanaba, M. and Sheil, D. (2007). Finding and promoting a local conservation consensus in a globally important tropical forest landscape. *Biodiversity and Conservation* **16**(1), 137–151.

Philips, O. L. (1996). Some quantitative methods for analyzing ethnobotanical knowledge. In *Selected Guidelines for Ethnobotanical Research: A Field Manual*, ed. M.N. Alexiades. USA: The New York Botanical Garden, pp. 171–197.

Pye-Smith, C. (2005). Biodiversity: a new perspective. *New Scientist*, 10 December 2005, 50.

Sassen, M. and Jum, C. (2007). Assessing local perspectives in a forested landscape in Central Cameroon. *Forest, Trees and Livelihoods* **17**(1), 23–42.

Sassen, M. and Wan, M. (2006). *Biodiversity and Local Priorities in a Community Near the Ivindo National Park. Makokou, Gabon.* Research report published online by the Centre for International Forestry Research (CIFOR), available at http://www.cifor.cgiar.org/mla.

Sheil, D. and Wunder, S. (2002). The value of tropical forest to local communities: complications, caveats and cautions. *Conservation Ecology* **6**(2), 9. Available at: http://www.consecol.org/vol6/iss2/art9.

Sheil, D., Puri, R., Basuki, I. *et al.* (2003). *Exploring Biological Diversity, Environment and Local People's Perspectives in Forest Landscapes.* Bogor: CIFOR. Revised and Updated Edition – also in Indonesian, French and Spanish. Available at http:www.cifor.cgiar.org/mla.

Sheil, D. and Boissière, M. (2006). People may be the best allies in conservation. *Nature* **440**, 868.

Sheil, D. and Liswanti, N. (2006). Scoring the importance of tropical forest landscapes with local people: patterns and insights. *Environmental Management* **38**(1), 126–36.

Sheil, D., Puri, R. K., Wan, M. *et al.* (2006). Recognizing local people's priorities for tropical forest biodiversity. *Ambio* **35**(1), 17–24.

Steinberg, P. F. (2005). From public concern to policy effectiveness: civic conservation in developing countries. *Journal of International Wildlife Law and Policy* **8**, 341–65.

Stoffle, R. W., Halmo, D. B. and Evans, M. J. (1990). Calculating the cultural significance of American Indian plants: paiute and Shoshone ethnobotany at Yucca Mountain, Nevada. *American Anthropologist* **92**(2), 416–432.

Turner, N. J. (1988). 'The importance of a rose': Evaluating the cultural significance of plants in Thompson and Lillooet interior Salish. *American Anthropologist* **90**, 272–290.

Van Der Meer, P. J., Bairaktari, C., de Groot, R. S., van Heist, M. and Schmerbeck, J. (2006). *Methodology for Assessing Benefits of Afforested Community and Forest Land.* Wageningen: ALTERRA.

Yance de Fretes (2006). Menggali Kekayaan Keanekaragaman Hayati Kawasan Mamberamo. *Tropika Indonesia* **10**(1), 8–11.

7

Participatory resources monitoring in SW China: lessons after five years

JEANNETTE VAN RIJSOORT, ZHANG JINFENG, MARLON TEN
HOONTE AND WANG LEI

Introduction

The opportunity to look at the effects of a participatory monitoring project several years after the end of a project is a rare one. This chapter does just that, by comparing project goals, experience one year after implementation, and five years later, in a project working with local communities in protected areas in the south-western province of Yunnan in China.

China's efforts in biodiversity conservation have increased in the last decade. China was one of the first countries to ratify the Convention on Biological Diversity (CBD) in 1992, and to formulate its National Biodiversity Conservation Action Plan (NBCAP) (Wang *et al.*, 2000). This plan specifically addresses the need to integrate conservation, development and local livelihoods, and to monitor the impacts of biodiversity conservation efforts. Its implementation has become, to a large extent, the responsibility of local government because of decentralizing reforms. Local government – county, township, and village committees – are mandated to formulate policies and develop regulations for natural resources management. They must, however, comply with the Chinese constitution and laws, and with higher level regulations and policies (Dupar and Badenoch, 2002). Consequently, national policies concerning land tenure, protected areas, agriculture development and rural cooperatives will have a great impact on implementation of the plan at local levels. However, support has not been provided for local institutions to develop sound environmental governance at village and township levels (Dupar and Badenoch, 2002).

It is in this context of weak institutional capacity to implement a decentralized NBCAP and related biodiversity monitoring systems, that we explore the

Taking Stock of Nature: Participatory Biodiversity Assessment for Policy, Planning and Practice, ed. Anna Lawrence. Published by Cambridge University Press. © Cambridge University Press 2010.

relevance and effect of participatory resource monitoring (PRM) and its contribution to environmental governance. It has been proposed that biodiversity monitoring can be a tool for improving environmental governance (Sheil, 2001). In this chapter we explore specifically whether and how local government staff are able to make use of national policies, and local rules and regulations, in participatory monitoring; and how environmental governance in Yunnan could be strengthened. We base this on the experience of local people and staff in two nature reserves. The three first authors were actively involved in different stages of the international project which supported these attempts, and the last author conducted an assessment five years after implementation of PRM.

Institutional context in which PRM was introduced

China has been in a process of shifts between devolution and re-centralization since the 1950s. In particular, forest and tree ownership has experienced frequent policy reversals (Table 7.1). Forests that were privately owned before 1949 were redistributed and collectivized (1950–1956), communized (1956–1980) and decollectivized (post-1980). Recently, with the 'Forest Tenure System Reform' (2006) more collective forests have been distributed to households. This high frequency of policy change has undermined farmers' confidence in policy (Liu, 2001). When farmers received control over resource use, they never knew for how long that would last before the policy would change again. This is why even favourable policies are looked upon with suspicion.

Since 2004, a new law on Protected Areas has been under discussion, which requires a review of legal systems regarding natural resources, including legal opportunities for developing co-management in parts of the nature reserves. With the approval of this law there will be a better legal opportunity to develop co-management of protected areas. A new law on rural cooperatives took effect on 1 July 2007, which encourages local governments to promote forest producer associations which can collectively employ forest guards, collectively manage, and harvest and market NTFPs (non-timber forest products).

Yunnan, where our case studies are located, has the largest total area of collective forests in China, and has a legislative framework that encourages community participation in biodiversity conservation and management (see Figure 7.1). The Yunnan Forestry Regulations (1987) stipulate that joint management systems by park administration and local people should be established for the nature reserves and community forests (see Box 7.1). The Yunnan Nature Reserve Rules and Regulations (1997) allow sustainable resource use by local people in specified parts of a nature reserve.

Table 7.1. *Policy dynamics and forest tenure changes in China (based on Liu, 2001; Miao and West, 2004; Xie Yan, 2004; Lu, 2002)*

Period	Description
< 1949	Tenure can be grouped into three broad categories: private forests by wealthy families, common forests by a social group, and state forests.
1950–1955	Land Reform Campaign: confiscation of private forests and common forests. Some were nationalized, the rest were redistributed to rural households. In Tibet and border areas of Yunnan, confiscated forests were all designated as common village property (due to political sensitivity). Elementary cooperatives (currently called 'natural villages') were established. Land is still privately owned, but elected leaders of the elementary cooperatives made management decisions.
End of 1956	Rural household lands merged to form advanced cooperatives (currently called 'administrative village'), amalgamating both private forestlands and those in elementary cooperatives, thus bringing private forestland ownership to an end. An advanced cooperative included hundreds of households and decision-making was further centralized.
1958	Great Leap Forward: landholding was aggregated further, by combining advanced cooperatives and transferring land ownership and decision-making to the commune (currently called 'township'). In the commune, the state appointed leadership and thus the Party managed and administered collective land use.
Early 1960s	The government reverted forestlands back to advanced and elementary cooperative management, respectively called 'production brigades' and 'production teams'. In Yunnan, the majority of collective forests were devolved to two levels: from communes to production teams (elementary cooperative/natural villages). Land ownership, however, remained collective.
1966–1976	Cultural Revolution: exacerbated forest mismanagement and deepened the insecurity surrounding rights to resources.
1981	Three Fixes: Private trees and forests emerge again.
	(1) Issuance of certificates to confirm forest resource tenure in hopes of stabilizing the sector.
	(2) Distribution of non-forested land to rural households as family plots (also called freehold mountains). The forestlands remain collectively owned, households have use and management rights.
	(3) Introduction of the Contract Responsibility System (for hills or mountains) in response to the Household Responsibility System in the agricultural sector. This system contracts mostly non-timber forests and fuelwood forests to households, but the natural or administrative village collective often retains some control of cutting and products.

1984	Forest Law: forest resources are divided between state and collective forests. State forest land is owned by the state and managed by state forest enterprises, while the collective forest land is owned and managed by rural collectives. Ambiguity surrounding the definition of 'collective' is the root of many ownership and policy conflicts. The Law reinforced the earlier 'three fix' policy by allowing for private use rights to trees.
1992	Four Wastelands Auction Policy: individuals are permitted to contract and lease degraded lands. The contractor possesses use rights for the land and the resources developed on the land.
1994	Regulations of Nature Reserves; rules for Nature Reserves endorsed by State Council.
1998	Forest Law amended: Defines five classes of forests: protection forests, timber forests, economic forests, fuelwood forests and forests for special uses. Resource rights may last for up to 70 years, and are renewable. It also sets out a range of government financial incentives for private investment in management (e.g. cheap loans, tax breaks) and its intention to set up Forest Environmental Benefit Compensation Funds to encourage forest protection.
1998	National Forest Protection Programme (NFPP) (as part of the Great West Development Programme): (1) complete logging bans in upper Yangtze River and mid-to-upper Yellow River and diminish logging in state-owned forests; (2) reforestation and silvicultural treatments for particular forestlands; (3) provision of alternative employment and pensions of state enterprise employees. In many parts of China, including Yunnan, the logging ban was implemented by local governments in all natural forests, regardless of ownership. In some extreme cases, communities are even prohibited from accessing NTFPs and fuelwood. By denying the communities use of their forests, the NFPP has dramatically reduced their active management, induced illegal activities, and led to a shift from community protection patrols to policing by government forestry officials.
2000	Sloping Land Conversion Programme (or: Grain for Green Policy) The general concept of the programme was to convert cropland on steep slopes prone to erosion to forestland and grassland, compensating farmers with grain, money and saplings.
2001	Forest Ecosystem Compensation Programme (FECP): All entities, be they public or private, who generate direct economic benefits from ecological functions of forests are required to pay for these services and the funds raised will be earmarked for investment in maintaining the forest environment.
2006	Forest Tenure System Reform: more allocation of community forestland to households.
In prep	Law on Protected Areas: includes legal opportunities for developing co-management in parts of the nature reserves.
2007	Law on Rural Cooperatives.

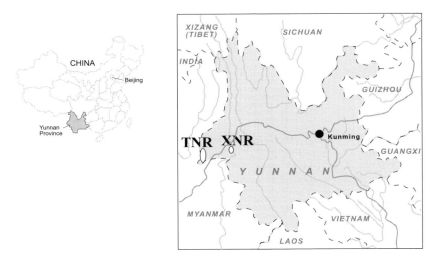

Figure 7.1 Location of Yunnan and project sites TNR (Tongbiguan Nature Reserve) and XNR (Xiaoheishan Nature Reserve) in China.

The Forest Conservation and Community Development Project (FCCDP) started in 1998, aiming to conserve (sub)tropical forest in Yunnan, through strengthening of the Yunnan Department of Forestry in conservation management skills, and sustainable socio-economic development of communities in and around nature reserves. Six (of approximately 150) nature reserves in Yunnan were selected during the first phase of the project. The project aimed at 'sustainable and participatory management of the six nature reserves and adjacent forestlands' linked with 'sustainable socio-economic development of communities in and around the six nature reserves' and institutional capacity building at provincial, prefecture and county level (FCCDP, 1998).

From 1998 to 2002 the project supported nature reserve staff to draft integrated management plans, using a series of participatory appraisal exercises with local stakeholders – local governments, village committees, villagers, private enterprises, county and township government departments. To support community development in the areas around the nature reserves, in the same period the project adopted a village planning approach, prepared community development plans, and set up village-based forest co-management committees. Nature reserve staff members were trained in awareness building and facilitation skills, and participatory rural appraisal (PRA) activities. In 2001, the project introduced PRM in two nature reserves, in order to test the feasibility of community-based resources monitoring.

Box 7.1. Co-management and sustainable use in the Yunnan Forestry and Nature Reserve regulations

Yunnan Nature Reserves Management Regulations (1997)

- 'Sustainable use and management of forest and wildlife resources' is permitted in the experimental area of the nature reserve (Article 12).

- 'On the premise of not destroying natural resources, the native people inside the nature reserve may engage in plantation, raising and other activities in the experimental areas, under the arrangement and direction of the nature reserve management department' (Article 16).

Yunnan Forestry and Wildlife Reserves Rules and Regulations (1987)

'The government at different levels should further define the responsibilities for forestry production and management, the right, obligation and benefit of the owner and manager/user of the forest and forest land, to improve production, technical service and forest management. (. . .) A sound joint management responsibility system should be established for the nature reserve mountain and the mountain contracted to the local household. (. . .) The forest management measures and afforestation requirement should be defined' (Article 4).

At this stage, the project team realized that wider implementation of the results from pilot villages would be difficult without project support, and started discussing a new project focus on management of a buffer zone. Commonly, this concept is understood to refer to 'a zone, peripheral to a national park or equivalent reserve, where restrictions are placed upon resource use or special development measures are undertaken to enhance the conservation value of the area' (Sayer, 1991). Because the buffer zone was not formally designated, it was referred to in the project as 'adjacent area'. The project assisted local governments in writing and implementing 'Adjacent-area Management Plans' (AMPs) during the period 2001–2004. The process of drafting the plans needed the active participation, discussion and collaboration of all stakeholders having an interest in the use of natural resources. It also integrated various governmental programmes. Stakeholder representatives received training to conduct awareness building and PRA activities in preparation of site-specific situation analysis reports validated in a facilitated stakeholders' meeting. Adjacent-area Management Committees (AMCs) representing all stakeholders and chaired by the county vice-governors, were in charge of AMP formulation in facilitated workshops elaborating logical frameworks. The plans formed the basis for negotiation on strategies not only with FCCDP, but also with (inter)national projects and NGOs (Hoonte ten *et al.*, 2004).

The change in project focus provoked a decentralization of responsibilities for project implementation at county, township and village level, and a change in short-term objectives. PRM was initiated at the time that the strategy of the project changed to Adjacent-Area Management Planning. While PRM was still a village-based activity, the project had moved to piloting AMP in other nature reserves. Later in the process, AMP was also initiated in the nature reserves where PRM was already being implemented.

Rationale for developing a participatory tool for biodiversity monitoring

Three reasons guided the project team in their decision to start a pilot PRM in two nature reserves.

- PRM could strengthen local environmental governance: by involving local people and staff in monitoring biodiversity, they would have the information basis to propose management actions, including the adaptation of local rules and regulations for resource use.
- In the draft integrated management plans of both nature reserves, local staff identified the need to involve local inhabitants in the conservation and management of forest resources, either because extensive collective forests occurred inside the nature reserve or because local livelihoods depended on NTFPs.
- PRM could provide a complementary system to two ongoing project monitoring activities: a scientific monitoring system implemented by provincial research institutes and an improved patrolling system involving nature reserve staff and forest guards recruited from the villages. The project team recognized that in some cases, scientific monitoring might take too much time and investment to respond to the urgent needs for management.

PRM approach

The project selected two nature reserves for PRM implementation (Box 7.2) to represent distinctive biodiversity and social contexts and to respond to staff interest in using PRM for their management plans. Within each nature reserve, the project selected six villages for PRM implementation. Assuming that participatory forest monitoring is only meaningful where forests are directly

---

Box 7.2. Main biodiversity and socio-economic characteristics of the pilot nature reserves

Tongbiguan Provincial Nature Reserve (TNR) in Dehong Prefecture covers in total nearly 30 700 ha, consisting of three sections in three different counties. About 18 000 residents (of whom more than half are Jingpo, Dai, Lisu and De'ang minorities) live in and around the reserve. It was established in 1986 for the protection of sub-tropical seasonal rainforest including *Shorea assamica* and *Dipterocarpus turbinatus* trees, and fauna including gaur (*Bos gaurus*), leaf monkey (*Presbytis phayrei*), and the IUCN Red-Listed elephant (*Elephas maximus*), common leopard (*Panthera pardus*), tiger (*P. tigris*), and slow loris (*Nycticebus coucang*). The Ruili section, where PRM took place, covers 21 840.5 ha and includes 9200 residents in 2350 families. Annual per capita income is around $90, mainly from agriculture, animal husbandry and forestry (plantations of coffee, fruit trees, birch (for timber and fuel wood) and bamboo) (FCCDP, 2000).

Xiaoheishan Provincial Nature Reserve (XNR) in Baoshan Prefecture covers 16 000 ha. It was established in 1995 to conserve the mountainous broadleaf forests, especially the tree fern forests, including key species such as tree fern (*Cyathea spinulosa*), wild rice (*Oryza meyeriana*), and fauna including leaf monkey (*Presbytis phayrei*), and the IUCN Red-Listed common leopard (*Panthera pardus*) and slow loris (*Nycticebus coucang*). The reserve is also an important watershed area. Unlike many other reserves, collective forests account for 74% of the reserve. Over 77 000 people live around the reserve (mainly Han, but also some Dai, Lisu and Yi minorities). Annual per capita income is around $45, mainly from agriculture, animal husbandry and forestry (plantations of tea, walnut, *Taiwania flousiana* (for timber) and bamboo) (FCCDP, 1999).

---

linked to people's livelihoods and where resource pressure requires urgent management actions, villages were selected for (1) high dependence on forests in and around the nature reserve for village livelihoods, and (2) unsustainable resource use. A third criterion was (3) representativeness of the area's geographical condition, enabling replication of PRM if the method turned out to be successful.

The project identified as primary stakeholders the villagers and the nature reserve and forestry staff. The expectations of both groups for PRM were identified at the start of the PRM (Table 7.2). In general, the villagers had a

Table 7.2. *Benefits and problems of participatory resources monitoring as perceived by participants in the 2001 evaluation workshop (adapted from van Rijsoort and Zhang, 2005)*

	Benefits	Problems
Technical	– **Protection (of resources used, wildlife that eat 'bad' animals, insects that pollinate flowers to get fruits, water, wildlife and plants to promote tourism)** – **Problem solving related to lack of wood and other resources** – **Prevention and control: of pests, diseases, fire, wildlife damage** – **Decision-making: to improve rules and regulations which are not suitable to actual situation** – **Evaluation: to assess whether forest conservation activities are successful** – *Villagers will understand benefits from certain species, like timber, water, NTFPs*	– **Lack of manpower and funds** – **Lack of knowledge and skills** – **Our suggestions may not be adopted by the management department** – **Accuracy: results may not be correct** – **Different views of villagers and staff towards resources (i.e. use and conservation respectively)** – *We may be restricted in grazing, logging and other resource use*
Social	– **Awareness raising and capacity building: of villagers and staff** – **Increase participation of villagers in conservation** – **Improve communication between villagers and staff** – *Supervise the work of villagers* – *Increase work efficiency when villagers provide information* – *Reduce workload of staff when villagers are involved*	– **Different languages impede good communication** – **Many people with different ideas are difficult to manage** – **Conflicts will arise when illegal cases happen** – **Accessibility difficult in rainy season** – *The work is optional, so hard to manage*

Key. **Bold**: benefits and problems identified by both villagers and staff. *Italics*: those only identified by staff. Plain text: those identified just by villagers.

direct stake, as they depend on forest resources for their livelihoods. Local professionals (foresters and conservation staff) also had a direct stake as they expect to obtain information from villagers that would support their conservation work. Secondary stakeholders included project staff (providing financial and technical assistance), and county and township government (responsible for supervising forest management, advocating sustainable resource management, and developing local livelihoods).

The PRM team was composed of four villagers, chosen by the village leader. Ideally, the members of this team should represent the heterogeneity of forest users and perceptions in the village. As it was the first time that such a participatory role in forest monitoring was developed in these villages, we believed it was better to follow the villagers' idea of representation. This included the village leader (or his representative the administrator), a woman representative, a forest guard (a villager that is appointed by the forestry station to patrol the village forests) and a person that can read and write. One nature reserve or forestry staff member was appointed to each PRM team to provide support, especially in data analysis and communication to higher levels.

To develop the monitoring approach, project staff facilitated a three-day workshop in each nature reserve in 2001, with the village PRM team, some government staff from the nature reserve and forestry stations, and project officials. The project staff believed it was too early to engage the county and township government at this stage. The idea was that the PRM should first generate good experience before the county and township government could become interested. The project facilitators used the participatory exercises elaborated in Abbot and Guijt (1998) as an inspiration to develop the workshop's exercises. These resulted in PRM objectives, monitoring targets, indicators and methods, and a monitoring calendar indicating responsibilities and timing of activities.

The workshop participants agreed on the following objectives for PRM:

- improved conservation and sustainable resource use in collective forests and nature reserve;
- improved local economy through sustainable resource use;
- improved knowledge among villagers and staff on resources abundance, distribution, value and use;
- improved capacity of villagers and staff to plan and conduct monitoring and to analyse reasons for change;
- improved relationships between villagers and staff, and among villagers.

As it is impossible to monitor all species, the facilitators invited the participants to select specific species, resources and land uses as monitoring targets from a list of resources previously established in village meetings. Participants in both nature reserves identified resources used for their livelihoods, as well as water, plantation areas and wildlife, either positively (because of their 'good ecological function' or cultural value), or negatively (because they cause damage to crops and livestock).

The workshop participants chose very simple methods for PRM: interviews with village forest guards and resource users to obtain information on resource trends, forest walks (to assess resource abundance), and direct observation (for wildlife damage and land use). Indicators ranged from 'easy or hard to see', quality of resources and habitats, frequency of wildlife damage, extent and scale of damage, total area of plantation and growth conditions. A full description of the method is provided in van Rijsoort and Zhang (2005). The intention of the project facilitators was to keep it as simple as possible, so that villagers could easily understand and integrate it into their daily work.

Participants agreed on an annual meeting for staff and villagers jointly to analyse the findings and to formulate suggestions for new management actions to address the identified problems. In data interpretation, the perspectives of both local people and staff are valuable. Staff can help to explain results, point out possible errors in data collection, and determine actions needed to mitigate the problems. In this instance they were also able to report proposed management actions beyond village level to the relevant authorities.

Methods for PRM evaluation

To evaluate PRM after one year of implementation, and adjust the methodology, the project organized a workshop with the PRM teams in September 2002. The workshop facilitators and participants were the same as those in the PRM planning workshop. The workshop approach was also similar: participants were given the opportunity to adjust parts of the PRM methodology on the basis of their experience with one-year implementation.

In November 2006, the project organized a field survey in all PRM villages to assess the status of PRM implementation after five years. The project staff and PRM facilitators developed a checklist, and the fourth author conducted the survey. He met with members of the PRM team in each of the PRM villages. In addition to those involved in the one year evaluations, in each village he interviewed nature reserve staff and two or three villagers who had not been members of the PRM team.

Outcome of PRM evaluation in 2002

The 2002 PRM evaluation is described in more detail in van Rijsoort and Zhang (2005). Here we present a summary of the relevant points for comparison with the 2006 evaluation.

Process

In the one-year evaluation workshop, each team presented detailed findings on resource abundance, land use changes, and wildlife damage. The villagers showed their motivation for PRM by recording findings regularly and by suggesting management actions in village meetings with staff. They also felt that they understood PRM better, and proposed adjusting some of the monitoring targets. For example, they decided to abandon monitoring some species because they had ascertained that they were abundant and not therefore of concern, while others were cultivated. The evaluation indicated villagers' keen interest in monitoring, as well as their sense of ownership. They expressed a need for more support by the nature reserve and forestry staff, especially in data interpretation. The staff themselves complained that this was difficult, as it was additional to their regular work, and community work is not specifically part of their job description. The county and township governments were not directly involved in PRM since the activity was limited to village level and not reported to higher levels.

Value and perceptions

The monitoring targets selected by the villagers in 2001 to some extent reflect the values they hold towards forests. These include consumption values (various resources), but also biodiversity values (wildlife, landscape and land use). These values were apparently still prevalent after one year as the villagers only proposed minor adjustments, such as deleting very abundant and planted resources from the monitoring target list.

Management actions

In the 2002 evaluation, the PRM teams linked the observed changes in forest resources to possible causes. These formed the basis for the following proposals for changing management.

1. The observed decline in abundance of medicinal plants was attributed to unsustainable collection, habitat destruction, encroachment by sugarcane (in Tongbiguan Nature Reserve) and high market values for medicinal plants such as *Dendrobium nobile*. The teams suggested management actions ranging from (unspecified) habitat management, cultivation of medicinal plants, promotion of sustainable collection methods, and regulation of purchases by herb dealers.

2. Similarly, they found other resources to be declining (specifically, wild fruits and fuel wood), and suggested restricting collection, as well as more cultivation, enhanced propaganda, and law enforcement.

3. Other resources were found to be increasing in abundance – wild vegetables, fodder, fungi, and bees. In these cases the teams proposed sustainable collection from the wild, with a Green Food Factory for wild vegetables, if external support were available.

4. To tackle the problem of wildlife damage, PRM teams suggested improving natural habitats, planting forage in home-gardens, and seeking compensation.

5. The suggestions of the PRM teams for improved land use included pest and disease control, to introduce mixed forestry, and restrictions on free grazing.

It is interesting that even within this defined geographic area we found differences in approach to PRM in the two case studies. In general the community team in Xiaoheishan listed more creative management suggestions than Tongbiguan, which in turn often suggested more restrictive rules. For example, in responding to a perceived decrease in fish, the Xiaoheishan team suggested establishing a fish pond, whereas Tongbiguan suggested a ban on the use of electricity in fishing. In response to a perceived increase in fungi, Xiaoheishan suggested allowing sustainable collection, whereas Tongbiguan suggested further habitat protection. The predominantly Jingpo and Dai people of Tongbiguan are more isolated; the access that Xiaoheishan residents have to information, cultural changes and formal education gives them greater confidence in linking findings to action, and in proposing co-operative solutions to management problems.

Management actions which require only the adaptation of village rules (e.g. restricting collection) are within the power and capacity of the villagers themselves and were therefore more commonly recommended and implemented. The villagers stated during the 2002 evaluation that as a result of PRM they were more involved in management decision-making, and had drafted location-specific rules and regulations, which would be more acceptable by local people. In addition local staff supported the cultivation of a medicinal orchid (*Dendrobium nobile*). These were in fact the only proposals that were implemented as they did not need external support. The lack of implementation of other proposals may have contributed to later loss of motivation.

Social change

After one year of PRM, there was an indication that it might contribute to social change as villagers and staff came closer together. For example in

Tongbiguan staff recognized that villagers could play a valuable role in constructing a botanical garden by using their indigenous knowledge on species and their distribution. Staff in both nature reserves recognized that local villagers have knowledge on distribution, use values, and occasionally 'ecological' knowledge, which the staff sometimes lack. Through PRM, staff and villagers held more discussions together, for example during the forest walk, village meetings, and data analysis. To be able to answer villagers' questions, the staff felt a need for more training in ecology and sustainable resource use. Villagers also felt empowered as they were more involved in management decision-making; owing to PRM they drafted more location-specific rules and regulations, which would be more acceptable by local people.

Outcome in 2006

Despite all these rather positive developments in the first year, the survey in November 2006 indicated that none of the suggested management actions have been taken up beyond village level, and that no village is now using PRM. All PRM teams in the two nature reserves stopped in 2003 or 2004, i.e. after two or three years. In this section, we analyse the results of this follow-up survey.

Values and perceptions

The evaluation explored the values of PRM team members, other villagers, and local staff in relation to the forest. In general, all three groups in both nature reserves value the forests highly for water and soil protection (50%–83% of PRM teams and other villagers). Use values are also mentioned by all three groups, but here there are differences between staff and villagers: staff in Tongbiguan only mention timber, fuel wood and one specific medicinal plant in the consumption category, while villagers value the forest for medicinal herbs (67%), fodder, vegetables and fruits, wildlife, as a water source and contribution to a better environment. Staff on the other hand valued the forest for migratory birds and wildlife. In Xiaoheishan the villagers attribute little value to scenic or wildlife values, but value vegetables and fruit (67% of non-PRM villagers), medicinal herbs, fungi, fodder, wildlife, fish and soil enrichment. By contrast the staff did value scenery, climate regulation and wildlife, but not the uses mentioned by the villagers. These use values were similar to those perceived in 2002 and 2001, but there was a new emphasis on water and soil conservation in 2006, which may have been influenced by propaganda on water and soil conservation by the government.

Differences were also noticed between PRM team members and non-PRM villagers: in Xiaoheishan the non-PRM villagers attribute relatively more value to planting conditions and fodders, but this is not reflected in the Tongbiguan group.

There are also differences between the two nature reserves. In comparison to Xiaoheishan, the respondents in Tongbiguan list more values, reflecting the stronger connection of the Jingpo and Dai ethnic groups with their forest, the better condition of their forest and their greater dependence on the forest in their daily lives.

Proposed management actions

To obtain new suggestions for management actions after five years, the 2006 survey invited villagers to express '*what they would do differently if they were in charge of management*'. The answers of the PRM teams and the rest of the villagers are taken together as there were few differences between them.

Of the 14 different management actions suggested by all respondents, only two were mentioned by both nature reserves: agroforestry and planting eco-nomic trees. The other management suggestions differ between the two nature reserves. Xiaoheishan villagers desire further improvement of the rules and regulations (62%) and strengthening of co-management and awareness (both 38%), whereas Tongbiguan villagers see more reason in scientific manage-ment (75%), selective logging (50%) and more strict punishment (42%). This difference is consistent with the findings of the 2002 evaluation.

The implementation of national and local policies in the areas adjacent to the nature reserves seems favourable for some of the suggested management actions. The new ideas compared to 2002 concerning 'agro-forestry' and 'co-management' expressed by the villagers reflect prevalent local government policies rather than a result of the participatory resources monitoring.

In general the villagers perceive that forest resources have improved. Only a few were able to suggest causes for these improvements, but those who did all listed national policies as the major cause. PRM implementation was also mentioned by all, but this answer may have been provided out of courtesy, as PRM stopped after two to three years. In Xiaoheishan the villagers (but not staff) also attribute improvement to local rules and regulations, and biogas pits.

Respondents in Xiaoheishan, who are more in touch with current politi-cal trends such as the introduction of democracy, seem to be confident that they can use PRM as a basis to propose forest management changes to decision-makers. The apparent increase in room for negotiation on forest management between government and local communities may also be due to the fact that the Xiaoheishan nature reserves consist of 75% collective forests. In Tongbiguan, however, a more top-down political culture prevails amongst the indigenous groups. Most villages and even staff claim that they 'follow orders', that they have nothing to say and decisions are made at higher levels. All but one villager reported that this is the same as five years ago. Tongbiguan staff, for example, commented during the 2006 survey that *'PRM cannot change management decisions, they are taken by the relevant authorities', 'PRM is just a reference'* and *'Results of PRM cannot really change villagers' lives'.*

Social change

The survey in 2006 inquired about changes in social and economic conditions in general. No distinct differences between the PRM team and the other villagers can be observed. In both nature reserves villagers unanimously declared that relationships among themselves and with staff had improved. Almost all villagers say their income has increased. Health has also improved according to around 80% of all respondents. In Xiaoheishan all villagers state that their perceptions towards forests and wildlife dynamics have improved, as has their self-confidence in forest management. In Tongbiguan, on the other hand, less than half of the villagers state this. Half of the villagers in Xiaoheishan, but only 20% in Tongbiguan, believe their decision-making power has increased.

In both nature reserves, respondents perceive governmental policies and propaganda as the main causes for improvement of their socio-economic condition. As with the causes of resource improvement, project activities are also credited, but less frequently.

Costs and benefits

Costs and benefits as perceived by the PRM teams determine the sustainability of the monitoring activity. The 2006 survey shows that the potential obstacles identified in 2001 (Table 7.2) to a large extent became reality. There were no explicit differences between the responses of PRM villagers and of other villagers. In both nature reserves wildlife damage and time (opportunity cost of farm work) are major costs. Currently, many villagers go out for migratory work, so labour is scarce. Tongbiguan villagers also mentioned conflicts between villagers and leaders, and among villagers who received different benefits.

Conversely, the benefits identified in 2001 (Table 7.2) were not widely perceived in 2006. Only few could suggest what benefits PRM would bring them.
Most responses related to benefits of conservation in general. In Tongbiguan
the two PRM teams mentioned: '*less hunting*', '*dependence on fuel wood is
decreased*', but four out of six other villagers could not answer this question.

Why has PRM not been sustainable?

The cases described here were based on initially enthusiastic participation
of villagers, keen interest in participatory monitoring activities, and careful
transfer of skills to do monitoring, but the success of PRM lasted only for a
short time. What are the reasons for this? In this section we use our long-term
experience of the project in both nature reserves to reflect on the findings from
the assessments, and attempt to identify and explain some of the reasons why
PRM did not prove to be sustainable.

1. Lack of motivation

To implement PRM, villagers need to perceive benefits from the results. In both
pilot sites, motivation fell after two or three years for several reasons, only one
of which is inherent in the monitoring itself.

- No important changes in abundance or quality of resources have been
  observed in such a short timeframe. The monitoring team has therefore
  lost interest as the task became monotonous and repetitive.
- During the first year of implementation, PRM teams received financial support whereas in the second year no budget was made available for activities
  outside the new project framework of AMP.
- Motivation for monitoring is directly related to the capacity to implement
  it. Villagers doubt their capacity in monitoring and analysing data and have
  expressed the need for external support from staff and experts to help them
  in building capacity and self-confidence.
- External support from local government is needed to put management suggestions into action; regular support has been lacking in this case.
- Absence of secure tenure rights negatively influences the motivation for
  PRM. Although the Yunnan rules and regulations for nature reserve management state that some use of NTFPs inside the nature reserve is allowed
  if done in a sustainable way, this is not acknowledged by the nature reserve
  managers. The villagers themselves place little trust in these policies, because
  of the frequent changes mentioned above.

2. Management staff do not perceive monitoring and the involvement of local people as a management tool

Although China's decentralizing reforms allocated rights and responsibilities to lower levels, participatory approaches were rather new in Yunnan in 2001. The project aimed to strengthen local institutions for sound environmental governance at various government levels, but the staff still find it difficult to involve local people in management systems. They do not perceive monitoring as a management tool but as an external controlling system to be conducted by experts. Consequently, they do not judge the concept of PRM on its merits; they are not convinced that villagers could contribute to the analysis of the current situation as a basis for management decision-making.

3. Changing socio-economic environment

The project is working in a changing environment as China's economy develops rapidly and the national and local governments invest in rural infrastructure, income generation and creation of job opportunities. Government policies and technical training programmes implemented in the areas adjacent to both nature reserves stimulated a significant improvement in villagers' socio-economic situation. In 2001 the project selected the pilot villages for PRM on the basis of their dependence on the forest resources for their livelihood. However, the 2006 survey data indicate a sharp decline in forest dependency. Some villagers declared that they did '*not have time to go into the forest so often, because agricultural work takes too much time*'. In addition, many people also migrate out for work.

4. Lack of institutionalization

A final explanation for the failure of PRM, and one that we consider to be particularly important, is the fact that it has never been institutionalized in local government practices. Although local governments were considered to be secondary stakeholders, they felt no responsibility for PRM (considered 'a project activity') since they were not involved. Whatever the results of PRM, no channel existed to pass it to the government meeting-table. As we have seen, few management suggestions by the villagers were taken up by the responsible management offices and put into practice. In turn, the management offices apparently have difficulties in asking for technical and financial support if those management actions are not part of regular governmental programmes.

Furthermore, the project itself shifted its focus from a village planning approach to area management, which directly affected the PRM experiment. Currently, the AMP strategies are in their implementation stage and most governments encourage forest co-management activities as part of their plans. PRM could therefore become an integral (institutionalized) activity within the co-management activities. Being institutionalized in government programmes, the relevant authorities could then decide on technical and financial support needed for the implementation of management suggestions derived from PRM. The institutionalization might also create an opportunity to link PRM with scientific biodiversity monitoring and patrolling, two other activities to be steered by the nature reserve and forest co-management committee.

Can these problems be overcome in the future?

Ultimately, this chapter asks how PRM can contribute to environmental governance in a devolved policy context. The linkages between local institutions and governance, and forest conservation and use, have often been overlooked in policy debates in China (Weyerhaeuser, Kahrl and Su, 2006). Over the past two decades, China has introduced forest resources management reforms aiming to protect forests and enhance rural livelihoods. As part of these reforms, some powers over forestry management have been decentralized to village-level institutions. However, this decentralization has so far failed to give local communities adequate control over forest resources, and when powers are given, they can be easily taken away. Elected local village leaders remain accountable and subject to higher-level government authorities. This is particularly true among the minority groups in Yunnan, where communities remain embedded in paternalistic administrative relations (Xu and Ribot, 2004).

The security of access rights directly affects the way that resources are valued. A study in Nepal found that the same species and habitats were valued in different ways according to whether they were on private farmland, forest land with secure access rights, or land with contested rights (Lawrence *et al.*, 2006). The new national Law on Protected Areas might increase security of resource use rights within the nature reserve as it legalizes co-management in parts of the nature reserve. The emerging co-management associations, resulting from the new Law on Rural Cooperatives, might adopt PRM activities as an operational system for drafting the local co-management agreements on sustainable use of natural resources inside the nature reserve, while empowering communities with an appropriate monitoring system of this agreement.

Although policy dynamics and uncertainties impede the success of partic-ipatory monitoring and management, it has been suggested that human and social capital are more important (Birner and Wittmer, 2002).

> Human capital includes individual capacity, training, human health, values and leadership. It also includes non-formal skills associated with experience carrying out a particular task and indigenous knowledge about an area. Health status and commitment are other aspects of human capital important for communities. Social capital in a community is defined as collective norms and networks of reciprocity and mutual trust that contribute to working together for mutual benefit (Flora, 1997).

Social capital also includes villagers' ability to access people and resources at higher levels of government, and therefore also relates to good leadership. Furthermore, Schanz (2002) states that participatory monitoring will be sus-tainable only if it leads to the creation or adaptation of 'discursive institutions', that is, institutional arrangements, through which various stakeholders can continuously exchange and interact. In this case study we found that villagers' suggestions were not taken up by local governments; and the PRM teams and activities did not last long after the project stopped funding their activities. Rel-evant government agencies did not take over the funding since they considered the activities 'project-owned'. Building 'discursive institutions' could increase the likelihood that what is learned or suggested will also inform management decisions. Moreover, the social process in discursive institutions is at least as important as the technical or managerial outcomes (Schanz, 2002). This was not taken into account during the development of PRM in 2001. The AMP might serve as a discursive institution having the potential to promote legislation and participatory planning and management approaches by government structures (Pimbert, 2004).

Conclusions

Though the local villagers were initially enthusiastic in implementing biodiver-sity monitoring, the success didn't last for more than two or three years. This is because of a lack of motivation, the fact that monitoring is not viewed upon as a forest management tool, villagers do not have a true role in this manage-ment, and the monitoring activity has not been institutionalized. These lessons may apply to any situation where participatory biodiversity monitoring is being implemented. It is therefore crucial that at the start of developing participatory monitoring, these factors are taken into consideration. Long-term tenure rights should be secured, technical and management support should be identified at the start and ensured throughout the process. Sustainable benefits from monitoring should be generated, e.g. through implementing management decisions. There is a need for a forum to take villagers' suggestions to local government levels. Developing a participatory monitoring method should go hand in hand with advocating new ways of thinking and sensitizing local government and villagers for bottom-up and participatory approaches in forest management. The responsible government authorities should be involved in the development and coordination of PRM in order to enable institutionalization. This is especially the case in China, where little activities can be sustained without government support.

A more specific lesson for the Chinese context, or for any country in transition, is that the changing socio-economic conditions also impact on the success of participatory forest resources monitoring. If dependence on the forest declines and the socio-economic situation improves, monitoring becomes an extra burden, and motivation declines. Consequently, involving local villagers in monitoring of forest resources is only meaningful in areas where local livelihoods are for a great part based on the local use of forest resources and where management actions are urgently needed.

Acknowledgements

This chapter resulted from research initiated in 2001 within the framework of a Sino-Dutch funded Forest Conservation and Community Development Project. We would like to thank the Directors of the project for their contribution to facilitating this research. We also would like to thank all villagers and nature reserve management and forestry staff participating in PRM for sharing their knowledge, enthusiasm and opinions. We are grateful to Dr Anna Lawrence for her multiple editing of earlier drafts.

REFERENCES

Abbot, J. and Guijt, I. (1998). Changing views on change: participatory approaches to monitoring the environment. *SARL Discussion paper No. 2*.

Birner, R. and Wittmer, H. (2002). Converting social capital into political capital: how do local communities gain political influence? A theoretical approach and empirical evidence from Thailand and Columbia. Paper submitted to the 8th Biennial Conference of the International Association for the Study of Common Property (IASCP) "*Constituting the Commons: Crafting Sustainable Commons in the New Millennium*".

Dupar, M. and Badenoch, N. (2002). *Environment, Livelihoods, and Local Institutions. Decentralization in Mainland Southwest Asia*. World Resources Institute, Washington D.C., USA.

FCCDP (1998). Inception Report. Yunnan Provincial Forestry Department, Yunnan, China – DGIS, Ministry of Foreign Affairs, The Netherlands.

FCCDP (1999). The Formulation Team of the PIMAP Xiaoheishan Nature Reserve Management Office, Longling County Forestry Bureau, Gaoligong Mountain Nature Reserve Management Division, Baoshan Prefecture; Preliminary Integrated Management Plan of the Province level Xiaoheishan Nature Reserve, Yunnan Province, P.R. of China. Baoshan Prefecture, July 1999.

FCCDP (2000). The Formulation Team of the PIMAP Dehong Management Division; Preliminary Integrated Management Plan of the Province level Tongbiguan Nature Reserve, Yunnan Province, P.R. of China: Dehong Prefecture, Nov. 2000.

Flora, C. B. (1997). Enhancing community capitals: the optimization equation. *Rural Development News* **21**(1) 1–2. Available at: http://www.ag.iastate.edu/centers/rdev/newsletter/mar97/enhance.comm.cap.html

Hoonte, M. ten; H. Bartsch, Xu, Y. and Wu, X.F. (2004). Adjacent-Area Management Planning in practice. Forest Conservation and Community Development Project, Kunming. In *China's Protected Areas*, eds. Xie Yan, Wang Sung, and Peter Schei. China Council for International Cooperation on Environment and Development (Phase III), pp. 539–550.

Lawrence, A., Paudel, K. C, Barnes R, and Malla, Y. B. (2006). Adaptive value of participatory biodiversity monitoring in community forestry. *Environmental Conservation* **33**(4), 325–334.

Liu, D. (2001). Tenure and management of non-state forests in China since 1950. A historical review. *Environmental History* **6**(2), 239–263.

Lu, Wenming (2002). *Getting the Private Sector to Work for the Public Good; Instruments for Sustainable Private Sector Forestry in China*. Chinese Academy of Forestry.

Miao, G. and West, R. A. (2004). Chinese collective forestlands: contributions and constraints. *International Forestry Review* **6**(3–4), 282–296.

Pimbert, M. (2004). *Institutionalizing Participation and People-Centered Processes in Natural Resource Management*. Research and publication highlights. Institutional Institute for Environment and Development (IIED) and the Institute of Development Studies

Rijsoort, J. van, and Zhang, J. F. (2005). Participatory resource monitoring as a means for promoting social change in Yunnan, China. *Biodiversity and Conservation* **14**, 2543–2573.

Sayer, J. (1991). *Rainforest Buffer Zone: Guidelines for Protected Area Managers*. Newbury, UK: IUCN, The Nature Conservation Bureau Ltd, 94 pp.

Schanz, H. (2002). National forest programmes as discursive institutions. *Forest Policy and Economics* **4**, 269–279.

Sheil, D. (2001). Conservation and biodiversity monitoring in the tropics: realities, priorities and distractions. *Conservation Biology* **15**, 1179–1182.

Wang, S., Wang, X. P., Xie, Y. *et al.* (2000). Developing and implementing national biodiversity strategy and action plan: lessons from China. *Proceedings of the 1st Workshop on National Biodiversity Strategies and Action Plans in Northeast and East Central Asia*. Experiences and Lessons. 26–28 April 2000, Beijing, China. Biodiversity Planning Support Programme, UNDP-UNEP. Available at: http://bpsp-neca.brim.ac.cn/calendars/workshop-1/9.html

Weyerhaeuser, H., Kahrl, F. and Su, Y. (2006). Ensuring a future for collective forestry in China's Southwest: adding human and social capital to policy reforms. *Forest Policy and Economics* **8**(4), 375–385.

Xie Yan (2004). Review on the management system of China's nature reserves. In *China's Protected Areas*, eds. Xie Yan, Wang Sung, Peter Schei. China Council for International Cooperation on Environment and Development (Phase III), pp. 315–340.

Xu, J. and Ribot, J. C. (2004). Decentralization and accountability in forest management: as case from Yunnan, Southwest China. *The European Journal of Development Research* **18**(1), 153–173.

Yunnan Forestry and Wildlife Reserves Rules and Regulations (1987). Issued by Yunnan Provincial Government on October 6, 1987.

Yunnan Nature Reserve Management Regulations (1997). Issued by the 8th People's Congress of Yunnan on December 3, 1997.

8

Forest inventory in Nepal – technical power or social empowerment?

JANE HULL, HEMANT OJHA AND KRISHNA PRASAD PAUDEL

Community forestry in Nepal has long been considered a leading model of participatory forest management, whereby the state hands over national forest to be managed by local Community Forest User Groups (CFUGs). This development has been well documented (Hobley, 1996; Poffenberger, 2000; Ojha *et al.*, 2006) with particularly keen attention to the social issues of organization, livelihoods impact and equity. However, the trend in Nepal follows a global tendency, as attention has shifted more recently to the technical details of forest management (Lawrence, 2007). Furthermore, as participatory approaches to natural resource management proliferate, initial enthusiasm has been tempered by the challenges of both scaling up participatory practice amongst the stakeholders who govern and use the resources (Sukwong, 1998) and developing the policy and institutional framework to support such approaches.

In this chapter we explore the negotiation of responses to both these shifts, through the process of developing and implementing the government-approved forest inventory guidelines for community forestry in Nepal (Ministry of Forests and Soil Conservation, 2000; Department of Forests, 2004). We focus on the process and how the results were experienced by different stakeholders – national and district staff from the Department of Forests, members of non-governmental organizations (NGOs) representing civil society, and CFUGs. We examine the knowledge, roles and involvement of these stakeholders in the development of the inventory guidelines. We show that recognition of different values is often counteracted by the dominance of the technical mindset of those with power over the process (Backstrand, 2004; Ojha, 2006), and that the exchange of knowledge and values can often be experienced as threatening.

Taking Stock of Nature: Participatory Biodiversity Assessment for Policy, Planning and Practice, ed. Anna Lawrence. Published by Cambridge University Press. © Cambridge University Press 2010.

The case is interesting as it examines the implementation of inventory across a whole country, not just at local level. Great controversy arose when these forest inventory guidelines were introduced. Concerns ranged from practical implementation of the guidelines, to accusations that forest inventory was a way for the government to strengthen its control over community forestry. This controversy stemmed particularly from the different degrees of participation and roles of stakeholders in the process, based on the knowledge they held or were perceived to hold. In particular, NGOs were excluded from the process of developing guidelines, as they were perceived not to hold knowledge on scientific forest management.

We consider why forest inventory was introduced. We then consider why the introduction was so controversial. We examine the extent to which the contested nature of the inventory helped improve policy and practice through a resulting revision of the guidelines. We finally draw out lessons for wider implementation of tools for participatory monitoring and assessment of biodiversity.

We do this by analysing stakeholders' roles in the process. This is based on research conducted since the introduction of the forest inventory guidelines in 2000, using content analysis of different inventory guidelines and semi-structured interviews with stakeholders. We find the concept of 'knowledge culture' a useful analytical tool. It is expressed in a range of literature and at different theoretical and practical levels, but can be briefly summarized as follows. Different stakeholders have access to different information about the resource – in this case a community forest (Powell, 2006). They also have different ways of internalizing information for it to become knowledge. Different stakeholders also have differential power over a situation and can use knowledge to negotiate their role in a situation. 'Knowledge culture' is the way that a type of stakeholder has been able to gain, develop and use knowledge. This is influenced through their daily cultural situation such as through formal technical training, or through daily experience in a particular place, etc.

A 'clash of knowledge cultures' can occur in negotiations between different stakeholders over use of resources – such as the community forest. The implementation of inventory in a participatory natural resource management situation particularly crystalizes the issues of interactions between different stakeholders, with different knowledges and different power over a situation. This is because decisions on resource management are based on a form of resource assessment (forest inventory) which produces information. Yet inventory comes out of one particular knowledge culture – that of the technically trained resource manager. Therefore it is easier for those stakeholders coming from that knowledge culture to engage with it – which becomes challenging in a participatory situation with many different stakeholders.

The authors have all been involved in community forestry in Nepal – Hemant Ojha and Krishna Paudel are both Nepali nationals with long experience as foresters, civil society activists in a research organization (Forest Action) and latterly as PhD students. Jane Hull (neé Bryden) worked on a community forestry project (2000–2001) and researched the involvement of stakeholders in forest inventory for her MSc dissertation (Bryden, 2002). This chapter draws on the views of respondents to her survey of the different stakeholders involved in developing and using the inventory guidelines.

Nepal's community forestry programme and stakeholders

Community forestry in Nepal emerged out of the failure of the nationalization programme of the 1950s, during which forests became noticeably degraded (Gautam, Shivakoti and Webb, 2004). By the 1970s, government foresters realized that the Department of Forests could not manage national forests alone. They encouraged communities to manage the forest for national benefit (Talbott and Khadka, 1994), initially through handover of degraded forest to local government units, the village panchayats. This was not popular or successful because authority over the forest remained with the panchayat political leaders who promoted their own interests (Malla, 2001); this prevented power from being devolved down to households that depend daily on the forest for products. Over the next 20 years the condition of community forests generally improved. However, this occurred because the panchayats protected the forests, rather than applying technical forest management (Branney and Yadav, 1998; Shrestha and Amatya, 2000; Mahapatra, 2001).

Community forestry in Nepal was formalized through the Forest Act (1993) and Regulations (1995), after a long process to institutionalize the organizations and skills required for participatory forest management. These included testing of participatory methods through bilateral projects, developing the Community Forestry section of the Department of Forests and training government foresters in community forestry methodologies. Once this occurred, focus moved to pressing social issues of equity, as members with more political or financial power ('elites') dominated the plans and decisions of many CFUGs (Agarwal, 2001; Ojha, 2002).

At local level there are various stakeholders involved in the community forest. The main stakeholder is the CFUG. As of March 2006, there were 14 258 CFUGs established across the country, managing over 1.18 million ha of forests and involving more than 1 640 000 households (CFD, 2006). Each CFUG has a constitution setting out rules for operating the CFUG. The full CFUG meets at

Table 8.1. *Stakeholders' roles in community forestry (CF)*

Stakeholder	Role in CF	Dominant knowledge culture
Forest User Group (CFUG) (Local)	Manager and user of the forest	Local/'Indigenous'
Ranger (Local)	Facilitator, leads CFUG through the handover process, giving technical advice	Basic technical
District Forest Officer (DFO) (District)	Approver of forest handover through checking Constitution and Operational plan	Technical
Department of Forests (DoF) (National)	CF deliverer through implementing policy (developed by Ministry of Forests)	Technical
NGO (National and District)	CFUG support – mainly seen as focused on social aspects	Mainly social, but some starting to undertake technical roles
Bilateral (National and International)	Developer of new ideas, financer of CF	Technical and social

least annually with committee meetings and management activities in between. Rangers (junior technical staff of the District Forest Office) facilitate participatory discussion with the CFUG. The results of discussion on the forest resources and demands for products are collated by the Ranger to form the Operational Plan (management plan for the forest).

Finally the District Forest Officer (DFO) approves the handover of community forests based on both formal criteria stated in the Forest Act (ability and willingness of CFUGs to manage the forest) and informal criteria (such as per capita forest area, and prescribed harvesting levels). This can all add up to a slow and frustrating process for CFUGs. Yet as community forestry is a national programme of the Department of Forests (DoF), the DFO is accountable to senior DoF colleagues, rather than to CFUGs.

Altogether a large number of local and national stakeholders, including bilateral forestry projects and NGO activists, are involved in the community forestry process. Table 8.1 summarizes the roles of these various stakeholders and their interactions when implementing community forestry. These relationships can become complex as the stakeholders have different knowledge cultures guiding their understanding and use of the community forest.

Recent policy changes suggest a more complicated picture of community forestry than has been heralded internationally (Timsina, Ohja and Paudel, 2004). While the 1993 Act and 1995 Regulations were developed in a relatively open and participatory manner, international respondents report that the level of consultation in policy development has subsequently fallen. Ojha *et al.* (unpublished data) conclude that most recent policy decisions have involved only limited discussion with a narrow range of national stakeholders. The views and knowledge of DoF officials dominated the processes. In particular NGOs were angered over an attempt to quickly push through the proposed Second Amendment to the 1993 Act without much consultation (Ojha *et al.*, unpublished data). The amendment was intended to impose taxes on CFUGs and was seen as curtailing their rights. The proposed amendment was withdrawn, but according to international respondents, the strong reaction of NGOs made the DoF reluctant to include them in further policy debates. The subsequent introduction of forest inventory proved controversial, in an increasingly fraught policy environment where trust had been reduced between stakeholders holding different knowledge (Britt, 2001; Shrestha, 2001).

The call for scientific forest inventory

Before 2000, social issues such as equity of benefit sharing had dominated the operation of CFUGs. However, in 1997, technical management questions were highlighted for the first time. CFUGs, having protected the forest, wanted to gain products and income. One CFUG tested its right to harvest trees from its forest and challenged the earlier protectionist approach to forest management (Malla, 2001; Pokharel and Nurse 2004; Pokharel *et al.*, 2006). Timber harvesting in Nepal is below the sustainable extraction limit of scientific forest management (Ojha and Bhatterai, 2001; Pokharel and Nurse, 2004). This move reflected the improvement in the condition of many community forests and the desire to use forest products to enhance livelihoods.

The relevant DFO disagreed with the CFUG's harvesting operation and the case reached the Supreme Court – where the CFUG won. The DoF responded by introducing forest inventory as a compulsory part of the forest handover process, to ensure appropriate silvicultural management. In theory, a supportive framework was already in place for participatory forest inventory, because community forestry is approved on the basis of a Constitution and Operational Plan, developed through a participatory process with CFUGs led by DFO Rangers.

To explore further why the government introduced inventory, we need to understand the nature of inventory, the technical training and knowledge culture of foresters and their dominant role in the process. Forest inventory is a technical tool used by foresters to measure the availability of forest resources (mainly timber). This information can help users better understand their resource and make more effective decisions about future management practice. There are various scientifically agreed methods for undertaking forest inventory, based on sampling techniques and tree volume estimations to calculate sustainable yields (Philip, 1994). However, methods also exist to measure a wider range of products within the forest (Stockdale and Corbett, 1999; Lawrence *et al.*, 2006; Vickers, 2006), particularly those of economic value.

Conventional forest inventory produces quantitative information about the forest based on accepted scientific knowledge and practice. Participatory methods often favour qualitative results and patterns, which recognize local knowledge about the forest. Lawrence (2002) found that technical foresters tend to emphasize conventional inventory methods, whereas non-foresters highlight more innovative approaches looking at a broader range of products. Indeed participatory forest inventory involves far more than just ensuring Rangers and CFUGs can use scientific methods in forest inventory. These stakeholders also need to understand how to interpret and use the results – turning information into knowledge. This is often challenging when inventory is imposed from a different knowledge culture, that of the technically trained forester.

Branney, Malla and Neupane (2000) note that without an objective quantitative basis for forest resource assessment, forest management practices tend to be conservative, biased towards restricting the use of resources. Other supporters of participatory approaches argue that users do not need highly technical information to manage the forest (Jackson and Ingles, 1998). However the participation of local communities in inventory is important, as 'problem-solvers must be directly involved in generating the knowledge they require' (Samoff and Stromquist, 2001, p. 654). Stockdale and Corbett (1999) highlight the importance of local people understanding the *concepts* of inventory, rather than understanding techniques and calculations. They suggest that forest technicians and a small team of trained local people can carry out inventory, and that the important factor is community control over the *use of* results. Carter (1996) sees the experts' role as providing recommendations based on data analysis, from which users choose their management action.

International experience, therefore, suggests a division of responsibilities among stakeholders, and recognition that scientific forest inventory methods are not necessarily ideal for participatory approaches. Yet the DoF staff were technically trained so they responded to calls to increase production, with a scientific approach to forest inventory. From their point of view, the CFUGs (who needed support to increase production) did not hold the scientific knowledge to implement the suggested methods. However, this rationale was contested, particularly by NGOs involved in a clash of knowledge cultures. This is explored further after outlining the process of developing forest inventory guidelines.

Developing the inventory guidelines – technocratic domination

By the time the DoF came to develop participatory inventory guidelines, various bilateral projects had already developed inventory methods for the districts they were working in (Amartya, 1999; Rai, aus der Beek and Dangal 2000a; 2000b; NACRMP, 2002), following valid scientific approaches (Bryden, 2002), generally in a participatory manner. The DoF viewed bilaterals as forums for testing new ideas such as introducing technical aspects into community forestry, but being the first to develop compulsory national guidelines, they did not want to adopt an existing bilateral approach. Instead, the task team who developed the national guidelines in 2000 consisted of technically qualified DoF foresters, who led the process, working with bilateral projects.

In 2000, DoF staff took a narrow view of other stakeholders' involvement, and allocated roles based upon its own perceptions of the roles of stakeholders in community forestry generally (Table 8.2). NGO participation was however not considered necessary, as the development of inventory is seen as a technical issue. NGOs were not seen to hold such knowledge:

> NGOs don't have much technical expertise – they are knocking the objectives of the inventory (interview with DFO staff member, July 2002).

For example CFUGs and Rangers, who implement community forestry locally, were only involved in field tests, because DoF staff viewed them as the implementers of inventory at field level. CFUGs were not invited to question the content or rationale for introduction of the inventory at national level. The resulting guidelines proved difficult to implement, however, and led to an outcry from NGOs about both content and process – issues which will be examined in more detail below. On the other hand, more positive outcomes of the process included raised awareness in the DoF of the need for more intensive management of forests and for more dynamic knowledge to support community forestry (Ojha, 2002).

Table 8.2. *Comparison of stakeholder's roles in community forestry and inventory (CF)*

Stakeholder	Role in CF	Role in Inventory
CFUG (Local)	Manager and user of the forest	Field assistant
Ranger (Local)	Facilitator, leads CFUG through the handover process, giving technical advice	Leads CFUG through the inventory process
DFO (District)	Approval of forest handover through checking Constitution and Operational plan	Approves forest handover and approves inventory results
DoF (National)	CF deliverer through implementing policy (developed by Ministry of Forests)	Led task team to devise forest inventory guidelines
NGO (National and District)	CFUG support – mainly seen as focused on social aspects	No formal role in forest inventory
Bilateral (National and International)	Developer of new ideas, financer of CF	Consulted by task team in preparation of forest inventory guidelines

Revising the inventory guidelines – from technocratic domination to limited deliberation

Once the first national inventory guidelines were published in 2000, non-DoF stakeholders, expressed strong concerns about them, based on questions ranging from practical implementation to issues of power (Singh, 2000; Britt 2001; Dhital, Paudel and Ojha, 2003). CFUGs were generally unable to carry out the inventory as prescribed in the guidelines. There was national resistance from NGOs, with calls to revise the inventory guidelines. Eventually in response, new guidelines were completed in 2004 (Department of Forests, 2004), which to an extent addressed these criticisms. Table 8.3 compares the criticisms of the 2000 guidelines with the 2004 changes.

The revised guidelines explicitly state that they are intended to meet the needs of CFUGs and their facilitators (Department of Forests, 2004: vii), through the following principles:

Table 8.3. *Concerns over the 2000 guidelines and developments in the revision process*

Concern	Evidence from the 2000 guidelines and their implementation	Response in the 2004 guidelines
Guidelines too difficult for semi-literate CFUGs to carry out	Guidelines printed in English	Printed in Nepali with more diagrams
Whilst Rangers can carry out inventory, they do not have skills to suggest appropriate management from results	Many Operational Plans had similar prescriptions and clauses for quite different forests	Section included on interpreting results and outlining how they could be linked to management strategies
Guidelines are focused on timber. However, CFUGs also have daily need of non-timber forest products (NTFPs) including fodder and fuelwood	Guidelines focused on traditional methods for measuring timber	Reference to other non-timber forest products e.g. fuelwood, grass and medicinal herbs. However, much less comprehensive than timber sections, and point to other publications
Inventory slows down handover of community forests – especially without skilled rangers to facilitate the process	Slowdown in handover of new community forests, plus slowdown in revision of existing operational plans after first five years. Failure to revise the plan means CFUG loses legal control of the forest	Refer to facilitators to implement inventory – defined more broadly than Rangers, and specifically include NGOs
Inventory is a tool for greater government control over community forestry	No government documentation supports this view. In the strained policy context, NGOs highlighted the slowing handover of community forests and examples such as introduction of taxation on community forest products	A technical document which does not deal with the political concerns surrounding inventory
Participation in the process of developing guidelines limited to those who the DoF perceives as holding technical knowledge, as inventory framed as a technical issue by DoF	Only DoF and bilateral foresters involved. NGOs deliberately excluded as not seen to hold technical knowledge	Only DoF and bilateral foresters in the drafting team, but NGOs consulted at national level. No CFUGs involved. Again difficult to challenge the DoF's position

active participation of CFUGs in the inventory process,

flexible and simple process,

possibility of engaging (non-government) service providers to facilitate
    inventory with CFUGs,

integration of indigenous and scientific knowledge,

emphasis on methods that can be used by disadvantaged groups,

inclusion of timber and NTFPs.

Of course, a revised document does not indicate change in practice. Since
the introduction of the revised guidelines, the Maoist conflict in Nepal intensified significantly with severe implications for community forestry (Paudel
and Kattel, 2006). Forests became contested domains and meetings were often
interrupted for political purposes. These troubles occurred over and above
the practical issues outlined above. There has not yet been field research
on the implementation of the revised guidelines so it cannot yet be claimed that
the new guidelines have had a widespread positive impact for local level stakeholders. However, their revision did allow broader stakeholder involvement and
a more deliberative form of participation in the national policy process.

Reconciling different knowledges in participation

Brown *et al.* (2002a) note that participatory forest management is a knowledge intensive process. This is particularly so with inventory as it can give
opportunity to develop new knowledge by combining scientific forestry with
local knowledge of the forest (Ojha and Bhattarai, 2001). We consider three
concerns over the introduction of inventory worth examining in more detail, to
demonstrate the challenges of working with different knowledges in participatory situations: first, capacity of the CFUGs to carry out inventory; second, the
focus on timber; and third, the concern over whether inventory was introduced
to increase control over community forestry.

As communities move from protection to utilization of forests the demands
for technical support increase (Brown *et al.* 2002b). The DoF did not fully
consider the ability and capacity of CFUGs to carry out inventory. Whilst
it could be argued that the capacity of CFUGs was addressed by the initial
guidelines using a prescriptive step-by-step approach focusing on one method,
these were published in English. Foresters considered that this step-by-step
approach undermined their own professional ability to decide the appropriate
method for each context. Yet Dhital *et al.* (2003) found that on average there
were only two Rangers per district who had the skills to facilitate inventory

with CFUGs. Some Rangers said they had never used inventory methods taught in their college courses (Livelihoods and Forestry Project, 2004).

The revised inventory guidelines are now published in Nepali, and give broad guidance to allow inventory facilitators to decide the most appropriate methods. But at over 50 pages long they are a daunting read for CFUG members.

There are signs that inventory implementation will be better supported in future. Initially Rangers were intended to be the main facilitators, reflecting the DoF view of itself as not only the regulator, but also the service provider to CFUGs. The DoF has now recognized the need to train others in inventory. The Livelihoods and Forestry Project (2004) outlined how they have supported training of 'Local Resource Persons' to do forestry inventory with CFUGs. This ensures that skills remain in the community. Local facilitators generally come with social skills, but once trained can help the CFUG use the Operational Plan for forest management. This is an important step forward, as it recognizes the need to support communities in carrying out inventory from an unfamiliar knowledge culture.

The second concern is the focus on timber in the 2000 guidelines. The initial demand, which stimulated the DoF to develop national inventory guidelines, was indeed a CFUG wanting to harvest timber. Trees are more commercially valuable in situations where the CFUG wants a return from their community forest. However, CFUGs also have daily need of NTFPs including fodder and fuelwood. Trees are instead used for occasions such as house construction or financial insurance against unexpected need.

In the initial guidelines, non-timber products such as fuelwood, leaf litter or medicinal plants were excluded despite being more important than timber in daily livelihoods (Ojha and Bhattarai, 2001). This reflects the training and knowledge culture of technical foresters, as scientific forest management, and inventory, traditionally focus on timber. Foresters therefore automatically responded to the CFUGs request for support by suggesting a timber focused inventory. This ignored the real need for support for NTFP harvesting and management. Yet technical foresters do not have experience in measuring NTFPs. The DoF had the confidence to develop their own timber-focused guidelines, but not for NTFPs. The revised guidelines refer back to methods for medicinal herb inventory developed by the Nepal Swiss Community forestry Project (2001).

Because timber is valuable, the focus also increased NGO concerns that the government was using the timber focus of inventory to strengthen control over community forests:

The focus on timber is in the interest of the Forest Department (NGO staff member, July 2002).

This claim elicits sensitive responses from government foresters, who have a legitimate interest in inventory because they must ensure that CFUG operational plans allow sustainable forest management (Paudel and Ojha, 2007). In fact, control by foresters occurs indirectly, because a lack of Rangers trained to facilitate inventory slows down both the handover process (Ojha, 2002) and the revision of operational plans, which is required every five years. This can lead to the suspension of CFUG use rights (Paudel and Ojha, 2007). Slow handover weakens trust between the government forester and communities (Ojha, 2002).

> The introduction of inventory guidelines has a negative implication. People have some doubt on the government intention, despite trust-building going on in the past ten years. People think the government will ask for the forest back (NGO staff member, July 2002).

Framing inventory as a technical issue could be seen as a way to exclude NGOs representing civil society, as foresters with technical knowledge try to reassert control over community forestry. Conversely the reaction of social-focused NGOs to their exclusion could also be interpreted as concern over loss of their role.

> There is a conflict between the technical and the social in community forestry. The sociologists see the threat to their profession that technical things are coming up (bilateral project worker).

Ojha (2002) found that technical foresters lack understanding of the wider social and political implications of the forest inventory guidelines, which reflects their technical knowledge culture. Yet in the broader context of apparent exclusion of certain stakeholders from policy debate, it is inevitable that NGOs viewed the introduction of forest inventory with suspicion.

Scaling up participatory forest inventory – taking knowledge into account

Nepal, with its long experience of community forestry, should be an ideal place to scale up participatory monitoring – in this case through forest inventory. Sheil and Lawrence (2004), having examined a broad sweep of participatory monitoring methods, suggest that 'political support for decentralization, community forestry and community-based conservation might provide a fertile environment for larger scale action'. Yet the three concerns examined above (CFUG capacity, timber focus and increased government control) show that there is much to be done to ensure that this becomes effective. The link between these concerns centres on the challenge of supporting effective discussion between different knowledge cultures in a participatory situation.

Three knowledge cultures interact here – the technical knowledge of the foresters focused in scientific forest management, the local knowledge of the CFUGs focused on 'use values' of the forest, and the social knowledge of the NGOs. Technical experts often develop their knowledge from a theoretical basis, in contrast to the CFUGs' practical context-specific and problem-orientated knowledge (Ohja *et al.*, 2007).

Notably, it was the NGOs who highlighted the inventory controversy rather than the CFUGs, who arguably had most to lose through the slowdown of community forestry. This highlights a communication gap between CFUGs and technical foresters. It also shows that the NGOs' social knowledge allowed them to both understand the social implications of imposing one form of knowledge on another, and to use this to highlight their own exclusion from the process.

Knowledge is information that has been processed by an individual to make it meaningful to their situation (Samoff and Stromquist, 2001; Powell, 2006). Inventory produces information, which only becomes knowledge when understood, adapted and used by stakeholders. The difference between scientific and local knowledge is often expressed as a dichotomy, which can be unhelpful as it reflects romantic views of rural societies and stifles adaptation of knowledge within a society (Agrawal, 1995). Gronow (1995, quoted in Carter, 1996, p. 3) expresses a pragmatic understanding, noting how users often have good knowledge of individual tree species, but need systematic information on their distribution in the forest to manage the resource. The inventory process in Nepal could lead to a synergy between local and scientific forms of knowledge, particularly now that it includes a broader range of products.

In this case the use of technical language has limited the potential for synergy in participatory processes by giving power to stakeholders with technical knowledge. In Nepal's situation, Nightingale (2005, p. 581) argued that 'the promotion of expert knowledge and professional practices in Community Forestry is often used as a somewhat contradictory vehicle for educated elites to retain control over forest management, thus undermining some of the key objectives of the program'. Samoff and Stromquist (2001, p. 639) consider that 'Official knowledge collectors will have important but often invisible authority over what is to be regarded as knowledge and over constructs used to organise it' but that this process can 'be obscured by the mystique of science and scientific method'. The generation of such knowledge is often portrayed as a technical rather than political process. Our study shows how the choice of methodology can be critiqued within the circles of technical professionals, yet the role of technical methods cannot be questioned either by those technical stakeholders, or by non-technical stakeholders. This reflects a wider tendency in development to talk in technical terms (Cleaver, 2001), rather than recognizing that there are 'more subtle issues at stake involving power and knowledge transactions and role negotiations' (Biggs and Smith, 1998, p. 241).

In developing participatory assessment methods it is therefore important to ask for whom such methods are developed and whose knowledge is involved in the preparation of guidelines. One team working in Nepal conclude that 'Participatory monitoring is a powerful approach that can improve the effectiveness of information gathering and help people understand the reasons for certain management decisions' (Tucker *et al.*, 2005, p. 23). This reflects a very functional view of participation – where resource users are not in control of defining of what is measured and how. Users' participation can help speed measurement but can increase their dependency. For example illiterate forest users are dependent on others as inventory information is recorded in a written management plan (Hodge and Chitrakar, 1999).

These inventory guidelines have not particularly benefited CFUGs. Their community forest tenure has been threatened by lack of facilitation for the inventory process. Yet the importance of retaining tenure explains why CFUGs will engage in the unfamiliar knowledge culture of inventory, even to the extent of paying charges to get inventory completed (Paudel and Ojha, 2007).

This need for CFUGs to have appropriate support in undertaking inventory is crucial. This is particularly important to note when considering how participatory inventory can be effectively supported as part of a national programme.

Different stakeholders have unequal opportunities for creating and utilizing knowledge (Bourdieu, 1998). To overcome this, Ojha (2006) considers the approach of deliberative participation to be worth applying to forest management. Deliberation assumes that participation is only fully effective if it moves beyond implementing functional tasks to the political process of empowering those who directly use and manage the resource, through interaction and dialogue. Opportunities for deliberation can occur in situations of 'crisis', for example when attempts to implement practical solutions, such as forest inventory, fail. In this study, it required the outcry of the social NGOs for the revision process to occur. Such crisis highlights the disconnection between the embedded knowledge of those with power over the situation and the actual situation. Crisis brings challenge, which here uncovered the dominance of the technocratic mindsets of forest officials and impact of that on the practical issues involved in undertaking inventory.

Lawrence *et al.* (2006) found that assessment was an unfamiliar and potentially threatening concept for CFUGs. Yet an intensive process of questioning and discussion was facilitated between CFUG members, researchers and DFO staff. Researchers used expressed values to prepare a framework for discussion between those holding different knowledges. This discussion allowed stakeholders to better understand each other's positions and what they valued in the forest. CFUGs were given the space to include their views. When DFO staff could not answer questions, the discursive format allowed them to suggest experimentation, rather than lose professional standing. Values were not just revealed, but also influenced and changed – though through an intensive process.

Alternatively, deliberation can take place in a more planned and relaxed way. So, in this case, deliberation is where both scientifically trained foresters and CFUGs engage in dialogue to learn about and adapt to each others' approaches to forest management. For deliberation to occur, CFUGs and forest officials have to participate in equitable discussion, negotiating local and scientific knowledge that best fits local needs. Foresters should support rather than dictate the CFUG's decision-making process (Ojha, 2006). This requires skilled facilitation and is possible where there is intensive project support for individual CFUGs (Lawrence *et al.*, 2006; Vickers, 2006), but the resource implications of this when scaling up nationally are significant.

Conclusions

This case study demonstrates the challenges of devising methods for participatory monitoring and assessment of biodiversity for a national programme, which take into account interactions between different kinds of knowledge. Implementing scientific forest management may be helpful in some participatory forestry management contexts, but it requires users to participate in an unfamiliar knowledge culture and appropriate support mechanisms need to be in place, particularly if scaling up its use across a country.

The technocratic viewpoint considers that scientific training generally allows foresters to take decisions over a particular management situation where science is needed, such as forest management. However, when enhancing deliberation in participatory approaches, scientists are expected to advise users on various options for management rather than taking management decisions themselves. The movement from instrumental to deliberative participation challenges embedded power structures and requires some form of transformation. This only occurs when there is strong resistance from civil society, in this case stimulated by the backlog of operation plan revision and the slowdown of community forestry.

The 2000 guidelines further fuelled broader mistrust between the techno-cratic DoF and socially focused NGOs, with passive resistance from CFUGs. However, some controversy could have been avoided had there not generally been an increasingly non-consultative approach to policy-making. The process made assumptions over what knowledge was required for stakeholders to par-ticipate in discussions over forest inventory, specifically excluding those with only social knowledge.

The conflict ensuing from the initial inventory guidelines prompted the DoF to initiate a revision process. Again the task force primarily comprised DoF and bilateral project officials. Yet the process did allow more space for deliberative discussion (Ojha, 2006), and consultation with a wider range of stakeholders.

There is a growing reflexivity within the DoF that allows space for those outside the DoF to engage in policy development. However, the DoF must consider whether it can remain a service provider for forest inventory, whether it should focus on policy-making and regulation. The training of local social facilitators to support the forest inventory process is a positive move, with inventory skills retained in the area and easier engagement with the CFUG.

Forest inventory in this case has come to signify more than just the mea-surement of forest resources. It has uncovered far wider issues of control in participatory natural resource situations, particularly the tendency for control to be held by technically trained personnel. The case highlights the need for political deliberation at all levels of natural resource governance in devising participatory methodologies as the broader policy process must be trusted, transparent and inclusive. Participatory monitoring and assessment of biodi-versity will only work if issues of power are given as much consideration as technical issues, with recognition of the different knowledge held by stake-holders at the heart of the process.

Acknowledgements

Thanks to Anna Lawrence for her support in preparing this chapter. Thanks also to colleagues in Nepal who were interviewed during the research for this chapter.

REFERENCES

Agrawal, A. (1995). Dismantling the divide between indigenous and scientific knowl-edge. *Development and Change* **26**(3), 413–439.

Agrawal, B. (2001). Participatory exclusions, community forestry, and gender: an anal-ysis for South Asia and a conceptual framework. *World Development* **29**(10), 1623–1648.

Amartya, D. B. (1999). *Technical Aspects on Community Forestry Production Training Manual*. Kathmandu, Nepal: Biodiversity Support Program, 14 pp.

Backstrand, K. (2004). Scientisation vs. civic expertise in environmental governance: ecofeminist, eco-modern and post-modern responses. *Environmental Politics* **13**(4), 695–714.

Biggs, S. and Smith, G. (1998). Beyond methodologies; coalition building for participatory technology development. *World Development* **6**(2), 239–248.

Bourdieu, P. (1998). *Practical Reason: On the Theory of Action*. Cambridge: Polity Press, 168 pp.

Branney, P. and Yadav, K. P. (1998). *Changes in Community Forest Condition and Management 1994–1998: Analysis of Information from the Forest Resource Assessment Study and Socio-economic Study in the Koshi Hills*. Kathmandu, Nepal: Nepal-UK Community Forestry Project (NUKCFP).

Branney, P., Malla Y. B. and Neupane, H. R. (2000). Learning by doing: participatory research with forest user groups in Nepal. In *Forestry, Forest Users And Research: New Ways Of Learning*, ed. A. Lawrence. Wageningen: ETFRN, 187 pp.

Britt, C. (2001). Mixed signals and government orders: the problem of on-again, off-again community forestry policy. *Forest, Trees and People Newsletter* **45**, 29–33.

Brown, D., Malla, Y. M., Schreckenberg, K. and Springate-Baginski, O. (2002a). From supervising 'subjects' to supporting 'citizens': recent developments in community forestry in Asia and Africa. *Natural Resources Perspectives Paper* **75**. London: Overseas Development Institute, 4 pp.

Brown, D., Shepherd, G., Schreckenberg, K. and Wells, A. (2002b). Forestry as an Entry Point for Governance Reform. *Forestry Briefing Paper 1*. London: Overseas Development Institute, 6 pp.

Bryden, J. (2002). Measuring Trees for Whom? The Role of Forest Inventory in Nepal's Community Forestry Programme. Unpublished MSc dissertation, University of Oxford, 102 pp.

Carter, J. (1996). *Recent Approaches to Participatory Forest Resource Assessment. Rural Development Forestry Study Guide 2*. London: Overseas Development Institute, 322 pp.

Cleaver, F. (2001). Institutions, agency and the limitations of participatory approaches to development. In *Participation – the New Tyranny?* B. Cooke and U. Kothari, eds. London: Zed Books, 207 pp.

Community Forestry Division (CFD). (2006). *Current Status of Community Forestry in Nepal*, 50 pp. Available at: http://www.forestrynepal.org/current-status-of-community-forestry-in-nepal

Dhital, N., Paudel, K. and Ojha, H. (2003). Inventory related problems and opportunities in community forestry: findings of a survey. *Journal of Forest and Livelihood* **2**(2), 62–66.

Department of Forests (2004). *Community Forest Resource Inventory Guidelines* (in Nepali – English translation used). Department of Forests, Kathmandu, Nepal, 63 pp.

Gautam, A. R., Shivakoti, G. P. and Webb, E. L. (2004). A review of forest policies, institutions, and changes in the resource condition in Nepal. *International Forestry Review* **6**(2), 136–148.

Hobley, M. (1996). Participatory forestry: the process of change in India and Nepal. *Rural Development Forestry Study Guide 3*. London: Overseas Development Institute, 337 pp.

Hodge, R. and Chitraker, R. (1999). *Literacy, Communication and Community Participation – Report of Baseline Study in 4 Forest User Group Areas, Dhankuta District, Nepal*. Kathmandu: CLPN.

Jackson, W. and Ingles, A. (1998). *Participatory Techniques for Community Forestry – A Field Manual*. Australian Aid for International Development, Gland, Switzerland: IUCN, WWF, 124 pp.

Lawrence, A. (2002). *Participatory Monitoring and Evaluation of Biodiversity: a Summary of an Internet Discussion*. Available at www.etfrn.org/etfrn/workshop/biodiversity/index.html

Lawrence, A. (2007). Beyond the second generation: towards adaptiveness in participatory forest management. *CABI Reviews: Perspectives in Agriculture, Veterinary Science, Nutrition and Natural Resources* 2(28), 1–15.

Lawrence, A., Paudel, K., Barnes, R. and Malla, Y. (2006). Adaptive value of participatory biodiversity monitoring in community forestry, Nepal. *Environmental Conservation* 33(4), 325–334.

Livelihoods and Forestry Project (2004). Innovations for sustainable services – training local people in forestry techniques. *Good Practice Papers*, 24 pp. Livelihoods and Forestry Project, Kathmandu, Nepal. Available at http://www.lfp.org.np/publications.php?id=14

Mahapatra, R. (2001). Betrayed: Nepal's forest bureaucracy prepares for the funerals of the much hailed community forest management programme. *Down to Earth* 9, 20–24. Available at http://www.downtoearth.org.in/archive.asp?year=2001

Malla, Y. B. (2001). Changing policies and the persistence of patron–client relations in Nepal: stakeholders' responses to changes in forest policies. *Environmental History* 6(2), 287–307.

Ministry of Forests and Soil Conservation (2000). *Guidelines for Inventory of Community Forests*. Kathmandu, Nepal: Ministry of Forests and Soil Conservation, 13 pp.

Nepal Australia Community Resource Management Project (NACRMP). (2002). Module 5 Participatory Forest Resource Assessment and Analysis. In *Training of Trainers Manual*. Kathmandu, Nepal: Nepal Australia Community Resource Management Project, 84 pp.

Nepal Swiss Community Forestry Project (2001). *Participatory Inventory Guidelines for Non-Timber Forest Product*. Kathmandu: SDC, 74 pp.

Nightingale, A. (2005). "The Experts Taught Us All We Know": professionalism and knowledge in Nepalese community forestry. *Antipode* 37(3), 581–604.

Ojha, H. R (2002). *A Critical Assessment of Scientific and Political Dimensions of the Issue of Community Forests Inventory in Nepal: A Policy Discussion Note*. Kathmandu, Nepal: Forest Action, 6 pp. Available at http://www.forestaction.org/publications/6_Discussion%20Papers/6_6.pdf

Ojha, H. (2006). Techno-bureaucratic doxa and challenges for deliberative governance: the case of community forestry policy and practice in Nepal. *Policy and Society* 25(2), 151–204.

Ojha, H. R and Bhattarai, B. (2001). Understanding community perspectives of silvicultural practices in the middle hills of Nepal. *Forest Trees and People Newsletter* **44**, 55–61.

Ojha, H., Timsina, N., Khanel, D. and Cameron, J. (2006) *Deliberation in Environmental Governance: The Case of Forest Policy Making in Nepal*. School of Development Studies, University of East Anglia, Norwich, UK, 21 pp. Available at http://www.forestaction.org/pdf/forestpo.pdf

Ojha, H., Paudel, K. P., Timsina, N. P. and Chhetri, R. B. (2007). Deliberative knowledge interface: lessons and policy implications. In Ohja, H. R., Timsina, N. P., Chhetri, R. B. and Paudel, K. P., eds, *Knowledge Systems Interface in Natural Resource Governance – Case Studies from Nepal*. Forest Action, Kathmandu, Nepal, 160 pp.

Paudel, K. P. and Kattel, B. (2006). Caught in the crossfire: forest-dependent poor people in Nepal. *Journal of Forest and Livelihood* **5**(1), 14–21.

Paudel, K. P. and Ohja, H. (2007). Contested knowledge and reconciliation in Nepal's community forestry – a case of forest inventory policy. In Ohja, H. R., Timsina, N. P., Chhetri, R. B. and Paudel, K. P., eds., *Knowledge Systems Interface in Natural Resource Governance – Case Studies from Nepal*. Kathmandu, Nepal: Forest Action, 160 pp.

Philip, M. S. (1994). *Measuring Trees and Forests*, 2nd edn. Wallingford: CAB International, 310 pp.

Powell, M. (2006). Which knowledge? Whose reality? An overview of knowledge used in the development sector. *Development in Practice* **16**(6), 518–532.

Poffenberger, M., ed. (2000). *Communities and Forest Management in South Asia – A Regional Profile of the Working Group on Community Involvement in Forest Management*. Switzerland: IUCN, 162 pp.

Pokharel, B. and Nurse, N. (2004). Forests and people's livelihood: benefiting the poor in community forestry. *Journal of Forest and Livelihood* **4**(1), 19–29.

Pokharel, B., Paudel, D., Branney, P., Khatri, D. B. and Nurse, N. (2006). Reconstructing the concept of forest based enterprise development in Nepal: towards a pro-poor approach. *Journal of Forest and Livelihood* **5**(1), 53–65.

Rai, C. B., aus der Beek, R. and Dangal, S. P. (2000a). *Simple Participatory Forest Inventory and Data Analysis*. Kathmandu, Nepal: Nepal Swiss Community Forestry Project, 70 pp.

Rai, C., aus der Beek, R. and Dangal, S. (2000b). *Participatory Forest Resource Assessment – a Guideline for Forest Management Operational Plan*. Kathmandu, Nepal: Nepal-Swiss Community Forestry Project.

Samoff, J. and Stromquist, N. P. (2001). Managing knowledge and storing wisdom? New forms of foreign aid? *Development and Change*, **32**, 631–656.

Sheil, D. and Lawrence, A. (2004). Tropical biologists, local people and conservation: new opportunities for collaboration. *Trends in Ecology and Evolution*, **19**, pp. 634–638.

Shrestha, K. and Amatya, D. (2000). Protection verses Active Management of Community Forests. Issue Paper 1 in *Community Forestry in Nepal: Proceedings of the Workshop on Community based Forest Resource Management*. Joint Technical Review Committee Kathmandu, Nepal, pp. 3–17.

Shrestha, N. K. (2001). The backlash – recent policy changes undermine user control of community forests in Nepal. *Forest Trees and People Newsletter* **44**, 62–65.

Singh, V. P. (2000). *Comment on Inventory Guidelines to Community Forest.* Unpublished paper. Kathmandu, Nepal, 5 pp.

Stockdale, M. C. and Corbett, J. M. S. (1999). Participatory inventory – a field manual written with special reference to Indonesia. *Oxford Forestry Institute Tropical Forestry Papers* **38**, 383 pp.

Sukwong, S. (1998). Foreword in Victor, M., Lang, C. and Bornmeier, J. *Community Forestry at a Crossroads: Reflections and Future Directions in the Development of Community Forestry.* Proceedings of an International Seminar held in Bangkok, Thailand 17th–19th July 1997. RECOFTC Report No 16. Bangkok, Thailand, 324 pp.

Talbott, K and Khadka, S. (1994). Handing it over – an analysis of the legal and policy framework of community forestry. In *Nepal WRI Cases in Development.* Washington D.C.: World Resources Institute, 20 pp.

Timsina, N, Ohja, H. and Paudel, K. P. (2004). *Deliberative Governance and Public Sphere: A reflection on Nepal's Community Forestry 1997–2004.* Fourth National Workshop on Community Forestry. Kathmandu, Nepal: Department of Forestry, Nepal.

Tucker, G., Bubb P., de Heer M. *et al.* (2005). *Guidelines for Biodiversity Assessment and Monitoring for Protected Areas.* Kathmandu, Nepal: KMTNC, 132 pp. Available at http://www.unepwcmc.org/collaborations/BCBMAN/PDF/PA_Guidelines_BMA.pdf

Vickers, B. (2006). *Community Forestry: An Opportunity for Participatory Biodiversity Monitoring*, 10 pp. Available at http://www.recoftc.org/site/index.php?id=324

9

Perceptions of landscape change in British Columbia's Northwest: implications for biodiversity and participatory management

JOHN LEWIS

Introduction

Throughout British Columbia (BC), as elsewhere in North America, debates surrounding biodiversity and landscape conservation have deepened as a result of the efforts of government and non-governmental organizations to establish large protected areas and limit the activities of resource development interests (such as timber companies and mining corporations) in ecologically sensitive landscapes. Such plans ultimately attempt to restore natural ecosystems by limiting human activity within selected areas and by restoring ecological processes such as fire, flooding, and erosion. Support for these plans is often the most strident in urbanized areas where people are least affected by concerns for the loss of socio-economic well-being and cultural identity. In BC's remote forested landscapes, which have contributed significantly to the identity of First Nations[1] and non-aboriginal residents alike, residents express opposition towards any conservation strategy that purports to remove humans as an agent of change in the natural landscape. Even conservationists are beginning to question whether 'naturalistic' approaches to landscape management conflict with the conservation of biodiversity and traditional landscapes (Hull and Robertson, 2000).

Owing in part to the reaction of local residents to nature conservation and landscape restoration strategies, the government of BC has begun to pay increasing attention to stakeholders' concerns by introducing and experimenting with innovative methods of public participation. However, they still face the challenge of working with competing values in decision-making processes. This is

[1] The aboriginal or indigenous people of Canada are referred to as First Nations.

Taking Stock of Nature: Participatory Biodiversity Assessment for Policy, Planning and Practice, ed. Anna Lawrence. Published by Cambridge University Press. © Cambridge University Press 2010.

particularly the case when values are rooted in unique and unfamiliar world-views, such as First Nations' culturally and spiritually based conceptions of nature and natural resources.

At another level, numerous studies in the broad field of landscape perception research have demonstrated that, in general, people tend to prefer landscapes that are predominantly natural over those that are largely built or modified (Kellert, 1997). It might be reasonable to conclude that people will tend to prefer those landscapes that are the most natural and biologically rich. However, this may not be the case (Kaplan and Kaplan, 1989). In his investigation of preferences for modified savanna landscapes, Gobster (1994, 1995) concludes that the biophysical processes on which environmental preferences are predicated may also promote preferences that are less than amenable to the protection of biological diversity. In her seminal work on the cultural basis for landscape preference, Nassauer (1995) suggests that the human preference for natural settings is tempered by North American cultural norms for neatness, which in turn equates with good management or stewardship of the land. In such a context, natural and more biodiverse landscapes may be viewed as untended and poorly managed (Thayer, 1989).

Multiple and poorly understood environmental values, combined with expectations of landscape management that may compete with biodiversity objectives, present significant challenges for those wishing to promote biologically diverse landscapes. To enhance our understanding of these challenges, this chapter examines the First Nations and non-aboriginal perspectives on landscape change and landscape conservation in BC's upper Skeena Valley. The first part sets the context by describing the pre- and post-contact history of the upper Skeena Valley landscapes, and posits that the relatively recent European settlement, with the attendant influx of agriculture, industrial timber management, recreation development and urbanization, is only the latest stage in a long history of landscape change. Biophysical changes that can be linked to social processes of acculturation, depopulation and resource exploitation have altered or eliminated historic patterns of indigenous land-use and, in turn, affected the appearance and ecology of the landscape.

The second part draws on interviews with First Nations and non-aboriginal residents of the Skeena Valley to assess their perceptions of the region's landscape history and what future changes will mean to them. Beyond inter-cultural perspectives on the meaning of nature and landscape change, study participants provided lengthy commentaries on the cultural appropriateness of particular landscape conditions, and conceptions of landscape care or 'visible stewardship'. The significance of these findings for pluralistic approaches to

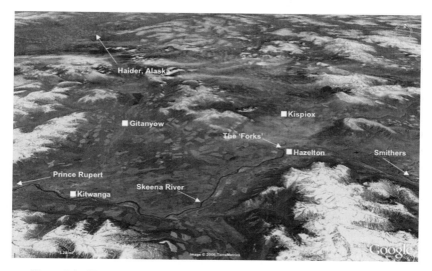

Figure 9.1. Upper Skeena communities and landscape setting (image courtesy of Google Earth).

biodiversity conservation and landscape management are addressed in the concluding discussion.

Research setting and landscape history

Situated below the Alaska panhandle, the landscapes of the upper Skeena Valley are exceptionally diverse (Figure 9.1). The environment through which much of the Skeena River passes is very mountainous, and only in the immediate vicinity of the river is there any level land. Mountain slopes and valley floors are heavily timbered, and only on the central plateau of the Skeena's eastern tributaries (i.e. the Kispiox and Bulkley rivers) near Hazelton is there any open grazing country. Both historic First Nations and more recent Euro-Canadian settlements have concentrated along the southern extent of the river at or near major river confluences. Stretching from Kitwanga in the west to Hazelton in the east, the upper Skeena Valley lowlands are the site of small-scale agriculture (mostly grazing and hay production), vast deciduous forests of cottonwood, poplar and aspen; and village and town settlements. This is the heart of the Gitksan territories, as well as the confluence of the Skeena and Bulkley rivers where the natural endowments of access to BC's coast and interior by way of two major river corridors and a relatively mild climate has made this part of the Northwest a natural choice for habitation, as well as a vital nexus for trade among coastal and interior First Nations peoples.

By most accounts, human induced landscape change in the Pacific Northwest is a relatively recent occurrence as, it is believed, the indigenous inhabitants did not improve, cultivate or enhance the productivity of their landscape prior to European contact (Benedict, 1934; Flanagan, 2000). There is, however, a growing body of evidence suggesting that the pre-contact people of the region did in fact engage in some form of landscape modification. There is clear evidence among much of the coast and interior of BC (Gottesfeld-Johnson, 1994; Turner, 1999), Alberta (Lewis, H., 1988), Washington, Oregon and California (Lewis, H., 1973; Agee, 1993) for the indigenous cultivation of black huckleberry (*Vaccinium membranaceum*), low-bush blueberry (*Vaccinium caespitosum*), thimbleberry (*Rubus parviflorus*), soap berry (*Sheperdia canadensis*) and other traditional food plants through the controlled but large-scale use of fire.

Although the forest environments of the Northwest are host to a rich variety of plant and wildlife resources, their availability varies considerably both seasonally and geographically. The theory is that, to overcome naturally occurring resource and nutritional deficits, the pre-contact First Nations in the Northwest modified existing plant communities to provide nearby villages with staple foods that would otherwise have been dispersed too widely to permit surplus accumulation. The extent to which this is true is still contested (Baker, 2000; Lepofsky *et al.*, 2003), but there is a growing consensus among fire ecologists and ethnoecologists that, prior to European settlement, regular burning did maintain or expand shrub and grassland ecosystems (Lewis, H., 1973; Agee, 1993; Anderson, 1993; Boyd, 1999; Johnson, 1999; Lewis and Ferguson, 1999; Bonnicksen, 2000; Peacock and Turner, 2000).

Throughout the nineteenth and twentieth centuries, visible evidence of First Nations plant cultivation gradually waned as population pressures from European diseases, introduced agricultural crops such as potatoes, and fire prohibitions in the 1940s by the BC Forest Service put a stop to most traditional landscape burning practices (Parminter, 1995; Figure 9.2). By the 1970s, timber management had replaced indigenous plant cultivation and natural fire disturbance as the dominant sources of landscape change, as the demand for wood products from BC's remote Northwest exploded. Forestry officials in BC's Northwest shifted from the more conservative selective harvesting methods prevalent during the inter-war and immediate post-war periods to a more aggressive and 'efficient' approach based on clearcutting (Weetman *et al.*, 1990).

The legacy of this management philosophy has produced large and often highly visible clearcut areas on mountainsides, lakeshores and roadsides

Figure 9.2. A photograph of the village of Kispiox taken in 1948, showing the western side of a portion of Skeena range. From interviews conducted in 2005, Gitksan elders identified light-coloured areas as two berry patches maintained by their parents and grandparents using controlled burns. The size, elevation and western aspect is typical of many black huckleberry patches within the Gitksan territories. Regrowth of the forest canopy over the past six decades has rendered these patches indistinguishable from the surrounding forest matrix (image courtesy of the BC Archives, Photo # I-21896).

(Figure 9.3) making forest management among the most visible and hotly contested issues in the Northwest during the past two decades. The rapid liquidation of old growth forests in the region led to local and internationally driven preservation pressure that suppressed annual harvests in the Skeena and other regions of the province. Although timber management will not completely disappear from the upper Skeena, change is likely to be a continuing part of the region's landscapes through the advent of a different economic sector, one that does not extract resources in the conventional sense. This new sector finds intrinsic, marketable values in the lofty mountains, majestic views, and sprawling 'pristine' forests that have become valuable both to exurban migrants and roving tourists alike. The same landscapes that were once regarded as difficult to conquer are now valued for hiking, skiing, camping, hunting and fishing, or simply living 'close to nature' (Chipeniuk, 2004). The influx of new residents and visitors to the region comes with expectations that impact the landscape. At

Figure 9.3. The visible remains of clearcuts from the region's period of intensive
timber management in the 1970s and 1980s (photo by the author).

a general level, the expectations of tourists and newcomers are for landscapes
that are 'natural' or unmodified by the kinds of land-uses that were characteristic of the Northwest's history. Such expectations have pitted recent migrants
against long-time residents (First Nations and Euro-Canadian alike) who characterize natural settings as 'unproductive' to the extent that they fail to provide
the kinds of material benefits that have historically sustained Northwest communities. Ultimately, the landscape transformations that are occurring in the
Skeena Valley are causing many to worry about a new host of impacts and conflicts – loss of livelihood, overcrowding, habitat reduction, and incompatible
land-uses.

Methods

This chapter is based on a case study that used a hybrid combination of qualitative research methods and more quantitative preference-testing analytical
methods, consistent with recommendations by Elmendorf and Luloff (2001).
The exploratory and inductive nature of qualitative inquiry uses an iterative
process where data collection is guided by the findings of the research process,
and theory is generated from the data as the investigation proceeds. I used a
purposive sampling strategy (Johnson, 1990; Henderson, 1991), and sought

people who are known by members of their community to be concerned about the current and future condition of the region's forests, and who may play an active role in expressing their concerns through formal channels (such as public meetings, citizen committees and newspapers), as well as informal (such as coffee klatches and social clubs). Implicitly, I sought participants who would be at ease with the research experience, and be comfortable in articulating their perceptions of the world in a way that genuinely reflects their ideas and beliefs. From an initial list of 35 participants based on key informant and network referrals, and personal introductions, 30 people consented to participate (15 First Nations and 15 Euro-Canadians, reflecting their roughly equal representation in the broader community).

I used a form of photo-elicitation (Ball and Smith, 1992; Harper, 1994) in my interviews with the upper Skeena participants. Since its first documented use in the late 1950s (Collier and Collier, 1957), photo-elicitation has remained a straightforward method to understand and employ. It involves using photographs, videos or other graphic images (e.g. drawings or paintings) to invoke comments, memory and discussion in the course of a semi-structured interview. The strength of the technique rests in the power of images to invite people to take the lead in an inquiry, to render full use of their expertise. Psychologically, the stimulus materials act as a third party in the interviews, shifting the focus of attention and pressure away from the participant as the subject of questioning. In effect, both the participant and the interviewer engage the photographs together, and the role of the participant shifts from research subject to that of co-investigator in discovering answers to questions posed in relation to the photographs. The participant's role can be seen as that of an expert guide leading the researcher through the content of the pictures. The incentive to take on this role often comes from the fact that people have a fascination with settings or visual information that they know intimately, and a common compulsion to express that knowledge (Collier and Collier, 1957).

The use of images had two further advantages. The main objective of this research was to gauge public preferences for different modified landscapes, and a carefully chosen set of images was a more efficient method of gathering this information than taking 30 participants into the field to discuss landscape settings that are in various stages of disturbance, and separated by large distances. Visual simulation techniques also allowed me to depict and elicit preferences for modified landscape conditions that no longer exist, as well as future conditions that are not yet part of the Skeena Valley landscape. I identified the power of landscape simulation to turn the clock back and represent historical landscape conditions as one means of capturing information about traditional land-management practices that are quickly disappearing from the Skeena landscape and the collective memories of the Gitksan community.

(a)

(b)

(c)

Figure 9.4. Aboriginal Fire Management Simulations.

Existing-condition photography was obtained from three viewpoints identified with community members, which represented sites that are both accessible
and familiar to most upper Skeena residents (Sheppard, 1989; 2001a). Four
landscape change scenarios were simulated for each viewpoint location, making 12 images in total (Figures 9.4–9.7), representing possible future conditions
in the upper Skeena's forested landscapes (Table 9.1).

Figure 9.5. Industrial Timber Management Simulations.

Interviews began with a general discussion of the participants' perceptions of their environment and relationship to the forest landscape. Participants were then shown the simulations of the alternative forest conditions. The interview prompted discussion of important landscape features and evaluations of the alternative conditions. I recorded and transcribed the interviews and, together

(a)

(b)

(c)

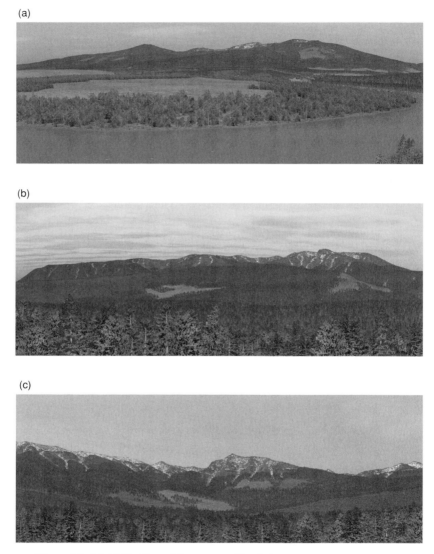

Figure 9.6. Multi-Use Forest Management Simulations.

with my field notes, analysed the transcripts using a form of qualitative content analysis based on the Constant Comparative Method (Glaser and Strauss, 1967; Goetz and LeCompte, 1984). Interview transcripts were returned to the participants, and community members were invited to review interpretations of the data for accuracy.

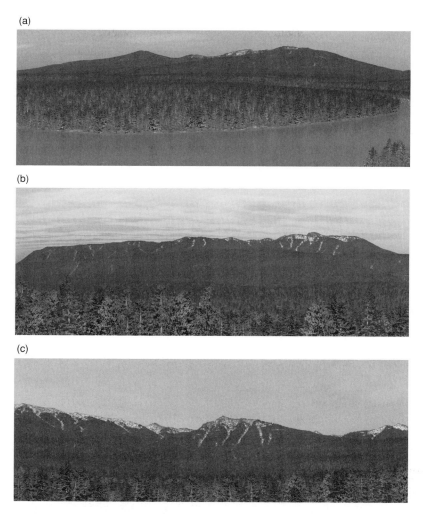

(a)

(b)

(c)

Figure 9.7. Natural Condition Simulations.

Results

The participants were able to describe at length the factors that influenced their appraisals of the simulated landscape conditions. In general, three dominant themes appeared to affect their judgements:

(1) perceived balance of impacts;
(2) perceived cultural disturbance;
(3) perceived care or 'visible stewardship'.

Table 9.1. *Landscape scenario conditions*

Scenario title	Management	Data sources	Landscape appearance
1. Aboriginal Fire Management	Reintroduction of traditional burning by local First Nations for ethnobotanical food products (e.g. berries, root crops, wildlife browse)	Interview data with Gitksan elders. Archival photography	More heterogeneous than current conditions, 'savanna-like'
2. Industrial Timber Management	Large-scale clearcutting reintroduced to suppress beetle infestations and control 'decadent' overmature stands	Recent photography. GIS vegetation datasets	Heavily impacted landscape. Large, geometric openings in the forest canopy
3. Multi-Use Forest Management	Smaller-scale timber management with more natural – i.e. less geometric – openings	GIS vegetation datasets. Consultation with local forest ecology experts	Emulates natural disturbance patterns. Designed to meet timber, range, riparian, and ethnobotanical products management objectives
4. Natural Condition	Replacement of timber management with non-extractive recreational land-uses	GIS vegetation datasets	A homogeneous landscape dominated by continuous forest cover with no visible evidence of human disturbance

Table 9.2 *Illustrative 'balance of impacts' comments*

Issues	Dimensions	Illustrative comments
Balance of impacts	Material livelihood	If that's a trapline, and if it's your trapline, you'd be pretty well heartbroken
	Scenic quality	. . . you've got a larger visual impact because of the clearcuts
	Habitat	. . . it doesn't provide the wildlife with the shelter they require
	Erosion	. . . when it rains a lot of it slides, and a lot of the sand and mud goes into the rivers
	Resource waste	. . . you see nice stuff just chucked away because they can't be bothered . . . to clean up
	Scale	These I didn't like because the clearcuts were too big
	Public relations	There's less visual impact, it's better public relations
	Care	. . . it would be nice to see that these areas are being cared for

Balance of impacts

The way that the participants engaged in evaluating the simulated landscapes was in effect a complex evaluation of multiple consequences. I have summarized these in eight themes (Table 9.2), which illustrate how the participants generally considered a change from a scenic quality standpoint, but are also fundamentally concerned about what is right for nature (erosion potential, habitat protection, etc.) and humans (material livelihood, resource waste, public relations, etc.). It was difficult to ascertain whether the participants realized that they were conducting a form of mental trade-off analysis, but the complexity of their evaluations and effort to consider multiple issues within the context of a single response was clear.

FN14[2]: That's what strikes me first about this picture. It's not very cosmetic, but they've left the mountainsides alone. It's all a matter of, if you're looking at it just like fibre, fibre, fibre then that's no good. There would be massive seepage into the creeks, and stuff like that. I've seen a lot of grazelands up the Kispiox Valley where

---

[2] Alphanumeric codes have been used to safeguard the anonymity of the participants. The ethnicity of the participants is coded as either FN (First Nations) or EC (Euro-Canadian). The numeric suffix refers to the order in which the participant was interviewed and allows the researcher to identify the participant.

there's absolutely no in-stream vegetation, and the fish populations there have just been decimated. And here, what if you want to go shoot a moose, or what if you just want to walk through a nice forest? Yeah, there's other values there besides the fibre. (Similar comments expressed by five other participants.)

For many participants, the large-scale harvest patterns depicted by the Industrial and, to some extent, the Multi-Use scenarios (see Table 9.1) reflected the management style that predominated in the region during the past 30 years and failed to balance important forest attributes. Comments pertaining to both conditions reflected a common tension between conflicting material uses of the forest – e.g. the forest as a source of economic timber wealth, subsistence or non-timber forest products – and comments that addressed either the scenic quality of the landscape or its intrinsic importance for wildlife and aquatic habitat. The following is an example.

EC11: ... to me, you've got a larger visual impact because of the clearcuts, and then for wildlife. If you have smaller clearcuts it's better for wildlife ... and just for public relations too. (Similar comments expressed by seven other participants.)

Whilst I had anticipated comments of this sort for the Industrial condition, I was more surprised by such evaluations of the Multi-Use scenarios. Despite the 'naturalistic' appearance of the harvest openings, several participants focused on the large openings and effectively dismissed the attempt to soften the visual imprint through patch retention, smaller openings (40 hectares and less), as well as irregular and feathered edges. In effect, they argued that 'a clearcut's a clearcut'.

FN10: I'm a little more comfortable with this [Multi-Use scenario], but not much. These are still clearcuts. (Similar comments expressed by six other participants.)

More directly, a group of First Nations and Euro-Canadian participants who depend on the forest for income from trapping, argued that clearcutting in any form, whether in geometric or naturalistic patterns, represents a threat to their material livelihoods. The Industrial and Multi-Use scenarios provide insufficient cover for small fur-bearing animals, and the degree to which the conditions destroy habitat or render valued species vulnerable to higher levels of predation from other animals or recreational hunters clearly affected their judgements.

FN1: if that's a trapline, and if it's your trapline, you'd be pretty well heartbroken. Like I say, the animals don't go in anything that's charcoaled or if there's nothing there to feed on.

EC8: if you do this, you're asking for trouble. This isn't going to stay anyways. It's all just going to get washed out. We harvest and eat a lot of fish up here and this is one of the places they come up to lay their eggs. (Similar comments expressed by six other participants.)

This evidence shows that rural communities are fairly sophisticated in the breadth of issues that define their approach to forest management. Ultimately, in order to address the multiple concerns that influence their judgements, forest managers will need to approach forest communities with more than a technical manual or template approach to landscape management. They will need to consider the biophysical setting, prior land-use history, and the cultural context in which the landscape modification is proposed, as discussed in the next section.

Perceptions of cultural disturbance

Participant evaluations of the burnt portions of the Multi-Use and Pre-Industrial scenarios elicited a particularly interesting range of opinions, from those focusing on material considerations, to expressions of concern or support rooted in competing notions of cultural identity. Comments that favoured the burn treatments were generally of two types. The first emphasized the material benefits associated with the management of non-timber products, underscoring both the dietary and potential economic benefits that the community may realize from the cultivation of berries and other forest-based food products (e.g. wild mushrooms). In many cases, however, this view was qualified by reflections on the scale of the disturbances and the practical necessity of large berry patches for small communities.

EC4: ... it's pretty positive, I think. You're feeding people, and it's local and it's high quality. But boy it looks like a big burnt area. (Similar comments expressed by eight other participants.)

The second group of positive comments suggested that ethnicity mediates landscape appraisals. For some of the First Nations participants, the reintroduction of berry cultivation would not only be conducive to a healthier lifestyle, but would also reinforce culturally based patterns of land-use.

FN12: it's cultural, and it's cultural in that the Gitksan, and in other areas the Wetsuweten, have through the generations made use of non-timber forest resources. I think it's important that we continue to have access to those values, to those activities, to those areas within our own traditional lands. (Similar comments expressed by five other participants.)

In part, the reintroduction of aboriginal burning to the upper Skeena valley may serve as a marker of First Nations culture through the visible imprint that traditional land-uses may leave on the landscape. On a more abstract level, the action of harvesting traditional food plants is capable of forging intimate bonds between settings and people who possess a distinct ethnic identity (Lewis and Sheppard, 2005). In effect, people who have historically been rooted to and derived their livelihood from the land will often characterize their relationship with the landscape in terms of 'the earth is part of us' or 'we are the land, and the land is us' (Lewis, 2000). These sentiments tended to be a common refrain among the First Nations participants.

For other participants, ethnicity considerations were indicated in views that ethnobotanical products management by local First Nations would be a wasteful use of resources. Euro-Canadian participants who remain actively employed in the local forest industry provided the most vocal expressions of opposition to the burn treatments. However, their assessments were initially positive. Most of them quickly recognized the indications of burning in the simulations and concluded that these were clearcuts that had subsequently been broadcast burned.[3]

> EC9: I think it's an acceptable management tool. Fire has always been a natural part of forest disturbance up here anyway. (Similar comments expressed by four other participants.)

However, these assessments changed when they were informed that the burn patterns reflected aboriginal food plant cultivation rather than timber management. The handful of Euro-Canadian participants who had formerly supported the use of fire as a silvicultural tool, appeared to base their concerns on the appropriateness of *aboriginal* burning and, in particular, on the competence of First Nations as fire managers.

> EC9: I think that it's not two hundred years ago now, that we know enough and there's enough value in that timber that it would be stupid to burn it just to make some huckleberries. You see I take issue with the idea that anything the Indians do is just automatically good because they're so in touch with the land because they're Indians. (Similar comments expressed by four other participants.)

This noteworthy reversal of opinion by the Euro-Canadian participants seems to be rooted in both competing and archaic notions of cultural identity ('they

---

[3] A prescribed burning technique used by foresters to break down coarse woody material following a harvest and prepare the site for restocking.

are our forests to manage and no longer belong to the "Indians"'), and concern about reintroducing forest management practices that have unknown risks.

On the other hand, some participants offered interesting suggestions on the potential for non-timber products management as a visible marker of active use and care for the forest landscape.

> EC14: Well when it's clearcut, companies just come in, take the logs and then just disappear. At least this way, with people on the land harvesting and tending to the berry patches, people may actually start caring for these areas. (Similar comments expressed by three other participants.)

Conventional timber management suffers from the public perception that, once the resource has been removed from the land, little (visible) interest or effort is expended into caring for the landscape to ensure that it will remain healthy and productive. As one participant described it, forestry appears to be characterized by a 'make a quick dollar and just grab it and run' (FN7) style of land management. Cultivating non-timber resources may be one means of providing a continuous stream of benefits from the landscape while the timber 'crop' grows, which ultimately places people on the land throughout the rotation and provides a visible human presence that reflects ongoing stewardship and care. This approach to 'Visible Stewardship' (Sheppard, 2001b) is discussed in more detail in the next section.

Perceptions of care or visible stewardship

For many of the participants, the Natural scenario was the clear favourite. In general, the high aesthetic value of an untouched landscape combined with considerations of fish and wildlife habitat integrity over the long term were clear factors in the participants' evaluations.

> FN1: That's the way it's supposed to look like. That way the animals can roam their own country out there.
> EC5: This is what I like. It's better for wildlife and I think it's just much nicer to look at.

In a more abstract sense, several participants couched their preference for the natural condition in terms of the spiritual and restorative benefits of a landscape that is undamaged or, as one participant stated, an environment that is 'whole'.

> FN4: I like this one because this is the kind of place where I'd like to go when something's troubling me, to find healing.

EC2: All the good stuff is still there ... I remember we used to go out to Kisegas, you could almost feel the people there, the old people. It was like, that's spiritual. And that's what I like about this place.

These comments echoed some of the findings from the environmental preference literature, which posit that people generally prefer landscapes where there is no visible imprint of human disturbance (Benson and Ulrich, 1981; Abello and Bernaldez, 1986; Kaplan and Kaplan, 1989). Moreover, pristine settings are generally regarded as more conducive to personal and psychological restoration, where contact with nature has been empirically demonstrated to promote restoration from psychophysical stress (Ulrich, 1979, 1981; Ulrich *et al.*, 1991) and mental fatigue (Kaplan and Talbot, 1983; Hartig, Mang and Evans, 1991). Finding spiritual and psychological fulfilment from nature in its most natural, sublime condition is something that European cultures have only recently rediscovered. The eco-tourism industry in BC and elsewhere is founded on the principle that people derive considerable pleasure and, on occasion, spiritual fulfilment from observing plant and animal life in a 'pristine' condition. This is not intended to equate First Nations with eco-tourists, but I am suggesting that BC's First Nations derive significant aesthetic and spiritual enjoyment from environments that are teeming with a variety of plant and wildlife; a pleasure which many people in European and Euro-Canadian culture share in-kind.

Despite the overwhelming preference for natural landscapes, most participants expressed a pragmatism that affirmed the need for forest management largely to maintain the region's standard of living, without returning to the conditions of the past 20 to 30 years. There was an unambiguous sense that forest management will remain an important part of the upper Skeena's economic future, and that 'pristine' landscapes such as those depicted by the Natural scenario do not reflect the social and economic reality of the region.

FN5: I would prefer this, but it's not natural the way we live nowadays. You know. You have to create employment, you have to live. (Similar comments expressed by seven other participants.)

However, recognizing the need for timber management of some form, a consistent statement made in reference to the Industrial and Multi-Use scenarios was the degree to which they failed to demonstrate proper care for the forest.

FN10: I think all this multiple-use stuff needs to be done with care because even the thinning where they do selective logging, because of things like mushrooms and medicinal plants, treat them with respect. (Similar comments expressed by four other participants.)

When pressed to explain how they would recognize a carefully managed forest, some First Nations pointed to the burn treatments in the Multi-Use and Pre-Industrial scenarios (see Table 9.1) to suggest that the smaller patchwork pattern of burning approximated the traditional practice of rotating burn treatments.

> FN4: When the old people did this [i.e. burn for berries] they used to burn off one area and leave the area nearby to grow and produce berries. Kind of like they do on a farm, you know, they would rotate the crop. Why can't forestry do that? Why do they have to take everything and leave nothing behind for the other plants and animals? (Similar comments expressed by four other participants.)

There is some ethnographic evidence that aboriginal berry patches were managed according to a rotating system of applying fire to a subsection of a much larger berry producing area (Trusler, 2002). Only after a 'sub-patch' had reached its peak production capability would it be burned (usually after five to 10 years of production), allowing the rhizome base beneath the soil to sprout more vigorous and productive shoots. While recently burned areas regenerate and reach a subsequent phase of peak production, adjacent areas that were burned three to five years earlier are fully productive and harvested for their fruit crop. In this manner, berry cultivation areas are maintained in a constant state of food production. From the perspective of some First Nations participants, emulating this pattern of traditional land management would embody 'care' to the extent that the disturbances are smaller than conventional harvest openings, the periodic burning of over-mature vegetation returns nutrients to the soil and, moreover, a regular and more sustained presence on the landscape may suggest that the forest is actively being tended.

> EC15: Why not just get people out there looking after the land? I mean, if you have people involved in looking after their backyard wouldn't that go a long way towards making people feel better about how the forest is managed?

For many of the First Nations and Euro-Canadian participants, selective stem removal represented the most obvious and preferred approach to careful land management. However, some Euro-Canadian participants expressed views that were consistent with their First Nations counterparts in that a sustained and visible human presence on the landscape would embody care. Among this group, suggestions for how to accomplish this varied from erecting built structures (e.g. silvicultural camps or growth monitoring stations) to direct community involvement in the restoration of damaged landscapes or recently harvested areas.

> EC14: ... it might be good to see some kind of building or permanent camp set up in areas that have been disturbed. That way you could see that someone is looking after the area. (Similar comments expressed by five other participants.)

These comments indicate a clear recognition that humans are dependent on the environment and that some visible alteration of the forest is to be both expected and regarded as part of the 'natural condition'. Indeed, as one participant remarked, upon coming to the region 40 years ago, the desire to see untrammelled nature was tempered after several years by the realization that, whether for timber, grazing lands or berries, human beings have in various ways transformed the landscapes of the Skeena valley for generations.

> EC15: I guess when I came here as a young guy I expected to see more of a wilderness, and it really got to me, you know, how the forest was being abused. But I guess with age I've either just mellowed or come to the realization that using the forest is what makes this area tick. (Similar comments expressed by two other participants.)

Second, where participants express a desire to see forest management conducted according to a standard of care, that standard may have its basis in familiar or culturally recognizable patterns of land stewardship. For instance, for some First Nations participants, care is implicit in the traditional pattern of berry patch rotation. Similarly, for the Euro-Canadian participants, care is seen largely through built structures and people present on and actively tending to the land, perhaps reflecting a more European conception of agricultural management.

Discussion: implications for landscape planning and research

A few basic caveats need to be stated before interpreting these exploratory study results. Based as it is on a small purposively selected sample, and a limited number of scenarios, the results cannot necessarily be statistically generalized to other communities in BC. Clearly, more work is needed to develop a deeper understanding of how the Gitksan and their Euro-Canadian neighbours perceive landscape change.

Nevertheless the methodological attention to eliminating bias means that these findings are worthy of attention. Some patterns of landscape evaluation are clear and broadly consistent with other forest landscape evaluation studies (Kruger, 2005). For instance, the study shows that multiple factors are brought to bear in the evaluation of alternative landscape conditions. The complexity of participant appraisals is reflected in the attention to visual factors, but they also care about how natural and human communities will be affected by landscape alterations. Sustaining multiple values in landscape management is an important principle in the management of BC's Crown forests, and the salience of balanced use to the Skeena participants reinforces its significance. No matter how new harvesting patterns are applied, they will need to address multiple and locally salient contextual issues regarding cumulative effects, the impact on unique resources, the location and extent of harvest operations, and the effect on subsistence resources (Lewis, 2006). The latter consideration seems to carry particular weight in the Northwest, as the importance of subsistence (fish, wildlife and plant) harvests to the resident First Nations and Euro-Canadian populations recurs in the interview comments. The future direction of landscape management in the upper Skeena will require careful attention to its effects on the integrity of these important values.

Landscape management in the Skeena Valley will carry with it significant trade-offs between desirable and undesirable outcomes. Further complicating matters for landscape managers is the finding that landscape appraisals may depend to an important degree on the type of knowledge that is activated at the moment of judgement. This was most clearly demonstrated by the Euro-Canadian forest workers who shifted their generally favourable assessments of the simulated burn treatments when they learnt that the conditions reflected traditional patterns of aboriginal berry cultivation than a conventional silvicultural practice. In effect, the same landscape condition can be associated with different responses depending on the particular knowledge that is contextually activated at the moment of judgement. From disciplines as disparate as political science and resource management, there is growing body of research that documents the effects of information on preference judgements (Davidson *et al.*, 1985; Althaus, 1998; Kearney, 2001; Ribe, 2006). By including larger participant samples and more diverse landscape types, future studies may gain more insight into the dynamic between landscape appraisals, knowledge, information and other contextual factors.

A more unambiguous finding is the notion that landscapes communicate. A fundamental aspect of this is that people seek information when they experience a landscape (Nassauer, 1995; Sheppard, 2001b). In effect, from natural as well as relatively developed or urbanized landscapes, people 'expect to see the look of human intention' and, in particular the degree to which a landscape is perceived to be well cared for. For the Skeena Valley participants, there was a clear desire to see that forest companies and the provincial government are managing the forest with care.

FN13: I'd like to see more care in how they design the blocks, the cutblocks, or how they take measures to protect riparian areas which, this has wildlife.

While the finding that people desire to see signs of human intention in the landscape is not new, I did not expect to find that participants preferred forest landscapes with a visible human presence such as through built structures in forest openings, or indications of short-term cultivation and management (e.g. rotating harvest and 'fallow' patches with interim uses such as berry cultivation). For the First Nations respondents, preferences for the latter form of visible stewardship were rooted in a culturally recognizable form of land management. This finding resonates with Nassauer's hypothesis that standards of care are predicated on culturally based expectations and recognizable patterns of landscape form (Nassauer, 1995).

On a more tacit level, interpretations of the simulated landscapes appeared to be based on culturally or personally salient motivations and needs. In other words, what people know about a landscape and the conditions that they prefer may be driven by their material or experiential needs. The degree to which landscape changes complement (or conflict with) conceptions of cultural identity, requirements for spiritual or psychological restoration, employment or recreational uses of the forest, appear to be subtle (or occasionally explicit) factors in appraisals of the landscape scenarios. For landscape managers, the complexities of balancing these factors need some practical support. If researchers can understand what stakeholders are looking for, they can enable landscape managers to design approaches that align with needs, and which allow human presence on the landscape to co-exist with or even complement biodiversity goals. Visual 'what-if' exercises of the imagination (Ervin, 1992; Lewis and Sheppard, 2005) using photo-realistic simulations of the kind used in this study hold significant promise as a means of eliciting the motivational or needs-based filters that individuals use in their evaluations of landscape condition.

Landscape designers may not need to look too broadly for novel landscape patterns. Future research may seek to explore preferences for patterns of interim cultivation in the forest landscape similar to the small-scale burn patches maintained by the First Nations in the Skeena region for berry cultivation. In addition to providing a visible marker of human intention that to some of the study participants suggested visible stewardship, this land-use pattern may have implications for biodiversity as well. In effect, disturbance is one of the principal factors that influences biodiversity in a landscape and, as a major historical form of landscape disturbance in the Skeena region, traditional plant management activities can affect which species occur in a particular location as well as the relative abundance of those species. Disturbances such as those created by the Gitksan people tended to be occasional and spatially focused (Trusler, 2002; Lewis, 2006) which has the effect of creating mosaics, thereby increasing habitat diversity within a landscape and, in turn, species diversity.

While introducing proto-agricultural techniques to the Skeena landscape may advance biodiversity goals and simultaneously satisfy local desires for the look of sustained human intention in the landscape, it would be naïve to expect that reintroducing such practices would be straightforward. Such techniques may not be feasible today when traditional lands are now controlled by government and industrial interests, when traditional methods of land management and subsistence have been largely replaced by dependence on mainstream sources of food, and where the widespread management of the forest with pesticides and herbicides has made the consumption of naturally occurring plant materials hazardous. Clearly, additional research and creative thinking is required to explore and identify other (perhaps similar) landscape patterns that bridge human landscape needs and biodiversity goals. The complex relationship between landscape preference and biodiversity highlights the important role that the social sciences and environmental design can play in the management of landscape resources. Landscape research is an important component of participatory landscape management, including both community values and behavioural practices in the management of landscapes.

REFERENCES

Abello, R. P. and Bernaldez, F. G. (1986). Landscape preference and personality. *Landscape and Urban Planning* **13**, 1928.

Althaus, S. L. (1998). Information effects in collective preferences. *American Political Science Review* **92**(3), 545–558.

Agee, J. (1993). *Fire Ecology of Pacific Northwest Forests*. Washington, D.C.: Island Press.

Anderson, M. (1993). Native Californians as ancient and contemporary cultivators. In *Before the Wilderness: Environmental Management by Native Californians*, ed. M. Anderson and T. Blackburn. New York, NY: Ballena Press, pp. 151–174.

Baker, W. (2000). Fires and climate in forested landscapes of the Rocky Mountains. In *Fire Regimes and Climatic Change in Temperate Ecosystems of the Western Americas*, ed. T. Veblen, G. Montenegro, W. Baker, and T. Swetnam. New York, NY: Springer-Verlag, pp. 120–157.

Ball, M. and Smith, G. (1992). *Analysing Visual Data* (Qualitative Research Methods Series, Vol. 24). Newbury Park, CA: Sage Publications.

Benedict, R. (1934). *Patterns of Culture*. Boston, MA: Houghton Mifflin.

Benson, R. and Ulrich, J. (1981). *Visual Impacts of Forest Management: Findings of Public Preferences*. USDA Forest Service INT-262; 14 pp.

Bonnickson, T. (2000). *America's Ancient Forests: From the Ice Age to the Age of Discovery*. London: John Wiley and Sons.

Boyd, R. (1999). Strategies of Indian Burning in the Willamette Valley. In *Indians, Fire and the Land in the Pacific Northwest*, ed. R. Boyd. Corvallis, OR: Oregon State University Press, pp. 94–138.

Chipeniuk, R. (2004). Planning for amenity migration in Canada: current capacities of interior British Columbian mountain communities. *Mountain Research and Development* **24**(4), 327–335.

Collier, J. and Collier, M. (1957). *Visual Anthropology: Photography as a Research Method*. Holt, Rinehart and Wiston.

Davidson, A. R., Yantis, S., Norwood, M. and Montano, D. E. (1985). Amount of information about the attitude-object and attitude-behavior consistency. *Journal of Personality and Social Psychology* **45**, 997–1009.

Elmendorf, W. and Luloff, A. (2001). Using qualitative data collection methods when planning for community forests. *Journal of Arboriculture* **27**(3), 139–151.

Ervin, S. (1992). Using computers to ask 'What If?'. *Landscape Architecture*, October, 25–29.

Flanagan, T. (2000). *First Nations? Second Thoughts*. Montreal, QC: McGill-Queen's University Press.

Glaser, B. and Strauss, A. (1967). *The Discovery of Grounded Theory: Strategies for Qualitative Research*. Chicago, IL: Aldine.

Gobster, P. H. (1994). The aesthetic experience of sustainable forest ecosystems. In: Covington W. W. and Debano, L. F. (eds.) *Sustainable Ecological Systems: Implementing an Ecological Approach to Land Management*, 12–15 July 1993, Flagstaff Arizona. General Technical Report RM247. Fort Collins, CO: US Dept of Agriculture, Forest Service, Rocky Mountain Forest and Range Experiment Station, pp. 246–255.

Gobster, P. H. (1995). Aldo Leopold's ecological esthetic: integrating esthetic and biodiversity values. *Journal of Forestry* **93**(2), 6–10.

Goetz, J. and LeCompte, M. (1984). *Ethnography and Qualitative Design in Educational Research*. Orlando, FL: Academic Press.

Gottesfeld-Johnson, L. (1994). Aboriginal burning for vegetation management in Northwest British Columbia. *Human Ecology* **22**, 171–188.

Harper, D. (1994). On the authority of the image: visual methods at the crossroads. In *Handbook of Qualitative Research*, ed. N. Denzin and Y. Lincoln. Thousand Oaks, CA: Sage Publications, pp. 403–412.

Hartig, T., Mang, M. and Evans, G. W. (1991). Restorative effects of natural environment experiences. *Environment and Behavior* **23**(1), 3–26.

Henderson, K. (1991). *Dimensions of Choice: A Qualitative Approach to Recreation, Parks and Leisure Research*. State College, PA: Venture Publishing.

Hull, B. and Robertson, D. (2000). Which nature? In *Restoring Nature: Perspectives from the Humanities and Social Sciences,* ed. P. Gobster and B. Hull. Washington, D.C.: Island Press, pp. 299–307.

Johnson, J. (1990). *Selecting Ethnographic Informants*. London: Sage Publications.

Johnson, L. (1999). Aboriginal burning for vegetation management in Northwest British Columbia. In *Indians, Fire and the Land in the Pacific Northwest*, ed. R. Boyd. Corvallis, OR: Oregon State University Press, pp. 238–254.

Kaplan, R. and Kaplan, S. (1989). *The Experience of Nature: a Psychological Perspective*. Cambridge: Cambridge University Press.

Kaplan, S. and Talbot, J. F. (1983). Psychological benefits of a wilderness experience. In: Altman, I. and Wohlwill, J. F. (eds.) *Behavior and the Natural Environment*. New York: Plenum, pp. 163–203.

Kearney, A. R. (2001). Effects of an informational intervention on public reactions to clear-cutting. *Society and Natural Resources* **14**(9), 777–790.

Kellert, S. R. (1997). *Kinship to Mastery: Biophilia in Human Evolution and Development.* Washington, D.C.: Island Press.

Kruger, L. (2005). Community and landscape change in southeast Alaska. *Landscape and Urban Planning* **72**, 235–249.

Lepofsky, D., Heyerdahl, E., Lertzman, K., Schaepe, D. and Mierendorf, B. (2003). Historical meadow dynamics in Southwest British Columbia: a multidisciplinary analysis. *Conservation Ecology* **7**(3), 5–22.

Lewis, H. (1973). *Patterns of Burning in California: Ecology and Ethnohistory.* Ballena Press Anthropological Papers 1. Ramona, CA: Ballena Press.

Lewis, H. (1988). Yards, corridors and mosaics: how to burn a boreal forest. *Human Ecology* **16**(1), 57–77.

Lewis, H. and Ferguson, T. (1999). Yards, corridors and mosaics. In *Indians, Fire and the Land in the Pacific Northwest,* ed. R. Boyd. Corvallis, OR:. Oregon State University Press, pp. 57–77.

Lewis, J. (2000). Ancient Values, New Technology: emerging methods for integrating cultural values in forest management. Master of Science, University of British Columbia.

Lewis, J. (2006). Culture and the forested landscape: inter and intra cultural perceptions of modified forest landscapes. Ph.D. dissertation, University of British Columbia, Vancouver.

Lewis, J. and Sheppard, S. R. J. (2005). Ancient values, new challenges: indigenous spiritual perceptions of landscapes and forest management. *Society and Natural Resources* **18**(10), 907–920.

Nassauer, J. (1995). Messy ecosystems, orderly frames. *Landscape Journal* **14**(2), 161–170.

Parminter, J. (1995). *Human Influence on Landscape Pattern in the Pacific Region: Impacts of Burning by First Nations and Early European Settlers.* Presented at the Landscape Ecology Symposium, 76th Annual Meeting of the Pacific Division, American Association for the Advancement of Science. Vancouver, BC, June 20, 1995.

Peacock, S. and Turner, N. (2000). 'Just Like a Garden': traditional resource management and biodiversity conservation in the interior plateau of British Columbia. In *Biodiversity and Native America,* ed. P. Minnis, W. Elisens. Tulsa, OK: University of Oklahoma Press, pp. 133–179.

Ribe, R. (2006). Perceptions of forestry alternatives in the US Pacific Northwest: information effects and acceptability distribution analysis. *Journal of Environmental Psychology* **26**(2), 100–115.

Sheppard, S. (1989). *Visual Simulation: A User's Guide for Architects, Engineers, and Planners.* New York, NY: Van Nostrand Reinhold.

Sheppard, S. (2001a). Guidance for crystal ball gazers: developing a code of ethics for landscape visualization. *Landscape and Urban Planning* **54**, 183–199.

Sheppard, S. (2001b). Beyond visual resource management: emerging theories of an ecological aesthetic and visible stewardship. In *Forests and Landscapes: Linking Ecology, Sustainability, and Aesthetics,* ed. S. Sheppard and H. Harshaw, IUFRO Research Series. Wallingford, UK: CABI, pp. 149–172.

Thayer, R. L. (1989). The experience of sustainable landscapes. *Landscape Journal* **8**, 101–110.

Trusler, S. (2002). Footsteps among the berries: the ecology and fire history of traditional Gitksan and Wet'suwet'en huckleberry sites. Master of Science, University of Northern British Columbia.

Turner, N. (1999). 'Time to Burn': traditional use of fire to enhance resource production by aboriginal peoples in British Columbia. In *Indians, Fire and the Land in the Pacific Northwest*, ed. R. Boyd. Corvallis, OR: Oregon State University Press, pp. 185–218.

Ulrich, R. S. (1979). Visual landscapes and psychological well-being. *Landscape Research* **4**(1), 17–23.

Ulrich, R. S. (1981). Natural versus urban scenes: some psychophysiological effects. *Effects and Behaviour* **13**, 523–556.

Ulrich, R. S., Simons, R. F., Losito, B. D. *et al.* (1991). Stress recovery during exposure to natural and urban environments. *Journal of Environmental Psychology* **11**, 201–230.

Weetman, G., Panozzo, E., Jull, M. and Marek, K. (1990). *An Assessment of Opportunities for Alternative Silvicultural Systems in the SBS, ICH and ESSF Biogeoclimatic Zones of the Prince Rupert Forest Region*. Contract Report, British Columbia Ministry of Forests, Prince Rupert Forest Region, Smithers, B.C., March 1990.

10

How thousands planned for a billion: lessons from India on decentralized, participatory planning

SEEMA BHATT AND TEJASWINI APTE

As a signatory of the Convention on Biological Diversity, India is obliged to produce a National Biodiversity Strategy and Action Plan (NBSAP). The broad purpose of the NBSAP process was to produce an action plan to help conserve India's unique biodiversity, facilitate the sustainable use of biological resources, and ensure the equitable sharing of benefits from this use. Moving away from the conventional top-down method whereby a group of experts is appointed to write the plan, the process of developing the NBSAP was intended to be transparent and participatory, accommodating points of view from diverse interest groups such as village level organizations and movements, NGOs, academicians and scientists, government officers from various line agencies, the private sector, the armed forces and politicians. The thinking behind this was that since biodiversity affects all of society, as many people as possible from a wide range of social sectors should be offered the opportunity to contribute to planning for its conservation.

The core group, appointed by the Ministry of Environment and Forests, Government of India (MoEF, GoI), to co-ordinate the process, made a conscious attempt to move away from the dominant trend of centralized planning. Several thousand people, spread all over the country and from different walks of life and backgrounds, including women and men from local communities, were involved in participatory planning at local, state and national levels, and used flexible and innovative methodologies for preparing strategies and action plans.

Despite the support provided by the MoEF, GoI to the NBSAP process, in a rather unexpected turn of events, the NBSAP document submitted to the Government of India had not been officially approved by June 2007, over three years after being submitted to the government. The reasons for this turn of

Taking Stock of Nature: Participatory Biodiversity Assessment for Policy, Planning and Practice, ed. Anna Lawrence. Published by Cambridge University Press. © Cambridge University Press 2010.

events are discussed in the concluding sections. Independently, however, local implementation of several of the strategies and action plans is underway.

This chapter incorporates both 'insider' and 'outsider' perspectives of the NBSAP process. One of the authors (Bhatt) was a member of the core group of the NBSAP process, while the other (Apte) conducted an independent review of the participatory tools and methodologies used, after the process was complete (Apte, 2005). This focused on four states (Karnataka, Sikkim, Andhra Pradesh and Maharashtra), and was based on field trips and about 200 interviews. Information, quotes and analysis on the participatory tools, local implementation and positive spin-offs are based on this study.

Biological diversity in India

India represents a wide spectrum of biological, cultural and geographic diversity. It is one of the world's megadiversity countries (Verma, Arora and Rai, 2006). This is primarily because of the confluence of three major biogeographic zones, i.e. the Indo-Malayan, the Eurasian and the Afro-Tropical. India contains over 8.1% of the world's biodiversity on 2.4% of the Earth's surface. An estimated 47 000 plant species identified represent 11% of the world's flora (GoI, MoEF, 1999). India is considered one of the world's eight centres of origin of cultivated plants. India's faunal wealth is equally diverse. An estimated 89 450 animal species represent 7% of the world's fauna. Domestication of animals from time immemorial has also resulted in diverse species of livestock, poultry and other animal breeds.

The country's ecological diversity is matched by its cultural diversity. The Anthropological Survey of India identifies 91 eco-cultural zones in India inhabited by 4635 communities, speaking 325 languages/dialects (Singh, 1992). It is estimated that 67.7 million of the 220 or so million Indigenous-Tribal people in the world live in India, constituting 8% of the country's population distributed among 461 tribes (IAITPTF, 1998).

Dependence on natural resources

Over 70% of India's population lives in rural areas and depends, in varying degrees, on natural resources for survival. Forests are a mainstay for tribals and rural poor; one estimate suggests that 60% of forest products are consumed as food or as a nutritional supplement by forest dwellers (Khare, 1998), and another states that about 30% of the diet of tribal groups living in and around the forests of the State of Maharashtra is from forest products (World Bank, 1993). It is estimated that ethnic communities use over 7500 species of plants for human and veterinary healthcare across the country (Shankar, 1998). Seventy percent of rural and 50% of urban people still use fuel wood for cooking purposes, most of which comes from forests (Saigal, Agarwal and Campbell, 1996). Biomass harvests from common land account for up to 23% of household income from all sources (Rangachari and Mukherji, 2000). Seventy percent of India's population relies on traditional medicine and traditional healthcare systems. Furthermore, many plants and animals are used for cultural purposes. Among auspicious plants and flowers offered in temples are *Hibiscus* offered to the goddess *Kali*, and flowers of *Euphorbia ligularia* to *Manasa*. Select animal species are considered sacred as they are *vahanas* or vehicles of deities and are hence venerated. For example, the bull is associated with Lord *Shiva* and the rat with the elephant God, *Ganesha* (TPCG and Kalpavriksh, 2005).

The framework for preparing India's National Biodiversity Strategy and Action Plan (NBSAP)

The need for a broad global framework for the conservation of biodiversity resulted in the Convention on Biological Diversity (CBD) at the United Nations' Conference on Environment and Development held at Rio de Janeiro in 1992. The CBD came into force on 29 December 1993. India became a signatory to the CBD in June 1992. Article 6 of the CBD requires parties to the Convention to prepare National Biodiversity Strategy and Action Plans (NBSAPs), as the main instruments for implementation of the CBD at a national level. The process to prepare India's NBSAP was started under this mandate.

Between 1994 and 1997, the Ministry of Environment and Forests (MoEF) consulted with representatives from ministries, governmental agencies, NGOs, and academics to discuss the formulation of a national action plan on biodiversity. In 1997, as a result of a series of consultations and drafts by two expert committees, the MoEF brought out a National Policy and Macro-level Action Strategy on Biodiversity. This became a policy statement in 1999. Concurrently, the MoEF applied to the United Nations Development Programme (UNDP) in March 1998, for a grant to formulate the NBSAP, sanctioned in March 1999.

Following consultations, the original structure of the plan preparation process was reviewed in 1999. The expert committees suggested a decentralized approach with state level consultations, and wider participation, involving central ministries and agencies other than the MoEF and state governments, developing grassroots conservation strategies, and considering socio-economic dimensions of biodiversity conservation (Taneja and Kothari, 2002).

NBSAP Sites

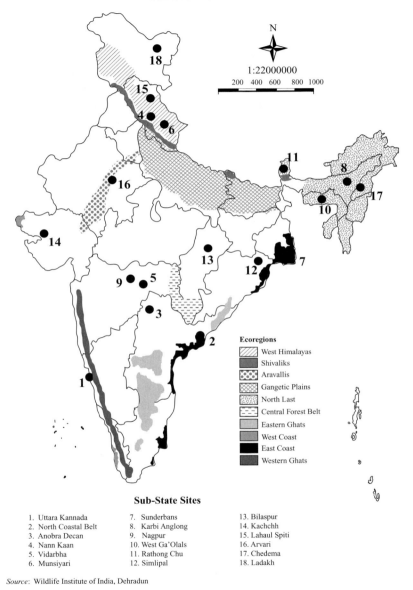

Figure 10.1. Selected eco-regions and sub-state sites.

Ecoregions

- West Himalayas
- Shivaliks
- Aravallis
- Gangetic Plains
- North Last
- Central Forest Belt
- Eastern Ghats
- West Coast
- East Coast
- Western Ghats

Sub-State Sites

1. Uttara Kannada	7. Sunderbans	13. Bilaspur
2. North Coastal Belt	8. Karbi Anglong	14. Kachchh
3. Anobra Decan	9. Nagpur	15. Lahaul Spiti
4. Nann Kaan	10. West Ga'Olals	16. Arvari
5. Vidarbha	11. Rathong Chu	17. Chedema
6. Munsiyari	12. Simlipal	18. Ladakh

Source: Wildlife Institute of India, Dehradun

In an unusual move, the MoEF decided to request an independent, non-governmental body to carry out the technical co-ordination of the process. Although the MoEF had a (relatively recent) record of consulting civil society organizations, this was the first time that an NGO was invited to independently design and execute a national planning process. After examining proposals invited and received from a number of NGOs and institutions, the MoEF assigned the technical execution of the project to Kalpavriksh, a 27-year old NGO based in Pune and Delhi. Kalpavriksh is a non-profit organization established in 1979 and works on environmental awareness, campaigns, litigation, research, and other areas on local, national and global levels. Kalpavriksh, in turn, established a 15-member Technical and Policy Core Group (TPCG). Although the process was headed by the MoEF, in practice the NGO had an unprecedented level of independence from the MoEF during the planning process.

The TPCG expertise included community-based conservation, agro-biodiversity, forestry, gender and livelihood issues, community-based enterprise, relevant laws, biotechnology, tribal (*adivasi*) rights, medicinal plants and local health traditions, wildlife conservation, and oceanography. The TPCG's mandate was to conceptualize and co-ordinate the preparation of the NBSAP.

In addition to this, the MoEF set up a National Steering Committee comprising senior officials of the MoEF, representatives from different ministries of the central government related to biodiversity and four NGO experts. The chairperson of the Steering Committee was the Secretary or the Additional Secretary of the MoEF. The National Steering Committee was meant to play an advisory role and guide the process. It was scheduled to meet once every six months to be briefed on the progress of the NBSAP, take key decisions and provide guidance.

The broad purpose of the NBSAP process was similar to that of the CBD: to produce an implementable action plan that would work towards the conservation of India's vast biodiversity, livelihood security, sustainable utilization of biological resources, and equitable decision-making on access to such resources and benefits from them (Taneja and Kothari, 2002).

The initial project document signed with the MoEF and UNDP prescribed action plans at national and state levels. The MoEF, UNDP, Kalpavriksh and the TPCG agreed that independent, 'standalone' Biodiversity Strategy and Action Plans (BSAPs) should be prepared at state level, which would then feed into preparation of the national plan. Plans were prepared for all 33 states and union territories; 18 sub-state sites; 10 interstate eco-regions (Figure 10.1); and 13 themes relating to biodiversity at the national level (for example, domesticated biodiversity; micro-organic diversity). In addition 35 sub-thematic reviews (for example, home gardens as a sub-theme of domesticated biodiversity) were prepared. A TPCG member was assigned to: (i) ensure that the priorities and recommendations from various BSAPs were reflected adequately in the national level strategies and (ii) incorporate new or innovative strategies from the BSAPs into the National Plan.

A local executing agency (usually an NGO, academic or government institution) was responsible for preparing each plan, and eliciting wide public participation for gaining planning inputs. TPCG members proposed agencies for approval by the MoEF, based on relevant expertise. However, the final decision rested with the state government. Only 20 out of 33 accepted the TPCG/MoEF recommendation. Most of the others nominated the State Department of Environment or the State Forest Department.

Further variations developed in the extent of decentralized planning across states, depending on the planning strategies developed by executing agencies. In Karnataka, for example, the focus was on decentralized gathering of information and suggestions, while the planning document itself was put together at a centralized state level. In other places, such as Sikkim or North Coastal Andhra Pradesh, there was a focus on eliciting direct local inputs into village-level plans. In the sub-state site of Nagpur (Maharashtra state), the focus was on gathering and collating scientific data and baseline information to formulate a general city strategy. However across all states, putting the actual plan together at state or sub-state level was necessarily a centralized activity. For instance, in Sikkim, though the co-ordinators facilitated the preparation of 39 local village-specific plans, the co-ordinators collated all inputs from across the state into a single plan for Sikkim.

The approach of the TPCG was that the *process* of preparing the NBSAP was as important as the *product*, thereby creating spin-offs such as capacity building, biodiversity awareness, and local enthusiasm for implementing the recommendations. An important point to note, however, is that implementation was not part of the mandate of the NBSAP process, which focused purely on preparing plans; implementation was to come later through subsequent government action.

The TPCG attempted to make the process transparent and open to diverse points of view. All meeting minutes and other working documents on the NBSAP were placed on the public website until January 2002. The TPCG also recommended to coordinating agencies that conflicting views during the planning process should be recorded and strategies to resolve the conflict of views should be incorporated into the plan. It was difficult to monitor the

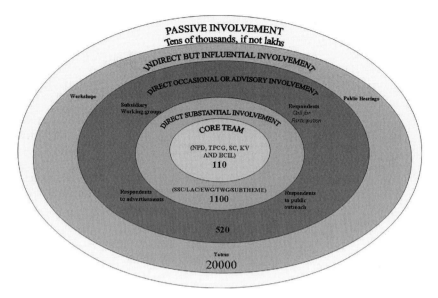

Figure 10.2. Concentric circle of participation. 1 lakh = 100 000.

extent to which states took this on board although some cases suggest that not all dissenting views were incorporated into BSAPs.

The involvement of people in terms of numbers and organization is summarized in Figure 10.2.

Tools used to elicit people's participation in the planning process

Very early in the process, the TPCG produced a simple brochure, 'Call for Participation' (CFP), which described the NBSAP process and invited public participation. It was printed centrally in 16 regional Indian languages, and locally in four further languages. Approximately 30 000 copies were distributed across the country. Many who responded became members of executing committees and even co-ordinators. Other media tools and activities included posters, calendars, a website and magazine/newspaper articles.

Executing agencies were free to develop their own tools and strategies to elicit people's participation in the planning process, as well as to raise general awareness about biodiversity. As a supporting measure and to kick-start the process, the TPCG suggested the use of tools such as Public Hearings and Biodiversity Festivals, but executing agencies were encouraged to develop the details locally. The resulting range of tools included a mixture of awareness raising tools and information gathering tools: public hearings; biodiversity

Table 10.1. *The function of different participatory tools used in the NBSAP* process

Tool	Information gathering	Raising awareness about biodiversity and about the NBSAP process	Eliciting direct inputs into planning
Radio series	•	•	
School biodiversity registers	•	•	
Biodiversity festivals		•	• (only in Deccan sub-state plan)
Written questionnaires	•		
Public hearings and meetings	•	•	• (only in some states)
State, regional and national-level workshops	•		• (in some workshops)
Village-level micro-planning	•	•	•
NBSAP website		•	
Calendar		•	
Posters		•	
Call for participation	•	•	
Brochure			
Print articles		•	
Boat races		•	

festivals; written questionnaires and surveys; micro-planning at village level; school biodiversity registers; interactive radio programmes; boat races and national and regional workshops (Table 10.1). Media tools played a supporting role in reaching out to people and encouraging participation. These tools were not necessarily used in any particular order, but instead combined in ways that seemed appropriate to local co-ordinators. Each state independently decided on what combination of tools to use, in order to fulfil different functions and reach out to different social sectors.

Many of the tools were developed and tested experimentally during this process. This section describes some of these tools to illustrate the diversity of methods used for preparing the plans, and analyses their strengths, weaknesses and impacts.

Public hearings: an example from Sikkim

For the state level plans, Public Hearings and meetings were used by several states as a way of eliciting public inputs into the planning process. The process in the north-eastern state of Sikkim was among the most successful in terms of eliciting grassroots community participation through public meetings. The executing agency for Sikkim was the State Forest Department, which worked in close collaboration with a grassroots NGO based in the Rathong Chu Valley, the Khangchendzonga Conservation Committee (KCC).

Thirty-nine Public Hearings were held in rural areas to create 39 Community Strategy and Action Plans (CSAPs). About 60 people (including about 20 women) from six to seven villages attended each Hearing, covering one or two *Gram Panchayats* (Village Councils). In most cases, separate plans were prepared by men and women to bring out gender-based interests, and then combined in a CSAP. A co-ordinating team comprising of Forest Department and NGO members conducted the Public Hearings over one to two days. After each Hearing a summary of the CSAP was printed out and given to the community. The co-ordinating agency tabulated these 39 CSAPs to produce one CSAP for the state of Sikkim. Separately, a government strategy and action plan (GSAP) contained information about government schemes relevant to biodiversity conservation and livelihood security. Finally, the CSAP was combined with the GSAP to produce a single action plan for the State: the idea was to present the community action plan along with concrete possibilities for its implementation through existing government schemes.

A planning tool called, 'Appreciative Participatory Planning and Action' (APPA) (The Mountain Institute, 2000) was used in these meetings. APPA focuses on discovering and building on the strengths of a community, using four steps: Discovery, Dream, Design, and Delivery. In the Discovery stage community members collectively drew a map showing resources in the vicinity. In the Dream stage they discussed and prepared a Dream Map of the village in the future. In the Design stage they discussed and mapped micro-strategies required to make the dreams a reality (e.g. afforestation or footpath construction). The Delivery stage is the implementation stage, which was not built into the NBSAP process. In some places this became a point of frustration, but also of creativity, when those involved in developing the plans decided to implement them as well.

Strengths of this approach, according to villagers, are that it:

- consolidated scattered conservation knowledge held by various community members, and generated collective information;

- was organized by a local NGO, KCC, which already had a good rapport with local communities, so villagers were encouraged to speak more freely. The Forest Department (which villagers can find intimidating) mainly helped with logistics and inputs on technical points such as forest laws.

Nevertheless a serious weakness was poor follow-up and information dissemination. Most villages were not provided with copies of their village's CSAP, which was taken by the co-ordinating agency for inclusion in the state plan. At the end of each meeting the villagers were only given a summarized printout of their CSAP in English since software was not available in the local language (Nepali). This impeded 'ownership' and local-level initiatives for implementation. The Khecheopalri Lake community did possess a copy of its CSAP, and a *Panchayat* member visited government departments in the state capital Gangtok, carrying the CSAP with him and demanding for it to be implemented (unfortunately no official was interested). And where implementation of the Sikkim BSAP *had* happened at the time of the independent review two years after the Public Hearings, most village interviewees were not aware of this, leading to disillusionment and the feeling that 'nothing was happening'.

Women's participation in Sikkim was weak, as it was all over the country. Even when women attended meetings they hardly spoke. Efforts to improve women's participation included providing posters at places where women tend to congregate, such as the dairy co-operative; reserving a location at meetings for women to sit together (thereby enhancing their confidence to speak) and inviting older women who tend to be more vocal, so that younger women could convey their points through them. Despite these measures, women's participation remained relatively low, and separate women's meetings gained better results. As one interviewee said, 'whenever there is a meeting, they always tell me to tell my husband to come to the meeting. But no-one tells me to come!' (Apte, 2005).

Biodiversity festivals: examples from Andhra Pradesh and Sikkim

Among the most innovative tools used in the NBSAP process were biodiversity festivals, organized by several executing agencies. These were used mainly for raising awareness about both biodiversity and the NBSAP. Each had a local flavour and catered to local requirements and customs. In the Deccan sub-state site in the southern state of Andhra Pradesh, a mobile agricultural biodiversity festival on a bullock cart procession travelled through 62 villages over 32 days. Seventy-five varieties of traditional seeds were used to decorate the carts. The carts also carried an exhibition of foods cooked using traditional crops. Crop diversity was celebrated with singing and dancing as the procession moved along and entered each village. Unlike festivals held in other states, this one was also used to hold a public meeting in each village to gain planning inputs from farmers. About 20 000 farmers participated in the meetings and an estimated 50 000 people saw the exhibition.

In Sikkim the biodiversity festival in Yuksam village in the Rathong Chu Valley attracted about 250 people from neighbouring villages. Stall displays and cultural programmes by local villagers included seed, forest produce and handicraft displays, a skit about the pollution of a local stream, folk songs and dances, and a play about the religious significance of the Rathong Chu valley, a sacred landscape. Interspersed among the cultural items were explanations of CSAPs that had been prepared during village Public Hearings. The displays also included several working models made from locally available material such as mud, plastic, pebbles and cotton, to demonstrate environmental issues.

An enthusiastic response to these festivals is indicated in the independent review, which highlighted success through creating nostalgia at increasingly rare forms of biodiversity, and developing local pride in local produce – thus providing inspiration to conserve local biodiversity. It also helped to provide a holistic picture of resource wealth rather than a daily, 'scattered' encountering of biological resources. Great attention was given to making these festivals as accessible as possible, and creating a festive atmosphere of celebrating biodiversity.

Interactive radio drama: an example from Karnataka

The BSAP process in the southern state of Karnataka used a series of 14 weekly radio programmes both to gather information from the public and to raise biodiversity awareness. Radio breaks the barrier of literacy and reaches remote corners of the State even where there is no electricity. An innovative programme format wove together grassroots interviews in field locations, with a scripted, fictitious drama recorded in the studio. The producers of the programme identified locations with interesting activities related to themes such as sacred rivers or crop diversity. For example, for the episode on crop diversity, the producers visited locations where minor millets were being documented, to interview grassroots communities. In the studio, actors played the roles of two fictitious characters travelling through the state, meeting people and discussing local biodiversity with them (here the grassroots interviews were woven into the dramatization). The dramatization included humour, folk music and songs recorded during field visits, and avoided scientific jargon.

Each programme focused on a different theme, and was followed the next week by a discussion programme with a panel of experts talking about the previous weeks' theme. Importantly, the series was flexible and interactive. The producers travelled to places suggested by listeners, and developed situations where the interviews could be integrated into the story. 'For example, to record the crop variety programme we had gone to a village where harvesting was going on. We had our dinner there and spent the night there. So the same thing was introduced into the [drama] script – where the characters have their dinner and sample different varieties of food, which shows the crop variety available in the area' (Radio producer, in Apte, 2005). Listeners were asked to send in letters with thematic information – the medicinal plants episode, for instance, requested listeners to send in information about locally found medicinal plants. This information was later used in preparing the Karnataka state plan.

The series proved very popular – about 9.4 million people heard it, and about 800 people sent letters, some with photographs. It took six weeks to read and analyse the information in the letters, which could not be assimilated into the plan as effectively as if the response had been anticipated.

Positive spin-offs of the NBSAP process

From the outset of the process, the core team encouraged the executing agencies to consider their local, state, eco-regional, or thematic plan processes as relatively independent. As a result, many organizations started independent implementation measures, often without the executing agencies, even before the national plan process was over. In addition, four or five states have committed to taking the state-level action plans forward, as part of the work of their newly set up State Biodiversity Boards. Some, including Sikkim and Madhya Pradesh, have already implemented elements of their plans.

These spin-offs from the NBSAP process can be broadly classified into three categories: capacity building, awareness raising and local implementation of plan recommendations. All three categories feed into a larger outcome, namely the creation of political spaces, institutional capacities and individual capabilities for people to engage in and influence biodiversity conservation and livelihood security. Below are examples of some of the positive outcomes of the NBSAP process.

Local implementation of plan recommendations

The North Coastal Andhra BSAP recommended that traditional *Adivasi* festivals should include discussions and exhibitions on biodiversity. In 2002 the *Adivasi* communities volunteered to incorporate biodiversity concerns into their annual *Angarada Devta* (Angarada God) festival at Neradivalasa village in the Angarada Hill Region of the Eastern Ghats. More than 600 people attended the festival, which included a biodiversity exhibition, discussions on natural resource management as well as discussions to further refine the BSAP (even though the official BSAP planning process was over). *Adivasi* women who had earlier attended BSAP meetings were more vocal in the discussions, some even volunteering to report on their group discussions – a concrete sign of capacity building and raising of confidence and awareness. Some *Adivasi* network representatives also felt that the NBSAP process had improved their skills at organizing and conducting workshops.

In Sikkim one of the plan recommendations was to implement garbage management and reduce yak grazing in Khangchendzonga National Park (KNP). Garbage management was taken up by KCC through a UNDP project in 2004, while in the same year reduction of yak grazing was taken up by the Forest Department in collaboration with KCC and The Mountain Institute (TMI), through the Khangchendzonga Biosphere Reserve (KBR) programme. After consultations and training programmes with the graziers, and an inventory of grazing yaks, numbers in the Rathong Chu area of KNP fell from 1248 in 2004 to 520 in 2006. TMI provided ex-herders with facilities for better sanitation, vegetable farming and village dairies; income opportunities as guides on a new tourist trek from Yambong to Singalila, and appointments as *Himal Rakshaks* (Honorary Mountain Guardians) to monitor alpine landscapes (Sandeep Tambe, Sikkim Forest Department, personal communication, January 2007).

On a larger scale, as executing agency of the Karnataka BSAP, the influential Centre for Ecological Sciences was able to incorporate many of the BSAP's recommendations into the Karnataka State of the Environment Report (a separate report which was submitted to the state government). This was an instance where the NBSAP process was able to feed into, and achieve synergy with, another official process, thus increasing the chances of its recommendations being officially implemented. A facilitator of the Uttar Kannada sub-state site in Karnataka felt that the NBSAP process had a direct positive impact on the discussions held for preparing the State of the Environment Report: 'People were already awakened [through the Uttar Kannada BSAP] and they came forward with more concrete and studied recommendations'.

Capacity building

The independent review showed that capacity building was one of the strongest outcomes of the NBSAP process, according to people from sectors as diverse as NGOs, tribal networks, students, teachers and government institutions.

Karnataka's planning process included the creation of School Biodiversity Registers (SBRs) with dozens of teachers and hundreds of students. Each SBR documented biodiversity and related knowledge such as memories of local biodiversity, in 1 sq km around the school, through field studies and interaction with the local community. The executing agency provided training to teachers and distributed prizes for the best SBRs. The teachers interviewed felt that the exercise had contributed greatly to their knowledge and experience, as well as to students who unexpectedly proved to be very enthusiastic about preparing the SBRs. A teacher in Nagpur, Maharashtra, where (more modest) NBSAP projects at school level also proved popular, felt it was a myth that students are only interested in watching television; on the contrary, teachers need to be more proactive in devising interesting projects, such as the NBSAP projects, to create enthusiasm among students.

Small NGOs in various states felt that participation in NBSAP activities helped to build up and strengthen networks, provided exposure to new information and provided an opportunity to consolidate ideas. For example an NGO in Srikakulam district, North Coastal Andhra Pradesh, pointed to the development of a more holistic approach to biodiversity among its network of 35 NGOs: 'We have now understood [environment] in an integrated way. Earlier we tried to work in a sectoral way, like only soil conservation or forestry. Now, the impact of NBSAP is, that we are integrating all conservation practices like forest conservation, livestock, human resources and traditional practices. This integration concept came [to us] due to the concept of biodiversity conservation... Earlier we used to talk about environment. Now we are talking about biodiversity' (Apte, 2005).

In Sikkim the Forest Department used its NBSAP experience in a subsequent planning process for the utilization and conservation of medicinal plants, with the Foundation for Revitalisation of Local Health Traditions (FRLHT). A similar format of village level consultations was used, with improvements. As a key facilitator noted, 'in the Sikkim BSAP about 90% of our effort went in conducting Public Hearings, because it was very new for us. So we had very little time left for analysing the outputs of the meetings. For FRLHT we ensured that part of the team was doing Public Hearings, and part of the team was focused only on writing and analysing the outputs. So the report for FRLHT is technically much stronger' (Apte, 2005).

There were other ways in which the Forest Department benefited from the NBSAP process: about 50 Forest Department staff were involved in the village level Public Hearings during which interested officers learned about microplanning. The final Public Hearing was conducted by Forest Department staff members who had learned the techniques from the NGO, KCC. This was a valuable outcome of the process since often state Forest Departments do not have a large amount of expertise or experience in participatory skills.

Awareness raising

The radio drama series broadcast in Karnataka had very positive spin-offs in terms of awareness raising. Firstly, it created awareness within All India Radio in Karnataka regarding the potential of science series: 'we are delighted by these [listener] statistics as a theme like biodiversity has interested so many millions of listeners. Generally for science programmes the clientele expected is small, as illiterates do not evince much interest in science programmes' (Centre for Ecological Sciences, 2002). The series was also the first time that All India Radio in Karnataka had used the medium to collect information and utilize it, as opposed to being simply a 'one-way' channel for education. Secondly, owing to the popularity of the series, All India Radio repeated it in an Education Branch programme as a public service (but without the requests for letters). Thirdly, the series inspired other institutions to request similar series for educational purposes; a series on wildlife was subsequently created with a similar format of two characters travelling through national parks in Karnataka. Finally, a mark of the success of the show was the selection of one of the producers as a 'Woman Who Made the City Proud' in a prize-giving organized by The Hindu, a national newspaper, on International Women's Day in 2002.

Political problems: finalizing the National Plan

The national level document, originally called the draft National Action Plan, was built on 70 draft biodiversity strategy and action plans (BSAPs) at sub-state, state, eco-regional, and thematic levels, produced during the NBSAP process; 31 draft sub-thematic reviews commissioned or voluntarily offered during the NBSAP process; and a large number of secondary sources, including previous official national-level documents. After an extensive assessment by co-ordinating agencies, sub-thematic reviewers, and other partners of the NBSAP process, as also a few hundred other institutions, experts, government officials, NGOs, and activists, the first draft was produced in October 2002, and finalized after feedback (from a range of people who had contributed to the plan and others in relevant fields) and subsequent drafts, in mid 2003. The TPCG understood that this final draft would then be considered for approval as the National Biodiversity Strategy and Action Plan.

Unexpectedly, however, in January 2004 the MoEF told the TPCG that the final draft could only be published as a Final Technical Report. In May 2004, without any intimation to Kalpavriksh (the technical co-ordinating agency) or the TPCG, the MoEF further changed its position and refused to sanction the publication of the draft even as a Final Technical Report. Informally, the TPCG learned that the Ministry was not comfortable with some parts of the report, but no official explanation was given. In March 2005, the MoEF wrote to Kalpavriksh asking it not to publish, or in any form make publicly available, the draft report submitted in December 2003.

These decisions were a shock to members of the TPCG. In its dismissal of the report, the MoEF ignored the energy and inputs that thousands of people had put into the decentralized and transparent planning process commissioned by the MoEF itself. Over a period of a year and a half, the MoEF's stance underwent dramatic transformations, from denying it had ever accepted the report as a 'draft NBSAP', to denying its acceptance of the document as a Final Technical Report, to finally rejecting it altogether.

Eventually in 2005 Kalpavriksh, in consultation with the TPCG, decided to publish the report (that had been submitted to the MoEF in December 2003) as the Final Technical Report of NBSAP (in the form agreed to by the MoEF in writing, in early 2004) (TPCG and Kalpavriksh, 2005). This was to avoid further delaying public access to the information, analysis and recommendations contained in the report, and to the hundred-odd other outputs of the planning process, on an accompanying CD. As of June 2007 the report submitted to the MoEF had still not been accepted and nor had the MoEF come up with its own official plan.

Why this turn of events?

Despite considerable questioning from the public through newspaper reports as well as letters and emails to the MoEF, the MoEF did not give a clear, public explanation for its rejection of the NBSAP report (in complete contrast to the open and transparent process followed throughout the NBSAP planning phase). In a written response to a Parliamentary Question, the MoEF stated that the plan contained inaccuracies and would embarrass India internationally, but it neither listed these inaccuracies to the TPCG, nor attempted to negotiate any changes (Ministry of Environment and Forests, 2004).

This turn of events seems less puzzling when seen as one symptom of a wider and growing malaise in India's recent environmental governance, which gives primacy to economic growth and investment over environmental conservation and people's livelihoods. The Final Technical Report argues that the root of

India's biodiversity crisis is a fundamentally flawed development process that favours and puts decision-making in the hands of a small elite, at the expense of marginalized social sectors that rely on natural resources for their livelihoods. The Final Technical Report, with its pro-environment, pro-people's livelihood recommendations, does not fit in with the current paradigm of environmental governance and was, perhaps, therefore not officially acceptable.

Since the process was stalled, the environmental community in India has questioned what really went wrong and what could have been done better. Many feel there was not enough lobbying to begin with, to get politically powerful sectors on board. If the TPCG had perceived the need to get key politicians to 'buy into' the process from the very beginning, then there could have been more effort put into engaging with this lobby. Members of the TPCG contacted a few select politicians to garner support after the MoEF had rejected the Final Technical Report. These politicians were of the view that the entire process of getting the final report to be accepted by the government could have been handled better by engaging with politicians from the very beginning and getting their support. There was no clear political strategy in place to involve politically powerful sectors, and therefore the effort that went into engaging with them was disproportionately little, especially as compared to the effort that went into securing the participation of sectors like grassroots communities, NGOs and academics. In the need to prioritize target groups, some politically important sectors such as politicians and industry received little attention.

Emerging lessons and conclusion

Balancing limited resources with ambitious plans

The planning process for the formulation of India's NBSAP was the most ambitious environmental participatory planning process undertaken in the country, in terms of scale and decentralization. It was also highly innovative and creative and succeeded to a large extent in reaching out to the marginalized people whose very existence depends on biodiversity. Carrying out an exercise on this scale requires both time and resources. The project was allocated less than a million US dollars distributed amongst 71 executing agencies. Each state received US $9000–11 000, and each sub-state, thematic or eco-regional site received US $1000–2300 for a two to three year planning process. This limitation, however, gave rise to innovative methods to raise additional resources.

Reliance on voluntary activity was a key feature of the NBSAP process. During the independent review several interviewees mentioned that the 'spirit' of the process was in its voluntary nature, which often created a sense of local 'ownership' of the process. Executing agencies were requested to extend the money received as much as possible through their own resources. Many TPCG members who had been contracted to do a week's work per month for two years, for fairly low fees, eventually put in almost daily work for three years for no extra remuneration. About 70% of the North Coastal Andhra Pradesh sub-state site, for example, was funded by local groups or individuals in the form of personal travel costs, voluntary work or food (though a few executing agencies worked mainly within the budget allocated to them).

On the other hand, the ambitious nature of the project, given the limited budget, also undermined some key elements of the process by stretching resources to their limits, for example, by hiring only a part-time media campaign manager to co-ordinate a national media campaign. Another example is in the sub-state site of Uttar Kannada where a shortage of human resources meant that the executing agency could not widely distribute awareness-raising tools such as newsletters and calendars, and could not develop a strategy for a local media campaign.

Need for more orientation

Many innovative methods were used during this process and were successful in eliciting a response from a wide range of people. However, an important lesson learnt is that special inputs in the form of orientation sessions are important to ensure that people understand the use of participatory tools. For example, the need for greater involvement of women and underprivileged sections of society was emphasized by the TPCG from the very beginning. It was only after the first national workshop that the TPCG realized that most executing agencies had little idea of how to actually implement this. Orientation programmes in different regions were subsequently organized to address this lacuna, but it became clear that more extensive orientation would have been beneficial.

Challenge of implementation and raising expectations

It was difficult to explain to grassroots stakeholders that there was no guarantee of implementation built into the NBSAP process. Villagers did not relate to the idea of planning elaborately for something without the guarantee of it being implemented. A related challenge at the grassroots lay in explaining what the NBSAP was all about, and how exactly inputs from the grassroots, such as from village-level Public Hearings, would feed into the NBSAP process. The formation of state and sub-state plans which would eventually feed into a national plan, all without guarantee of implementation, were abstract concepts which proved difficult to explain in the space of one or two meetings. Tools such as flow charts or maps are needed for communicating abstract concepts such as the movement of information from the grassroots to the state level to the national level. A member of the TPCG commented, 'such tools were not there. With hindsight, that could have been done. It may be an urban bias. We assume that people know what is 'India' or 'government'. But for some people Delhi is a different country, or just a vague idea.' (Apte, 2005).

Need for a clear political strategy

It was unfortunate that the results of an open, public and democratic process were taken out of the public domain, leaving the fate of the Final Technical Report unclear at the time of writing (June 2007). But perhaps the most critical lesson learnt is the importance of politically astute positioning of a process of this scale within the larger political process. It was crucial for politicians and bureaucrats to have understood the relevance of biodiversity conservation in terms of ensuring the livelihood security of marginalized people. In the present political scenario where decentralization and *Panchayati Raj* Institutions (Local Governance Institutions) are being recognized and promoted, the recommendations from the NBSAP are extremely relevant. However, not enough effort was made to highlight this aspect to the political lobby.

Process vs product

In this context of ambiguity over the outcome, the TPCG's emphasis that the process of putting the plan together was as important as the final product, emerges as one of the primary strengths of the NBSAP process. The process itself has resulted in several positive outcomes such as capacity building and increased awareness of biodiversity issues. Local actors are attempting to implement many strategies and actions recommended at various levels. Some states have taken ownership of their plans and are putting them into practice. Various networks were established as a result of the NBSAP process and have the potential to function effectively towards the conservation and sustainable use of biodiversity, if sustained by local initiative.

The Indian NBSAP process was the first of its kind. An internal evaluation report noted: 'One major problem that had faced the coordinating teams at the start of NBSAP was the lack of any previous nation-wide exercise of this scale and magnitude, in India or elsewhere, from which lessons could be learnt. A number of the design elements were therefore new or without precedence, and it was inevitable that some of them would come unstuck' (Kothari *et al.*, 2002). As a pioneering effort in terms of its large scale, participatory and decentralized operations, the NBSAP process offers many valuable lessons and models for future participatory planning processes, within and outside India, particularly since the NBSAP experience has been extensively documented and analysed by NBSAP team members as well as outsiders.

Acknowledgements

We would like to acknowledge the efforts of all those who participated in this unique process.

REFERENCES

Apte, T. (2005). *An Activist Approach to Biodiversity Planning: A Handbook of Participatory Tools Used to Prepare India's National Biodiversity Strategy and Action Plan*. London: International Institute of Environment and Development. Available at: http://www.policy-powertools.org/related/NBSAP.html.

Centre for Ecological Sciences. (2002). Annexure H: Letter to Centre for Ecological Sciences from All India Radio Deputy Director. In *Karnataka State Biodiversity Strategy and Action Plan*, Vols. 1 and 2. Bangalore: Centre for Ecological Sciences, Indian Institute of Science.

GoI, MoEF (1999). *National Policy and Macrolevel Action Strategy on Biodiversity*. New Delhi: Ministry of Environment and Forests, Government of India.

IAITPTF (1998). *Adivasi/ Indigenous Peoples in India – A Brief Situationer*. New Delhi: International Alliance of Indigenous and Tribal Peoples of the Tropical Forests, South Asia Region.

Khare, A. (1998). Community-based conservation in India. In *Communities and Conservation: Natural Resource Management in South and Central Asia*, eds. A. Kothari, N. Pathak, R. V. Anuradha and B. Taneja. New Delhi: Sage Publications.

Kothari, A. with Padmanabhan, S., Kohli, K., Singh, K. *et al.* (2002). National Biodiversity Strategy and Action Plan: Did we achieve what we wanted to? In *Workshop Papers. Final Workshop, New Delhi, Dec. 20–23, 2002*. New Delhi: Ministry of Environment and Forests, Government of India.

Ministry of Environment and Forests. (2004). Short Notice Question Dy. No. 15 regarding National Biodiversity Strategy and Action Plan (NBSAP). No. SNQ 15/III/XIV/2004-Q. Dated 16th December. New Delhi: Lok Sabha Secretariat (Question Branch).

Rangachari, C. S. and Mukherji, S. D. (2000). *Old Roots, New Shoots. A Study of Joint Forest Management in Andhra Pradesh*. New Delhi: Winrock International and Ford Foundation.

Saigal, S., Agarwal, C. and Campbell, J. (1996). *Sustaining Joint Forest Management: The Role of Non-timber Forest Products. Monograph*. New Delhi: Society for Promotion of Wastelands Development.

Shankar, D. (1998). Conserving a community resource: medicinal plants. In *Communities and Conservation: Natural Resource Management in South and Central Asia*, eds. A. Kothari, N. Pathak, R. V. Anuradha and B. Taneja. New Delhi: Sage Publications.

Singh, K. S. (1992). *People of India: An Introduction*. Calcutta: Anthropological Survey of India and Laurens and Co.

Taneja, B. and Kothari, A. (2002). Indian case study. In *Biodiversity Planning in Asia*, ed. J. C. Reid. Sri Lanka: IUCN.

The Mountain Institute (2000). *Resource Kit for Community-Based Tourism for Conservation and Development*. Nepal: The Mountain Institute. Available at: www.mountain.org.

TPCG and Kalpavriksh (2005). *Securing India's Future: Final Technical Report of the National Biodiversity Strategy and Action Plan*. Prepared by the NBSAP Technical and Policy Core Group. Delhi/Pune: Kalpavriksh.

Verma, D. D., Arora, S. and Rai, R. K. (2006). *Perspectives on Biodiversity: A Vision for Megadiverse Countries*. New Delhi: Ministry of Environment and Forests, Government of India.

World Bank (1993). *India: Policies and Issues in Forest Sector Development*. Report No. 10965-IN. New Delhi: World Bank.

11

Inside monitoring: a comparison of bird monitoring groups in Slovenia and the United Kingdom

SANDRA BELL, MARIELLA MARZANO AND DAN PODJED

Throughout the member states of the European Union a large number of volunteers work alone on biodiversity monitoring across a range of species and habitats. They send their records to electronic databases via nature-based websites and sometimes talk to one another via discussion boards. One recently established example is the UK phenology network (http://www.phenology.org.uk). However, most volunteer monitoring programmes are embedded in the many and varied nature-based organizations in Europe, in particular those associations dedicated to members' interest in specific taxonomic groups of flora and fauna.

Our chapter explores the contribution these organizations make to monitoring biodiversity by focusing on two case studies of highly productive ornithological associations – the regional Northumberland and Tyneside Bird Club (NTBC) operating at the county level in the north-east of England and the Birdwatching and Bird Study Association of Slovenia (Društvo za opazovanje in proučevanje ptic – DOPPS), a national organization.

The two organizations show similarities and differences. DOPPS is a relatively young organization, with strong links to the global environmental NGO, BirdLife International, which unites over 2 500 000 members of different bird organizations worldwide, with more than 4000 staff working on conservation projects (BirdLife, 2007). DOPPS has carved out an influential position in the field of environmental governance within the small, newly emerged nation state of Slovenia. NTBC is an older, county level (i.e. sub-national) organization. It is linked to environmental governance at national level by members' participation in surveys devised by NGOs like the British Trust for Ornithology (BTO), an organization that studiously avoids a campaigning stance. The BTO's mission

Taking Stock of Nature: Participatory Biodiversity Assessment for Policy, Planning and Practice, ed. Anna Lawrence. Published by Cambridge University Press. © Cambridge University Press 2010.

is to 'promote and encourage the wider understanding, appreciation and conservation of birds' through scientifically rigorous research in field ornithology.[1] Participation in these surveys ultimately links members of the NTBC to government agencies such as the Joint Nature Conservation Committee (JNCC), Environment Agency (EA) and the Department for Environment, Food and Rural Affairs (DEFRA) through the BTO's reporting mechanisms.

Both organizations have some reservations relating to the amount of information they can collect and process to help inform decision-making and policy processes. In DOPPS volunteer recorders are currently overstretched and in the NTBC there are worries about sufficient numbers of young people coming through to replace older members in the future. Participants in our research point to the intensity of planning and work involved in bird recording programmes. As well as demanding intimate (spatial and temporal) knowledge of their own localities, and the natural and social histories of these places, as one informant highlights, '[there are] increased demands in terms of the standards of work that is done, in terms of ensuring that coverage is complete, ensuring that the method, the design and analysis are done correctly . . . nowadays you wouldn't embark on any piece of ecological research without substantial planning from the statistical point of view' (BTO official).

Our evidence suggests that volunteers are currently willing and able to meet exacting contemporary standards. But questions arise about how volunteer monitors can continue to meet the growing requirement for data without overtaxing people's willingness and ability to participate, now and in the future. One answer lies in understanding the significance of nature-based leisure activities like birdwatching for participants (Lawrence and Turnhout, 2005; Lawrence, 2006). Knowledgeable birdwatchers claim a well-deserved reputation for passionate enthusiasm and all-consuming dedication (Cocker, 2001). Liep's study of birdwatching in Denmark (Liep, 2001) describes the inner gratification that comes from discovering and observing birds. Our research confirms Liep's observation that the overwhelming enthusiasm for birds is the most powerful motivating force for birders to keep careful records. But Liep also notes a strong set of motivations attached to the social aspects of birdwatching. His study focuses on competition between birders whose main objective is to see rare birds, but even here he finds 'common intimacy built up through year-long acquaintance, and practical competence in bird identification' (Liep, 2001, p. 12).

---

[1] The British Trust for Ornithology (BTO) funds its work through a combination of membership and donations, contracts, largely with government bodies (e.g. Joint Nature Conservation Committee, Environment Agency, etc.) and through partnerships with industry, private consultancies, other NGOs such as the RSPB and universities. See website www.bto.org

Specialist birdwatchers are taking part in what Stebbins calls serious leisure (Stebbins, 1992). The term refers to activities that require practitioners to attain expert knowledge and skills; where psychological rewards are balanced against considerable high costs in terms of time, effort and perseverance; and where participants find opportunities for camaraderie and collaboration. Nature associations, of the kind featured here, provide vital socio-cultural contexts for the pursuit of serious leisure. They offer encouragement and support to volunteer monitors, unavailable to the solitary naturalist, as well as providing institutional access points for governmental and other organizations looking for data on biodiversity.

Our case studies focus on three specific issues. The first relates to ways in which the members of the organizations contribute to scientific monitoring of birds and their habitats through recording aspects of local birdlife. The second seeks links between local and national perspectives, whereby data collected by members of organizations are networked through partnerships with governmental agencies either directly or through larger NGOs. Finally, we ask how local and/or interest based collectives build social capital to create the confidence and enduring commitment essential to sustaining reliable biodiversity monitoring programmes.

Social capital

As voluntary organizations, the success of nature associations relies heavily on the depth and durability of the social capital they generate and draw upon. By social capital we mean the degrees of trust, co-operation, collective confidence, adherence to shared objectives, combined efforts to the realization of achievable goals and the affect of these relationships on members' participation. We also ask how these factors influence the sentiments and commitments that prompt members to take part in voluntary biological recording.

The term social capital is controversial, partly because it emanates from different and often contradictory sociological perspectives (Portes, 1998). The greatest contrast in its application exists between the communitarian approaches to social capital represented by Putnam (2000) and Coleman (1988) for whom it is a means towards social integration, and that of the French thinker Bourdieu (1986). Bourdieu's instrumental view of social networks sets social capital alongside cultural and economic capital as one of three strategic devices to be mobilized in 'an arena of struggle' for social power (Blackshaw and Long, 2005, p. 251).

While Bourdieu thus seeks to dispose of a narrowly economic conception of capital, Pawar complains that social capital is a contradictory phrase precisely because the terms *social* and *capital* 'have contrasting features, capital being antisocial and exploitative' (Pawar, 2006, p. 222). Instead Pawar advocates that the phrase social capital be substituted for its constituent phrases that include trust, networks and collective action. He also proposes one suitable substitute phrase could be 'social capacity' – a term relevant to our examination of the potential for nature based associations to create supportive frameworks and meaningful contexts for people's participation in voluntary monitoring activities.

In his review and application of the concept of social capital Adger develops a framework 'that classifies social capital as bonding or networking and highlights the relationship of these aspects of social capital as oppositional or synergistic to the state' (2003, p. 389). Bonding social capital depends on informal relations, based on kinship, friendship or locality. It represents the processes by which people share knowledge, risk and claims for reciprocity. Networking social capital is made up of 'economic and other ties that are external to the group' and is more formal in character (2003, p. 392). These ideas are helpful in clarifying the characteristics of relationships within groups and those between nature based associations and external individuals or organizations, such as sponsors or recipients of the data that they produce.

Methods

Research with members of the Northumberland and Tyneside Bird Club (NTBC) and the Birdwatching and Bird Study Association of Slovenia (DOPPS) was carried out in 2006 within a much larger European Union funded Sixth Framework Programme project, EuMon (EU-wide Monitoring Methods and Systems of Surveillance for Species and Habitats of Community Interest). The EuMon[2] project aims to provide a European framework to standardize, focus and co-ordinate existing monitoring programmes by comparing and integrating methods and monitoring schemes of species and habitats of community interests.

A section of the project is devoted to studying the position and roles undertaken by amateur naturalists in monitoring programmes. Part of this section involves qualitative exploratory research using ethnographic field methods, such as open interviews and participant observation, in a total of eight organizations in different EU member states. Five of the selected organizations were ornithological, including the two featured here. Subsequent analysis used grounded theory, theory generated from the data rather than imposed on it

---

[2] http://eumon.ckff.si

(Glaser and Strauss, 1967). The coded data were searched for emergent patterns, using a series of validity checks (Miles and Huberman, 1994). The material on Slovenian and UK ornithological organizations is subjected to comparative analysis to identify similarities and differences in context, structure, organization, purpose, style, values and practices.

Slovenia

When Slovenia was still a part of the Socialist Federation of Yugoslavia most people considered the collective expression of nature appreciation to be contained within traditional outdoor activities such as hunting and fishing. In comparison with other Yugoslav Republics and the communist countries of Central and Eastern Europe during the 1970s and 1980s nature conservation in Slovenia was considered progressive and 'quite *avant garde* even by Western standards' (Elliott and Udovč, 2005). During the period immediately after independence Slovenian citizens came to regard the varied biogeography of their country as a badge of distinction that set it apart from the other former Yugoslavian states. In a bid to develop foreign tourism the country with its 'exceptional natural diversity and natural values' was conceived as the 'true nature park of Europe' (Mršić, 1997, p. 108). The national tourism marketing campaign adopted a lime tree leaf as its logo and presented Slovenia as 'an idyllic country, full of natural beauties and surrounded by a wreath of mountains' (Kučan, 1998, p. 212).

Upon its constitutional transformation into a separate nation state, Slovenia ratified the Convention on Biological Diversity (CBD) and in 2002 the government adopted its Biodiversity Conservation Strategy (MESP, 2002) which emphasizes the aesthetic, cultural and intrinsic value of nature (2002, p. 13). The strategy document mentions the contribution of 'volunteer work' to conservation, even though (apart from activities by members of fishing and hunting associations) the rates for nature volunteering in Slovenia are low. In a public opinion survey (Kirn, 2004, p. 270) more than 95% of respondents claim not to belong to any environmental organization. However, in the years from 1993 to 2000 membership of organizations dedicated to nature conservation rose from 3.7% to 4.2% (*ibid.*) which shows a slight change of Slovene attitude to organized environmental and nature protection. Meanwhile the government's commitment to the maintenance of biodiversity deepens with Slovenia's entry to the European Union, and its consequent undertaking to fulfil the requirements of the EU's Natura 2000 network initiative, which is designed on the basis of the Habitats Directive of 1992 and complements the Birds Directive of 1979, to protect the most threatened habitats and species across Europe (Natura, 2007).

Slovenia's independence and EU accession has inflated demand for biological data so those capable of producing it are sought after by government agencies.

Birdwatching in Slovenia as a culturally sanctioned activity has a relatively brief history, even though the scientific interest in ornithology has deeper roots and can be traced back to at least the seventeenth century (Gregori, 1976). A former president and secretary of DOPPS recalled in an interview how at the start of his own career as a birdwatcher in the 1980s his interest was treated by others as 'almost as a mental illness'. He observes that it is only during the past two decades that birdwatching has become 'an approximately normal thing' achieving the level of public acceptability accorded to other outdoor activities like mountaineering, mushroom picking, fishing or hunting. It was during the early post-independence period of the 'greening' of Slovenia described above that the social acceptability of birdwatching increased.

Bird watching and bird study association of Slovenia (DOPPS)

DOPPS was founded in 1979 after previous attempts by a handful of professional and amateur ornithologists to collect data for an ornithological atlas of nesting birds in Slovenia failed. The ornithologists ascribed their failure to the random and unsystematic nature of their data, concluding that the atlas project required concerted effort within an organizational structure. A year later the first issue of the association's journal, *Acrocephalus*, was published and in the following decade the society put most of its efforts into the systematic collection of data for a series of atlases. In 1995, four years after Slovenia's independence, DOPPS published *The Ornithological Atlas of Slovenia* (Geister, 1995) to which 87 birdwatchers contributed data. In the preface to the atlas, editor and founder member of DOPPS, Iztok Geister, stressed the relevance of volunteer ornithological recording and research for the construction of Slovenian identity. He described the publication of ornithological atlases as 'a cultural act of every nation' asserting that 'for small countries like ours such projects are even more important because they place us alongside larger, more important nations that consider them to be inevitable and necessary' (Geister, 1995, p. 25).

In 1988 DOPPS was included in the newly established Association of Yugoslav Ornithological Societies (ZODJ) which became a national section of the International Council for Bird Preservation (now BirdLife International) during the following year. Also during this early period of DOPPS' evolution the first local section was founded, at Maribor in eastern Slovenia. When Slovenia seceded from the Republic of Yugoslavia in 1991 DOPPS withdrew from the Association of Yugoslav Ornithological Societies and continued to operate at the Slovenian national level. The disintegration of socialist Yugoslavia tore apart ZODJ causing DOPPS to seek fresh links via BirdLife, a movement paralleled by the new state's search for international connections, via institutions like the EU and NATO.

DOPPS became the Slovenian representative within BirdLife International in 1996, acceding to fully authorized membership in 2001. The partnership with BirdLife grew ever closer so that in 2007 a former director of DOPPS states in a follow-up interview for our research: 'We are BirdLife and we share everything we do'. Certainly, DOPPS have become influential within BirdLife. For example, it was through the promptings of DOPPS that BirdLife set up an informal working group to lobby against plans to build wind turbines at Volovja Slope (Volovja reber), an important bird migration flight path in Slovenia. Growth in public approval and interest in ornithology has enabled DOPPS to develop a visible profile through its international connections, publications and conservation campaigns. In addition DOPPS proved its worth by becoming heavily involved in the identification of Special Protected Areas for the development of Slovenia's Natura 2000 programme during and after accession to the EU in 2004.

As these events demonstrate, the evolution of DOPPS is aligned to the emergence of Slovenia as an independent state. DOPPS subsequently consolidated a partnership with the government when it was granted a concession to restore and manage a valuable nature reserve at Škocjan Bay (Škocjanski zatok). The partnership with the government was unique among NGOs acting in the field of nature conservation in Slovenia. Furthermore, DOPPS succeeded in obtaining an ongoing sponsorship agreement with Mobitel, the largest mobile telecommunications company in Slovenia.[3] The organization also secured European funding towards the restoration project at Škocjan Bay. These developments led DOPPS towards a gradual increase in numbers of paid staff, beginning with the appointment of a secretary in 1994, a director in 1999 and rising to a current figure of eighteen. As will be discussed later, this trend towards professionalization has caused ripples of concern among section of the membership. People worry that the ethos of altruism they judge to have been responsible for the association's early efflorescence – often described as 'the spirit of the society' – is nowadays compromised.

Nevertheless, DOPPS' success in securing European Union funding for its conservation activities is an important source of satisfaction for members,

---

[3] The co-operation with this sponsor in fact led to the expansion of the society in the late 1990s and to a sudden, but only temporary, increase of membership to 2000 members after a handy field guide *Birds of Slovenia* (Müller and Vrezec, 1998) was sent to all subscribers of the company's mobile telephone.

especially in view of the shifting cultural context where conservation has become increasingly associated with national identity. At the same time as advancing its national credentials, DOPPS gradually spread its roots at local level with four local branches, a youth section and a total membership of approximately 750 individuals.

However, continuing demands for DOPPS' services stretch the organization's resource base and highlight its shortage of volunteers. Of DOPPS' 750 members, only 50 are fully active volunteers, approximately 200 are less active, 18 are paid professionals while the remaining 500 tend to be passive members, who pay their fees and receive the popular bird magazine, *World of Birds (Svet ptic)*, launched by DOPPS in 2000. The contribution of the 50 most active volunteers is therefore thinly spread across various voluntary monitoring activities, including counts for the new ornithological atlas, a winter water bird census, a number of species counts, as well as habitat-restoration projects.

United Kingdom

According to Allen's classic social history, *The Naturalist in Britain* (1976), the origins of popular interest in natural history reach as far back as the seventeenth century with the formation of the first botanical societies, followed in the early eighteenth century by societies for the study of butterflies and insects. Although these sorts of societies declined during the middle years of the century, the popularity of collecting all sorts of natural history specimens grew, together with the availability of natural history books. The revival of generalist and specialist nature associations continued to spread throughout the country during the nineteenth and early twentieth centuries (Allen, 1976).

Wide sections of the general public demonstrated an interest in birds from at least the start of the twentieth century. From then on public interest in ornithology in the UK grew apace. Even during the war years between 1939 and 1944 membership of the British Trust for Ornithology (BTO) 'very nearly doubled' (Allen, 1976, p. 266). During the post-war era a new wave of amateur birdwatchers sought to observe birds in a range of habitats beyond the confines of parks and gardens (Moss, 2004, p. 191). Rising interest was marked by a boom in the publication of books and broadcasts about birdwatching. Particularly significant were the creation of comprehensive yet accessible field guides and better optics. (Moss, 2004, pp. 172–212).

Despite these promising developments, Moss describes how in the 1960s and 1970s British birders found theirs was 'not a passion you freely admitted to' (Moss, 2004, p. 332), especially within the masculine cultures of the industrial north-east of England where 'keeping racing pigeons was an honourable pursuit, but watching wild birds was regarded with contempt' (Moss, 2004, p. 333). However, these attitudes changed rapidly, under the influence of new products and services, access to mobility, communication via the internet and television programmes featuring well known broadcasters. By the time the mines of the north-east coalfields closed in the 1980s and 1990s 'a number of miners used their redundancy cash to buy binoculars and telescopes so that they could take up birding' (*ibid.*).

It was during the 1990s that the British state began to organize and regulate around the concept of biodiversity, or what had previously been though of as 'the variety of life' (Marren, 2002: 254). Only two years after the UK government became a signatory to the Convention on Biological Diversity (CBD) in 1992, civil servants produced four White Papers (proposals for discussion by parliament) including one which was to become the UK Biodiversity Action Plan (BAP). Around the same time a consortium of nature-based NGOs, representing a total membership of two million British citizens, published their own ideas in a document entitled *Biodiversity Challenge*, which Marren describes as 'one of the milestones on the journey of the voluntary bodies from amateur natural history societies to partners in environmental policy-making' (Marren, 2002, p. 256).

By the end of the decade the UK BAP and its local offshoots (Local Biodiversity Plans – LBAPs), together with the Local Agenda 21 programmes that emerged from the 1992 United Nations Rio Conference, were supporting an impetus to 'broaden participation in conservation, and environmental policy-making more generally' (Ellis and Waterton, 2004, p. 97), even if this was most visible at the rhetorical rather than practical level (Baldoumas, 2003). These developments greatly increased demand for biological recording that far outstripped the capacity of professional scientists to satisfy (Lawrence, this volume). Large amounts of data are now required to meet the UK government's obligations enshrined in a range of treaties and conventions, including the EU's Natura 2000 programme, and other associated targets. Much of this information originates among members of nature-based associations like the NTBC.

Northumberland and Tyneside Bird Club

The NTBC was founded in 1958 as a break-away group from the generalist Natural History Society of Northumberland. Its original core members wanted to create an organization with a focus on ornithological field activities. The constitutional aims of the club were, and remain, focused on the promotion of ornithology in the local area, including commitment to engage in 'scientific work' and the production of comprehensive reports on the county's avifauna. From the outset the NTBC was field-based and published monthly bulletins reporting bird sightings by members. The evolution of the club was marked by growing professionalization, as reflected in the style and sophistication of its organizational activities and publications.

The monthly bulletins, and their synthesis into an annual report, are composed of data returned to a compiler by members using record cards, detailing bird species, numbers, location and behaviour. Among the club's committee members, who are elected for a six-year period, is the office of County Recorder. The County Recorder is supported by a Records Committee who scrutinize records of rare or unusual sightings. The County Recorder's work in cataloguing the record cards sent in by members is assisted by half a dozen 'writers' who are allocated record cards according to the section of the bulletin for which they are responsible. Members submit their cards to a deadline each month. The names of all contributors are listed in the bulletin and interviews reveal this to be an important source of personal satisfaction. The total number of cards amassed since the club's founding is currently calculated to number around half a million. They are held in the archives of a regional natural history museum.

Members have also contributed to the production of two atlases. These massive publications meet exacting scientific standards, are fully illustrated, and maintain the highest level of print production. The first, on breeding birds of Northumberland (Day, Hodgson and Rossiter, 1995), resulted from a survey conducted in association with the BTO. The second, *The Atlas of Wintering Birds in Northumberland* (Day and Hodgson, 2003), cites contributions from 134 members and was produced entirely within the club. The relatively high costs of both these publications were supported through donations, legacies and sponsorship from the commercial and non-commercial sectors.

Not all current members of the NTBC return completed record cards, a fact that provokes disapproval from the rest because 'the bird club needs every bit of information about birds'. Indeed, much of this activity is undertaken by a relatively small proportion of the NTBC membership (around 24%–40% of members, depending on the month). Some very regular birdwatchers do not submit record cards, others do so by proxy (forwarding information to a colleague who completes a record card on their behalf), and still others are thought to avoid the cards because they lack confidence in making the necessary species descriptions. Concerns about the depletion of records are particularly evident when thoughts turn to the future. In interviews members frequently mention their anxieties about the lack of young people coming forward to replace 'old hands' of many years' standing. The old hands proclaim their readiness to train apprentices to ensure the long-term future of their club and its legacy of continuous recording with which they so closely identify. They blame the absence of interest among young people on a host of social changes, such as the rise of computer-based leisure activities and parental reluctance to allow children to roam.

Many specific bird surveys are undertaken by the bird club, such as controlled tetrad surveys (regular timed counts of species in specific areas at specific times of day), region-specific counts (synchronized and thus requiring a large number of observers) and species counts (normally three species are chosen a year in order to encourage a full record submission). Government and non-government organizations – most frequently the BTO – request volunteers from the bird club to take part in surveys and recording.

The BTO retains a system of regional representatives, who are also volunteers, to help recruit amateur ornithologists for surveys. The current BTO County Representative for Northumberland is a member of NTBC and attends the club's meetings, encouraging participation in specific types of surveys that focus on particular species, on breeding birds, or on birds associated with certain types of habitat (e.g. scarce woodland birds). He is highly regarded by other NTBC members as a persuasive, even charismatic character: 'I mean even the most horrendous survey, he can sell it to the club because of the way he is'.

Interestingly, some potentially valuable information can go unrecorded because many birdwatchers rarely record common birds unless they appear in large numbers or at an unusual site. One interviewee gave an example: people are unlikely to record a Dunnock (*Prunella modularis*), which is amongst the most common bird species in Northumberland, because 'it is just a bird'. However, via the NTBC monthly bulletin, members are also encouraged to send in *full* listings of all bird species from specific sites throughout the year in order to track the seasonal movements and distribution patterns of non-migratory birds. In an attempt to counter the problem of under-representation, the BTO now run a new project known as BirdTrack, which primarily traces the arrival of migrants through its specially designed website. There is even discussion that county records be submitted directly to BirdTrack instead of via record cards submitted to the club. The County Recorder would then be able to receive these records (which will still belong to the Club) from the BTO.

Not all NTBC members are convinced that they will be able to retain ownership and control over the Northumberland data once they have been submitted to BirdTrack. As well as its responsibility for providing an annual record of birdlife in the county, 'information about birds' is a valuable resource to the NTBC on a number of levels. The NTBC sells its data to consultancies and other institutions engaged in creating environmental impact assessments for planning applications and business expansion plans. Additionally, experienced members, especially those with years of serial records of a particular area, are consulted by local authorities and other bodies involved in scoping exercises to judge the desirability, or possibility, of certain sites for development projects. One NTBC member considered that he and others in the club, though unpaid volunteers, wielded considerable influence via these informal channels: 'There are battles we lose, but I think over the years, we've probably influenced a lot of decisions. I mean the [name of development] has been modified'.

Amateurs, volunteers and serious leisure

Glover and Hemmingway (2005) argue that leisure is a lubricant for social capital because it holds the potential for people to create deep and enduring ties. This is certainly detectable in our descriptions of DOPPS and NTBC where social capital exists in the strength of ties between members as bonding social capital, and as networking capital through alignments with related organizations.

In our introduction we refer to Stebbins' characterization of the sort of pursuits undertaken by active members of DOPPS and NTBC as serious leisure. Serious leisure 'is the systematic pursuit of an amateur, hobbyist or voluntary activity that participants find so substantial and interesting, that in the typical case, they launch themselves on a career centred on acquiring and expressing its special skills, knowledge and experience' (Stebbins, 1992, p. 3; Stebbins, 2001, p. 3). Birdwatchers who undertake monitoring activities are usually both amateurs and volunteers and Stebbins remarks that his three categories, or ideal types, are often found to overlap (Stebbins, 2001, p. 126).

Stebbins proposes that a defining feature of amateur activities consists of participants being locked into a system of relations linking professionals, amateurs and their publics (2001, p. 5). Among hobbyists the professional *alter ego* is absent, but its presence in other focal interest activities creates amateurs. Volunteering, which may or may not be a part of being an amateur, is defined by Stebbins as a 'helpful activity that is engaged in not primarily for financial gain and not by coercion or mandate' (*ibid.*).

Serious leisure practitioners are additionally characterized by their pursuit of leisure careers. An individual's leisure career may unfold in a variety of ways, but progress is dependent on the development of skill, knowledge and expertize. The achievement of status is related to stages in career progression, because status is based on other people's recognition of the level of an individual's accomplishments. Most important are the opinions of proximate fellows, and to a lesser extent a wider public who inhabit the same 'social world' (Stebbins, 2001, p. 8). Social worlds emerge out of the unique ethos that grows up around the expression of a serious leisure pursuit. These are 'diffuse and amorphous constellations' centred on the serious leisure interest. They are rarely heavily bureaucratized, mediated by communications media and marked by special sets of values, beliefs, moral principles, performance standards and similar shared representations (Stebbins, 2001, pp. 7–8).

The social world of birdwatching extends across national boundaries, as is clear from DOPPS' close relationship with BirdLife International, and in a different way by the frequency with which NTBC members travel abroad for birdwatching vacations. The dispersed social world of birdwatching is inhabited by more or less dedicated birders – which would include the 500 passive members of DOPPS and the NTBC members who attend only the occasional talk – together with special interest media, such as magazines and websites, e-mail chat groups or events like the annual UK Bird Fair.

People with high-status recognition – be it in the confines of the club or the wider social birding world – are capable of motivating fellow birdwatchers to take part in monitoring activities. Or, as exemplified by the NTBC member who is also the BTO Regional Representative, of urging volunteer recorders towards more difficult and strenuous monitoring activities. While competition for status may risk creating division through envy, questions of status can also assist in maintaining loyalty. Members of NTBC refer to high-status members as 'good birders' and take pride in their club because they perceive it as embracing an unusually large percentage of members who are 'good birders'. Similarly, within DOPPS the most active and skilled volunteers derive their status from a willingness to share information and expertise with less experienced members.

Status based on reputation is not only a question of how well one performs as an ornithologist, but also how well one performs as a member of a moral community: the two are entwined. Birds are not merely an entry into the world of nature, or an object of study and pleasure. Within the context of bird-based organizations they are the catalyst for human sociality.

Glover and Hemmingway note 'sociability is a central component of leisure, both structurally and motivationally' (2005, p. 397). DOPPS members enjoy field trips, camps, working together on habitat-restoration projects, lectures and meetings that often end with a trip to a bar where ornithological debates are continued in a less formal atmosphere. The President of a local section explained about the cohesive function of such informal exchanges of knowledge, 'many of them think they are not good enough at ornithology for their opinion to be taken into consideration. Therefore they rather stay quiet. But then they drink "two times two" [two glasses of alcohol] and they become more open and not afraid to talk'. NTBC members prize the sociability of their club, with its meetings, informal gatherings in the field, organized trips and long-standing, close friendships among small groups within the wider membership.

Anti-social behaviour is identified in two main ways. First is failing, or even worse wilfully refusing, to learn from fellow bird enthusiasts. It is a badge of honour and sign of a 'good birder' to exhibit a willingness to learn from one's peers. Second is the denial of information to fellow birders about the whereabouts of 'good birds'. People discovered not to have shared information about sighted birds gain a negative reputation for being 'suppressors'. Anyone who makes a rare sighting is expected to use their mobile telephone to notify colleagues so they can decide whether or not to rush to the scene. Failure to announce a rare sighting contravenes the unwritten codes of birdwatching.

Donnelly (1994) suggests the social and cultural values prevalent among birdwatchers render the activity extraordinarily dependent on trust between participants. The authenticity of ornithological data depends on the validity of claims that certain birds have been sighted at certain times and places. Hence, for an individual birdwatcher 'the construction of an appropriate subcultural identity involves the development of a reputation for reliability' (1994, p. 235). Various devices involving the scrutiny of records by experienced birdwatchers are employed to ensure their accuracy. But the acceptability of records frequently depends on assessment of a person's trustworthiness founded on reputation. Doubts about authenticity are likely to be greatest when the recorder is a novice or someone with a dubious reputation for false sightings.

New members of DOPPS and NTBC gradually accumulate recognition among experienced members of 'being trustworthy', an honour that is acknowledged when the records they produce contribute to the organization's projects or publications. One younger member of DOPPS explained to us: 'If I say "I saw that bird!" they trust me as much as they would trust someone with a PhD. That means a lot to me!'. Another member proudly described how data from his personal birdwatching log were used in designing a flood protection plan. His data were selected on the basis of trust by a more experienced and renowned member of DOPPS: 'He knew he could trust the data'.

Members perceive shared trust and egalitarianism to have formed crucial elements of DOPPS' culture since the organization's inception. However, those stable elements are threatened with erosion by the gradual professionalization of the society, beginning in the mid 1990s. Although professionalization was probably inevitable for the survival and expansion of DOPPS within Slovenia's new social and political climate, it transformed the 'basic assumptions' of the organization, especially the conception of voluntarism (Schein, 1992, pp. 21–26). Prior to professionalization, data were treated as a gift from a member to the organization as well as to nature itself (cf. Ellis and Waterton, 2005). But when DOPPS began to receive external funding, commoditizing the data exchange process, altruism was perceived to diminish.

It is useful to recall Stebbins' theory that amateurs are structurally linked inter-dependently to professionals. Stebbins reminds us that 'the early history of many contemporary professions was made up exclusively of amateurs, the only people practising the profession in their day' (1992, p. 9). This is certainly true of naturalists who once pursued their activities without professionals to refer to. They could not therefore hold a conception of themselves as amateurs. However, according to Stebbins emergent professionalism is paralleled by emergent amateurism, in particular among those he refers to as 'modern amateurs' whose relationship with professionals is not the same as that of ordinary lay people (1992, p. 35). Contemporary working patterns allow amateurs time to become experts and to regularly deploy their core skills and knowledge. It is the pursuit of professional standards that distinguishes modern amateurs from their predecessors – the well-to-do collectors and naturalists of the eighteenth and nineteenth centuries (Stebbins, 1992, p. 42).

The situation in DOPPS is certainly not a straightforward clash between professional experts and amateur ornithologists with less expertise: some members of staff were previously volunteers themselves. Almost all employees volunteer for bird counts in addition to their paid work and, as one long-term member of DOPPS pointed out with some irony, the professional staff work so many long hours that they make an extra voluntary contribution by default. Tensions originate in pressures brought about by the degree of systematization and administration necessitated by the receipt of the EU Life Programme funding, the task of managing a wildlife reserve and demands from the national government for processed as opposed to raw data. Professionals are often recruited from among the most active and enthusiastic volunteers. Raising the numbers of professionals is beneficial for activities like those referred to above, but weakens DOPPS' volunteer base since the volunteer turned professional has less time for volunteering. Professionalization is thus sometimes seen as threatening the integrity of the organization. The president of DOPPS' supervisory board told us that when long-term volunteers turned into professionals 'the volunteer side lost the engine that made it run'.

People react nervously if they begin to detect the weakening of vital bonding social capital in their organizations. Long-term active members of DOPPS yearn for what they feel to have been the more egalitarian early days of the association, while both employees and volunteers are worried that over-professionalization might alienate voluntary participants. The current president remarked: 'We can't say "You did it. We don't need you anymore." ' . . . . The volunteer is not a slave to exploit. He or she is worth the same – or even more – than an employee'. Here DOPPS' president asserts a moral dimension – something fraternal and fundamentally levelling – within the pursuit of ornithology that appears less endangered within the NTBC, where there are no paid employees and professionalization is restricted to setting standards for members to aspire to. Nevertheless, there are anxieties about relations with professionals in partner organizations, as revealed in reservations held by some members about handing over their monthly records to the BTO ornithologists via the BirdTrack scheme.

Birdwatching and social capital

It is a salient feature of both DOPPS and NTBC that members' commitment to the serious leisure pursuit of birdwatching is harnessed and organized in ways that contribute significantly towards scientific monitoring. Organizations like DOPPS and NTBC act as arenas in which data are produced and processed.

The production of data depends upon members' mutual passion for birds which creates strong ties of bonding capital. As collectives these ornithological organizations are more than the sum of their individual parts. Each organization is made up of the relationships between those parts and provides a structure that frames each person's bird recording activities. The importance of trust in the two organizations stresses the role of bonding social capital in maintaining institutional viability and attractiveness. The sustainability of DOPPS and NTBC is therefore based primarily on the nature of the internal connections between individual members, including volunteer monitors and members who do not take part in monitoring. These factors relate to Adger's (2003) ideas about bonding social capital being founded on friendship. In our examples fellowship spawns loyalty and collaboration.

We have also examined relations with external institutions, invoking Adger's networking capital, which he claims to be weaker, because they are less dependent on face to face interactions (*ibid*. p. 392). In our examples, key relationships that entail networking social capital are DOPPS' partnerships with BirdLife and with the Slovenian government, as well as NTBC's connection with the BTO.

In the case of DOPPS networking capital brought great benefits in boosting its public credentials through involvement with a high-profile international NGO and through the Slovenian government handing over management of an important specially protected area. However, tension has been generated around degrees of professionalization, provoking members of DOPPS at all levels to express concern over negative impacts these alliances may have on precious bonding social capital. There are worries about the fate of the 'spirit of the organization', which members identify as responsible for safely steering

DOPPS from its inception through the societal upheavals of Slovenia's recent past. In the NTBC rumblings of discontent occur among a portion of the membership about some programmes promoted by its main networking institution the BTO. The new BirdTrack scheme has prompted debate about control and ownership of the data volunteers collect. The example of DOPPS suggests that professonalization can interfere with internal cohesion, while that of the NTBC suggests gaps where misunderstandings can occur between organizations based on volunteering and those that operate entirely through professional personnel using rational bureaucratic methods and assumptions.

Our two case studies demonstrate that nature-based organizations can make a large contribution to monitoring biodiversity by harnessing the energies of a committed section of their membership. If this degree of productivity is to be sustained then attention has to be paid not only to those motivations of volunteers traceable to their emotional connections with nature. The relationships they have with one another and with the wider social world of bird watching are equally relevant for the sustainability of biodiversity monitoring programmes.

Acknowledgements

We would like to thank the NTBC, DOPPS and BTO for spending time with us to explain how their organizations work and to give us some insight into the art of birdwatching.

REFERENCES

Adger, W. N. (2003). Social capital, collective action and adaptation to climate change. *Economic Geography* **79**(4), 387–404.

Allen, D. E. (1976). *The Naturalist in Britain: A Social History*. London: Allen Lane.

Baldoumas, A. (2003). A role for volunteers in biodiversity interest intermediation. In *Why Involve Volunteers in Biodiversity Monitoring? Summary of the BioWatch UK workshop, 20th October 2003. BioWatch UK Workshop*, eds. S. Gillett and A. Lawrence. Oxford, UK. Available at http://www.eci.ox.ac.uk/research/humaneco/biowatch.php.

BirdLife (2007). *BirdLife Global Partnership*. On-line: http://www.birdlife.org/worldwide/global/index.html.

Blackshaw, T. and Long, J. (2005). What's the big idea? A critical exploration of the concept of social capital and its incorporation into leisure policy discourse. *Leisure Studies* **24**(3), 239–258.

Bourdieu, P. (1986). The forms of capital. In *Handbook of Theory and Research for the Sociology of Education*, ed. J. Richardson. New York.: Greenwood, pp. 241–258.

Cocker, M. (2001). *Birders: Tales of a Tribe*. New York: Atlantic Monthly Press.

Coleman, J. S. (1988). Social capital in the creation of human capital. *American Journal of Sociology* **94** (Suppl.), S94–S120.

Day, J. C., Hodgson, M. S. and Rossiter, B. N., eds. (1995). *The Atlas of Breeding Birds in Northumbria*. Newcastle-upon-Tyne: Northumberland and Tyneside Bird Club.

Day, J. C. and Hodgson, M. S., eds. (2003). *The Atlas of Wintering Birds in Northumbria*. Newcastle-upon-Tyne: Northumberland and Tyneside Bird Club.

Donnelly, P. (1994). Take my word for it: trust in the context of birding and mountaineering. *Qualitative Sociology* **17**(3), 215–241.

Elliott, C. and Udovč, A. (2005). Nature conservation and spatial planning in Slovenia: continuity in transition. *Land Use Policy* **22**(3), 265–276.

Ellis, R. and Waterton, C. (2004). Environmental citizenship in the making: the participation of volunteer naturalists in UK biological recording and biodiversity policy. *Science and Public Policy* **31**(1), 95–105.

Ellis, R. and Waterton, C. (2005). Caught between the cartographic and the ethnographic imagination; the whereabouts of amateurs, professionals, and nature in knowing biodiversity. *Environment and Planning D: Society and Space* **23**, 673–693.

Geister, I. (ed.) (1995). *Ornitološki atlas Slovenije: Razširjenost gnezdilk (Ornithological Atlas of Slovenia)*. Ljubljana: DZS.

Glaser, B. G. and Strauss, A. L. (1967). *The Discovery of Grounded Theory: Strategy for Qualitative Research*. New York: Aldine.

Glover, T. and Hemmingway, J. L. (2005). Locating leisure in the social capital literature. *Journal of Leisure Research* **37**(4), 387–401.

Gregori, J. (1976). Ornitologija na ozemlju današnje Slovenije do leta 1926. *Proteus* **38**(7), 244–246.

Kirn, A. (2004). *Narava, družba, ekološka zavest*. Ljubljana: Fakulteta za družbene vede.

Kučan, A. (1998). *Krajina kot nacionalni simbol. (Landscape as a National Symbol.)* Ljubljana: Znanstveno in publicistično središče.

Liep, J. (2001). Airbourne kula. The appropriation of birds by Danish ornithologists. *Anthropology Today* **17**(5), 10–15.

Lawrence, A. (2006). 'No personal motive?' Volunteers, biodiversity, and the false dichotomies of participation. *Ethics, Place and Environment* **9**(3), 279–298.

Lawrence, A. and Turnhout, C. (2005). *Personal meaning in the public space: the bureaucratisation of biodiversity data in the UK and the Netherlands*. Paper presented at the RGS-IBG Annual conference, London. Available at http://www.eci.ox.ac.uk/pdfdownload/human_ecology/lawrenceturnhout_2005.pdf (accessed April 3 2005).

Marren, P. (2002). *Nature Conservation: A Review of the Conservation of Wildlife in Britain 1950–2001*. London: HarperCollins.

MESP (2002). *Strategija ohranjanja biotske raznovrstnosti v Sloveniji. (Biodiversity Conservation Strategy of Slovenia.)* Ljubljana: Ministry of the Environment and Spatial Planning of Republic Slovenia.

Miles, M. B. and Huberman, A. M. (1994). *Qualitative Data Analysis*. Newbury Park, CA: Sage.

Moss, S. (2004). *A Bird in the Bush: A Social History of Birdwatching*. London: Aurum Press.

Mršić, N. (1997). *Biotska raznovrstnost v Sloveniji: Slovenija – "vroča točka" Evrope. (Biotic Diversity in Slovenia: Slovenia – the "Hot Spot" of Europe.)* Ljubljana: Ministry of the Environment and Spatial Planning of Republic Slovenia.

Müller, W. and Vrezec, A. (1998). *Ptice Slovenije: Mali priročnik (Birds of Slovenia: A Short Guide)*. Ljubljana: DOPPS.

Natura (2007). 'What is Natura 2000?' Natura 2000 Networking Programme. On-line: http://www.natura.org/about.html.

Pawar, M. (2006). "Social" "Capital"? *The Social Science Journal* **43**(2), 211–226.

Portes, A. (1998). Social capital: its origins and applications in modern sociology. *Annual Review of Sociology* **24**, 1–24.

Putnam, R. D. (2000). *Bowling Alone: The Collapse and Revival of American Community*. New York: Simon and Schuster.

Schein, Edgar H. (1992). *Organizational Culture and Leadership*. 2nd edn. San Francisco: Jossey-Bass Publishers.

Stebbins, R. A. (1992). *Amateurs, Professionals, and Serious Leisure*. Montreal and Kingston: McGill-Queen's University Press.

Stebbins, R. A. (2001). *New Directions in the Theory and Research of Serious Leisure*. Lewiston NY: Edwin Mellen Press.

12

The personal and political of volunteers' data: towards a national biodiversity database for the UK

ANNA LAWRENCE

Britain has an exceptional tradition of natural history societies and amateur naturalists who collect data about species distributions, frequency and behaviour (Bell *et al.*, this volume). This chapter examines an attempt to harness the data for a wider range of purposes, and the ways in which different actors have perceived and responded to this. Many of the volunteers have a strong personal attachment to their data, and to the ways in which they hope that it will be used. When powerful organizations become involved in managing the data, the volunteers can perceive threats and opportunities for the value of their data. The chapter considers the need to balance these emotional and political aspects in developing an effective national data management system. It is based on a cross-cutting analysis of research into the processes behind biodiversity action plans and biological recording, conducted over several years in the UK (Gillett and Lawrence, 2003; Lawrence, 2005; Lawrence, 2006; Lawrence and Molteno in press; Lawrence and Turnhout, 2005). The chapter draws on interviews with volunteers and professionals involved in the complex organizational landscape that has evolved around biological data collection and sharing, descriptions of the process on websites and in reports, and on presentations made at the annual National Biodiversity Network conferences.

The supply side: growth of biological recording

Biological recording, or the collection of data about the distribution and abundance of species, has a long history in Britain, going back to the leisure time of country vicars in the eighteenth century (Moss, 2004). The nineteenth century

Taking Stock of Nature: Participatory Biodiversity Assessment for Policy, Planning and Practice, ed. Anna Lawrence. Published by Cambridge University Press. © Cambridge University Press 2010.

saw the establishment of natural history societies and recording societies to share field trips and records of species distributions. Among many others, the Botanical Society of the British Isles was founded in 1836, the Royal Society for the Protection of Birds in 1889, and the British Bryological Society founded in 1896 for the study of mosses. The trend continued into the twentieth century. The British Trust for Ornithology (BTO) was founded in 1932, as a 'clearing house for bird-watching results' (Nicholson, 1931), and the Mammal Society in 1954 to 'link amateurs and professionals in promoting the study of mammals' (Flowerdew, 2004).

All of them emphasize the importance of amateur members who collect data. They also advertise their contribution to policy and conservation practice. For example, Butterfly Conservation, founded in 1968, now with several thousand volunteers participating in surveys, is explicit about its role of lobbying government. The BTO is one of the most successful. Over the last 40 years it has:

> monitored populations of the commoner 35–50% of species of British breeding birds. [As a result] the widespread declines in farmland birds that occurred in the last quarter of the 20th century [have been] brought to the attention of conservation scientists, campaigners, policy-makers, politicians and the public. From this ... have stemmed policies aimed at reducing the problems and a commitment by government to halt the declines.
>
> *(Greenwood, 2003)*

Rare birds and plants can be difficult to identify; and even the more common insects may be misidentified by non-experts. The recording societies and schemes have therefore developed a system of quality control, whereby every county or vice-county is assigned a Recorder, who verifies unusual or unreliable records. This Vice-County, or County, Recorder, is acknowledged as an expert by her or his peers.

Recently, however, numbers of expert amateur recorders have been declining (Hopkins and Freckleton, 2002) and in a broadsheet British newspaper Bowler, (2003) goes so far as to note:

> Sadly, fewer and fewer people are joining amateur natural history societies, while existing memberships are ageing. ... many of the old natural history societies are almost moribund, having ceased to hold meetings.

Yet the overall recording effort for the second *Atlas of the British Flora* increased from the work for the first atlas during 1930–1969, to that of the *New Atlas of the British Flora* for which data were gathered during 1987–1999. For the *New Atlas*, over 1600 volunteers visited over 3800 squares

(10 × 10 km), producing a cumulative database of 9 million records (Preston *et al.*, 2002). In total, a quasi-government report estimated that over 60 000 volunteers were active in biological recording in the mid 1990s (Burnett, Copp and Harding, 1995).

The importance of volunteers is reflected in government indicators of progress towards the target agreed at the World Summit on Sustainable Development (Johannesburg 2002) to significantly reduce biodiversity loss by 2010, and the European Commission target of halting biodiversity loss by the same date. Under the heading 'Education and public understanding', one target is 'volunteer time spent in citizen science activity'. Data based on the RSPB's Big Garden Birdwatch and the UK Phenology Network showed increases in volunteer time in 2003 and 2008 (DEFRA, 2006a).

So specialist amateurs are on the decline while more generalist volunteers and environmental enthusiasts are on the rise. This brings with it new concerns about quality control. Even more complicated, however, are the developments in cross-cutting data flows, and overlapping data collection organizations. These have arisen as the situation moves from a supply-led to a demand-led one.

From supply to demand: data needs in policy context

Since the 1990s the relationship between recorders and government has changed. The recording societies and conservation NGOs still aim to influence policy, but now the government is also actively seeking the data produced by the volunteers. Demand has increased for two reasons: spatial planning law has evolved to take more account of environmental impact, including biodiversity; and the 1992 UN Convention on Biological Diversity (CBD), followed by the European Commission's Habitats and Species Directives and the UK Biodiversity Action Plan (UKBAP), bring considerable reporting obligations (Battersby and Greenwood, 2004; Warren and Witter, 2002). The two strands interweave to form local data needs related to spatial planning applications, and national data needs related to reporting. In addition, legislation on freedom of access to environmental information has affected data flows between suppliers and the public.

The new data demands began with the Wildlife and Countryside Act of 1981, which provided new levels of protection for listed species. Because planning regulations are implemented by local government, this placed a new onus on the local authorities to be aware of threats to protected species and habitats. Biological data used in this way can be used to prioritize areas for conservation designations, or prevent an inappropriate housing development (Key, 1993).

In response, some local authorities established or supported a Local Record Centre (LRC, also known in some counties as Environmental Record Centre, or Biological Record Centre) (Palmer, 2004). Some were established by county museum services, others by wildlife trusts or other non-government conservation organizations. LRCs have been defined as a 'not-for-profit service run in partnership for the public benefit, which collects, collates, manages and disseminates information of known quality relating to the wildlife, wildlife sites and habitats for a defined geographical area' (NFBR, 2002). However, there was no statutory requirement to establish them, and so scale varies and coverage is still incomplete. The Strategic Business Plan for Biological Recording in Scotland notes:

> There is no Local Record Centre coverage for two thirds of Scotland, meaning a huge amount of locally recorded biological data has nowhere to go, creating a negative feedback for all but the most enthusiastic of recorders. The Central Scotland Record Centre holds upward of 120,000 records. This records centre has been out of business for three years, and the records sit on a computer in an unverified and currently unusable state.
>
> *(BRISC, 2006)*

Many LRCs were under-resourced for decades. As one respondent explained, the LRC network was developed initially on the ground in response to local needs, and was not resourced centrally. It was often up to museum biologists to find funding, and many of them had little experience or training in this field, so they set up records centres with scarce financial support. However, the growing local government requirements for biodiversity data – to check planning applications, and to report against local government performance indicators – means that local authorities now provide financial support to the LRCs.

Separately, and also struggling with funding, the UKBAP was developed between 1994 and 1996. It established a new more target-based approach to conservation, enshrined in 391 Species Action Plans and 45 Habitat Action Plans (DEFRA, 2006b), all of which had to be monitored. These original lists of priority species and habitats were chosen quickly and pragmatically, and have now been revised and expanded, using clearer criteria that combine international status and level of decline in the UK (DEFRA, 2007a; Lawrence and Molteno, in press). These priority lists are influential in terms of government requirements for data.

The requirements have been strengthened with the new biodiversity 'duty'. In 2004 the Scottish Parliament passed the Nature Conservation (Scotland) Act 2004, giving all public bodies in Scotland a duty to 'further the conservation of biodiversity' as they carry out their work. (Biodiversity Scotland, 2008). In England and Wales, the Natural Environment and Rural Communities Act of 2006 gives all local authorities and public bodies a duty to 'have regard to the purpose of conserving biodiversity' (DEFRA, 2007c).

Recent developments in international policy support the public availability of environmental information, particularly through national policies mandated by the Aarhus Convention on Access to Information, Public Participation in Decision-making and Access to Justice in Environmental Matters. It came into law as Directive 2003/4/EC on public access to environmental information, implemented by member states in 2005 (Hartley and Wood, 2005). The UK response included the revised Environmental Information Regulations (EIR) on public access to environmental information held by government bodies.

A key issue is that, as planning regulations have increasingly required bio-diversity data to be taken into account, a market has arisen for those data. Consultants pay the record centres for access to biological records of pro-tected species. Many of those records have been collected by unpaid recorders, whose motivation is often related to personal kudos or environmental concern, and who do not want to lose control over the use of their records. Payment for records supports the administration of the LRCs, but the managers have to maintain a delicate balance between income derived from consultants, and records derived from volunteers. If the volunteers perceive that their records are being used inappropriately by stakeholders who have access to them, they may withhold their data. This is the crux of the struggles that have arisen over data sharing, as we see in the next section.

A national network

By the beginning of the twenty-first century there were, in addition to the 60 000 plus volunteers, a wide range of organizations to be taken into account including recording societies and schemes, local record centres, and conser-vation NGOs who sought to involve members of the public in surveying the more easily recognizable species. All of them were producing data, for a range of motivations and aspirations. These data were in demand from the national government, local authorities and members of the public. Some of these sources started to be perceived as being in competition with each other.

> You could look at it as two separate worlds ... LRCs are getting the lion's share of the funding, while traditional recording schemes are suffering.
> *[Chairman of national recording society, 2004]*
> Sometimes it's inevitable, if the national scheme doesn't have the resources or the will to make data available locally, to send it back to the LRC, the only thing we

can do is say to people, yes send it to the records centre and send it to the national scheme. But what we try and do is we go to the national scheme and say please can we have the data for our county. Because there are 57 counties, they have to cut their data up into 57 places and make sure it goes back to the counties and most of them don't want to do that.

[Interview with LRC manager, 2006]

Many of these actors began to see a need for co-ordination. Two developments in particular triggered this: the UKBAP with its national reporting needs, and a quasi-government report written by experienced recorders, *Biological Recording in the UK* (Burnett, Copp and Harding, 1995). The latter called on the stakeholders to 'secure the recognition of the need for a national system' and to 'prepare design specifications for a metadatabase of biological recording based on standardised metarecords.'

Conservation NGOs, rather than recording societies, took a key role in initiating this. The Wildlife Trusts in the UK are a network of county-based conservation NGOs which build up their own property base of nature reserves. They collect biodiversity data on their own sites for management purposes. They saw value in a national biodiversity network, based on countrywide coverage of LRCs. The Royal Society for the Protection of Birds (RSPB), which was also involved, has a large national membership but unlike the BTO is not primarily a recording society.

So, in 2000, the National Biodiversity Network (NBN) was set up as a charitable trust, jointly by government nature conservation agencies and two of the largest conservation NGOs in the UK (NBN, 2006). This early involvement of the conservation NGOs was politically important, but perhaps contributed to a feeling that the plan excluded recorders from the natural history societies and schemes. The NBN Trust was formed in recognition of the need for the Network to be overseen independently from any of its founding partner organizations, and the Trustees focused on the practical value of the Network.

The NBN idea could not be simpler: capture wildlife data once in a standard electronic form; integrate data from different sources; and use the internet to enable data to be used many times in different ways by as many people as possible.

(NBN, 2006)

The simplicity of this idea is emphasized by NBN officers.

It was really to provide a conduit for data. It doesn't hold or own any data at all. The data is all owned or held by the individual organisations.

[interview with NBN Trustee, 2006]

This simplicity, however, overlooked the politics of data collection, founded on the historical and local identities of the recording societies and LRCs, and the emotional attachment that recorders have with their data. While the Burnett report was 'essentially a grassroots product' and the NBN was 'designed to be an open partnership', it quickly ran into unexpected reservations or outright hostility.

Initial resistance

Recorders are emotionally connected with their species and their data. As one official commented, this applies even to experts (many of who collect data voluntarily in their spare time):

> Of course experts are not only scientifically connected with their field and their group and their taxa, but they also have a strong personal connection with that, so they want it to be conserved, they think it matters. That's great, it's harnessed a huge amount of enthusiasm [interview with national biodiversity policy adviser, 2006]
>
> We take photographs of people and things we love, and we cherish those photographs, well the records are the same thing [. . .] I would never want anybody to draw moustaches on my photographs, you know, or to use them or not to love them [. . .]And so they're emotionally attached to it, and I think that we lose that and we forget that.
>
> *[interview with county biodiversity officer, Scotland, 2004]*

For LRC officers, this means that data management depends on maintaining good relationships with the recorders and recording societies:

> [At county level] it's a community. The NBN has taken out the whole relationship. They have assumed the LRCs will provide the data. But the recorders in [my county] would be upset if I passed on the data, it would completely ruin the relationship.
>
> *[interview with county LRC manager, England, 2004]*

Those working at local level recognised the importance of personal contacts, and to them it seemed that the NBN overrode those. Resentments were translated into conspiracy theories.

> A little group of men all got together, and they formed a steering committee . . . and then one day the NBN was born, and they presented it, fully handed out to the record centres without any consultation and it pretty much said "You will hand over all of your data to us" . . . It was top down, by people you can't contact that are scientists and professionals, and that you just don't know who's doing what.
>
> *[interview with county biodiversity officer, Scotland, 2004]*

The contrast with the description given by the NBN officer, of a 'grassroots product' and an 'open partnership' could hardly be greater. What could have gone wrong? To some extent the scale and complexity of data flows in the UK made it impossible to consult and inform all the stakeholders. Combined with the bureaucratic approach taken by the NBN, this meant it was a struggle to make everyone feel involved.

> Because they are bureaucrats they tend to think of things in terms of control from above, and so it was very important to keep reminding them that they were in a genuine partnership, not a legal one, but a genuine, mutual interest partnership to get this thing set up.
>
> *[interview with NBN trustee, March 2006]*

A more serious oversight was to miss the personal meaning that people attach to their recording activities, their connection with the organisms they observed, their hopes and aspirations for the use of the data, and the importance of local scale (Lawrence, 2005). One interview after another emphasized the importance of trust between recorders and users of data, or the absence of trust as a reason for withholding data.

Two other factors stoked the flames, factors which pulled in opposite directions: the increasing commercial significance of data, and the EIRs. The divisive feelings were often expressed as funding issues. Those LRCs dependent on consultants' payments for data felt threatened by the NBN – as they saw it, the consultants would simply be able to go to the national website and download the data for free. What had the NBN ever done for them, they wondered? Meanwhile their friends and competitors, the recording societies, saw no funds coming their way, and felt sidelined. Many of their more expert members worried that data would be available to unscrupulous individuals keen to find locations of rare plants or threatened bird species for illegal purposes.

In this delicate situation, the new legislation on freedom of information could hardly have come at a worse time. One NBN trustee described the EIRs as a 'sledgehammer', and noted that they 'cut across fragile and developing relationships between an already slightly sceptical voluntary sector and the NBN'. Again, suspicions were raised by lack of consultation. Most of the political attention to the EIRs focused on the public benefits of knowing about pollution sources and levels; the *disadvantages* of public access to biodiversity data had not been considered and recorders found that policy decisions had been formulated before they had realized the process was taking place. The National Federation of Biological Recording (which represents LRCs and recording societies) had a blunt reaction:

> The fundamental cornerstone of [the LRCs'] ability to [make information available] is **trust** between them and their data suppliers [. . .] which is **in jeopardy ...** There is a very real danger [of] wholesale **withdrawal of existing**

records ... breakdown of trust between landowners and LRC's [and] **wholesale plundering of data** for commercial purposes.

(NFBR, 2004, emphasis in original)

The cost to the NBN was enormous. The EIRs were already approved, and the only option left was to influence the way they were interpreted. The DEFRA guidance on exceptions to the public right of access to environmental information now makes clear that

> The Aarhus Convention, which contains the origins of the Directive on which the EIRs are based, protected information volunteered by a third party and required their consent to disclose it. Its purpose is to encourage the free flow of information from private persons to the government in order to protect the environment.
>
> *(DEFRA, 2007b)*

However, that was not clear to the recorders in 2004, and contributed to the difficult birth of the NBN.

Addressing the issues

Four years on, the situation had eased. As of 31 July 2008, the NBN Gateway (the web portal for accessing the database) announces 'There are currently 30,386,785 species records available on the NBN Gateway from 264 different datasets'. Data coverage and access is described as 'infinitely better than two years ago' by an NBN officer. Clearly, some organizations have been convinced it is a good thing.

The NBN conference in November 2007 was a showcase of partnerships between the NBN and LRCs or national recording societies. Whilst it is unlikely that the die-hard sceptics were present, the programme was an impressive range of case studies of developing relationships and data flow. It was clear that mutual perceptions had improved:

> LRCs once struggled to find a place and be sustainable and have now turned the corner.
>
> *[Keith Porter, Natural England, speaking at the 2007 NBN Conference]*

> We are the NBN. It's us talking to each other.
>
> *[Tim Corner, Bristol Environmental Records Centre, speaking at the 2007 NBN Conference]*

Many presenters were frank about their early doubts. There was overall a positive tone, bordering on the (self) congratulatory, but tensions were still detectable.

We have to remind some people it's a partnership not a competition.
And we still hear – 'why should I put my records on the NBN? I don't trust them.'
[Keith Porter, Natural England, speaking at the 2007 NBN Conference]

When the NBN wants 'our data', it's not 'our data', we are the custodians, and we're held back by individual personalities. A lot of people need more persuasion.
[comment from the audience, 2007 NBN Conference]

Some people still seem to think that data is power and as long as they have control over it they might make some money. But they are in a minority and we're finding ways round it.
[Steve Cham, British Dragonfly Society, speaking at the 2007 NBN Conference]

The politics of these tensions was also still evident, and polarizations between recording societies and LRCs emerged at times, as for example in the exchange after a presentation about the Dragonfly Recording Scheme (DRS):

DRS: most dragonfly records come to us so it's in the LRC's interest to share data. The LRC would lose out if it doesn't exchange readily.
Audience question: But won't the dragonflies lose out as they won't be taken into account in planning applications?

Since 2004 NBN staff and partners have done a great deal of work, both in developing relationships and in developing the technology to improve access and labelling of recorders' data. Workshops and national conferences have been a key part of the communication. But the 2007 conference showed above all that working one-to-one with individual LRCs and recording societies, to build confidence and positive experiences, is central to turning around negative perceptions and resistance.

As one NBN officer explained, their message has focused on the potential benefits to the partner, in helping them overcome the conflicting demands to fulfil their duty to disseminate data under the EIRs, and support their existence financially through the sale of data. The technology of the NBN is a great attraction: it acts as a 'shop window' for the LRCs, but also allows them to control access to the data. LRCs can show off the existence of their data, but require consultants to come directly to them to buy it.

Tim Corner from the Bristol Environmental Records Centre (BRERC) drew perhaps most attention at the 2007 conference. As he said at the start of his talk, BRERC's attitude used to be 'we provide full and free access to data to anyone in the world – except the NBN of course!' The NBN was perceived as a threat. BRERC now has nearly two million records on the Gateway.

How has this transition happened? Central to the success is the commercial interest of the record centre. Corner summarized the results in terms of income, data quality, professional satisfaction, status and relations. Income from consultants has approximately doubled, because they become more aware of the existence of the data through the NBN, and in England government support has also increased as a result of participating in the NBN. The quality of data has improved through contact with national experts, and, contrary to fears, some recorders have become more motivated to contribute by seeing their records on the NBN. BRERC and NBN are communicating clearly on issues of data accuracy, duplication of records and names. Public inquiries have also doubled, and BRERC staff report an improvement in status, and professional recognition.

In England, the future of the LRCs and their relationship with the NBN has started to look more secure. In 2008 they signed a three year memorandum of understanding with Natural England, the government agency responsible for biodiversity conservation. This provides funding to the LRCs to develop and hold data on habitats and species; and, importantly, requires them to feed data into the NBN.

Next steps

There was much attention at the 2007 NBN conference to 'keeping up with the times'. The guidance on implementing the EIRs, and the positive experiences of the past few years, have done much to calm fears about inappropriate data access, and data managers now routinely develop data exchange agreements with recorders, to make these aspects explicit.

Attention now is focused on efficiency, quality and technology. The experience of setting up the NBN has highlighted multiple and overlapping data flows, and the emergence of the LRC network now has to mesh with the more traditional data-gathering practices of the recording societies. This will help move towards complete UK coverage and a nationally consistent dataset, as well as maintaining current effort to allow analysis of change over time:

> Change is the most powerful piece of information any of us can use to talk to politicians.
>
> *[Keith Porter]*

At the same time, as more recorders from a wider range of backgrounds become involved, there are new concerns about data quality. Validation of species identification, for example, is an increasing challenge as increasing use of on-line surveys allows a wider public to contribute.

This challenge is associated with the wider one of information technology. Others have commented how changes in web-based technology have profoundly influenced participation and size of biological databases (Firbank *et al.*, 2003; Gouveia *et al.*, 2004). It does, however, bring challenges. Recorders who were happy to keep notes on cards or in notebooks can be discouraged by the task of data entry into computers, and there are calls for funded posts to support the specialist demands of computerized data exchange. Interviews and the 2007 NBN conference provided numerous cases where societies or LRCs had developed their own software, for example automated spreadsheets that made data entry easier. Issues arise over duplication of effort, or incompatibility of results. This area of recording, at least, seems to be a specialist one where paid posts will be required.

Other factors may affect the significance of voluntary recorders in the emerging structures. From an *ad hoc* process based on historically diverse and overlapping social groupings, we are now seeing an organized and structured arrangement of local and national government and non-government stakeholders. The NBN has been one catalyst for this process, along with revisions to the UKBAP itself (Lawrence and Molteno, in press). The wider context of a shift to thinking about ecosystem services has stimulated a change in focus to habitat data rather than species data. These data are more often collected by professionals than by volunteers because of the systematic and structured approach required (T. Butterworth, Natural England, personal communication). Volunteers will still be part of the picture, but the balance of interests may shift. These trends do not undermine however the important of the lessons learnt in the process of developing the NBN.

Conclusions

The experience of setting up the NBN has been fascinatingly human in its complexity and evolution. Its success depends on the motivation and good will of the (mostly voluntary) recorders. Attention to their motivations, perceptions and values is therefore essential. From the social point of view, the key lesson is that data represent power, but they also represent emotions and personal meaning.

Some of the start-up challenges that the NBN confronted were undoubtedly linked to communication in what had become a highly complex institutional landscape. New organizations, scales, types of volunteer, and data markets were all emerging. Recording schemes and societies, some with more than a century of history, were no longer the only actors in the field; the LRCs worked in a different way and with different purposes. The arrival of legislation that cut across the apparent interests of the recorders caused further consternation.

Looking back over eight years the development is remarkable. Apart from the technological advances, and accumulation of data that make the NBN Gateway a valuable biodiversity information tool, the NBN has negotiated its way through these social issues, succeeding through the shared enthusiasm and commitment of recorders and their underlying concern that data should be used to good effect. There has been a huge communication effort, helped by the fact that many individuals are members of several of the organizations involved (so NBN officers, for example, have experience as LRC managers, and also record voluntarily in their spare time). Above all, the strategy of developing partnerships with specific recording societies and LRCs, to provide concrete experience of data sharing, has provided the most convincing evidence to other recorders. The annual NBN conferences have supported a growing sense of combined purpose. It is this commitment to communication, building positive experience and willingness to reflect openly, that has underpinned the transformation of the national biodiversity network in the UK.

Acknowledgements

This chapter builds on work conducted while the author was a research fellow at the Environmental Change Institute, University of Oxford. I am grateful to Diana Liverman for an enlightened attitude to supporting exploratory research. Additional research was supported through a grant from the Netherlands, held in collaboration with Esther Turnhout, University of Wageningen. Many thanks to Tom Butterworth of Natural England for valuable comments on an earlier version of this chapter.

REFERENCES

Battersby, J. E. and J. J. D. Greenwood. (2004). Monitoring terrestrial mammals in the UK: past, present and future, using lessons from the bird world. *Mammal Review* **34**, 3–29.

Biodiversity Scotland (2008). Biodiversity Duty for Public Bodies. Scottish Government. Available at http://www.biodiversityscotland.gov.uk/pageType2.php?id=6&type=2&navID=28

Bowler, P. (2003). Identity crisis. In *The Guardian*, pp. 8–9. London.

BRISC (2006). *Biological Recording in Scotland: Strategic Business Plan 2006 – 2016.* Available at: http://www.brisc.org.uk/StrategicPlan06–16.pdf.

Burnett, J., C. Copp, and P. Harding (1995). *Biological Recording in the UK: Present Practice and Future Development.* Coordinating Commission for Biological Recording. Ruislip, England.

DEFRA (2006a). *Biodiversity Indicators – Working with the Grain of Nature – Taking it Forward: Volume II. Measuring Progress on the England Biodiversity Strategy:*

2006 Assessment. London: DEFRA. Available at: http://www.parliament.uk/documents/upload/postpn312.pdf.

DEFRA (2006b). *The UK Biodiversity Action Plan: Highlights of the 2005 Reporting Round*. Available at: http://www.defra.gov.uk/wildlife-countryside/pdfs/biodiversity/uk-bap-report.pdf#search=%22lbaps%20reporting%20round%202005%22.

DEFRA (2007a). *Conserving Biodiversity in a Changing Climate: Guidance on Building Capacity to Adapt*. London: DEFRA. Available at: http://www.ukbap.org.uk/Library/BRIG/CBCCGuidance.pdf.

DEFRA (2007b). *Environmental Information Regulations: Exceptions*. Available at http://www.defra.gov.uk/corporate/opengov/eir/guidance/full-guidance/pdf/guidance-7.pdf

DEFRA (2007c). *Guidance for Public Authorities on Implementing the Biodiversity Duty*. Available at http://www.defra.gov.uk/wildlife-countryside/pdfs/biodiversity/pa-guid-english.pdf

Firbank, L. G., C. J. Barr, R. G. H. Bunce *et al.* (2003). Assessing stock and change in land cover and biodiversity in GB: an introduction to Countryside Survey 2000. *Journal of Environmental Management* **67**, 207–218.

Flowerdew, J. R. (2004). Advances in the conservation of British mammals, 1954–2004: 50 years of progress with the Mammal Society. *Mammal Review* **34**, 169–210.

Gillett, S. and A. Lawrence, editors (2003). *Why Involve Volunteers in Biodiversity Monitoring? Summary of the BioWatch UK workshop, 20th October 2003. BioWatch UK Workshop*. Oxford, UK. Available at: http://www.eci.ox.ac.uk/research/humaneco/biowatch.php

Gouveia, C., A. Fonseca, A. Camara, and F. Ferreira (2004). Promoting the use of environmental data collected by concerned citizens through information and communication technologies. *Journal of Environmental Management* **71**, 135–154.

Greenwood, J. J. D. (2003). The monitoring of British breeding birds: a success story for conservation science? *Science of the Total Environment* **310**, 221–230.

Hartley, N. and C. Wood. (2005). Public participation in environmental impact assessment – implementing the Aarhus Convention. *Environmental Impact Assessment Review* **25**, 319–340.

Hopkins, G. W. and R. P. Freckleton (2002). Declines in the numbers of amateur and professional taxonomists: implications for conservation. *Animal Conservation* **5**, 245–249.

Key, R. S. (1993). The use of biological records to protect a Thames grazing marsh of national importance for invertebrates. In *The Proceedings of the NFBR Conference: Crises and Biological Records*, eds. A. Spalding and C. French, pp. 20–22. Redruth, Cornwall: Institute of Cornish Studies, University of Exeter.

Lawrence, A. (2005). Reluctant citizens? The disjuncture between participatory biological monitoring and participatory environmental governance. *Paper presented at the International Sociology Conference 'Environment, Knowledge and Democracy' 6–7 July 2005, Faculte des Sciences de Luminy, Marseilles, 2005*. Available at: http://www.eci.ox.ac.uk/research/humaneco/downloads/lawrence_marseille.PDF

Lawrence, A. (2006). "No Personal Motive?" Volunteers, biodiversity and the false dichotomies of participation. *Ethics, Place and Environment* **9**, 279–298.

Lawrence, A. and S. Molteno, in press. From rationalism to reflexivity? Reflections on change in the UK Biodiversity Action Plan. In *Reflexive Governance for Global Public Goods*, eds. E. Brousseau, T. Dedeurwaerdere and B. Siebenhüner. MIT Press.

Lawrence, A. and E. Turnhout (2005). Personal meaning in the public space: the bureaucratization of biodiversity data in the UK and the Netherlands. *RGS-IBG Annual Conference, London, 2005.*

Moss, S. (2004). *A Bird in the Bush: a Social History of Birdwatching.* London: Aurum.

NBN (2006). *The NBN concept,* vol. 2007. Available at www.nbn.org.uk

NFBR (2002). *The Status of Local Records Centres in the UK, 2002.* National Federation for Biological Recording. Available at www.nfbr.org.uk

NFBR (2004). *LRCs and the Draft Environmental Information Regulations Code of Practice.* National Federation of Biological Recording. Available at www.nfbr.org.uk/html/lrcs.html

Nicholson, E. (1931). *The Art of Bird-Watching.* London: Witherby.

Palmer, C. (2004). Functions of museums and record centres and how they have changed. Paper presented at the NFBR Conference. *National Federation of Biological Recorders Conference, 2–3 July 2004, Cardiff, 2004.*

Preston, C. D., M. G. Telfer, H. R. Arnold *et al.* (2002). *The Changing Flora of the UK.* London: DEFRA. Available at: www.defra.gov.uk/wildlife-countryside/ewd/flora/FlorainUK.pdf

Warren, R. D. and M. S. Witter. (2002). Monitoring trends in bat populations through roost surveys: methods and data from *Rhinolophus hipposideros. Biological Conservation* **105**, 255–261.

13

Improving forest management through participatory monitoring: a comparative case study of four community-based forestry organizations in the Western United States

HEIDI L. BALLARD, VICTORIA STURTEVANT AND
MARIA E. FERNANDEZ-GIMENEZ

Introduction

Community-based forestry (CBF) in the United States (USA) has taken a variety of forms, as resource-dependent communities attempt to balance local social, ecological and economic needs with the preferences of stakeholders outside the community. Although CBF is about more than biodiversity, stakeholders value it for different reasons. This has inspired some community-based organizations to use participatory biodiversity monitoring to assess the impacts of alternative forest restoration activities, address conflicting goals among stakeholders, restore trust and build community in rural areas undergoing rapid demographic and economic changes.

In this chapter we examine such projects in four CBF organizations (CBFOs) that participated in the Ford Community-Based Forestry Demonstration Program. First, we provide background information on community-based forestry in the USA, and some of the theories that informed this research. Then we present the ecological and social contexts and stewardship strategies of our four case study sites, followed by a detailed account of one participatory monitoring project undertaken by each group and the ecological and social outcomes. Finally, we discuss key challenges including the sustainability and replicability of these efforts.

Community-based forestry in the USA

The sustained yield model was the dominant forest management model in the twentieth century, focused on maximizing timber yields in perpetuity (Cortner

Taking Stock of Nature: Participatory Biodiversity Assessment for Policy, Planning and Practice, ed. Anna Lawrence. Published by Cambridge University Press. © Cambridge University Press 2010.

and Moote, 1994). However, forestry has undergone a profound transformation since the 1980s. In the western states, where much forested land is owned by the federal government, well-publicized environmental conflicts have effectively shut down timber production on federal lands. Globalization of the forest products industry has resulted in increased timber imports from overseas and disinvestment from forested lands and industries (World Forest Institute, 2004). Caught in the legislative and judicial battles between government agencies and powerful interest groups, rural communities have often had no voice in decisions that directly affect their livelihoods and well-being, and are cut off from the very resources that sustained their communities (Kusel and Adler, 2003; Sturtevant and Donoghue, 2007).

Furthermore, while the amount of forest cover in the USA has remained stable for several decades, the quality of forests has deteriorated (The Heinz Center, 2002; UNEP, 1999). As forest industries divest their lands, rural communities lose a source of livelihood and ecological systems suffer from 'cut and run' practices or conversion to development that fragments landscapes and attracts urban refugees (Hansen *et al.*, 2002; World Forest Institute, 2003). In many areas of the Western USA recently, wildfires have been abnormally severe owing in part to nearly 100 years of active forest fire suppression – a practice that is now acknowledged to jeopardize long-term forest health (Agee and Skinner, 2005; Pyne, 2004).

In response, community-based forestry (CBF) has emerged in the USA within the past two decades. Whilst it takes many forms, a shared tenet is that local communities are more likely than centralized government agencies or timber industries to be invested in sustainable management of forest assets that they depend upon directly (Child and Lyman, 2005). CBFOs complement, strengthen and sometimes replace the roles of government forestry agencies where decreasing staff and funding have led to a loss of management capacity (Cheng *et al.*, 2006).

Community participation in forest monitoring is therefore a response to cuts in government-sponsored monitoring programmes, the growing need for information on local environmental changes, increasing recognition by public lands agencies of the value and importance of including stakeholders in management processes, and a growing desire on the part of citizens to participate in management decisions that affect them (Moir and Block, 2001; Weber, 2003). The combination of data needs, declining agency resources, and increasing agency and community commitments to meaningful stakeholder participation opens the door for CBFOs to play a role in building local capacity to meet both restoration and monitoring needs.

Despite these opportunities, CBFOs in the USA face several obstacles (Cheng *et al.*, 2006). Their rural communities are often geographically, politically, economically and culturally isolated, and lack political and scientific legitimacy among established institutions. In cases where collaboration with public agencies is required, CBFOs must deal with unstable policy and agency operating environments. National environmental groups remain suspicious about rural people's commitment to stewardship on federal lands, contending that CBF efforts unfairly and illegally give disproportionate consideration to local stakeholders' preferences at the expense of national constituencies (Coggins, 1999; McCloskey, 1999). The increasing pressures for land development as more people move from urban areas into rural communities cause increases in cultural diversity and conflicting values among rural residents. Finally, CBFOs find it difficult to demonstrate their success in forest restoration, as measurable ecological impacts are not always immediately evident. The magnitude of the measurement challenge and the importance of overcoming it highlight the potential long-term significance of participatory monitoring by CBF groups. In the near term, participatory monitoring by CBF groups may play a key role in helping communities forge common understanding and experience among individuals who hold conflicting values or cultural norms. This chapter examines the evidence for these aspirations.

Community-based science

Community-based forestry in the USA seeks to move forest resource management from a top-down regulatory model to focus on community-based stewardship that engages citizens and experts in dialogue and learning about the complex and uncertain relationships within ecosystems. Civic science (Lee, 1993; Shannon and Antypas, 1996) refers to the democratization of science and its reorientation towards public dialogue and interpretation. Community science (Carr, 2004), takes an even more inclusive and radical approach, focusing on the interaction of community and scientific knowledge systems to address community-defined problems. These approaches challenge the traditional stance of science as objective knowledge situated outside of, rather than within, society. In these case studies, we assess the extent to which the potential ecological and social benefits of participatory monitoring have been realized by these CBFOs, explore the challenges they faced in implementing participatory monitoring, and describe how they used participatory monitoring as a means to integrate diverse forms of knowledge.

The Ford Community-Based Forestry Demonstration Project

Despite the growing literature on CBF in the USA (Aspen Institute, 2005; Baker and Kusel, 2003), few case studies keep pace with the theoretical debates about its efficacy and sustainability. Our chapter redresses this by focusing on four case studies. The US Ford Community-Based Forestry Demonstration Project applies the principles of community forestry in a context of land tenure arrangements very different from most other countries where it is practised. To both support CBF in the USA and to learn about how CBF can be an effective alternative to forest management and community development, the Ford CBF Demonstration Project funded 13 CBFOs for five years beginning in 1999. The 13 CBF groups typify different ways in which community organizations approach community-based forestry. They include membership organizations that serve a network of small private forest landowners in the Northeast and Southeast, organizations working with ethnically diverse communities of Latino forest workers in the Pacific Northwest or African American forest landowners in the Southeast, and organizations that work to facilitate forest restoration activities on federally owned public lands in the West.

In the last year of the Ford Community-Based Forestry Demonstration programme (2004), we were invited to research the experiences of the demonstration projects, focusing on the ecological inventory, monitoring and assessment activities. We collected data using a combination of on-site interviews and participant observation, telephone interviews, and document review. We visited each site at least once for three to five days of interviews and field tours, followed by visits as participant observers in monitoring activities. All of the leaders from the demonstration projects contributed to identifying key research questions, provided input and feedback on the research at key points throughout the process, and on several occasions participated in the interpretation of preliminary results.

Introduction to the four case studies

Ecological and social context

The four community-based organizations discussed in this chapter are the Jobs and Biodiversity Coalition (JBC) in Silver City, New Mexico; the Public Lands Partnership (PLP) in Delta, Colorado; Wallowa Resources (WR) in Joseph, Oregon; and the Watershed Research and Training Center (WRTC) in Hayfork, California. They are all located in coniferous forest-dominated landscapes in the US West, managed primarily by federal agencies. They all have significant

Table 13.1. *Ecological and social contexts of the four community forestry organizations*

	Jobs and Biodiversity Coalition (JBC)	Public Lands Partnership (PLP)	Wallowa Resources (WR)	Watershed Research and Training Center (WRTC)
Location	Silver City, New Mexico (Eastern New Mexico)	Delta, Colorado (Western Colorado)	Joseph, Oregon (Northeastern Oregon)	Hayfork, California (Northern California)
Ecological setting	Southwestern ponderosa pine forests	Western conifer forests, piñon-juniper woodlands, sagebrush-grassland rangelands	Western conifer forests, riparian habitat, rare native prairie rangelands	California mixed conifer forests, with some ponderosa pine, oak savannas and early-successional shrublands
Ecological threats	Altered fire regimes, poor logging practices	Altered fire regimes, non-native invasive species, habitat loss and fragmentation, erosion	Altered fire and flood regimes, non-native invasive species, habitat loss and degradation, fragmentation	Habitat degradation, altered fire regimes, history of poor logging practices
Land ownership setting	Public lands	Primarily public lands	Primarily public and some private lands	Primarily public lands and some private lands
Socio-economic setting	Formerly timber and mining-dependent, now low socio-economic levels, historic Spanish land grants	Rapid demographic change, increase in retirees, tourism and exurban development	Community in transition; cultural conflict over land and natural resource use; loss of middle class	Community in decline, increasing poverty
Socio-economic threats	Limited timber production on federal land; mine closures	Declining economic viability of land-based livelihoods	Limited timber production on federal land; declining institutional capacity	Limited timber production; mill closures; declining institutional capacity
Ethnic composition	Anglo, Hispano and Latino, Native American	Anglo and growing Hispano	Primarily Anglo, some Native American	Primarily Anglo, some Native American and Latino

natural assets; they work in productive, diverse, and often resilient ecosystems, and their landscapes encompass several large areas of intact, unfragmented habitat in public and private ownership. They all experience similar threats to ecosystems and livelihoods (Table 13.1), but had sufficient human and social capital to spawn and support a collaborative, community-based forestry organization to address the intertwined ecological and social challenges facing many western forests.

All four groups work in systems transformed by altered fire regimes, especially in forest types at lower elevations and on drier sites. Extensive, high-severity fires such as the 1987 fire in Hayfork, California, were a departure from the historic fire regime in the region (Agee and Skinner, 2005; Taylor and Skinner, 2003). Although fire is increasingly recognized as an important natural disturbance regime in many western forests, fires that burn more intensely and over larger areas than was historically typical threaten forest communities with loss of life and property, as well as lost income from forest products. In three of the four cases (PLP, WR and JBC), development has brought landscape fragmentation, habitat degradation and increasing populations of invasive, non-native plant species. These threaten the ecosystems, biodiversity and land-based livelihoods such as ranching, which play an important part in the local culture and economy of the communities where WR and PLP are located (Hansen *et al.*, 2002).

In the southwestern sites (PLP and JBC), invasive species such as cheatgrass (*Bromus tectorum*) are also associated with the increase in extensive, stand-replacing fires in ponderosa pine forest and piñon-juniper woodlands (Arno and Fiedler, 2005). Finally, past forest-management practices (fire-suppression, high-grading) significantly altered the structure and composition of forest stands in the study areas, affecting habitat quality for threatened and sensitive wildlife species (Hessburg, Agee and Franklin, 2005). Such impacts on habitat for species such as the northern spotted owl and salmon in the Pacific Northwest led to the infamous 'timber wars' of the early 1990s, and ultimately a dramatic change in forest management policy that reduced harvesting activities from nearly 10 billion board feet (bbf) off of federal forest lands to 3 bbf in 2000 (Arabis and Bowersox, 2004). Salvage logging emerged as a second hot-button issue in the mid 1990s, triggered by the increasing frequency, intensity and spatial extent of forest fires in the western USA, coupled with the loss of access to green timber as a result of changing forest policy. Proponents argued that salvage timber sales cleaned up the forests for replanting, reduced danger from falling snags, and allowed some economic benefit from the charred forest with modest ecological impacts. Opponents believed that the negative ecological impacts were underestimated and were deeply suspicious of policies that proposed expedited approval of salvage sales on public lands. Heated debate continues over the impacts of salvage logging (Beschta *et al.*, 2004) and appropriate methods for restoring stand structures and fire regimes of fire-adapted forests (Agee and Skinner, 2005, Noss *et al.*, 2006).

These polarizing conflicts over forest values and management formed the political and social context for the emergence of our four CBF case studies. In Wallowa County, where WR is located, effigies of regional environmental leaders were publicly burned and US Forest Service (USFS) facilities threatened with arson. Like Wallowa, the community of Hayfork suffered the loss of its local mill in the aftermath of the spotted owl decision, leaving this small remote forest community reeling and its children dependent on the free lunch programme in the public school (Danks, 2000). JBC and PLP stakeholders held widely diverging views on forest restoration goals and methods, and the acceptability of salvage logging after fires, creating conflicts in those regions. Active timber management on many public forests in the southwest ground to a near halt under the burden of environmental litigation and appeals challenging everything from grazing practices to salvage logging proposals.

These conditions gave rise to a new kind of community-based organization: community forestry organizations that sought to reconcile local land-based economic and social development with ecological stewardship and restoration of vulnerable or degraded forests, by bringing together diverse stakeholders to seek a common vision for their forests and communities.

Monitoring goals and projects

The four organizations shared a common goal of creating learning communities to better address the complex array of forest health and forest livelihood issues. They explicitly focused on the participation of local resource users whenever possible in inventory, monitoring and assessment. These participatory monitoring projects took two general forms: projects supported, co-ordinated, designed and/or implemented by the CBF organization solely; and projects in collaboration with federal and/or state agencies to highlight local goals, concerns and knowledge. The four organizations differed, however, in their ecological and social goals, and stewardship strategies and activities (Table 13.2). These differences influenced the range of monitoring projects implemented and the particular benefits, challenges and lessons learned.

Overall, the four CBF groups conducted 18 participatory monitoring and assessment projects which included watershed assessments, compliance and effectiveness monitoring for forest stand thinning treatments and salvage logging, invasive plant species inventory and monitoring, and non-timber forest

Table 13.2. *Social setting and goals, ecological goals and stewardship strategies of the four community forestry groups*

	JBC	PLP	WR	WRTC
Social goals	Build trust and support from environmental organizations and USFS for forest restoration prescriptions Create jobs from small diameter wood utilization Reduce conflict	Facilitate constructive dialogue about public land management Participate in public land management decision making Increase awareness of interdependence of local economies and landscapes Increase civic engagement and social learning	Build trust and support in community and USFS for forest restoration prescriptions Training, education and outreach Build contractor capacity and create jobs Civic science and social learning	Address conflict Build relationships among organizations and agencies Build contractor capacity Support traditional resource-based economy Civic science and social learning
Ecological goals	Achieve historic ponderosa pine forest structure and function through restoration rather than 'standard' fuel reduction Create wildlife habitat	Enhance and maintain diverse, healthy and viable environments Restore the link between livelihoods and the land	Understand and maintain natural variation Address causes as well as symptoms of degradation Use adaptive management Restore the link between livelihoods and the forest	Reduce risk of catastrophic fire Wildlife habitat enhancement Restore the link between livelihoods and the forest Use adaptive management
Stewardship strategies and activities	Natural process and restoration treatments on FS lands Small diameter wood utilization to provide markets for poles removed in treatments Monitoring of impacts of forest restoration treatments	Large-scale habitat restoration Small-scale experimental restoration projects Negotiation and monitoring of USFS projects Documentation of local ecological knowledge Fostering place attachment Forum for collaboration Participate in USFS planning process	Assessment and inventory Restoration and management projects (including fuel reduction) Monitoring, adaptive management and research Education (Grades K-12 and college level) Job generation	Manage public and private lands as a matrix of multiple patches with different goals, some wildlife, some fuels reduction Negotiation of USFS projects stewardship contracts Monitoring and adaptive management Community Fire Plan Forest products and jobs

product inventories. We found that local people (non-timber forest product harvesters, ranchers, loggers, Native American tribes, and other long-time resource
users, as well as other local residents) were involved in some way in all of the
18 projects studied, and that their local ecological knowledge contributed in
some way to the project outcome (management decisions) or products (reports
or manuals disseminated to outside organizations).

Strategies to involve local people

We describe briefly the monitoring programs of each group and then examine
in detail one specific project from each case. For each case, the socio-economic
and ecological settings and goals of the group (Table 13.1) influenced the monitoring objectives, stakeholders involved, methods and findings of the projects
studied (Table 13.2).

Watershed Research and Training Center's Post Mountain collaborative stewardship project

The WRTC in northern California implemented a variety of inventory and
monitoring projects over the course of the five years of the Ford CBF Demonstration Program. Early on they developed an Ecosystem Management Training
program for local people, particularly out-of-work loggers and mill workers,
to conduct inventory and monitoring of species and habitats of special concern
for federal agencies in the area using agency-designed protocols. In contrast,
the Chopsticks Project was designed and conducted solely by WRTC staff and
local residents to monitor the impacts of forest thinning and slash[1] treatments
on USFS land. Results surprisingly showed that a particularly popular treatment of the slash caused more damage to the soils than the thinning equipment.
WRTC used these results in the design of subsequent thinning projects on
USFS lands. Finally, WRTC co-ordinated a non-timber forest product (NTFP)
inventory and research project on National Forest lands with local medicinal
plant harvesters. They collaboratively designed and conducted the project to
identify the location and quantity of medicinal NTFP species, many threatened
or endangered, and assess the impacts of harvest. The results demonstrated that
several species existed in greater abundance and across a broader range than
previously documented, and that harvest had less impact on plant populations,
for several species, than previously believed.

---

[1] Cut branches and stems that remain after thinning.

Wallowa Resources' Upper Joseph Creek Watershed Assessment project

In northeastern Oregon WR also co-ordinated a number of assessment and monitoring projects with private landowners and public agencies. Several projects contracted with local people familiar with the landscape to monitor effectiveness of restoration methods in aspen stands and land bird habitat, primarily on private lands, and to build trust and credibility for WR. The results showed that fencing used to exclude herbivores (cattle and wildlife) was effective for aspen regeneration, but harmed some target bird species, and led to increased landowner participation in habitat restoration activities.

WR's Weed Monitoring programme tracks weed infestations in Wallowa County in a collaborative effort with agencies, The Nature Conservancy, and residents and ranchers, aiming to learn which mechanical and chemical treatments are most effective. The collaborative has been able to make recommendations about herbicide types, application timing and rates, and biocontrol insect releases, with local people's observations providing key data.

In a project similar to WRTC's Chopsticks Project, WR's Buck Stewardship Project included compliance and effectiveness monitoring to determine the impacts on soil compaction and ground vegetation of their forest stand thinning treatments. Designed by the USFS personnel, a consulting scientist, and WR staff and conducted by local contractors, the results showed no negative effects from 'light-on-the-land' logging treatments. This information reassured regional environmental organizations that logging treatments could be done without harm to soils.

In another example, Wallowa Resources arranged to conduct surveys for the federal agencies of threatened species, particularly lynx, grouse and eagles, through contracts with local people. These people have intimate local knowledge of the area, but are were not involved in setting the survey objectives, designing the methods, or analysing the results.

In 2003, WR completed the Upper Joseph Creek Watershed Assessment (UJCWA) on 174 000 acres of mountainous forest and grasslands across a patchwork of private and federal public lands. WR had wanted to develop a long-term restoration programme for the watershed as a whole but found that sound biophysical data was not available from federal agencies nor private landowners. WR therefore began working with the agencies and private landowners to design a complete watershed assessment to generate information needed for management on a watershed scale. They co-ordinated sub-committees for five resource categories: forest, range, riparian, wildlife and road/recreation use. Each included at least one local person with expertise in the resource in question (for example, a cattle rancher on the range committee, a forester on the forest committee, a hunter/tracker on the wildlife committee). In some cases a Nez Perce tribal member participated in the committees. In addition, one or more federal and state agency staff members, environmental interest groups, and professional scientists were also on committees. These committees designed the assessment protocol, collected the field data, and participated in analysing the results.

The results, analysis and preliminary recommendations from all five resource committees were presented as part of the Community Planning Process at an 'Integration Workshop' in March 2003. Participants then developed broader integrated recommendations for priority restoration project areas in the watershed. WR staff characterized this as a key component of the project, as the local ranchers and other resource users played an important 'ground-truthing' role when it was time to interpret the ecological data. Further, participants defined a framework for ongoing multiparty monitoring of project activities within the watershed, as well as longer-term monitoring of ecosystem functioning. The whole project involved over 70 residents and agency personnel, with 30 people working intensively on the resource sub-committees. At the time of writing, 115 acres in various forest management and riparian restoration projects had been completed on the watershed as a result of the UJCWA. Particularly, several USFS staff described how the information and recommendations that resulted from the UJCWA has been instrumental in prioritizing projects on the National Forest.

Public Lands Partnership's Burn Canyon project

A wildfire in 2002 scorched over 50 000 acres of oak and ponderosa pine woodlands in the foothills of the southern Rocky Mountains in western Colorado. As with many of the catastrophic fires that have ravaged Western US forests, debates immediately erupted between local community members who might benefit economically from salvage logging of the burned area, and environmental organizations concerned about environmental impacts of salvage logging. The PLP took this opportunity to facilitate a dialogue among community members, environmental groups and federal agencies through meetings and workshops to discuss Burn Canyon ecosystem health and management. Environmentalists eventually agreed not to appeal the salvage logging project if monitoring were implemented to assess the ecological effects of salvage logging. The diverse participants nominated scientists to help clarify the group's monitoring objectives, identify appropriate indicators, and craft a monitoring protocol the group could implement on its own, with participation from local interests and citizens. A retired USFS employee (and environmentalist) volunteered to collect data, which were analysed by a university researcher, who then presented the analysis at meetings of the Monitoring Working Group. The group discussed their interpretation of the data and planned to present their findings to a broader community meeting.

Through the course of the Burn Canyon monitoring project, PLP served as a conduit for voicing the concerns, values and knowledge of resource users to agencies in a genuine listening forum. PLP emphasized the participation of local people not only in planning and protocol development but also in data interpretation, enhanced by their experiential and observational knowledge. For example, ranchers with permits to graze on the burned public lands observed the spread of exotic species, loss of water and increased sediment after the fire, but also increased presence of wildlife in the salvage logging areas. Monitoring demonstrated little difference in effect on soils or most understorey plant species abundance and diversity in the logged and un-logged areas, but showed an invasive species (cheatgrass) is more abundant in logged areas. This information may influence invasive plant management, and PLP hopes to apply its learning from this project to other community-based monitoring projects in the area.

Jobs and Biodiversity Coalition's Mill Site project

The JBC in eastern New Mexico has designed and implemented two forest stand thinning treatments in order to reduce fuel loads and risk of catastrophic fire, on the Mill Creek Site on the Gila National Forest, including effectiveness monitoring to quantify thinning treatments and measure impacts on understorey plants and soils. In both cases, a local person served as monitoring co-ordinator and collaborated with the high school science teacher to train selected students to collect data. Thus far the data show that the treatments are effective in achieving the desired basal area (volume of remaining trees), which allays concerns of both the USFS and environmental organizations, and furthermore that treatments cause little change to understorey plants or soils. The information was included in reports for federal agencies and regional groups working with the Collaborative Forest Restoration Project of the Forest Service in the Southwest. JBC has used the information to iteratively design other forest stand thinning projects.

In 2002, the JBC began work with the USFS's Collaborative Forest Restoration Program (CFRP) to develop a forest thinning treatment for one unit (68 acres) of the Gila National Forest, aiming to create forest structure that allowed low-intensity fire to burn through the stands, restoring historic fire-adapted ecosystem processes. A major concern was to minimize ground disturbance and soil compaction, and to create habitat for wildlife. JBC leaders wanted to determine if they could achieve the basal area desired by the USFS but also create more clumping of trees considered to be effective wildlife habitat. A monitoring co-ordinator hired by CFRP worked with the JBC leaders to adapt an existing monitoring protocol for ponderosa pine forest common across the region. Indicators corresponding to changes in forest structure include tree density, species composition, size, basal area, canopy cover. Indicators for wildlife habitat included snags (standing dead trees used by wildlife) and downed logs. Ground vegetation was also measured, since fine fuels are needed to carry a surface fire and provide cover for wildlife. High school students were trained to collect data over three summers under supervision of the monitoring co-ordinator. Data collection therefore cost only the co-ordinator's salary, while students were educated about methods and local ecology.

The results were compiled and analysed by the monitoring co-ordinator. They showed that the basal area desired by the USFS was achieved using JBC treatment methods while also leave clumps of trees for wildlife. They also found little effect on soils or understorey cover. This information was presented in a report to the JBC leaders, the other groups participating in the CFRP, regional environmental groups and the USFS, and was used to design other thinning projects conducted by JBC on National Forest lands.

It is interesting that JBC used formal data to verify what they believed they already knew about the impacts of their work in the woods. However, while the Forest Service and environmentalists agree on the overall objective of restoring a fire-adapted ecosystem, debate continues on the appropriate basal area required to achieve this goal. JBC has tended to look very carefully within an individual stand, whereas the USFS looks at variation among stands across a large landscape. According to the JBC leaders, the multiparty discussions about designing and monitoring their restoration project were more important than the monitoring data because of the trust built between parties.

Ecological benefits of participatory monitoring for four CBF groups

For the four projects described above, it is generally too early in the process to determine the long-term ecological benefits as measured on the ground. However, CBFOs used the knowledge gained through participatory monitoring in several ways. Each of the CBF groups used written reports or field tours to help design their next monitoring projects and, in most cases, to design future management activities, effectively closing the loop in an adaptive management framework. As one WRTC staff member explained, 'What we did at Chopsticks changed the prescriptions . . . we had enough decision space to change based on what we learned. That was pretty fun'.

In all cases, the monitoring information was provided to the federal management agencies working with the CBF groups, and in some cases agencies altered their land management plans and projects. The ecological implications of the assessment project are easier to identify than those of the monitoring projects, as the assessment provided a snapshot in time that can be used to plan projects immediately, whereas monitoring projects have been going on for a short time, or are localized and site-specific so it is more difficult to see ways in which this information was acted upon.

Social benefits of participatory monitoring by four CBF Groups

For all four CBF monitoring projects, participants emphasized the important changes and improvements in social relationships and institutional relationships between the CBF group, the public lands agencies and the environmental groups. Bliss *et al.*, (2001) explains that 'By engaging citizens to work together on shared objectives, monitoring can help build "social capital", cooperative, interdependent relationships that comprise the foundation of community'. In rural areas experiencing dramatic demographic changes creating communities with very diverse land use values, building social capital can be crucial. In addition, because the CBF groups specifically focused on including local people in monitoring projects and explicitly valuing local knowledge, social relationships between CBF groups and scientists, whether university or agency scientists, were created or enhanced. Local knowledge was incorporated into monitoring reports to agencies and environmental groups where it generally hasn't been included before, further strengthening these relationships.

Monitoring helped local participants to appreciate the complexity of ecosystems and the difficulty of obtaining complete and reliable data. Several participants in the PLP projects described how they increased local people's understanding of the scientific process and of the ecosystem of which they were a part 'The environmentalists knew that salvaging timber was going to be damaging . . . and the . . . timber industry [opinion]) was that salvage logging had no impact at all. What we see is, . . . it's right in the middle, it's not either. It's not a huge impact, but there is an impact'.

CBFOs used participatory monitoring as a community-building strategy to alter social attitudes and assumptions as well as build trust. A WR staff member pointed out that once the various stakeholders went into the forest and worked on the UJCWA together, opinions converged based on data they could all use, rather than (as previously) competing data sets and science. Several CBFO staff saw participatory monitoring as a direct and tangible way to 're-connect' people with the land in a way that had not been accomplished by the standard protocol of stakeholder meetings conducted with paper flip charts and presentations projected onto a screen.

Trust was also built between the CBFOs and the agencies and environmentalists, even where this was not the explicit goal of the monitoring project. A JBC participant talked of the importance of the collaborative aspect of project design and monitoring in building trust and credibility with outside environmental groups. Previously it had been common for the regional environmental groups to sue the USFS to stop similar forest thinning projects. The process used by JBC, in which an environmental group leader was involved in designing the monitoring project, helped avert any law suits on their forest thinning projects. The monitoring data JBC gathered was also important in maintaining credibility with the USFS, since it showed that the JBC project met the standards of the typical agency forest stand thinning prescriptions.

Incorporating local ecological knowledge

The manner in which local knowledge holders were involved varied across projects and influenced how their knowledge was incorporated. Some approaches were consistent with those reported in the literature (Moller *et al.*, 2004; Wilson *et al.*, 2006). For example, WRTC, WR and PLP each formed monitoring committees or advisory groups in some of their projects, made up of scientists, managers and communities members with local knowledge (cf. Fernandez-Gimenez, Huntington and Frost, 2006). However, in five of the 18 projects, local people were involved only in data collection, following protocols they did not design (e.g. WR's lynx, grouse and eagle surveys). In five projects, the primary source of local knowledge was the CBF group's staff members. For example, JBC's leaders set the objectives and design of the Mill Creek Projects, along with USFS personnel, while local high school students (who were fairly unfamiliar with the ecology of the landscape) and their teacher collected the data. In this case, 'local knowledge' is represented by a very small and self-selected group of locals.

However, the remaining eight projects included a combination of local people collecting data, large contributions of local knowledge from CBF staff, and/or explicit and direct involvement of local people in the planning, assessment and interpretation of monitoring results of their stewardship projects.

These projects exhibited most clearly the explicit use of local ecological knowledge through the participation in most phases of a variety of knowledge holders. Two projects documented local ecological knowledge as a primary focus of the project; PLP conducted an oral history project to document local residents' and ranchers' knowledge of land use history and effects of fire; and WRTC collaborated with local harvesters of medicinal plants to conduct a NTFP inventory of the neighbouring Trinity-Shasta National Forests. Finally, five projects sought out participants or representatives from local Native American tribes and attempted to incorporate traditional ecological knowledge (TEK) into the project. Members of several California Indian tribes were involved in WRTC's NTFP inventory, and WR ensured that Nez Perce tribal members were on several resource sub-committees of the UJCWA.

In all cases, rather than seeing scientists and managers use local people for token local ecological knowledge, we saw local people in CBF groups hiring scientists and facilitating monitoring projects on their own terms. This kind of power-sharing was consistent with the findings of Fernandez-Gimenez *et al.* (2006) in the Alaskan Beluga Whale Committee, and contrasts with experiences of typical power relations between locals and scientists (Nadasdy, 1999).

Challenges and costs of participatory monitoring

Challenges to participatory monitoring by CBFOs fall into several categories: resources, participation and communication, and technical and institutional hurdles. Funding, time and labour were often the limiting resources in conducting any kind of monitoring, and since participatory monitoring took more time, it often demanded more funding and labour, as well. In several cases, a large amount of CBF staff time was required to work with local people, or grants had to be raised solely for the purpose of monitoring.

One of the concerns about efforts to integrate knowledge is whether or not the local community members really benefit from the project or are just being co-opted by outside groups, whether federal agencies, environmental groups, or research scientists (Fernandez-Gimenez *et al.*, 2006; Nadasdy, 1999). One important way that the local community can benefit is by learning of the results of the monitoring work. Overall, most CBF groups communicated monitoring results formally or informally to the people involved with the group, and in some cases, to the broader community. The efforts that CBF groups make to share their information compare favourably with those of public land management agencies like the USFS and BLM, which often do not communicate monitoring data at all, except perhaps to permittees or contractors directly affected by the results. However, one CBFO staffer admitted that in general, the group's monitoring results were not well communicated; sometimes the contractor who collected the data only gave one public lecture. A major constraint to formal communication back to the community was lack of funding.

On the whole, few of the CBF groups enlisted a large portion of their local communities to participate in the monitoring projects, so new knowledge, skills and wages were not widely distributed. Much of the work was conducted by CBF staff who were former resource professionals and were trained to do the monitoring work. In JBC's area, the community includes many Hispano residents, none of whom participated in the monitoring project. Several of the CBFOs described difficulty in getting or maintaining participation by key stake-holders (e.g. environmental groups, Native American tribes, some agencies), over-reliance on specific individuals (e.g. a dedicated volunteer with specific knowledge, a visiting scientist), and the general difficulty in mobilizing and maintaining long-term volunteer commitment to monitoring.

The CBFOs all described their struggle to determine an acceptable level of scientific rigour for community monitoring projects, an issue that plagues many citizen monitoring programmes in the USA (Nicholson, Ryan and Hodgkins, 2002). CBF organizations often lacked technical expertise in monitoring design and protocols; to address this they all worked with consultants and researchers to help them design monitoring projects and analyse data. For WR and WRTC, working across several agency jurisdictions created the challenge of differing monitoring methods among agencies. Furthermore, involving many people in monitoring design occasionally led to confusion about the objectives and protocols for the project.

Issues of sustainability and replicability

For many of these CBF groups, participatory monitoring addresses issues of sustainability by increasing the local capacity of people to work with scientists, to gain scientific knowledge for their own use, to use science to communicate to outside groups about what their land management outcomes are, and to integrate their own local knowledge with conventional scientific knowledge to ultimately manage the forests better. Monitoring therefore contributes to the sustainability of these CBFOs. However, almost all the projects only last as long as the grant funding. Two groups, JBC and WR, have designated a full-time staff member to co-ordinating monitoring projects for several years, whose sole charge is to develop and conduct monitoring projects for the group. WR has integrated a monitoring component into almost every project, prioritizing science as a bridge between conflicting stakeholder groups, such that monitoring and assessment have become part of their standard operating procedure. WRTC and PLP have similarly prioritized monitoring as an integral part of what they do, but remain dependent on grant funding.

Recruiting volunteer participants in monitoring projects is a continual and uphill task. The main active volunteer in PLP's Burn Canyon monitoring project is elderly and there are no new recruits to succeed him. In the larger picture, some question the sustainability of the CBF groups themselves, because they rely on enthusiastic, knowledgeable leaders who continually renew the community's commitment to creative approaches to improved forest management, monitoring, and economic development. These leaders are all working to build human resources and capacity within their organizations to continue innovating. For example, while WRTC and WR may have relied on one very capable executive director early on, both organizations now have multiple long-serving leaders in each area of focus for the groups, such as education and outreach, monitoring, and forest management activities.

The sustainability of these projects also lies in their relationships with other organizations. Many of the monitoring projects were catalysed by environmental groups seeking evidence to address their concerns about the forest management activities of the CBF group and agencies; however, the environmentalists often did not follow-through by participating in the entire monitoring process. If monitoring is a priority for these environmental groups, it may be necessary for them to contribute more to the process and funding of monitoring projects by CBF groups in the future to help ensure that CBF stewardship projects include a monitoring component.

Such projects may also require more collaboration with agencies for their ability to contribute infrastructure and scientific capacity and prioritization by agencies. Nearly all the projects described above had USFS personnel on the monitoring committee.

In examining the projects across the four cases, it became clear that they operate best at small scales and in very site-specific ways. This has implications for whether their participatory monitoring projects could be replicated in other sites or contexts. On the whole, these projects provide many lessons but perhaps should not be used as templates. However, if we look at the more general goals of the projects and the roles played by each organization, several projects could be used as models to guide other monitoring projects in similar contexts. For example, the approach used by WR to assemble resource sub-committees in their UJCWA is a potential model for other groups working at a landscape scale with multiple resources and multiple stakeholders.

In addition to being models themselves, the groups used models from other community-based natural resource management programmes with similar vegetation. For their Mill Site monitoring projects, JBC used handbooks produced by the USFS CFRP used throughout the southwest in areas dominated by ponderosa pine forest. The WRTC used a very structured process created by Wondolleck and Yaffee (2000) to facilitate the Post Mountain Collaborative Stewardship monitoring sub-committee, whereby the group created their own definition of forest health, and identified objectives, criteria, indicators and measures for their monitoring plan. This formation of a monitoring committee could be used as a model for groups working across a patchwork of private and federal forest lands in the West.

Conclusions and implications

For these four case examples of participatory monitoring in the USA, the social outcomes and processes of the monitoring projects have been as important as the ecological information produced. Participatory monitoring brought together conventional scientists and local people to share and integrate their knowledge of the forest, probably providing a more complete picture of the effects of resource management. This improved the information available but also laid the foundation for continued co-learning about the ecosystem for scientists and local people. Collaboration on the monitoring projects across multiple stakeholder groups allowed people from within and outside the local area to come to a common understanding about how the ecosystem functioned, how different forest management treatments affected the understorey and soils, and how multiple visions of forest use and conservation could be accommodated. Improving forest management through participatory monitoring may therefore come not as much from the biological information gathered, but from the social relationships built and processes that occur along the way.

These social outcomes of CBFOs' monitoring have implications when placed in an international context and when compared with participatory monitoring in developing countries. The Ford CBFO projects are located in areas of the USA defined by poverty, lack of access to state services, and dependence on natural resources; to some degree their situation is similar to those in developing countries. While all of these projects have conservation of biodiversity as a major goal, the participatory monitoring by these CBF groups was not driven by conservation organizations from outside the community. Instead, it was driven by rural development organizations from inside the community. In this way, biodiversity and ecological monitoring were a *vehicle* for these organizations to prove that their community-based forestry approaches to rural economic development is effective. The monitoring was often used to communicate the benign environmental impact of their activities to environ-mental groups and public lands agencies, and to communicate the economic viability of the projects to the agencies and local community.

The implications of this participatory monitoring for the conservation of biodiversity on a large scale may be slight. On a small scale, however, this work may slowly be changing the way public agencies, environmental groups, and rural communities in the USA learn about and conduct forest management. Small-scale, site-specific monitoring, with participation from local resource users, youth, environmentalists, and scientists, is a vast improvement over the former system, where either no monitoring was done, or done over such a large landscape at a coarse level that information couldn't be used at the stand level or for management decisions. Participatory monitoring by CBFOs has changed the social, political, and economic relationships between these small rural communities, environmental organizations and federal lands agencies. In every case, the federal lands agencies have become more collaborative and responsive to innovative forest restoration and management practices as a result of CBFO-facilitated monitoring projects. Forest restoration projects have moved forward without litigation from environmental groups in unprecedented ways, partly because of the process and products of the participatory monitoring projects. By enacting community science and civic science, CBF groups may be slowly democratizing the way public lands agencies conduct and use science to manage their forests.

Acknowledgements

We are grateful to the staff and partners of the five community-based organi-zations who contributed their expertise, time and energy participating in this research. We would also like to thank the Ford Foundation Community-Based Forestry Demonstration Program for funding the research on which this chapter was based.

REFERENCES

Agee, J. K. and Skinner, C. N. (2005). Basic principles of forest fuel reduction treat-ments. *Forest Ecology and Management* **211**, 83–96.

Arabis, K. and Bowersox, J. (2004). *Forest Futures: Science, Politics, and Policy for the Next Century*. Lanham: Rowman and Littlefield Publishers.

Arno, S. F. and Fiedler, C. E. (2005). *Mimicking Nature's Fire*. Washington, D.C.: Island Press.

Aspen Institute (2005). *Growth Rings: Communities and Trees*. Washington, D.C.: Aspen Insitute.

Baker, M. and Kusel, J. (2003). *Community Forestry in the United States: Past Practice, Crafting the Future*. Washington, D.C.: Island Press.

Beschta, R. L., Rhodes, J. R., Kauggman, J. B. *et al.* (2004). Postfire management on the forested public lands of the western United States. *Conservation Biology* **18**(4), 957–967.

Bliss, J., Aplet, G., Hartzell, C. *et al.* (2001). Community-based ecosystem monitoring. *Journal of Sustainable Forestry* **12**(3–4), 143–167.

Carr, A. J. L. (2004). Why do we all need community science. *Society and Natural Resources* **17**, 841–849.

Cheng, A. S., Fernandez-Gimenez M. E., Ballard H. L. *et al.* (2006). *Ford Foundation Community-Based Forestry Demonstration Program Research Component Final Report*. New York: Ford Foundation.

Child, B. and Lyman, M. W. (2005). Introduction: natural resources as community assets. In *Natural Resources as Community Assets: Lessons from Two Continents*, eds. B. Child and M. W. Lyman. Madison, WI: Sand County Foundation.

Coggins, G. C. (1999). Regulating federal natural resources: a summary case against devolved collaboration. *Ecology Law Quarterly* **25**, 602–610.

Cortner, H. J. and Moote, M. A. (1994). Trends and issues in land and water resources management: Setting the agenda for change. *Environmental Management* **18**(2), 167–173.

Danks, C. (2000). Community forestry initiatives for the creation of sustainable rural livelihoods: a case from North America. *Unasylva* **51**(202), 53–63.

Fernandez-Gimenez, M. E., Huntington, H. P. and Frost, K. J. (2006). Integration or cooptation? Traditional knowledge and science in the Alaska Beluga whale committee. *Environmental Conservation* **33**(4), 306–315.

Hansen, A. J., Rasker, R., Maxwell, B. *et al.* (2002). Ecological causes and consequences of demographic change in the New West. *BioScience* **52**(2), 151–162.

The Heinz Center (2002). *The State of the Nation's Ecosystems*. Cambridge, England: Cambridge University Press.

Hessburg, P. F., Agee, J. K. and Franklin, J. F. (2005). Dry forests and wildland fires of the inland Northwest USA: contrasting the landscape ecology of the pre-settlement and modern eras. *Forest Ecology and Management* **211**, 117–139.

Kusel, J. and Adler, E. (eds.) (2003). *Forest Communities, Community Forests: Struggles and Successes in Rebuilding Communities and Forests*. Landham, MD: Rowman and Littlefield.

Lee, K. N. (1993). *Compass and Gyroscope, Integrating Science and Politics for the Environment*. Washington, D.C.: Island Press.

McCloskey, M. (1999). Local communities and the management of public forests. *Ecology Law Quarterly* **25**(4), 624–629.

Moir, W. H. and Block, W. M. (2001). Adaptive management on public lands in the United States: commitment or rhetoric. *Environmental Management* **28**(2), 141–148.

Moller, H., Berkes, F., O'Brian Lyver, P. and Kislalioglu, M., eds. (2004). Combining science and traditional ecological knowledge: monitoring populations for co-management. *Ecology and Society*, **9**.

Nadasdy, P. (1999). The politics of TEK: power and the integration of knowledge. *Arctic Anthropology* **36**, 1–18.

Nicholson, E., Ryan, J. and Hodgkins, D. (2002). Community data – where does the value lie? Assessing confidence limits of community collected water quality data. *Water Science and Technology* **45**, 193–200.

Noss, R. F., Franklin, J. F., Baker, W. L., Schoennagel, T. and Moyle, P. B. (2006). Managing fire-prone forests in the western United States. *Frontiers in Ecology and the Environment* **4**(9), 481–487.

Pyne, S. J. (2004). *Tending Fire: Coping with Americia's Wildland Fires*. Washington D.C.: Island Press.

Shannon, M. A. and Antypas, A. R. (1996). Civic science is democracy in action. *Northwest Science* **70**(1), 66–69.

Sturtevant, V. E. and Donoghue, E. M. (2007). Forest community connections: continuity and change. In *Forest Community Connections*, eds. V. E. Sturtevant and E. M. Donoghue. Washington D.C.: Resources for the Future.

Taylor, A. H. and Skinner, C. N. (2003). Spatial patterns and controls on historical fire regimes and forest structure in the Klamath Mountains. *Ecological Applications* **13**(3), 704–719.

UNEP (1999). *Global Environment Outlook 2000*. New York: United Nations Environment Programme.

Weber, E. P. (2003). *Bringing Society Back In*. Cambridge, MA: The MIT Press.

Wilson, D. C., Raakjaer J. *et al.* (2006). Local ecological knowledge and practical fisheries management in the tropics: a policy brief. *Marine Policy* **30**, 794–801.

Wondolleck, J. M. and Yaffee, S. L. (2000). *Making Collaboration Work: Lessons from Innovation in Natural Resource Management*. Washington, D.C.: Island Press.

World Forest Institute (2003). *Who Will Own the Forest? Origins and Implications of Changing Ownership*. Portland, OR: World Forest Institute.

World Forest Institute (2004). *Who Will Own the Forest? Globalization and Consolidation Effects on Forests*. Portland, OR: World Forestry Institute.

Index

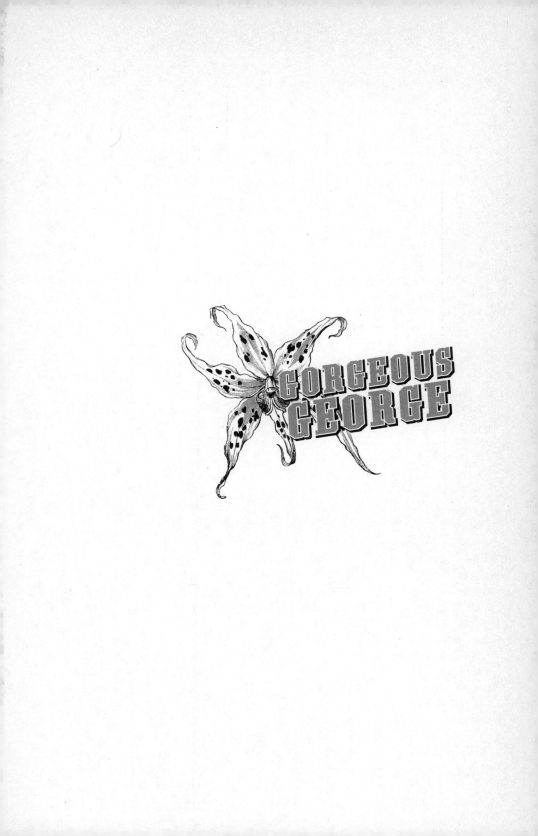

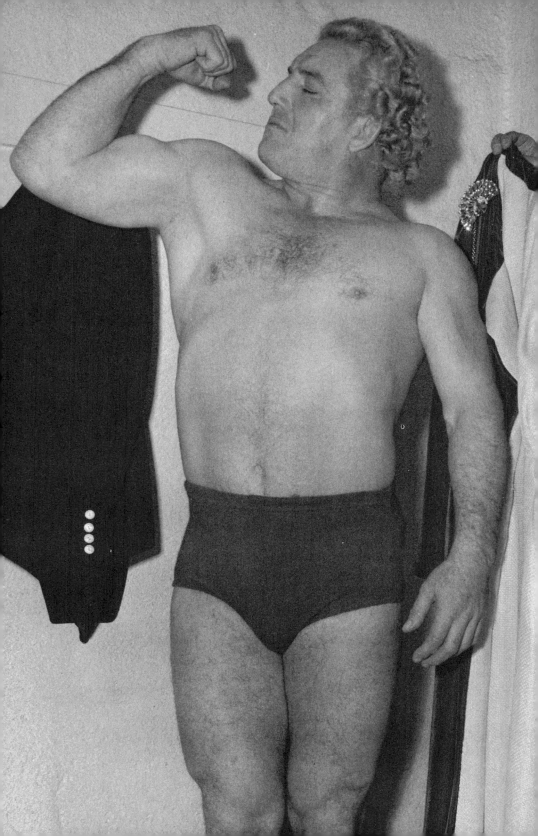

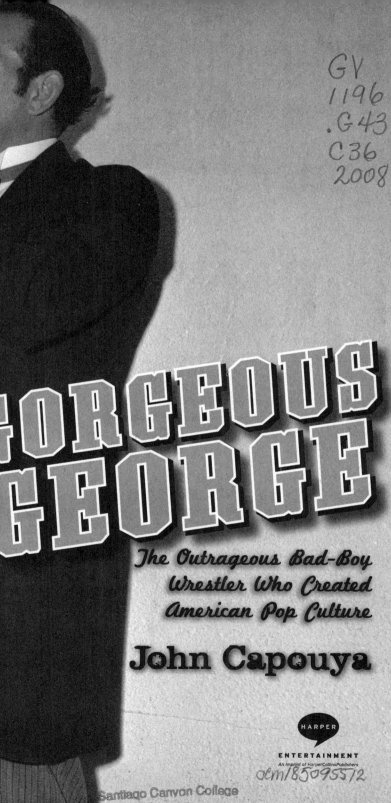

GORGEOUS GEORGE

The Outrageous Bad-Boy
Wrestler Who Created
American Pop Culture

John Capouya

HARPER

ENTERTAINMENT
An Imprint of HarperCollinsPublishers

HarperCollins books may be purchased for educational, business, or sales promotional use. For information please write: Special Markets Department, HarperCollins Publishers, 10 East 53rd Street, New York, NY 10022.

FIRST EDITION

Designed by Timothy Shaner, nightanddaydesign.biz

Library of Congress Cataloging-in-Publication Data

Capouya, John, 1956–

Gorgeous George : the outrageous bad-boy wrestler who created american pop culture / John Capouya — 1st ed.

    p. cm.

ISBN 978-0-06-117303-5

1. George, Gorgeous, 1915–1963.   2. Wrestlers—United States—Biography.   I. Title.

GV1196.G43C36 2008

796.812092—dc22   2007051749

[B]

08 09 10 11 12 WTC/RRD 10 9 8 7 6 5 4 3 2 1

To my mother and father

ON THE
GORGEOUS ONE:

"A mighty spirit. Crossing paths with Gorgeous George was all the recognition and encouragement I would need for years to come."
—BOB DYLAN

"The capes I wear? That came from the rassler, Gorgeous George. Seeing him on TV helped to create the James Brown you see onstage."
—JAMES BROWN, THE LATE GODFATHER OF SOUL

"I saw fifteen thousand people comin' to see this man get beat. And his talking did it. I said this is a gooood idea!"
—MUHAMMAD ALI

"I don't know if I was made for television, or television was made for me."
—GORGEOUS GEORGE

CONTENTS

PRELUDE

There was time, the wrestler thought, for one last look in the mirror. It was a thought that came to him often; not just out of vanity, but due also to a lingering disbelief at what he saw there.

A few short years ago, he saw George Wagner. His hair was dark, nearly black. He was handsome with rugged features, a muscular athlete in his twenties with strongly defined biceps, a broad back, and imposing V-shaped thighs. In the late 1930s and early 1940s he looked earnest and uncomplicated, like an ambitious professional wrestler— not the biggest at five-foot-nine or -ten and 185 pounds—who's trying hard but hasn't quite made it yet. His good looks and appealing mien made him a "babyface," the wrestling term for the grappler who plays the good guy in the ring, as opposed to the villain, or "heel." Like all wrestlers of that era, he wore plain dark trunks and black shoes.

On this night in 1949 he sees Gorgeous George. Standing before a full-length mirror in the locker room at the Olympic Auditorium in Los Angeles, the man has been transformed. He still carries the same Wagner body, but now it's covered, made practically irrelevant, by his shining, floor-length, quilted pink satin robe. The lining and lapels are a contrasting bright yellow silk; on the robe's shoulders are epaulets of glimmering sequins. A writer here tonight to write a feature on George for *Sport* magazine declares that "Any woman in town would give her teeth for it." Around his throat George has wrapped a scarf, also silk, shiny, and pink. Peeking out from under the robe's bottom hem are his small, almost dainty, size-eight-and-a-half feet in white patent-leather wrestling boots.

His hair, too, is strikingly—wildly—different. What was short, dark, and straight is now a shrieking platinum blond, long on the sides and in the back. It's set in a woman's hairdo of myriad curls and waves known as the "marcel." Every wrestling fan and practically anyone with a television set knows that this style was created for him by Frank and Joseph of Hollywood. George has a big head; as generations of actors and news anchors will go on to prove, this is an asset on the TV screen. With the halo of bright curls surrounding it, his head looks positively massive, floating above the bright pink expanse of his robe. Through oversight or intention his eyebrows are still dark, though that odd detail may be the least startling thing about him.

His demeanor, his affect, is jarringly different. Gone is the determined seriousness, the willingness and eagerness to please. Still watching himself in the mirror, George draws himself up higher, puffing out his chest and cocking his head upward in a parody of imperial haughtiness. He's become some queenly brute, a pampered, pompous glamour puss with a world-class attitude. Gorgeous George now insists on being introduced in the arenas as the Toast of the Coast and the Sensation of the Nation; he also likes to be called the Human Orchid, a sobriquet meant to indicate that he's a flower of rare and delicate beauty. Fittingly, the prima donna of the mats will appear on the TV show *Queen for a Day*. Soon he will codify this transformation by legally changing his name from George Wagner to Gorgeous George. Between the black-haired nights of the past and tonight's post–World War II platinum spectacle, another change has taken place as well: Unlike his previous incarnation, the Gorgeous One is a rich and famous man.

Now thirty-five years old, George the sissified brute has become the ultimate wrestling villain, the (questionable) man the fans love to hate. When he parades slowly and regally to the ring a bit later, his bearing is disdainful amid the fans' catcalls, whistles, and boos, that of an exalted personage who, through some misfortune, finds himself among the basest commoners. "Peasants!" he spits out. The "mat addicts," as the sporting press likes to call them, hurl wadded-up programs, peanuts, coins, and even lit cigarettes at the heel. When he reaches the border around the ring, the apron, George turns and faces his tormentors. "You're all ignorant peasants!" he informs them, waving his right arm away dismissively. For good measure he declares: "You're beneath contempt!" This brings absolute roars from the crowd.

Back in the locker room, before George's entrance, a taller, thinner, balding man appears in the mirror behind him, wearing a long black morning coat with tails. This mustachioed gentleman plays the role of manservant or valet, a dignified Jeeves-like character who goes by the name Jeffrey Jefferies. Over the years there will be many different valets, including several iterations of Jefferies, before George turns the helpmate role over to his second wife. He calls her his "valette," pronounced *val-et-tay,* which he blithely tells everyone is the "correct French way to say it." The valet helps settle the gleaming satin robe across the wrestler's broad shoulders. George tells reporters, who breathlessly relay this information to the public, that he has eighty-eight of these custom-made creations. It's the valet's job—privilege, really—to keep a chart of which ones the master wears when, so he doesn't appear in the same finery twice in any one venue. One night it's the silver lamé and the next it might be the lace number, the one with apple blossoms sewn on its bodice, or the gown with the protruding bustle made of lavender turkey feathers. Or perhaps one of several gowns trimmed with ermine at the cuffs and collars. George recently held forth before a throng of reporters on just which furs might be adequate to grace the Gorgeous corpus. "Mink is so mediocre," he declared. "I will wear nothing less than ermine on my ring robes." He explained further that "I owe it to my fans to wear nothing but the most costly and resplendent outfits money can buy."

Tonight's action is being broadcast live on KTLA, the most-watched station in Los Angeles, and will later be distributed on kinescope, a sixteen-millimeter film of a television broadcast, to cities across the country. Television announcer Dick Lane tells the viewers at home that George pays as much as $1,900 for a single robe. Like the number of robes in his collection, this is a huge exaggeration, but no matter. An American audience still predisposed to believe what it hears—still wanting to believe it, perhaps—is mightily impressed. In 1949, a new car costs $1,650, and gasoline is twenty-six cents a gallon.

Now Jefferies begins to fix George's curls, a blond Medusa's mass, in place with what look like gold-colored bobby pins. However, His Gorgeousness insists these *objets* be called Georgie pins—who, pray tell, is Bobby? At his countless public appearances George will hand them out by way of inducting fans into the Gorgeous George Fan Club. But before relinquishing the trinket he makes the recipient raise his right hand and repeat this oath:

> *I solemnly swear and promise I will*
> *never confuse this gold Georgie pin*
> *with a common, ordinary bobby pin,*
> *so help me, Gorgeous George.*

President Truman's wife, Bess, is reportedly among those who have taken the oath.

Catching the valet's eye in the mirror, George grins at his boyhood friend Jacob Brown, aka Jefferies. "Okay, Jake," he says, "let's go to work." His voice isn't high or thin, exactly, just more than the resonating chamber formed by his barrel chest would indicate. "Time to give the people what they want." The Olympic, built on L.A.'s Grand Avenue for the 1932 Olympic Games, is already full to its 10,500 capacity. Because Gorgeous George is headlining tonight, the crowd contains many more women than usual, and in the clamor for the Georgie pins they are the most vocal. George's vain posturing makes the male "crunch customers" furious, but women, especially older women, are his biggest fans—to them he's an extremely sensitive, misunderstood lad the other brutes should stop picking on.

An announcement rings out over the PA system: "Ladies and gentlemen, Gorgeous George is coming!" The fans, men and women both formally dressed to today's eyes, stir excitedly; they've already waited through the undercard, four or five preliminary matches, and they're primed for the main event. They want George. However, the next thing the audience will see is not George—not yet—but rather Jefferies walking stiffly erect down the long center aisle toward the ring. His expression is completely deadpan, his movements slow and dignified. Not so the crowd, which erupts in laughter at his progress. In front of him Jefferies carries a big silver tray; on it rests a whisk broom, along with some other accoutrements his master might need, including perfume and smelling salts. Between falls the valet will serve tea from it.

George's opponent is already in the ring, waiting, wearing some nondescript outfit, the kind George used to wear. When the wrestling begins—when Gorgeous George finally deigns to wrestle—the heel will turn impressively athletic, startlingly fast as he moves from one side of the ring to another. Though it's not entirely called for in these rigged contests, he does know how to wrestle. Tonight's script calls for George to play the cowardly heel, and he is ready to answer with kidney punches and eye gouges and other dastardly tricks. George will win, but even more than usual in these fixed bouts, the outcome isn't really the point, and George's opponent could be anyone. The main event, what the people paid to see, is Gorgeous George, the strutting star of TV they're thrilled to watch on their new home screens. Tonight the Olympic fans get to experience him live and in the flesh, to take in his grand entrance and outrageous appearance, his over-the-top flamboyance—his Gorgeosity.

The next announcement booms out through the speakers: "Ladies and gentlemen, Gorgeous George is here!" But the top of the main aisle is still empty; the headliner hasn't come just yet. He's still ensconced in front of the locker-room mirror. At times, and this is one of them, even the Gorgeous One is taken aback. He can't help but marvel at all that's happened to him—what he's made happen, rather. "We've come a long way, Sweetie," he'll say to his wife Betty.

Now he looks a little closer into the Olympic glass, scrutinizing this new image, his created second self. The vanity he exudes as Gorgeous George is not entirely an act; throughout his life George Wagner will let few reflective surfaces pass by unexamined. Gazing at his reflection, this transformed man, now a "Human Orchid," tries to bring back to his mind's eye what he used to see there. But he can't, really; George Wagner is gone. Besides, Gorgeous George likes what he sees, likes it very much. He gives up the search and the moment is quickly past. In the mirror the wrestling diva smiles.

G.G.

ACT ONE

"I don't know if I was made for television, or television was made for me."

—Gorgeous George

Chapter 1

"THE BIGGEST THING ON TV"

More than a half century later, Gorgeous George in all his vainglory remains a bizarre sight. The combination of those feminine robes and ornate hairdo with his masculine features—including a somewhat bulbous nose, broken several times in the ring—is confounding and, perhaps because of that, strangely compelling. Not to mention hilarious. Back in the 1940s, however, for any man, let alone an athlete, to willingly present himself as a loud, perfumed dandy crossbred with a dowager, and a sissified coward to boot, was stranger still; nearly unthinkable. To Americans of that era, George and his Gorgeous ways were truly outrageous—just the reaction the wrestler wanted.

In his heyday the strutting wrestler would be chauffeured around the country in long Cadillac and Packard limousines painted orchid, a shade of lavender, to match his namesake flower. In the early, struggling years before, however, he and his young wife, Betty Hanson, careened around the country in a secondhand sedan, as excited as they were flat broke. George Wagner the handsome babyface wasn't enough of a drawing card, so as they raced to make it to the next arena they improvised on the fly, Betty pushing for more provocative stunts and

George putting them all inimitably across. A tiny woman, less than five feet tall, she was his orchid muse and impish co-conspirator. Betty made his first luxurious robes, dyed his hair that champagne-tinted blond, and she may even have coined that fateful nickname, Gorgeous George. Together they created George's outrageous identity out of thin air, instinct, and imagination.

To make himself sublimely ridiculous took courage, and what's more, he and Betty did it all on their own. Unlike the Hollywood movie stars Gorgeous George would later rub egos with, he had no studios supplying him with scripts and directors, or choosing his parts. A feisty "usherette" at a Eugene, Oregon, movie theater, and a cocky roughneck who barely made it to high school in Houston, they became the writers, directors, publicity agents, wardrobe supervisors, and key grips of their own feature presentation, auteurs in orchid.

After World War II, America was adjusting, re-forming and reassembling itself into what exactly no one knew. But it clearly was going to be different, something new. Then television came and took hold, and Gorgeous George did as much as any single person to ensure that new device became a fixture. He, along with Milton Berle and the lovable Kukla, Fran, and Ollie, were the first true stars of the medium that would change American life, and in that transformation the transformed George became a national celebrity. Just as legions perched eagerly near their radios during the 1930s to follow Seabiscuit's epic races, millions of postwar Americans gathered—as families, everyone from grandparents to newborns—in front of their massive TV consoles and tiny screens, laughing, hooting, and shaking their heads in disbelief at the Gorgeous One, entranced by the new technology that brought him and their living rooms so vividly to life.

With television showcasing George's antics, his wacky confreres, and numerous imitators, professional wrestling became hugely popular, an improbably successful industry. In this, the grunt-and-groan game's golden age, matches aired every night of the week in what is now called prime time. After all the war's mortal damage, it seemed the country was ready for a cathartic release and a harmless good time. Television, that amazing new appliance, delivered them, with wrestling supplying many of the belly laughs. "The boys," as the wrestling promoters called their workers, became well-paid entertainers, and George became the Sensation of the Nation. In 1949 the *Washington Post* declared NO DOUBT OF IT: GEE GEE'S THE BIGGEST THING IN TV.

In the dozen or so years that followed World War II, he was ubiquitous: Everyone knew Gorgeous George. The *Los Angeles Times* reported that many women there were having their hair done in a Gorgeous homage. Popular comedians of the day, including Red Skelton, Jack Benny, and Bob Hope, told Gorgeous jokes. Songs were written about him, including one (lyrics by Borget, music by Joseph Furio) with this chorus:

> *His wavy hair, his dainty air*
> *Are every mama's pride and joy.*
> *He's such a pet, you can't forget*
> *Gorgeous George is just the darlin'est boy*
> *His eau de fleur, his manicure*
> *The way he struts so cute and coy*
> *Will show you why you can't deny*
> *Gorgeous George is just a bundle of joy.*

He reinvented himself, in a unique iteration of our national idea. George Wagner, child of the Great Depression, used his wit and prodigious will, then bent his broad back to create a better destiny. In another classic American scenario, his showmanship, catchy moniker, and the outré persona he played to the hilt transformed this poor boy into one of the country's highest-paid entertainers. As a youngster, he'd wrestled with his friends in a sawdust pile on the banks of a Houston bayou, and they'd split the change thrown by passersby. By the time he was thirty-five he was taking in $100,000 a year, the same amount the legendary Joe DiMaggio made playing baseball for the Yankees. (One newspaper headline dubbed George "Gorgeous Moneybags.") An astonishing percentage of those boyhood buddies became professional wrestlers, too, and after he became a star George would loyally find them work, insisting to promoters who wanted the Gorgeous One that they book his friends as well.

His success was at once hard-earned and an amazing fluke, something that could only have happened when it did. Even more unlikely, and less understood, is Gorgeous George's remarkable influence. James Brown, the late, great soul singer and entertainer, saw George's shimmering robes as a young man and was moved to add more splendor and flourish to his shows. The sequined capes and lush robes he wore onstage? "That came from the rassler Gorgeous George," he said. For more than fifty years Brown used this glittering array in his legendary live performances, and each night the Godfather of Soul also had a faithful valet attend to him onstage.

Muhammad Ali sat right next to Gorgeous George and heard him declaim on his wrestling superiority and "manly beauty." This was in 1961, when the boxer was just nineteen years old and his name was still Cassius Clay. Then Clay, a manly beauty himself, went to the matches at George's invitation and saw him inflame a sellout crowd with his boastful arrogance. The fans were there, the boxer realized, "to see this man get beat. And his talking did it." As Muhammad Ali, the lethal braggart, his most frequent and strident proclamations were "I am the prettiest" and "I am the greatest!" Few realize how closely those boasts echo the great wrestler's song of himself—they were vintage Gorgeousness.

Clearly, Gorgeous George's flamboyant showmanship didn't take hold with his other most prominent student, Bob Dylan. Instead, a chance encounter with the wrestler when the teenage Robert Zimmerman was a distinctly unpromising musician in Hibbing, Minnesota, convinced him that he could succeed as a performer, that he, too, had the charismatic gifts—Dylan called them "lightning and vitality"—that the Gorgeous One so clearly overflowed with. To him George was "a mighty spirit." Like George Wagner and Cassius Clay, Robert Zimmerman reincarnated himself, changing his name and taking on the persona of a troubadour poet, a Dylan.

Three Gorgeous disciples, among the most important American cultural figures of the twentieth century, they changed sports and entertainment, and more, inspiring countless heirs, descendants, and imitators. They had it in them, of course; George didn't grant them their genius. All of these men freely acknowledged, though, that the wrestler helped draw out their gifts and give shape to their artistry. Gorgeous George, the greatest, silliest practitioner of a faux, lowbrow sport—whose work seemed so utterly, intentionally unedifying—can reasonably be called a forgotten father of our popular culture.

When George Wagner grew up watching movie cowboy Tom Mix and screen detective Bulldog Drummond, male American icons were heroes and good guys. Villains, almost never. A remarkable man, worthy of our attention and devotion, was stoic and brave—like Sergeant York, the deeply religious World War I combat hero. That was the prevailing model of masculine virtue in entertainment as well, and Gary Cooper, the man who played Sergeant York in the movies, took on those qualities in the public imagination. A real man was also humble and unfailingly modest, like another hero Cooper portrayed, baseball slugger Lou Gehrig, in *Pride of the Yankees*. After World War II, General Dwight D. Eisenhower was elected president, and one of his most admired traits was that even he, the conquering hero on a world stage, was a steadfastly modest man.

Not George. He made a spectacle of himself when that word was still a term of disapproval. The strutting showman shouted "Look at me!" with his whole being, issuing an irresistible invitation to share in his self-infatuation—or to condemn him for it. Gorgeous George certainly didn't invent the pervasive culture of narcissism that followed him, but he may well have been a catalyst, a powerful accelerant. He was an avatar of conspicuous consumption well before that term became cliché, spending and showing off wildly in a country just coming out of wartime rationing. Immodesty personified, he put on a visually dazzling display, then praised himself for it. Along with his pupil Muhammad Ali, George helped make antipathy currency and infamy a profitable path to fame, something today's athletes, hip-hoppers, and marketers clearly understand. And yet the wrestling audiences also came to love the Human Orchid, or at least the way he so reliably, thrillingly provoked them. As one perceptive writer noted at the time, they hated him with affection.

Just as daring in his day, the gussied-up Human Orchid was also one of the first male celebrities to flaunt a sexually ambiguous, quasi-effeminate, vaguely gay persona, and to profit nicely from it. In a 1948 story on the Gorgeous George phenomenon *Newsweek* magazine noted that "both in and out of the ring he affects a . . . swishy manner, and effeminate fragrance." At that time any hint of femininity in a man was scorned and, except in a few bohemian enclaves, homosexuality considered depraved. Against this backdrop George strutted into women's beauty parlors, reporters in tow, and cheekily demanded to have his hair marcelled. He and Betty sensed a change in sensibilities, one that meant the American public was willing to be engaged—both enraged and entertained—by a man who flitted to the ring, as George described his saucy stroll. Filmmaker John Waters said it was Gorgeous George's silly, scary gender-bending that led him to create his own bizarre characters, including those played by Divine, the wrestler-size cross-dresser who starred in *Pink Flamingos, Female Trouble,* and *Hairspray.*

When the wrestling began, however, George became a battling macho athlete, taking punishment and dishing out pain with nary a swish audible or visible. A *Playboy* magazine writer would later dub him a "killer fruitcake," and it was the way George synthesized those two conflicting meanings, his shifting mixture of butch and belle, that made him unique, *sui gorgeous.* From Little Richard and Liberace— who a furious George claimed "stole my whole act, including the candelabra!"—in the 1950s to David Bowie and Boy George decades later, many other entertainers have transgressed successfully in the sexual arena. This line of provocateurs may have become a full circle in the late 1990s when Stephanie Bellars, a minimally dressed woman with maximal breasts, wrestled professionally under the name Gorgeous George.

Earlier than most, George and Betty saw the value in shock value; indeed, the young couple helped put it there. They were masters of publicity, too; before the words *media* and *hype* were in use, much less combined, George and Betty understood that a press-pleasing persona, spin, and savvy public relations were the ultimate submission holds. Their success presaged the day tennis star Andre Agassi famously declared, in a television commercial for Canon cameras, that "Image is everything."

George's fame outlasted his marriage to Betty, but his good fortune did not. After his spectacular rise he would arc downward just as steeply, then die young—he was not yet fifty years old. When he died in Los Angeles in 1963 the city council adjourned to show its respect and passed a resolution honoring his memory. Gorgeous George is buried under a small bronze plaque in Valhalla Memorial Park in North Hollywood, near a much bigger monument to Oliver Hardy. Just before his death George Wagner—by then he was legally, completely Gorgeous George—gave an interview from his hospital bed. In it he described the night at the Olympic Auditorium in Los Angeles when he felt his transformation was complete and the rise of the Human Orchid assured.

"I'll never forget my first walk down the aisle when my hair was blond, and I was trailed by the haunting scent of perfume," he said fondly. On that occasion the Gorgeous One wore a purple or orchid-colored robe, festooned with cloth flowers sewn onto the flashy fabric. "When I flitted down that aisle," George continued, "I got the biggest ovation of my life. They couldn't announce the match. The announcer burst out laughing, but I didn't mind. I was a sensation."

Chapter 2

HARRISBURG RATS

Gorgeous George reveled in slinging hooey—in making himself fabulous, he became a dedicated fabulist. "I'm actually a trained psychologist," he told reporters and his more gullible acquaintances. This specialized background, he explained, gave him great insight into, and mental mastery over, his less sophisticated ring opponents, whom he referred to as "the brutes." Sporting scribes of the day, whose obsession with facts was easily surpassed by the value they placed on entertaining copy, passed this whopper along verbatim and it's had remarkable staying power: A 1998 A&E television documentary on professional wrestling, for instance, appears to have swallowed it whole.

Like the original hard-wrestling George Wagner, the unvarnished truth lacked a certain gloss. What people really wanted, he found, was something more lustrous, and George would masterfully shine them on. He didn't introduce blarney and ballyhoo into pro wrestling; in the grunt-and-groan game, as in the traveling carnivals that spawned it, lies, exaggerations, and misdirection were not just habitual but fundamental. George simply raised them to their highest exponents. No subject, it seems, was too trivial to be shucked or jived. George insisted he was born in Seward, Nebraska, while his birth certificate makes clear that George Raymond Wagner first stepped between the worldly ropes in Butte, Nebraska, on March 24, 1915. He was the firstborn son of Howard James Wagner, twenty-three years old, and Bessie May Francis, nineteen, and the family lived in Phoenix, a nearby farming community. In the next five years the Wagners moved several times within Nebraska and in Iowa, and George's brother Elmer was born. Carl, the youngest and last child, came along three years later.

In his private life George was less of a liar, but not necessarily more of a revealer. He didn't record things, including, to his detriment, his income and expenses. He kept no journals or diaries and neither his wife Betty nor his daughter, Carol, could remember getting so much as a postcard from him during his twenty years or so on the road. He was a caller; he phoned. George and Betty talked about *her* past and childhood, but never his. Married to him for more than thirteen years, she never knew when George's mother died, for example, or whether the Wagners went to church. She only knew that he grew up in Houston.

Actually, it was Harrisburg, Texas. In 1925, when the Wagners moved to what is now a neighborhood in Houston's East End, Harrisburg was its own city of roughly 3,500 people. John Richardson Harris, a New Yorker, founded it in 1824 on the subtropical, swampy acres where Bray's Bayou met the Buffalo Bayou, which ran south and east to the Gulf of Mexico. Houston was an outgrowth of that city created twelve years later by two more New Yorkers, the Allen brothers, who bought the land to the northwest along the bayou. Lumber and cotton made the area's first great fortunes and then, just after the turn of the century, oil was discovered at Spindletop, about ninety miles east of Houston, and Humble Field, twenty miles north. The Buffalo Bayou was dredged to create a deeper shipping channel, and the new oil companies built refineries along its banks, including some at the wide mouth bordering Harrisburg. Other industries set up floating shop there as well.

The Wagners' house on Avenue E was less than a five-minute walk from the bayou. Just three or four blocks in the other direction the streetcar line ran into Houston from a triangular turnaround between Broadway, Harrisburg's main drag, and Eighty-first Street. Few people owned private cars, so everyone—workers, shoppers, and students—relied on the streetcars; the fare was seven cents, or four tokens for a quarter. With their metal antennae reaching for the wires above, the enclosed orange cars hummed along, past Sallee's Music Store, an A&P, the Boulevard movie theater, and the Wayside Café. Private jitneys, Ford Model T touring cars often crammed with seven people, were also popular, and they cost only five cents (*jitney* was slang for a nickel). In December 1927 Houston annexed Harrisburg and the streetcars were gradually replaced by buses; by that time the fare was a dime.

Like the other thirty houses crowded into their short block on Avenue E, George's home was a one-story, wooden structure with a peaked roof just high enough for an attic or half floor above the living space. Two stone steps in front were framed by wooden columns. This was a shotgun house, a plain narrow rectangle set with the short end toward the street; there were no sidewalks. The neighbors' houses were much the same, and chickens roamed the backyards. When Howard and Bessie Wagner and the three boys moved to Harrisburg, these houses were fairly new, thrown up roughly ten years before by the Ship Channel Lumber and Building Company to accommodate the influx of industrial workers near their waterfront jobs. The Wagners' had electric lights, water, and gas, but it was tiny: The five of them (and later, one of Howard's nephews) lived in what can't have been more than six hundred square feet.

The shotguns lay practically on top of one another, so families created a little privacy by hammering up wooden fences between the houses, and more came from the surging green growth that surrounded them. Hanging vines, palm trees, and tropical fronds flourished in the dank, near-permanent humidity, along with rubber trees, birds-of-paradise with their orange flowers and pointy green stalks, elephant ears, and pecan trees, the neighborhood's tallest feature. Their dark brown trunks shot up two or three times as high as the houses, and their branches were gnarly, scraggly, and stuck out at odd angles, making the trees look both majestic and bedraggled. Sound still carried through this jungle but at least it blocked neighbors' views.

In the fall, when George walked to school—or somewhere he liked better—he'd kick pecan nuts aside and crunch the husks under his feet. He wore a white T-shirt and cotton dungarees, or knickers, the three-quarter-length pants many younger boys wore in the 1920s. When he got a little older and graduated to white button-down shirts, George would roll the sleeves up to show off his biceps. Cotton was plentiful and light, and there were no synthetic fabrics or permanent press yet, so in class pictures from the local schools, Deede Junior High and Milby High, George's generation looks bright, eager, and thoroughly wrinkled. Despite the summer heat that would drive Harrisburg families to sleep outside, enduring the mosquitoes just to feel a breeze, boys' haircuts were surprisingly long, with some bulk to them, closer to Edwardian looks or the Beatles' mop tops than to the 1950s buzz. George wore his dark brown hair longish and side-parted, swept back from his broad face and brown eyes.

When the Wagners arrived in Harrisburg, half the families there and in the adjacent neighborhood, Magnolia Park, were Mexican-American, considered "non-white." The white locals included many German-American families, like Howard Wagner's. Harrisburg wasn't as strictly segregated racially as some other neighborhoods; there was one black-owned café that everyone patronized, for example. But black children went to the Negro schools, and plans for a Southern Pacific Railroad station were rejected by the city because blacks and whites would have used the same entrances to board the trains. When George began his pro wrestling career roughly fifteen years later, a state law still forbade Caucasians and "Africans" from boxing or wrestling against one another. Some two thousand Ku Klux Klan members from the Houston area held their hooded meetings on the prairie in nearby Bellaire, Texas. Beyond their racial and religious agendas, they strongly backed Prohibition in 1920.

George would never be temperate, but he was tolerant; none of his contemporaries remembered him ever uttering a racist remark. In their low-caste subculture, black and white wrestlers often felt more solidarity with one another than they did with the promoters or the "marks," the paying customers. Egotists and independent contractors all, they tended to fixate on their own fortunes and were less interested in anyone else's melanin content, and that was true of George.

George's dad—Poppa Wagner, as he was known—was a house painter, though he was never listed in the city's business directory, which seems to indicate that he didn't own a company. The other fathers on their block (mothers didn't work) included riggers and pump men at the refineries, tool-plant and construction hands, a carpenter, a baker, and a sanitation truck driver. They all worked with their hands and their sons expected to do the same. Six-day, forty-eight-hour weeks were the minimum a man could expect to put in; logging fifty-four to sixty hours a week was more common and a good many people worked even longer. But work there was, and the residents of Harrisburg were grateful.

Cherie Dupre, George's second wife, didn't get a complete account of her husband's upbringing either, but she did glean this much: "It was very hard, very deprived." Three children wasn't a lot in that era, but Howard Wagner had trouble supporting them all. They moved once or twice to other rentals in their first few Harrisburg years, and had a brief sojourn in Houston Heights, but returned to Avenue E in 1929. They stayed the longest at number 7834, and this was the smallest, meanest house of all, barely wider than two of today's cars parked side by side. Howard paid sixteen dollars a month in rent and sometimes had difficulty raising it, while the median for all Houston families was twenty-eight dollars, and for Negro families it was over eighteen. So the Wagners' was indeed a low estate. They never had a phone, but they were one of the few houses in their area with a "radio set," as they were known. Why would they buy this seeming luxury?

Bessie needed it, desperately. When George was five or six, it seems, she was stricken with a crippling malady. A small, slender woman with sharp features and reddish-brown hair, Bessie suffered near-constant pain and was bedridden for long stretches, unable to walk. The radio, tuned in to KPRC (the last three letters stood for *ports, railroads,* and *cotton*), was Bessie's link to the outside world. She had chronic articular rheumatism, now known as chronic rheumatoid arthritis: an extremely painful swelling of the joints that may also attack the muscles, ligaments, cartilage, tendons, and even the heart valves. As one early medical text, *The Eclectic Practice of Medicine,* put it: "The ligaments, tendons, and muscles . . . may so change their structure as to leave little resemblance to their original condition." At times, it continued, "the tenderness and pain are exquisite." As seems to have been the case with George's mother, the chronic pain and sleeplessness often led to depression. Today this condition is better treated with anti-inflammatory drugs, among others, and physical therapy; in Bessie's day doctors and lay healers recommended bed rest, taking the waters at hot springs; a vegetarian diet; and herbal remedies based on *Apocynum,* known as dogbane.

As soon as he was able, George, the oldest, was charged with caring for his bed-bound mother, feeding her, changing bandages, and emptying bedpans. He not only had to witness his mother's suffering, and to be utterly unable to relieve it, but was to some extent imprisoned by it. He served willingly and genuinely wanted to help both his mother and his father, but it's no wonder that as a boy, he wanted to escape whenever he could, taking the five-minute walk east on dirt paths to the banks of the Buffalo Bayou. Along the water, which looked swamp green in the sun and turned steel blue when skies were overcast, George and his pals easily found enough muck and mischief to fill their days.

Best of all, Brady's Island, a good-size circular patch of undeveloped land, was just a quick wade offshore. On the far side of the island the ship channel ran northwest or left to the Port of Houston, and right, southeast, to the Gulf. Beyond the island on the far bank lay a derelict barge the locals called the *Old Gray Ghost.* Bootleggers had staked out part of the island for brewing their illegal hootch, but there was still plenty of room for George and his buddies to clear a patch of sandy ground, roughly twenty by twenty feet, to form a wrestling ring. There were no posts, ropes, or mats, of course, but the soft soil did cushion their falls. In between bouts they'd swap or gamble for wrestling trading cards (these usually came as premiums with candy or cigarettes), featuring grappling heroes like Frank Gotch and George Hackenschmidt and listing their signature throws and holds.

The Brady's Island gang called themselves the Harrisburg Rats, as in wharf rats. They were tough kids and loyal to the tribe. Many if not most of them wound up as professional wrestlers, including Johnny and Jimmy James, who wrestled as "Jesse" James, Chester "Chesty" Hayes, and Sterling Davis, whose *nom de ring* was Dizzy Davis. Jacob Brown—the future valet Jefferies—who lived about two miles inland on Avenue Q, never had full Rat status, but was another wrestling buddy and became the closest friend in George's life. Another early mat adversary, Jack Hunter, would serve as a valet, too; he was "my man Jackson."

On Brady's Island they were just a long stone's throw from some of their houses, but somehow crossing the water—when George was in junior high school they made a primitive walkway out of old planks— made them feel that they'd escaped to their own enclave. Here, where the tang of the refineries hung in the air a little sharper, the dense green foliage and the scraggly southern pines that sank their roots into the bayou also shielded the goings-on from pesky parents or truant officers. George got his toughness from the intramural tussles there and what he remembered as frequent fistfights with other groups of Harrisburg boys. The other gang hailing from, say, Avenue F instead of E, was reason enough to brawl.

When George was ten or twelve he first learned to perform to a crowd, and that he was good at it. The James brothers' father, a Greek who had likely changed his name to make life easier for his sons, had a fruit stand near the edge of the bayou. As he stood hawking with his back to the water, Johnny, Jimmy, George, and the other Rats would wrestle off to one side in a pile of sawdust left by a former sawmill. The wilder their throws and rougher their falls, George saw, the more coins passersby would toss them. The more change that came clinking down, the more wrestling cards he could buy, or tickets to see Dizzy Dean pitch for the Houston "Buffs" or Buffaloes, the minor-league baseball team, at their stadium on Jefferson Street. The boys also loved movies, taking them in at one of downtown Houston's ornate movie palaces such as the Majestic or the Isis, or a cheaper Harrisburg venue.

They didn't wrestle in the Harrisburg schools, which only fielded teams in football and basket ball (which was spelled with two words). As a teenager, George got wrestling instruction at a local YMCA. Besides the classic holds—the quarter, half, and full nelsons, the cradle, the cross face—and escape moves—including sit-outs and the bridge-out—he learned to get behind the other grappler for leverage, and how technique could amplify his natural strength. In one of his more sober and truthful later pronouncements, George would tell reporters: "It's all about leverage and balance." Even as he became Gorgeous, strutting more and doing less actual grappling, the other wrestlers could still tell immediately that he'd had this amateur training. "He was fast, he was nimble, and he knew what he was doing," said Don Leo Jonathan, a six-foot-six, three-hundred-pound heavyweight from Utah who went a few falls with the Gorgeous One.

As a teenager, George was tall for his age and thickly muscled, especially through the trunk and back. Even before he'd learned any wrestling techniques, he took on his schoolmates one day in a nearby lot and threw fourteen of them, one after another. Or at least George said he did. Soon, though, the king of the hill's growth would stall and his advantage began to vanish. Though as a pro he'd often be billed as six-foot-one or six-foot-two and up to 235 pounds, he never actually grew beyond the five-foot-nine or -ten he reached in high school, and at his heaviest, 190 or so, he was still puny for a heavyweight.

George wasn't the biggest or oldest Rat and he didn't dominate overtly. But something in his face, an open and expressive rectangle, in the glint of his brown eyes, and in his stance toward the world made this particular kid stand out. It could have been the kind of distinction that lands boys in reform school. There was a feral male intensity to him, and even more restless energy than his pals had; no doubt wrestling was a providential outlet. Yet he also carried a charismatic charge and a love of comradeship that made the others naturally fall in with him, ready to join the fun he was bound to create. He always wanted to stand out. "Even as a boy," he said later, "I didn't want to look like anyone else when I walked down the street. I wanted people to notice me." He even claimed that "I used to wear knickers just so the other kids would tease me and pick a fight," but that was likely just a Georgian line. In his late teens, perhaps after the handsome tough had begun to get some attention from girls, he wore a cocky grin, and whether the confidence he projected was genuine or compensatory, it was convincing.

By all accounts Poppa Wagner was easygoing, a placid man. He didn't raise his voice, didn't curse, and met his misfortunes with a rueful smile. He was a good-size man; growing up in the Midwest, he took down many a comer in "Indian wrestling," and he enjoyed teaching that style to George. While his son would puff himself up, however, trying to loom larger than he was, Howard stood with diffidence. When he reached his forties, a ripe middle age back then, his light brown hair retreated behind his largish ears and George's dad came to look strikingly like the post–World War II Dwight D. Eisenhower (just two years older). Betty, who immediately bonded with George's dad, called him "a big ol' country sweetheart." Poppa Wagner may have felt he needed to be a buffer, to try to soothe his afflicted wife, while softening the impact her illness had on the boys. She could be a very affectionate mother, but through no fault of her own, her moods were wildly variable, shooting up and down with her suffering. While Poppa Wagner seemed to want little and ask less for himself, Bessie was, in her helplessness, ever demanding.

If his parents are rendered in just these broad strokes, George combined their traits with great symmetry: A manual laborer, he would doggedly ply the same trade his whole working life without complaint. As the Gorgeous One, though, he was an ultrasensitive character with womanish traits, who lived within his own wants and emotions—a special-needs diva. Yet that reading doesn't do any of them, or human complexity, justice. George loved his well-meaning dad but couldn't stomach his passivity, the lack of imagination that left Howard resigned to his fate, including his family's life of poverty. The son would rather have died than accept the short end or meager rations; and in some ways, he did. George would define himself in opposition to Bessie, too: She was physically trapped, confined, so he would spend his entire life on the move. He'd have homes and marriages but he'd never fully inhabit them. She had few if any choices and her fate was dictated by implacable external forces; George would vehemently make his own decisions and break every rule. Wrestling, the métier he chose, is the transgressor's Eden: All the supposed strictures, and the boundaries of the ring, are made to be broken, and the referee exists only to be defied.

Bessie couldn't parent George fully, yet she inspired him. When his mother was able to sew, George sat on her bed with her and threaded her embroidery needles. This, he once said, was his first exposure to finery and color, and he was enchanted. Having seen her create beauty, George would prize it and pursue it for himself. As a teenager, he remembered, "I used to stop in front of a clothing store and look at the suits in the window." But, typically, George didn't crave the suits on display; he thought he could do better. "They all looked drab," he said, "and I'd imagine that if I ever got money I'd have them made up to my taste—green and purple suits, black suits with white buttons, dark red, turquoise blue . . ." As he sat with her in her illness, George also absorbed Bessie's desire for a different life, taking on his mother's conviction that she and her children deserved something better. No doubt the radio, her other faithful companion and link to the world outside her bedroom, helped her to envision it. From her imaginings and longings, his own took shape.

Chapter 3

ON THE CARNY GAME

When George was fourteen, the Great Depression crushed expectations and turned the national economy to ashes. Houston wasn't as poorly off as many other areas of the country; no banks failed there during the 1930s, for example, and the rest of America still depended on it for oil. By 1933, though, the huge grain elevator standing near the channel banks, a looming landmark, stood empty. Industrial employment cratered and wouldn't return to pre-Depression numbers until 1939. Life changed in the details as well. At least one streetcar company had to open a credit department; too many people were unable to scrape together the change to pay their fares. Some of the movie theaters began accepting IOUs, though they were presumably not foolish enough to accept them from George and his cadre of Rats. Some of the wrestling cards at the City Auditorium turned into food drives: Bring canned goods and get in free, with the food donated to the needy. Poppa Wagner's painting business, never lucrative, dried up as houses were left to crack, peel, and fade. It's not known whether Howard went to the Hampshaw Building downtown to apply for Mayor Walter E. Monteith's emergency relief checks, but the need was certainly there.

Then, at 1:00 A.M. on October 8, 1932, Bessie died. She was just thirty-six years old. George was seventeen, Elmer thirteen, and Carl not quite ten. She most likely got an infection in one or more of her joints and couldn't fight it off with her compromised immune system. (Penicillin, the first antibiotic, wasn't in use until the 1940s.) Bessie was buried in Forest Park Cemetery. George was bereft; now he would never get the attention from Bessie he'd craved. But he was liberated as well; he would not be tied down any longer. It seems that he'd already dropped out of Milby High School, about a mile and a half down Broadway from the Wagner house. (While enrolled there, he worked as a gas-station filling attendant after school.) His records are lost, though, and Milby, two stories of beige brick that are still in use, didn't produce yearbooks when George attended—in the Depression there was no money for such nonessentials.

George was sharp, a quick study, but never bookish. He had a hard time sitting still, and one can easily picture him mouthing off in class to get attention, then resenting the resulting discipline. Since he often cut classes, leaving school was easy. At the same time he didn't enjoy the alternatives. With so many experienced workers and family men unemployed, work was hard to find, so George couldn't be choosy. For a while he machined metal parts at Reed Drill Bits alongside his buddy Jake Brown. He wrecked cars with a crowbar; sacked cement at the bottom of a conveyor belt in a construction pit; and chopped cotton in the wet Houston heat. It was punishing work that tore at the sinews and ripped muscle from bone. George's hands, small but powerful with strong, stubby fingers, took a beating, and he came home with cuts, scrapes, and livid bruises.

He was a willing worker, taking odd shifts and often holding two or more jobs. Even then he had prodigious energy and stamina, a seemingly inherent advantage in life's competitions that would always serve him. Like many highly successful people, George could simply keep going—keep talking, keep wrestling, keep driving, keep working—when others had to stop or drop. Nonetheless, he was greatly relieved to find easier, whiter-collar work downtown at the Houston Typewriter Exchange at 408 Fannin Street. Later he would tell reporters that he repaired the Coronas and L.C. Smith machines—"No fatigue at the end of the day!" their slogan promised—but it's hard to imagine George had the patience for this close work, manipulating the delicate rods and hammers. A better guess is that he delivered typewriters and installed replacement ribbons in offices as needed, a service the Exchange offered its customers at no extra charge.

One of the Houston newspapers ran a feature on this shop, and George kept this yellowing clipping for the rest of his life in a scrapbook with wooden covers, bound with leather straps. The photo accompanying that story shows nine Exchange employees, "part of the force," as the caption calls it. George is the youngest-looking and the least formally dressed; he and one other man are the only ones without jackets and ties. He's wearing his hair fairly short and slicked back now, still parted on the left; his ears look big and they're protruding a bit, which may be an early sign of wrestling damage. The sleeves on the white sport shirt he wears are short enough to show off his biceps, and in the ranks of nine white men facing the camera, George has managed to place himself out in front and squarely in the middle of the image. The others seem to want to look professionally serious; George's cheek-creasing grin is easily the biggest smile. After all the ink spilled on him when he was the Gorgeous One, why did he keep this modest piece for so long? It may have marked the first time he'd improved his situation with his mind, carving out a better place for himself than the berth Fate seemed to be preparing.

All along he did everything a young wrestler could do to improve his skills, make a name, and scrape up a couple of dollars. He'd won some amateur tournaments as a 150-pounder and fairly often a Lions or Elks Club would call for a few high schoolers to put on a Saturday wrestling exhibition, after which the boys would get sandwiches, plus a little money. A man named Hill had a Harrisburg blacksmith shop and also owned the Broadway movie theater. Upstairs there was a stage and some seats, and Hill put on matches there for the local workingmen. They'd drink, yell, stomp their feet on the wooden floor, and bet money they couldn't afford to lose on the anonymous and carelessly matched kids whaling away in front of them. Once Hill even brought in a bear, and some lunatics wrestled it, too.

As far as we know, George stuck to human contests. The mats spread over the stage were thin and the falls hurt, but he'd come away with the equivalent of two or three days' wages at one of his other jobs, and the take increased when he managed to get a successful side bet down on himself. During Prohibition, George, Johnny and Jimmy James, and other Rats also wrestled in speakeasies, throwing one another around for the drinkers' amusement. Some older man usually played Fagin, finding the combatants, refereeing the bouts, and pocketing most of the money.

Late in his school years George began to pal around with Glen Price, one of three brothers who may actually have been worse off financially than the Wagner boys, and who lived with their aunt over the RB Department Store, at the corner of Broadway and the LaPorte Highway. Glen was two years older than George and handsome, slender but well built, with a smile that slayed the girls, who were just beginning to matter to George. In and out of the Brady's Island wrestling pit, the six-foot-four Glen was serious competition, and George saw that to hold his own he needed to provide a clear alternative. Glen was soft-spoken and a bit shy, so the shorter, stockier boy became even bolder and cockier around him.

The Price brothers owned one beat-up truck among them (they also shared one good suit of clothes), and many a hot Harrisburg night, Glen would commandeer the truck and run the streets with George. These two, along with the odd Rat or Price brother, would cram into the truck and head for the Sylvan Beach Amusement Park, about a half hour away in La Porte, on the shores of Trinity Bay. Often a traveling carnival had pitched its tents there, and for George, the carnival was the true seducer.

George, Glen, and their entourage walked down the dirt and patchy grass midway through a carnival configuration that hadn't changed much since before the Civil War. They moved past the canvas tents with the front flaps pinned back and the close clutter of wooden booths offering games of chance, smelling the fried food and grease and hearing the barkers' cries, until they reached a conspicuously closed tent that housed the girlie show or striptease act. Signs and more barkers out front promised all sorts of salacious sights and lurid acts, which were seldom delivered. Close by was the "ten-in-one show," another tent or a long stall offering a combination of "geek" acts, such as a fat lady, a midget, some abnormal animals, and maybe a sword swallower. Again, the come-on was a bit misleading, as there were commonly fewer than ten acts, but the name stuck.

At the end of the midway sat one of the biggest tents, up to forty by sixty feet, with a banner announcing the Athletic Show—the carnies called it the "AT show." Often the outsides of these tents were painted with colorful pictures showing two boxers in their old-fashioned, bare-knuckled and fists-raised stance, as well as two wrestlers grappling. Out front stood the chest-high bally stand, a sort of podium, and behind it a barker yelling out his inducements, or ballyhoo. To further yank the strolling customers' attention his way, the barker might have a bell he'd hit with a hammer, or set off a siren; when wrestler Johnny Buff ran his AT show in Washington State after the Second World War, they scraped a car axle over the rivets on an old metal water tank to make an ungodly noise. "Okay, ladies and gentlemen, right down here, come see live professional wrestling, these are bone-crushing men who are famous all over the world . . ." This was the hook for the exhibition wrestling, in which two carnies took on each other. What drew in George and Glen, though, were the challenge matches.

"Okay, you tough guys out there," this barker shouted, "let's see if any of you can stay in the ring with our man. It only costs a quarter to try, and if you can last for ten minutes, we'll give you five bucks! Yeah, you, over there with the pretty girl hanging on your arm, you think you're man enough? What about you, farm boy? You can push those cows around, why don't you step up here and try pushing a man around? Who'll raise their hand?" No takers meant no show, so there would always be a "stick" in the crowd, a confederate who'd take up the challenge if needed. Often the stick would win, pocketing the five dollars in front of the crowd and giving the marks ideas of victory.

George came as close to standing idly by as he did to his advanced psychology degree. With his wrestling buddies egging him on, he stepped into the tent through the pinned-up flaps. The first thing he noticed was that the ring was smaller than usual, maybe fourteen by fourteen. "A smaller ring makes the action look faster," Buff explained. The ring surface was lightly padded plywood, raised a foot or two off the ground on a base of two-by-fours and steel springs, and topped with a none-too-clean mat. Off to one side hung a rough canvas curtain; that was the dressing room.

The carny wrestlers were grown men and tough; often they doubled as the strongmen, lifting, bending, and ripping things before the amazed crowds. Some of these feats were even real. Most of the yokels, the local farm boys or oil riggers, were no threat. The carny's goal—and the true art involved here—was to beat the mark while convincing him he'd barely lost, and could win a rematch. Or to entice his friend looking on to step up with what he thought was a real shot at revenge. The crowd naturally took the side of the local, and some could even be enticed to bet their loyalties against other carnies salted in among the paying customers.

George, who didn't weigh more than 170 pounds at this point, was giving away size and experience. At the same time he would have been an enormous handful for anyone who took him on: young, strong, and fearless, with the wrestling know-how that most suckers lacked. There's reason to think he won—once. According to published accounts, George beat the house in a seven-minute carnival match when he was seventeen. His YMCA wrestling coach, who happened to be in the audience, saw him pocket his pay afterward. When George went up to greet him after the match, the coach wouldn't shake his hand. "You're not an amateur anymore," he told him. "You're a professional."

The home team losing was not unheard of. At times a pro wrestler who wasn't working elsewhere that night would strip off his shirt, climb in against the strongman, and take him down before the carny crowd could react. If their man in the ring had time, he'd try to come to a hurriedly whispered accommodation with the pro. "Let's make this last and make it look good," he'd tell the outsider. "You win this one, and I'll win the rematch, and we'll take care of you afterward." But wrestlers on the carny weren't in the business of giving away money, and all knew some painful, effective moves they'd resort to should a challenger start to get the best of them. The next time George stepped in and created an emergency, steps would have been taken.

When the two men locked up, standing and holding on to each other's shoulders or arms as they tried to gain leverage, the inside man might put the kid in an innocuous-looking headlock. George's friends and all the other spectators couldn't see the protruding knuckle jammed into his eye and the referee, another house employee, conveniently saw nothing either. The pain was enormous, and the natural reaction—an irresistible instinct, really—would make George raise his hands to his face. As his arms began to come up, his body was exposed, and the carny man would dive underneath, reach out with both arms, and yank George's legs out from under him, putting him on his back. The ref would quickly count George out: "One, two, three. Pin!" If George really got an advantage, the carny might go for the more drastic "sleeper hold," also disguised as a headlock. In this variation, the holder slips one forearm down over the enemy's neck and applies pressure to the carotid artery, cutting off the blood and oxygen supply and rendering him unconscious. When he came back to clarity, he'd be on his back, defeated.

George didn't stay a sucker for long; he learned the game quickly. If innocence was lost, he didn't miss it. Like his forsaken amateur standing, purity had no payoff and thus no utility. He wanted in. Being an insider, part of a secret society, was a thrill. That carny tinge of illegitimacy, the nefarious, made it even more irresistible. He got to know some of the carny wrestlers and worked some rigged matches with them: win a few, throw a few. A rigged game? So what. George already believed, or at least suspected, that life wasn't quite fair. The point, then, was not to be the luckless loser, not to get played. It wasn't a moral decision, anyway, but more like a hormonal imperative. For George, carnival wrestling was an adrenaline rush, powerfully addictive. He liked winning his real, amateur matches, the thrill of suddenly summoning all your strength, and having it proved superior. But there was another kind of contest here, and winning at it meant more to him. As Thomas Hackett observes in *Slaphappy,* his book about twenty-first-century professional wrestling, the real competition in this game is the one for attention. That's the battle George waged at the carnivals, and as Gorgeous George, he would reign triumphant, undefeated.

Confined by the carnival tent, heat built in the atmosphere, intensified by the crowd. The noise fifty or sixty people made rang out like that of hundreds. And they sat so close, George could make out the young boys' high-pitched encouragement and the adult men's deeper shouts. "Look out!" "Get him, son!" Or: "You're done for now, kid!" In the fast action of the smaller ring there was no room to maneuver away from the opponent, no time to look up and catch your breath. But even as he kept his eyes squarely on his partner, George could visualize the crowd's reactions in his mind's eye: women clutching two-handed at their dates' biceps when the grappling turned its most violent, men shaking their fists, swearing and laughing, and both sexes loosening, unbuttoning, and rolling up their clothes in the shared heat, a simulacrum of the wrestlers' sweaty, bare-chested immodesty. Even as part of his mind stayed with the give-and-take of the match, he could hear and sense the people all around him reacting to his every move. It felt, despite the presence—or at times, even the preeminence—of the other wrestler, as if all eyes were on George.

He'd never felt anything like this, and he responded like a born performer. The crowd's reactions fired warmth in his gut that spread through his whole body. He'd act out more, louder, throw his body around even harder. The teenage girls, young brides and mothers in their twenties, women who usually had to be dragged into the wrestling tents by their dates and husbands, seemed to scream louder when young Wagner was in the ring, the carny operators noticed. The laborers in overalls and office workers in straw hats and linen sport coats bet more heavily, both for and against.

One night some carnies who'd gotten to know him asked the nineteen-year-old George to referee. He wasn't supposed to do much, just create the impression by his presence that the night's matches were regulated and thus "fair." But the carnies didn't realize that the role of neutral third party was one George was constitutionally incapable of playing. When "Texas Red" Allen took on an off-duty policeman who happened to be a friend of George's, the guest ref didn't stick to the script. At one point the wrestlers locked up in a corner with George's buddy pushed backward into the turnbuckle, the metal coupling that joins the ropes. George approached and instructed Red to break the hold. When he didn't comply, George leaned in and tried to pry him away. Instead of cooperating, the older man got annoyed with this punk who was overplaying his part, and threw an elbow that just whizzed by George's nose and would have broken it had it struck.

Angry—but also delighted that his role was becoming more important—George found the talent for improvisation that would help make his career. He bent down, his longish hair falling in strands in front of his eyes, and grabbed Texas Red with both arms. George then lifted him up off the mat and slung him across his broad back like a sack of cotton, then hurled him—his limbs splaying outward like a cartoon character's in flight—over the ropes and out of the ring, where he landed on spectators' laps in the front row. Their bench cracked in half at the impact, spilling fans, popcorn, and drinks onto the dirt floor in a tangle with the stunned wrestler. George grinned his cocky grin and strutted just a little, quick-wittedly announcing that "Texas Red has been disqualified for leaving the ring," and raising his friend's hand as the winner. The crowd, at least the part that hadn't been struck by the flying grappler, roared and laughed in delight. How Red felt was not recorded.

God, he loved it. George began to wonder about wrestling professionally. Some guys made real money at it, he knew; why not him? His
ability and antics, including the Red-tossing episode, got him noticed
and he soon gained entrée to the small-time Houston promoters. They
offered him work wrestling opening matches—the first and shortest
one on each night's card—in small towns within driving distance of
the city. This was the professional game's lowest echelon but the pros
nonetheless, so George jumped at the chance (while keeping his day
job at the Typewriter Exchange). He may have wrestled some under
the name of Elmer Schmitt, either to increase his appeal to pockets of
German-Americans, or simply to avoid being confused with another
grappler named Wagner. After a one-fall, fifteen-minute tussle with
some other wild-eyed rookie, George would leave the Legion hall,
school auditorium, or makeshift arena with three to five dollars, mi-
nus his expenses. All the boys, including the headliners or "main
eventers," paid for their own travel, gear, and professional licenses.
Luckily the travel wasn't far and life's essentials were cheap, with
prices still depressed along with the economy. Gas was ten cents a gallon, and five or six of the strapping wrestlers would share a cramped
car ride, reimbursing the owner a penny a mile. Sometimes the gang
was all there, when one or more of the Rats were booked on the same
small-time cards.

One Texas summer night George was standing just inside the
door to the wrestlers' dressing room, a term that promises more than
the real room delivered: A couple of wooden benches and a collection
of nails driven into the wall serving as lockers. This might have been
in Conroe or Brenham. He was pleased; in his opening match George
had pinned his opponent's shoulders to the mat for the requisite three
seconds and the win. (In the preliminary bouts, one pin or fall carried
the day; the semifinal and headline matches generally required a wrestler to win two out of a possible three falls. If a wrestler couldn't continue due to injury or exhaustion, his opponent was awarded a fall as
well, and referees could also award falls to the victims of especially
egregious fouls.) After their matches he and the other Rats would stay

to watch the older, more experienced boys work the rest of the card. Still excited, George was chatting eagerly with one of his buddies about their next booking while a local newspaper reporter stood nearby, waiting to interview one of the headliners still in the shower. Just then an older wrestler who was passing by on his way out heard something he didn't like. *"Kayfabe, kayfabe,"* he hissed at George under his breath. Crestfallen, George quickly shut his trap.

Kayfabe is carnival slang, part of the coded language hucksters, con men, and wrestlers used among themselves to work their subterfuge and exclude the clueless marks. In this lingo, resembling pig latin, *kayfabe* referred both to the game's professional secrets and to the code of silence surrounding them; like the Mafia's *omerta*. "If someone on the inside said 'Kayfabe, kayfabe,' to you, it meant 'Hey, there's an outsider around,'" said Don Arnold, a Southern California babyface who wrestled with George in the 1950s. "'Don't talk about our business in front of others, don't give out information that could blow our cover. Wrestling's always on the up-and-up. Isn't it?'"

Well, no. American professional wrestling matches hadn't been legitimate contests since the 1880s, perhaps since the Civil War. Perversely, for decades after the fix was in and wrestling became an entertainment, the matches were nonetheless long and boring. Before 1910 or so promoters usually offered just a main event and one "prelim" with local boys. To create a full evening's amusement, they needed the main event to last two hours or more, and a truly contested match ran the risk of ending in minutes. In one infamous encounter between Ed "Strangler" Lewis and Joe Stecher, the first fall took two hours and the third went four, the whole match lasting longer than a baseball doubleheader. Worse, in entertainment terms, for much of that time the two wrestlers were lying around, inert, with one in the other's headlock. The promoters had fans convinced that a long contest signaled competitiveness and skilled, "scientific wrestling," but only true aficionados could appreciate this drawn-out exchange of sweat. Much of the interest in these matches lay in the heavy betting that accompanied them.

Then wrestling looked again to the carnivals, where matches with fixed outcomes began, and saw anew how taking the competition out of things there allowed acrobatics and dramatics to flourish. Feigned violence, in which both "opponents" know what's coming, can be much more high-flying and spectacular than the real, unpredictable—and therefore dangerous—thing. Promoters also put time limits on matches and hired more wrestlers to fill their bills. Afterward legitimate bouts existed only to settle personal scores and these happened in private. They were called "shooting" matches, or just "shoots," and the ones with predetermined outcomes were "working" matches or "works." The boys were also called workers, and being called a good worker was high industry praise. Don Arnold made his name in a pair of dynamic matches with the great champion Lou Thesz. In the early going of each one the older Thesz tested the 230-pound Arnold with some real grappling moves to see if he had the skill to respond. Then, after five or ten minutes, Thesz would lean in and say, "Okay, let's work." That meant: "Let's play. It's time to start acting, and get this match's prearranged scenario under way."

Controlling the results enabled promoters to give certain wrestlers a "push," building career momentum and an audience by ensuring a string of victories. Crowd-drawing rivalries were created the same way: A heavy favorite would unexpectedly lose, for example, or an especially controversial, "unfair" outcome produced, both of which would inevitably lead to a lucrative rematch. To help professionalize the look of the sport the promoters also looked to boxing—hard to imagine as a source of legitimacy today—borrowing the rope-enclosed ring and the striped-shirted referee, neither of which exists in amateur wrestling.

As George Wagner found when he entered the business in the 1930s, show-business wrestling presents a unique quandary to its athletes. In every other sport you can advance by beating the competition, but not here. Instead of winning, the currency is "getting heat," drawing a reaction from the fans, performing in a way that will get more of them to come out next time—to see you, whether you're the heroic babyface or the despicable heel. If you draw better, your percentage of the gate receipts translates into more dollars, and if you sustain it, the promoters will raise your percentage. (Usually only the featured performers or headliners got a split, while those on the undercard, lower on the bill, were paid a minimal, fixed amount.)

But the marks couldn't know where the real competition lay, and no one in the grunt-and-groan game was about to tell. Vigilance had to be maintained. (Kayfabe was finally blown for good in 1989 when Linda McMahon, the wife of World Wrestling Entertainment owner Vince McMahon, testified to the New Jersey legislature that wrestling wasn't a sport but "sports entertainment." Their purpose was to avoid taxes and regulation that apply to real athletic contests.) To keep up appearances the boys, who often drove from town to town with the colleagues they supposedly hated and would try to kill in the ring that night, stopped a mile or so from the arenas and dropped some wrestlers off where they could get a taxi. That way, the "bitter rivals" wouldn't be seen arriving together.

When the promoters told them who the winners were to be that night, each pair of dance partners would put their heads together in the locker room to choreograph. The designated loser was known as the "jobber" or "put-over guy"—he'd do the job, which was putting the other guy over. He might ask the chosen winner, "What's your finishing move?" meaning: What crowd-pleasing maneuver do you want to use to end this match? If one of the pair hadn't worked in the area before, he might ask, "What do they like here?" or, "What haven't these people seen?"

Once the ending and a few maneuvers were agreed upon, much of what happened in the ring was improvised. Usually the heel was the lead dancer, as his heinous deeds and the excruciating retribution he suffered dictated the flow. Cooperation made the dance. "If you are going into a body slam," said Pete Burr, who wrestled out of Syracuse in the 1950s, including with Gorgeous George, "you aren't just going to grab a guy that is 250 to 300 pounds, pick him up and flop him. He has to push off your leg, jump a little, help get you started. Once he gets the momentum going you can lift him and all, but you need to work together."

After his youthful faux pas, George vehemently kept to the code of kayfabe. In his 1950 profile of the Gorgeous One in *American Mercury* magazine, writer Ted Shane recounted, "I got up my courage and asked George, 'Is wrestling fixed?'

"'You might,' George said haughtily, 'also ask me if I enter false income tax returns or if I beat my wife. To the best of my knowledge I have never engaged in any fraudulent bout . . . everybody in there is trying to kill me.'"

Even with his friends and drinking buddies, "George would get pretty upset when he heard anything about it being fixed or rigged up for him to win," said Ernie Serfas, who owned the wrestler's favorite Los Angeles saloon. "And he would never admit it. Never." George taught Betty some of the secret language the wrestlers used, calling it "double-talk." One night in the late 1950s George and his daughter, Carol, were leaving a restaurant in Hollywood, and as they approached a driveway a car came out too fast and too near for George. He said something sharp to the driver in double-talk—and the man stopped and answered back using the same lingo. It turned out he'd been in the game, too.

Chapter 4

POSSUMS AND HOOK SCISSORS

In 1933 Texas repealed its alcohol ban, Houston's first legal beer in thirteen years flowed from the new Gulf Brewing Company plant, and whiskey ran from the cask. Shortly thereafter, when George was almost nineteen, local promoter Morris Sigel gave him his break into the bigger-time. Sigel put on regular Friday-night cards at the City Auditorium downtown for more than forty years. He called George into his office in the Milam Building, a block or so away, and booked him on a January 26, 1934, card. To George the Auditorium was a palace, and when the building opened in 1910, that's how it was intended: as a landmark cultural center and monument to Houston sophistication. The massive brown stone facade, facing the Auditorium Hotel across the street, had three central arches above the entrances, surrounded by decorative brickwork. This was Houston's Carnegie Hall, not some carnival midway or hick town.

On other nights of the week higher-toned performers filled the dressing rooms and held the stage, including orchestras and ballet troupes. But on Fridays rude and crude wrestling moved the turn-stiles, and a good seat could be had for fifty cents. The ring was set up in the middle of the main floor, after some seats had been removed—

and the ones that remained were real wooden seats, not splintery benches or spindly folding chairs. The ceiling soared several stories above the orchestra seating, and the stage was draped with a heavy velvet curtain. Most impressive to George, the place held four thousand people, more than the entire population of Harrisburg.

During the period of George's first Auditorium matches, the Houston papers—the *Chronicle, Post,* and *Press*—were full of bitter Depression truths. NO AGREEMENT IS REACHED IN OIL STRIKE read one headline; another said MEAT WORKERS WALKOUT CONTINUES. In yet another labor conflict, "a group of armed guards employed by the Southern Steamship Company . . . opened fire on a group of striking longshoremen, wounding four persons." More period ugliness, from Newton, Texas, about 150 miles northeast of Houston, was summed up this way: NEGRO FOUND WITH WHITE GIRL IS HANGED.

Dollars were thin but Houstonians still spent on entertainment, the slighter the better. Shirley Temple cutesied around with Adolphe Menjou in *Little Miss Marker,* and Will Rogers, in the feel-good *Mr. Skitch,* was opening at the Majestic. Bessie Wagner's radio station, KPRC, aired the "droll humor" of blackface comedians Molasses and January. Gangsters were front-page news, and took on a decided populist appeal. Shortly after George's pro wrestling debut the *Post* blared: BARROW SPEEDS TOWARD DALLAS. Clyde Barrow, wanted for six killings and a slew of robberies along with his cigar-smoking moll, Bonnie Parker, had just broken six men out of a prison near Huntsville in "a spectacular machine gun raid."

Babe Ruth's New York swats were tracked all the way in Houston, as were the fights of world heavyweight boxing champion Max Baer. Wrestling coverage was especially fulsome—the sports sections ran grappling results from St. Louis and New York—and boosterish. Two days or more before a Sigel card at the Auditorium, the city's papers would begin a series of preview or "run-up" stories on the matches, explaining with great brio why this grappler wanted dearly to rack revenge on that one; what vicious holds each might employ; why the action was certain to be hot, heavy, and hopefully, bloody. In a city eager for diversion, the Friday-night lines at the Auditorium snaked around the block from the Louisiana Avenue entrance and up Texas Avenue.

The biggest names to wrestle at the Aud in the 1930s were Strangler Lewis and Jim Londos. A Greek, Londos was known not just for his prowess but also for his handsome face and perfectly proportioned physique; Greek-god comparisons were commonplace. Though his was a decidedly masculine beauty, the attention paid to Londos's pleasing appearance—a new phenomenon in sports—might certainly have registered with the future Gorgeous One. But when George Wagner was coming up, the man on top in Houston was Whiskers Savage (real name Eddie Civil). Supposedly from Boone County, Kentucky, he also went by Leo Daniel Boone Savage, and his gimmick was the hillbilly act. He sported a big, scraggly beard, wore overalls over his trunks, and over his shoulder he carried a "toe sack," the burlap sack that potatoes were sold in. It was full of hillbilly necessities like a moonshine jug and live possums. George no doubt cast a calculating eye on the impact Savage's gimmicks, elaborate for that time, had on the crowds and the cash receipts. He wouldn't have been awed. More likely, he thought, *Possums? I can do better than that.*

In its run-up to George's first Auditorium card, the *Post* doesn't even mention him or his opening match; it may have been a last-minute replacement or addition by Sigel. In the main event, Paul Jones, "Houston hook scissor star," beat Dynamite Joe Cox, "rough New York matman," in two straight falls. Last and least, the next day's papers noted that "In the opening match between local middleweights, Billy Smith defeated George Wagner after 19 minutes . . . although at the time of the fall Wagner had a hook scissors on Smith. Smith reached up and pulled Wagner's head and shoulders to the mat before Wagner could break away."

In the scissors you trap your opponent between your legs—they're the blades—and squeeze, usually around the torso or stomach. You're usually sitting up; ideally you're behind him, and he's sitting or prone. The hook, said Tommy Fooshee, who refereed in Houston and other southern cities in the 1950s, comes when you bend one leg and stick that foot behind your other knee, then pull on the foot with your hands to cinch down even harder. Paul Jones, the main-eventer on the night of George's debut, used it as his finishing move, and on this night the rookie used it, too. Was this an early glimpse of George the appropriator, who would take elements from friends, competitors, and anyone else who'd succeeded, when he created his Gorgeous act? Despite bad weather, a reported crowd of about two thousand turned out. Even allowing for a friendly count and George's going on first, he likely performed for ten times as many people that night as he had ever done before.

It took him six months to appear before that kind of crowd again. When he worked the Auditorium next, in June, George was once again relegated to the opening match, the eight-fifteen curtain-raiser, and the last paragraph of the next day's report: "Ernie Mulhausen, bouncing Houston middleweight, scored a one-fall win over George Wagner, winning in 16 minutes with a series of flying mares." This maneuver, a wrestling staple, is a throw in which Ernie, let's say, grabs George by the wrist—or the arm, or the hair—turns his back to George, then flips him over his shoulder onto the mat. It looks flashy: The flippee is airborne, and hits the mat with a very satisfying *whomp*. But since he falls squarely on his back, it's safe. George later made the flying mare a specialty, and as preeminent wrestling historian and former promoter J Michael Kenyon observed, he used it to great effect "in both directions." By that, Kenyon meant "either throwing his own man or, even better, being thrown, because he could catapult himself so high, with his long hair flying, and so far as to make it look as though the other fellow had thrown him 15–20 feet."

Back in 1934, however, brief stints as Ernie Mulhausen's flying mare earned George five dollars or so and precious little ink. One story referred to him as "Wagoner" and the writers dwelled longer on promoter Sigel's homemade air-conditioning system. "With the hot spell still present," said the *Post*, "a corps of ice men will begin dragging 300-pound slabs of the cold stuff into the Auditorium and sliding them into the ventilating tunnels." Afterward, the move was judged a success: "The tons of ice [were] a big help to both wrestlers and spectators." George kept working one or more day jobs, still living at home with his father; Elmer, who was attending Milby; and Carl, who went by the nickname Buddy. Though he was still a part-time pro, his career quickly took on more bounce. Whatever nervousness he had felt during his debut matches at Sigel's opera house quickly vanished and the promoters at Houston's grittier arenas started using him as well. The Wagner kid had a live body, they saw. His athleticism was a cut above, such that he could easily do a kip-up, for example: Lying on the mat on his back after being thrown down, drawing his legs back toward his face, then torquing them forward and down with such force that, along with the thrust of his head, neck, and back, he propelled himself suddenly upright, all the way to standing.

It wasn't just that George could do things in the ring others couldn't. Somehow, what he did was more dynamic. When another young, strong wrestler rolled or jumped or reacted to being struck, the fans saw movement, but when George did the same thing, it was *action*. The energy he put out in the ring didn't die there but was transmitted, felt palpably, all the way up in the balcony. Later this would hold true in the much longer transmissions of television. Live or in the living room, he could put it across to the fans. In these early years his antennae got more sensitive, too, his entertainer's feel for the crowd more acute. He'd sense a reaction from the fans and then, in less time than it would take a conscious thought to form and that intention to get carried out, he'd give them another jolt—either the same move over again or an immediately improvised variation—of the same juice.

In 1935 he piled up some important firsts: on October 14, he beat Tiger Mudd in two straight falls—his first recorded win. Another semi-final, this one on the regular Wednesday-night card at Harrisburg's Boulevard Arena, earned him his first headline, albeit after a semicolon: BULL HANNA TOSSES GONZALES IN THREE FALLS; WAGNER WINS. He beat Happy Jack Beaty, "after 20 minutes of fast wrestling."

Outside the arenas, in daylight, Houston was beginning to find its way out of the Depression. The city was getting a push of sorts: Jesse H. Jones, a prominent banker and businessman, was chairman of the federal Reconstruction Finance Corporation and steered dollars and jobs toward Harris County. New intracoastal canals linked Houston with the Mississippi River navigational system and helped the economy rebound. The word *recovery* began to be heard, and ladies' fashions looked more opulent than they had in years. "Ostrich plumes once again will do their share to enhance the pulchritude and charms of the chic woman," the *Press* announced. A dozen years later those feathers would enhance the pulchritude and charms of the Gorgeous One.

Just as things began to improve, George decided to clear out. He'd wanted to leave since his mother died, but didn't know where or how he could earn his keep. In 1936 a veteran wrestler from Atlanta—probably Karl von Hoffman—came to town, and was impressed by young Wagner. He had pull with a Georgia promoter, he told George, and could get him regular work there. George was ready to make it as a full-time pro wrestler, one of the boys. He could feel it—his skills were sharpening and he was filling out, getting stronger and tipping in closer to 180. No more backbreaking, no-collar jobs for him; or rather, he'd only do the kind of backbreaking labor he loved.

When he told Poppa Wagner of the offer, the father feared for his son and tried to dissuade him. "Don't go, George," he pleaded. "It's a hard game to get into. You'll be home in a month, broke and all beat up. Stay here and come into the painting business with me." Elmer did just that, but George wanted more. He bought a bus ticket and packed up his scant gear and belongings, including the heavy woolen tights that some wrestlers still wore in the ring. George didn't like them; after the tights got soaked with sweat, they weighed three or four pounds, and he felt they slowed him down. But if the Atlanta men wore them, he'd fit in. He'd called the Atlanta promoter and the man confirmed what von Hoffman had said: There was plenty of work, and he'd find George a cheap place to flop. George would train with the more experienced local boys, and they'd teach him all he needed to know. With their help, he'd be on his way.

Instead, they nearly murdered him.

Chapter 5

A HURTING BUSINESS

Then as now the wrestling game was clannish and rough, and the promoters ran their territories like lordly fiefdoms. The boys, as their nickname makes clear, were the serfs. In the tradition of oppressed classes everywhere, they took it out on one another. Every territory had a "hooker," an experienced worker with real wrestling skills, a repertoire of painful, crippling holds called hooks—and a mean streak. If someone dared try to win a match he was supposed to lose, for example, the promoter would send a hooker to teach him a lesson. The bosses would also settle business disputes among them by vicarious combat, commanding their best hookers to fight until one man couldn't continue. In this medieval form of justice, one that made perfect sense to all involved, the winning wrestler's might established his boss's right. In St. Louis, where Lou Thesz learned the business, the administrator of pain was his teacher, George Tragos. In his memoir, *Hooker,* Thesz describes how Tragos cleared up one ring misunderstanding: "George hooked one of the kid's arms with a double wristlock, and jammed it home. It tore the ligaments, tendons and muscles in one motion. I am sure the ambulance had no trouble finding the arena, because the kid was screaming at the top of his lungs."

When a new boy came to town, the hooker, or anyone handy who didn't mind hurting people, would initiate him in his first practice session. Johnny Buff, who had his introductory hazing about fifteen years after George's, remembers it with seared clarity. When he got out of high school in Seattle, he approached a local promoter, Jack Ryan, who laughed at the 145-pound Buff, but told him the boys worked out at the Eagles Club on Saturdays, Tuesdays, and Thursdays. When he got there to find an old mat laid down in the balcony of the gym, Buff was matched with Russ Rogers, a 220-pounder whose day job was at the phone company. "He was pretty tough," Buff remembered, without rancor. "He took me in and broke four of my ribs almost immediately." That was a Tuesday. On Thursday, Buff was all taped up and couldn't take a deep breath. But he showed up at the Elks Club anyway, three times a week, until he healed. In so doing, Buff passed the test. "If you come back, they teach you. If you don't, you didn't want to wrestle anyhow."

George never saw it coming. He didn't name any names, but in later interviews he made it clear that, as fresh meat, he got his pounding. Like other fraternity hazers, the boys easily justified their brutality: They'd taken their beatings, too, hadn't they? Then, too, George's brand of cockiness might have inspired more than the usual reprisals. Instead of controlling their strength as they usually did, for instance, they might grab George by the arm and whip him into a turnbuckle, full force. The rough treatment continued during the couple of dozen matches he worked in the Atlanta area—against his friend Karl von Hoffman, who went by "Count" von Hoffman there, Wild Bill Collins, John Mauldin, and Mex McClain, among others—in the summer of 1936. "They do little unkind things like trying to break your toes and fingers," George later explained. The scariest part of this mistreatment, he added, was that "your hands are your breadwinners." Taking time off to heal a torn calf muscle or a cracked rib meant you didn't earn. Of course, no one had health insurance, either.

In the finest moment of its most elevated hour, wrestling's always been a dirty, hurting business. Back then staph infections were frequent, picked up from the smeared, grimy mats, and they caused wrestlers' bodies to break out in hideous boils. Trachoma, a contagious eye infection, was another occupational hazard. The folk remedy in use was rubbing the eyes with a blue stone, which was probably closer to a superstition than a therapy. Strangler Lewis was only one of the wrestlers blinded by this disease; in the ring he could see only the vague shape of his opponent.

Even with a script, any actor can slip, forget a blocking or a line—and on this stage that kind of mistake meant loosened teeth, a broken nose, or cracked vertebrae. A "potato" was a hard punch that accidentally landed. Normally the agony the boys acted out in their "crippling submission holds" was feigned, but if a wrestler found himself in real pain, the coded signal to his partner to ease up was tapping him quickly two times on the arm or leg. The "bumps," the falls the wrestlers intended to take, were hard, too, and the injuries real. Years of pounding on the mats and one another wearing no protective gear took its toll. Ears painfully swollen with fluid from ruptured blood vessels—cauliflower ears—were another occupational hazard, one the boys shared with boxers. That's where today's old-time wrestlers' alumni association, the Cauliflower Alley Club, gets its name. When the boys who've survived into their seventies and eighties arrive for their annual conventions in Las Vegas, they sway a little, clanking in on their metal hips and knees.

Nonetheless, George stuck. Even as the self-indulgent starlet he later became, he remained a stoic in this one way: He took the bumps and the pain, accepting them as facts of wrestling life and the means to his personal ends. In Atlanta, he managed to stay relatively healthy, and to get work two or three nights a week as the promoter had promised. If only he hadn't insisted on eating. As a "prelim boy," George got a flat, puny fee. Even for those who earned a percentage, the payoffs were whatever the promoter decided to fork over, since there was no on-the-spot accounting or transparency in this cash-only business. George could have argued at times that a full house seemed to warrant more than his few crumpled dollar bills, but that would just have gotten him blackballed by that night's promoter and, once the latter got on the phone or the telegraph wires, the rest of the territory. So George took what he was offered.

Sometimes a carload of wrestlers would drive all night in dangerous weather to get the next booking only to find that the hail or floods or snow they'd just skittered through had caused the matches to be canceled. Once again, there was no pay for no work. So they were "doubly screwed," as Thesz described it: out their time, the transportation and hotel costs, and marooned in some Nowheresville. (Triply screwed might be more accurate.) Now the "jerks" or the "jumps"— the travel times and distances between matches—were much longer than George was used to; in Houston, he'd gone home every night. Later in his career, especially after the $25 billion Federal Highway Program of 1956 created so many smooth interstates, George would ride in limousine style, but he never forgot the earlier rides, the hundreds of thousands of miles ridden on sagging shocks, trying with those early, dimmer headlights to find the right side of some dark, unmarked two-lane road. "The jumps aren't so bad when you've got a good car and the roads are good," he told a Tacoma reporter in the 1950s. "I remember the days when we'd go long distances crowded in a jalopy—and then get paid maybe $3.50 for a night's work."

These were those days. "Many a time I lay hungry and broke, and wished I was home," George said. "The only thing that kept me from hitchhiking back was what my father said to me, that I wouldn't make it as a wrestler." Fortunately life was still cheap, and almost sustainable. Hotel rooms ran as little as one dollar and the boys told George where to find "tourist homes," where families took in guests for that amount or less and, for fifty cents more, would lay out a big farmer's breakfast. Hopes of willing farmers' daughters sprang eternal, and anecdotally, at least, they materialized.

George was getting an education but he wasn't exactly moving up. Most of the work he got was "out of my class," he said, meaning that he, a light heavyweight, was matched with much bigger opponents. They'd smother him and make it tougher for him to show his stuff the way he could with a faster man. More significantly, the local promoters weren't giving him much of a buildup. Most nights he was in the openers, and once the promoters and fans start to think of you as a prelim boy or "underneath boy" (since you were at the bottom of the cards), he knew, it's hard to change their minds. So in September of 1936 George went to New York, where Jimmy James was already doing well, even working some main events billed as "Jesse James, outstanding light-heavyweight grappler from Hollywood." George took the train; at least he'd moved up in class from the bus he'd rode in on.

The city was teeming and incredibly noisy, not just with its seven million inhabitants, twice the population at the turn of the century, but also with torrents of horn-blaring cars. The great George Washington Bridge, the just-opened Triboro Bridge, and the Lincoln Tunnel, opened in 1937 with a fifty-cent toll, sent ever-increasing numbers of cars, buses, and delivery trucks swooping into Manhattan. Traffic lights had only recently come into widespread use and obeying them was not yet a habit. Actually, it's still not . . .

George wasn't fazed by Gotham, however. He didn't mind crowds; getting jostled was nothing to him; and he liked looking at millions of women. What's more, George tended to move through life in a bubble of preoccupied self-interest. Things and people outside that sphere—whatever didn't impact him directly by serving his career for good or ill, providing him pleasure or pain—faded into an innocuous background. He had a narrow focus, as do many ambitious performers and artists. Just the same, he looked before he stepped off a curb.

Much of the city's explosive population growth had come from immigrants: Irish, Italians, Russian Jews, German Jews, and a big contingent of German gentiles. The Fatherland was frequently on page one of the *Times*, the *Sun*, the *Post*, the *News*, and certainly all the German-language papers when George arrived, a month or so after the infamous 1936 Olympic Games in Berlin. Not everyone thought Chancellor Hitler had been humiliated by the victories of black American Jesse Owens over the Aryans. That October,

American Olympic Committee chairman Avery Brundage gave a German Day speech in New York, telling the audience that "Uncle Sam could learn some things from Hitler's Germany." After his remarks, the *Post* reported, "Boy Scouts of German American parentage solemnly gave the Nazi salute. Then their elders, 20,000 of them, as solemnly followed suit."

To appeal to the *"volks"* packing Yorkville and Washington Heights, George was dubbed "George Wagner of Germany." The promoters here, including Jack Curley, who ran the most prestigious arenas—Madison Square Garden at Fiftieth Street and Eighth Avenue and the Hippodrome on Sixth Avenue—felt the boys didn't need elaborate gimmicks to get over. They just played the ethnic card. George's opponents were all clearly typed: Abe Goldberg and Sammy Stein; Ali Baba the Turk; Gino Martinelli; Danno O'Mahoney; John Gudiski the Pole, "King Kong, from Abyssinia"; Henry Piers of Holland; and Tommy Nilan, the Australian Kangaroo. Chief Little Wolf, "the Navajo Indian," didn't have a big constituency; his appeal was as an "exotic." Another exotic, Chief Chewchki, the Gypsy, expressed his people's unique character and customs, the papers explained, by spitting water on himself and eating spectators' straw hats.

New York's immigrant stew formed a huge and enthusiastic wrestling audience, supporting at least one card in Manhattan and another in the boroughs every night of the week. George the German got himself booked at the New York Coliseum at Tremont Ave and 177th Street in the Bronx, Ridgewood Grove in Brooklyn, in Queens, and in Irvington and Camden, New Jersey. By mid-1937 he was working almost nightly, in much greater demand than he'd been in his Atlanta days. Most of his dates were in the smaller arenas, but he did make it to the Hippodrome in Manhattan, where he drew Zimba Parker in the opener, in front of two thousand fans. Year later, when he came back to New York a wrestling celebrity, George "arrived in LaGuardia Field with all the pomp of a motion picture star," as one paper put it. This time, however, he was probably living in a tenement walk-up, sharing digs with

James or other wrestlers, eating poorly and showering with cold water. But here again, his focus served him; he was studying for success.

George went home briefly—not as broke and beaten as his father had feared, but not exactly in triumph either. He may have gone to meet Poppa Wagner's new wife, Eulah; the couple now lived with Buddy in her house on Foster Street. When he returned the front pages were consumed with the search for Amelia Earhart, the aviator who'd been lost on her attempted round-the-world flight. The sports pages, however, were given over to heavyweight boxing champion James J. Braddock. What a story: Down-and-out, trying to feed his wife and kids on twenty-four dollars a month in relief payments, plus whatever shifts he could beg as a longshoreman, he had taken the title from Max Baer in a ten-to-one upset. Now he was about to defend it against the Brown Bomber, Joe Louis. Braddock, an Irish-American born in New York City and living right across the Hudson River in New Jersey, represented perfectly the strain of athletic heroism the American public and the pretelevision media were prepared to embrace. Braddock was stoic (he once fought with a broken hand), hardworking ("he does eight miles of roadwork every morning," reported the *Sun*), and though in his interviews he showed a sardonic wit, he was still hailed as—and may well have been—humble, self-deprecating, and sincere. This was exactly the image the arrogant Gorgeous George character would later shatter. If Braddock was the Depression's Cinderella Man, George was the postwar era's wicked stepmother.

George more likely took his transformational cues from Braddock's opponent and polar opposite, the former champion Max Baer. Just as the self-infatuated George would later do, Baer made boasts his trademark, calling himself "the world's greatest fighter and the world's greatest lover." He was only champion for a year; the handsome dark-haired playboy was equally famous for his high living, free spending, and flashy dress. Baer showed up for one fight dressed like an English nobleman, accompanied by a chauffeur and a footman, in a sixteen-cylinder limousine. Sports and society pages never failed to note upon his arrival for a fight that Baer had brought ten trunks with him, filled with bespoke suits, just as they would later regale readers with tales of George's eighty-eight sumptuous robes.

Always available and eminently quotable, Baer was mostly a lovable bad boy, but to the press he was openly contemptuous of his opponents, declaring that "they aren't fit to lick my boots." A decade later, when the great wrestler would deign to speak about his foes, George was equally disparaging, and he heaped scorn on the fans for good measure. However, while Baer may well have made an impression on young and struggling George Wagner, he was by no means a Gorgeous template. The boxer, or his public self, was a dandy, but completely manly. George's flirting with the effeminate would require an entirely different level of daring.

The big-city fans, George had learned, really liked light heavies and their faster, more acrobatic style. He particularly noticed the way they took to Jesse James. George's striking-looking Harrisburg buddy had jet-black hair parted on one side, a hawk nose, and prominent biceps. Overall, he was skinny, not chunky like George; in today's parlance, George was buff while Jesse was cut. And James was fast. The papers all praised his "whirlwind style." George recognized through Jesse the appeal of the handsome hunk; indeed, a few years later Wagner's hair seems to have darkened from brown to jet black, worn in a glistening side part, which quite became him in a Rudolph Valentino sort of way. Even though he'd been called "the Houston Flash," George recognized that he'd never be as fast as James and the other "speed merchants." He was a canny pragmatist, candid (with himself) about his own limitations. So, just as he'd repositioned himself in relation to Glen Price's Harrisburg charm, George took another tack. Handily, this retrofitting fit right in with what some of the more experienced boys in New York were trying to teach him.

When they weren't busy beating him up, the Atlanta workers had shown George how to fall as spectacularly, and as safely, as possible. In New York, he learned more about showmanship, the art that went with the wrestler's craft: Pacing, variety, modifying the tempo for dramatic effect—what musicians call dynamics. "Slow down," the older men told him in their workouts, after seeing him pour on one athletic move after another. "What you need to do," they explained, "is hit your high spot," meaning one of his showiest moves. "Then *before* you do the next thing, give your partner time to react and really sell the last one to the crowd. If you let him, he can do his half of the work, and the marks get a little time to absorb what you just did, too."

This would take a while to sink in, but in his prime George became much more of a minimalist, putting over fewer well-timed moves and reactions. Both performance wrestling in general and the Gorgeous persona in particular involved the broadest kind of acting—George and his ring opponents resembled a squawking Punch-and-Judy show—but there was undeniable subtlety in the way he played his exaggerated role: The haughty, perfectly calibrated cock of his head when the roiling crowd began to show its displeasure; the truly stricken look on his face as he reeled backward on rubber legs, absorbing a supposedly devastating blow. As the Gorgeous One, he became a withholding tease, making the fans beg, or near-riot, before he graced them with his presence. He'd send Jefferies out first for his elaborate manservant rituals, which took a good ten minutes, and then he'd have the PA announcer tell the waiting crowd: "Ladies and gentlemen, Gorgeous George refuses to enter the arena until everyone is standing, in a show of respect for the Human Orchid." The fans' curses and howls showed more fury than respect—but just the same, he had them.

It's not just what you do that gets you noticed, George was beginning to realize, it's how you do it. The opposing narratives constructed around Jim Braddock and Max Baer may also have given him a nascent sense that who you actually are isn't paramount—it's who you *seem to be,* the image you project, that people respond to. And that's not immutable, but something you can change and control. At this point he was still meeting expectations, giving the mat addicts what they were accustomed to. "They want a babyface German? Fine, I'm a handsome Kraut." It would take another imaginative leap for him to understand that people didn't just want their expectations fulfilled, that they might react even more strongly to something they'd never seen, or someone who not only defied expectations but completely violated them. To see the value of the outrageous and then to act on it—to become it—George would need more help, a different kind of push.

Chapter 6

HIS GORGEOUS MUSE

They were married in a wrestling ring, in Eugene, Oregon, on February 23, 1939. As George intended, the local paper, the *Register Guard,* was entranced by this stunt and began excitedly covering the Thursday-night nuptials at the National Guard armory weeks in advance. One story hailed the ring wedding as a combined society and sports event for the area's wrestling partisans and "Lane County's 400"—meaning the families whose lumber wealth qualified them as prominent. A combined wedding announcement and wrestling card the paper published read:

WEDDING BELLS, GRUNTS AND GROANS
Feature Wrestling Card at Armory Thursday

Main Event: Bulldog Jackson and Tony Garibaldi
vs. George Wagner and Harry Elliott, team match

Wedding Ceremony: Geo. Wagner and Betty Hanson

Opener: Jack Kaiser vs. Jimmy Londes

Referee: Vern Clark

The bride, Elizabeth Hanson, was born in Kelso, Washington, in 1913, the younger daughter of Clyde and Elsie Hanson. Betty grew up in rural Oregon, for the most part in Creswell, with her sister, Eve, who was five years older. Their mother was short and plump, with beautiful dark curly hair she passed on to Betty. Clyde, who drove logging trains and raised turkeys on a small farm—called a ranch in this part of the country—was also quite short. The "bioengineered" result: Betty was tiny. Though in later years she'd claim "five feet, almost," her true altitude was more like four-foot-nine or -ten. When she met George, she weighed ninety-five pounds. Coincidentally or not, the next woman George would marry, Cherie Dupre, was also tiny, well under five feet. In what was clearly not a coincidence, both were lookers.

Betty's parents were low-key, warm, and peaceable people. Mother, as her daughters always called her (Betty's children would call their mother that, too, never "Mom" or "Ma"), was especially patient. Betty could not remember being spanked or Elsie even raising her voice. Through some combination or aberration of nature and nurture, however, Betty was sharp and fast, impatient with constraint, eager to get places and do things—just like George. A handful from the beginning, Betty had no use for school. What she would later remember about the little building that held the elementary grades through high school in Central Point, Oregon, was her feeling of irritation. She'd try to sit still and do what she was told, but not too hard. "I was bratty," Betty said in later years, "because I hated every minute of it."

Her father was gone a lot, driving trains laden with cut timber from the logging camps to Butte Falls, Medford, and other nearby towns. Despite his absences or because of them, Betty was crazy about Daddy. "I thought an awful lot of him, and he thought an awful lot of me," is how she put it. By the time she was in seventh grade or so, Betty would sit in school, bored to death but alert for the sound of the train. Her father would blow a special pattern on the train whistle to let her know he was coming. As soon as she heard it, she'd simply get up and leave class, cut across a field, and go home to put on her blue jeans (girls had to wear dresses to school in those days). From there she'd hurl herself down a steep hill, sliding on her backside, the stiff denim slick on the grass, down to the railroad tracks where her father had stopped his train to take on water.

The firemen, who kept the engine stoked with wood, all knew her and they'd wave when they saw her coming. When she came inside the cab, Clyde would get up out of his engineer's seat and stand next to her while she ran the engine the way he'd taught her, pulling the ten or twelve cars loaded high with logs. She knew how to go forward and reverse, skills that very few girls in the early 1920s would have asked to learn, or been allowed to. After high school Betty went to a business college in nearby Medford and learned bookkeeping, typing, and shorthand, what young women who wanted careers did in those days. She got a car, a little two-door Chevrolet coupé, and left Mother and Daddy on the turkey ranch, moving into Eugene, the biggest nearby city. Betty worked as a store cashier for a while, dated a few young men but didn't get too serious, and still saw a lot of her parents. A few years later she got a job at the State Theater down the street from her rented room, where she was both cashier and "usherette." She liked the job and the movies but not the uniforms she and the other girls had to wear. Echoing George when he saw the suits in the windows of Houston department stores, Betty thought she could do better.

Elsie was an accomplished seamstress and she'd shown her daughter how to make fancy little dresses for her dolls. So, working on her own time and using her own money—and without asking anyone's permission—Betty replaced the plain white blouses and straight black pants all the usherettes wore with more colorful custom-made attire. "I made cute blouses with big puff sleeves and wide-legged pants with straps that went over the shoulder," she remembered. When queried as to whether the other girls liked her handiwork, she seemed taken aback that the question could even be asked. "Of course they did."

Betty had been working at the theater for about a year when

George Wagner strolled in to the picture show, toward the end of 1938. The projectionist at the movie theater, name of Bob, had met George at the armory matches and invited him to catch a show for free. (Then as always George had the knack of collecting people who would do things for him.) At twenty-three, he was feeling confident about himself and his prospects. Certainly, other pro athletes were doing vastly better. Joe DiMaggio, just six months older than George, was about to sign a new contract with the Yankees for $25,000, while the wrestler was probably making one tenth that. Still, $2,500 was two and a half times the national average and five times what the first minimum wage, just enacted, of twenty-five cents an hour would bring in on an annual basis. George had other reasons for contentment as well: He wasn't sacking any more cement and he punched no man's clock—he was young, strong, and making a living at the game he loved.

He looked good doing it, too. When the wrestler showed up that evening, the petite dark-haired cashier with the striking greenish eyes noticed him immediately—one good-looker responded viscerally to the other. "I thought he was a very handsome man," she said. "With beautiful dark hair. And muscles." The young man dressed nicely, too. Nothing fancy, but his slacks and sport shirt were well chosen; he clearly paid attention to his appearance. And to hers. Right away, the larger of the dark beauties asked the smaller one out, and he got his first taste of Betty's independent sass. "No," she said, "I won't go out with you, I don't know you." But after a couple more tries, with Bob vouching for young Wagner, she relented.

Their first dates were doubles: Betty went with Bob and his girlfriend to watch George wrestle, then they all went out to dinner. Very soon it was just the two of them, going out dancing. Two local wrestlers owned the down-home Glenwood Tavern in Springfield, where a steak sandwich with a soft drink cost thirty-five cents and the chicken in a basket was fifty cents, served without silverware. "Be Yourself," the menu advised, meaning use your hands. After their simple dinners, the two hit the floor, Betty wearing flattering dresses she'd made herself. George, it turned out, was a very good dancer, light on his feet, and she especially noticed his "beautiful, soft hands." Big-band swing—Benny Goodman, Glenn Miller—was the musical rage across the country, but there wasn't much of it in Eugene, so she and George ended up doing a lot of ballroom dancing, including waltzes and fox-trots.

Dancing was practically the only socially acceptable way for unmarried men and women to touch one another in public. The fox-trot didn't lend itself to much contact with its slow-slow, quick-quick pattern of steps, but during a waltz or other, more deliberate dance, Betty would lean into George, the top of her head just coming up to his breastbone, her face turned so her pale white cheek rested against his shirtfront. He smelled good, she thought. Holding her, George looked enormous, and on some inchoate level, that pleased him.

"After a couple of months," Betty said, "I guess we just fell in love." In the beginning she'd been seeing another young man at more or less the same time—Bart, the brother of one of the girls working at the theater. Betty chose George, and dispatched Bart. "Ooh, he didn't like it," Betty said, her eyes widening as she recalled the scene. "He threw a hysterical fit." George took an apartment four or five blocks away from her room and they saw a lot of each other for a couple of months. Then George went out of town for a few weeks, wrestling in Oklahoma. On the night he returned George was walking her home when he asked, "How about we get married right away?" Betty kept her equilibrium, or at least that's the way she told the story. "All right," she responded. "Now or later, it doesn't matter to me."

Betty would make George gorgeous. She sewed his spectacular finery, creating beauty in front of him as his mother did with her embroidery. She dressed the wrestler as she had the State Theater ushers and even her girlhood dolls, then put the curls and the color in his dark, straight hair. George would never be tamed, but when he was with Betty, he was remarkably compliant, deferring to this slightly older woman (she was twenty-six when they married; George was twenty-three) in ways that were quite unusual given the sexual politics of those times. Perhaps his service to his mother led George to accept

a certain level of female direction. Betty pushed, coddled, and capti-
vated him all at once, exciting and reassuring him in just the right ad-
mixture.

Betty claimed she responded calmly to his marriage proposal, but
she was excited enough about George's courting her to save a menu
from the Glenwood for the next seventy years. To her, George was a
strong man, with a strong personality, who shared her energy and eagerness for life, her adventurous sense of fun. In many ways he was
the opposite of her beloved, contained daddy. But in George, Betty
also found a man who, like Clyde Hanson, would sometimes let her
drive the train.

George had made his way out to Oregon after his New York stint,
arriving there in January of 1938. In the Northwest wrestling territory,
grapplers George's size were classed as middleweights; more importantly, the lumberjacks and salmon fishermen who filled the armories
and Legion halls liked fast action, favoring the more nimble and acrobatic workers. Here the good guys or babyfaces were known as "cleanies," and the heels were the "meanies." Like his counterparts in Atlanta
and New York, promoter Herb Owen took the handsome Wagner for
a natural cleanie and George certainly didn't object to being touted for
his good looks and "scientific" ring technique.

Billed for unknown promotional reasons as "George Wagner of
Chicago," he quickly got work in Salem, at Portland's Labor Temple,
and most of all in the National Guard armory on East Seventh Avenue
in downtown Eugene, a few blocks west of the Union Pacific railroad
tracks and, just beyond them, the Willamette River. In the next year
he would wrestle as many as 200 to 250 times, including a monthlong
trip to Oklahoma. Owen pushed the newcomer heavily and the local
fans were taken with George's athleticism and showmanship. At one
of his first Thursday-night armory matches, before a crowd of two
thousand, the *Register Guard* reported, "the newcomer left the fans
breathless as he demonstrated holds that have never been seen here . . .
The Chicago lad, built like a Greek god, is a true wrestling stylist. He
boasts a pair of 'rubber' legs that allow him to bounce around and

jump at unbelievable heights." Another story quickly pronounced him "one of the finest cleanies ever to appear here."

George liked his technique as well, but the realist in him noticed that sportswriters in Oregon were among the freest with superlatives. Here as elsewhere the scribes were compensated by the promoters to make sure wrestling was amply covered, and their payoffs went well beyond bottles of Christmas Scotch. Some newspapermen were hired to write press releases, which they then turned into their stories, and others were simply handed envelopes of cash. The Eugene writers and editors showed great enthusiasm, and it seems to have been at least partially genuine. In May George was partnered with fellow cleanie Al Szasz in a tag-team match. The two meanies, reprobates that they were, both attacked George at once—the rules clearly state that tag partners must alternate—and each got him in a leg scissors. Szasz came to the rescue, grabbing each heel by the hair and peeling them off George, only to reveal that George had both meanies tied into a "double Indian death lock," in which they were quickly pinned. This was entertaining wrestling, no doubt. To the *Register Guard,* though, it was *"the most thrilling and spectacular finish in local mat history."*

Here, too, ethnic identity and national rivalries were used to gin up fan interest. The United States' involvement in World War II was still a few years off, but by this time enough was known about Germany's National Socialists for Curley Donchin, "the Jewish lad from Philadelphia," and his ring opponent, "Baron von Hoffman, the German villain," to be billed as "natural enemies." Mixing stereotypes furiously, one anonymous writer (these wrestling stories usually weren't bylined) described Donchin as "the Philadelphia Jew with the Irish temper." The blood feud or "bitter personal hatred" between two wrestlers was another classic ploy, and George immediately got one going with "the lantern-jawed Mick," Pat O'Dowdy. The wild-eyed Irishman, as he was also known, took to calling George "prison puss," and young Wagner was properly contemptuous of his new archenemy. Asked about some threat from the Irishman before a match with José Rodriguez, George yawned and said, "I'll probably have my hands full

with this Spic without bothering about O'Dowdy." In March of 1938
"George Wagner, the people's choice," won the Pacific Coast middleweight title by beating Jack Lipscomb at the armory in front of three
thousand rabid fans. After surviving a cowardly attack from his enemy, O'Dowdy, who rushed him from the stands, George walked out
with the studded championship belt, only to lose that "coveted gon-
falon" to O'Dowdy a week or two later. And so it went.

George had a new publicity photograph taken, unveiling a much
more glamorous look. In it his hair is jet black and lies flat, parted on
the left and neatly tucked behind his ears. His bare, hairless chest is
oiled and he's got his arms crossed just below his pectorals, popping
them out and upward as if boosted by a push-up bra. His clenched fists
sit under his upper arms, making his biceps and triceps bulge. George
looks off into the distance, to his left, not at the camera. It's a posed
beauty shot, more Clara Bow than bone-bending grappler, and very
unlike the mug shots the other wrestlers handed out. George's upper
lip always had a striking Cupid's bow in the middle, but now this
prized feminine double curve is strikingly prominent. Movie actresses
of that era exaggerated their bows with lip liner; could George have
done that, too?

Night after night, though, the pretty boy took his lumps in the
ring. The roughneck fans demanded violent action, responding most
viscerally to the sight of spilled blood, which the writers called "the
claret." George injured a hip (and missed a few paydays as a result) in
losing to Gust Johnson when he overshot his run at the Swede and
flew over the ropes and crashed down on the armory floor. In later
years the apron, the area around the ring, would be padded, but in
George's day it was concrete or bare hardwood. He couldn't hesitate,
though—willingness to hurl oneself onto bone-breaking surfaces is
what separated the boys in the ring from the men in the stands. These
were the moves that got heat, the highlights the writers hailed in their
next day's accounts. After another Wagner loss, a "humiliating defeat"
by George Becker, *Register Guard* sports editor Dick Strite celebrated
the way George suffered for his art: "Catching Wagner by the wrist,

Becker whipped his opponent into the ropes and charged into the opposite strands to gain momentum to *the most smashing crash of human
flesh this writer has ever seen."*

In tracing George and Betty's alchemy, it's nigh impossible to tell
who was the sorcerer and who was the apprentice. Betty took credit
for most of their innovations. "I pushed, and he did it," she liked to say.
However, she gave him all the kudos for their first outrageous scheme,
getting married in the wrestling ring. George hesitated to ask at first,
thinking his bride-to-be might object; he hadn't known her all that
long. She said yes immediately. "I could see it was going to be great
publicity." Her parents must have been startled but they didn't object
to the unconventional nuptials. They liked George a lot, and with
their daughter still single at twenty-six, late in the game in those days,
they were probably relieved as well. George's father and brothers
couldn't make the long trip from Houston, so he and Betty planned to
go see them on their honeymoon, combining that visit with a wrestling
tour. The ceremony would not be a religious one. Betty and George
thought the local ministers might view a wrestling wedding with
some skepticism, and engaged a justice of the peace instead.

Promoter Herb Owen and his allies at the newspaper beat the
drum for weeks beforehand. As part of the buildup, George lost his Pacific Coast light-heavyweight title—middleweights were now known
as light-heavies—to Bulldog Jackson. Afterward the Bulldog told the
world: "I guess I gave that mug a wedding present, eh?" George responded by insisting that their team match at the wedding be "winner
take all." As far as the fans knew, the victor would take home the entire
purse.

As sometimes happens with important events, Betty remembered
her wedding as a blur. It was over practically before she knew it; unlike George's wrestling match, the marriage was scheduled for only
one fall. Betty and her mother made her dress together, working evenings in the living room at the turkey ranch. It was a long white gown
with panels of tulle or white net, and it had a white veil of the same
material. Even the fans in the back of the house could see the way its

tucks showed off her tiny waist and other curves, and the white halo around her head made her dark hair look even more lustrous. She carried a bouquet of pink roses and sweet peas, and her daddy gave her away. One of the things she remembered more clearly afterward was the line of potted plants and flowers along the aisle floor leading to the ring, and then the flower arrangements—tulips and acacia, with local heather—arranged around the mat surface. That raised, altarless square sat in the center of the brick armory, surrounded by rows of wooden seats and, above, the balcony. Unsure whether wedding or wrestling etiquette prevailed, the fans rose to their feet when she appeared at the top of the aisle, and began to applaud.

George, used to the public eye and in his element, could take a mental step back, and better observe his stunt realized. Just the thought that others were paying to see him get married instead of shelling out himself gave him a little kick of glee. He stood waiting for Betty in the ring in his black tuxedo, joined by Bob, the projectionist who'd introduced them, his best man, and Dee Esta, the maid of honor, a friend of Betty's and fellow usherette. Promoter Owen's sons, Elton and Don, served as ushers. George surveyed the crowd, and he could see immediately that there were far more spectators jamming into the arena than the two thousand or so who normally came to the Thursday night matches. Close to thirty-five hundred, out of a Eugene population of twenty-three thousand, paid to attend. George's grin grew a little wider; he'd negotiated a higher-than-usual percentage of the gate with Owen. When he heard the people begin to clap, then turned and caught sight of Betty, though, his vision narrowed, and the surroundings disappeared for him, too.

The justice of the peace, Mr. Kennedy, played it straight, and the couple likewise behaved. In short order, the "I do's" were spoken, to more applause from the standing fans. Betty left the ring and sat down, still in her wedding dress, in one of the front rows with her parents, along with Eve and her children. George went down to the dressing rooms in the armory basement and put on his wrestling gear. He and Harry Elliott, a wrestler and frequent referee, were the cleanies, taking on meanies Tony Garibaldi ("the Italian mat villain and two-fisted slugger who throws caution and ethics to the wind") and sworn Wagner foe Bulldog Jackson.

The *Register Guard* sent their society writer, Catherine Taylor, to cover the event, giving the wrestling scribes the day off. Judging from her long story the next day, "Wedding Bells Ring at Armory Mat Match," she had never attended a wrestling match before. She called the boys "players" and the falls "rounds," but she just as clearly enjoyed the assignment. The meanies she likened to "two primitive animals" who put on "an exhibition of the cruelest and most obnoxious tussling that can be imagined . . . with no sense of fair play." When George and Jackson plummeted out of the ring together, she observed, they fell into the lap of a woman "who wore a lovely high-crowned black hat with a red feather." The woman's male companion slapped the meanie, and the melee continued.

The match went the distance, three falls, the groom's team prevailing "much to the delight of the crowd which was by this time surging about the ring in great excitement." After the wrestling and a quick shower for George, Herb Owen hosted a small reception for Mr. and Mrs. Wagner in a room off to the side of the main auditorium, serving coffee and wedding cake. The mood was one of jollity and relief: The tag teaming of bride and groom and the wrestling had both gone according to plan, and the turnstiles had turned in very satisfying fashion. The conversation turned to the honeymoon. Betty and George had bought a new car—well, a used one—a beige Ford sedan, since Betty's coupé was too small for them and their luggage. They were headed for points south: Los Angeles, then El Paso, to Houston to meet George's family, and then to a series of matches booked in Mexico.

On the same day the *Register Guard* reported their wedding, it ran a regular column reporting the doings of local families. Mr. and Mrs. Vern Keahy would be vacationing at the Grand Canyon, this edition noted, and from there would travel to the World's Fair, in Flushing Meadow, New York. The theme of that exhibition was "Building the

World of Tomorrow." What role the gigantic fourteen-ton typewriter displayed by Underwood (its ribbon was a hundred feet long) would play in the future remains unclear. However a genuine technological breakthrough was showcased at the RCA Pavilion. President Franklin D. Roosevelt gave an address at the Fair, and was simultaneously seen and heard elsewhere. Not later, as in a newsreel, but just as it happened. Not just his voice, either, which radio listeners were accustomed to, but his image and movements as well, conveyed by a transmitter atop the Empire State Building. Since this new system sent things seen over distances, it was called "tele-vision."

Another prominent story that day told of a painful, career-threatening injury to one of the country's most beloved athletes. Seabiscuit had come up lame earlier, and had just been pulled from the $100,000 Santa Anita Handicap. The five-year-old had beaten War Admiral at Pimlico in their famed match race the year before, and the American public had thrilled to the Biscuit's every bit of news, from what he was or wasn't eating to his animal companions. There were Seabiscuit songs, hats, and board games—transcending sports, the horse became a cultural icon. Ten years later George had songs written in his honor and dolls created in his image; he also became a societal touchstone.

The proud horse and the overly proud wrestler were very different phenomena, however: Culturally as well as biologically, they belonged to different species. The Biscuit was the plucky, lovable underdog, his skills, mettle, and even his looks denigrated, before he was gloriously redeemed. In real life George's rise from rags to riches followed a similarly heartwarming trajectory, but in his Gorgeous public persona he was the preening overdog, an arrogant winner who admitted neither struggle nor sincerity. George's message was that nice guys *should* finish last; they're suckers, and worse, they're boring. Seabiscuit was all heart, the mute horse a variation on the strong, silent type. George was all mouth; he wouldn't shut up.

Their paths to fame were different, too. Seabiscuit actually had to beat those other horses to the finish line, while George's triumph had little to do with athletic competition and everything to do with the entertainer's art. At that game, George won in a romp; it was literally and figuratively no contest. Between the Depression and the victorious muscle flexing of post–World War II America, there was a sensibility shift. Rather than embracing a gallant, galloping horse, the country was fascinated by a braying, preening man in short pants.

Chapter 7

SWERVES AND CURVES

On their way south the honeymooners stopped in Los Angeles, where Betty met Jesse James, and they stayed a night or two in his Hollywood apartment. The next couple of months were spent zooming around the Southwest: Tucson, Phoenix, Yuma, Albuquerque, then east to El Paso, then west again. They shared the driving, but often it was Betty at the wheel while George slept in the backseat. Air-conditioning in cars debuted in 1939 when Packard offered it as a $274 option—but the driver had to stop the car and disconnect the compressor belt from the engine. It didn't matter; their heap didn't have it. Neither of them minded, they just kept the windows down and their clothing minimal. As she zoomed along, wearing shorts and a short-sleeved top, warm air swirling around her bare legs, Betty saw and felt the high desert for the first time, and fell in love with it—the sand, the wind, and during the amazingly clear nights, the stars. Later they'd move to similar territory in Beaumont, California, which sat high in the San Gorgonio Mountain Pass, near the Mojave.

One hot afternoon the newlyweds were speeding through the desert, on a stretch of terrain so flat it seemed they could see twenty miles in front of them. At the horizon, though, it suddenly began to get dark. Peering through the top of their windshield, they couldn't see clouds anymore, just a horizontal swath of sky where the lights had gone out. The closer they got to it, the darker the day became, and George, who was driving, slowed down. "What is it?" Betty asked. "I don't know, Sweetie," he answered, looking up, too. Then they saw white hail bouncing off the black road, still a good way ahead of them, but approaching fast. George braked some more, then pulled off the road altogether, stopping on the edge of the sand. Mesmerized, they watched, the car still sitting in the hot sunlight, as the dark sky and the hail kept coming closer, then closer still. George turned off the car and at first there was silence; then the sound of the stones on the pavement got louder, like a rushing waterfall, only staccato at the same time.

Moving at the same moment, George and Betty reached to roll up their windows, then waited for the onslaught to pound their hood and roof. They held hands. *Will hail like that break the windshield?* Betty wondered. The dark sky and the white sheet descending from it kept coming toward them—and then the hail suddenly stopped moving horizontally even as it continued to roil vertically. The hailstones skittered off the pavement just a car length in front of them, but came no closer. In a few quick minutes the storm emptied itself, and the downpour stopped. The road in front of them began to lighten and the darkness receded. Sitting silently next to each other in the front seat, they watched as the narrow shaft of sunlight they'd been sitting in expanded to the horizon.

To keep in training, George did his roadwork during the heat of the day, running along the two-lane highways in his plain black trunks and wrestling shoes. (He was a smoker, but the cigarettes didn't seem to affect his stamina.) George ran bare-chested; as Betty later reported, laughing at her husband's vanity, "George never wore a shirt if he didn't have to." When he began to run, she drove ahead, parked in the shade a mile or two up the road, and waited for him to catch up. Sometimes when she saw him appear in the rearview mirror, gasping for breath with the sweat pouring off his chest, she'd wait until he was almost at the car, then gun the motor and drive off again, spraying him with red dust that clung to his soaked torso. Without turning around to look back, Betty would give him a little cheery wave with her free arm as she pulled away. George laughed, too, still panting and trying to catch his breath, and he'd wave back. She'd wait for him another half mile ahead, and this time she'd let him in.

They crossed the border into Mexico, where George's first dates were in Monterrey. His quickness and athletic style pleased the fans of *lucha libre*, or free fighting, the fast, acrobatic variant of pro wrestling that still prevails there. Later, when he was Gorgeous, he'd be hailed in Mexico as "Jorge El Magnífico." One night on their honeymoon, though, George's pay from the previous match had gotten lost in translation, and he refused to go on. "I'm not wrestling until I get my money!" he yelled angrily, shaking off the arena workers who were hanging on his arms and trying to lead him to the ring. With the fans, the promoter, and the opposing wrestler's camp all threatening violence, guns were drawn by the Guardia Civil soldiers patrolling the ring's perimeter. It's unclear whether the firearms were pointed at George or at the shouting, stomping crowd.

The nervous promoter hurriedly found Betty in her ringside seat. Go get your car, he told her, and wait by a certain exit. "As soon as George comes out that door," he said, "get going and get out of town." George deemed it wiser to wrestle, so Betty spent a nerve-racking half hour before he came through the doorway—still in his trunks, unshowered, and clutching his duffel bag in one hand. He jumped in and they sped off, not only blowing town but leaving Mexico and sprinting to Laredo, Texas. They escaped with their skin intact, but they did so without any payment—for either date.

In Houston, Betty finally met Poppa Wagner, Elmer, and Buddy. George didn't take his new wife to see any of his childhood homes or haunts, and she didn't ask. George's dad was living with his second wife, Eulah, in her neat little white one-story house, much like the ones George had grown up in, though in a different working-class neighborhood. Betty took to Poppa Wagner immediately, but, somewhat predictably, she and Eulah did not warm to each other. In the future, when Poppa Wagner and Eulah would visit George and Betty in California, he'd stay for months but his wife would go back to Houston after a few days. And on this visit, the newlyweds stayed with friends. They stopped by to see Mr. James, Johnny and Jimmy's father, whose fruit stand George had wrestled next to as a boy, and he welcomed them with a home-cooked Greek feast.

Mostly they drove, hustling day and night to cover the long distances between arenas and the cheap hotels the wrestlers frequented, hitting Amarillo, Oklahoma City, Little Rock, and Springfield, Missouri in the later stages of this ten-month extended honeymoon. If he could get the work, George wrestled five nights a week, and at times they barely made it to the next date, George changing in the backseat while Betty drove, screeching into the parking lot with minutes to spare. In less hurried arrivals she prepared his wrestling bag for him, packing everything he'd need: trunks, socks, wrestling shoes, towels, and the like.

This gave her an opening for what the wrestlers called a "swerve." Swerves were practical jokes, much prized and pulled often. The cruder the stunts, the better the boys liked them, though Betty's were more restrained. At one of the couple's stops she found time to shop during the day, so she went to a sewing store and picked up some frilly white lace, imported from France. While George was making arrangements with the local promoter in the afternoon, she sewed ringlets of the stuff around both legs of his wrestling trunks, then packed them away in his bag. When it was time for him to leave for the arena in the evening, she handed it to him with a smile. "Here you are, dear," she said sweetly. "It's all ready for you."

George got to the locker room and innocently pulled out the bizarre garment in front of all the boys. It now resembled gym shorts that had been involved in a tragic accident with some women's lingerie. He held the trunks out at arm's length in front of him, staring uncomprehendingly while the wrestlers hooted and pointed, calling everyone's attention to the frilled thing Wagner had in his hands.

"Look at Mr. Fancy Pants!"

"Hey, sweetheart, nice drawers! You free tonight?"

Then George grinned as he realized he'd been swerved. Betty's stock immediately shot up among the boys; they knew she was pretty, but pulling off a stunt like this earned her a very different kind of esteem. This foray, as well as Betty's leaving George in the dust while he did his roadwork, were almost certainly payback for some earlier pranks of his. Once, while they were still courting in Oregon, they went dancing at a nearby honky-tonk. At the end of one song, George dipped his partner, taking Betty in his arms and lowering her all the way down until her back touched the floor. Then, instead of lifting her back to standing in the typical finale, he simply let go and left her there, lying on the barroom floor. As he walked away back toward their table, he threw her a wink.

Their constant one-upmanship kept them laughing and gave them a mischievous bond. Betty loved being caught up in George's special energy, especially when he brought it to bear on her alone. In it, she shone. In their quieter moments, she remembered, he was solicitous and accommodating. George craved attention, yet he knew how to give it as well. He may have transferred the intense focus he had on his mother as a boy, and sought the rapport the two of them had shared with his wife.

Toward the end of 1939 George and Betty made their way to Columbus, Ohio. They rented half of a house they shared with wrestler Cyclone Mackey (real name Corbin Massey) and his wife, Geraldine, and George went to work for promoter Al Haft. The driving got shorter and saner as they cycled between Columbus and the arenas in Lima, Marion, Fort Wayne, Zanesville, Elyria, and Toledo. Their expenses were lower, too, with fewer hotels and more home-cooked meals. But they still couldn't quite make ends meet, much less get ahead. "The truth is," Betty said ruefully, "we were pretty broke by the time we hit El Paso," one of their first honeymoon stops. As happens so consistently, love failed to pay a single bill.

George thought he'd gotten his next big break when promoter

Hugh Nichols agreed to book him in Los Angeles later that year at Hollywood Legion Stadium. This white-painted 1921 building on El Centro sat six thousand or more fans in pitched seats. But in two separate stints that year, George couldn't get much traction with the fans, nor, one senses, a real push from Nichols. After one June loss in an opener, the *Los Angeles Daily News* dismissed Betty's husband with this imagery: "Yukon Jake, fresh from his fishing trip in the hinterlands, threw George Wagner around as if he were a rainbow trout on the end of his line."

During these L.A. sojourns George and Betty became good friends with Dangerous Danny McShain, a very successful heel, and his wife, Nola. McShain was a charismatic black Irishman, about seven or eight years older than George, with a barrel chest and a thin dark villain's mustache. In the ring McShain had a great dynamism and a piratical appeal; many wrestling historians consider him one of the game's greatest showmen. Quick to laugh and to provoke laughter over the dinners the two couples shared, he looked exceedingly dapper and seemed to be enjoying himself immensely in his double-breasted white suits. Danny's finery made George's neat slacks and sport shirts look a bit boyish. Though he and Betty would remain friends with Danny and Nola for a long time, their differences in status at that time were glaring.

George wrestled McShain at the armory in Eugene that June, and the two were billed, naturally, as "bitter enemies." The *Register Guard,* an ever-reliable cheerleader, predicted beforehand that promoter Owen could expect "the largest crowd since Hector was a pup." George the cleanie won, or rather he "battered the villain from one side of the ring to the other," and the dastardly McShain even got a "lusty drop-kick from a ringside spectator" in the process. To keep the feud going afterward George proclaimed himself unsatisfied with the victory, saying that McShain had deprived him of a title match he deserved back in L.A. On one level this was just the usual ballyhoo, yet there was a current of real envy in his lament. "Who wouldn't be mad?" George told the reporters at his locker after the match. "The guy built a $20,000 home in Los Angeles and has three new cars. I'd like to get a chance at that kind of money."

Six months in Hawaii put the struggling couple in a much better frame of mind. In this idyll George wrestled often, the promoter found them cheap lodgings right near the beach, and they lived on fresh fish. Best of all there was no travel, as all the matches were in Honolulu. That left plenty of time for George and Betty to try to out-tan each other; she won, turning a nut brown. Wearing a fairly modest one-piece with her hair tied back, Betty stood on George's stomach as he did sit-ups on a towel. Together they charmed the local press. For one beach photo shoot Betty added high heels to her bathing costume and let her curls down. She struck a model's pose, standing with the front leg slightly bent, and hung on George's arm with both hands. Squinting toward the camera in the sun, his hair wet and slicked back, George wore what looked like an early version of a white Speedo, and his thigh muscles bulged.

Betty found some white satin in a fabric shop and made herself a knee-length skirt, a blouse, and a short jacket, on the back of which she sewed WAGNER in black letters. She put white bows in her hair and wore low-heeled white boots to match—for some reason, in later years she'd be adamant that they weren't cowgirl boots, but some other, nonwestern style. She became George's "second" or aide-de-camp at the matches, adding considerable visual appeal and a novelty twist for the appreciative fans. Relaxed and loose, the two experimented, giving an out-of-town tryout to some of the tomfoolery that would later become the Gorgeous act. "I fixed a tray with perfumes and powders and some other goop on it, and there was a tiny spray bottle, too," Betty said. "And I wore that white outfit. I'd walk up to the ring with the tray and sit on the edge and hand him those things and he'd take them and use them. We just did it three or four times for laughs."

It went over: George frequently got top billing and set a local attendance record of six thousand for a match with Hawaiian Ben Pilar. After a good long run, they came back to Oregon. The press there heralded the coming of "Betty the Second" to the matches, but she never appeared. "I just didn't feel like it," she said, citing a reason that to her always seemed more than sufficient. Without his attractive second George went back to relying on his athleticism and stunts to get heat. Against Taro Ito, a "pudgy Japanese matman," George used those powerful thighs to leap straight up and over Ito's head as he stood in the middle of the ring, then grabbed him from behind for a press and the fall. In July he crawled under the ring, then came up from the other side to surprise and flatten Bulldog Jackson. In September of 1941 George won the Pacific Coast light-heavyweight title from Jack Kiser, which soon got him elevated to "world's champion" in promoters' parlance. Fans turned out reliably, if in modest numbers, to see good-looking good guy Wagner perform at the Oregon arenas—though now they had to drive there on rationed gasoline.

The Japanese Imperial Navy had just bombed Pearl Harbor, little more than ten miles from where George and Betty stayed on Oahu, and the country was at war. The next attack, it was feared, could come anywhere at any time, so nighttime blackouts immediately went into effect all the way up the West Coast, even in Eugene, sixty miles inland. Within months George and Betty had their first ration books, issued by the national Office of Price Administration. They could only buy allotted amounts of gasoline, sugar, butter, meat, coffee, and other staples by tearing stamps out of their books. That is, if those things were available at all. Chicken-wire fencing, an Oregon farm essential, was rationed, too, and rubber tires—crucial in the itinerant wrestling business—were especially tough to come by. Manufactured cigarettes were mostly reserved for the troops, so George's Chesterfields were scarce and he, like millions of other Americans, learned to roll his own.

In Creswell, Eugene, and everywhere the couple went, they saw houses with red-and-white banners in the front windows, and in the center of each rectangular flag was a blue star, signifying that the family living there had a son in the service. Some of these service banners, as they were known, had two or more stars on them, and soon the gold stars began to appear, sewn onto the blue. Each of those signaled a soldier who would never return. The United States had become a nation of soldiers—sixteen million men and women would serve. Many wrestlers and other athletes enlisted, including Joe Louis, who joined a segregated army and served in the same unit as Jackie Robinson. Baseball's Joe DiMaggio, Ted Williams, Bob Feller, and Hank Greenberg served, among many others, along with golf great Sam Snead.

George reported to Lane County induction centers many times, took his physicals (at the first one he weighed in at 185 and was measured at just five-foot-eight and a half), and got his serial number. Yet he never served. For five years he was granted one deferment after another, including a mysterious 4-F exemption, meaning he was unfit for military service for "physical, mental or moral reasons." George never explained this and Betty's recollection was hazy; she thought George might have gotten out of serving by claiming he was claustrophobic. Among the surviving wrestling old-timers, the presumption is that George went down to his local draft board, showed them his effeminate routine—"acted like a fruit," as one former colleague put it—and was dismissed as a homosexual. But during the war years, George had yet to swish.

The wrestling game, though diminished during wartime, adapted and survived. In Eugene, Herb Owen, who was charging around fifty cents per seat and seventy-five cents for ringside, established earlier starting times so fans could get home before the blackouts began. One ten-man battle royal, a free-for-all in which the last man standing was declared the winner, was combined with an intricate bidding scheme that managed to fill the house and sell ten thousand dollars' worth of bonds for "Uncle Sam's war chest" in a single evening. George got to continue working when many others didn't, but whatever momentum his career was gathering was lost in May of 1942 when he shattered an ankle in the ring. He had to sit out a few months, earning nothing. George and Betty stayed with Mother and Daddy Hanson at their turkey ranch while he convalesced and she helped out with the chores. At twenty-seven George was still filling out and he put on some more weight during his inactivity, hitting his high-water mark of 190 or so.

From then on he'd be classed as a junior heavyweight. More importantly, Team Wagner had time to sit and think, to ponder their future, which soon became a brood. The couple wanted to start a family, but were barely feeding two people on George's wrestling take, even with Betty eating like a particularly figure-conscious bird.

"You know I'm working as hard as I can, Sweetie," George said dejectedly one evening at the turkey ranch. "And now with this darn ankle . . ." (Even before he made his genteel refinement a commercial calling card, George never swore in front of ladies.) "I know, George," Betty said, trying to reassure him. They had to do better, but how? As they fretted and schemed, they may well have thought about Danny McShain, the success he was having, and the affluent lifestyle he and Nola had shown them in L.A. After some more silent consideration Betty rendered her judgment. "You just can't wrestle like this anymore," she told him. "There's not enough work and you're not really making the big money.

"You're too clean a wrestler, George," she concluded, looking right at him and pronouncing on his career—on their lives—with her customary confidence. *"Let's make it dirty."*

From her lips, as it were, to Muhammad Ali's ear. Twenty years later the boxer, with George urging him on, also chose a villain's role. In the prewar years, however, when George and Betty began to create their version of the antihero, very little in American culture suggested they'd be rewarded, especially outside the wrestling world. Even there, while heels including McShain, Red Berry, Ted "King Kong" Cox, Dirty Dick Raines, and Ivan Rasputin made main-event money, the promoters knew their audiences well enough to make clean, admirable Lou Thesz the perennial champion. Remarkably, the heel Betty and George invented would triumph in the culture at large, where the square-jawed, well-intentioned, courageous, and upstanding man still ruled.

Back in the early 1940s it was clear who the worthies were: They wore the white hats. The Lone Ranger lived only to serve, first on his radio show and then on television, from 1949 to 1957. Silver's owner and Tonto's employer didn't drink or smoke, for purity's sake and also to prepare himself "to fight when necessary for what is right." What's more, this leading man didn't want any reward for his good deeds, nor, in what now seems a quaint anachronism, any recognition—he even wore a mask to prevent it. For American boys, this was the prevailing fantasy and for grown men the ideal way of being. Not incidentally, it was also the way to succeed. Like Seabiscuit, the Ranger was both an icon and a franchise, spawning movies, comics, novels, toys, and games. The Masked Man's upright ride was a potent cultural force for almost all of George's career—in a sense, he was what George and Betty were up against.

For a bad man to take on a heroic good guy was clearly a losing battle: Villains were necessary as plot devices but essentially existed to be conquered. They weren't leading men; they were put-over boys. The public could laugh along with madcap rule-breakers like the Marx Brothers and enjoy the (harmless) misanthropy of W. C. Fields, but America wasn't yet ready to root for a true malefactor or empathize with a protagonist whose flaws ran too deep. The comic-book crime fighter Batman, who first appeared in 1939, had a vengeful streak and a following, but the preeminent hunk of rectitude was Superman. The Man of Steel, another contemporary of George's who debuted in 1938, was the ultimate babyface. Like the Lone Ranger he was selfless; he even sacrificed love and the possibility of life with Lois Lane for the common good. Many babyface wrestlers would mimic him, pushing out their pumped-up chests and striking noble, chin-thrusting poses; one, bodybuilder Walter Podolak, took the name Golden Superman.

The Gorgeous One and Superman were titans in juxtaposition— what a shame the two never met in the ring. Actually, they might have. In 1959 George Reeves, who played Clark Kent and his alter ego on TV, announced he was considering going into professional wrestling. He'd wrestled as an amateur at Pasadena City College as a light-heavyweight, and Reeves could see the billing already, he said: "Superman, the Man of Steel vs. Gorgeous George."

In their daring reinvention George and Betty would surpass the merely dirty (as would Clay/Ali). Ultimately, the couple found, it's as one-dimensional, and thus as limiting, as "clean." They reimagined and expanded heelishness into a villainy that was much more nuanced and complex. In so doing they redefined the role that the bad guy, the other who is always with us, gets to play, and in their hands the villain grew to the hero's size. This gamble by two playful twentysomethings arguably changed what it means to be a star, and who gets to become one. Of course they never thought of it that way. "We were just having fun," Betty said, adding a pet expression that dates back to her girl-hood in the 1920s. "I tell you, we had more fun than a picnic."

ACT TWO

"After I saw Gorgeous George,
and realized he had added a special
flamboyance to his matches,
[that] helped to create the James
Brown you see onstage."

—The Godfather of Soul

Chapter 8

MEAN OLD GEORGE

Dirty called. George had to unleash the beast, to transform himself from handsome cleanie to despicable thug, and he'd been a babyface his whole career. It was a leap, yet not a problem. The scowl, the sneer—and especially the strut—came quickly, naturally. He still held the Pacific Coast light-heavyweight title, but with the cooperation of the promoters and the press, he soon became known as a crybaby, whiner, and a cheat. And Georgie the bad boy began to do "little unkind things." George lustily eye-gouged ("Foul!" the fans and writers cried), kidney-punched ("Despicable!"), and hammered his opponents with his closed fist ("Totally uncalled for!"). A "vicious stranglehold" he invented was quickly ruled illegal, and he lost a series of matches on fouls and disqualifications. In 1942 the *Register Guard* doubted before one title defense "if the champion will have a backer outside of his immediate family." By the end of that year the paper was sadly forced to announce his expulsion from the cleanie ranks.

When Wagner the "mat gangster" took on a local warrior on furlough from the army, Sergeant Babe Smallinski, and crushed him with a stomping hammerlock, some of the fans screamed at George for not serving his country. "You took a 4-F, a healthy wrestler like you? You coward! Shame!" George got a white-hot feud going with Walter Achiu, an Asian-American whose surname earned him the nickname Sneeze. "You dirty rotten half-breed so and so!" George yelled at him in the ring. "I'll teach you to put your stinking hands on me. And behind my back, too. Just like a stinking Jap!" The heel's appeal to the racism and suspicion aimed at the Japanese enemy—and Japanese-Americans—fell apart, though, when it was pointed out that Achiu was of Chinese descent. Undeterred, George quickly changed his tune. "I'll either get another match with that Chink," he vowed in the locker room afterward, "or I'll get the hell back to Hollywood, where they know how to treat you like a white man." One bloody grudger with Achiu in Salem was a winner-take-all event, and after the Sneeze won, the promoter counted out "$1,000 in cold but cuddlesome cash" into his hand at ringside, with George forced to watch the payoff. Such an approving roar went up at Wagner's humiliation that "the roof tried to leave the bop hall."

He and Betty began distributing a new photo to the press. Instead of the poised beauty pose, this was an action shot, in which the former oiled matinee idol with bulging muscles had been replaced by an almost unrecognizable wild man, a snarling ruffian in black trunks. "Desperate George Wagner," one caption called him. His straight black hair, once short and neat, now fell messily down over his eyes and onto the sides of his face as he crouched aggressively in a grappling stance, left arm outstretched to claw an imaginary enemy, right fist cocked. His lips curled back, baring his teeth in a fierce grimace. Suddenly he looked most unhandsome, bound to displease.

The heel turn played. "Mean Old George," as Betty dubbed his new incarnation, was booked solidly in Oregon arenas, and worked in front of bigger crowds. Through his strenuous efforts, good looks, and athleticism, George had carried off the babyface role, but as the offender, the depraved ne'er-do-well, he easily, instinctively, infuriated the fans. After George lost his title to Herb Parks, the *Register Guard* captured the new dynamic neatly, reporting that "Wagner lost some friends, but assured himself of a larger following of spectators who will pay on the line to see him licked." This is exactly the approach that George would suggest to Cassius Clay twenty years later. At times, repentant George appeared. "I'll admit my temper got the best of me and that I've turned rough at times," he told a reporter plaintively. He longed to win his way back into the hearts of spectators, he declared, "if the fans will let me." But by that point no one really wanted baby-face George back.

Though he intentionally provoked them, George wasn't completely prepared for the fans' reaction. *"They really hate me,"* he realized early on, seeing the men's reddened faces at ringside and hearing their bellowed threats and insults. "Coward!" they'd scream, along with the most primal shout of all, directed at his morally superior opponent: "Kill him!" At first he laughed with Betty, even a bit scornfully, at how easily the marks' emotions were manipulated. The next revelation didn't amuse him a bit: *"They'll hurt me if they can."* All the fist shaking and cursing, the wadded-up programs, newspapers, pennies, and buttons thrown his way didn't worry him, nor did the lit cigarettes. But the hurled pop bottles, which thankfully were few, could split your scalp.

The ends of matches were the most dangerous moments, when crowds sometimes rushed to ringside to vent their fury. Once in 1943 George the sore loser was protesting his defeat by Tony Ross at Eugene's Pearl Street Arena. To make his feelings clear, he went after the referee (Elton Owen, the promoter's son, who also wrestled) with a few haymakers. That got one fan's blood up—strangely enough, it was a man with a wooden hand—and he climbed into the ring. Bent over the prostrate Owen, George had his back to the enraged fan and the crowd was so loud, he didn't hear him approach. In a matter of seconds, the man struck George several times in the head and face with his wooden prosthesis, cutting him badly. Holding both arms out in front of him as a battering ram, with blood streaming down from his hairline, George barreled his way to the dressing room, pushing aside more irate fans in his way. When they saw the blood on his face, and the anger there, they stepped aside.

Another night at the armory in Salem, George had Tony Ross

down in a corner, stomping him fiendishly, when eight or ten fans rushed the ring. Suddenly George saw a glint at the edge of his gaze—one man was brandishing a knife. After a short struggle, the ushers and off-duty policemen working security subdued the knife wielder and quelled the riot.

Good guys never had these days at the office, George thought to himself. Once again, though, he would take the pain; he was willing to risk his scalp and sacrifice his body to get ahead. After the Pearl Street bloodletting, Team Wagner told the press that George was demanding police protection to and from the dressing room before his next match, a "grudger" against Elton Owen. As George and Betty intended, this special treatment only infuriated the fans further. "Thousands of fans will flock miles" to see Wagner get his comeuppance, the *Register Guard* declared.

George and Betty were renting a tiny ranch, complete with a few turkeys, outside of Eugene and Poppa Wagner came up and stayed with them for a time. Then, one wet and chilly wartime winter, they moved to Portland, living on Northwest Fifteenth Avenue, not far from the Willamette River. George was working the docks by day and wrestling at night in Portland, Salem, Medford, and Eugene. (His jobs there and across the Columbia River in Vancouver, Washington, were considered national defense work and earned him at least one of his deferments.) Betty punched the clock in the shipyards, too, though not particularly hard. She sat high on her perch in the nice warm chart house, handing out nautical maps and other papers. George and his buddies, including some fellow wrestlers, would come in and eat their bag lunches with her, then head back out into the freezing rain. In the afternoons she'd wave merrily to him as he'd pass by her window, bundled up, breath steaming from his nose and mouth. His ears turned pink and those beautiful soft hands were getting red and raw through his soaked work gloves. Meanwhile, Betty purred by the heater. "I never even went out there to see what George was doing," she reported. "Why go out in the cold?"

By this time George was often at the top of the cards and earning up to fifty dollars for a main-event match—pretty rich, he thought, for a couple hours' work. He and Betty were each making another forty a week or so in their defense jobs, and for a short time the young couple was flush. But the true luxury the war afforded them was the time and space to invent, to create. The pure heel routine would pale eventually, they knew. Newly mean George gave a terrific rendition, but the fans had seen eye gouging before. What could get the fans even more worked up; how to better bring the heat? Maybe it wasn't something else he could *do,* they thought, but what he could become. Toward the end of 1943 they took their first Gorgeous step.

Betty's white satin outfit had caused quite a stir in Hawaii, she reminded George. True, that reaction had a lot to do with the way she filled the fabric, but now they wondered: What if they dressed up George? Wouldn't a working-class audience, making do on wartime rations, resent anyone who made a display of luxury, who clearly had the goods? Why, they'd hate George even before he threw his first kidney punch! George and his wife weren't sociologists or pollsters, and their calculations weren't all that fine. The provocations they devised were based on a shared love of mischief and a keen, intuitive sense of what the market wouldn't bear. Wittingly or no, they chose a sensitive area in which to experiment. Clothing, always a powerful and emotional symbol, was scarce and the restrictions on it severe. The heels on women's shoes were limited to one inch to save material, and due to fabric shortages, men's suits now came with a vest and only one pair of pants instead of two. Suits hanging unworn in absent servicemen's closets were tailored into women's outfits, some with the shoulder pads still inside, and those reconstituted suits became a signature 1940s style.

They never acknowledged it, but Danny McShain may have been an early influence here, too. The strutting Irishman was known for his gaudy outer wear, though he favored short jackets instead of robes. They were often quite hideous: One shiny jacket had high, padded shoulders and puffy, paisley-patterned sleeves, with DANNY inscribed in gold letters running down one side of his chest and MCSHAIN down the other. The robes Betty made for George would far surpass their friend's outfits, but it seems likely that the two young image makers began in part by following his garish lead.

Betty and Elsie, her seamstress mother, bought yards of a shimmering deep blue satin fabric and fashioned a long capelike raiment with a wide, circular skirt as its lower half, festooned across the chest and shoulders with silver sequins. To hear the Gorgeous One tell it later, the Portland promoter refused at first to let him wear this feminine frippery at the Labor Temple, a union hall that also hosted sporting events. "Wear that in my place of business?" he roared. "Certainly not! You're a wrestling dame!" George also maintained that unruly fans grabbed his new robe and tore it to shreds, costing him $250. Of course the promoter would have been in on the stunt from the outset, and the homemade robe cost nothing like that sum. What actually took place at the unveiling of the first Gorgeous robe was more likely this:

The Labor Temple, a brick building on Fourth Street near Alder, was arranged inside like a theater, so the ring was set up in front, on a raised stage. It held about 1,500 in wooden seats, on the floor level and in the balcony above. On a Monday, there would probably be fewer than 800 paying fans. Portland's armory, that city's Friday-night venue, held twice that amount and drew a better-behaved crowd; the Temple was where the rowdies went. The seats rose steeply and the balcony loomed close, practically on top of the stage, so fans felt near the action, almost a part of it, and thus, entitled to participate. In these close quarters heat didn't dissipate, it intensified.

The ratty dressing rooms were downstairs, reached by a narrow spiral staircase that was really more of a corkscrewed ladder. That stairway was so tight, especially for the broad-shouldered grapplers, that George clutched his precious new robe in front of him as he clambered up, lest he scrape it against the walls in passing. Then he put on the satin creation, which draped him down to his shins. He puffed out his chest and began his strut down the aisle. The fans responded with catcalls, hisses, and jeers. Some of the more beer-sodden marks threw things, but mostly paper; no Coke bottles. The beautiful blue prop was doing its inciteful job, but what drove the audience truly crazy that night had more to do with the wrestler's art. The lessons he'd absorbed on timing and showmanship—about slowing down and selling his moves more fully—all came together in a flow of improvisations. George climbed through the ropes, hearing the mat addicts' wrath, and in that moment he decided to bow to the crowd, turning and facing them in all four directions. The blue-collar audience understood this was no sincere homage, that they were being mocked. Men in denim work shirts and rough corduroy pants stood up and yelled insults, "Sissy!" and "Momma's Boy!" prominent among them. "Who do you think you are?" they demanded.

After the introductions, and more lusty booing, it was time to take off the robe. "I folded it carefully, and placed it in my corner on the stool," George said. Very carefully. And *very* slowly. And at that, the loggers, lumberjacks, truck drivers, fishermen, and their companions went completely berserk. "Did you see that, George?" Betty asked him excitedly later that night. He'd seen. It wasn't just the robe, they marveled together; it was the *folding* of it, the meticulous care shown to his snobbish finery, that had the fans screaming their leathery lungs out.

"The more they yelled, the more time I took," George continued, relishing the memory. He'd left the robe and moved to the center of the ring, but now he thought better of it. George went back to his corner and picked the robe up again, refolding it even more deliberately, as the crowd stomped their feet in anger, the referee gestured impatiently for him to wrestle, and his opponent fumed. (Tellingly, in later years no one was sure who George's opponent was that night; as would happen often, George and his Gorgeousness made that person irrelevant.) In complete control now, he improvised further, coming up with more extemporaneous vamps. "I sneered," he said, and then he added an inimitable and crucial fillip, a slight, silent head movement that powered his snobbish portrayal, and drove the cascading waves of boos even higher. He identified this signature move with one of his most felicitous phrases, too, saying: "I gave them the high nose."

Some said Betty fueled the fires as well, that when the first cat-calls directed at her husband rang out, she took exception at ringside and called a bellowing fan a few choice names. He returned the insults, or she thought he did, so she hauled off and slapped him right in the kisser. "No, no, that doesn't sound like me," was her nondenial denial.

The robe was silk dynamite; it got heat from the fans and ink from the press beyond their imaginings. Immediately Betty began to create more glittering objects of derision. Her vision was bright, to say the least: She saw and sewed in Technicolor. One night in 1944 George swaggered forth in Salem's Ferry Street Gardens wearing a flaming red gown, lined with white satin, tied at the waist with a matching white sash, and topped off at the shoulders with white epaulets. "Georgie turned the joint on its ear with his usual and hilarious kimono-folding act," the *Salem Statesman* reported. "How he did take care of folding that gem!"

Soon George sashayed forth in a green satin number, worn with matching green trunks. For a tiff with Buck Davidson, George was a vision in white brocaded satin, lined with baby-blue silk. To complete the ensemble he carried a baby-blue towel and wore blue shorts with white panels sewn on the sides. George also let it be known that he had insured his new "collection of priceless robes" for five thousand dollars. Working solo and at times with her mother's help, Betty scissored and stitched furiously to keep him in new finery. When the two of them traveled together over the next few years, she'd pack five robes per trip along with a tiny black Singer sewing machine. After they checked in to a hotel, she'd run out to a drapery shop to find more satin or other materials, then she'd do alterations on the hotel-room floor—shortening a long robe into a midlength cape, changing linings, adding sparkles or sequins—so he'd never appear in the same outfit twice at any venue.

George's white satin robe trimmed in silver, wrote *Register Guard* reporter Rolla J. Crick, "would put Caesar to shame." Mr. Crick noted that this report would be his last before he reported to Uncle Sam's army. After Wagner took that night's first fall, Crick wrote, "Pompous

George strutted about the ring like little Lord Fauntleroy as much as if to say, 'Am I not a clever boy?' The crowd evidently didn't agree with his opinion judging from the amount of boos and jeers hurled at him."

George was now taking up to ten full minutes to fold and refold his robe every time out, and the gimmick showed no sign of weakening. He was main-eventing now, packing crunch customers into the bicep bins. One showdown with Walter (Sneeze) Achiu had Ferry Street Garden customers standing in the aisles and another hundred were turned away. On his next match in Eugene the SRO sign was put out again. George issued forth in black velvet with a yellow silk lining and gold sequins on his shoulders. After beating Herb Parks he was escorted from the ring by four policemen while George crowed, "Clear the track for the great Wagner!"

Behind that SRO sign lay an unexpected push, a collateral advantage Betty and George hadn't counted on. The male spectators were in compliance; they hated the heel with the fancy robes, just as they were supposed to. It was the women at the arenas who surprised the young impresarios. They *loved* the robes, loved George, and couldn't wait to see what he'd be wearing next. To find out, many demanded to be taken to the matches, so when Georgie appeared, attendance soared. In the winter of 1944 the *Register Guard* remarked on how "the women go for that Wagner man." This crossover appeal to the "soprano fans" would sustain him for the rest of his career. In 1948, after George drew the biggest wrestling crowd in years to San Francisco's Coliseum Bowl, the next day's paper declared that "Last night you could not have taken the little lady to see Hodiak [actor John Hodiak, who starred in several World War II pictures] or [Clark] Gable. You're darn right, she wanted to see Gorgeous George." Women turned out to see his wild outfits and sensitive-flower act, while men came to see his demise. At least those were the ostensible reasons; on another unspoken level, the male fans clearly enjoyed his outrageous drag act, too, and no doubt some of the ladies responded to the cathartic bloodletting in George's matches as well.

Back from a trip to Hollywood, George now insisted on being called "The Toast of the Coast." (A short time earlier he had proclaimed himself "The Body Beautiful.") An earlier feud with Elton Owen was resumed, allowing that grappler to complain to reporters that "I'm getting tired of that Hollywood panty-waist. Every time he returns from California he acts like one of those big-shots of the films." And as with many other bits of wrestling hyperbole, there was some truth to that, too. George's momentum was building and he did not shy away from that fact.

His new costuming also gave George the opportunity for one of his better swerves. He was booked at the Portland Armory with Danny McShain and Betty had spent all afternoon on an especially tricky robe renovation. She came to the arena that night, dressed for the dinner they'd have with Danny and his wife afterward. Betty was sitting ringside with Nola when the announcer called McShain's name. Out came the handsome heel—wearing George's shiny robe! As he came into the ring Danny twirled around, then opened up the robe, looking directly at Betty with a grin that only she understood, as if to say, "So, what do you think? How do I look?" Then George came strolling out, casually bare-chested with just a towel draped over his shoulder, and gave her a wink and a grin. Betty had to admit, they'd put one over on her. "I couldn't really say anything with all the people around me," she remembered. "I just said, 'Oh!' Really, I almost cried."

"A swerve a day keeps the blues away," George used to tell Jake Brown, his devoted friend and valet. Which blues he had or whence they came, he didn't say.

Chapter 9

SOUL BROTHERS

It was the robes that made young James Brown a believer, and then a follower. Every time the younger man (born in 1933) saw Gorgeous George, the wrestler was draped in a different outer layer, another dazzling style in a new jazzy hue. The robes reminded the aspiring singer of the capes worn by superheroes in his beloved comic books. Overall, Brown was drawn to the strutting wrestler—physically, energetically, they seemed to come from the same foundry. Only skin color set them drastically apart. Like the man and entertainer Brown would become, George was not that big or tall, but a dynamo, a muscular athlete with fast, tiny feet, an oversize head, and a wild hairstyle that only he would dare to wear. Brown loved the titles George bestowed on himself, too; this man clearly knew he was special, and he let everyone else know it. The younger entertainer would create his own set of superlative nicknames—the Godfather of Soul, Mr. Dynamite, and the Hardest Working Man in Show Business—and what's more, live up to them.

The late Brown, who passed away in 2006, had the same needful drive and ambition that young Wagner did. He came up hard, as he put it, so poor he was once sent home from school in North Carolina for being "insufficiently dressed." Like George he lost his mother, but much earlier, and in an even more devastating way: He was abandoned by her at four years old. Brown had thick features and extremely dark skin in an era in which many whites and blacks saw those as ugly. On the side of Augusta, Georgia, he grew up on—Niggertown— Brown's shade was known as a "low complexion." Looking pretty and dressing sharp would be inordinately important to him as an adult, as it was to George.

Brown never finished seventh grade, and just like the lightly educated George, he was a tough businessman and great moneymaker, shrewd about publicity, and foolish when it came to holding on to a dollar. Before they found their callings and their ways out of poverty, both young men worked at menial jobs: Brown shined shoes for three or five cents a pair. "I never did get to a dime," he said. He also delivered groceries, danced for tips on the street, and broke into cars, for which he went to prison at age sixteen.

In all likelihood, there was no television for inmates in Georgia prisons, circa 1949, but a good house of ill repute might well have had a set. Brown probably first caught sight of George some evening at his aunt Honey's two-story bawdy house, a combination whorehouse and gambling den, where he was sent to live at about age seven. Or he may not have seen the celebrity wrestler perform until he got out of the jail on Fourth Street at age nineteen. When he did, Brown wasn't just impressed, but analytical as well. He wanted to be a famous entertainer, a star like George, and he studied the Gorgeous act very carefully.

He began to develop his legendary live act—Brown called these performances "spectacles"—while he was singing in Bobby Byrd's Gospel Starlighters, which became James Brown's rhythm-and-blues group, the Famous Flames. His showmanship, he explained in his memoir, *I Feel Good,* came from three important influences. Only one was musical: Louis Jordan and his Tympany Five, whom Brown admired for their immaculate style as well as their musical technique. Second, growing up, he was entranced by the bold colors and action-packed panels of comic books, reading every one he could get his hands on.

The third element was "the rassler, Gorgeous George, one of the great early stars of live TV [who] added a special flamboyance to his matches." George's act was a riot of gaudy color as well, and after Brown saw the Gorgeous One twirl and curtsy in his fancy robes, he explained, he added a towel to his act. He used it like a preacher, to wipe away sweat and as a prop, to flourish and twirl. Soon, though, Brown had his own robes, mostly shorter capes, of red sequins, or shiny gold fabric with his name inscribed in rhinestones on the back. Brown claimed that Elvis Presley took to wearing capes after seeing his fine drapery; if his account is believed, then Gorgeous George indirectly influenced the King as well.

In 1956 Brown had his first big hit, "Please Please Please," and for fifty years thereafter the climax of his live shows came during this song. In this defining moment there was another nod to George: The Godfather employed a valet, like Jefferies, to achieve what he called "maximum dramatic effect."

"*Ba-by, you did me wrong . . . You took my love, and now you're gone . . .*" As JB the despairing lover sings, he is suddenly overcome by loss, TKO'd by love gone wrong. He staggers away from the audience and drops to his knees, then collapses to the floor. He can't go on—singing or, it seems, even living. From the wings comes a light-skinned black man in a white tuxedo and red bow tie. The "Cape Man," Danny Ray, bears a lush covering that he drapes over the tormented singer's back. As solicitous as Jefferies of his master's well-being, the Cape Man puts a comforting arm across Brown's shoulders. Suddenly the tortured singer stirs, as if to get back up and into the fray. The valet tries to hold him back, but no, JB can't be held back—he's got to go on! The performer struggles to his feet, shrugging the cape off his shoulders, and returns to face the audience at the front of the stage. Once again he sings, screams, shrieks, and shouts, pleading to the love of his life. "*Please . . . please . . . please . . . please.*"

Often this ritual was repeated two or three times with a different cape in each reprise; the song could go on for thirty-five to forty minutes. Brown was so identified with these showmanship techniques that, to honor the singer at the Grammy Awards ceremony following his death, the valet Ray walked out onstage and silently hung a glittering cape on a singerless microphone stand.

Brown used eye-catching props, broad gestures, and physical pantomime to tell his story, and it was as unsubtle and primal as a grappling narrative of good and evil. The emotions JB conveyed were as extreme as George's exaggerated portrayals of arrogance and fear, and the soul singer's melodrama, a cathartic arc of suffering and redemption, could have easily taken place in a wrestling ring. The two men's images were skillfully crafted and the entertainment they produced was in many ways sophisticated, yet their work was fundamentally raw as well, based in sweat, phenomenal energy, and determination. Brown, a boxer, was as physical and athletic at his craft as Wagner; at times his knees would be bloody at the end of a show. They both shouted and declaimed, in victory and in loss, and their effort and intensity made them utterly compelling—they gave it up and turned it loose.

One specialized in tough truth telling ("a woman got to use what she got to get just what she wants") and the other in fabulous lies, but both were fervid in getting their messages out: The Godfather and the Gorgeous One would be heard. As a consequence, perhaps, they both had trouble listening. Each adopted a highly sexual persona, though George put a confounding feminine cover on his muscled body, masculine boasts, and athletic prowess. The Godfather's tight pants and chest-swelling ruffled shirts, as well as his shouted pronouncements about men, women, and love, were pure machismo. Vanity they shared, along with idiosyncratic ideas of male beauty—very few, if any, other men have spent as much time as these two in curlers and under the hair dryer.

When he spoke about George he emphasized showmanship, yet Brown no doubt absorbed what Muhammad Ali would also take to heart: The way the Gorgeous One defied expectations and insisted on living on his own terms. George got up and did *his thing,* and he certainly didn't take no mess. He said it loud; he was George and he was inordinately proud. Most likely James Brown would never have been denied or dictated to, whether he'd seen the rassler or not. But until black pride and anger exploded in the United States in the 1960s, that kind of assertiveness in African-Americans had to stay underground. Decades before James Brown became a man, for example, Jack Johnson the boxer was boastful and showy, including in his appreciation of white women. In his time such "unforgivable blackness," as the title of a recent documentary about him termed it, would not go unpunished. (Convicted on trumped-up morals charges in 1913, he was jailed and went into exile.) Brown became an outspoken civil rights activist, a black capitalist, and, in a stand that made sense only to him, a supporter of Richard Nixon. His lifelong drive for self-determination, for self-definition, was necessarily different from George's—his was that of a black man living in America. But the ethos and the images were similar. Before he became Super Bad, James Brown saw that quality brought to life by a man who had the essential, forgivable whiteness to get away with it, strutting in a Gorgeous robe.

This transference fits a pattern of mutual influencing, a racial give-and-take, that has always enriched American culture. Before George suggested flamboyant possibilities to Brown, he may have in turn been influenced by the extravagant black preachers who traveled the South in the 1920s and 1930s. Daddy Grace, also known as Sweet Daddy Grace, wore his fingernails long and painted in bright colors, flashed expensive rings, and drove fancy cars. He also made grandiose pronouncements such as, "I am the boyfriend of the world." (Another African-American preacher from that era, Father Divine, did him one better by simply declaring that he was God.) Could young George Wagner, still developing his taste for what he thought of as the finer things, have seen one of these grandees drive by in loud, luxurious style one day while he stood on Fannin Street in Houston? Might he have heard any of them on the radio, exalting themselves as they praised God? If he did, George would have remembered.

In their lives as well as their performances, James Brown and George Wagner went further than others would dare or care to. These strong, flawed men held nothing back, for better and often for worse. (Brown had several problematic marriages and legal, financial, and drug woes.) They had deep blues and strong demons, but created redemptive thrills, a joy they could possess only briefly themselves but passed more lastingly to others. These two American originals died more than forty years apart, and both went out in Gorgeous style. The Godfather's coffin was reportedly made of twenty-four-karat gold, and it arrived at the Apollo Theater in Harlem for a viewing in a white carriage drawn by two white Percherons wearing plumed headdresses. Later, at his Augusta funeral, James Brown wore a black suit with sequined lapels over a fire-engine-red shirt and a black bow tie. On his feet he wore black pumps topped with more sparkling sequins.

Chapter 10
A "HOME MAN"

The baby in the dresser drawer cried and cried. A little girl, less than a month old, her face was red and contorted into a grimace by her bawling. George and Betty stood near, craning over the wooden dresser with the bottom drawer pulled out. Inside the baby lay on her back on a pillow, moving her tiny arms and legs as if to generate more power for her wails. Tiny Betty was in her nightdress with a bathrobe over it; burly George wore pajamas and slippers. The new parents looked at the baby, then back at each other, baffled and helpless.

Like their spontaneous approach to the wrestling business, their parenthood had an impromptu feel to it. Parts of it had been planned: They'd been working and living in Tulsa for a time and Betty told a doctor there, Dr. Shapiro, that she and George wanted children but hadn't conceived. He worked with a home for unwed mothers, as those institutions were called, in nearby Ada, Oklahoma, and thought he could help the Wagners adopt. They told him they'd take a boy or a girl. When Dr. Shapiro called a few months later, at Christmas in 1944, they'd made their way back to Oregon. He told them a little girl would soon be born at the home; the mother was a sixteen-year-old and the father some since-disappeared soldier. Did they want her, and if so, could they come and get her immediately? Betty and George were more than willing to drive the two thousand miles—four thousand round-trip—on their balding tires, but there was a war on. Gas was still strictly rationed, and they were using up their allotment just going back and forth from Eugene to Portland to Salem for matches. They just didn't see how they could get to Tulsa and create their new family. At the eleventh hour, the boys—friends and rivals who'd traded punches, bruises, and blood with George—came through. The wrestlers and their wives got out their own ration books, tore out as many gas stamps as they could possibly spare, and gave them to Betty and George.

So now they had her, and they called her Carol Sue. But neither of them really knew much about babies and none of their parents were close by; they were winging it. The couple had rented the hotel room for a month to stay close to Dr. Shapiro, and they'd figured out how to make a crib of the dresser. But they couldn't seem to calm the baby or stop its screaming and crying. They fretted some more, paced again. Finally, in the middle of the cold Oklahoma night, Betty went downstairs to use the hotel phone and called Dr. Shapiro. He came. A slender, dark-haired man about George's height, he'd thrown an overcoat over his own pajamas. As the parents stood anxiously by, the young doctor examined Carol thoughtfully, asked a few questions. The last one did it.

"How often are you feeding her?" he asked.

"We're giving her a bottle about every four or five hours," Betty replied.

"There you have it," the doctor said evenly, without losing any of his patience. *"She's hungry.* Feed her every two hours. Starting right now."

"Oh. Well, okay, then. Thanks."

Dr. Shapiro put his hat back on, buttoned up his overcoat over his sleepwear, and went back out into the cold.

The abashed but somewhat wiser parents made the long trip back to Oregon, cradling Carol in their arms in the car or making a bed for her on the backseat. They had a wonderful trip, staying with all the wrestlers they knew along the way. When they stopped in restaurants, folks inside heated bottles and mixed formula for them, and dispensed advice. A little more than a year later, they were back for a rematch. It was April of 1946 and the war was finally over. Wrestling regrouped as many of its top workers returned from the service, including Lou Thesz. George was working in Tulsa again for promoter Sam Avey and they were renting half of a big two-story house from a woman who let her apartments to a shifting cast of wrestlers. Betty, George, and Carol had the downstairs and Antone "Ripper" Leone, "the roaring French-Canadian," and his wife had the upstairs. One day when George was on the road, Betty was helping the landlady hang some new curtains upstairs in the Leones' place. She was standing on a table to reach the curtain rod when she suddenly began to hemorrhage, blood pouring out from under her dress.

She was rushed to the hospital; Leone and his wife took care of Carol. Dr. Shapiro performed surgery, including a hysterectomy, and when he came to see Betty the next day, she sighed and asked, "I won't ever have kids now, will I?" Rather than answer directly, he excused himself and came back five minutes later holding a newborn boy, just hours alive. A local married woman had gotten pregnant while her serviceman husband was away, and she couldn't keep him. "You can have this young man, Betty," Dr. Shapiro told her. "Would you like him?" She seems to have said yes without asking George; in any case, Don was the answer.

George couldn't match that surprise, but he retaliated as best he could. One day he came back to the house in Tulsa and opened his wrestling bag to show Betty and Carol the bulldog puppy inside. "They were going to get rid of her, so I brought her home," he said. They named her Judy and George spent a good deal of time training her; the two of them clicked. Judy must have felt his special energy, too, for she learned tricks and obedience that went far beyond sitting and staying. When George told the dog, "Say your prayers," Judy would pad over to a wooden chair, put her forelegs up on the seat, then bow her head down and rest it on her paws. George could balance a small piece of steak right on her snout and the dog wouldn't touch it until he told her, "Okay."

Mr. and Mrs. Wagner bought a trailer, a good-size caravan with small windows near the tops of both sides. Not an Airstream, the silvery lozenge-shaped kind of trailer; this was closer to a brown railroad car towed behind their car. In the window set into the narrow metal door hung a white curtain. Inside it was quite ample, including a living room they stepped down into, a kitchen, and two bedrooms. Pat Gray, a local girl with curly dark hair like Betty's, became their nanny. She wasn't even eighteen yet, working in a Tulsa dress store for fifty cents an hour, and traveling with this family seemed like a whole lot more fun to her, with room and board thrown in. Carol, around fourteen months old with blond hair that was almost white, couldn't say Pat yet, so she called her "Tat."

The parents bought a canvas canopy with white piping along its scalloped edges and a folding wooden fence to corral the kids. They loaded up the car and trailer with the two adults, the nanny, two kids, the dog, plus teddy bears, potty chairs, and the like, and off they went, from one wrestling date to the next. On warm summer days they'd stop by a river, have a picnic, and let the kids play. Toward evening they'd find a trailer camp, and within thirty minutes the canopy was up and the fence was erected, making a shady place to sit and an enclosed playpen. They'd set up a small table with wooden chairs, including a high chair, outside the trailer's door as well.

Wearing white blouses and knee-length skirts that seem today like very formal parenting wear, Betty bathed the two little naked kids together in a big washtub on the grass. George would help sometimes, donning his wrestling trunks for this wet event. She did the cooking and George dug in; to keep his weight down he occasionally ran behind the trailer as he had on their honeymoon. With Pat to watch the children, Betty accompanied George to the arenas some nights, and the nanny also gave the young couple the freedom to occasionally go out to dinner by themselves. Whenever they found a place to dance in the nearest town, they'd dress up, and to Pat, George, now thirty-one, and Betty, thirty-three, looked very adult, very glamorous.

On other evenings Betty fashioned George's robes, laying the fabric out on the floor in the trailer's living room then shooing Carol off when she inevitably ran onto it to play. These months they spent traveling together with the trailer, Betty said, were the best times of their marriage. "That's when George and I were the closest." George shared those feelings, or something akin to them. To Pat, he was very much a "home man," someone who wanted to be with his family as much as possible. When they were parked in and around Columbus, Ohio, George would drive all night after wrestling in Canada to get back to them. He was proud of his burgeoning family, and of his ability to support them. George wasn't bossy, though, like a lot of other men, Pat noticed; he pretty much let Betty run things.

One day Pat came into the trailer's kitchen and saw him leaning down and reaching under the sink and behind the garbage canister with the step-on handle. He was stashing a liquor bottle. George wasn't embarrassed at being seen; he just closed the cabinet door, looked at the nanny calmly, and said: "Don't tell Betty."

Chapter 11

THE BLOND BOMBSHELL

As they zoomed from Little Rock to Oklahoma City, some 350 miles, there was no time to stop. Betty slid over close to George on the front seat as he drove, gazing intently at his head and hair. (They'd left the children temporarily with her mother in Oregon.) Once she decided on her approach, she reached up with both hands, grabbed little fistfuls of his mane, and twisted them clockwise around her forefingers, fixing the curls with oversize black bobby pins. Later, she'd remove the pins and brush out a froth of waves, beauty-parlor smooth. In their speeding salon, however, hairdressing could get rough. "Ow! Take it easy, Sweetie!" George would exclaim, jerking his head away if she twisted a curl too tight or inadvertently jabbed him with one of her pins. "Sit still, George!" would be her retort. Sometimes when he pulled back, the car would lurch across the two-lane blacktop, but somehow they always got back between the white lines and made it to the arenas intact. On days like this, when the two of them worked and made fun together, they felt close.

Draping George in garish splendor—and calling him the Body Beautiful and the Gorgeous—was clearly working. Not one to stand pat, Betty wondered: How could they take things even further? By making him even prettier, she decided, adding something that would rankle the fans *after* George took off his robes. She talked him into letting his dark brown hair grow long, and began to fix it in elaborate pin-curled styles, creating dense layers of waves in the front, on the sides, and in the back of his oversize head. "He was very quick to catch on to any of the crazy ideas I came up with," she said. "He'd go right along."

One reason George may have acquiesced so easily is that before he met Betty, he'd befriended an Irishman in Columbus, Ohio, named Wilbur Finran. This wrestler's gimmick was impersonating a British nobleman, calling himself Lord Patrick Lansdowne. As George would later acknowledge in private, Lansdowne was an accomplished pioneer of the haughty-heel persona. Finran stopped touring for the most part around 1941, concentrating instead on running his taverns and restaurants, so he missed the postwar television exposure that made George a national figure. Or, given the agile 175-pounder's skill and showmanship, it might be more accurate to say that TV missed him. Finran contracted ALS, Lou Gehrig's disease, and died in 1959 at the age of fifty-four. The Gorgeous act would incorporate several of the older man's innovations, including the use of entrance music. Lansdowne used "God Save the King" on his haughty march, while George was partial to "Pomp and Circumstance." The puffed-up lord also sported a monocle and wore a long, curly coif, so George had seen hair used successfully to attract attention.

With his adventurous hair treatment, though, Lansdowne was trying to evoke the lords of yore, men of the manor in an era already past. George's stylings, by contrast, were of the moment, and even more strikingly, they were decidedly feminine. Betty created her own versions of pin-curled styles made famous by the reigning movie sirens: Betty Grable, the blond knockout and World War II pinup; green-eyed beauty Gene Tierney (she'd just played her signature role in the 1944 film *Laura*); and Ginger Rogers. In Betty's view, though, she wasn't making George look feminine, much less playing intentionally with gender or sexuality. They just needed him to be more Gorgeous.

George went along with her next inspiration, too, one of the few he regretted. Betty came across some tinted hair sprays, and promptly bought them in loud hues of red, green, and purple, as well as baby blue. When she explained her idea, Betty was full of excitement. "We'll dye your hair every night to match your robe!" she told him. On this gimmick's opening night, she went with him to the dressing room and gave him a good shellacking in baby blue, the same color as his satin outfit. The couple hadn't quite thought through what would happen when George began to wrestle, and then to sweat. Little drops of blue bubbled up from his scalp, appeared on his forehead and neck, then ran down onto his chest, leaving blue streaks. Then he mixed it up with his opponent some more, and in the groping and grabbing, his hair and sweaty chest rubbed against the other boy. Now he was blue, too, in runny smears and blotches. And when the stuff got into either wrestler's eyes, it stung. The fans loved it, and George took it in stride. But the straight man didn't appreciate the gag, complaining to the promoter and telling George and Betty afterward, "Don't do that again." So that experiment was shelved.

Beyond the robes, the curls, and the various forms of goop, there was another element crucial to George's success that neither he nor Betty could take full credit for. They did anyway, naturally. When George became famous, press accounts usually attributed his mellifluous moniker to a smitten female fan in Oregon, who gasped upon seeing him, then dreamily breathed her flattering description. Betty maintained that this fan-ette, as a woman attending the matches was sometimes referred to, was her. She was sitting ringside at the armory in Eugene one night with her mother when George entered the ring in one of his new resplendent robes, found Betty in the stands, and gave her a wink. Then he twirled completely around to give everyone in the arena a good look at him and the ice-blue satin vestment he was wearing, raising his arms to show the white satin lining. As he did Betty, impressed with both her creations on display, said, "Oh, look, Mother, he's gorgeous!" Then, she said, it hit her: "That's it—Gorgeous George!"

George also claimed at various points to have thought up the so-briquet himself; others say the handle was first applied to him by *Register Guard* sports editor Dick Strite. The first print reference to him as George "Gorgeous" Wagner came in 1940; by '42 or '43 the given name and the adjective were reversed, and over time the last name was dropped. Whoever coined it, the name was kismet. It rolls off the tongue; there's an irresistibly catchy ring to it. Other Georges before and since profited from this stickiness, including French boxer Georges Carpentier, heavyweight world champion in 1914; George Sisler, 1920s baseball star for the St. Louis Browns, George Cafego, 1930s college football star; and George Senesky, a high-scoring basketball player in the 1940s. More recently Gorgeous has been applied to actor George Clooney and, a bit ironically, to balding, left-wing British MP George Galloway. If George Wagner had called himself Handsome George or Wagner the Great, would he ever have become the Toast of the Coast, the Human Orchid, the Sensation of the Nation? One doubts it.

After the blue-hair debacle, George and Betty quickly regained their creative stride. Within a year or so after adopting Carol and Don, they invented the rest of the Gorgeous act, each gimmick building on the previous ones as the two dared and egged each other on. Their next innovation was perhaps the most potent image maker of all. His soigné hairdo's had prettified George, and signaled the requisite vanity. Yet with his dark hair, the effect remained somewhat subdued. The shockingly bright blond color the couple went to next was transformative—it made George a bombshell. It sounds very simple in retrospect, but at the time the Gorgeous hair was a shocking novelty, causing a coiffure furor that may have been surpassed only by the Beatles' 1960s moptops.

Men weren't bombshells in George's era, they simply weren't. Female tresses could be remarked on, but male hair was supposed to be innocuous and irrelevant. President Truman's, like every other male's, was short, neat, side-parted. Yes, it was thinning and graying a bit, but the idea that he might take remedial steps had not yet been born. Clairol would not release its first coloring product for men—Great

Day, it was called—for another twenty years, and there were no hair weaves or scalp plugs, no Rogaine or Propecia. Some Hollywood leading men dyed their hair or wore toupées, but they would never have wanted those facts to emerge. George's hair emerged.

It was blatant, it shrieked. In the black-and-white photos the newspapers ran of George, his dark hair sometimes faded into a muddy blur, but the blond locks popped off the page. His new do called attention to its own artificiality as it invited onlookers in on the joke. George and Betty didn't lighten his dark eyebrows, and the contrast between them and his newly light hair also had a subtly jarring effect. The results were triumphant in their ridiculousness. Ted Lewin, one of three wrestling brothers from New York, was putting himself through art school, and he later became an illustrator of children's books. So he had an eye for faces. He remembered coming into the locker room in Reading, Pennsylvania, one night and seeing George "sitting there with his blond curls, and his big, rugged face. He had a tough face, a square jaw, a very manly face with all these silly curls around it. The whole thing was really very funny."

Betty did it herself at first, beginning in Columbus sometime in 1946. Then, toward the end of 1947, George and Betty were in L.A. for a few months and they turned the coloring and styling over to "Frank and Joseph of Hollywood." Those two gentlemen, who would work with George for more than ten years, also taught Betty how to maintain his *blondeur* on the road. Surpassing what mere pin curls could do, the hairdressers elevated George's styling to the "marcel." This method, invented by Marcel Grateau, a Parisian *artiste des cheveux,* in the 1870s, used heated irons or tongs to create intricate flowing waves, which were often gathered at the top of the head and held by pins. This created a dramatic upswept look, fit for a queen.

Almost immediately, bleached blond hair became de rigueur for wrestling heels and they've used it ever since to show their villainy. Buddy Rogers, a contemporary of George's, was one of the first; others include Classy Fred Blassie, Ric Flair, Dusty Rhodes, Johnny Valentine, the Fargo Brothers, Superstar Billy Graham, and in the 1970s and

1980s, Jesse "The Body" Ventura and Hulk Hogan (though the Hulkster was at times a babyface). For the length of George's career, this gimmick never failed to get attention. In 1948 *Time* magazine ran a piece on George's burgeoning stardom, entitled "Catcalls and Curls," and it described his hair as "an improbable pale blond." One newspaper account called him "a blond O'Cedar mop with a new marcel." A cheeky Memphis columnist wrote that "Gorgeous George will flounce in on June 9. The celebrated tragedian plans spurious strife with Daniel McShain, and we, for at least one, will be right glad to see his peroxide plume . . ." Embedded in the copy were two black-and-white photos. One showed the "celebrated tragedian," shot from above, revealing the climactic consummation of swirls and curls on the top of his dome. This image was captioned simply "George." The picture next to it showed a counterpart, with a long mop of white hair falling down from his crown, obscuring his eyes and ears and revealing only a black button nose. That second picture was labeled "Sheep Dog."

It wasn't just the peroxide; George was also hitting his stride as a performing poseur, fleshing out the Gorgeous persona. His rhetoric took on a grandiloquent tone and greater dramatic sweep, while he gave reporters quotable soliloquies on his hair. "I have six different styles," he announced a couple of years after his first marcel: "The Rococo, the Bird of Paradise, the Gorgeous George Swirl, the Gorgeous George Swagger, the Television Flair and the Frank and Joseph Special. My favorite, of course, is the Frank and Joseph Special. Unfortunately, it can't be copied and I usually am forced to resort to one of the other five when I'm away from Hollywood." Later, it was another variation that pleased him the most: The Hellenic look, also by Frank and Joseph. "With Grecian contours."

George began scheduling his interviews at women's beauty parlors in each town he visited. He'd hold forth while getting his hair marcelled under the hot croquignole machines, which was always good for a few column inches. When asked why he didn't simply go to a barber like other men, the Gorgeous One shuddered delicately. "I've always loathed the atmosphere of the barber shop," he confided. "Barbers are crude and unsympathetic and apt to talk about such uncouth things as boxing and baseball. They have no sense of the esthetic." The time he logged in salons became another point of pride. "There have been women who have been in the same beauty parlor more than I have," he acknowledged later in his career. "But I have been touched up in all parts of the world. I have had beauty treatments in Africa, Australia, Hong Kong, Honolulu, Mexico, Canada, and in most cities of the United States."

Soon she would stop traveling with George to stay home with the children, but at this point Betty still wanted in on the act. When she accompanied him on the road now, she met with the press also, donning a white smock and working on George's hair in his hotel room, in front of each city's sports reporters. They told the press she was his personal hairdresser, Miss Betty, of Frank and Joseph's. Why tell the truth when a ruse will do? George would treat her like the help, too, ignoring or ordering her around just like a fussy client. Later they'd laugh; the couple had seen the scribes trying to find out how many hotel rooms the two had rented. "Aren't you his wife?" they'd ask, baffled. "No, I'm Miss Betty."

After a Gorgeous win in Long Beach, California, a local writer described him leaving the ring "with a straight-fall victory, and a head of curls awry and writhing like the Medusa's." To George and Betty, the Medusa effect was another unanticipated bonus. The soprano fans, especially, were turning out to see his glorious plumage. But what the crowd most lusted for, it turned out, was to see George's elaborate, pretentious hairstyle *ruined*. Defeated. Deflated. To see his locks, as the same writer once described them, "resembling a bowl of discouraged corn flakes." The wrestling showman saw this immediately, and made the great undoing a mandatory part of the act. "The first thing you had to do when you locked horns with him," remembered Ted Lewin, "was mess up his hair. You just grabbed it, roughed it up with your hands. Then he'd leap up and stamp his feet and scream—he'd raise hell for the next twenty minutes. You didn't have to do anything, just go back and stand in the corner while he raised hell. And the audience went absolutely crazy."

George also used this routine defilement to showcase his sensitive nature, the delicate vulnerability that he increasingly emphasized to the public. In an interview with *Pan,* the magazine of the Pan Pacific Auditorium, a boxing and wrestling venue in L.A., George addressed the difficulties—the *trauma*—brought on by his newfound fabulousness. "Since I've gone blond," he complained "the other wrestlers all call me light-headed and taunt me more than ever. They can't help being jealous, but must they be so rude?" As he talked, the magazine relayed, "Matdom's No. 1 pin-up boy [was] running a comb through his honey-hued tresses." George further explained that it was the ribald remarks of his opponents that provoked his tantrums and ring violence. He'd abide by the rules, he professed, if "the boys only wouldn't be so rough and muss up my hair!" Through the vehicle of his bleached blond hair, Gorgeous George exposed his wounded outer child. And a complicated child it was.

That hair was George's totem, the symbol of his potency. Losing it dramatically, fifteen years and thousands of treatments after he first went blond, meant the end of his career. In one unexpected place, though, George's identifier is still extant. At his home in Franklin Square on Long Island, wrestling expert and collector John Pantozzi keeps a lock of Gorgeous hair. George's second wife, Cherie, sold it to him (he can't remember for how much), along with some photographs and a brooch in the 1990s. He also offered her $1,500 for one of George's robes, but she turned it down. Cherie sent the snipped-off bleached blond hair to Pantozzi in a rectangular cardboard box, the kind necklaces come in, on some cotton padding. Today it rests, like a jewel, under a glass case.

In the middle of 1946 the Wagner family and modest entourage—consisting of one nanny and one dog—piled in the trailer for a Texas tour. They saw Poppa Wagner and Eulah, and George's youngest brother, Buddy, squired Pat around for a while and even asked her to marry him. He was good-looking, a younger, trimmer version of George, but he was also unemployed. Whatever the reasons, Pat declined. George wrestled a series of action-packed matches in Houston,

Dallas, and Galveston with his childhood friend Sterling "Dizzy" Davis. He was also sporting gaudier-than-usual kimonos in the ring, so the two of them came up with a series of "Robe vs. Robe" matches, in which the loser would have to surrender his vestment immediately after the final fall. Dizzy announced that he would set George's robe on fire then and there, while George thought greater humiliation would lie in having his vanquished opponent's robe altered by his Hollywood tailors and added to his sartorial harem. The matches were big draws and good paydays, with each man winning in turn, yet somehow no one's robes were actually destroyed in the public eye.

On this swing George added another member to his entourage, unveiling the next stage in the evolution of the Gorgeous act. By adding this new personage, George (and this was his idea, not Betty's) opened up more dramatic possibilities for stunts, brawls, folderol, and all manner of ring nonsense. Tonally, this human gimmick took the mock pomposity of his performance to a higher level, and with it the masterwork was nearly complete. A *Houston Chronicle* headline put fans on notice, declaring that GORGEOUS GEORGE CARRIES VALET ON WRESTLING JAUNTS. George would have a second or attendant with him, it was explained, who was charged with the care of his eighty-eight fabulous robes, which the proud owner had insured for $10,000. This first valet was Thomas Ross, who may have been another of George's Houston pals. "My man Thomas," it was immediately remarked, bore a striking resemblance to Thomas E. Dewey, the Republican governor of New York who famously would *not* defeat Harry Truman in the 1948 presidential election. He had the same dark, slightly wavy hair and mustache and bushy eyebrows that angled sharply upward—the valet and the politician certainly resembled each other as much as, say, George and the sheepdog.

Within six months, though, George and Betty swung through Texas again and this time the wrestler sought out Jacob Brown, his boyhood friend from Avenue Q. Jake, immediately dubbed "my man Jefferies," was the best-known gentleman's gentleman and the one who stayed in service the longest, from 1947 to 1952. Jake had served two and a half years with the 30th Air Service Squadron in the Western Pacific before being discharged as Corporal Brown, with $300 in mustering-out pay in his pocket. He was working in a Houston department store when George rescued him; Jake and his wife, Beulah, promptly bought a trailer like George and Betty's and followed those two back to Santa Monica, where they lived near their friends and employers. Betty and Jake, George's better halves or his enabling counterparts, bonded instantly. For some reason she always called him by his stage name, or her abbreviation of it; to her, he was Jeff or "my Jeff."

The valet's role would be embellished over the years, but the essentials were there from the start. In one of their early matches together, when George took on Enrique Torres at the Auditorium in Houston, the Gorgeous One was introduced with great fanfare over the PA system. First to appear, though, at the top of one aisle, was Jefferies, dressed formally in gray pin-striped trousers and a gray vest under a long-tailed black morning coat. He also wore a thin black mustache. As he ankled deliberately to the ring the valet bore a large gilded box in front of him on a matching tray. Once inside the ropes, he opened the box with great ceremony, removed a small whisk broom, then stood at the ready. A loud march, played on a scratchy phonograph record, began to blare through the speakers, and George, gloriously blond and berobed, strutted in. At least once he experimented with a cane, twirling it on the way down the aisle, then surrendering it to the valet, but that prop soon went the way of the blue hair.

Now came the ever-so-deliberate folding of the robe, with Jefferies standing just inside the ropes, arms outstretched and his torso inclined forward from the waist to receive it. When he did, the valet would make an obsequious bow or three, as if to thank the overseer for the privilege of serving him. The snobbish presumption of George having an underling drew howls of derision from the 3,500 or so fans. Then the match got under way and Jefferies positioned himself just outside the ring and directly facing George, never taking his eyes off him to acknowledge the crowd or any other distraction. Like Judy the dog, he showed his devotion, remaining focused—fixated—on George the master.

When the gown came off, George's flowing blond mane now gave him the appearance of a rare and wild animal. Indeed, one writer, overflowing with alliterative ardor, called him the Percheron of Pulchritude. As he grappled with Torres, his elaborate hairdo naturally toppled into ruin, much to the delight of the Houston fans. Between falls Jefferies served George tea from a silver tea set or merely primped his hair, holding up a large silver-framed mirror afterward so George could approve these repairs. Jake, subtly snooty, was a master of the deadpan, underplaying in perfect complement to George's histrionics. A less powerful, and less boastful, athlete than the rest of the Harrisburg gang, he found his most authentic role as George's man in service. Though neither Jake nor Jefferies was a fighter, at times the valet was nonetheless drawn into the uncouth.

In Atchison, Kansas, the heel Wild Red Berry got to play babyface for one night. The squat, five-foot-eight former boxer hailed from Pittsburg, Kansas, which made him the local favorite, and George the invading hellion. After a few action-packed falls, Berry won, pinning George with his signature move, the Gilligan Twist. Gorgeous and Jefferies sulked in their corner for a bit as the verdict was pronounced, then turned as one and rushed at Berry, knocking the referee to the mat as they charged. This unsanctioned tag team pummeled Berry as he covered up in his corner, George whaling away with his fists and Jefferies windmilling the huge mirror with both hands. Berry's camp and a few incensed mat addicts rushed the ring, coming to their champion's aid, and the melee was on.

That set up the sold-out rematch. George wasn't concerned about Berry or his own safety, he let it be known, but he was upset at the mauling his manservant had received. "Jefferies is the only person capable of giving me a decent wave set and I just dare any of these bruisers to harm a hair on his head," he threatened, adding that he considered the Atchison citizenry "an uncouth band of peasants."

George was now spending considerably more time entertaining

and much less actually wrestling. Yet, he noted thoughtfully, the showbiz stuff was making him stand out more and more from the other boys, who were looking increasingly drab in comparison. No one, least of all the promoters, was complaining about the changing ratio of posturing to spine bending, the ascendancy of gimmicks over action. From here on, George would always have a valet with him. Through shrewd hiring and astute tutoring, they all displayed a deft dramatic touch. The essential absurdity of their role helped enormously. The valets played scaredy-cats, who usually ran away from any possible altercation, so seeing them buffeted by enraged opponents was part of the fun. As Jefferies, Jake Brown took innumerable hits to the noggin with the tray he bore to the ring, his own totem used against him to the delight of the rowdy crowds. Fussily polite, the gentleman's gentlemen served in a rude realm, trying to impose order where there was none—and furthermore, where no one desired any. In vain they whisked, neatened, and freshened, oblivious amid the chaos. The hapless valets portrayed dignity in the den of indignity; hence the hilarity.

George kept them on for practical as well as theatrical reasons. Though he certainly did not have anything like eighty-eight robes, he did have trunks full of wardrobe, which needed maintaining. Betty taught the valets how to press the finery and touch up George's tinted locks. As the master got more work, that meant more driving, something he was relieved to turn over to his employees. He needed the help, and in truth, he craved the companionship; he didn't do well on his own. Bookings were picking up and he now commanded a bigger slice of the gate receipts, maybe 10 percent. Later, when George was at the height of his popularity, he would demand that the promoters pay his valets themselves; the majordomos got paid the same as the boys working on the undercard.

Other wrestlers, including Lord Lansdowne, had used valets, seconds, and managers before. George co-opted and improved on that riff, making it his own. Similarly, Dizzy Davis had been known as Gardenia Davis at one point, when he threw those flowers to the fans.

He was working in Mexico then, and when George asked his permission to try the flower gimmick in the United States, he said, "Sure, go ahead. But it'll never work in the States." George would later disprove that, with orchids. Appropriation is how wrestling, and much of art and entertainment, evolves. (One man George inspired, Bob Dylan, was an especially egregious borrower, beginning with his early Woody Guthrie impersonation or homage, his early patterning after Ramblin' Jack Elliott, and his name, which he took from Dylan Thomas.) George and Betty almost certainly took ideas from and were swayed by others; some of this was conscious, and some may not have been. Then they put their own imprimatur on their friends' and competitors' best moves, creating an original work. Then, after the wrestler synthesized all these hooks and gimmicks, he put them across in performance like no one else, before or since.

Chapter 12

THE WRESTLING SET

"So, Sweetie, what do you think?"

It was evening and George was standing on the terrace of a three-story white stucco house in Windsor Hills, the Los Angeles neighborhood just north of Inglewood. Betty was seated in one of the rattan patio chairs, facing him. Beyond George she could see the lights of the city, all the way to Santa Monica, and then on to the Pacific. On his head her husband wore his now-habitual tam, a knit beret that covered his long blond curls when he wasn't working, or having his hair done at the beauty parlor. George had on a red Hawaiian shirt over his slacks, and its boxy drape suited his big-chested frame, she thought approvingly. He'd taken to wearing aloha shirts before the war when they lived in Honolulu and now they were in style Stateside after men serving in the Pacific theater brought them home. Shortages of fabric and dye over with, men's clothes were longer and looser, and brighter shades were favored—anything but khaki or army green. When George got more dressed up, he was partial to the sharkskin suits and gaudy hand-painted ties that were also in postwar vogue. Some had palm trees painted on them; others, desert landscapes or New York skyscrapers. George especially liked the ones with flowers.

He'd found this vacant house and brought Betty up for a twilight tour, walking her like a realtor through the empty rooms: the entrance hall, the kitchen off to the left, and the big front room with huge windows that also showed beautiful views. Down a few steps there was a bedroom for Don, and on yet another level, one for Carol, along with a second bathroom and a den that was forty feet long. That room had the sliding-glass doors Don would later run into and shatter, but emerge from unhurt. Behind the house was a big backyard that looked down on La Brea Avenue. The terrace, which faced the opposite way, hung out over a steep drop, suspended in the air over all the shimmering lights.

What did she think? First Betty had a half-conscious realization that made her smile. *He brought me up here at twilight on purpose; it's exactly the right time to show the place off.* Her second, more fully formed thought was that his strategy was working. The house was pretty grand and the terrace and views . . . "It's like fairyland," she told him. He came and sat down with her and they talked quietly for a while. It started to get cool, and darker. In the privacy of the terrace it seemed to George and Betty that they were far away from everyone else and all that they saw, very much alone together.

They'd been living in Hawthorne, about six miles south, with the kids and Pat. This house gave them lots more room in a nicer neighborhood. Of all the places he and Betty lived together, this one, his choice, was George's favorite. It was big, classy, and showed that he was getting places. This Gorgeous George person they'd invented was becoming someone to reckon with. When he and Betty came to L.A. late in 1947, the promoters had gotten word from their brethren of George's increased drawing power in Texas, St. Louis, and elsewhere. This time he was booked not just into the smaller arenas like Legion Stadium and Ocean Park, but finally into L.A.'s premier pit, the Olympic Auditorium, on Grand Avenue between Eighth Street and Washington Boulevard. A couple, Cal and Aileen Eaton, ran this boxing and wrestling venue, and the Olympic would be George's redoubt for the best part of his career.

In one of his early matches there, George flew out of his corner as the opening bell sounded, leaped straight up in the air, and dropkicked Reginald Siki into the land of no light, winning in just twelve seconds. (This was unusual; perhaps one of the combatants had another booking across town to get to.) Remarkably, this abbreviated match didn't leave the crowd feeling cheated; the throng of 9,600 felt it had gotten its money's worth from George's finery and preliminary antics alone. He was Gorgeous George now, billed here as "a new personality in wrestling," with no connection made to the George Wagner who'd toiled in L.A. many times before. "The goon who dresses like Beau Brummell," also known as "the gorilla with glamour," was an instant box-office attraction.

Almost as soon as he acquired his beautiful new home, though, George essentially abandoned it. The Gorgeous One was in demand, and there was money to be made in other territories. He was on the road for five or six weeks at a time, then home for just a few days. Carol Sue, who went by Susie in those days, was old enough to start school there, but what she remembers more clearly is missing him. They all did. When Betty knew George was on his way home, she'd sing a version of "Santa Claus Is Coming to Town" to the kids, but with Gorgeous George substituting for Saint Nick. *"You better watch out, you better not cry, better watch out, I'm telling you why . . ."* After a while she'd just start humming it, and they knew.

Absence was his strongest parental trait, but when he was home George was an affectionate father. While some parents are apt to fudge unpleasant truths with their children or to sugarcoat, George was strikingly, painfully honest. "I'm not going to tell you there's a Santa Claus," he said to Carol when she was still very young. "Because there isn't." One morning George threw a tam on over his blond tangles and drove her to see the doctor. He was in a good mood, relaxed, just back from a profitable trip. As they sat together in the waiting room, the blond four- or five-year-old with a gap between her front teeth wore an orange skirt, a white embroidered top, and a matching orange ribbon nestled in the part of her hair. Betty had dressed her brightly and cheerfully, but her young face was fearful. As the slender little girl sat with her brick house of a father, she clenched one or two of his fingers in her hand. Turning to face him, she asked, "Daddy, if I have to get a shot, will it hurt?" George looked her right in the eye and replied evenly, "Yes, Susie, it will."

When he began to make real money, George hired a business manager, a wrestling booking agent named Johnny Doyle. George either thought his new status called for it, or recognized that neither he nor Betty had any discernible financial acumen. The manager paid the mortgage and the other bills. Betty had no idea how much George was earning; she only knew that for practically the first time, there was enough. She wrote checks without worrying. When she said, "George, we need this," or "Hey, George, can I have that?" he'd say, "Sure, do what you want."

He did what he wanted as well. George might have chosen a Ford sedan, say, to transport himself and Jefferies around the country. The four-door Super Deluxe would have set him back about $1,255. Instead George went for a 75 Series Fleetwood, an enlongated, seven-passenger limousine with jump seats in the back—the biggest Cadillac available. For a frequent traveler such as George, with a lot of gear, this land yacht could almost be construed as practical, but he really bought it to make a statement. This was the kind of car the swells drove, he reckoned. And he suddenly had an image to maintain, or inflate. For this shot of swagger, George shelled out about $5,000.

Betty was never a spender like her husband, and had no particular yen when it came to cars. She was intrigued, though, with the idea of buying one of the newfangled television sets she'd heard about. RCA made one that cost $350. It was like a radio, only the programs came with pictures as well. Someone else said it was like having movies right in your living room.

When Bert Sugar, boxing analyst and former editor of *The Ring* magazine, was growing up, his parents ran an appliance store on F

Street in Washington, D.C. When the Sugars closed their store for the night, they left their dazzling new entertainment machines turned on, facing outward so the flickering screens were visible through the storefront windows. "People would stand three-deep out there on the sidewalk to watch whatever was on, just to see television," Sugar remembers. By 1948 or '49 the Sugars added outdoor loudspeakers so their sidewalk patrons could fully appreciate their favorite broadcast every Tuesday night, the wrestling shows from Baltimore. Sellers of receiver sets all over the country used similar techniques to entice customers, though most found they didn't need speakers; just leaving the sets on and tuned to wrestling was enough. Some took an even easier, lower-tech approach: After hours they simply taped photos of Gorgeous George over their television screens and let the public gaze in on him.

As best as can be determined, the Gorgeous One first strutted into a televised wrestling ring at the Olympic Auditorium in November 1947; Sam Menacker was most likely the opponent. When his image appeared on the tiny black-and-white screen, heat became electric. (A half century later *Entertainment Weekly* declared George's TV debut one of "The 100 Greatest Moments in Television," ranking it No. 45 on that list.) Looking back, it seems there was truth as well as hubris in one of George's most grandiose declarations, his take on this new delivery system for Gorgeousness. Assuming a deliberating posture—arms folded, with one hand to his chin—he would muse thoughtfully as he pondered a conundrum. "I don't know if I was made for television," said Gorgeous George, "or television was made for me."

Certainly, in the early days of the new medium, television and wrestling formed a spectacularly successful union. This electronic convergence was long and fruitful, combining all the best attributes of a love match and an arranged marriage. The two partners had complementary strengths and shored up each other's weaknesses. There was affection between the spouses, and both sides made out well financially—everyone's needs were met. Of the couple, wrestling was definitely the older, more experienced partner; in the years immediately following World War II, television was still very young and knew nothing of the world.

Not long after NBC showed President Roosevelt speaking at the 1939 World's Fair—the one Betty and George's neighbors in Eugene visited—broadcasting was virtually shut down until the war ended. In 1946 it resumed with CBS and ABC the second and third networks and Dumont, a manufacturer of TV sets, the fourth. These were still small regional outfits showing a limited hodgepodge of programs. Often the broadcasters took nights off and went dark, including on Saturday nights when, it was thought, Americans had better things to do.

In its infancy television was a very tentative and chancy business. RCA, the Radio Corporation of America, issued the 630TS model television in 1946, but sold only ten thousand or so that year at $350 apiece. The Model T of televisions, it was twenty-six inches wide by fifteen inches high with a miniature screen in the center, flanked on both sides by covered speakers. It looked, not surprisingly, like a radio. This appliance clearly had some novelty and entertainment value, but no one knew if the American public would take to the flickering invader. Movie mogul Darryl F. Zanuck famously gave it six months, saying: "People will soon get tired of staring at a plywood box every night." Advertisers, habituated to radio and newspapers, were skeptical, so they were often given free time, and that helped make early broadcasting a money pit. Programmers, network executives, and station owners were simultaneously breaking ground and anxiously hedging their bets. Like American business at the advent of the Internet, they knew they had to be involved—lest TV turn out to be the next big thing—but didn't want to overinvest in case Zanuck was proved correct.

The strategy most settled on was ginning up cheap content with mass appeal. Original programming, including dramas, was costly to produce, and while variety shows like Milton Berle's, Ted Mack's *Original Amateur Hour,* and those hosted by Ed Sullivan and Arthur Godfrey were extremely popular, they required an investment in talent. Quiz shows were an early, low-budget offering, but sitcoms didn't make any real impact until 1951 or so, when *I Love Lucy* debuted, and the heydays of the western and the hospital drama (*Dr. Kildare* et al) were still to come. Sport was a natural solution and brought in TV's first mass audience, when just shy of four million viewers watched the 1947 World Series. With TV sets still an expensive rarity, almost 90 percent of those folks watched the Series in bars.

The sports leagues had already built their audiences and their schedules were set; they could supply ready-made airwave filler. Starting in 1946, NBC let the *Gillette Cavalcade of Sports* go on for hours, two nights a week. For programmers, wrestling was the easiest solution: All a broadcast required was one fixed camera pointed at the ring, a few extra lights, and one out-of-work actor to serve as the announcer. Promoters would accept small fees for the rights to broadcast from their arenas; to them it was extra revenue with very little extra effort. Baseball and football presented much greater technical challenges with the need to follow the ball, and boxing matches, though easy to shoot, couldn't be counted on to fill the required time slots. The pesky fighters insisted on knocking each other out at unpredictable intervals. In addition, boxing's champs and top contenders fought only a few times a year, so they weren't helpful very often.

Wrestling, on the other hand, was a plastic material, something you could really work with. Their biggest stars, including George, would work as often as you wanted them to. Promoters could make the matches go as long or short as needed. And the grunt-and-groan game was all about mass, never mind the class. As a result, wrestling was slathered across early prime-time schedules the way reality shows and forensic sleuthing are sixty years later. When wrestling shows began to air, however, they did so with very little competition—instead of hundreds of cable and satellite channels, most areas received three or four stations and there were no remote-control devices to make changing channels easy. As a result, wrestling on TV was endlessly available and all but inescapable.

In 1948 NBC offered wrestling on Tuesday nights, and ABC gave over half its evening schedule to it on Wednesdays, where it remained for most of the next six years. Dumont, the network with the shallowest pockets, aired two hours of wrestling on both Thursday and Friday nights. The latter show originated in New York's Jamaica Arena, with Dennis James, later the host of *Name That Tune* and *The Nighttime Price Is Right,* at the microphone. Beginning in 1949, Dumont carried the action from Chicago's Marigold Arena, with Jack Brickhouse announcing. That show ran for nearly six years as well—apparently, America *didn't* have anything better to do on Saturday nights.

Local stations, at least as needful of cheap programming as the networks, beamed out even more matches. In Los Angeles, German-born engineer Klaus Landsberg ran the first commercial station west of the Mississippi, KTLA, and Channel 5 quickly became the market's number one station, and the seat of George's broadcast kingdom. TV-set owners in L.A. were invited to a televised wrestling orgy: broadcasts six nights a week, Monday through Saturday, on five different stations. So voracious was the demand, and abundant the supply, that Channel 13 came back on Sunday mornings with *Wrestling Workouts.* This was *practice,* mind you. For staged matches.

Before the networks became truly national, broadcasting coast-to-coast, in 1951, wrestling and other programming was distributed via the kinescope. This was filmed by a movie camera pointed at the TV screen, a technique Kodak pioneered in 1947, allowing audiences all over the country to watch what had been broadcast live in some other locale. Kinescoping was so widespread that at one point the TV industry actually used more film than the movie business. For wrestling and the boys, this was a huge gift, free exposure to vastly greater audiences. Now they could be seen on every set in the land.

Boxing had its moments, despite its unpredictability—*Pabst Blue Ribbon Bouts* aired Wednesday nights for many years on CBS. And baseball and football broadcasts were regular fodder, too. Yet it's almost impossible to overstate the degree to which early television was inundated by, and identified with, the maim-and-maul game. It was wrestling hegemony, with Gorgeous George rampant. Paul "The Butcher" Vachon, was a six-foot-one, 280-pound heel who, along with his brother Maurice, "The Mad Dog," grew up watching wrestling in Quebec during these early years of television. When people talked about buying a TV back then, he remembers, "they said they were gonna get themselves a 'wrestling set.'"

As it turned out, Americans were not just entertained by that plywood box, they were *enchanted* by it. TV was . . . miraculous, really. You got to choose how you wanted to be amused each night, or to be amused many times over by turning the knob from Channel 2 all the way up to Channel 13. Amazingly, no matter how many different programs you watched, there was no extra cost. As history has since confirmed, Americans like nothing better than an all-you-can-consume buffet. *Masterpiece Theater* it wasn't. Some tonier programming, such as *Actors Studio* and the *Philco TV Playhouse* aired almost from the beginning, as did some well-done journalism. But especially as television spread beyond the big cities, the most popular fare was just that: of the people. Sweating, joking, falling, talking so fast and loud the spittle flew from his mouth, Milton Berle—Uncle Miltie—the star of the hit *Texaco Star Theater,* was crude and often lewd. A former vaudevillian and burlesque veteran, he would do anything for a laugh as long as it was undignified.

Whether it was "good" or "clean" is questionable, but wrestling was indisputably fun. Most vitally, it was fun for all. As more families acquired sets, they began to tune in together at home, rather than going out to taverns or bars. The console models, and "combo" sets, which had a phonograph and radio built in, were massive pieces of furniture, with ten- or twelve-inch screens at most. When the entire family piled into the living room to watch, it helped to sit as close as possible. Quaint as it now seems, there was only one set per household, so togetherness was assured.

Wrestling's visceral action, simple story lines, and primitive drama—the compelling narrative question of who will kick the bejesus out of whom—gave no one trying to follow it any trouble. As the National Football League has also shown, a violent spectacle in a confined space transmits quite well in this medium. Match action was wild and woolly, with the compelling chaos of a good cartoon (*Crusader Rabbit,* the first animated series produced just for TV—debuted in 1949, as did the Roadrunner and Wile E. Coyote), so the youngsters laughed along with the older folks. In 1950 more than 10 million Americans had been born abroad and three-quarters of them were over forty-five; these were the grandparents from the old countries, and many grew up speaking a language other than English. As they found to their delight, you didn't have to talk American that well to follow grappling and groping, or to appreciate the Gorgeousness of George.

Television would later be described as a "cool medium," but in the beginning Americans didn't see it that way at all. They weren't yet used to sitting passively in front of their entertainments, something we've since raised to a fine art. When the TV set showed, say, the supremely athletic Lou Thesz versus the handsome ladykiller Baron Michele Leone, the whole household partook loudly and rowdily, just like the fans in the arenas. (This stylish heel was a different Leone, not Antone, the Wagners' housemate in Tulsa.) When George the magnificent came on, the dads and grandfathers would shake their fists and yell at him to "Quit fighting dirty! He's cheating!" Mom and Grandmom, on the other hand, might bellow at his opponent to "Leave Georgie alone! Stop picking on him!"

From the start, women were a substantial part of the wrestling audience. An early survey by Woodbury College in California showed wrestling was easily that state's favorite TV sport, and that older women preferred it five to one. *Wrestling and TV Sports* magazine noted that female viewers were partial to announcer Dennis James because "he talks confidentially, not to the male TV viewers, but to ma and the rest of the girls." The patriarchs, some with Schlitz in hand to re-create the tavern atmosphere, held forth knowledgeably on the holds, techniques, and abilities of the boys at work. (Men reportedly favored the more technical approach used by New York announcer Bill Johnston.) Older children tried out their own versions of body slams and submission holds on their luckless siblings. Everyone in the living room had, and freely exercised, the right to yell at any offending family member, or guest, should they improperly stray: *"Hey, stop blocking the set!"* And back in what now seems an intentionally naive era, anyone who dared suggest that wrestling was a fake was met with rage, indignation, and complete denial. That heresy invited banishment from the room, or from the house altogether.

In 1947 there were just 180,000 TV sets made in this country, but the following year that number was close to a million, and then in 1949 production tripled—60,000 sets were sold every week. In roughly four years, TV went from nonexistent to a four-and-a-half-hours-a-day habit for those fortunate, plugged-in owners. And while many have since decried the sleeper hold television has on the collective American neck, at that time it was still hailed as a wholesome family activity—TV was still a babyface.

Some accomplished wrestlers shriveled under the TV lights and froze in the camera's eye. These stiffs, as Lou Thesz called them, had to quit the business or try to make a living working only nontelevised bouts. With George, the opposite occurred. His charismatic energy was transmitted fully to the small screen, losing none of its intensity. Those platinum locks, his overopulent wardrobe, and eye-opening antics made him the most recognizable and memorable of the new mat celebrities. TV announcers chuckled and played along appreciatively as they narrated all the stages of George's arena folderol. Yet almost all of what set him apart—George's looks, rituals, and mimed hauteur, as well as his ring acrobatics—was easily apprehended as pure visuals and motion. If the sound couldn't be heard in a bar, for example, his Gorgeosity still came through.

A bit later, when TV announcers began doing interviews with the wrestlers before and after matches, George proved himself bombastically adept as well. When the camera zoomed in during these spots, his big talking head filled the picture and George's expressive face was captivating in close-up. He sent out special signals, it seemed, on frequencies only he could transmit. If Gorgeous George didn't make television great, as he proclaimed, he certainly made great television. Watching him strut and wrestle, then strut some more, was more fun than a picnic.

Chapter 13

RING RATS
AND CADILLACS

During those early years of television, the sweet spot of his career, George essentially lived with Jake Brown, spending more time with his loyal Jefferies than he did with Betty and the children. All those nights at the arenas and then the hotels and bars, and through the interminable driving, they were together. From 1947 until 1952 or thereabouts, Jake woke him up in the morning; Jake dressed him before the matches; Jake fixed his hair; Jake took care of all the bills, checks, and tips; Jake made sure they got to the next mat palace on time. In a sense, the manservant took on another wifely duty as well: Jake loved George.

Born in 1917, he was two years younger than his friend, the second of Leon and Molly Brown's four boys. The parents ran a neighborhood grocery in Houston, and raised their children as observant Jews, keeping kosher. George wouldn't talk about his early childhood, but the adult Jake was a little more forthcoming. One of Jacob's most searing memories was of his father forcing him to hold one of his brothers still so Leon could beat him. Terrified, young Jacob put all his hope in his mother, Molly. Like George, Jacob dropped out of Milby High School early, after tenth grade, to help support his family. He was working as a machinist at Reed Roller Bit in Houston when he was inducted into the army in August of 1943. During his two years, four months, and three days of service, he wrote fervent declarations of filial love. In one entitled "Memories," he wrote:

Send me the pressure of your hand,
The glance that says you understand.
Send me the love that's in your heart,
So you and I will never part.
Through the years alone of suffering and strife,
You will always be the light of my life.
And when this is over and the victory is won,
I'll hurry home to you, Mother, your loving son.

Very soon after his return, however, Molly Brown died of stomach cancer (her husband was already deceased, from complications of diabetes). Jake, who was working in a Houston department store, recovered enough to marry a woman named Beulah Mae Crosson in July of 1947. She was from Illinois and seven years younger; somewhat surprisingly, she was a Baptist. Then George and Betty took Jake on as the valet, and he and Beulah followed them to Southern California, where they bought property in Culver City. Their first daughter, Elizabeth—named after George's Elizabeth—was born in 1948 and her sister, Brenda, in 1951. Beulah was tall, over five-foot-eight (when Jake met her in Dallas, she was working as a model), and her blue eyes and dark hair made her strikingly attractive. She was also domineering, unhappy, and at times unstable. Jake feared her anger but resisted only passively: He escaped with George.

George treated him like an equal, not an employee, yet Jake was in thrall to him as well and his devotion countenanced all George's faults. Their years together—"When I was with George," as Jake always put it—was the best time he ever had, he told his daughters. They'd known each other forever, grown up poor during painful boyhoods, and both lost their mothers too soon. George couldn't be faithful to women, but he was loyal to men, most of all to Jake. Beyond those similarities the two men were complementary opposites, down to their appearance: George beefy and blond, Jake lean and dark. Jake was gentle where George was rough, and quiet amid his friend's blare. Despite all his opportunities and his unhappy marriage—and much to the amazement of the other wrestling men—Jake was faithful to Beulah.

Their wrestling life was essentially nocturnal. After the matches ended at 10 or 11 P.M., groups of boys piled back into their cars and careened through the night to get to the next booking. The leading cause of death in this business wasn't ring falls or attacks by deranged fans, but car accidents. When you did get to the next town, you'd be exhausted, recalled John Lakey, a New Zealander who wrestled here as Jack Carter beginning in 1948. "Not much enthusiasm to spare. But you had to be a trouper." He finally quit the game when he fell asleep at the wheel one night on the way from Detroit back to Chicago. Most shrugged when that happened, and kept going.

It didn't help that many of the boys thought nothing of drinking at the wheel. The owner of the car called the shots; Killer Kowalski, for one, never let anyone drink or smoke in his car. But most didn't impose any such bans. There were few illicit drugs to be had, much less steroids, but there were boozers aplenty. Paul Vachon, the Butcher, had his last drink twenty-five years ago, downing twenty-four bottles of King's beer in a motel room in Edmonton, Alberta, in a final binge. When he was out on the road in the 1950s, though, beer wasn't considered drinking but rather healthy rehydration. Vachon explains the hundred-mile rule: "One six-pack per 100 miles. If you had to go a couple hundred miles, it was two six-packs." Per person, of course.

Once, when Dick Beyer was driving through the South with Sky Hi Lee, he noticed that Lee's car stank for days—or rather, nights—on end. He'd seen that Lee kept a bottle of whiskey on the front seat between them and pulled on it frequently, but this odor was different. Finally, he asked Lee, "What's that smell?" Sky Hi reached up and flipped down his windshield visor, showing the Destroyer the huge head of garlic hidden behind it. "If we get pulled over," he told his passenger, "I'll take a big bite of the garlic so they don't smell the whiskey on my breath." At that time, though, law enforcement on drinking and driving was light, especially if you were a wrestling celebrity. A couple of free tickets usually made any such problems disappear.

Jake Brown was a drinker, too, but just beer, and he didn't imbibe every day. Thankfully, he was a sober driver. When he was home his drinking drove Beulah crazy, but then, as someone who knew them both remarked, she was already crazy.

Usually, he and George took off by themselves after the matches, but at other times they'd stay overnight, eating and drinking with the boys. Even in his most successful times, George never high-hatted the other wrestlers—the Gorgeous act was just for the ring and the marks. He loved their company and they his. George told jokes, did card tricks (he could throw a card at a wall and make it stick), bought drinks, and slapped backs. He was a physical man in a physical business. When George started horsing around, remembered one of his drinking buddies, and he grabbed your arm or shoulder, you could feel how powerful his muscles were under the loose clothes.

Like other persuasive public men, George had a way of engaging others, of being squarely, fully with them, such that they both felt included and wanted to be included. The boys, who had considerable egos of their own and might have resented his success, still considered him one of the brethren. Yet in some ways he stood apart. No one else traveled by chauffeur-driven limousine, for one. More importantly, George had his ineffable current, the quality that allowed him to cannily, intentionally diminish his natural handsomeness and still become a star, and that overshadowed his impressive athletic ability. Ted Lewin, the babyface who became an illustrator, worked with George just once, when he was nineteen or twenty years old. "I had so many matches over fifteen years," he said, "and I don't remember one from the other. I remember this one, though, because of Gorgeous George. You see him perform and he's bigger than life, then when you get in his company in the dressing room, he still had that quality about him.

Other guys were great wrestlers and great workers, but they just didn't have that star power."

George drank a good bit, and at times he would fight, both of which the boys heartily endorsed. Jody Hamilton, who wrestled as the Assassin, once said approvingly, "George never weighed over 190 pounds and yet I saw him deck a 300-pound truck driver in a bar in the old Claridge Hotel in St. Louis. He dropped him colder than a wedge." After they wrestled, the boys usually hit a local bar or three. Frequently, some inebriated patron would recognize one of them, or just react to his size, and say something along the lines of, "You think you're tough, big guy?" Almost invariably, he did, and fights followed. Marks would also confront the boys with the accusation that their game was fixed. The wrestlers' first response was usually rhetorical. "The guy who wins a match makes more money than the guy who loses," they'd say. "So why would I ever go in the tank?" Untrue, but eminently reasonable. At times, though, fans would keep insisting the fix was in and then another kind of argument came into play. Killer Kowalski once found himself sitting at a saloon table next to three businessmen in suits and ties when one of them looked over and declared, "Wrestling's all a fake." Kowalski got up, grabbed him, lifted him up, and slammed him down on the table headfirst, whereupon the executive sensibly lost consciousness. Kowalski turned to his friends and said, "Is that a fake? Now get him the hell out of here and don't come back."

Their travel schedules were tight, but the boys always made time for their groupies, whom they charmingly called "ring rats," or simply rats. Wrestlers weren't the most attractive lot, but they were big, strong men, and as Don Arnold, a beneficiary of this dynamic, points out, they were becoming TV stars, which had its own powerful pull. Then, too, some women liked the fact that tonight's date would be almost assuredly gone tomorrow. A mating routine evolved. On a cool 1950s night in San Bernardino, let's say, Arnold is making his way from the arena to his car. At twenty-seven the blue-eyed lifeguard with a weight lifter's build is an up-and-coming babyface, and to his delight he's starting to make real money. Arnold's taken a shower after the night's exertions, he's feeling good about life, and would like to feel even better. As he strolls into the parking lot with his duffel bag in one hand, a ring of fans forms around him. Arnold horses around with some of the kids, putting them in headlocks or lifting them overhead in a military press, and he signs a few autograph books. There are young women in the little throng, too, some with their husbands or dates, some not. One kind is more interesting than the other.

Arnold turns toward one of them, a dark-haired girl in a skirt and white blouse who has a certain air. She looks kind of sassy, somehow, and the signals she's sending, he's receiving. He turns toward her, they chat, and then she asks, "How long will you be in town?" Or she might be even more direct: "Where are you staying?" If he didn't like the way she looked, he'd say, "I'm not staying, I'm leaving town tonight." But this isn't one of those times. "I'm at the So-and-So Hotel," he tells her, "and I'll be there at eleven."

In this boys' club, locker-room humor prevailed. Much discussion revolved around the size of Antonino Rocca's penis, said to be the biggest in wrestling. According to some of the boys, Rocca would leave the locker-room door open at times to let potential ring rats get a look at his main-eventer. Lou Thesz, who possessed a more elevated wit, said of Rocca, an Argentine of Italian ancestry, that "blessing him in the jockstrap was the Lord's way of compensating for not giving him any brains."

Early in his career, George worked out in local gyms in the afternoons whenever he could, but as his stardom grew he no longer had the time, and fitness was no longer essential to his act. Even if he'd continued, no amount of muscular armor would have made the game safe. Cracked ribs were so common as to not be worth talking about, said Don Leo Jonathan, who wrestled for roughly thirty years before a severe back injury forced him to retire. In a construct that rivaled the sayings of baseball's Yogi Berra, he estimated that "Sixty percent of the guys was mostly 50 percent of the time hurt." One night George came to Phoenix's Madison Square Garden with a badly sprained ankle, using a crutch and Jake's help to get from the car to the dressing room. Rod Fenton, the promoter, had a doctor already there, and after he examined the ankle the doctor conferred with Fenton in private. "I wouldn't have him do anything with that, I'd just wrap that sucker up and send him home," he said.

"We can't do that," Fenton replied. "We've got the house full and people are waiting to see him."

The two men went back to the dressing room and offered George a needle, a numbing shot. "If you're careful," the doctor said, "you can get through the match." George was game, and of course he wanted to get paid. "All right," he said, "I'll give it a try." Twenty minutes or so after the shot he was standing on the foot, then pushing on it hard. *Hey, this isn't so bad,* he thought to himself. With his opponent looking out for his injured ankle, George not only got through the match but tore the house down. The next morning in his hotel room, though, George woke up in agony. He couldn't put any weight on the foot at all; when he tried to get up and touched the floor, he fell back on the bed, screaming. Then he called Fenton, at 6 A.M., and cursed a filthy blue streak that impressed even Jake, who'd heard George angry before.

Wrestling was becoming family television fare, but the Romans in the arenas still went berserk at the sight of gladiatorial blood. The subset of wrestlers known as "blade men" gave theirs intentionally. To get heat, a boy would conceal an eighth-of-an-inch razor blade on a wrist or finger, fixing it there with tape. When his opponent slammed him face-first into a turnbuckle, he'd put a hand to his forehead, drawing the cutting tool across it and opening up a slash that gushed crimson. When the crowd saw the blood, or "juice," running down his face and neck and staining the mat below, it let out a primal roar. A star like George would never have to resort to blading or "getting color," as it was also known. But quite a few others did, their foreheads gradually becoming hatch-marked with tiny whitish scars.

Just as they had during George's Oregon years, ticket-buying fans around the country felt they'd bought a heel's license themselves, and got their money's worth by screaming, cursing, throwing things, and at times more. Late in the wrestling boom that George and television touched off, an up-and-coming young reporter for the *New York Times* named Gay Talese wrote: "Next to rock 'n' roll addicts, Dodger baseball fans and untipped taxicab drivers, perhaps the most violently expressive citizens to be found these days are those who pay to watch wrestling matches." He noted that at most Madison Square Garden sporting events there were five New York City policemen on duty. However, an upcoming wrestling show required twenty patrolmen and two sergeants.

Classy Freddie Blassie once felt a pain in his leg midmatch, and looked down to see a knife protruding from his calf. He also had his Lincoln Continental set on fire in San Bernardino, California. Cars were a frequent target. Tom Drake worked as a babyface called the Wrestling Sergeant, out of Fort Benning, Georgia. If a visiting heel worked him over too badly, some of Drake's fellow soldiers would go out and turn his car over, smashing the headlights and windshield. Or they might destroy another car they mistakenly thought belonged to the offending wrestler.

One memorable night in 1949 George threw Jim Mitchell, the Black Panther, out of the ring into the first row of seats at the Olympic Auditorium. Then, when the Panther tried to climb back in, George kicked him in the face, and he crashed onto the typewriters on press row. The referee signaled that the battered Panther couldn't continue, George was declared the winner, and the Olympic fans took it the wrong way. First a huge man, sitting close, threw off his coat, climbed into the ring, and charged George. The wrestler, sensing a real threat, cut his theatrical strutting and gloating short, and crouched down in a combat stance. George sidestepped neatly, then flipped the man over his shoulder. But rather than stopping to appreciate this display of hand-to-hand technique, tens more irate fans poured into the ring, and as the *Los Angeles Times* report said, "a general free-for-all ensued. The fighting spread from the ring into the aisles and seats and even continued outside the building." Both George and Mitchell were scratched, cut, and bruised, but neither went to the hospital. However, in the me-lee Mr. C. M. Bullard of Azusa was stabbed in the right shoulder and a friend suffered a broken thumb when he came to Bullard's aid. Thirty-one-year-old Miss Norma Romero was struck in the eye with a blackjack before scores of additional police officers called in could re-store order.

The men in the wrestling audiences were the most dangerous, but the soprano fans also bore watching. "Women, for some strange rea-son, often go berserk," observed *New York Times* writer Sam Boal. "The villain especially is in danger and women specialize in taking off high-heeled slippers and beating the poor man heavily about the head. Or sometimes they just yank out his hair." Dick Beyer, the Destroyer, never forgot his match against Gorgeous George in Birmingham, Ala-bama, due mainly to one particular woman at ringside. "She was standing on a chair and cheering and screaming for me—while nurs-ing a baby."

What exactly happened between one female fan and the Gorgeous One in the summer of 1948 isn't clear. But their one-fall dustup, which took place in the Ocean Park Arena in Santa Monica, made headlines all the way across the country. The *Washington Post* ran a version of a United Press wire-service story on the heel's latest outrage: "Gorgeous George, a perfumed wrestler of daintiness and refinement, was sued by a grandmother today for forgetting his manners and bopping her on the kisser."

Mrs. Elsie Alexander, forty-eight, got a half-nelson on the wrestler with a suit for $35,000. "The attack," she announced, "was malicious and without provocation."

Mrs. Alexander, who weighed in at 150 pounds, began the evening peacefully, eating her popcorn in a back-row seat. That night the Gor-geous One wore a robe of gold lamé with a red satin lining, and for some reason, he had gone back to the ill-advised blue hair. Mrs. Alex-ander was amazed by this. Her exact quote was: "Humph! Last time I saw him rassle his hair was blond." At the end of the match she rushed to the ring, intrigued, to take a closer look. When she did so, Mrs. A.

alleged, George bopped her on the button. "Wham!" the wire service story said, explaining the concussive event.

"Since then," the grandmother said, "I've suffered headaches, dizziness and have been under a doctor's care." George denied it vociferously, maintaining he never laid a perfumed paw on her. Even for wrestling's ur-heel, actually punching an elderly lady in the face would have been bad form. Older women were a vital part of his constituency, and outside the arenas George was conspicuously chivalrous and solicitous with them. Once he was having dinner with wrestler Pete Burr in Buffalo and they were approached by two of the local boy's former grammar school teachers. The famous wrestler immediately stood, kissed elderly hands, chatted, flattered, and bestowed Georgie pins. "What a gentleman," the ladies said to each other afterward. "And he has advanced degrees in psychology, too, imagine that . . ." The alleged kisser-bopping incident may have been a put-up job or publicity stunt, and it's also possible that, while Americans were not nearly as litigious in 1948 as they later became, this was a frivolous lawsuit on Granny's part. (No outcome was recorded.)

In the television era more boys could do well, even outearning some other professional athletes. In 1948 Bob Geigel had a chance to play for the Chicago Cardinals of the National Football League, earning $4,800 a season; instead he became a babyface and made $28,000, working his way up to $45,000 or $50,000 in the 1950s. One way he and his peers were able to accomplish this was by working all the time: Geigel wrestled fifty-one weeks a year, taking one week off to hunt and fish. In the late 1940s New York state law actually forbade wrestlers to grapple more than four nights a week for health reasons. Besides George, Lou Thesz, Antonino ("Argentina") Rocca, and Baron Michele Leone, very few wrestlers were getting rich. That's why they traveled four or five to a car and many of their meals were roadside "baloney blowouts." The Fabulous Moolah, the late Lillian Ellison, said she often drove all night to get to her next booking, then slept in her car to save money.

When their pockets were light, the boys often felt the hands of the promoters at work. Cal and Aileen Eaton, the couple who ran the Olympic Auditorium in Los Angeles, were fair, the wrestlers thought, but most of the other promoters would cheat them anytime they could. In a cash business in which the promoters counted the receipts, that was fairly easy. Lou Thesz said of Toots Mondt, who ran a New York promotion: "You couldn't trust him with a dog's dinner. He'd go through the wrestlers' pay envelopes and take out fives, tens, and twenties, saying, 'Ah, that's too much for that guy' . . . the whole operation was being controlled by a thief."

They loved it, of course, despite the grinding pace, the weaselly promoters, the blood they shed and left behind. The rigors the boys faced only confirmed that they were tougher than everyone else, feeding their egos. Wrestlers in George's day were among the luckiest of performers, hams who constantly got work in front of responsive audiences. Though in some ways they were pawns of the promoters, "there was really a lot of freedom, a lot of improvisation to what we did," said Don Arnold. How many would-be actors and athletes would trade their eyeteeth, as the saying goes, for such a creative outlet and a similar level of exposure? Usually, that's a rhetorical question. But in this wrestling era, the boys actually got to make that bargain.

Chapter 14

GEORGE VS. GEORGE

After the World War, wrestlers and promoters saw night after night just how much the public craved being entertained. With the fear and pain of that long effort eased, returning troops as well as relieved civilians were ready for a harmless hoot or two, and the kind of thrills that held no real danger. Rationing was finally over, too, and folks had money to spend, at least enough to purchase gasoline, wrestling tickets, popcorn, and the right to act silly. Television's coming was perfectly timed to meet that need for excitement and release.

At the same time this was no longer a nation of innocent farmers. Four hundred thousand of America's soldiers had died, and the survivors had seen and done things in the war they would find hard to forget. This wasn't a nation of cynics, by any means, but balanced on a moral cusp. In that equipoise, amusement-seeking Americans were ready, as they might not have been beforehand, to embrace a not-too-heinous villain, a man who embodied some complexity and contradictions—just as they did. The Gorgeous One made it clear how highly he thought of himself, that he thought only of himself, and he broke every rule he could find, Suddenly that was an engaging possibility—still a bit scandalous, certainly, but not completely contemptible. Americans had just shared sacrifice; collectivism had been lived at its limits. In a natural reversal, individuals began to think of themselves a little more that way. On one level George tantalized with his egotism, challenging viewers to stop pretending that they'd never thought as he did—never dreamed of standing out and acting out, never felt the impulse to put themselves first. More overtly, he offered Americans the opportunity to condemn him for his unabashed selfishness, denying that emerging part of themselves. Today it's a given, but at that time Americans were just working up the nerve to admit it: There's a little Gorgeous George in all of us.

Six months after his first televised match, *Time* ran a story on the TV wrestling phenomenon, calling George "the newest, slickest, most popular performer of them all." In Buffalo, 11,845 fans had just jammed the Memorial Auditorium to see the outrageous performer in person. He drew 20,000 in Cleveland and 18,000 in Toronto, attendance figures unheard of for wrestling. In Hollywood, the *Time* story also related, some taverns and restaurants trying to attract customers with their new television sets were changing their tactics. Formerly, they'd put out signs with just the single word TELEVISION. Now, *Time* said, "They put out signs reading, GORGEOUS GEORGE, TELEVISION, HERE TONIGHT."

Their forces joined, George and television changed the wrestling game as they gave it new life. Earlier generations of fans had been enticed with gimmicks such as mud wrestling, offered in male and female varieties. There were ice-cream matches, like the tussle between Joe Reno and Roughhouse Ross in 250 gallons of vanilla, chocolate, and strawberry. On Michigan's upper peninsula you had the fruit-for-all known as the Blueberry Bowl. In a "Good Housekeeping match," opponents beat and slashed at each other with various household appliances, including toasters and electric mixers. Now that grunt and groan was a successful arm of show business, however, different entertainment values prevailed. For the boys, grappling technique wasn't a major asset anymore, and an imposing physique was no longer sufficient. Instead, wrestlers with highly developed characters, eye-catching visual displays, and "acting" ability were in demand. As the novelty of

Gorgeous George proved such a good drawing card, the boys and promoters furiously invented their own increasingly wacky personalities,
in hopes of replicating his success.

Out came the Gorilla, wheeled to the ring in a cage while he
roared and shook the bars, and the Bat, who dressed in black from
head to foot and pretended to suck opponents' blood. Professor Roy
Shire wore a cap and gown to the ring. Ricki Starr, a friend of George's,
developed an act that could only have flown after the Gorgeous One
flitted. Starr, who'd actually had ballet training, appeared in a pink
tutu and would leap across the ring in jetés and rush at opponents up
on the tips of his toe shoes.

Lord Leslie Carlton worked a faux-royal act, similar to Lord
Lansdowne's. Killer Kowalski was also quite successful, though more
of a throwback. A pure heel, he made his bones when he accidentally
tore off Yukon Eric's cauliflower ear in the ring. The referee said that
when he picked it up and put it in his pocket, it was still quivering. The
ethnic or national villain—like the German Hans Schmidt, actually a
French-Canadian—continued to play well after World War II. Later
the Nazi heels would morph into Russians and then Iranians, including the Iron Sheik.

Few of these characters could match George's ornate silliness,
however, or the sincerity of his pose. While some of the other wrestlers were clearly playacting in their ring roles, and even seemed a little embarrassed, George clearly identified with and completely
inhabited his character. He'd found the role he was born to play, and
this was intrinsic to his success: more convinced, he was more convincing. Now, thanks to television, he could impress millions of fans
in a single night, and the response to his new, Gorgeous self continued
to grow. Before the cathode-ray glow came on in American living
rooms, George and Betty's ring creation was a well-known success, *for
a wrestler*. After the great illumination no one, including those two,
could tell where his success might find its limits—were there any limits for TV stars?

Then George suddenly felt he could lose all he'd worked for, just as stunningly as he'd attained it. He heard the alarming, infuriating news from one worried friend, then another, and next in a phone call from a loyal promoter: Others were stealing his act, inhabiting the same Gorgeous character.

George hated very few people; he got angry, but his fury didn't have the requisite stamina. What's more, in the pragmatic, transactional way he viewed the world, hating or not hating wasn't a very useful construct. But for promoter Jack Pfefer, George made a thorough exception. Pfefer (born Jacob) was a tiny man, five-foot-two, with an unruly mass of black hair. He came to this country in 1921 from Poland, then part of the Russian empire, and began promoting wrestling three years later. In the mid-1930s Pfefer fell out with his partners and showed just how fierce and vindictive an enemy he could be. He exposed all the inner workings of wrestling's fakery to Dan Parker, sports editor of New York's *Daily Mirror,* who wrote a series of exposés. Wrestling lived to pretend another day, however, as did Pfefer. When he returned to the business, he specialized in what he called his Angels, huge men—and the occasional woman—mostly foreigners, with congenital deformities and misshapen heads. He dubbed them the Swedish Angel, the Lady Angel, and so on. "I love my freaks," he told *Collier's* magazine. "I am very proud of some of my monstrosities."

He had bad breath and bad manners, rarely smiled, and, for what it's worth, never married. The promoter constantly felt himself ill-used and complained bitterly to his peers, wheedling, threatening, gossiping, and always at the ready to retaliate for some perceived offense. "I can smell and feel there is a lot of cunning going on," he wrote to St. Louis promoter Sam Muchnick. "Believe me, I can see what's cooking far ahead, more than all the wise guys together. I am always far sighted in the smelling game and that is why I am still around punching and holding my own." For anyone prepared to dislike Pfefer, there were many points of purchase. Some of the disdain for Pfefer among the wrestlers and the press was tinged with anti-Semitism; he was almost always described as "the wily Russian Jew." But much of it was earned.

A 1939 letter from George's buddy Jesse James to the promoter shows the most likely source of Wagner and Pfefer's enmity. Stating his case matter-of-factly on stationery from the Hotel Padre in Hollywood, Jesse wrote:

> Dear Jack,
> Every time you write to me you ask me when I intend to come back to N.Y. I want you to know the reason I never did come back to you was because of the $240 that you still owe me, and you still owe Billy Raeburn over $300.
>
> Now, Jack, if you will promise to treat me right, and pay me back the $240 I'll come back and work for you, otherwise I'll never come back. You may let me know in return mail what is what. Sincerely,
>
> Jesse

That was a good deal of money in 1939, and it seems Pfefer pulled something similar with another Harrisburg Rat. George's response was not nearly as reasoned as James's. Their climactic dispute took place in the promoter's New York office in the Times Building and the argument ended with George reaching into his wrestling bag, pulling out his sweaty, smelly jockstrap, and rubbing it in the little man's face. Years later, when George became such a gate attraction, Pfefer sought his revenge. He hired a series of imitators, had them copy George and Betty's gimmicks, and promoted his boys as Gorgeous George. The most successful was Gorgeous George Grant, aka Danny Sheffield, who was wrestling in L.A. as Darling Danny in 1949. A promoter there had already dyed Sheffield's hair blond in imitation of George when Pfefer recruited him, and together the two undertook a blatant theft. Grant strutted to the ring in fancy robes, to the tune of "Pomp and Circumstance." He used a series of valets, including Sir Charles and a midget called Mister Jeffrey. Grant's wife, Christine, put his bleached blond hair up in pin curls; he posed for publicity photographs in beauty parlors and was promoted as "The Original Hollywood Dandy," "The Toast of the Nation," and "The Original Platinum Blond." Grant split with Pfefer in 1966 but continued to use the same gimmicks up until the early 1970s. Before he retired he was "saved," as Grant termed his religious conversion, and became a preacher as well as a wrestler, but he never repented or renounced his imitation of George.

In 1948, when George Wagner was still very much on the rise, the *Los Angeles Times* noted that Gorgeous George was "a sobriquet now apparently affected, like the name Santa Claus, by various practitioners." Gorgeous George Arena strutted on three-inch platform heels and claimed he used the act before George, beginning in 1936. His valets sprayed Evening in Paris. Gorgeous George Winchell ("Dutch" Schweigert) was another strike at George launched by Pfefer from Toledo in the late 1940s. The promoter kept it up for practically the entirety of the original George's career, trying both to ruin him and to cash in on his moneymaking prowess.

The real George Wagner was beside himself. Sure, he'd used some of Lord Lansdowne's gimmicks, George reasoned, but he and Betty added plenty of their own—and he wasn't *calling himself* Lord Lansdowne, taking money out of the man's pocket. This threat was a dangerous one, he knew, especially when he learned that the impostors were not just stealing his act but undercutting him as well; they were working for much less money. Arizona promoter Rod Fenton wouldn't book the pretenders, but others did. George knew how the business worked. What if the rest of the promoters decided, as they were inclined to, that the cheaper alternative was the better one? He began billing himself as "The Original Gorgeous George"—but some of the fakers quickly imitated *that* as well.

In public, though, George didn't show his concern. In an interview, he admitted he'd been "complaining rather severely about some of the second rate wrestlers who were trying to copy my style. It burned me up to see a young punk strutting around the ring, wearing a shabby robe, hair dyed grotesquely in what he thought was a reasonable facsimile of me." But then, he recounted, his good friend Eddie

Cantor set him straight. The comedian, singer, and actor, one of the country's most popular entertainers from the 1930s to the '50s, was an early booster, giving the wrestler important exposure on his hit radio show, *Time to Smile*.

"George, if you see a singer on the stage on his knees and singing 'Mammy,' you don't think about that singer, do you?" Cantor asked.

"No," George replied, shrugging his shoulders. "I think of Al Jolson."

"That's it, Gorgeous," said Cantor. "Imitation is the highest form of compliment. No matter who it is up there in the ring, imitating you, the audience will always remember the one and only Gorgeous George."

The promoters tried hard to keep the Gorgeous Ones apart, but they occasionally crossed paths. When he and George Wagner did, George Grant acknowledged, "We never got along too good. If I walked into a bar and he was already there, I'd walk out." Once, in October 1956, though, they were booked against each other in the National Guard Armory in Pocatello, Idaho. Promoter Jack Reynolds put up posters all over town: "Gorgeous Hair vs. Gorgeous Hair . . . Gorgeous Robe vs. Gorgeous Robe . . . Gorgeous George Wagner vs. Gorgeous George Grant!"

Grant was apprehensive, but when he got to the locker room, George Wagner was calm and professional. There was money to be made, after all, and George had a harder time holding a grudge against another worker, a member of his own tribe, than he did against promoters, the wrestlers' historical enemies. "Hey, kid," he said amicably to Grant, who was about ten years his junior, "what are we going to do tonight?"

"Anything you want, George," Grant replied hastily. (The promoter hadn't predetermined this match's outcome.) George Wagner was generous; he was leaving for Australia soon, so he didn't mind losing, he told Grant. Neither man had brought his valet, so it was one-on-one. They both strutted to the ring in their Gorgeous robes as "Pomp and Circumstance" played. When the bell rang the two Georges with heads of blond curls approached each other in the same stance, both with their legs bent and their arms extended—the pair resembled Groucho Marx confronting himself in the mirror in *Duck Soup*.

Not content with his Gorgeous frauds, Pfefer initiated another assault on George in the late 1940s, using a former policeman from New Jersey named Herman Rohde. Six years younger than George, he was both a weapon for Pfefer and, in his own right, the Gorgeous One's greatest rival as a performer. First he was Dutch Rohde, then became Buddy Rogers, taking the name of a popular star of 1920s silent films. When Pfefer began booking him, Rogers peroxided his hair blond, though he kept his short, and took to wearing shiny capes and shorter jackets. He was the arrogant, sneering heel without George's aristocratic airs and more complex grooming refinements. Rogers was also a terrific worker, a handsome hunk with the athleticism to pour on one "flying move," or airborne stunt, after another. He couldn't really wrestle at all, but he had the ineffable kinetic knack, as George did, for creating excitement. With Pfefer he took the nickname "Nature Boy," after the song that was a huge hit in 1948 for Nat King Cole and Frank Sinatra, who covered it the same year. (Wrestling wasn't the only endeavor in which success bred imitation.)

In June 1948 Pfefer wrote to Hugh Nichols, the promoter at the Hollywood Legion Stadium. "Here is what I want you to do: To make the gorgeous guy look like a lemon, and you can be sure after the first showing of the Nature Boy, Buddy Rogers, they will think nothing more but of Rogers." A *Newsweek* story on the real Human Orchid clearly understood Pfefer's intent. "Imitators are mushrooming all over the country," it said of George. "A few miles away in Hollywood is a gladiator who has picked his act clean. He is billed as Nature Boy, Buddy Rogers, World's Champion, a triple steal of misnomery."

George made his living fooling people, but he was usually honest with himself. He knew Rogers meant real trouble, and tried to strike back. He called Sam Muchnick in St. Louis, who was fighting with Lou Thesz's rival outfit for control of that city's wrestling promotions. George said he wouldn't perform for the other bunch, and might come in for Muchnick—if the promoter didn't use Buddy Rogers. In the end, Muchnick couldn't pass up booking Nature Boy and he brought him his first sellout at Kiel Auditorium, drawing 10,651 fans. In retaliation George came to St. Louis and packed them in for Thesz.

Like the scorpion who has to sting—it's his nature—Pfefer was soon threatening to double-cross Muchnick. They patched it up and then, just as inevitably, Pfefer and Rogers had had their own falling-out. Nature Boy decamped without any notice in 1951. Furious, Pfefer had flyers printed up denouncing Rogers and paid to have them plastered up wherever he wrestled. Rogers continued to do well, and like George, he was imitated—or, more charitably, he inspired wrestling homage— for decades (he died in 1992). His most notable modern descendant is Nature Boy Ric Flair.

George's rendition of himself was too good. It's also possible that the demand for Gorgeousness he and Betty created was so great it could sustain more than one supplier. In any case, Jack Pfefer's sabotage could never derail George's success in any satisfactory way, not with television giving him such an unprecedented push. Pfefer's imitation Georges did make him a good deal of money, as did his Angels and troupes of lady wrestlers, and he continued to promote and to punch back at his enemies real and imagined until 1967. Pfefer did get one measure of revenge: He outlived George, dying in 1974 at age seventy-nine. His hatred never abated. The promoter kept fat files of clippings and correspondence on almost all the people he did business with. A few of these manila files bore the stenciled image of a black cat on the outside, meaning Pfefer wished those people ill—and the Gorgeous George file bore that curse mark. Inside it Pfefer kept something to help him gloat, a photograph that ran in *Boxing Illustrated* showing George slumped in defeat after his last match, awaiting the indignity that followed.

Chapter 15

"THEY LOVED ME IN NEW YORK"

"If they don't give this guy Gorgeous George an Oscar for the best supporting role of 1947, then Hollywood is rottener than Denmark ever was," wrote Braven Dyer of the *Los Angeles Times*. "Gorgeous George is a wrestler. In fact, he's THE Wrestler.

"And if you don't think he had the best supporting role of the year, ask [promoters] Cal Eaton of the Olympic; Mike Hirsch of Ocean Park and Hugh Nichols of Hollywood. Gorgeous George has supported them like nobody's business." Dyer also decided that Gorgeous George would be known from now on as G.G. "to save wear and tear on my typewriter." Some of George's friends had already begun to call him that, as would his second wife, Cherie. Betty always called him George.

He'd conquered California, Texas, and most of the Midwest. To become the sensation of the nation as more than just a boastful nickname, though, George needed to extend his reach eastward. He'd already done well in Boston and Montreal and now, he told Betty, the showcase match he'd booked in New York's Madison Square Garden would strengthen his hold: He'd be the toast of a second coast. This was in February 1949, and for the dozen years previous the Garden hadn't hosted a single maim-and-maul event. The place held eighteen thousand and wrestling couldn't fill that kind of space. Promoter Bill Johnston expected the Gorgeous One to change all that, counting on a crowd of twelve thousand for George's main event with Ernie Dusek. *The Ring* magazine, which devoted a good many pages to "News of the Mat World" in addition to boxing, predicted a turnout of fifteen thousand. Ticket prices were scaled higher to meet the anticipated demand and ringside seats went for an unprecedented $7.50 a pop. George's negotiated 13 percent of the gate would mean an enormous payoff.

La Guardia was no longer the mayor but newly an airport, so when George's flight landed, it was at La Guardia Field. He was met at the bottom of the plane's exit steps by a bevy of models with their hair dyed champagne blond to match George's, and as he made his way across the tarmac two lines of flower girls facing each other tossed rose petals in his path. Surprisingly, George declined to be interviewed upon his arrival but had his valet, Jackson Hunter on this trip, issue a statement to the assembled press. "I am overwhelmed by the tremendous reception," came the uncharacteristically humble proclamation. "Please assure my fans that I will do my best not to let them down Tuesday evening at the Garden." With that the two were whisked away by limousine to the Park Sheraton.

Promoter Bill Johnston gave the match a big push, and the New York papers did their part as well. One preview showed a photo of George labeled "The Aromatic Kid Himself." He was shown bent over deeply from the waist. "Bow . . . or Curtsy?" asked the caption. Dusek, a skilled worker and normally a good draw in his own right, was tersely identified as "the Omaha, Nebraska wildcat," if at all. The match was scheduled for Tuesday night, February 22, Washington's birthday, and George took this to be a good sign. He often invoked the other George in his exhortations to the press; if someone suggested that his long curly hairstyles were feminine, for instance, he'd explode in indignation. "That's ridiculous! If you knew anything about history you would never say that. Why, the father of our country and 18 other presidents wore their hair long, and that's why I do, too." He'd first noticed this, he added, when he was very young, while engaged in the intense scrutiny of a dollar bill. George also called one of his most lavish and striking robes "The George Washington." Made of shimmering, bluish-purple satin, it bore lace trim and rows of hammered silver buttons on the front, mimicking a military tunic, but with a decidedly nonmilitary A-line swell at the bottom of the skirt.

The day before the match, George was upbeat and confident. He went shopping on Fifth Avenue, strolling along with Jack, and he didn't stint, buying himself some more gaudy threads. Reporters tagged along, naturally. He paid for his and Jack's new finery by peeling bills off a fat roll that had recently made a home in his pocket. One observer noticed how few images of George Washington it contained. (Andrew Jackson and Benjamin Franklin wore their hair long, too.)

In the Garden locker room, though, George's confidence cratered. On this rainy Tuesday night, before one of the most important matches of his career, he was assailed by a rare failure of nerve. He'd gotten there early for once, and as he sat on a rough wooden bench in front of the metal lockers, his nerves were jangling. Doubt showed on his furrowed face, surrounded by the blond curls. He sat hunched over, forearms on top of his thighs, wearing his aqua-blue trunks, white wrestling shoes, and white bobby socks. Soon he'd put on the white silk robe festooned with lace and pink roses all the way around the hem. His hands, the ones Betty admired when they were courting, were clasped between his knees. Just a few years earlier, on the Northwest docks, they were the reddened, rough hands of a workingman. Later, as Gorgeous George did even more swishing and less actual grappling, they would become the soft, white paws of the pampered. Tonight they were somewhere in between and just now, he saw, they were trembling.

At times George suffered from claustrophobia; it wasn't just a word he'd used on the Oregon draft boards. There were seven preliminary bouts, many more than usual, on Johnston's special card, all of them twenty minutes long. With so many boys working, the damp, sweaty locker room was much more crowded than usual and he began to feel short of air. It had been a long time since George thought of his father, and the warning Poppa Wagner had given him about wrestling, that the son would soon come home broken and poor. George had used that well-intended but fearful remark as motivation, but when it came to him now it brought not energizing anger but an enervating dread. The Gorgeous act was working great in L.A., but this wasn't L.A. *What if they don't buy it here?* George thought. *What if they think I'm just some fairy?*

As the preliminary matches dragged on George reached out to another older gentleman with whom he'd have a long and complicated relationship: Jack Daniel's. George gestured to one of the ring boys, or locker-room attendants, and gave him three dollars, telling him to run out and buy him a pint, and keep the fifty cents change. While the kid was away, George and Jackson finished getting dressed, the valet donning his Prince Albert coat, striped trousers, and a pea-green vest. His balding pate was shiny with sweat; Hunter had never performed in an arena remotely this size and he was as nervous as George. When the ring boy returned with their bourbon, they each took a few belts. Then they could hear that the match before theirs had ended; they were on. George was feeling better now, if not quite back to his usual cockiness. "Well, Jack, here goes nothing," he said, standing up and looking at his Gorgeous self in the mirror. Then he grinned a quick grin and clapped those hands once in front of his chest. "Okay," said the platinum ingenue of a wrestling man. "Let's go to work." With that he strode from the room.

New York was not amused. At all. To begin with, hardly anyone showed up. WRESTLING FOLLIES PLAY TO ONLY 4,197, read the *Times* headline. Beyond that sufficiently disastrous fact, the New York fans, and especially the city's sporting scribes, had a severe allergic reaction to the Gorgeous act. Jack Hunter conquered his nerves and acquitted himself well, getting the biggest laughs of the night on the way to the ring, though they quickly dissipated in the cavernous, mostly empty arena. Then "Pomp and Circumstance" rang out and soon George began his strut down the longest aisle he'd ever seen. He kept his arms folded across his chest and his nose imperiously high as he went, the light sparkling off his white satin robe.

Nothing. Oh, there were a few derisive jeers, a few catcalls and "yoo-hoo" hoots. But this audience of first-timers—those who'd never seen George live before, usually the most reactive of fans—showed no shock and very little interest. George sneered his best sarcastic sneer, strutted a little harder, and flitted even more flittingly. Still nothing. When he got to the edge of the ring, he saw the ranks of fedora-wearing, note-taking writers along press row. Seated in his customary spot on the Forty-ninth Street side was Al Buck of the *Post,* whom George knew bore one of New York's most influential bylines. A pudgy, balding, and sallow man in his mid forties—he had the "saloon tan," as it was known—Buck was puffing on his ubiquitous cigarette and the smoke partially obscured his face. George could only get a quick impression, but from what the wrestler could glimpse, Buck wasn't finding anything very funny.

George won over exactly one person in the house: Hatpin Mary, a middle-aged scourge named for her habit of skewering wrestlers unwise enough to blunder into her area, Loge Section 36. George bowed in her direction when he got to the ring and she took it as tribute, waving her arms and cheering him in return. The rest of the paying customers booed in a desultory way all the way to the one-fall windup, when George threw Dusek with a series of headlocks he was calling Gorgeous George Specials. He didn't get heat; they booed because they found the action and the denouement unconvincing. It was the worst possible reaction. The fans didn't fall for him, and they didn't hate him—the Garden crowd just found him ridiculous.

In the most balanced of the next day's accounts (there were no favorable ones), *Times* sportswriter James P. Dawson called the match "good, clean fun" and described George's coiffeur as one "any damsel might envy." However, he also noted the "guffaws, boos and jeers" from the onlookers. "Technically a succession of five headlocks and a body hold finished Dusek," he informed readers, "but that was incidental, like the bout itself."

"Gorgeous George flopped," Al Buck wrote in the *Post*. "The act wasn't good theater, and what there was to it was stolen by Jackson, a bit player." His conclusion: "It was the first wrestling show held at the Garden in 12 years. An equal period of time is likely to elapse before another one is attempted." Even *The Ring* piled on in its next monthly issue, calling the match one of the biggest flops in the history of sports. "Ringsiders were disgusted," wrote Stanley Weston, by "a dollar show being passed off as a $7.50 Madison Square Garden attraction." The press coverage was so surprisingly vituperative that *Newsweek* told its national audience about those reactions, in a piece entitled "Garden Gorgonzola." In it the *New York Telegraph*'s Alton Cook was quoted saying: "I made one mistake. I cleaned my glasses."

Why all the vitriol? Carelessly, George wasn't in top shape and that showed. One New York scribe wrote that the removal of George's robe "exposed a potbellied freak in aquamarine trunks." (That must have hurt.) His lack of conditioning may have made some of the supposed mayhem look more feigned than usual. Other scribes resented that wrestling, with TV its accomplice, had become pure show business, no longer the noble, manly art they once thought it was. Arthur Daley, a well-known *Times* sports columnist, was the most strident. "Once upon a time there were real wrestlers like George Hackenschmidt and Frank Gotch," he waxed, though whether or not he realized it, their matches were works as well. "But the buffoons and the clowns took over from them . . ." His conclusion: "If Gorgeous George has not killed wrestling in New York for good and for all, the sport is hardy enough to survive a direct hit by an atomic bomb. It was a most insufferable and obnoxious performance."

In this indictment and others there was also an element of regional rivalry. Horse racing's eastern establishment and the attendant press had dismissed Seabiscuit and his California owner, Charles Howard, in much the same way. New Yorkers were predisposed to reject the flamboyant West Coast phenomenon that was George. "The gorgeous one . . . is something of an idol in Hollywood's film colony," columnist Daley noted with disdain. "California, here he comes! You can have him." Al Buck also noted in his screed that George was "made in Hollywood, where he is reported to be a tremendous success. He should return there without delay."

George was shaken. This setback was unsettling in itself, and worse, it also exposed the utter fragility of his wrestling success. Heat was not just elusive but frighteningly arbitrary—hadn't he done as good a job as ever putting across the same act? In the extended print beating he administered, Daley described a point in the match when "the glamour, if any, had gone and the show had degenerated into just a tugging match between a couple of sweaty creatures." But isn't that what wrestling always is, at bottom? For a boy or an act to go over, the audience has to agree that it's more than that, to become complicit in the farce and the ballyhoo. The fans' and newspapers' refusal, the way they suddenly withdrew their cooperation, was an alarming first that could not, for George's sake, become a trend. If it did, all the success he'd had so far would dissolve, and he'd be back on the undercard.

"It was kind of a rough go," George told Betty over the phone. When he got home, he'd explain. In public, though, the Gorgeous One, his business manager, Johnny Doyle, and the L.A. promoters instinctively knew how to respond to this defeat. Their tactic, the big, blithe lie, has since proved its usefulness in many areas of American life. With no Internet watchdogs giving instant lie to its claims, the next edition of the Olympic Auditorium program trumpeted that "George is back after another great Eastern tour. He's even more popular in New York today, [and] his recent tour of that section proved this statement. One thing George can always say: 'They loved me in New York.'"

Chapter 16

PACKING THEM IN LIKE MARSHMALLOWS

Gorgeous George was coming to town, Betty told the children after she hung up the phone. He was returning from New York, having wrestled a good many dates on the way back, and traveling the last leg by train. She'd arranged to drive down and pick him up the next morning. He sounded a little down, Betty thought; he might have still been upset by that night at Madison Square Garden. She felt, not for the first time, that underneath the surface her husband was an insecure man. A swerve might cheer him up. In any case, just meeting him at the station, running the dutiful spousal errand, seemed lacking in flavor, so she gave the chauffeur the next day off. By this time they employed not only a driver but also a housekeeper and a maid. Pat, the longtime nanny, had married Virgil Gray, Cyclone Mackey's stepson, with Betty and George hosting the wedding, and she was now a friend and frequent visitor.

Betty borrowed the driver's visored cap and somehow got herself up in an extra-small dark green chauffeur's uniform. Early the next day she drove between the rows of palm trees on Alameda Street to L.A.'s Union Passenger Terminal. The beige station gleamed yellowish in the sunny California morning, and with its tiled roof, inlaid arches and tall clock tower, it looked like a Spanish church attached to a monastery. Betty stood by the car, at the beginning of the concrete walkway. Between her and the main entrance gathered a small group of reporters who had been alerted to the return of the Gorgeous One.

Then he appeared, resplendent in a pink silk shirt, lime-green slacks, and two-tone, brown-and-white shoes. Coming from the cooler north after a date in San Francisco, he still had a white scarf hanging loosely around his neck and a camel-hair coat draped over his shoulders. Had anyone else made these fashion choices they might have been regrettable, but on him it all looked good. As he swaggered forward, his hair tucked under a tam, he didn't notice the chauffeur waiting, and turned his attention to the writers. After he answered a few questions, Betty approached, lengthening her stride and marching upright, giving her best approximation of a male liveried servant's march. When she got close, she tugged at her cap in a saluted greeting, adding a little servile nod of her head. She'd taken him completely by surprise, but the showman didn't flinch. With no hesitation or sign of recognition, George nodded briskly and handed her the bag he was carrying—porters were toting the rest of the trunks and valises—and strode silently ahead of her to the car. There he waited by the back door for the chauffeur to catch up and open it, after which the master climbed in. Betty, not uttering a word herself, deposited the bag on the front passenger seat, then came deliberately around and got behind the wheel. Without so much as a glance behind her, she gunned the big engine and drove off. The two didn't even greet each other until they were well out of sight. After they'd laughed and caught up a little, George leaned back in his seat and added a last line to the gag. "Home, Betty," he said.

Home at this point was a ranch they'd bought in Beaumont, a town of three or four thousand people roughly eighty miles east of Los Angeles, high up in the San Gorgonio Mountains near the San Bernardino National Forest. George filled her in on his Madison Square Garden debacle. He'd had a long trip home in which to reframe it in more favorable, ego-soothing terms. After all the wrestling he'd done, he knew how to fall. Promoter Johnston, who'd shelled out $6,000 to rent the Garden, lost about $1,500 on the night, but George's share of the gate still made a darn good payday, he told Betty. If they want to call it a "bomb" or a "flopperoo," George said, he would gladly tank again. In fact, this "sweaty creature," as he'd been labeled, took home more than $1,800 from that one thirty-minute tugging match when, across the country, John and Jane Doe's annual household income was something like $3,100.

Still, it stung. When he wrestled next at the Olympic Auditorium a few nights later, the Orchid arrived with a little extra determination. He would show everyone—hadn't he done that his entire career, his entire life? This was his bop hall, where Gorgeous George had become a sensation two years before, and these marks were his people. The Los Angeles fans, who'd come to know him on the KTLA broadcasts, were primed, too. George was still new enough to surprise them, yet they were familiar enough with him to expect a raucous good time. Gorgeous was billed elsewhere in the country as the Hollywood Invader, they knew, and the Toast of the Coast. That made him their champion, and the villain they had the greatest right to hate. On this Wednesday night in early 1949, George had been honing his craft for fifteen years and refining the Gorgeous persona for the last two. He was ready to deliver the performance of his life, and the fans would get every bit of what they came for: Gorgeous George, at the top of his outrageous game.

The Olympic was a massive cinder-block rectangle, painted white with maroon-brown trim, at Eighth Street and Grand Avenue. The roof, though not clearly visible from the street, formed a half dome; a sign easily seen from the adjacent parking lots declared this the LARGEST BOXING AND WRESTLING ARENA IN THE WORLD, SEATING 10,400. Over the marquee loomed a huge color mural of a boxer. Cal and Aileen Eaton, the couple running the Olympic, claimed they led the nation in wrestling attendance the year before, 1948, drawing more than 300,000 through the turnstiles. Of course, as Mike LeBell, her son and his stepson, who later took over the promotion there, admitted, "We lied a little about things like that." He said the 10,400 capacity was really more like 10,052, and others put it at 9,900. Regardless, it was one of the country's premier mat palaces. In other words, something of a dump. Like wrestling itself, the Olympic had a shiny facade and a grandiose line of patter, but in its heart and bowels it was a grimy sweatshop, a much-beloved bucket of blood.

George sits in the lower-level locker room, with Jake Brown standing by, taking a robe out of its garment bag, under one bare lightbulb. The room itself, more concrete blocks painted white, is tiny, maybe six feet by eight feet. Besides the beat-up metal lockers, nails driven into a wooden lath at eye level serve as the coatrack. Uncovered pipes run above and the occasional porcelain sink juts from the walls. When his opponent, Bobby Managoff, comes into the room, George doesn't get up. He stays sprawled, wearing just his trunks and socks, in a metal folding chair in front of the lockers, reflected in the frameless mirror on the opposite wall. But he gives Managoff (real name, Robert Manoogian Jr.) a friendly grin and sticks out his hand. George likes Managoff and considers him a good worker, trained by his father, an Armenian who went by Big Yusiff. Later in the year George will land Bobby Jr. a role in his wrestling flick.

"Hi, Bobby," he says with a laugh. "I hear you're going to put me over tonight." Cal Eaton wants them to go the distance, three falls with a one-hour time limit, and Gorgeous is to be the winner. "George," says Managoff, who stands to get a hefty payoff after this main event, "it will be my pleasure." The two put their heads together briefly and talk about different moves they'll use. Managoff is a dropkick man: He leaps straight up, turns his body sideways, and slams his opponent's chest with the soles of both feet. (Antonino Rocca became a great box-office attraction with this as his signature move. A former acrobat with no wrestling training, he was a great leaper, and wrestled barefoot.)

As George looks at Managoff, three years his junior, he sees a strongly built, dark-haired fellow with bushy eyebrows, about his size but a little darker-complected. The writer from *Sport* magazine here tonight to write a feature about George—"Goldilocks of Grappling"—calls Managoff "a nice-looking Armenian boy . . . with a back as broad as a good garage." The guileless earnestness he projects makes Managoff the perfect babyface to go against this egotistical heel. In a sense tonight's headline match pits a version of the younger George Wagner—strong, willing, with fewer sharp edges—against his new Gorgeous self. Cal Eaton's expecting a sellout or something close. Ringside tickets are four dollars, and the next ten rows behind them, called the "club circle," go for three. A crowd this size requires forty ushers to work the narrow aisles and the man by the VIP entrance on the west side of the building reports that Rita Moreno and Eddie Cantor are on the celebrity list.

Now George stands up and the lanky valet comes over to help George into his robe. Jake is a couple of inches taller than his boss and boyhood friend. But in his tight waistcoat the valet, who weighed 185 when he went into the army, appears even thinner next to George, whose stocky silhouette is widened further by his billowing robes. Tonight Jake is sporting a kelly-green vest and matching bow tie over his white shirt with a stiff, pointed Gladstone collar, along with the dark butler's morning coat, pin-striped trousers, and black patent-leather shoes. At other times he wears a light purple or orchid-colored ensemble. His black hair is already receding from his forehead though he's just thirty-two, brushed back in front and tufting out a little on both sides, just north of his largish ears. In his act he is deadpan, never smiling, but as he grins now while approaching George, he reveals long, fanglike incisors.

The robe Jake holds in front of him is a shiny, floor-length, quilted pink satin beauty. The lining and lapels are a contrasting bright yellow silk; on the robe's shoulders are epaulets of glimmering silver sequins. This is either one of Betty's last efforts—she stood down from robe making when the children required more of her time—or created by Kay Cantonwine, the daughter of George's buddy and fellow wrestler Howard "The Hangman" Cantonwine. From the end of her high school years into the mid-1950s she fashioned many of the Gorgeous

One's robes. The *Los Angeles Times* dubbed her "the Betsy Ross of the mat world."

Working from a woman's size-sixteen pattern, Kay and her mother, Gertrude, would spend a couple of weeks on each one, working from one of Betty's ideas or their own flights of fancy. The younger woman, who made clothing and swimwear design her profession, ordered the fabrics from a specialty shop in New York. George would come by their house on Harvard Street in South Central L.A. to try on each new showy wrapper, always in a bit of a hurry. George would drape the new gown over his street clothes and suddenly he'd assume the Gorgeous persona, swelling himself up and stalking the Cantonwines' front hall in front of the full-length mirror. At times Kay worried that she'd gone too far. Would George reject the robe with a bulging bustle of turkey feathers that protruded from the Gorgeous posterior? Or the two pink fans she'd made for him to swish around his body, fashioned with stripper Gypsy Rose Lee in mind? She needn't have been concerned. As Betty had told her, with George no design was too lurid, no feminine touch too effeminate. "Do you love it?" Kay would ask. "I sure do," George always replied. Then, just as suddenly as he'd gotten in character, he'd deflate himself, reverting back to just George, remove the new robe, and he'd be off.

Managoff left the locker room, gone to enter the ring, where he joins the nameless, faceless, stripe-shirted referee and the longtime Olympic announcer Jimmy Lennon (uncle to the singing Lennon Sisters). Like the other boys, Managoff takes a narrow passageway from the locker rooms and climbs up a small stairway that emerges just in front of the ring. That truncated arrival won't do for George, of course; he has a much longer, grander entrance in mind. The undercard's over and by now even the late arrivals have taken their places. As one sportswriter describes them, the fans are now "as jam-packed as marshmallows in a box."

"Behind you and all around you, you can feel the expectant stirring welling up in the crowd," Hannibal Coons writes in *Sport*. The announcement that George is coming has already boomed out over the PA system more than once. Back in the locker room Jeff gives the Gorgeous robe one last tug, smoothing a pink padded shoulder as they both stand facing the locker-room mirror. The wrestler has a pink satin scarf draped around his neck that matches his gown and falls down over the contrasting yellow lapels. Smiling at his friend in the mirror, Jeff gives him a little pat on his satin-covered back. "Ready, George?" he asks. His boss answers with a businesslike nod—that is, as businesslike as you can be if you're a burly man wearing a dress with your dyed blond hair done up in an intricate woman's hairdo. "Let's go to work," Gorgeous George Wagner says, in his surprisingly high, nasal voice. "Time to give the people what they want."

Jefferies walks stiffly erect down the long center aisle toward the ring, a spotlight illuminating his progress. As he proceeds, carrying a big silver tray in both hands in front of his chest, his movements are slow and solemn, deliberate and dignified—"aloof as a cake of Life-buoy," in the words of another witty grappling writer. Not so the crowd, which begins to laugh as the valet descends the aisle. Bending low, Jefferies steps through the ropes and enters the ring, whereupon he deposits the silver tray on the canvas surface. He approaches this, and all his tasks, with reverence. Now Jefferies stoops and removes from his tray a large chrome-plated spray gun with a pump handle. He brandishes it in the air, and the paying customers hoot and laugh some more. His instrument looks like a bicycle pump; it's commonly known as a Flit gun for the plant insecticide it often contains. But this gleaming version holds a strong sweet-smelling perfume. George tells the press, and TV announcer Dick Lane gleefully relays tonight, that it's a special mixture, "Chanel Number 10." No. Five's good enough for other people, George says grandly, but "why be half safe?"

With great concentration, Jefferies sprays the entire twenty-by-twenty ring floor—the Gorgeous One's white-shod footsies must not touch anything malodorous or unclean. "Around the ring he dashes," writes the thoroughly entertained reporter from the *Long Beach Democrat*. "Spraying here, and spraying there. Spraying all over and everywhere. Like an insane housewife knocking off flies with a Flit gun in her kitchen." Now the valet makes a move with the spray gun toward Managoff, as if to decontaminate him as well, but the black-haired grappler raises a cocked fist, snarling, and Jefferies hastily retreats. There's more laughter in the stands at this pantomime.

The spray-gun gimmick, which replaced the whisk broom, may have been born of George's early experiences with dirty, infectious mats. He said, and it could even have been true, that he began disinfecting the ring to avoid getting boils and other contagions. When the fans gave him heat in response—George did the decontaminating himself in the early days—he made the fumigant a fixture. (At one point George and Betty discussed wafting floral perfume through the Olympic's ventilation system but apparently this early biological weapon was never put to use.) The perfume spritzing by George's valets, including Cherie, became an enduring signature, one of the most memorable parts of the Gorgeous act.

Now the valet removes a square of cherry-red carpet from the tray. Dick Lane tells the 1949 viewing audience, seeing all this in black and white, that it's a "a beautiful cerise color." Jefferies places this rug on the floor near the tray; George will stand on it after he makes his entrance. With a flourish the valet removes another square and places it near the first. This one is mink, and it will hold the folded, precious robe off the mat once George has consented to its removal. (Apparently mink, while not luxurious enough to cover the Sensational body, is adequate to cushion his kimonos.)

His preparations complete, George's man Friday stands by the rugs and awaits his master's arrival. "By this time the excitement is pretty much tense," Coons reports, "with much confused babble and neck-craning." He can appreciate the delay, the tease. In his piece he calls George "a well-muscled and remarkable man who could have given P. T. Barnum three Tom Thumbs and licked him as a showman in straight falls." Just now the PA system booms again, but with a different message: "Ladies and gentlemen, Gorgeous George is here!"

The majority of the audience stands up immediately. The spectators twist and crane this way and that, trying to catch their first glimpse of the star attraction. In George's crowd, roughly 35 percent are soprano fans; it seems the writer who called him "the answer to a maiden's prayer, as well as a matron's," was not mistaken. Most if not all of the women are here with male companions, and they're dressed up for a night on the town. Many wear hats, some of which have veils, and all the fan-ettes wear blouses, skirts, and hose; no woman wears pants. Some of the men have on suits and ties, though the ties are generally loosened. For these gents, hats are the norm. Above ringside the men are less swank, with more of a working-class Angeleno look to them. From the haze hovering over the ring lights, it's clear that from the front rows to the upper balcony, where the seating is rows of wooden benches, smoking is both allowed and enjoyed.

One middle-aged woman leaps up from her seat. "Land's sakes, look!" she shouts. The popcorn man and the soda-pop vendors are temporarily out of business, as the fans are riveted to the coming of George. "Look, there he is!" someone else shouts. "He's in pink tonight!" Heads swivel as the Gorgeous One appears at the top of the main aisle, standing stock-still, hands on hips, head cocked back, taking in the entire Olympic laid out before him, a mighty lord surveying his realm from on high. To get to their seats the fans have walked upstairs to the concession level and the mezzanine doors. From there it's an extremely steep drop down the aisles and the rows of seats (they have arms, a rare luxury in wrestling arenas) to the ring, which sits in a pit at the very bottom. The balcony looms, stacked right on top of the lower levels and the ring. In these upper reaches there's a small section cordoned off with wire mesh on three sides. This is "the cage," where the wrestlers' wives or friends of the promoters can sit if they need protection from the raucous crowds.

The Olympic's a vast vertical cone with the ring the narrow tip at the bottom. Under the domed roof, the ceiling is at least a hundred feet above the ring. At balcony level a grid of lights is suspended over the ring, hanging from thick cables. Right now, though, it's completely dark—except for the one spotlight on the Gorgeous One, glimmering when it touches his shiny pinkness and glinting off the gold-mesh hairnet he's wearing, covering the marcel. The standing crowd gives out a collective gasp, a loud "aaah." In some ways, this first glimpse of George is *the* moment of the evening. It's not enough to call it an entrance; one writer deems it "his manifestation." The impact that George creates by simply showing up overpowers anything most wrestlers can do in the ring. That same scribe sees the humor in the grand arrival, and senses its import. "There, statued in the pose of a Greek god, and looking very much like the berries, stands the Hubba-Hubba He-man of the 20th century," he writes. "Yes, Gorgeous George has just crashed in upon the scene."

The coronation march begins to blare, and George takes his first steps down the aisle, the dainty white boots rasping a bit on the corrugated metal covering that concrete path. At first he's greeted mostly by clapping, laughter, and cheers. This is his home turf and Los Angeles appreciates a spectacle. "George, you're gorgeous!" shouts one smitten lady. He knew that already, so George sees no need to acknowledge her encouragement. Instead he's giving everyone, including his partisans, the elevated proboscis as he parades slowly, exuding imperial arrogance. Some boos and hisses issue in response, and as they do disdain transfigures George's face. He starts to sway more side to side as he walks and his parading gait broadens into the Gorgeous strut. "And, oh, my, what a strut," another reporter remarks. "If only this man had been born in the barnyard. What a rooster he would have made."

More catcalls, more whistles. "Hey, Gruesome, Bobby's gonna murder you!" jeers another fan, a middle-aged woman who shakes her fist at George as she stands next to her husband, who's giving her a look of surprise mixed with some wariness. To this point the Sensation's temper has not been truly tried, so he responds mildly, merely observing with a look in her direction that "I told you not to come down tonight, Mother." Another wit shouts, "Hey, Myrtle!" reacting to the extravagant display of finery, vanity, and coiffure—to George's feminine side. George the fabulous fop is strutting, but it can also be seen as a coy sashaying. It can't be denied: There is some hen in this rooster.

Jefferies bends at the waist and pulls two ropes apart so George can step through, gathering his skirts in both hands as he stoops and enters the ring. The wrestler wipes his booties on the patch of cerise carpet, then strides to the center of the mat and bows in all four directions. Wait: The Gorgeous knees are bending—is his bow really a curtsy? Some in the crowd clearly think so; the laughter and hooting both dial up a notch or two in volume. George paces around the ring, peering at the mat surface intently and sniffing. Something displeases him. "Uh-oh, Georgie isn't happy," Dick Lane says, chuckling on the air. It seems Jefferies has not fumigated properly; he missed some spots. George remonstrates with him, pointing vehemently at several areas. Stricken by his failure, the valet scurries over and sprays some more with the overgrown atomizer. Satisfied for now, George repairs to his corner. Managoff still stands waiting in his corner, and the ring announcer is likewise inactive. They might as well be napping, buying an ice-cold pop, or missing altogether, as no one's paying them the slightest bit of attention.

Now George, still standing, consents to Jefferies removing the gold-mesh hairnet, called a snood. Under it George's locks are held in place with the gold-colored Georgie pins. Now, with a great show of deference and obsequiousness, the valet begins taking them out. "Those pins are gold-plated and very expensive," Lane informs the TV audience. "George has them made especially at $85 the half-pound." Jefferies returns a handful of the Georgie pins to the master, who shakes out his newly liberated locks, looking, as Coons describes him, "like a lordly Spaniel." Now the wrestler stalks around the ring, peering out into the crowd to see who might deserve a Gorgeous souvenir. Women wave wildly, trying to catch his eye. "Throw it here, George! Give one to me!"' A fair number of men are standing and waving, too, including some who were booing him lustily minutes earlier. When he flips the pins into the crowd, mild scuffles break out over them.

Jimmy Lennon moves to take the microphone suspended by its cord over the center of the ring. "In this corner," he intones, gesturing at George's opponent with one tuxedoed arm, "at 225 pounds, from

Chicago, Illinois, the former heavyweight champion of the world, Bobby Managoff!" There's a good smattering of applause and Managoff takes a step toward the ring's center and gives a friendly wave to the crowd. Managoff wears nondescript black trunks and black calf-high wrestling boots over white socks. His robe is a terry bathrobe, dark and wrinkled. It looks like a garment his grandfather might have died in.

"And in this corner," the ring announcer continues, turning to face the opposite corner, his voice rising: "The Toast of the Coast . . . The Sensation of the Nation . . . The Human Orchid . . . Gorgeous George!" Boos, catcalls, and hoots rain down from all levels of the tornado-shaped house, with a good many laughs and cheers mixed in. George nods at the booming response as if he's accepting just tribute from a rapt and loving people. The referee calls both wrestlers to the center of the ring, goes over a few rules, and then, as always, he checks each combatant for concealed weapons and any overoiling of the body, which would give him an unfair slipperiness advantage. This requires that the wrestlers open any garments they might be wearing to allow the inspection. The ref runs his hands over Managoff's body without incident, but when the official reaches toward George, the heel isn't having it. *"Take your filthy hands off me!"* he roars, so loudly that the referee actually takes a step backward. The crowd roars again in response. This refusal to be glommed by grubby mortals is another signature moment, one the fans come to expect yet never fail to respond to. Aghast at the plebeian contamination, George gestures urgently to Jefferies, who rushes over and sprays the ref's hands with Chanel Number 10. Only now will George submit to being touched.

To allow the examination, he raises both arms to the sides and holds the pink robe open wide, like a butterfly with its wings extended, exposing the corpus delectable for all to see. He's wearing tight white trunks and pink socks under his white boots. George still has his muscles but his body's thicker now and there's not as much definition; his torso barely narrows from his shoulders to his waist. The Gorgeous flesh is pale, and by today's standards, he's even got a bit of a potbelly.

Yet no one here doubts he's gorgeous, least of all him. Back in his corner, George allows Jefferies to remove the shimmering robe, which he then folds and places carefully on the mink square. Without the billowing cloth surrounding him, George's head looks even bigger in relation to his body.

Fifteen or twenty minutes have elapsed since George first struck his entrance pose, with nary a grunt, groan, or grapple. Now, finally, the bell rings, the referee waves both wrestlers to the center of the ring, and the match commences. Managoff rushes forward to engage in the middle of the ring. Following the locker-room discussion with George, he makes the classic opening move: trying to get his hands on the Gorgeous curls. Horrified, George skitters away, circling counterclockwise then darting into corners, up on his toes, his hands up in front of him to fend off any contact, those platinum locks fanning out behind his head as he moves. The crowd knows that of all the unkind things the other boys do, this dismays George the most. "Oh, no! No!" he protests pleadingly as Managoff pursues him, then ducks behind the referee for cover. "Stop him!" he yells at the faceless ref. "Don't let him mess up my hair!" But the official offers no quarter. "Wrestle on!" he commands. Managoff straightens up from his crouch and bellows at George to "Come and fight, darn it!" In the crowd some fans stand up, too, irate at Georgie's shameful behavior. "Sissy!" they yell. "Coward!"

Thirty-five and increasingly well fed, George is still athletic and his speed can still surprise. On his back and in "danger" of being pinned, he goes to the kip-up, launching himself upright without using his hands. As he lands back on his feet and dances a few more quick steps, the crowd roars in appreciation. "Whoa, Nellie!" exclaims Dick Lane. This is this pet expression, which will become part of the American colloquial vocabulary. A few minutes later, after getting thrown across the ring, George sells the move by landing loudly on his back, then bouncing up onto his shoulders so they're supporting his body, his torso and legs sticking straight up in the air. Now he adds a flourish, corkscrewing his upside-down body rapidly in what looks like a classic version of a 1980s break-dancing move.

Now it's George who's unkind: He throws Managoff out of the ring a couple times, kicks him when he's down, rams him into the corner posts, punches him in the kidneys—then denies it to the remonstrating ref, demonstrating in broad, slow motion how he actually hit the babyface with the heel of his open hand, which is legal. When he gets Managoff down on his back for an instant, George starts screaming at the ref to call it a pin and award him the first fall. "What kind of a referee are you, anyway?" he bellows. "There, count—he's down!"

He eye-gouges. He hits Managoff as they break. If Managoff starts to gain any advantage, dastardly George steps one foot outside the ropes, which brings him a reprieve, a halt in the action for an automatic ten-count. Jeers and shouts fill the air, and the classic exhortation is aimed at the babyface: "Kill him!" With an increasingly fast series of body slams, George wins the first fall.

Normally this is the time to visit the restroom and stock up at the concession stands, but experienced George watchers know to stick around. A wooden stool is produced in his corner for Himself to rest on (all the other wrestlers stand between falls). A woman in the crowd yells, "George, you look like a scrubwoman!" In truth, his hair is a mess, completely disheveled. That calls for Jefferies, who reappears with his tray, and uses a comb to touch up the marcel. It's the Frank and Joseph Special, the one that sweeps up so dramatically in the back when pinned. The valet can't restore that glory, but manages to reestablish a semblance of order. He hands George a hand mirror in a gilded frame to inspect the results, then goes behind him to massage his shoulders. George looks, and seems, satisfied. More than satisfied, in fact.

Now the valet pours him a nice cup of hot tea from a matching silver service. George, breathing hard, manages to take a few sips to put over the gimmick as the Charming Chest continues to heave. Suddenly George is on his feet, bawling furiously at Jefferies. "Uh-oh," Dick Lane translates for the TV audience, "it looks like Georgie's spied a speck of something in his tea!" Enraged, George hauls off and slaps Jefferies, who staggers backward. His master then aims a savage kick at his backside, but misses, and the audience erupts again at this slapstick. Finally, with much bowing and scraping, the stricken servant gets his abject apologies accepted. Eager to serve again, the valet offers George some smelling salts, but he declines.

The second fall begins, and George quickly throws his friend Bobby to the canvas. As the babyface struggles to get back to his feet, shaking his head as if dazed, George taunts him, yelling, "Come on, get up, you rat!" For most of the second stanza, though, the babyface maintains the advantage; he needs to win the fall for the match to go the distance. He throws George out of the ring and onto the apron, and as the heel starts to climb back in, a striking, zaftig woman in a white ruffled blouse and dark skirt runs up to within three feet of him and yells, "Hey, George, your makeup's all messed up. Want some of mine?" She taunts him by offering him her purse, raising it in front of George and dangling it by the strap. George snarls—in a flash he's Desperate George Wagner of old, the wild man returned—and cocks his right fist back by his ear. But Beatrice, as the next day's *Times* calls her, is uncowed. She puts up her own dukes and advances on the Lovely. Faced with this confrontation, Georgie runs for cover, skedaddling back into the ring and hiding behind the referee.

Managoff slings George from one side of the ring to the other, where he rebounds, slingshot, off the ropes. In this part of the dance George shows one of the great staggers in grunt-and-groan history, reeling and stumbling as if barely able to keep his balance, mouth hanging open, eyes rolling in ersatz suffering. As George bounces off the ropes for the last time, Managoff jumps up and dropkicks him right in the chops. George falls "unconscious" to the mat and is counted out. Jefferies scuttles into their corner with the hand mirror again, but this time it's so George can check for missing teeth. Once again the valet tries to reshape his puddled curls with the comb, but this time George waves him away in disgust. Frank and Joseph's creation is just a ruined memory. This pains George bitterly, and lo, this bitterness turns to rage.

The bell rings for the third fall and George leaps up, grabs his wooden stool by one leg, raises it over his head, and takes off after Managoff. Jefferies and the ref restrain him and pry the stool out of his clutch, and this heinous attempt gets the crowd riled all over again. The referee has to stop the action for a few moments to clear the wrappers, bottle caps, and half-smoked cigars off the canvas. When combat resumes George suddenly clutches his chest and collapses down to the mat while hanging on to a rope with one arm. "No, no," he gasps at the advancing Managoff, the other arm up and out to keep the babyface away. It appears that after all this evening's stresses and indignities, George's delicate heart is giving out.

"Watch out here, son," Dick Lane warns the babyface over the air. Unheeding, Managoff stops his rush just as he reaches George's side, drops his arms to his sides, and gazes down with concern at the felled victim. Then, in an instant, the devious heel leaps up, grabs the babyface around the neck, and jumps into the air, throwing his legs out straight in front of him. As he leaps, he jerks Managoff's head viciously to the left with a convulsive wrench of both arms. Managoff's torso and then the rest of his body are yanked up into the air, and his legs flail helplessly out to the side. He's horizontal for a moment, airborne with George, who's hanging on to him like a rodeo bull rider, and then Managoff comes crashing down to the canvas, landing on his back with a shattering smack that's amplified by the microphones underneath the grappling floor. The innocent babyface has fallen, first for George's trickery and then to his signature finishing move, "the flying side headlock."

Managoff writhes desperately under George, trying to get his shoulders off the mat and escape the pin. Facedown on top of him, the Beauteous Beast grins maniacally as he senses an ill-gotten victory. That's the best kind. As George is fond of saying: "Win if you can, lose if you must, but always cheat." To make sure of items one and three, George reaches back with his right foot, finds the lowest rope, and pushes off with his white shoe to gain additional leverage. These fans know the rules and thousands—men and women—shoot to their feet again, pointing at George and screaming at the ref that he's cheating.

"Look at his foot, that's an illegal move!" "Foul!" George turns and gives the shouting fans a piece of his mind. "Shut up, you lousy stool pigeons!" Somehow the zebra-shirted arbiter manages not to see the infraction. He keeps counting Managoff out: "One . . . Two . . . Three. Pin." The match is over: Gorgeous George wins again!

This is so wrong. The booing builds to a cacophony of outrage and contempt that fills the Olympic and rings out for a good ten minutes—the lusty sound of ten thousand people exercising their constitutional right to vent spleen. Still sweating, his hair bedraggled, George struts around the ring in his shiny white trunks, raising his arms overhead in triumph, welcoming the abuse the mat addicts are spewing down on him, opening his arms wider and gesturing toward himself as if to embrace their rage. After a few minutes four off-duty cops approach, and escort George from the ring to the dressing room. Seeing the forces of order marshaled for the protection of the cheating heel rankles deeply, and in response fans bomb the ring with whatever debris they still have left to hurl. The injustice of it all is rank.

And yet so right. Everyone, even the adherents of the luckless babyface, looks happy leaving the Olympic tonight. The fans talk and laugh excitedly as they file back up the steep aisles, gesturing as they reenact this or that high spot. Back in the locker room, George is happy, too, relieved and reassured. The home crowd's reaction was just what he needed, completely washing away the hangover of doubt he's carried since New York.

Gratitude was not George's forte, but he would always have a special regard for the Olympic and the Los Angeles fans. Unlike the hostiles in Madison Square Garden, they understood Gorgeousness immediately, and for the better part of a decade they loved and hated him faithfully.

Tonight he's come through for them as well. Seen in person, George proved just as vain, arrogant, and eye-poppingly effeminate as he is on their home screens. Confoundingly, he's also shown them his wrestling athleticism and triumphed in this test of masculine power—he is indeed the Hubba-Hubba He-Man. This delighted and delighted-to-be-infuriated crowd got to meet the killer fruitcake in the flesh, if not close enough to touch, certainly near enough to insult or admire. When they show up at work the next morning, tonight's spectators won't tell their envious coworkers that they went to the wrestling at the Olympic. They'll say, "We saw Gorgeous George."

Chapter 17

KING STRUT

Attendance at boxing matches went down after it became possible to watch at home on television instead of going to the fights in person. Turnouts at horse-racing tracks dropped 30 percent from 1946 to '49. However, TV didn't hurt wrestling's live gate, as some promoters had feared—on the contrary, George's histrionics and the previously unimaginable exposure of television gave the wrestling business a breathtaking jolt. Especially in those first few years of broadcasting, viewers poured into the arenas to experience what they'd seen on the tube, and to meet those crazy characters in person. Between 1948 and 1955, approximately, the pro game enjoyed its greatest popularity in this country, a golden age equaled only in the era of Hulk Hogan and "Wrestlemania," the mid- to late 1980s. Promoters were so flush that they cut back on the cash-filled envelopes handed to sportswriters for their coverage; they didn't really need them anymore.

In 1950 twenty-four million admissions to wrestling matches were purchased for a cumulative take of $36 million, according to *American Mercury* magazine. That same year Major League Baseball, the respectable, aboveground national pastime, drew 17.5 million fans to its fourteen ballparks. Paul Zimmerman, sports editor of the *Los Angeles Times*, proclaimed baseball soundly beaten. "Wrestling has been taken into millions of parlors," he wrote. "It is safe to say that families, from kid to grandmothers, know more about double hammerlocks than double plays."

The *New York Times* ran a lavishly arted Sunday-magazine piece entitled "Big Boom in the Grunt and Groan Business." It began: "Upward of 3,000 huge men, and a few somewhat less huge women, right about now are looking forward to their most profitable season in the last twenty years . . . Audiences of 12,000 or 15,000 are not uncommon even in comparatively small towns. Wrestlers are being recognized on the streets just like movie stars. Their fees for shows have gone up. The 'groaning business' is happy."

Despite all the violence and the fakery in wrestling, there was barely a ripple of resistance. Once, in 1949, a group of parents voiced concern about "the consistency with which villainy triumphs over virtue on video," as *Washington Post* columnist Shirley Povich put it. Heels were defeating heroes, with George leading this miscreant charge. Was this any way to teach children that cheaters never prosper? But this moral qualm—Povich called it a "squawk"—quickly dissipated, and George's game grew unabated. "Television brought the Gorgeous One's pure corn into the home," Povich wrote, "and it apparently took root because the wrestling business was never so good."

In a story entitled "Gorgeous Georgeous," *Newsweek* declared that California TV dealers "now credit him with creating more sales than any other program on the line-of-sight." Since George was wrestling almost seven nights a week, the magazine added, "he gives set buyers plenty of return on their investment." By this time, however, television, that delivery system for Gorgeousness, had become a conduit that flowed in the other direction as well, rendering from the public unto George. Most, of that era's other TV stars, including Ed Sullivan and Arthur Godfrey, stayed tethered to the tube. That was where their fame was created and where they derived most of their income. George, on the other hand, made his living from live wrestling events, and every one of his televised matches served as a twenty-to-thirty-minute advertisement for his other, much more lucrative business. Since the Toast of the Coast's appeal had little to do with actual wrestling, he attracted the broadest audience, drawing those who cared nothing for the ring as well as the dedicated wrestling fans. "Pretty soon," Lou Thesz said, "promoters around the country were begging for George . . . knowing he'd bring out the curious as well as the regulars."

George and Betty began to demand 20 percent of each night's gate receipts (after the promoter took 20 percent off the top for overhead). Normally, the two main-eventers would receive 4 or 5 percent each, yet George commanded five times that. "And he was completely worth it," said the Butcher, Paul Vachon. "There was such a curiosity, everyone wanted to see him." Some promoters raised ticket prices, usually fifty cents or a dollar, when George appeared; other impresarios, such as Morris Sigel in Houston, made a loud point of it when ducats *didn't* get more expensive. One of his ads boasted: "There will be no increase in prices for next week's card which will feature Gorgeous George!"

Unlike the Hollywood actors and other star athletes of the day, who abstained from discussing their pay (leaving it to the press and their agents), George blasted about his earnings to anyone with a microphone or a notepad. As might be expected, though, George's pay reports served more to magnify than to clarify. In 1948 *Time* said George earned "upwards of $70,000 a year," which was probably close. Two years later the *American Mercury* said that only three of George's rivals—former heavyweight boxer Primo Carnera; Gene Stanlee, aka Mr. America; and Antonino Rocca—approached the $100,000-a-year mark, and that the Toast easily surpassed it. "I don't want to be a millionaire," George explained to writer Ted Shane. "I just want to live like one." He was getting there. The *Los Angeles Times* said George collected $160,000 for "unkinking his muscles and uncurling his hair," pointing out that the Human Orchid could also be called "The Human Billfold." When asked by a reporter to clear up these discrepancies, George told him to "take your pick."

A clearer light is shed on this by, of all people, the Hangman, Howard Cantonwine. A hard drinker and frequent brawler with a volcanic temper, when he became George's business manager around 1949, Cantonwine nonetheless kept careful records. His log and account book from that year indicate that the Gorgeous One was indeed hauling in over $100,000 a year, even after he paid his booking agent a 10 percent fee. In one short stretch of April nights, for example, George got paid $1,494 in St. Louis for beating Chief Don Eagle on a disqualification; $1,939.68 for a win over Gypsy Joe Dorsetti in Milwaukee; and just $459.08 in Wichita for a no-contest against Sonny Myers. Cantonwine almost always appeared lower down on the cards George worked, and made about $200 to $250 a week, extremely good money for a workingman.

That same year Hank Williams, the undisputed king of country music, made $92,500, according to his biographer, Paul Hemphill. A year later Joe DiMaggio, the Yankee Clipper, retired and walked away from his $100,000 salary, one of the highest in all "legitimate" sports. Movie stars like Spencer Tracy and William Holden made much more, but the *Washington Post* was nonetheless correct when it said of George that "in answer to cries of 'sissy' he laughs much of the way to the bank." Most of the time, that is. At others George whined that he wasn't getting to keep enough of the lucre, sighing that "If you net a million you can only keep $110,000 of it." It was true—for much of his career George's earnings placed him in the highest tax bracket, and that was the 90 percent tier. Since George worked in a cash business, though, he may have been able to submerge some of his income. Each night at the arenas, right after the receipts were counted, promoters literally paid the boys out of cigar boxes filled with crumpled bills. Dick Steinborn, a former wrestler whose father was a promoter, stood in the locker room at the Jamaica Arena in Queens, New York, one Friday night in 1949. After a televised match, with Dennis James as the announcer, Steinborn watched as his father counted out $1,155 in cash into George's perfumed paws. (The other boys on the card that night made $175 or $250, and were happy to get it, when, as Steinborn said, "regular people were making ninety dollars a week.") To consistently declare all that cuddlesome cash on one's income taxes seems like the act of a mark, jarringly out of place in the Gorgeous universe.

At least one person thought George made too much money. In 1949 Joseph L. Mankiewicz wrote and directed *Letter to Three Wives*, a film about suburban life and marriage, a new postwar subject. The film's strongest message, he said, had to do with Kirk Douglas's character, a schoolteacher who earned very little. This injustice was based in reality, Mankiewicz explained, and it rankled. "My father, Prof. Frank Mankiewicz, was himself an educator," the son said. "With his help I once could have made an assistant instructorship in English literature. If I had, I probably would have been earning for a year about half of what Gorgeous George gets for one wrestling match." (How Mankiewicz felt about the exorbitant pay scale in Hollywood, compared to teachers' earnings, wasn't included in the interview.)

Beyond the loot George won something else, a prize that he never complained about. He became a national celebrity, and his was a new kind of outsize, feeds-on-itself fame. From the late 1940s to the mid-1950s his image was so pervasive, and his silliness so addictive, that virtually everyone in the country—English speaking or not; interested in sports or indifferent; television owning or lacking—recognized Gorgeous George. George and Betty's timing was perfect: In their day we saw for the first time how TV exposure led to more print and radio publicity, which led to more packed arenas, which then occasioned more coverage. The cycle spun in widening circles until the media event that was George became news, which needed to be covered again. Before long George's fame outgrew wrestling and television, and became its own entity. He became famous not so much for what he did in either of those venues anymore, but simply for who and what he was—for being so famously Gorgeous George.

In March of 1948 Gorgeous George debuted his nightclub act at Slapsy Maxie's, an L.A. nightclub on Beverly Boulevard that he and

Betty frequented. More than once the owner, Maxie Rosenbloom, a former light-heavyweight boxing champion turned comedian, put on a wig and bathrobe and lampooned George while the couple was in the audience. On the nights when he was wrestling earlier in the evening, George would get his hair redone in a limo from Hollywood Legion Stadium or the Olympic, then take the stage at Maxie's. Sharing the bill with comedian Ben Blue, George didn't wrestle, dance, sing, or tell jokes. He just . . . acted Gorgeous, strutting to and fro wearing one of his robes, handing out some Georgie pins and answering a few questions in his dandified character. (He would work a similar act at the Silver Slipper in Las Vegas in the 1950s.) Just seeing George be George was what the cover charge bought the nightclub patrons, and that was enough.

George—or, rather, the Gorgeous George character—permeated the popular culture, even as he helped to shape it. When Eddie Cantor, also known as "Banjo Eyes" and "The Apostle of Pep," welcomed G.G. to his 10 P.M. radio show, George bellowed out: "I refuse to speak until my valet has fumigated this place. Jefferies!" Listeners then heard the *swish-swish* of the famous spray gun. Cantor then set George up with his line about Chanel Number 10, and there was a "surprise" intrusion by an upcoming opponent, the Mad Russian, who called George a "snooty patootie." This segment ended with Cantor asking his guest star: "There is one thing I always wanted to know. What makes you call yourself Gorgeous?"

To which George answered: "Honesty."

Lauritz Melchior, the opera star, was photographed kissing George's hand. In so doing, the world's reigning Wagnerian tenor may have spared himself the embarrassment of the Georgie Kiss. In this ritual the wrestler would take a lady's hand, bow gallantly, and bend over as if to buss the proffered paw. Instead, as the Gorgeous lips approached their presumed target, he'd flip his wrist over, then kiss the back of his own hand instead. George most famously pulled this stunt on Kim Novak at Chicago's Chez Paree Lounge, whereupon well-known *Tribune* columnist Herb Lyon wrote it up in his "Tower Ticker" column.

eorge Wagner

"Cleanie," not "meanie." The original George: a handsome black-haired babyface or good-guy wrestler, circa 1937. *Jack Pfefer Collection, University Libraries of Notre Dame.*

Left: **Team Wagner in Hawaii, 1941.** Here, Betty briefly became a part of the ring act, then went back to making mischief behind the scenes. *Courtesy of the George family.*

Above: **Ab work.** George does sit-ups on the Hawaiian beach, using a ninety-five-pound wifely weight for resistance. *Courtesy of the George family.*

Left: **Team Wagner expands.** George and Betty with Carol Sue and the just-adopted Don, most likely in Tulsa, 1946. *Courtesy of the George family.*

Below: **The transformation begins.** George in one of his early robes, around 1943. His smile hasn't yet given way to the trademark sneer. *Jack Pfefer Collection, University Libraries of Notre Dame.*

Robes Gallery

Left: **The Human Orchid.** Pinned to his layer cake of a gown are two pink Hawaiian orchids. The bejeweled dog collar adds another bizarre touch. © *Bettmann/CORBIS.*

Above: **Getting pinned.** George tossed his fans much sought-after souvenirs: "gold-plated" Georgie pins that held his intricate curls. *Courtesy of John Pantozzi.*

Left: **Satin Doll.** The haughty heel in his finest fabrics, ruffles, and lace. *Jack Pfefer Collection, University Libraries of Notre Dame.*

Above: **Chanel No. 10.** Jefferies sprays the ring with perfume, lest the Gorgeous One's delicate senses be offended by odor or the unclean. © *Bettmann/CORBIS.*

Below: **Ring action.** After all the preliminary strutting and sneering, the Pompous Prissy turned into a snarling beast, a surprisingly fast, high-flying athlete. *Courtesy of John Pantozzi.*

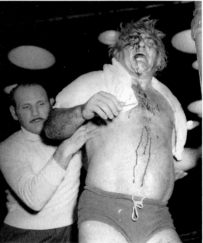

Above: **The "claret" flows.** Arena fans roared at the sight of blood. A subset of grapplers known as blade men cut themselves intentionally to get heat from the crowd. *Jack Pfefer Collection, University Libraries of Notre Dame.*

GORGEOUS GEORGE, JACK BENNY and VIOLIN.

Toast of the Coast. George with comedian Jack Benny (above), crooner Bing Crosby (below left) *[Jack Pfefer Collection, University Libraries of Notre Dame]*, and Burt Lancaster (below right), "The Killer," at a 1948 charity event in Santa Monica. Bob Hope stands in for Jefferies, assuming the role of George's valet. It seems there's a midmatch phone call for the master. *Courtesy of the George family.*

Left: **Made for TV.** G.G. at L.A.'s NBC station. In the foreground, his hairstylists, Frank and Joseph. While George is very much in his element, Poppa Wagner, left, is clearly uncomfortable in the spotlight.
Courtesy of the George family.

Below: **Pomp and Circumstance.** Parading to the ring, with entrance music blaring, at Madison Square Garden in 1949.
Photo by Hy Peskin / Time Life Pictures / Getty Images.

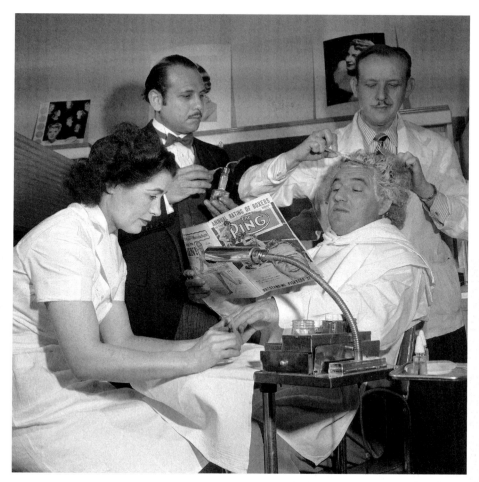

Above: **Time for my marcel.**
George claimed he'd had his
hair done in more beauty
parlors than any woman in
the world. Here he catches up
on the wrestling news while
getting a set and a manicure.
© *Bettmann/CORBIS.*

Right: **"I solemnly swear . . ."**
The Sensation inducts fans into
the Gorgeous George fan club,
which requires swearing that
"I will never confuse this gold
Georgie pin with an ordinary
bobby pin, so help me,
Gorgeous George." *Courtesy
of the George family.*

Left: **Like father . . .** Young Donnie, George and Betty's second adopted child, emulates his famous dad. *Courtesy of Dick Steinborn.*

Right: **Betty goes blond.** Borrowing her husband's fan, she poses at their home in Windsor Hills, California. Her hair was so naturally dark it took sixteen bleachings to get it to match George's platinum 'do. *Courtesy of the George family.*

Below left: **Turkey world.** George and Betty raised thirty thousand turkeys on their ranch in Beaumont, California—including a few dyed orchid, the same color as the couple's house and cars. *Courtesy of the George family.*

Below right: **Betty today.** George's muse and co-conspirator in 2006, more than sixty years after they invented Gorgeousness together. "I pushed, and he did it," she liked to say. *Courtesy of the author.*

Above: **Matinee idol.** George's one and only movie was released in 1949. George played himself—channeling Bette Davis and Tallulah Bankhead. *Courtesy of the author.*

Right: **Musical tribute.** George the cultural icon inspired popular songs. This ditty proclaimed that "his wavy hair and dainty air" made him "the darlin'est boy." *Courtesy of Brenda Cantonwine.*

Right: **Legally Gorgeous.** Betty helps George primp before his 1950 court appearance to have his name changed from George Wagner to Gorgeous George. *Los Angeles Times.*

Below: **The archenemy.** Promoter Jack Pfefer sent out his own wrestlers, dressed in fancy robes with their hair dyed blond, and billed them as Gorgeous George. *Jack Pfefer Collection, University Libraries of Notre Dame.*

Right: **Gorgeous George Grant.** He worked the gorgeous act and used a valet, another gimmick used by the original G.G. *Courtesy of Scott Teal.*

Left: **The "valette."** George's female valet—and second wife—former showgirl and dancer Cherie Dupre. *Courtesy of John Pantozzi.*

Right: **The stakes will be mighty high . . .** *Referee* magazine hyped the hair vs. mask match—if George lost, his curls would be shorn, and if the Destroyer lost, he'd finally be unmasked. *Courtesy of Tom Burke.*

Below right: **Still game.** The forty-seven-year-old George, in debt and looking for a quick payday, lets The Destroyer throw him from pillar to post to put the match across for the fans. *Courtesy of Tom Burke.*

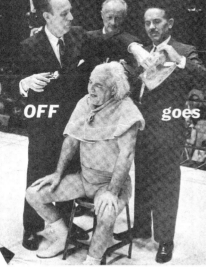

OFF goes

a world famous trademark

Above left: **The final indignity.** In 1962, George gets his gorgeous locks shaved off after losing a match to the masked Destroyer. *Courtesy of Tom Burke.*

Left: **Jesse "The Body" Ventura.** A flamboyant heel in the 1970s and '80s, Ventura took the trappings of Gorgeousness—all the way to the Minnesota governor's mansion. *Photofest.*

Above: **Hulkamania.** The charismatic Hulk Hogan in a tutu. Ever since George flitted and pranced, pro wrestling has continued to play with the feminine. *Time Life Pictures/Getty Images.*

Left: **Nature Boy.** Ric Flair, a wrestling descendant of George's rival Nature Boy Buddy Rogers, flaunted robes the Gorgeous One might have envied. *wrealano@aol.com.*

Above: **The hardest working man in showbiz.** James Brown was an athletic showman with caped finery and a valet, just like George. Brown said G.G. was one of the most important influences on his sensational live performances. *Michael Ochs Archives/Getty Images.*

Top right: **"I'm a bad, bad man!"** Muhammad Ali said George taught him to provoke and antagonize the fans, who would then pay to see someone shut his mouth. *Harry Benson/Getty Images.*

Bottom right: **"Shocking, scary, and silly."** That's how filmmaker John Waters remembers Gorgeous George. His outrageous movie characters, including Divine, right, are in some ways based on George. © *Fred W. McDarrah.*

Glam man. George in all his confounding, *sui gorgeous* glory. As the title of a 1978 Henry Winkler movie loosely based on G.G.'s life put it, he was The One and Only. *Jack Pfefer Collection, University Libraries of Notre Dame.*

At the Bachelors Ball in Los Angeles, a high-society costume party held at the Biltmore Bowl, Sharp Whitmore, a prominent lawyer, got much praise for his Gorgeous George portrayal. Gorgeous songs played on the radio, and then in the arenas before George's appearances. Jimmy Lennon, the singing ring announcer, recorded one such tune that began:

He has an armful of muscles and a head full of curls.
He wrestles with the fellows and he thrills all the girls.
A two-ton truck with a velvet sheen,
Gorgeous George is the man I mean.

He has a chest like a mountain and a face like a dream
He starts the women sighing and he makes the men scream.
A powerhouse fit for any queen,
Gorgeous George is the man I mean.

Let me tell you something:
You're not really in
If in your hair you don't wear
A gorgeous Georgie pin.

There never was any creature who had such a physique;
The population's clamoring for only a peek
At the man who can make them swoon or shriek,
Gor-geous, Gor-geous George.

Well-known comedians of the day, many of whose careers were also soaring thanks to television, told Gorgeous jokes. Jack Benny warned viewers that he was an ex-wrestler, known as the Body Beautiful, the predecessor of Gorgeous George, and hence not to be trifled with. On *The Red Skelton Show,* that radio and TV comic quipped: "If Gorgeous George had to pay taxes on what he *thinks* he's worth, he'd be broke." Bob Hope also riffed on the Gorgeous One in his syndicated newspaper column:

"George wants to join the Navy and have the world see *him*."

"His favorite hold is the full-dressed Nelson."

"George is so high class, instead of cauliflower ears, he has broccoli ears."

"His perfume is called Surrender—or I'll break your arm."

Hope's promotion of George preceded television. The former vaudevillian enjoyed wrestling, was tickled by the Gorgeous shtick, and had George on his hugely popular *Pepsodent Show,* a Tuesday-night radio program, quite a few times. So supportive of the wrestler was the comedian that, one night in 1948, Bob Hope went to work for the Sensation of the Nation.

Chapter 18

THE TOAST OF HOLLYWOOD

Bing Crosby was a clown. So, incongruously, was Gregory Peck, his perpetual earnestness hidden behind white pancake makeup, ludicrously big painted eyebrows, and the classic clown's indignity: a swollen red bulb affixed to his nose. Ronald Reagan, the thirty-seven-year-old war-movie actor and Chesterfield cigarette pitchman with the brown, wavy pompadour, was very much *in* character as a ringmaster, shining out his genial smile. On this September Saturday night more than two hundred Hollywood actors, radio personalities, and other celebrities gave a benefit performance on the grounds of L.A.'s Pan-Pacific Auditorium, replacing the regular employees of the Ringling Brothers Circus. The event raised some $175,000 (close to $1.5 million in today's dollars) to build a new wing at the St. John's Hospital in Santa Monica.

Hollywood gossip columnist Hedda Hopper was one of the principal organizers and she dressed as a toy soldier. With her blond hair tucked away underneath the earflaps of a stiff-brimmed black felt hat, she made her entrance dancing a little jig with Danny Kaye and Harpo Marx. Then Hopper banged out her next day's *Times* column on a typewriter, which sat on a big wooden desk, which was in turn anchored on the back of an elephant. Dan Dailey, nominated for the Best Actor Oscar that year for his performance in the musical *When My Baby Smiles at Me*, was a barker of sorts, drumming up visitors to the caged circus animals. Buster Keaton did a strongman parody, while William Powell, the debonair actor who'd already made his sixth *Thin Man* movie, played Punch and Judy alongside his third wife, Diana Lewis. "Filmland girls," as the next day's paper called them, sang, danced, rode horses or elephants, or "just walked around looking pretty." These starlets included World War II pinup queens Betty Grable and Lizabeth Scott, Maureen O'Sullivan, and Rosalind Russell. Jennifer Jones, the dark beauty who starred opposite Peck in *Duel in the Sun*, smoldered in a red velvet number as she was driven around the big tent in a chariot. The house band was led for the evening by trumpeter Harry James.

As Saturday evening turned into Sunday morning, cooling fog rolled in off the Pacific a few miles to the west and relieved the heat built up in the heavy canvas tents. Over the course of the event ten thousand people crammed inside. Even with three rings whirling at once, it took more than four and a half hours for all two hundred stars to be adored. In adherence to the unchanging hierarchy of show business, the biggest, top-billed star of the moment went on last. The benefit organizers' choice for their grand finale, shown nationwide the next week in the Hearst "News of the Day" newsreel, was a certain thirty-five-year-old wrestler with bleached blond hair.

The Pan-Pacific, on Beverly Boulevard in Los Angeles's Fairfax district, had a streamlined Art Moderne facade, from which jutted four tall, white towers shaped like tail fins. For the charity circus the facing parking lots had been covered with a collection of colorful tents, and now George walked rapidly toward them with his hairdressing team, Frank and Joseph, trying to keep up. He'd just flown in from Ohio, chartering his own plane and canceling some lucrative dates to make it. Normally, losing money held no interest for Howard and Bessie's boy, but the glory of closing this show made it irresistible to the Gorgeous ego.

Once he reached the tent serving as a dressing room, he was seated at a wooden table equipped with a good-size mirror, a white smock draped over his shoulders and chest. Elizabeth Arden did his makeup, and then Frank and Joseph applied themselves to his curls with all four hands. They were interrupted every minute, it seemed, by other stars stopping by to say hello, to pose with George for publicity pictures, and to satisfy their curiosity about the blond bombshell who was also a wrestling villain. Betty took a liking to Lucille Ball, who stopped by to introduce herself. Gary Cooper, all tanned and handsome six-foot-three of him, strolled in and loomed over George in a double-breasted suit. Gallant George stood up abruptly when Esther Williams, swimming champion and star of MGM's "aqua musicals," showed up, her reddish hair lustrous and her equally luxuriant figure on display in a revealing bathing suit. She laughed as George kissed her cheek, then pulled her into a mock headlock. Ray Milland came by to introduce himself, greeting the mat prima donna as George. "I don't know who you are, sir," he shot back jokingly at the star of *The Lost Weekend* and that year's *The Big Clock*, "but peasants usually refer to me as 'Gorgeous.'"

In the big top, tuxedo-clad Jimmy Lennon moved to the middle of the largest sawdust-covered ring. "Ladies and gentlemen," he intoned into the microphone. "It's time for the main event—the wrestling match of the century! The Killer of the screen faces off with The Killer of the ring!" Cheers rang out for the darkly handsome Burt Lancaster, starring just then as the murderous husband in *Sorry, Wrong Number*. He wore brown trunks and over them a flesh-colored robe. The referee was next to be introduced: Billy Curtis, the midget actor who played a Munchkin City official in *The Wizard of Oz*. The top of his pomaded dark hair reached Lancaster's lowest rib.

Then the lights went down and the tent, save the ring, was dark. "And now, here he is, ladies and gentlemen," Lennon resumed, sweeping one arm out to point up a long aisle between the rows of folding chairs. "The Toast of the Coast . . ." A man emerged: Bob Hope in a long black morning coat, a white carnation on his lapel, bearing in front of him a silver tray. The comedian had already starred in five "road movies" with Bing Crosby, but tonight he was here to serve George, and the Los Angeles audience recognized the impersonation in an instant: "He's playing Jefferies!"

Hope and Lancaster had rehearsed for two weeks, but they did so without George, who was out wrestling and earning until the last minute. So the two stars worked with Vic Holbrook, a wrestling friend of George's and an occasional valet, as a stand-in. When showtime came Hope flawlessly ran through the spray-gun routine—including an abortive attempt to disinfect the Killer. George then made his manifestation wearing a full-length yellow satin robe, trimmed at the elbows and cuffs with rings of white ermine.

Disrobed, George and Lancaster circled each other, glaring menacingly. The actor was several inches taller, lean and muscled; it was clear right away that Lancaster, who had once made his living as an acrobat, knew how to fall and roll. As he gained confidence and began to enjoy himself, he mugged, exaggerated, and overacted along with the master. Both men's backs took on a splotchy covering of sawdust. At one point George lifted Lancaster high over his shoulder and slammed him down. He was about to pin him when Hope approached the two-man tangle of arms, legs, and heads, holding a black telephone out in front of him, its cord trailing behind. In those days it was still a sizable instrument, and thus a more visible prop.

"Excuse me, Master," the valet said as the crowd chortled. "There's a call for you." George left off kneeling on Lancaster's chest to take the handset. After uttering a few quick sentences, he extended the phone toward his adversary. "It's for you." Lancaster took it and growled, "I'm busy, now, I can't talk!"

Then Lancaster got George in a near pin, and Hope flew to the rescue. He walloped the actor full in the face with a huge powder puff cached on the silver tray, and a pink cloud exploded around Lancaster's head. He staggered back, then turned toward Hope and shot him a furious look, full of Killer menace. Hope ran terrified and jumped into George's arms, the wrestler cradling his valet in front of his chest like a big, morning-coated baby. Then the incensed Lancaster, powder still caking his face, motioned to his corner, where two seconds had suddenly appeared. The two hulking men in double-breasted suits and fedoras—full gangster regalia—stalked toward Hope, who now cowered behind George's back. One of the thugs pulled a revolver from his waistband and raised it in the air. Suddenly all the lights in the tent went out. Shots rang out, *rat-tat-tat!* (Or were they rim shots by the house band's drummer?) The audience gasped.

Then, just as suddenly as they went out, the lights came back up and the band broke into a raucous jump tune, horns blaring. All the players, including the two gangsters, now smiling, began to dance. Hope dropped to his knees to make himself the same height as the tiny referee, and they circled the ring in a loopy waltz. George and Lancaster spun each other around in a fast-paced do-si-do, then ran up the main aisle together laughing, arm in arm.

At George's peak, the Gorgeous persona hung so thick in the atmosphere that it could be referenced, alluded to, or parodied, without even being named. In the 1951 Bugs Bunny cartoon entitled "Bunny Hugged," there appeared a vain wrestler who went by the alliterative name of Ravishing Ronald. Preceded to the ring by a leaping nymph, carried there on a covered silver tray by bare-chested men wearing fezzes, Ronald is finally revealed, wearing purple trunks around his tiny waist. His head is cartoonishly huge underneath his bright yellow hair and he's eating purple grapes. A harem girl sprays perfume. Ronald is even wearing a snood. His opponent, the massively muscled and ugly Crusher (wrestler Reggie Lisowski would have a long, successful run under that name), uses the hairnet to tie Ronald up with, then begins pounding him like an unloved drum. Bugs is Ravishing Ronald's valet, his Jefferies. "It's a living," he tells the camera with a shrug. When he sees his master getting thrashed, he exclaims: "Oh, bruddah, there goes my bread and buddah!" So the rabbit defeats the Crusher himself, with a strategy involving an anvil as well as the impersonation of a Jewish tailor.

Born in 1938, Bugs was a rascally brother to Gorgeous George's cartoonish character. Transgressive tricksters both, they defied as many conventions as possible (Bugs even defied gravity, among other laws of physics), talked insolent trash to everyone—and got away with it, always. Self-assured, self-reliant, and self-absorbed, they existed in their own worlds, autonomous regions of their own creation; they insisted on seeing things their ways. Cheerfully defiant and forever, improbably, unharmed, George and Bugs were both clearly having more fun than anyone else in their respective pictures.

At the opposite end of the pop-culture spectrum from these cool cats lived one well-meaning square named Andy Hardy, the hero of a Dell comic book and more than a dozen movies starring Mickey Rooney. This all-American male teenager was eager, adolescent, and innocent—he asked his father, Judge Hardy, how to *avoid* getting kissed by so many girls. He, too, had an encounter with a Gorgeous George stand-in. In comic strip Number 389, published in 1952, Andy runs afoul of a scowling grappler who wears his blond hair in a net and sports a long robe with white fur trim: Glamorous Gus. When Gus parades down the aisle of a wrestling arena, Andy accidentally trips Gus and a male fan wearing a bow tie taunts the wrestler, yelling, "S'matter, cutie boy? Won't your little footsies hold you up? Ho! Ho!"

Later, though, Gus, still wearing the hairnet outside the ring, proves himself a good egg and helps Andy reunite with his girlfriend, Polly. "If it hadn't been for Glamorous Gus, we might never have seen each other again!" pants Andy, clasping both her hands as they sit in his convertible jalopy. "I can't stand to even think about it, Andy!" is Polly's impassioned reply.

G.G. wasn't merely known; he signified. "Acting like Gorgeous George," "pulling a Gorgeous George," or someone "thinking he's Gorgeous George" all entered the common parlance. George became a ready symbol of the vain, the loud, and the attention-crazed, anything or anyone over-the-top. When Ethel Barrymore saw Laurence Olivier's Hamlet, she wasn't impressed, preferring her brother John's more subdued portrayal. Her hissed verdict on Olivier's rendition was: "Gorgeous George!"

In 1952 Katharine Hepburn was starring in *The Millionairess* on Broadway. Critic Bill Henry described her as looking fragile but charging around the stage, bellowing, taking stairs three steps at a time, and decking other actors. He summed up her scenery-chewing work by dubbing her "a feminine Gorgeous George." However, Henry added, her stage histrionics were creating a furor, and therefore interest. He concluded that "controversy must be better than talent—you can't buy a seat for the run of the play." A very George-ish notion.

Chapter 19

PURPLE MAJESTY

On a beautifully sharp blue-skied California afternoon, George sits smiling behind the wheel of a brand-new Packard convertible, top down. He's heading for home on Route 99, five or six miles outside Beaumont. The car he's steering with one meaty finger is the 1950 Packard Deluxe Coupe. He's just picked it up from the dealer, where the roadster—so low-slung it's said to embody "bathtub design"—has been painted a light purple, right down to the bands on the whitewall tires. George, between Cadillacs right now, owns another Packard he takes on the road with Jake Brown and his business manager Howard Cantonwine, the Hangman. That one's the Custom 8 Club Sedan, a massive limited-run land yacht with wide running boards. It's light purple, too—or, as he and Betty insist the color be properly called, orchid.

He turns off onto a smaller rural road, Cherry Valley Boulevard. The afternoon's warm, but here in the high desert the breeze coming in the open windows is cooling. George wears his version of casual wear: a bright yellow-and-black leopard-print, pajama-like outfit with matching top and trouser bottoms. He's resting his left arm on the window frame and his blond locks, sans tam today, stream behind him in the breeze. Off to his right runs a dark-railed wooden fence and George slows, then turns through its open gate into a semicircular dirt-and-gravel driveway. He's home, at the farm George and Betty moved to in 1950.

A few moments ago George drove past a sign advertising GORGEOUS GEORGE'S BROAD-BREASTED TURKEYS, and as he turns off the car in the driveway, then steps outside, he hears the low, constant burbling of the birds they're raising here. He can see them, too, in the huge farmyard behind the house and the fields across the road, thirty-five thousand turkeys scratching, bobbing, squawking, and teeming around the long, low wooden troughs holding their feed and water. Acres and acres are given over to—covered in—these dark-bodied, light-necked hordes. It seems an alien, gobbling planet. However, that's not the oddest aspect of this landscape.

Sitting fairly close to the road, the sprawling one-story farmhouse with the big picture window juts up from the sandy-colored earth the same bright purple as the cars. A short distance away sits Betty's parents' house and farther down another one, where her sister, Eve, and Eve's husband, Harold, live with their daughters, Sally and Nancy. Both of those homes are painted orchid, too. All the outbuildings on both sides of the road, including the brooder houses, where the chicks are kept, and the processing plant with its killing rooms, are orchid, in lurid contrast to the scrubby brown-and-gold hills behind. It's a bizarre Technicolor spectacle, like Dorothy's arrival in Oz, and just as in that movie the colors in this scene are so saturated they seem in need of correction, a dialing back toward reality. But that would spoil the fun.

Inside the little store and lunch counter—among his other accomplishments, George was a turkey-burger pioneer—there's a good chance that some of the birds, "Guaranteed Delicious and Hygienic," are orchid, too. For special promotions, Betty dunks them in purple vegetable dye. A second billboard along Cherry Valley announces in huge letters that TURPLE PURKEYS are for sale. Betty had no real reason to have the two first letters transposed, except her usual: Why have things bland when you can put some spice into them? Nearby supermarkets like Sage's and other customers who order birds get them delivered, in orchid-colored limousines.

It's unclear just how George and Betty came by their orchid fixation, but when they did, it was with total commitment. This obsession took in not just that lighter shade of purple, but the flower as well. She sewed cloth orchids in various colors onto several of his robes, and George, who was introduced as the Human Orchid, would sometimes carry real ones on his march to the ring, clasping them in front of him like a bride with a bouquet, then tossing them to deserving women in the audience. Occasionally he'd invite the sweetest-looking old lady he could find in the crowd to come into the ring, where he'd offer her one of the beautiful flowers. When the poor woman reached for her gift, he'd drop the orchid to the mat and grind it to pieces under his white-shod boot. "Just for fun," Betty explained. "You know, Mean Old George."

The turple purkey ranch they bought is quite a spread, one hundred acres of what George enjoys calling "prime real estate." When they bought it, he was as proud as Betty had ever seen him. Just outside the house, there's Betty's beloved cactus garden; the home itself, orchid-painted stucco, is 3,200 square feet, quite large for its day. Betty says with a laugh that she needs to pack a lunch when going from the entrance to the master-bedroom suite. A small piano sits in the roomy entrance hall, and in the kitchen all the cupboards are specially built low so Betty can easily reach them. Out back is the pool, the kids' domain, and inside, the adults entertain in a den, formerly a back porch, that Betty had enclosed in windows, with a bar, some stools, and some rattan furniture. A few years from now Betty will hold a party there for her parents' fiftieth anniversary.

Eve and Harold, experienced turkey farmers in Oregon, run the ranch for them, but Betty pitches in. She's too squeamish for the killing rooms and it's too cold in the giant freezers, so she works instead in the dressing room, as it's called, packaging the already processed birds. Turning turkeys purple is her specialty, though. One at a time she takes the birds out into the backyard and wrestles them into an old washtub filled with warm water and purple dye. She needs to massage the dye well into them, otherwise the oil under their feathers will make the orchid color run right off like the rain. They fight her, and since they're big birds and she's quite small, it's a struggle. Betty also does promotion, accompanying the driver when he makes his poultry deliveries; she puts on orchid pants, hands out Gorgeous George Broad-Breasted Turkeys decals, and pins baby orchids they have flown in from Hawaii on potential customers.

Carol, who's in the first grade, and Don, not yet in kindergarten, now look very much alike, even though they're not blood relatives. They have the same facial structure and both have a little gap between two upper front teeth. Those two and Sally and Nancy play with the yapping sheepdogs that herd the turkeys in and out of the fields, and they have horses, too. The menagerie doesn't stop there; for a while the family will also tend an alligator and a kangaroo; those two may have belonged to another of Cantonwine's managerial clients, a strongman who wrestled the gator and boxed the kangaroo in his act. At the exit of the semicircular drive sits a series of four or five raised turkey cages, a collection known as Celebrity Row. Each cage bears a metal nameplate: "Betty Grable" is in one cage, and "Tyrone Power" in another.

The orchid Packard George drove home today is a present for Betty. The surprise will be a good one, he thinks, standing in the driveway, but a swerve would be better. "Betty," he calls out, "I had an accident, I wrecked my car. Can you come out and take a look?" His wife bustles out of the house and into the driveway in jeans and a white shirt with the sleeves rolled up, a worried look on her face. Like the new car, Betty's had a dye job: Her hair is bleached bright blond in solidarity with George. It's naturally so dark that it took Frank and Joseph sixteen treatments to make the new color hold, she said. But right now that's the last thing on her mind. "George?" she calls out as she gets near. "Are you all right?"

"Surprise, Sweetie," he answers with a laugh and a grin, gesturing with one leopard-printed arm to the car. "I got you a little present—it's all yours." She bursts out laughing, then inspects the gleaming Packard outside and in. "George, I love it!" she exclaims, then gives him a hug. As he takes in the familiar feel of his wife's body in his arms, George looks out over Betty's head and surveys their purple realm. Life is good, he's thinking. He's winning. He's defied his father's prediction; he's a star. Everyone knows his name. "We're doing all right, aren't we, cutie?" George says to his wife of more than ten years, shaking his head at the improbability of it all. "We're riding high."

He'd always had a taste for the finer things, George liked to say, and now he could indulge it. Actually, he had a taste for the gaudy and the garish. Ostentation, in the forms of fancy cars and custom-made clothes, became the rule. Outside the arenas he dressed with a pimp's discretion; long before there was such a term, George was ghetto fabulous. His loud style was most likely part genuine penchant and another part calculation, as George was very aware of its impact on the marks and the press. In one of its stories on George, *Newsweek* said "his sartorial effects when not working at his trade are as blinding as his 80-odd robes of all hues and designs, and run to bright red jackets, yellow trousers and two-tone shoes." When he met with writer Ted Shane for his *American Mercury* profile, George wore a purple lounging suit with mottled pony-skin loafers. For yet another public appearance, it was duly reported, he chose olive-green slacks and a rust sport coat with a big yellow orchid pinned on the lapel, topped with a mink bow tie. (Perhaps it was actually ermine, given George's strong feelings about fur.) Carol couldn't ever remember seeing her dad in jeans. When George would drive to her school to pick her up, pulling up in an orchid luxury liner and wearing, say, the leopard-print lounge-wear, all her classmates who watched George on Channel 5, their wrestling station, would run outside to get a look, and she'd be embarrassed.

George was spendy but he could also be generous. He continued to see that his Houston wrestling buddies got work, negotiating with the promoters to include them on his cards. When George beat Jim Mitchell, the Black Panther, at the Olympic in August of 1949, for example, the Harrisburg Rat Chesty Hayes worked, too, drawing Sven Skagland. Ali Bey, the Terrible Turk, worked with George a good deal between 1950 and '55, sharing many a car ride up and down the California coast. He was a Greek, actually, name of Stephanides, a stubby five-foot-five man who weighed more than two hundred pounds, wore a fez, and was borne to the ring on a "flying carpet." The Turk was very impressed with George, he told his son, Andy. On nights when the house wasn't full (or when the promoters cheated the wrestlers more than usual), George would reach into his pocket and share his take with the lesser-paid boys on the undercard.

In his *Sport* magazine profile, Hannibal Coons addressed George's spending habits and fortune making, but the otherwise astute writer's interpretation of those patterns was diametrically wrong. "No one seems to know what George does with all the money he makes," Coons wrote. "It is fairly well established, however, that he hurls very little of it out the window." The wrestler's best hold, he claimed, was the grasp George had on his money, calling him "tighter than a two-dollar pair of shoes." The story went on to say that "George is cannily putting every nickel he makes into a big turkey ranch . . . Nobody will ever hold a benefit for this boy."

Once again, after George realized his vision of home—this orchid estate—he was mostly absent from it. Even when he wasn't on the road, he was out wrestling in California five or six nights a week, occasionally taping a TV bout in the morning and then wrestling again that same night. Like a coal miner he bent his body to the task; as his disciple James Brown would later describe himself, George was the hardest-working man in show business. Increasingly, he worked all day, too, and it was then that he may have done his best and most important digging. George assiduously, tirelessly courted the press, dazzling them into submission with good humor, good copy, and his prescient understanding of the value of publicity. (At this point it was mostly him generating the ballyhoo, as Betty, having done her part, stepped back and took care of the children.) When Jake Brown's wife,

Beulah, insisted Jake come off the road at one point, George managed to turn that into a promotable event. The Sensation called a friendly reporter, who wrote that George's "voice flowed through the phone like syrup across a waffle."

"It's about that wretched Jefferies," George told him. "I've had to sack the fellow. He failed to fumigate my hotel room and one of my finest scarlet caftans is a mass of wrinkles. You may give this news to the United Press and the Associated Press." Afterward, the story continued, "the wires were hot for hours."

During his matches he still got incendiary heat, but outside the arenas, in his myriad public appearances, fans almost always greeted him with admiration. In the light of day, no one jabbed him with hatpins or hurled lit cigarettes. When Gorgeous George got marcelled in S. W. Morrison in Portland in 1950, more than three hundred people crowded around the beauty-parlor windows, snarling traffic. The crowd was a mix of teenage and preteen girls—bobby-soxers, as they'd recently come to be called—older women, and very amused men. Five years later George and Cherie had dinner in a New York restaurant and were seated at a choice window table. A quarter hour later, though, the maître d' asked them to move—so many gawkers were pressing and leaning against the plate glass that the staff feared they would break it.

Like other celebrities, George developed tactics to cope with the conditions of fame. When he flew from California to New York to perform, for instance, he'd take an overnight TWA Constellation. The "Connie" made the trek in something like nine hours. Glad-hander and extrovert though he was, he still needed to get some sleep en route, so George launched a preemptive first strike. As soon as he boarded and began making his way down the aisle to first class, he'd stop and greet the other passengers—men and women all dressed up to fly—signing autographs, shooting the breeze, and posing for pictures. Once he'd given the public the encounters and souvenirs they craved, he could relax uninterrupted.

In Los Angeles, showing off the great show-off at your charity event made it stand out, and gracing it kept George in the gossip and society columns. At the Toys for Tots giveaway at Grauman's Chinese Theatre, George appeared with George Jessell, Broderick Crawford, Anne Baxter, and Gregory Peck. His marcelled locks shining, with a huge orchid pinned to his lapel, he posed for pictures while bussing brunette Private First Class Ramona Claypool of the Marine Corps Reserve on the cheek. As they grinned at the camera both held his donation to the tots, Gorgeous George dolls. Fittingly, the dolls, a fair overall likeness and accurate down to the dark eyebrows, had huge heads and relatively tiny robe-draped bodies. The miniature Georges also had white gloves on their tiny hands, an embellishment George didn't use in his act and might have done well with. Besides the dolls, George was also marketing a Gorgeous George strength belt for weight lifters, a G.G. replica bathrobe, and, on a chivalrous note, a self-defense book for women with his imprimatur.

The United States was at war again, in Korea, and George donated Christmas turkeys to L.A.'s navy and Marine Corps reservists. A crew of six GIs had just written to George from Korea, telling him they'd named their Sherman tank after him. "We have watched you wrestle on television and you pack a big wallop," the letter said. "We intend to pack a big wallop, too." With the American military bogged down in that conflict, Commander in Chief Truman decided not to run for reelection. Dwight Eisenhower, the dead ringer for George's dad, won the Republican nomination, while Truman threw his support behind Illinois governor Adlai Stevenson. Then, in March of 1952, George declared, announcing at a series of well-attended press conferences that he was running for president. "There's nothing novel in U.S. Presidents being wrestlers," he explained. "Washington went in for combat wrestling, Buchanan was a judo expert, Teddy Roosevelt wrestled hand-to-hand with William Muldoon before and after he got to the White House and Taft—why Taft was a wrestling champion at Yale. Abe Lincoln was a professional; he once earned $10 for a match." (There was even some truth scattered in among these claims.)

As he saw it, George was clearly the most qualified candidate. "Both Adlai and Ike are bald," he explained. "I firmly believe the head of our country should have hair on it." Surely the people would recognize this disparity, and vote accordingly. For his first act as president, George said, he would make over the Supreme Court justices, whose black robes struck him as unnecessarily grim and plain. Curiously, he is not found on record making what seems the most logical campaign promise: a turkey in every pot.

On yet another beautifully sunny California afternoon George, Betty, and their attorney appeared in an L.A. courthouse before Judge W. Turney Fox. For an occasion such as this, the leopard-print pajamas wouldn't do. The husband and wife spent time choosing his outfit and he shone in a dark violet single-breasted silk suit with a bold yellow shirt, a matching pocket hankie, and a gray silk tie painted with the image of an orchid. Georgie pins glinted gold from an especially intricate marcel. Oddly, for a ceremony that affected his legal, family, and marital status, he wasn't wearing his wedding ring. George the person would completely merge with his invented public persona: He was legally changing his name to Gorgeous George.

Betty, too, was elegant, very dressy in an orchid suit, white gloves, and a hat with a circular brim. Her hair shone newly blond along with her husband's. After some discussion of how changing their last name would affect Carol Sue and Donnie, the judge granted their petition. Before they went outside to pose for the throng of photographers, Betty stopped to reapply her red lipstick and redrape an ermine stole across her shoulders. Then George stood on the courthouse steps regaling the press with his arm around her. Betty leaned into him, half turned away from the cameras and gazing up at Mr. George. She reached up now and then to straighten a blond curl. Looking at him, touching him, smiling, the newly christened Mrs. George looked both glamorous and utterly devoted.

A few days later, though, when she heard him invoke his new name, Betty was heartsick. They were at home, on the turkey ranch in Beaumont, and her face fell as she overheard her husband talking to the children in the next room. "Don't call me Daddy anymore," he told them. "Call me Gorgeous."

ACT THREE

"I saw fifteen thousand people comin' to see this man get beat. And his talking did it. I said this is a gooood idea!"

—MUHAMMAD ALI

Chapter 20

"YOU'VE CHANGED ENOUGH"

Bring me another Jack Daniel's on the rocks, will ya, honey?" George was sitting at a blackjack table in the Silver Slipper, his favorite Las Vegas haunt. (A few years later he would ply his nightclub act there in the lounge.) It was three o'clock in the morning when he asked the waitress for his refill, or thereabouts; casinos famously have no clocks on their walls. This was a high-limit table, naturally. The wrestling celebrity was wearing a white open-neck sport shirt with black starbursts on it, lime-green slacks, and soft black loafers. In the way he did most everything these days—prodigiously—he was drinking, sweating, and losing.

He, along with Jake Brown and Hangman Cantonwine, were on their way home from a road trip; his two companions had already called it a night. They tried to get George to stop, Jake wheedling and Cantonwine making a more blustery argument to at least try another game, goddamn it! But their boss refused to quit while he was behind. The next morning, after another attempt to persuade him, they checked out from their rooms and flew home to L.A., leaving him behind. George was adamant: He'd stay and win his money back, then drive the purple land yacht home. He looked like he hadn't slept, droplets beading up on his meaty face.

A day or two later Betty was surprised and none too pleased to run into Jeff, as she always thought of him, by himself. "Where's George?" she demanded. The valet was evasive at first, but he could never withstand the force of her personality any better than he could George's. They'd left him in Vegas, he admitted, adding that he was worried, too. The last thing he'd seen that night was George, desperately trying to recoup, betting twenty thousand dollars on a single hand.

The next summer day was hot, with lots of sunshine, and Betty was wearing shorts. She was standing in the kitchen at the purple turkey ranch when she saw the Cadillac limo pull into the drive. She walked out the back door to meet George as he parked in front of the garage. He wore slacks and a T-shirt, with one of his tams covering his hair. He said hi, when he saw her approach, and that was all he had time for. George was still sitting in the driver's seat when Betty walked up to him and said, "I want a divorce."

He just looked at her. Betty turned around and walked back in the house, went to get the nanny, then drove her home. Then she and George sat down and tried to talk it over. They didn't get very far. "I've had it," Betty said. "I don't want any more. You can't do this kind of thing with two kids and a ranch to run." George said he'd do better; he would change. Betty's response just shot right out of her; she hadn't thought it through, yet it summed up all she was feeling when she told her husband: "You've changed enough."

Gambling was a young, if burgeoning, vice of George's, but he had others that were more fully matured. He'd always drunk a lot, for as long as Betty had known him. After Betty objected, in a series of conversations that strung out over years, George drank less at home (or drank in secret), and mostly saved his excess for the road. But as their lot improved so spectacularly, his drinking increased, both in frequency and volume. Most of the time he held his Jack Daniel's well. "Everyone knew he had a drinking problem, but he never got falling down," said John Hall, then an *L.A. Times* sportswriter who frequented the L.A. bar where George held court in the mid-1950s. He wasn't abusive to his wife or children when he drank, he simply became preoccupied, busy drinking. Like many serious drinkers, once his imbibing got under way and the alcohol took its chemical hold, that's where his attention went and his commitment truly lay. George was already an absentee father and husband; when he drank around his family, he was elsewhere at home, too.

Once he took Carol and Donnie to a drive-in and conked out in the back of the car while the kids watched the movie from the front seat. Don started looking around for the snacks their mother had packed for them, reached behind the seat, and came up with a quart bottle with some brown liquid left in it. He held it up, delighted with his find and eager to show off his knowledge of adult matters to his older sister. "Whiskey!" he exclaimed loudly. George snoozed through the whole episode.

"These things stay with you," said Carol as an adult. "I didn't like to be around him when he drank; I wanted our dad."

On another afternoon late in their marriage, George and Betty threw a turkey dinner at the ranch, charging wrestling fans a few dollars a head to come see the place (including the turkeys on Celebrity Row), meet George and some other wrestlers, and eat all the barbecued bird they could hold. Jesse and Johnny James were there, as was Danny McShain, with his second wife, Sallee. Off-duty policemen were hired as security and more on-duty officers had to drive out and help handle the car traffic that built up around the ranch. Hundreds of people showed up, but George didn't appear. By early evening the food was running out and the crowd milling in front of the makeshift stage in the backyard was demanding to see the Gorgeous One. Howard Cantonwine, the business manager, was boiling with anger, but otherwise none too helpful.

Jesse and Danny went back into the house to help Betty pour black coffee into George, who had passed out in the bedroom. Danny McShain asked his wife to take the mike and try to distract the fans. She wasn't an entertainer, but she was blond and curvaceous; the thinking was that at least the crowd would have something to look at. Eventually George made it to the stage, about three hours late. He'd needed help getting into a robe. He made a few remarks and strutted a little unsteadily and the crowd was satisfied. Betty was furious. "Of course she was," said Sallee. "George was drunk out of his skull."

He began to stay in character more offstage, when formerly he'd revert to just George. Ida Mae Martinez was just eighteen when she became a professional wrestler and early in her career she worked on the same card as George. He asked her to fix his hair before a match (for some reason he was without a valet). Happy to oblige, the young girl combed and, following his instructions, put the hairpins in his blond curls, which fell to just below his neck. Then she dropped one of his pins and said, "Whoops, I dropped the bobby pin." George turned on her, yelling, "That's a Georgie pin!" He was livid.

Later in life Betty consistently took the high road when asked about another of George's husbandly deficits. "If George was running around on me," she insisted, "I never knew about it." In her legal petition she alleged only the umbrella term *mental cruelty*. Those who knew George, however, especially the wrestlers who encountered him on the road, described him as the lead hound in a notoriously skirt-chasing pack. "He always had a couple of broads with him," said one former wrestler based on the East Coast. "When he flew in he'd start meeting them right at the airport, invite a dozen or so to a party later at his hotel, so that way, we could pick and choose, you know?"

Cherie, his next wife, either had a different experience from Betty or was more forthcoming. Was George faithful? she was asked in an interview with Canadian filmmakers Claude and Dale Barnes for their 2006 TV documentary *Gorgeous George*. "Well, not always, no," she said, looking away from the camera. "When I was expecting with our son, Gary," Cherie continued, "George had to go to Australia alone. I was in no fit condition. He got a little inebriated and called me to tell me"—here she changed to a deeper, drunken voice—"'Honey, I just dumped my ashes.' That was his way of saying he'd been with a woman.

I said, 'You didn't have to call me long distance, collect, from Australia to tell me *that!*' And I hung up."

With her, George seems to have used the same brutally honest approach he did with his children: Where his faithfulness was concerned, there was no Santa Claus. "He never lied to me about it," Cherie said. "I wish to hell he had lied sometimes. At least he was honest; he was an honest playboy." Cherie ventured that George's infidelities weren't entirely his fault. "He had many temptations with female fans when I wasn't traveling with him," she said. "He wasn't looking for women; they came to him. He had a million chances to be unfaithful." But George was hardly prey for corrupting huntresses. There was something excessive and compulsive about George's womanizing, as there was in his lust for alcohol. He ached for female touch and attention, needed this other rush of chemicals that was thrilling and also soothing, an intoxicating succor.

After George's death, Cherie said, "There were lots of women who claimed to be the mother of his children." She maintained bitterly that they were looking for money. During the writing of this book two women surfaced who maintained that they were George's illegitimate children. They were looking for information and from that, it seemed, some kind of solace; neither mentioned money. One woman said that while her mother was dating George she made her living in another rough-edged sport popular in that era, the roller derby.

Bob Kurtz, who runs a sports memorabilia store in Berkeley, California, got an unlikely insight into George's womanizing when he was just ten years old. A wrestling fanatic and junior autograph hound, he begged his mother for tickets when Gorgeous George came to the Oakland Auditorium. She came through in champion fashion: They had front-row seats at the end of an aisle; her friend had gotten the tickets. Then, after George pinned babyface Dennis Clary with the flying side headlock, Kurtz suddenly found himself heading back to the locker room, his mother's friend leading the way. There, a somewhat tired Orchid sat on a bench toweling off. He asked the youngster his name and how he'd liked the match. He'd loved it, Bobby told him, but he was disappointed not to have gotten a Georgie pin thrown to him before the match. "That's part of the show," G.G. told him. "I only throw them to women, especially older ones—they're my biggest fans. But you look like a really big fan, too, so how many pins do you want?"

"Three," Bobby figured. "One for me, one for my mother, and one for her friend." George laughed and said his mother's friend already had a bunch of them, not to worry. Kurtz went home buzzing with his memories. He was confused, though, as to how the woman came to own Georgie pins. His mother, in her infinite parental wisdom, decided to level with the ten-year-old. "You see, Bobby," she said, "George has a lady friend in many of the places where he wrestles, and she's his lady friend in Oakland." This was in 1951, when George was still married to Betty.

Another subtler breach had formed between Betty and George as well. She had found the Truth, as Jehovah's Witnesses call their faith. She'd been raised as a Christian, but young Betty was never happy with a God who would put you in a burning furnace forever if you sinned. Witnesses believe that hell is simply the grave, where we'll sleep until the Resurrection. Then everyone will be returned to the earth in a perfected form; their "flesh will be younger than youth." First Jesus must wrest this world from Satan, who now has dominion over it. Betty's face would glow as she explained to her children that, after the Resurrection, "there'll be no more hunger, no more hurt, no more tears."

It was Geraldine Massey, the wife of wrestler Corbin Massey (Cyclone Mackey), who helped bring her to the Truth. This was before the war, when the two couples were sharing a house in Columbus, and before George and Betty adopted Carol and Don. The Wagners were upstairs, the Masseys down, and when the two wrestlers were away, Betty would come downstairs in her slippers at night, along with Judy the bulldog. Geraldine was about ten years older than Betty's thirty-two, blondish, and at five-foot-three, a few inches taller. The two women would make coffee, then sit in their bathrobes, Judy between them, each reading from her own Bible and discussing it together. After George and Betty left Columbus and moved on to Tulsa and all the other territories, she'd find Kingdom Halls in the towns they stopped in and go to meetings, as the Witnesses call their services. When the Wagners lived in Windsor Hills the Masseys lived in Lancaster, California, so the two women were able to continue studying together. Geraldine, her sons Vance and Virgil; Pat, the Wagners' former nanny, who married Virgil; and Betty with her two children would all go to the Kingdom Halls. When he was young, Donnie was something of a Kingdom Hall prodigy, with a photographic memory or close to it; he could read an entire *Awake* magazine or *Watchtower*, then recite it.

George wanted to belong and, it seemed, to believe. Always a quick study, he learned the tenets and put in some time reading his Bible. He read very little else, rarely dallying with books, magazines, or newspapers, though he'd glance at stories on himself. To Betty it seemed that "George didn't have time. He was always busy, going here or there." George the pragmatist may also not have seen the payoff, the immediate benefit. When he'd call home to Beaumont from the road, though, he'd encourage his children to read the Bible, listen to their mother, and go to meetings. With his family George would sometimes attend assemblies, huge convocations of twenty-five thousand Witnesses or more, and several times he donated thousands of turkeys to help feed the gatherings. He absorbed enough of the Truth, and valued it enough, to teach it to his last girlfriend, Beverly Styles. It was always in his consciousness, Carol believed. But his grasp of other things, and the holds they had on him in return, proved stronger.

Once, after George's death, when she was in her late twenties, Carol was sunbathing at her home in Grants Pass, Oregon, and as she often did, she thought of her dad. An alarming thought suddenly came to her. *When he's resurrected, he's going to ask me if I ever tried to help Gary* [George's son with Cherie] *find the Truth about the Bible. And what am I going to say?* So she sent her half brother some books and a letter explaining their beliefs. But she never heard back from Gary.

When Betty told George she was through, he was shocked and sullen. After stewing for a day or two, he got angry. "I'll fix you," he threatened over the phone. "I'll take you to court, and I'll take everything." Mean Old George, indeed. Go ahead, she told him, contest the divorce. "I'll get everyone we know to come and testify about how you've behaved." That quieted him down quickly. In the settlement they arrived at in Riverside County Court, both parties agreed it was unwise to sell the ranch and divide the proceeds at that time; Betty and the children would continue to live there. She kept her Packard and the house trailer in which they'd spent some of their best moments. He got the Cadillac he was driving at that time, and all rights to the name Gorgeous George. George was to pay her $400 a week for child support. The divorce went through on September 23, 1952; they'd been married for thirteen years and seven months.

George's support payments were neither prompt nor frequent. In 1953 they came to a new arrangement in which Betty got all the income from the ranch to support the children instead of fixed payments by George. She also got the right to use the name "Gorgeous George Turkeys" in connection with that business. Those rights and that supposed income proved to be of scant worth, so Betty went to work as a cocktail waitress at a club called Pinky's in nearby Redlands. Since her shift started at 6 P.M., she was home when the children returned from school, and her sister, Eve, was right next door to look after them the rest of the night. Betty missed a lot of evening meetings at the Kingdom Hall, but it had to be done. She liked the work, and she made good money, too. "I was a damn good cocktail waitress," Betty said.

Betty's still alive, at this writing, still crackling with energy. She stayed on the West Coast, and when the first interview for this book was about to take place in her hometown, her end of the phone conversation went like this: "You're at the hotel? Good, stay there. I'll come right over." *Click.* Soon her fifteen-year-old red Plymouth Acclaim pulled neatly into a parking space. "I'll be ninety-three in January," Betty announced, "and I didn't make any mistakes driving over here, either." Her rich dark hair was now a bright white, piled in snowy curls on top of her head and over her ears. Her face was deeply wrinkled, but her green-brown eyes were still bright. She wore high heels on fancy occasions and shiny gold or silver slippers for most others, along with makeup and bangly gold jewelry. And Betty still favored the brightest shades in clothes, including orchid, the color of Gorgeousness.

She lived alone in a modest ranch house with a tiny, fluffy dog. After her divorce from George, Betty married again, and stayed with that man for twenty-five years until she outlived him, too. She never acquired much of an interest in what others might think—or she continued to delight in confounding their expectations. During her second marriage Betty adopted two more children, a boy and a girl. Her husband was reluctant; in fact, "he objected strongly," she said. "But I did it anyway." Sixty years after she first learned the Truth with Geraldine, Betty continued to go to meetings, attending by speakerphone when the weather was too inclement or she was feeling poorly. Because those of her faith don't believe in society's false governance, she's never voted in a public election. Her daughter Carol lived a few hours away, but Don left the family soon after he graduated from high school, reappearing just once in the late 1970s, and neither Carol nor Betty had heard from him in more than thirty years. He didn't stay with the Truth; he once told Betty, "It's too easy for me." His mother feared he'd fallen away into the world.

She stayed fond of George's memory and keeps pictures of the two of them in their outrageous finery on display in her home. "I thought a lot of George," she said, using the same locution she had when talking about her father. "We had some very good years, a lot of fun together. But then it all went to his head. He'd have a drink and he thought he *was* Gorgeous. I liked it in the ring, but at home I didn't want it. I wanted us to be a family." If she had the same choice again, though, Betty said, she wouldn't divorce George. She said this unbidden, during a ride to a favorite seafood restaurant. "In those days we didn't know what we know now about alcohol and treatment," she explained. "At the time, I didn't know what to do, I really didn't. I couldn't keep putting the kids through that. I just kept hoping he'd stop.

"In a way," she continued, "it's my fault." The white-haired woman's eyes welled up and she looked away, to her right, out the passenger-side window of the car moving up the Pacific coast. From time to time a long trailer truck loaded with timber, slender tree trunks with the bark still on, went by on the two-lane road, just as they did in the Oregon logging country she grew up in. "I made him Gorgeous," she said finally, "and he just couldn't handle it."

Chapter 21

WHAT BOB DYLAN SAW

When he left the turkey ranch, George moved his robes and supplies of ersatz-gold bobby pins into the House of Serfas, a favorite L.A. watering hole. A combination restaurant, saloon, and motel in Inglewood, it sat at the top of View Park Hill, where three good-size streets came together—the HOS motto was: "Where Stocker, LaBrea, Overhill, and Good Friends Meet." The thirty-two small units in back were mostly rented out to the Dodgers and Angels baseball players, and to other bar regulars when, as one of them, *L.A. Times* sportswriter John Hall, put it, "we were between wives."

Ernie Serfas, the Greek-American who owned the place with his brother Nick, was very proud of his heritage and a big wrestling fan; he'd grown up idolizing the Greek champion Jim Londos. Serfas was convinced that his buddy and excellent customer was Greek, too, on his mother's side. George had reeled off a couple of Greek phrases he'd learned from the James family back in Houston and embellished a bit to seal their kinship. "The Hill," as the House of Serfas was also known due to its location, was an early prototype for both the sports bar and the singles bar. The booths were red leather and behind the bar, instead of mirrors, Serfas had commissioned colorful paintings of voluptuous sirens enticing sailors to their doom, lit with a special blue light. All the baseball and football players, sportswriters, and other sharpies who frequented the place had a long-running home stand there with another L.A. team: the young women who came to the Hill to meet them. "It was a big meat market," said Hall with some satisfaction. "Some of the waitresses there were a part of it, too." Such was the female availability, Serfas said, that prostitutes couldn't do any business there. "I didn't want them, anyway," he said. "The sheriff in L.A. County then was a Greek, a good guy, and I wouldn't have wanted to embarrass him."

So as not to miss any of the good times, Bud Furillo, sports editor of the *Herald Examiner,* would call Mike LeBell at the Olympic and ask what was going to happen in the wrestling matches that night. Then he'd knock off two or three clever paragraphs about the results, file his story in the afternoon, and go right to the Hill after work. George was in his element here, friends with the deferential owners, surrounded by admiring men and willing women, in a booze dispensary where good ballyhoo was appreciated. When he was in town, he held court, standing with a glass of Jack Daniel's, dressed in a Hawaiian shirt and slacks, his Gorgeous hair pinned under a tam or beret. He told jokes, he did his card tricks, and Serfas said he saw George hypnotize people, too, though that could have been a work. George joined the poker games that went on in the motel rooms, and he dated a string of exotic dancers. In this, his stripper period, as one friend called it, George's dalliances were all brief.

George got more recognition than any of the ballplayers, but to him they were peers. On one occasion, though, George did remind the jocks of his star status. He bet a few Rams he was drinking with that he could bring one of their games at Memorial Coliseum to a halt. The seven footballers each put up $100 and George put up $700; Ernie held the money. George told Nick Serfas, who was occasionally playing the Jefferies role by then, to get out the monkey suit and fill the spray gun. That Sunday, about five minutes into the first quarter, George—in one of his outlandish robes, valet leading the way—

paraded up from the tunnel entrance to the Serfas brothers' seats, thirty-seven rows up. The fans stirred and someone yelled, "Look, it's Gorgeous George, he's at the game!" Soon the referees were looking up to find the source of the commotion, then some of the players did, too. Finally. Amid the chaos, one of the officials called time-out. "There goes our 700 bucks," said one of the betting Rams to another. Not entirely. When they all got back to the Hill that night and George collected, he dropped the folded bills on the bar and announced, "We're having a $1,400 party."

When he was in L.A., George still went to Beaumont fairly often to see the children. He and Betty would sit down and talk over coffee. They were still concerned about each other, and maybe more. A year or two after their divorce George told her he wanted to get back together. "We'll get married in the ring again, at the Olympic Auditorium!" he proposed, not one to overlook the publicity value of this reconciliation. She'd do it, Betty told George, if he would stay sober. He agreed, but three days later he was drunk again.

On the road at night he'd brood, alone in the capacious backseat of the purple limo, the valet driving while the dark miles went by outside the windows. At the arenas, though, he came alive. George still loved to perform and could lose himself in it, summoning his special energy. One day he pulled into Hibbing, Minnesota, a small town about seventy-five miles north of Duluth in the iron range, where that ore was extracted, in the northeast corner of the state. He was *on* that day, feeling fully Gorgeous, and a struggling teenage musician there felt his charge.

Robert Zimmerman was scuffling around his hometown, trying to find an audience along with a working identity. Not yet a folkie, he played Little Richard covers and had his own kinky hair piled high in what looked like a combination of the conk or "process" done on black hair and the pompadour worn by other singers he admired, including Elvis Presley. Hibbing High School was the home of the Blue Jackets, and during the talent-show portion of a mid-1950s Blue Jacket Jamboree, his classmates and the principal were shocked when quiet but intense Bobby Zimmerman stood up at the piano and banged out an amplified "Rock 'n' Roll Is Here to Stay" at top volume.

His father, Abe, was fairly well-off and well known in Hibbing—four hundred people attended Bobby's bar mitzvah at the Androy Hotel—but young Zimmerman felt very much an outsider, a nobody, especially when it came to his music. Tellingly, he attributed his lack of success not to his gratingly nasal voice but to social connections (presumably WASPier ones) the other bandleaders had that he lacked. His bands, the Shadow Blasters and the Golden Chords, could play at Collier's BBQ jam sessions, park pavilions, and store openings, "but those gigs didn't pay except maybe for expenses and sometimes not even that." Other singers kept stealing his backup bands, because they could pay and he couldn't. At a loss, Bobby talked to his father about joining the military, going to West Point. Abe told him not to bother; it took connections to get in there, too. His grandfather had this helpful suggestion: "Go work in the mines." It was a bleak time, he wrote in his memoir, *Chronicles: Volume One,* filled with "a lot of waiting, little acknowledgment, little affirmation."

Then Gorgeous George came to town. In all likelihood Bobby had seen him before on television; Abe and his brothers owned Micka Electric, an appliance and furniture store on Fifth Avenue. But it was in this live encounter that the Zimmerman kid would be transfixed and transformed; as Bob Dylan describes this life-altering event that's now half a century old, its power is still palpable. "I was playing on a makeshift platform in the lobby of the National Guard Armory," he recounted. This was the venue for "livestock shows and hockey games, circuses and boxing shows, traveling preacher revivals, country-and-western jamborees." Amid the Hibbing farmers and veterans and their wives and children milling about, he and his band played as loudly as they could. Yet, typically, "no one was paying much attention." Suddenly the doors burst open and in came "the great wrestler," as Dylan calls him.

"He roared in like the storm, didn't go through the backstage area, he came through the lobby of the building and he seemed like forty men. It was Gorgeous George, in all his magnificent glory. He had valets and was surrounded by women carrying roses, wore a majestic fur-lined gold cape and his long blond curls were flowing." Then the Gorgeous One aimed his "lightning and vitality" directly at the unformed artist in the corner. "He brushed by the makeshift stage and glanced towards the sound of the music. He didn't break stride, but he looked at me, eyes flashing with moonshine. He winked and seemed to mouth the phrase 'You're making it come alive.'"

Dylan couldn't be sure Gorgeous George really said that, or anything, to him. It made no difference. "It's what I thought I heard him say that mattered, and I never forgot it." It wasn't merely the wrestler's words, real or imagined, that electrified the singer, it was the man himself, his towering presence. A teacher at Hibbing High had asked his ninth-grade social-studies students what they hoped to become in life. Zimmerman stood up and announced, improbably, that he wanted to be "a star." Now, for the first time, he'd encountered one. Dylan calls him "a mighty spirit."

It was that look, the wink, the complicit communication from a king to an as-yet commoner, that moved him the most. From someone whose artistry had already been achieved to another who had yet to define his own, the look said: "I'm someone special. I'm not like everybody else. And I don't just accept that, I revel in it. I've got it, kid. *And you've got it, too.*" That message, Dylan writes, "was all the recognition and encouragement I would need for years to come." A decade or so later he'd have another inspiring encounter, with singer and civil rights activist Harry Belafonte. In both cases, Dylan said, he felt afterward "like I'd become anointed." To him George and Belafonte were both "that rare type of character that radiates greatness and you hope that some of it rubs off on you."

Soon thereafter, it did. After about a year and a half at the University of Minnesota in Minneapolis, Bobby Zimmerman got behind the wheel of a four-door '57 Chevy and drove to New York City. There he would tell the press entertaining lies worthy of Gorgeous George's, announcing blithely that he'd been raised by tramps and hoboes, not nice middle-class Jewish folks, and grown up riding the rails like Woody Guthrie. (To critic Greil Marcus, this Dylan, the fabulist trickster, evoked the world of carny hustlers, the place where George found his own hustler's vocation.) Soon Zimmerman began writing his own songs—and he became Bob Dylan. Just as George Wagner home-birthed Gorgeous George, the musician summoned a doppelgänger from inside himself. He wanted to be a poet, like Dylan Thomas, so he took that name, redefining his identity. Not long afterward, Cassius Clay, another transforming son of George, declared himself a prophet, Muhammad Ali, and told the world to honor his new name. Unlike George, Ali and Dylan would continue to morph and shape-shift in their careers and adult lives, changing personae several times each. The boxer became a war resister, among other things, and Dylan a Christian.

James Brown kept his birth name, but from an unwanted, unlovely Negro boy he also summoned someone new and more exalted: the Godfather of Soul, Soul Brother Number One. Decades later rappers changed their names and they, too, adopted theatrical personae: Curtis Jackson became 50 Cent and Marshall Mathers created the alter ego Eminem. Some acknowledged their musical and rhetorical debts to James Brown and others paid respect to Muhammad Ali, the Champ. One wonders, though, did any of them know they were also following a certain perfumed white gentleman, born in Butte, Nebraska, who wrestled and threw orchids to the ladies?

Chapter 22
THE COPPER-HAIRED CUTIE-PIE

George punched his friend in the face very hard. Howard Cantonwine, his business manager and traveling companion, reeled backward, blood dripping from his cut lip, then set himself and charged at George.

The Hangman was about George's height but a good deal bulkier, a legitimate 235 pounds, as opposed to an announced wrestling weight of 235. A big wide man with a big wide nose and equally broad jowls, he had jet-black hair slicked back on a diagonal, and his ears protruded a little, probably from mat damage. His nickname came from his signature move: He'd pin his opponent by the neck between two ring ropes, then yank on their feet in a supposed attempt to strangle. Fifteen years older than George, the Hangman was never a top draw, but he was well known in L.A. and Hollywood, appearing in two movies: *You Can't Have Everything* in 1937 and *Merry Go Round of 1938* with Bert Lahr. Howard and his wife, Gertrude, lived in Laguna Beach and he opened and folded a series of businesses in that area, including Cantonwine's Sport Palace, a bar/restaurant where Golden Glow beer went for fifteen cents a pop.

The red-faced Cantonwine was quick to anger: Once, when he felt his daughter Brenda's bed hadn't been made properly, he threw it out the window. Another day she came home from junior high school and saw her father, George, and Black Bart (another wrestler) facedown and unconscious on the rumpus-room floor. She called the police, but it turned out they were all just passed-out drunk. The reward for her concern was a bawling out for "causing trouble." Like George, Hangman drank the hard stuff. In their travels he sat up front with the valet, while George occupied the back. At dinnertime they'd find the best restaurant in town and devour great steaks; in keeping up with these two trenchermen, Jake put on weight, developing a paunch that outgrew George's modest protrusion. He'd have beer with his meals while the other two put away Scotch and bourbon.

Against the backdrop of heavy drinking, the trio's days and nights did not unfold in a smooth and orderly progression. Missteps, chaos, and recrimination played out at high volume. The three of them were zooming through the western desert in the middle of the night when George threw some trash out the window of the limo (if littering was considered a social sin back then, it didn't concern him). Then he saw that a diamond ring he'd just treated himself to had gone out with the detritus. "Stop the car!" he yelled at Jake. They drove back and searched for the ring under the headlights, but couldn't find the bauble. Cantonwine made some critical remarks; the words *idiotic* and *goddamn ring* might have been included. A drunken fury of shouting, cursing, and blaming ensued, then George threw the first punch, catching Hangman flush in the mouth. The two muscular athletes had at each other savagely, grappling, grunting, and sometimes landing punches. Jake just sat in the driver's seat with his feet out the open door and waited for them to exhaust themselves. Soon they did, separated, and each climbed back into his designated seat, muttering.

After his divorce, the boys noticed, George's drinking escalated. He complained to some of them that Betty was trying to break him financially. Their misogyny was reflexive and they easily believed that "she took him to the cleaners," as one of them put it. To others, though, George crowed, "I just gave her the ranch, so I made out great." He got to keep his six-figure wrestling earnings while she got turkey feed. In the past the more moderate Jake Brown had helped keep George in check, dragging and wheedling him away from potential barroom brawls. Yet the quieter, younger man was so entertained, so vicariously thrilled, by his friend's oversize aggression that he often just sat back and watched. That night in the bar, for example, when the two of them were sitting at a table with some young ladies George was attempting to charm. Toward that end, George stood up, unzipped his pants, and stirred his drink with his penis. He'd seen George do some crazy things, Jake told his wife when he returned home next, but that stunt left him stunned and silent. Apparently—unaccountably—the ladies *were* charmed.

When Cantonwine came on board the orchid limo in late 1948 or early 1949, whatever balance George and Jake maintained as a twosome was lost. The Hangman usually wrestled when George did, booked somewhere on the undercards. On another night they were heading westward out of New York after they'd both worked at Sunnyside Gardens in Queens when George and Cantonwine discovered that neither of them had collected that night's payoff. Again, the cry of "Stop the car!" rang out, and the two fought. As he drank more, with this kind of supervision in place, George began to miss dates, noshowing for some booked matches. When he did arrive on time, he might not be in any condition to perform. One night in the mid-1950s George was booked with Don Arnold in San Diego. They sat in the dressing room discussing the match beforehand, how the dance would play out. On Arnold's turf, George asked him, "What are the people here used to, what do they like to see?" As they talked, he was sipping from a container. Arnold thought it was brandy; in any case, George finished off a pint getting ready.

When their match got under way, George was wobbly and his reactions were off. "He was on the ropes and I was beating on him," Arnold remembered. "He kept sinking, so I had to hold him up *while* I beat on him." The match was supposed to go another twenty minutes, but Arnold leaned in close and told George, "Let's finish." The babyface's signature move was the airplane spin, in which he lifted the opponent onto his shoulders, then spun both of them around, faster and faster, finally hurling the luckless loser into a corner, where he'd slam loudly into the mat. That's what they'd agreed on in the locker room, but out of respect for the drunken legend, Arnold held off, and instead he took George down gently.

On better nights, though, George could still command an arena crowd, and his showman's instincts remained sharp. Booked against Lou Thesz, the reigning world champion, in Las Vegas, George somehow convinced the famed stripper Gypsy Rose Lee to briefly become part of the act. (This was still George's stripper period, but there's no evidence the two had any other kind of relationship.) Lee, real name Rose Louise Hovick, was in her forties at this point, but like George she could still get heat. Just after Thesz and George entered the ring and were introduced, Lee—an unannounced guest—sashayed down the same aisle in a low-cut, open-backed, tight-fitting red gown. With her dark hair, high forehead, and wide-set eyes, she looked a little like Mary Astor of *Maltese Falcon* fame, but with a lusher body and thicker lips. As she swayed she carried a single long-stemmed rose. Entering the brightly lit ring, Lee headed directly for George. She gave a little curtsy, presented her fellow Gorgeous One the rose, then kissed him on the cheek. George accepted the tribute, nodding his appreciation, and strolled around the ring, bringing the flower to his nose for the occasional sniff, lost in a reverie of self-regard.

Lee waited a moment or two to let George work the crowd, then strutted over to Thesz's corner. When she reached the dark-haired, ruggedly good-looking wrestler, she kissed him, too—but this smooch was on the lips, a long, steamy version that made the one she'd given George seem perfunctory and chaste. Thesz cooperated and then some, bending her backward in a Hollywood clinch. George did an equally broad double take when he spied the kiss, then flew into a rage. "Stop it! *That's disgusting!*" he yelled at the lip-lockers. He threw his rose to the mat and ground it to shreds under his boot, then stormed around the ring, shaking his head and gesturing wildly with his arms. This, his actions said, was simply too much. Finally he could take no more and he ran at Lee, drawing back his open hand as if to slap her face. Thesz, the gallant stalwart, jumped in front, protecting her, so George struck him instead, and the pitched battle was on. Thesz later gave George all the credit for driving the crowd wild; the fans were on their feet the entire match.

In the early 1950s Beulah Brown insisted that Jake come off the road and stay home, and he complied. He became a milkman for Alden Farms and barely missed a day of work in thirty years. But he mourned. Jake would come home by one in the afternoon and just sit on the back steps of the house in Culver City, doing nothing, looking out at no place in particular. He missed George, rubbing shoulders with celebrities, and he missed performing. It was easy to overlook, given his supporting role, but every time the Gorgeous One was in a main event or on television, his man Jefferies was in the bright lights, too. Some afternoons he'd drive the milk truck over to the Cantonwines' in Laguna Beach to visit with Gertie and her young girls. Or he'd go see Betty, Donnie, and Carol Sue all the way up in Beaumont. After he retired, he took trips by himself in a Winnebago. Sometimes he'd take his daughter Elizabeth, whom he called Beeb. After he'd had a few beers he'd start telling his stories, which invariably began, "When I was with George . . ."

After Jake, George worked some with Nick Serfas, the L.A. bar owner, as his gentleman's gentleman, including on a trip to Australia in 1956. There, the Gorgeous One drew traffic-stopping crowds upon his arrival at the Wynyard train station in Sydney. Nick, who'd been an amateur boxer, also came in handy in warding off that country's crunch customers, who were even more aggressive in rushing the ring than their U.S. counterparts. Thomas Ross, whose deadpan was hailed at Madison Square Garden, also came back from time to time to brandish the spray gun. A year or so after that Australia jaunt, though, George found his second wife and a different dimension to the Gorgeous act, both incarnated in Cherie Dupre.

She was twenty-nine at the time, working as a showgirl at the Silver

Slipper lounge, George's Las Vegas den, which was part of the New Frontier Casino. Cherie was tiny, four-foot-nine or so, with striking green eyes and lustrous red-brown hair. Her face was oval with a prominent expanse of forehead; she looked a good deal like Loretta Young, with whom she and G.G. would later become friends. Brief but not abbreviated, she still managed to be long-legged at her height and showed off those shapely gams, her entrée to a show-business career, and the rest of her with a forthright sexiness. One publicity photo from her show-dancer days pictured her in an extremely low-cut dress, open to just above the navel. "That was the come-hither look," Cherie said later. "The coquette."

She'd met George before when she dressed up some wrestling publicity pictures he was in, and when they ran into each other again, George was already thinking about adding some pulchritude to his act. He'd seen the reaction to Lillian Ellison, who became the Fabulous Moolah, earlier in her career when she was Slave Girl Moolah. As the sexy helpmate indentured to the Elephant Boy (Bill Olivas), she wore leopard-print sandals and a dress that fell off one shoulder, like the outfits Jane wore in the Tarzan movies. One of her challengers was Daisy May, the girl from L'il Abner's Dogpatch come to life (with one letter of her name changed), who wore extremely short, ragged shorts and a blouse tied across her midriff with a deeply plunging neckline. George needed a new valet, and he always needed female companionship.

A business proposition, he told Cherie—could she stop by his room after the show to discuss? (In her telling of this story she didn't suspect his interest went further, which seems uncharacteristically naive.) When she went to his hotel room, Cherie said, George was in a smoking jacket and in his cups, and he made some crude advances, which she rebuffed. As she walked back to the elevator and began urgently pushing the buttons, George followed her out into the hall, bellowing drunkenly and "calling me every foul name you can think of."

So she married him, naturally. After apologies and flowers were issued, she said, she agreed to become his valette. She took over the

Jefferies role and added her own flair, including but not limited to her showcasing those legs in fishnet hose that ran all the way up to her val-ette-tay's posterior. Above she wore a short black jacket; a white shirt with either a bow tie or a string tie; heavy, dark eye makeup; and bright red lipstick. One sportswriter particularly liked what he saw, leering in print at the "copper-haired cutie-pie, measurements 35-20-34."

After George's death, Cherie told interviewers he'd been twenty-eight years older than her, but the difference was really fourteen years. Cherie also maintained that during the first year or so she traveled with G.G., as she always called him, before they were married in Benson, Arizona, in October 1958, their relationship was professional and they "weren't intimate." But that was almost certainly a work. Cherie had two daughters, Shari and Bobbette, from a previous marriage, and in August of 1959 she and George had a son, Gary Wayne.

Unlike Betty, who operated mostly behind the scenes, Cherie loved to perform in the ring. She adopted the deadpan, dignified air of the male valets, never cracking a smile. George and some of the other boys tried to break her mask by whispering filthy comments into her ears that the marks couldn't hear, but she never wavered. As time went on Cherie boldly got involved in the stunts and brawls, and took some bumps and potatoes of her own. Once in Odessa, Texas, George had arranged with the local babyface that Cherie would bash him in the head with the spray gun. "I talked to him," George told his wife before the match. "He won't do anything to you, don't worry." So she clocked him, and as he was supposed to, the babyface went after George instead. However, an irate, inebriated fan charged the ring, threw a body block at Cherie, and cracked three of her ribs as she slammed into the turnbuckle.

Cherie also played a prominent role—a bigger one than she'd bargained for—in an infamous sequence of matches that began one Toronto evening in March 1959. George's tilt against hometown boy "Whipper" Billy Watson in the Maple Leaf Gardens began as usual, with the valette spritzing the ring with the fragrant odor of Chanel Number 10. However, this match, as advertised heavily by promoter Frank Tunney, carried an unprecedented gimmick: If he lost, Watson vowed, he would retire, a threat the besotted locals took as dire. If George lost, the result would be even more unthinkable: The famous peroxided locks would be immediately shorn in the ring. It's not clear why George would have agreed to lose this "hair match"; perhaps a substantial bonus payment did the trick. He succumbed to Watson's Canuck Commando, a variant on the sleeper hold, in front of fourteen thousand screaming fans, whereupon a wooden stool was placed in the middle of the ring. To save her master from the ignominy of the waiting barber, Cherie immediately sat down on the stool and refused to move. But the forces of order hauled her away and George, wearing just his white trunks and boots, was, as one Toronto paper described it, transformed into Yul Brynner, as Cherie sobbed uncontrollably. She gathered the clipped Gorgeous hair in a towel. It would be preserved in a special urn, the newspaper informed its readers, and then offered to the Smithsonian Institution in Washington. Immediately after the shearing George ran ashamedly from the ring, trying to cover up his shorn scalp with both arms. The next day's headline was GORGEOUS JUST ISN'T AFTER WHIP WINS, and the caption to the accompanying photo read: "Hi, Baldy!"

Very soon thereafter George was a celebrity guest on the popular TV game show *I've Got a Secret,* hosted at that point by Garry Moore. The celebrity panel—Bess Myerson, the former Miss America; actress Betsy Palmer, who was in *The Last Angry Man* that year; Bill Cullen, a future host of the show; and comedian Henry Morgan—couldn't guess George's secret: He was wearing a blond wig over his stubble, which Cherie ceremoniously removed for the audience and the stumped panel.

Of course there had to be a rematch with Whipper Watson, but George didn't have any marcel left to bet. So he put up Cherie's hair. She only agreed, she said, "because I was told G.G. would get the win somehow." But there was a double cross, either by the promoters or by

George betraying his red-haired wife. She was furious, struggling mightily against the men who held her for the clipping, and her surprise and anger appeared to be genuine. Unlike George, Cherie didn't get shaved completely, but her hair was shorn quite short; afterward she made the promoter buy her a human-hair wig.

Adding some sex appeal to his matches proved a good thing for George and it's still a wrestling staple. The classic combination is beefcake (the male wrestler) paired with cheesecake, a female "manager," preferably scantily clad. Once again George kept his relationship with his wife under wraps and in the ring they showed each other no affection, rarely touching. He acted the irascible master and she the long-suffering servant. As he did with Jefferies, George turned on this loyal helpmate in the ring. After a loss, he would blame her for his defeat, remonstrating with her and drawing back a fist; she'd counter by threatening him with the spray gun. This churlishness played well with the marks, making them angrier at George, but it also distanced the wrestler and the valette. In the subliminal script they acted out, her sexuality meant nothing to him; it was only for the crowd.

Cherie's presence created yet another facet in the Gorgeous One's already complex presentation, raising new questions and reviving familiar ones about the wrestler and just where his sexual loyalties might lie. Who or what was this queenly brute, really, this killer fruitcake? As Cherie noted, "George didn't really come off as gay," like Keith Franks, who wrestled as Adorable Adrian Adonis, or the bizarrely cross-dressed Adrian Street, both of whom effected less subtle "queer" personae in the ring. Yet George was also the furthest thing from a straitlaced macho man like Thesz. The Gorgeous One seemed neither completely manly nor wholly feminine. Instead, Cherie said perceptively, the Gorgeous persona was really something in between . . .

Chapter 23

BETWEEN A FLIT AND A MINCE

When George's fame reached a certain critical mass, he could no longer be denied the appropriate tribute: a Gorgeous George movie. Hedda Hopper, who kept the nation abreast of Gorgeous doings in her syndicated Hollywood column, called on the industry to "celluloid" him, and in 1949 Republic Pictures complied. That year Carol Reed's *The Third Man* with Orson Welles, *White Heat* with James Cagney, and *All the King's Men* with a bravura performance by Broderick Crawford were all released and they've since become film classics. Gorgeous George's first and only movie would not be joining them. *Alias the Champ* compares more favorably to another 1949 film attempting to cash in on an athlete's popularity, *The Story of Seabiscuit,* a racing saga into which the producers somehow managed to inject a teenage Shirley Temple.

Alias the Champ never aspired to cinematic grandeur, but at least Republic reconsidered the original title, *Pardon My Toehold.* When it was released, *Alias* played mostly as the second act in double features, and George's flick had a run in Mexico, where it was entitled *Jorge El Magnífico.* Reaction to this B picture was drily distilled in the *L.A. Times* sports pages when previewing a 1950 match: "Gorgeous George, who may win an Oscar for his performance in 'Alias the Champ'—and again, may not—will wrestle Lord Blears of England . . ."

It's a murder mystery with a wrestling backdrop, and six of G.G.'s ring buddies had roles. Hoodlums from New York are attempting to take over California's upstanding grunt-and-groan game, and when George won't play along, they frame him for murder. Homicide Lieutenant Ron Peterson, played by Robert Rockwell (of *Our Miss Brooks*) uses a replay of a kinescoped match to cleverly crack the case, with the help of George's lovely manager, Lorraine Connors. As might be expected, sparks of romance fly between the lieutenant and the manageress, but *Alias* is really a showcase for George, who plays himself quite naturally and confidently, holding the big screen. What's really remarkable about the film, though, is the high level of camp he reaches, seeming to channel Talullah Bankhead, Bette Davis, and Mae West in an arch and hilariously queenly turn.

"Beat it, Junior, you bore me," he tells the detective grandly at one point, flicking him away with one dangling wrist. Later he scornfully advises the lieutenant to "See my valet; he has a knack with children." (Jack Hunter got this screen role over Jake Brown, for some reason.) As George decamps—or demanifests—from one scene he stands in the doorway and gestures like a bossy dowager aunt for Audrey Long to accompany him. "Come, little one," he pronounces grandly. "It's time for my marcel."

Most American men in the postwar era hewed considerably closer to the ethos of machismo. In America's idea of itself and the images entertainment provided—including war movies such as *The Sands of Iwo Jima*, starring John Wayne, and *A Walk in the Sun*, with square-jawed Dana Andrews—this was a nation of conquering tough guys who'd fought and died in a just cause. If there were other ways of being a man, Americans didn't seem to want to know about them. In Hollywood, gay or bisexual stars' greatest fear was that they would be outed, for which the sentence, imposed immediately, was box-office death. The fictional world of detective stories and noir films, created before the war, was still influential, and in it contempt for anything queer was overt. In Raymond Chandler's novel *The Big Sleep*, Philip Marlowe takes a punch from a very handsome young man named Carol Lundgren and shrugs it off. "It was meant to be a hard one," he narrates, "but a pansy has no iron in his bones." The detective knocks the boy unconscious, but not before calling his older boyfriend a queen and a fag.

In this attitudinal landscape the apparition of a wrestling man with a feminine tinge, who exuded vanity—thought to be a female trait, and tolerable only in women—was quite a shock. Some sensed that the disturbance George caused was sexual in nature, and thus alarming. In Tacoma, Washington, public-safety commissioner James T. Kerr demanded that the local board of censors investigate G.G.'s matches. These performances, he felt, might constitute a threat to public morals. (No outcome was discoverable.) George was convincingly, even excessively heterosexual; of that there's no reasonable doubt. But since he raised the issue, many wondered. When Bob Hope and Burt Lancaster agreed to work with George at the charity circus, the first question they asked his stand-in, Vic Holbrook, was: Is George gay? Holbrook was astonished that two Hollywood showmen didn't recognize a performance when they saw one.

George clearly invited the curses and shouts of "Queer!" and "Sissy!" directed at him, becoming a lightning rod in the arenas. In his business any strong reaction was a good one; homophobia was just another form of heat. Yet, amid the indignation the crowds worked themselves into over George's taboo behavior, they admired his daring, too. A few onlookers may have been truly angry, but wider swaths of the postwar audiences enjoyed being startled by George in his certain, special ways. The electricity coming off the Gorgeous One's strutting form wasn't just garden-variety stimulation—that jolt, though powerful, was as old as pornography—but a new and ambiguous frisson, a much more subtle sensation. He invited onlookers to enjoy his thrilling transgressions, but only vicariously. So much of what Gorgeous George did and said set himself apart from the audience, and that positioning allowed the public to participate without endorsing him or becoming like him—whatever that meant, exactly. Being a "sissy"? A "fruit"? No, not them.

By determinedly keeping his family life a secret—a habit so ingrained it was noted in his obituaries—George kept his sexual identity as mysterious and open to interpretation as possible. In its profile of George, *Time* magazine seemed genuinely puzzled. "He doesn't seem to mind playing his swishy role," the writer noted. "But he steps out of character whenever anybody asks nosey questions about his wife and two kids. 'Let's leave the better half of my life outta this, yes?'" Though of course neither effeminacy nor cross-dressing is the same thing as homosexuality, George's drag turn compelled some to defend his heterosexual honor. Hannibal Coons, writing in *Sport* magazine, simply denied unequivocally that the wrestler acted effeminate. "George never uses a swishy voice or a swishy gesture. George is above that. His role is that of the powdered, beautifully dressed, ageless, worldly monarch." In 1948, the early days of Gorgeousness, a San Francisco paper ran a picture of George with his robe open and the caption "Not a Sissy Physique." When George wrestled Ernie Dusek at Madison Square Garden the next year, *New York Times* sports columnist Arthur Daley saw that he was only playacting—but found that as objectionable as the real thing. As the match unfolded, Daley wrote, "feelings of disgust grew in leaps and bounds . . . A display of effeminacy in a man, even simulated effeminacy, is nauseating and Gorgeous George has made himself over into a most revolting character."

The definition of what he did in his Gorgeous act can be parsed very fine, the degree of swishiness debated. George called it "flitting," as in "I flitted to the ring." Yet director John Waters, a gay man who was inspired by George, stressed that the wrestling diva didn't *mince*. It's an important distinction, Waters said: George had a queenly manner, yet "he wasn't a big mincing queen, a bad stereotype that a straight man would use to put others down, which would have been offensive." Whatever Gorgeous George was, or pretended to be, it wasn't gay per se. The Beautiful Bicep, as one scribe dubbed him, sent out deliberately mixed messages, and it was in this realm of uncertainty and contradictory possibilities that George did his most original work. *Newsweek* spoke to George's complexity, declaring that "this anomalous figure is a mass of incongruities, even to the epithets hurled at him from the gallery, such as: 'T'row de bum out.' Gorgeous George looks anything but a bum . . ."

As Gorgeous, George was a snob, a faux aristocrat who put on airs and derided the peasants. But he was also a manual laborer, and on some level, audiences must have known that George was really a working stiff, lampooning the rich and pretentious. He was a sniveling coward who ran away from conflict—and then he beat people up, absorbing pain and punishment in the next instant. He was a despised heel, yet even in the arenas, cauldrons in which George's villainy incited bellowed rage and thrown projectiles, he was in some ways beloved. He provoked the fans like no other, giving them license to match their bizarre behavior to his, and for that they were secretly grateful. As writer Al Geronomus acutely observed in a *Boxing Illustrated* piece, many in the wrestling audiences "jeered him with a smile and hated him with affection."

Most powerfully of all, he was effeminate and macho, butch and femme, gay and not gay; all of these things at once. At the end of Milton Berle's televised drag skits he always removed his wig or other female accoutrements, showing himself as a man. Similarly, George followed his prissy antics with the manly act of wrestling, and this transition probably served a similar function, un-womaning both performers. In addition, whatever gay possibilities did adhere to his girlie man act were divorced from any overt homosexuality, and thus less threatening. The boys wouldn't care to hear it, but in a sport in which two barely clothed and oiled men try to mount each other, there's a bit of a homoerotic subtext. However, as theater professor Sharon Mazer pointed out in her book *Professional Wrestling: Sport and Spectacle,* wrestling is "contact between men with built-in denials" that it's sexual.

More importantly, the wrestler earned a star entertainer's immunity. Gorgeous George was an accepted fact of life, practically an institution—if he was swishy, he was a celebrated swish. This may have served George well when the 1950s turned their most intolerant. The Red Scare and the congressional hearings fronted by Wisconsin senator Joseph McCarthy are usually thought of as a witch hunt intended to root out Communists in American government. But investigators were also obsessed with rooting out homosexuals. The Senate's "pervert inquiry," begun in 1950, purportedly found two hundred gays in the civil service and the military and many were dismissed for "sexual causes." In that climate, sexual insouciance in someone else—a civilian or a mark—might have gotten them punished. But George sailed on by. As he put it with characteristic bluntness, "I became so well known that people would say, 'There goes Gorgeous George,' instead of 'There goes a pansy.'"

His gender-bending was perfectly calibrated—titillating but not threatening—and once again his timing was excellent. In the postwar period Americans began to allow themselves slightly more open expressions of their intense, perennial curiosity about things done in the dark. The Kinsey Report, released in 1948, made thinking and talking about sexual mores respectable; it was scientific. In a more lurid, voyeuristic show of our fascination with sex and gender, the country became obsessed with a former World War II private from New York, George Jorgensen, who went to Denmark and came back in 1952 as Christine Jorgensen. One reporter in the swarms asked her if and where her former male genitalia had been preserved; suddenly a penis was front-page news. Jorgensen managed to live gracefully in her new incarnation, and even became a performer and entertainer; as George did, she played nightclub dates in Hollywood and Las Vegas.

Only once did George issue a direct denial of homosexuality. "I am not a you-know-what," he told an interviewer in 1951. "If you read history, you know that men wore curls and lace before women did." He might have made one other implicitly hetero statement in 1957 when he announced: "I am suing *Confidential* magazine for the unauthorized use of my name, which has been copyrighted, without my permission. I am seeking $250,000 in damages." It's not legally possible to copyright a name (he could have trademarked Gorgeous George,

228 · GORGEOUS GEORGE

but federal records indicate he didn't), so if there really was a suit, it went nowhere.

The reason for George's bluster, aside from the usual one, publicity, seems to be that he was mentioned in an article on Liberace, who was suing the magazine for $25 million over the same piece. The offending story was touted on the cover under a picture of the grinning pianist and singer, who showed perfect white teeth and wore a tiger-print bow tie. The headline read EXCLUSIVE: WHY LIBERACE'S THEME SONG SHOULD BE, "MAD ABOUT THE BOY!" *Confidential* detailed Liberace's pursuit of a young, "innocent" male publicist. "The sour note came when the Kandelabra Kid tried to turn public relations into private relations," the magazine noted in its trademark style. One such encounter, the writer said, had "all the lively action and wild comedy of a TV wrestling match. A referee certainly would have penalized the panting pianist for illegal holds." When a purring Liberace came after the "reluctant ballyhoo boy" a second time, the story recounted, "before you could say Gorgeous George, the pair were playing a return wrestling match."

Presumably, it was being mentioned in this gay context that angered George. Then again, George had never liked the panting pianist. He felt—and he complained loud and long—that "Liberace stole my entire act, including the candelabra!" G.G. maintained that he'd had his valets carry lit candelabra to the ring early in his career in Texas, though fire marshals had later forbidden the flaming prop. In all likelihood this wasn't true, but it's certainly possible that Liberace was influenced by the Gorgeous act. Though he became a star in 1944, the pianist never even dared to wear a white tuxedo instead of the traditional black onstage until 1952, and it wasn't until 1955, when George's fabulosity had been on national display for seven years or more, that Liberace first performed with a gold lamé jacket and tie, moving from there into glittering outfits of brocade and beads, and then into capes, and still later, wigs. Seeing George's success in the mainstream may have emboldened Liberace to make a glittering, queenie show of himself. Of course at the time most admirers of the singing pianist, including many older women, didn't know or wouldn't admit that their Lee was gay. To them Liberace was exquisitely sensitive, too much so for brutish men to understand—just the rationale many soprano fans used to explain their fealty to Gorgeous George.

The knowledge that George wasn't gay, and didn't act effeminate or cross-dress in private, begs the question: Where did he get the moves? How did the Harrisburg Rat and brawling wrestler learn his provocative performance art? His voguing seemed so natural, as if this was the real George or at least a real part of him. It's accepted lore in the wrestling world that Sterling "Dizzy" Davis, George's boyhood friend, was gay or bisexual, and that George accepted him without any difficulty. It's possible that George took more than the orchid gimmick from Dizzy (who'd used gardenias). More likely, though, he learned to flit in the big, bad city, where everyone goes to experience—or at least to brush up against—the forbidden and the extreme.

When George came to New York in the mid-1930s, Prohibition had only recently been repealed. During that period of banned vice, a culture emerged, especially in America's big cities, that was much more daring and permissive. In the 1920s white New Yorkers with money had gone up to Harlem to get their kicks at Negro nightclubs and brothels. By the early 1930s another marginalized culture broke out in "the Pansy Craze." Now New Yorkers went to Greenwich Village, and to Harlem again, to drink and watch gay comedians and singers like the campy wit Gene Malin, as well as "ambisextrous" female impersonators, including Ray Bourbon. Soon these acts were supplemented by a formerly underground event known as the drag ball. Blacks and whites attended these contests in Harlem at the Savoy Ballroom and the Rockland Palace, which held six thousand people. Mae West wrote a play called *The Drag*, which opened only in New Jersey due to legal problems stemming from her earlier Broadway play *Sex*. To cast this second one West auditioned fifty cross-dressing men she'd met at Paul & Joe's, a gay bar on West Ninth Street in the Village. The drags spread to the theater district around Times Square and other Manhattan arenas, some of which, including the St. Nicholas

Arena at Sixty-sixth Street and Columbus Avenue, also hosted wrestling.

At the drag balls gay men, stunningly transformed into the most exotic and outrageous women, would parade down a central runway. A panel of judges would declare one of them the most fabulous, the queen of the drag. Each contestant would take on a distinct and complete persona—one might be a Spanish señorita, another a Southern debutante at her coming-out party—and a new identity. Just like George and the boys in their ring characters, the draggers reinvented themselves, and then performed with high drama. These lovely and regal creations didn't mince, it should be noted: They strutted.

Everyone—or everyone in the nightlife, the show people, demimondes, and bon vivants—went to the drags. Men took their wives and dates. Slapsy Maxie Rosenbloom, the boxer who would later hire George to perform at his L.A. nightclub, was a habitué in those days. By the time George got to New York, after Repeal, another cultural shift was under way, a reversal that would again repress gays with "degeneracy laws." But the drags continued to be held, as long as the police were paid off sufficiently, and at them liquor was still being served, though it was now, less excitingly, legal. On an off night, would twenty-two-year-old George Wagner, a young wrestler with a taste for the outlandish and the first real money he'd ever made in his pockets, have gone to the drags? Quite likely. If he did, would he have taken mental notes on the gorgeous creatures he saw there? Almost certainly.

In the late 1940s, when George was becoming a national celebrity, a magazine called *Sports Week* attacked him in print. This hatchet job, by one Marty Berg, was headlined PHONY SISSY'S MAT FRAUD. "This George gee is positively the last word in rassle finesse," Berg hammered into his typewriter, "all because he has all the earmarks of what we kids used to call a 'sissy' . . . the mannerisms that go with a swish-boy. They went wild for him on the West Coast, where the sissy production runs high, anyway."

Gorgeous George used to be George Wagner, the story revealed, and showed a picture of him in the early, black-haired days. "He's emerged with a new look and that makes him a phony," Berg declared, "a bilker of the public," though how one could condemn a pro wrestler for adopting a ring persona at that point is hard to fathom. Berg then floats the notion that G.G. might have gotten the inspiration "for affecting the sissy business after he'd visited a 'drag' at the St. Nick in NY, where those shindigs used to be popular." The caption under the photo read "Pantywaist George."

Chapter 24

INTO THE DRINK

Betty heard about George's new wife, including a bit from him, and she was curious. One day she got word that he and Cherie were making a promotional appearance near the turkey ranch, lending their presence to the opening of a service station around Redlands. She didn't think of it as spying, exactly; Betty and her sister simply wanted to get a look at the new Mrs. George. She borrowed her hairdresser's car so George wouldn't recognize her purple Packard and watched through a store window across the street. Very few people came, and that led Betty to think of the time she'd attended a Jehovah's Witness assembly with him in the same area a few years earlier, when he'd been mobbed by kids and adults alike.

Betty watched as George handed out a few Georgie pins at the gas station. Then she saw Cherie and for a moment caught her breath. First, Betty thought she recognized her, that she'd seen her around Redlands before, maybe at Pinky's, where she was a cocktail waitress. And that raised certain suspicions. But mostly she was taken aback by Cherie's looks, her stature, the way she appeared standing next to George. "She was my size," Betty said, remembering that odd feeling. "She was pretty, too, I'll give her that, and she had a nice figure.

I mean, I couldn't help but notice the similarities. She could have been my sister." Betty didn't say anything to Eve.

Betty's sense was right, even more than she knew. George was trying to re-create what he'd lost. Just as he and Betty had done, George and Cherie bought a little camper trailer, pulling it behind their car as they traveled with their children—her two daughters and their infant son, Gary—to wrestling dates. Cherie called this time, early in their marriage, the fondest memory of her life with George, just as Betty did. "We camped at different parks, including a big one near Las Vegas," Cherie said. "Gary was in a little playpen, and I remember George romping and playing with his son and step-daughters. Other wrestlers were staying there, too; they'd have us over, then we'd have them over. It was a wonderful time that I'll never forget." Like the curator of a living diorama, George placed his new family members in the same tableau his former wife and children had occupied in his own happiest days. He left out only Judy the dog.

There were differences in the dynamics of the two families, certainly, and as even George must have realized on some level, he wasn't the same man. Cherie was tougher and harder-edged than Betty, which made her a more capable and more frequent adversary for George. She battled harder and could drink with George longer, due in part to her upbringing (her French parents had wine on the dinner table every night). George did maintain a certain continuity in his two marriages, however, bringing to the second the same deficits that helped ruin the first. He was still gambling, for one. When Gary was a toddler, George, Cherie, and the three children settled in Reseda, not far from Windsor Hills, in Los Angeles County. One night Cherie came home while a poker game was in progress at their house and saw her fur coat lying in the middle of the table. George had put it up as collateral.

Drunk or sober, George wasn't a lucky gambler. And, though he loved to show off his card tricks and manipulations, he wasn't a very good one. Once after wrestling in Nashville, with Cherie joining him in the ring, George lost all his earnings in Printers Alley, that city's

French Quarter. Cherie went to the casino the next day and threatened to sue them for taking advantage of George in his drunken condition, but got no satisfaction. They'd driven to Nashville in the camper
trailer (without the children on this trip), and when George was out
gambling that night, a small pack of wrestlers decided to pull a swerve
on the couple. Jessica Rogers, Penny Banner, the Fargo Brothers, and
Ray Stevens got together and moved the trailer to another spot. The
swerve worked: When George and Cherie got home early that morning, inebriated and infuriated, respectively, they were certainly surprised. And it took them a long, acrimonious while to find their
all-too-mobile home. When the wrestlers saw Cherie, still fuming, the
next morning and heard how badly her evening had gone beforehand,
none of them wanted to take any credit for the swerve. Instead, they
sympathized, then slunk away.

As Betty had done, Cherie began to stay home more, so George
used fill-in valets when he traveled. Without her along, he missed
dates, including one on a New York swing for promoter Vince McMahon Sr., and the state athletic commission suspended him. The demand for George had already begun to cool. Television was no longer
an exciting novelty but a less remarkable fact, and broadcasters were
trying to attract more upscale viewers and advertisers. By the mid-1950s
wrestling no longer aired much on the networks, shunted instead onto
local stations, where it would remain for decades. A younger cadre of
wrestlers, including Vern Gagne, Killer Kowalski, Pat O'Connor, Chief
Don Eagle, and Yukon Eric (he of the missing ear) had by now equaled
George in popularity, or surpassed him. The mention of George's
name, or a knowing reference to his arrogant personality, still drew
smiles to American faces, but he'd lost some of his power to outrage
and inflame. Now he was regarded with something more like
affection—Mean Old George had become Good Old George.

Tom Drake, the Wrestling Sergeant, who'd worked lucrative main
events with George in Georgia during the Korean War, encountered
him again in Jasper, Alabama, in 1960. Drake had just been elected to
the Alabama legislature; he would serve two terms as the speaker of

the house under Governor George Wallace. So he was now billed as the Wrestling Legislator. Drake noticed right away that George had developed quite a stomach; he'd lost muscle tone and put on weight. He still had the robes and the pins, but his fancy ring attire was looking a little worn. The headliner was driving himself on this trip, without a valet, and when he got to Jasper's old armory, he lacked the energy Drake remembered. He didn't need it. After everyone in the locker room got dressed, oiled, and pumped, the promoter came in and told them to stand down. No one had showed up; there weren't enough fans in the house to go on. The promoter gave George a few dollars for expenses and gas, and Drake and the others reached into their pockets as well.

Though they were fewer, on good nights he could still give the fans their money's worth. In 1961, at the very end of his career, he performed again at the Aqua Theater, on Green Lake in Seattle. Here the ring was surrounded by water, and a lifeguard or second referee circled the floating wrestling action in a rowboat, with a concrete grandstand facing the action on shore. Like the gun introduced early in a mystery that must go off at some point, the laws of drama demanded that the water come into play. It was a cool July evening, and by the time the main event got started around nine-thirty, a dip was less than appealing, but a deal was a deal. When George, wearing a billowing red satin number festooned with pink lace, was set to lose a fall to Leaping Leo Garibaldi, he still had the athleticism—and the willingness—to sell Leo's dropkick by hurling himself backward over the ropes and into the drink. When George hit the cold, twelve-foot-deep lake water, the alarmed announcer shouted: "He can't swim!" (He could.)

George still felt at home around the boys, and he hadn't lost his sense of humor. When George worked another small town with Drake, this one in Tennessee, a couple of the boys on the card had heard that he was afraid of snakes (he may have had a bad experience with one back in Harrisburg's Buffalo Bayou). After George's main event was over and he'd showered and changed, one of the local workers offered him a cigar. When he opened the cigar box, the wrestler's pet garter snake raised its head. It was just a tiny harmless thing, but George recoiled, jumping back into the metal lockers, yelling "God damn!" Then he had to laugh—they'd got him. On another night Cherie substituted beer for perfume in the spray gun and gave him a spritz in the ring, trying to get him to react out of character, and he appreciated that, too. But a swerve a day was no longer keeping the blues away.

If she hadn't known it before, Cherie soon learned her husband was "a full-blown alcoholic," as she described him. "He couldn't control it—one drink and he'd be off to the races." Cherie thought George used alcohol to fuel the outrageous behavior his Gorgeous persona constantly required. Without booze, she said, "he didn't really have the nerve to do those things." Betty never had an explanation beyond what she saw as George's fundamental insecurity; the reasons for his drinking never came up between them, just the results.

The forensics of alcoholism is always very speculative, especially at such a remove of time. It does run in families; however, there's no sign that drink was involved in George's mother's invalidism and death. Poppa Wagner seems to have lived a long life that, though not always easy, was uncomplicated by alcohol. He'd have a drink with Betty on the porch of the turkey ranch, but one was all he cared for. George was immersed in an alcohol-soaked business, where drinking was encouraged and considered manly. And life on the wrestling road led many to drink; it was rootless, lonely, and pain was a near constant.

It seems, though, that George was troubled before he became one of the boys. The Wagners were poorer than most, but George's true deprivation growing up would have been emotional, internal. His family life was dominated by Bessie's illness, which literally uprooted the family as they moved around the Midwest and to Houston in search of a cure. In the young firstborn son, the unspoken possibility of losing his mother must have created tremendous fear. When she was capable of it, Bessie was a loving mother to George, but she couldn't parent fully or consistently; *she* needed constant attention.

At times she was all but paralyzed and her arms and legs were suspended in canvas slings, used to move her so she wouldn't get bedsores. Cherie described this in a videotaped interview for the Canadian television documentary. An older woman, close to death from emphysema, Cherie interrupted herself frequently with fits of coughing. Her face was gaunt; as she talked, her own failing health seemed to stand in for George's mother's. Cherie demonstrated Bessie's incapacity for the camera by raising both arms high over her shoulders and dangling them as if suspended, her elbows bent, hands flopping limp. In this portrayal George's mother looked both a pathetic and a scary creature, incapable of embrace.

Instead, George may have gotten something more intermittent and contingent, closer to appreciation: sincere praise and gratitude from his parents for helping his invalid mother. When that happens, psychologists tell us, the result can be a narcissist, someone who comes to rely on—to require—admiration from others, the reflected glory the original Narcissus saw in the water. He may feel inadequate on some level but along with that comes a kind of grandiosity. His need for attention and approval becomes his right to have it: He deserves it. Artists, including the geniuses, are often narcissistic (as are elite athletes). They turn their need for admiration into creative achievement, and if they succeed, that gives them a certain social license to strut.

George wasn't a syndrome or a walking pathology, but he did create the life of the ultimate narcissist. He chose a profession based on calling attention to oneself, then devised the Gorgeous act, in which he shouted out his superiority. Television became an incredibly potent enabler, providing a whole new body of attention, which the narcissist confuses with love. George swam in it, and may have drowned in it. Cruelly, when adult George was given the love he needed as a child, by Betty, he couldn't fully accept it. He didn't know how to take it in, process it, and extract the benefit; he'd never had the practice.

In another emotional reading of his ring act, George, having seen his mother get the attention he craved, dolled himself up like her to get attention himself. Taken even further, he'd be angry at Bessie for her unintentional abandonment, and so he called down condemnation on her—that is, him in female form—from the rafters and the angry crowds. In this scenario, the valet, the little, loyal, ever-attentive helpmate, is George.

When the admiration in George's mirror was disrupted—the failure of his first marriage, and later, the public fever for him abating—his drinking accelerated. Alcohol was the second outside force he looked to for comfort that failed to love him back sufficiently. At first drinking reliably numbed the pain; then it didn't. After a while it caused him even more pain. But still he clung.

If his childhood did George damage, however, it was also his gift. The boy must have learned to read his mother's changing condition and availability very closely: "How is she feeling? What can she do and not do?" And, most fundamentally, "What can she give me?" He'd become very adept at getting her attention, working mightily to pull it toward himself through her suffering. As an adult, George could sense very acutely what drew people and what lost them, and his success as an entertainer was based on that ability. In his private life, he knew what to say and do to make women lovers and men loyal. That sounds coldly manipulative, but in life—in George—it produced warmth. He wanted to be liked, and became truly likable. Just as there was a tinge of genuine meanness in Mean Old George that made his ring villainy so compelling, there was real good in Good Old George.

Whatever led him to adopt his Gorgeous alter ego, changing identities as he did almost certainly contributed to George's downfall. Artists have to take risks, but this one can be especially unmooring. Consistently, some of those who create new personae—from Papa Hemingway, the Great White Writer, to Tupac Shakur, the thug— flounder trying to reconcile the old and the new, or to incorporate both in a single coherent self. The mainstream culture can reward those who shock us with the transgressive ideas they embody and portray, but often there's a price: These new, exaggerated selves no longer fit into life's constraints. It seems that George had the imagination and determination to make his Gorgeous leap, but couldn't continue to inhabit the extreme character he created. Ultimately, pitiably, he wasn't able to live with his first self or live up to his second. Nor could he overcome the power of the past.

Chapter 25

THE ORCHID AND THE BUTTERFLY

I am the greatest! I cannot be defeated! All my so-called opponents are afraid of me, and they're right to be afraid—because I am the king! I'm warning everybody right now: If this bum I'm fighting messes up the pretty waves in my hair, I'm going to kill him. I'll tear off his arm! And if that uneducated punk somehow manages to beat me, I'll crawl across the ring and cut off all my beautiful hair—and then I'll take the next jet to Russia! But that will never happen, because I am the greatest!"

It's George, of course, holding forth at a Las Vegas radio station in June of 1961. The bum he's about to grapple with is Fred Blassie, and the venue, the new Convention Center just off the Strip. As boastful rants go, it's a fine one, delivered with style and conviction. What sets it apart, however, is the audience, one particular listener. A much younger man, strong and athletic, he sits five or six feet away from George in the radio studio. He takes in the wrestler's words and energy, processing them with his own quick mind. In what will become an increasingly rare event, this younger athlete—he's a boxer—is quiet and still, smiling as he feels Gorgeous George's braggadocio at work on him even though he understands perfectly that it's a manufactured act, a gimmick. Perhaps he recognizes a like soul. The boxer's name is Cassius Clay.

The nineteen-year-old Clay and the forty-six-year-old Gorgeous One sit on either side of the radio host—it might be Charlie Swan, at either KORK or KLAS—at a long wooden table. A short, fat-headed microphone stands on the table in front of each man. Standing behind them with his back against the studio's rough cinder-block wall is Mel "Red" Greb, who's promoting both of their upcoming bouts. The promoter wears black-framed glasses and his red hair slicked back; he's about five-foot-seven and above him a huge wall clock counts off the minutes of the 1 P.M., half-hour show.

Clay has won a gold medal at the Rome Olympics, but he's unproven as a professional fighter. *Sports Illustrated* calls him "an unsophisticated Olympic gold medalist who hasn't run out of luck . . . physically and mentally immature." Even his own trainer, Angelo Dundee, tells the reporters, "I can run down a list of twenty things he does wrong." Clay's in Las Vegas for his seventh pro fight (he won all the previous ones relatively easily); his opponent is Kolo "Duke" Sabedong, a hulking six-foot-six Hawaiian. This fight tops a Monday-night card, when the new Convention Center cannot be put to any more lucrative use. Like all of Clay's matches to date, it won't be televised.

Today he wears dark slacks, an open-collared white shirt, and a blazer patterned with small black and white checks. His new clothes fit him well. At this age Clay is still quite slender; at 195 pounds he's grown since the Olympics, but shirtless in the ring a few nights later, his back looks almost concave. The young boxer's arms are long snakes; his eighty-inch wingspan will make the Ali jab deadly. His muscles are supple and distributed smoothly, without prominent bulging, over a six-foot-three frame. Over those muscles his light brown skin with its moist, slightly oily texture, has the color and surface tension of a well-made cigar. His features are symmetrical, his face handsome, and his smile is engaging. He's a superb athlete in top condition, and there's something more: Clay has his own special energy.

Like the man he'll become, Muhammad Ali, young Cassius

Marcellus Clay Jr. is singularly mutable: When he's excited, his voice is high, up in George's unexpected register, but at other, calmer times, it's a deep rumble. He alternates between spurts of dynamism and near lethargy, when he seems to be recharging his power supply. Clay is already being called cocky and brash for his prediction that he'll win the heavyweight championship of the world before he turns twenty-one. Many resent that claim—in this age, fight managers brag, not fighters. And black fighters' boasts are the least appreciated. Yet many who come in contact with him in these early days are struck by how quiet, soft-spoken, and respectful he is—shy, they say, especially around girls. This afternoon Clay is either in a low gear or, since he is interviewed first, he may not be fully warmed up. When asked about the outcome of his ten-rounder against the thirty-one-year-old Sabe-dong, he says fairly mildly that "somebody's got to go before the tenth, and you can bet it won't be me." Later he will remember: "I can't say I was humble, but I wasn't too loud."

George waits his turn, wearing his usual loud clash of colors and knit tam over his blond curls. Juxtaposed with the tall fighter, he looks wider and whiter than ever, and he appears, as indeed he is, more than twice as old. But he still has the force of his Gorgeousness. Asked again about his match with Blassie, George hunches forward over the microphone, with one forearm on either side of the device, and testifies on his own behalf. "I am the Gorgeous One! Not only am I the best wrestler, the most highly skilled, with the greatest technique, but I'm also the most beautiful wrestler who ever lived! That's why all these curs, these ignorant brutes, don't want to take me on—they're afraid of my brilliant style of wrestling. And they know that the fans only want to gaze upon my manly beauty." Clay knows it's a performance but still finds himself thinking, *Man, I want to see this fight. It don't matter if he wins or loses; I want to be there to see what happens.*

A night or two later the two appear together on KLAS-TV, Channel 8, the local CBS affiliate, on sports editor Dick Porter's segment, *In This Corner.* Afterward George, always affable with fellow athletes, invites the kid to come and see him work. "Red will bring you," he tells Cassius. "And come by the locker room after, and we'll talk." Maybe George sensed a like soul as well; he seems inordinately interested in the young boxer. "One more thing," he adds with a smile and a clap on the black man's back: "You can stop calling me 'sir.' Just call me Gorgeous."

Brash, young John F. Kennedy had just succeeded old, modest Ike, effectively archiving the 1950s and making the 1940s, when Gorgeous George came to stardom and television was new, seem positively archaic. JFK was promoted by his father, Joseph Kennedy, the Vince McMahon of American politics. The handsome president's youthful vitality was something of a work (outside the bedroom), as he had already been diagnosed with Addison's disease. But that fact didn't fit the forty-three-year-old babyface's image, so it was suppressed. In the televised presidential debates, broadcast to 70 million viewers, the ill-shaven, sweating Republican Richard Nixon seemed almost eager to play the heel.

The failed U.S. invasion of Cuba at the Bay of Pigs was just two months past; America's Red enemies and the nuclear threat they were thought to represent were ever-present preoccupations. Daringly, given that surround, Cassius Clay gave statements to the Las Vegas press the week of his fight there that generated this headline: YOUNG FIGHTER CLAIMS RUSSIANS NOT SO BAD: HE SAYS REDS, U.S. CAN BE FRIENDS.

At the Olympics, Clay told the reporters, he'd actually met a Red or two. "When we moved into the Olympic Village we found we were neighbors with the Russians," he said. "Some of them became friends for life." He continued with this apostate line, adding that he saw the same friendly attitudes among the athletes from the other Eastern-bloc countries. He saw no reason, Clay concluded, why East and West could not live together in peace. As Muhammad Ali, he would make a similar declaration about another of America's enemies. When resisting induction into the military during the war in Vietnam, he will famously say, "I got no quarrel with them Viet Cong."

Las Vegas was booming: The Convention Center, 515,000 square feet on forty-five acres, had begun to bring in name-tagged tourists from all over the country, joining the gamblers and nightlifers who'd come before. Delta and National airlines just announced that they will extend their routes to serve the city. Vegas casinos and clubs had only been integrated a year before, averting threatened protest marches and boycotts. Previously Las Vegas had been so harshly segregated that the city was called "the Mississippi of the West." In June 1961 that change was far from complete. Mel Greb booked rooms for Clay and his mother, Odessa Clay, at the Dunes in his own name, and when the hotel operators saw just who their guests were, they weren't happy and let the promoter know it.

Young Cassius hadn't yet rebelled against these kinds of racial realities, or let his opposition be known. He didn't want to alienate his syndicate of white Southern sponsors, surely, but he also didn't yet possess the consciousness and confidence to protest; he was only nineteen. (The myth of Clay throwing his Olympic gold medal into a river in disgust over racism in his native Louisville seems to have been just that.) When asked by Soviet reporters at the Olympics how he felt about representing a country that still denied him equal rights, in fact if not by law, he answered: "We have our best people working on that and the U.S. is still the greatest country in the world."

Sammy Davis Jr. was performing at the Sands, and now, in theory, he could stay there overnight. (The other Rat Pack members played "the fabulous Copa Room" just before and after Sammy did.) Milton Berle, who'd vied with George as the most popular star of early TV, was doing two shows a night at the Flamingo. All the competing nightlife notwithstanding, George's match with Classy Freddie Blassie was expected to fill the Convention Center on Friday night. Blassie, a Gorgeous George descendant—an arrogant, loudmouthed heel with bleached blond hair—was a skilled showman, too, with a real gift for projecting his heelishness and antagonizing the public. So convincing was he that George, at the end of his career and now evoking nostalgia in some wrestling fans, may well have been the babyface in their main event.

The Rotunda, the Convention Center's bowl-shaped arena, is designed to look like a spaceship; topped with an eight-story-high, gleaming silver-colored dome, it resembles a flying saucer come to Earth just east of Paradise Road. Inside, that shape means there are no pillars or other obstructions blocking views from any of the 4,400 upholstered seats. With portable seating added, it holds over 7,500. It's new, clean, and open—seeming to belong to another century than the old armories and legion halls, with their sagging, splintering seats, where George's career had begun almost thirty years earlier. Greb, who promoted boxing and wrestling in Las Vegas for more than thirty years, has constructed a remarkable card. For four, three, or two dollars, any mat fan willing to forgo the Rat Pack and other attractions will feast on the main event, George vs. Blassie (who has just announced that instead of Classy Freddie Blassie, fans should now call him "Frederick the Great"), and an undercard that includes Lou Thesz taking on Reggie Parks.

Cassius Clay doesn't know or care anything about wrestling; he's here to see George. Standing at the top of one aisle with Greb, he wears a slightly louder madras-plaid sport jacket, neatly creased khaki pants, and a yellow shirt. It's well after 10 P.M., nearing the end of a 108-degree day, before the main event gets started. The air-conditioned Rotunda is beginning to warm. Finally the arena lights go dark and the announcement booms through the loudspeakers: "Ladies and gentlemen, Gorgeous George is here!" A spotlight swings to catch him at the top of the main aisle, and the boxer sees Gorgeous George revealed in a voluptuous, formfitting red velvet gown that falls gracefully to the floor. The robe's shoulders are puffy with padding and the lining is white satin. It's only now that Clay gets his first glimpse of the Gorgeous hair; even from this distance he can make out the unnaturally bright blond color of the marcel. Until this instant Clay's face has worn the look of a bored teenager. Now his expression flashes into that of a young man being mightily—and best of all, transgressively—entertained, his eyes widening with something like glee.

The Sensation of the Nation begins to make his way to the ring, parading regally to the sounds of "Pomp and Circumstance." The boxer sees the fans stand up, hears them spewing insults and curses—he feels the heat. The inside of the spaceship is vibrating with noise and the stomping of feet, thrumming to George's provocative tune. George stops several times to give it back to the peasants, telling them just where they stand relative to contempt. "When he got to the ring, everyone *booed*," Muhammad Ali would later recount to Dundee, the trainer, and other confidants. "Oh, everybody just *booed* him. I looked around and I saw everybody was mad. *I was mad!* I saw 15,000 people coming to see this man get beat, and his talking did it. And I said, 'This is a *gooood* idea.'" More likely Clay saw five thousand people, but no matter: The lesson was clear. It was reinforced three nights later, at the same venue. Cassius Clay, the up-and-coming star of the Olympics, beat Duke Sabedong in ten rounds, winning a unanimous decision, and fewer than five hundred people showed up.

The Gorgeous match isn't that memorable, perhaps due to George's deteriorating fitness. It will be recorded as: "Gorgeous George drew Fred Blassie (dcor)." *Dcor* stands for "double count out of the ring," meaning both grapplers wound up fighting in the aisles, or running around outside the ring, for more than twenty seconds and were both disqualified. Of course the outcome is not the compelling part for those in attendance, including the boxer. When he and Greb, with a few of the promoter's sportswriter buddies in tow, reach the locker room afterward, George is getting dressed. Clay approaches and sticks out a big paw for the wrestler to shake. His smile is wide; he grins with a young man's delight. The budding showman understands viscerally what George has just shown him, and he acknowledges the older man's mastery.

George accepts the compliments with a nod and then begins to mentor the nineteen-year-old, teaching him the explicit lessons of what he's seen. Nearing the end of his run, George passes the torch.

This is one of his last acts of generosity and may be the most important of his life. "They tell me you can fight like a dream, kid," he says. "You just gotta have a gimmick, polish your act. Boxing, wrestling—it's all a show. You gotta get the crowd to react. You saw that crowd out there: Most of 'em hated me and the rest of 'em wanted to kiss me. The most important thing is, they all paid their money, and the place was full.

"You got your good looks, a great body, and you've got a good mouth on you. Talk about how pretty you are, tell 'em how great you are. And a lot of people will pay to see somebody shut your big mouth. So keep on bragging, keep on sassing, and *always be outrageous.*"

He doesn't say it but George, the canny gauge of heat, knows that as a black man Clay can be a truly provocative heel—millions of white folks would indeed want to see a loud, uppity Negro's mouth shut, his pretty face disfigured with bloody force. G.G. approves of the white boxing shoes Clay wears in the ring, just as he does. "The purists will hate you for it," he says from experience, "and besides, they make your feet look faster." On a roll, George wonders next if there's anything Cassius can do with his hair. It's black and neat, cut short . . . George tries, but can't quite picture the right improvement. "I don't know, kid," he concludes. "Think about it." He also tosses out the idea of Clay throwing roses to the crowd as George does with orchids.

Gorgeous George's last two ideas went nowhere, but his other parting shots clearly landed. Soon afterward, Clay took his cocky rhetoric to new, dramatic heights. He'd recited some rudimentary poetry on his return from Rome, but now he added a new gimmick: He would predict, in rhyme, the outcome of his matches, including the round in which he would defeat his opponent: "Old Archie Moore will fall in four!" This earned him much attention and disapproval, primarily from boxing writers and other traditionalists who preferred their fighters silent and compliant, like Joe Louis had been. Clay told blithe and grandiose lies; he ballyhooed. When he fought Doug Jones in New York in 1963, the city was in the midst of a newspaper strike. "I'm making an appointment to talk to President Kennedy, to see if he can't do something about it," Clay declared. The strike was a serious problem, he explained, in terms George would have approved, because "there's a lot of people who want to read about my fight and see my picture." Clay had called himself "the greatest" once or twice before he met George, but when he did, he immediately qualified that claim. "It's not ego," he explained. He just didn't see, in his boxing analysis, how any other fighter could beat him. Now, though, his boasts were personal, not just professional. He, Cassius Clay, *the man,* was the greatest, not just Clay the boxer. And others seeing him as egotistical was a *gooooood* thing.

Before February 1964 weigh-ins, especially for world championship fights, were relatively somber ceremonies. Then Cassius Clay stormed in before his title bout against Sonny Liston in Miami Beach, shouting that he would "kill that big, ugly bear!" He used props, too, those traditional wrestling devices: As he brayed at Liston he pounded an African walking stick loudly into the floor and Clay wore a special denim jacket that had BEAR HUNTIN' embroidered on the back. "I'm ready to rumble now!" he screamed, and charged toward the champion with six men restraining him. He caused such an uproar that the Miami Boxing Commission fined him $2,500 on the spot. Some present were convinced he had genuinely lost his mind. During his crazed explosion, though, Clay caught the eye of Sugar Ray Robinson, the former welterweight and middleweight champ, who was trying to calm him down. And Clay winked.

After a damaging sixth round, Sonny Liston sat on his stool in the corner, spat out his mouthpiece, and refused to keep fighting. Cassius Clay, who had just turned twenty-two, was the world champion. Wearing his white trunks and white shoes, he rushed around the ring, then stood on the ropes in one corner, holding both arms over his head, and unleashed a fervent torrent. "I am the greatest," he shouted out at the crowd as TV commentator Howard Cosell approached, microphone in hand, and tried to get in an interviewing word. "I'm the king of the world!" Clay ranted. "I am the king! I want everybody to bear witness: I shook up the world. I'm pretty! I'm a *bad man*! I can't be beat! I *must be* the greatest. I'm the prettiest thing that ever lived! I shook up the world!"

Immediately after that fight Clay announced his conversion to Islam. After a very brief time as Cassius X, he became Muhammad Ali. As Ali the Muslim, Ali the outspoken antiracist, and Ali the Vietnam war resister, he would take the role of the antihero or heel much further than George Wagner ever did. Society would react much more severely to his kind of "villainy"—race, politics, and the boxer's sense of his own destiny would see to that. Yet for years he gave credit to Gorgeous George, the white man, for schooling him in the liberating, self-aggrandizing swagger of the man you love to hate.

Roughly a decade after they met, though, Ali renounced his onetime mentor. "I made up my mind after seeing Gorgeous George to make people angry at me," he told the Associated Press in 1970. "I used to shoot off my mouth. But I don't have to speak that way anymore." He wasn't entirely done being Gorgeous, however: He arrived at the New Jersey publicity event in a brand-new, thirty-thousand-dollar maroon Rolls-Royce.

What George called himself, Ali truly was: A gorgeous man. Looks were tremendously important to both their public images (and no doubt, their images of themselves), as well as their success. While George played with femininity very broadly, the lethal Ali flirted a little as well. What other boxer—what other man—would boast that he "floated like a butterfly"? Ali didn't call himself handsome, though he had every right to. No, he insisted loudly that he was "pretty." Like George he used an adjective normally applied to scenery, objects, or women, a way of saying, in effect: "I'm so masculine that I can invoke feminine qualities and still be ultrapotent, a bad, redoubtable man." While George first showed his vain, feminine side before the matches, then turned more macho as he wrestled, Ali was both things at once.

The closest genetic match between the Orchid and the Butterfly may lie in their shared insistence on self-definition, on creating new identities and fulfilling destinies that *they* chose for themselves, and that only they could imagine. When the boxer was grilled about his affiliation with "the Black Muslims," which he pointed out was properly called the Nation of Islam, his response showed the younger man's sense of himself. "I don't have to be what you want me to be," Ali said, stating what could also have been George's credo. "I'm free to be what I want."

Over the years Ali and the two other most notable men influenced by George would occasionally intersect, and their auras overlap. James Brown, whom Ali had long admired, performed at the "Rumble in the Jungle," the championship fight against George Foreman in Zaire. Eight years earlier, Ali's draft status had just been reclassified as 1-A, meaning he'd have to decide whether to be inducted and possibly serve in Vietnam, or refuse and risk going to jail for his principles. Jack Newfield, investigative reporter and boxing writer, wrote in the *Nation* that during that first agonizing afternoon, Ali was humming a tune that showed what his decision might be: Bob Dylan's "Blowin' in the Wind."

Chapter 26

SHORN BY THE DESTROYER

Later in 1961, Gorgeous withdrew, exhausted, from a "death match" with Freddie Blassie. After one last loss to the balletic Ricki Starr in Long Beach, George retired in October of that year. He'd been a professional wrestler for twenty-seven years. As many entertainers, former athletes, and alcoholics have done, he opened a bar, the Gorgeous George Ringside, at 6230 Sepulveda in the San Fernando Valley. He quickly learned how hard it is to make money one glass of beer at a time, but he willingly put in long hours. Customers wanted to see the celebrity wrestler; that was the tavern's main draw, its gimmick. During all of those hours Jack Daniel's was always just an arm's length away. One night he came home loaded, and frustrated at the bar's wan receipts. The children were asleep and Cherie was in the bedroom. The door crashed open against the wall and George lurched in, holding the pot of stew she'd made in front of him by the handles. "You call this stew?" he bellowed. Then he flipped his wrists and dumped the whole thing—thankfully, it had cooled—on her head. She sat on the edge of the bed with the gravy and meat running down onto her nightdress and cried.

Everyone in the business knew "he had gotten into the bottle and couldn't get out," said Nick Bockwinkel, who was still learning wrestling then from his father, Warren. None of the boys tried to help George with his drinking problem, though, or even discussed it with him; in those days that just wasn't done. When he stopped by the Ringside to see George on his way to wrestle in Bakersfield, Don Leo Jonathan said, "I tried to cheer him up by talking about old times. I always tried to avoid bringing up his personal problems." George tried to quit drinking many times. It was during a dry spell that he asked Betty to marry him again. He even stayed sober for nine months or so while he owned the bar. As many temporarily dry drunks find, the world taken sober was an unsettling place. When he and Cherie went out, it took all his energy not to drink, and there was none left over with which to enjoy himself. And all their friends drank. Cherie would see beads of sweat breaking out on his forehead under the tam. Soon he'd say, "Let's get out of here."

George had lost touch with Donnie and Carol Sue, his visits and phone calls dwindling along with his support payments. Betty was remarried to a man she'd met while cocktail-waitressing at Pinky's and had moved down to Brawley, California, about 120 miles inland from San Diego. Carol stayed in Beaumont to finish high school, and the week before her senior year started, she got married to a nineteen-year-old boyfriend, a marriage that lasted only a year. At this point Betty wasn't encouraging her children to see George anymore, and Carol knew her father had failed in his responsibilities. But one day she woke up determined to reconnect with her father.

Carol and her young husband, a mechanic, drove their dark blue '57 Chevy to L.A. from Beaumont. The Ringside had two doors that opened outward, saloon style, and just inside them stood two life-size mannequins of G.G. with robes on. The walls were covered with photos of George with Hollywood celebrities. It was quite dark in the bar; there were few windows in the long, narrow room and the paneling was a dark brown shade. There he was, standing among the tables in the middle of the room, his hair still dyed blond because that's what the clientele expected. When she remembered this visit years later, Carol thought her father was wearing something orchid.

George was surprised, and delighted. She hadn't told him she was getting married, and that upset him, but he was gracious with her and warm to her new husband. He asked them to come to the house on Amigo Avenue in Reseda, about a half-hour drive, and have dinner with him, Cherie, Bobbette, Shari, and Gary. Carol hadn't met Cherie before, but it wasn't awkward at all; George's new wife was kind, she thought. The next morning they all had breakfast together at a bowling alley down the street. Carol recognized one of her pop idols there—not Elvis, her greatest heartthrob, but singer Jimmie Rodgers, whose hits included "Honeycomb" and "Kisses Sweeter Than Wine." She told her dad and George asked, "Would you like to meet him?" Carol was shy but nodded yes. George promptly went over and chatted him up, and Rodgers came over gladly. Whatever George's parental blunders had been, that morning he made his daughter happy. Soon thereafter, George, Cherie, and their family came to visit Carol and her husband in Beaumont. That was the last time Carol saw George alive.

Six months after he met Cassius Clay, George's liver began to fail. In January 1962 he was hospitalized for more than ten days. He lost a great deal of weight during his stay but began to feel considerably better, due in part to his inability to drink and smoke there. He gave an upbeat interview to sports columnist Sid Ziff of the *L.A. Times,* who wrote that even a year after retiring, the occupant of Room 601-A might still be one of the most famous men in America. George held court, wearing an orchid robe with four hand-painted flowers on the front, greeting a steady stream of visitors and even handing out Georgie pins. Being the center of attention again, albeit for less than desirable reasons, cheered him considerably.

In retrospect this interview seems a final, fond declaration by the Gorgeous One. "I wouldn't trade my career for anything in the world," George said. "I've shaken hands with two Presidents. I am a celebrity. I have found the life to be very satisfying." For the first time George allowed himself a tiny breach of kayfabe, a hint that wrestling was not the cutthroat competition he'd always insisted it was. "As a host in his tavern," Ziff wrote, "he is often asked whether wrestling isn't completely phony and all his matches faked. 'I think you have phony and fake misconstrued with showmanship,' he tells them sweetly."

George was working on a memoir, *The Loves and Lives of the Human Orchid,* collaborating with an actor named Joe DuVal. The *Hollywood Reporter* broke the news on its front page that producer Fred Gebhardt was set to film George's life story, based on the book, for the Four Crown production company. For some unfathomable reason, the work was to be retitled *The Eternal Nymph.* This movie went into eternal turnaround and the book manuscript, if there ever was one, has never come to light. At his release from the hospital, doctors gave George several medications and a strict dietary regimen to follow: no fatty food, no carbonated beverages, and above all, no alcohol. Failing to adhere, they warned him, could be fatal. George kept to it for a month or two until one night, out to dinner alone, he heard himself order a double Jack Daniel's and a big juicy steak. Rare.

Cherie divorced George in June of 1962, soon after the stew incident. The first marriage had lasted almost fourteen years and this one only three and a half. In her filing she alleged "that defendant has struck plaintiff and has stated on many occasions that he would kill plaintiff." She asked for a restraining order. In court their landlady, a Mrs. Evelyn Wengler, testified about the night she heard shouting at 7015 Amigo, then saw Mrs. George emerge from the house with her face bruised and two black eyes. Judge Leonard A. Deither decreed that all three children should remain with Cherie, though George got legal joint custody of his two-year-old son, Gary, and was directed to pay seventy-five dollars a week for his support. Cherie waived alimony, telling the judge that George was struggling in his new tavern business. "I don't want to be rough on him, even though it's been rough on me," she said charitably.

George's doings still made news, in Los Angeles and across the country, and the published reports surrounding his divorce employed a dry wit regarding wife beating that only men of that era could appreciate. One said Cherie "charged her grappler-husband with failing to see the difference between his wedding ring and the wrestling ring." Another noted that "the wife of Gorgeous George, the wrestler with the curly blond hair, was granted an interlocutory divorce decree yesterday on testimony that George used her as a sparring partner. They were married in 1958."

George moved back into the House of Serfas; there was always a room there for him. He let his hair go back to dark brown, dyeing it only for the occasional promotional appearance. John Hall, the sportswriter, had the motel room next door to George's. The walls were thin and late at night he could hear George hacking and retching from his smoking and other ills. These fits would go on for five or ten minutes at a time, and then he'd be quiet for a while.

The Ringside continued to lose money, despite its owner's celebrity. He missed support payments for Gary as well as the monthly $100 due to Betty for Don's support. Pleading poverty, he had his payments to Cherie reduced to $50 a week and then to $25. In yet another filing he admitted that he had missed the last seven payments to her. "My personal expenses were $611 [per month] and my personal debts amount to $7,795 and my business debts amount to $3,888. I cannot afford to continue to pay the child support. Otherwise, I will be forced out of business and lose my investment entirely." Based on that, his payments were reduced to $12.50 a week.

Nick Serfas, his friend and occasional valet, offered to lend him two thousand dollars. George was talking about going into the painting business—the very thing Poppa Wagner had urged his son to join him in a quarter century ago, the drab workaday existence George had spurned his entire life. In the end George rebelled again. "I can't do it," he told himself. "I won't." Besides his aversion to that kind of work, George realized that he didn't really know anything about the painting business, anyway. Bars he understood well, but only from the paying side. George called Dick Beyer, wrestling as the masked heel the Destroyer, and asked him to stop by the Ringside. Beyer took

Sepulveda to get to the arena in Bakersfield, so he drove up the next afternoon. As he walked through the double doors he saw the Gorgeous George mannequins and the walls plastered with photos of G.G. with the glitterati. The first thing that struck him, though, was that there was nobody in the place but George. "Where are your customers?" he asked, with his usual bluntness. "It's three in the afternoon, Dick, it's a slow time," George replied. "Come back anytime after five and it'll be packed." Beyer came back after he wrestled that night, around eleven, and there was still no one there.

On his first visit that afternoon the two men sat down at one of the tables. George wasn't drinking, Beyer noticed. "Dick, I want to have a match with you," he said. "We put up my hair versus your mask." In other words, whoever lost would have their identifying totem torn off, like a disgraced officer's epaulets. Beyer was sixteen years younger, fitter, and on the way up. He was the one in demand, and he knew he had the upper hand. "Well, that's fine, but you're gonna have to shave your head," he told George. "I know, I know," George replied. "That's all right. I need a payday. You gotta go sell this to Jules," meaning Jules Strongbow, the booker at the Olympic. Beyer, who grew up in the Gorgeous era (he began his career in 1954, as a babyface), was never a sentimentalist, yet even he was struck by the circumstances. "In the fifties George was *the king*," he said. "In the sixties he'd lost all his money, and he was asking me to get him a match. He was humbled, you would say, like a whipped dog." That assessment was accurate, if harsh, yet George's proposal was also pragmatic and shrewd. He wasn't a big draw anymore; Beyer was. George's hair wasn't putting any steaks on the table; losing it would.

Once decided, George was newly energized. He ballyhooed the match for two weeks beforehand, appearing with hairdressers Frank and Joseph. He'd also known in suggesting this match that the Destroyer was quite a good publicity hand, too. Beyer gave dozens of shouted—and masked, naturally—interviews in which he'd hold up a photo of an ugly bald man and yell, "See this, George? That's what you're gonna look like!" George's return got plenty of attention. The

L.A. papers alerted fans that "The masked Destroyer risks his world heavyweight mat title against the famed Orchid of wrestling." *Referee* magazine, which covered wrestling and boxing, put the upcoming match on the cover, along with two photos of George (and none of Beyer).

That Wednesday night in November of 1962, the hair vs. mask match was the main event, set to go two out of three falls, with a one-hour time limit. Attendance was 7,634; not a sellout by any means, but a good crowd in the biceps bin. "Pomp and Circumstance" rang out in the Olympic Auditorium for the last time. George couldn't afford to pay a valet anymore and the promoters wouldn't take on the extra expense, so he strutted down the metal walkway to the ring alone, then did his own spraying of Chanel Number 10. He wore his white boots and one of his favorite Kay Cantonwine creations, the Kiss of Fire, a robe in crimson nylon festooned with rhinestones and embroidered with glinting yellow thread, or, as George always described it, "eighteen karat gold." When he removed the robe his body looked thick but taut. By not drinking he had lost his paunch and his arm muscles still had definition. Instead of their customary champagne color, though, George's curls looked almost white and lacked sheen under the lights; he may have had to resort to a cheaper dye job. But the overall effect was something approaching Gorgeous.

The Destroyer was deeply tanned, much darker than the pale Gorgeous One, and he also wore white boots. They matched his white leather mask, which was trimmed in orange around the eyeholes and mouth hole. As arranged, George managed to win the first fall with the reverse cradle, rolling up and over Beyer, who was on top, for the pin. The older man, close to fifty, with countless hard miles on his chassis, was moving well; he could still sell the bumps and put the match across. Said Beyer approvingly, "He gave the people their money's worth." George twisted his knee inadvertently during the second fall, but kept performing, hamming it up through the pain. He hadn't wrestled in what seemed like forever; it was a respite and a joy to be back in the ring.

In the second stanza, the brutal Destroyer began to persecute George's left arm—twisting it, ripping it, pinning it to the mat, then jumping on it with both knees. The Destroyer was selling it, too: As he inflicted these savageries, he bellowed through his sinister-looking mouth hole. The crowd responded to the two showmen with cacophony, stomping and screaming. Under this mistreatment George lost the second fall and then quickly the third as well. The Destroyer's finishing move was a figure-four leg lock. Asked later to explain that maneuver, he replied tersely: "I bend the guy's leg 'til it looks like the number four." First he got George up on his shoulders, though, and took him for an airplane spin, followed by a slam to the mat, and then the figure four.

The referee held the Destroyer's arm up to signal his victory, and Beyer raised the other in exultation. The fans roared as Frank and Joseph entered the ring; now the vainglorious Orchid would have to suffer the ultimate indignity. George was genuinely exhausted now, and sat down on the metal folding chair in the middle of the ring with his chest heaving. He closed his eyes as the hairdressers draped a towel over his shoulders and began working away at his curls with shears, placing the shorn whitish-yellow snips in a plastic container. (There was no discussion this time of donating the hair to the Smithsonian.) Still fully in character, the Destroyer yelled, "Yeah, that's it! Shave him good!"

Then an untoward thing began to happen. The bloodthirsty crowd, including those who had been screaming earlier for George to get his comeuppance, fell practically silent. George was too tired to act anymore, so he just sat there stoically as Frank and Joseph denuded him, buzzing his stubble down to the skin with electric clippers. "Leave him alone!" yelled one man in the audience, and other cries of sympathy were heard. So moved were the fans, Boxing Illustrated reported, that many "couldn't bear to watch and quietly slipped out of the arena." By that point the Gorgeous One was completely bald, his massive head gleaming under the ring lights. Good Old George was now Poor Old George. Not everyone sympathized. A photograph taken at this moment was the image that George's enemy, promoter Jack Pfefer, kept and cherished in his Gorgeous George file. On it he scrawled (and misspelled): "The final end of a swolen headed drunk."

This wasn't quite the end. The hair vs. mask match had gone well: The gate was probably around twenty thousand dollars, with the two main-eventers receiving 8 percent each, or sixteen hundred. Wrestling's businessmen thought it could go well again, and promoter Hardy Kruskamp set up a rematch for December 11 in Long Beach. The parties had to wait several weeks for George to grow some stubble, so he could wager his hair again. The result was the same, of course. Beyer and George were professional enough to vary things: This time the Destroyer finished him off with an armlock. The crowd was smaller, and so was the payoff. For less than three thousand dollars, George had sold his Gorgeous hair, his difference maker, one of the inspired innovations that helped make his persona and his career. He never wrestled again.

Chapter 27
"THE SPORTS WORLD IS SADDENED"

When Christmas came in 1962, the ex-wrestler was so broke he tried to make young Gary a skateboard, a recent invention also known in California as a sidewalk surfer, instead of buying him one. He couldn't do it. In the spring of the following year George, behind on both support payments, sold the Ringside. The newspaper ad he ran called it the "most gorgeous beer bar in the Valley," adding: "Other commitments force quick sale." He showed up at the Cantonwines' house in Laguna Beach a few times, and money changed hands. The Hangman, always protective of George when he wasn't trying to kill him, told his daughter Brenda that his friend had come over to pay back some loans. Later she realized he was actually there to borrow more.

George moved out of the House of Serfas and into a flophouse on Hollywood Boulevard, where, in late 1963, his friend Woody Strode paid him a visit. Strode was a football star and decathlete at UCLA who became one of the first black players in the National Football League in 1946, a year before Jackie Robinson broke baseball's color line. He also wrestled; already a sports hero in Los Angeles, the handsome Strode was a natural babyface. He took up acting as well and is best known for his lead role in *Sergeant Rutledge* and his turn in the 1960 movie *Spartacus*. The imposing Strode—six-foot-four and a muscled two-hundred-plus pounds—played Draba, the gladiator with the net and trident whom Kirk Douglas refuses to kill in the arena. Along the way, Strode and George had wrestled with each other, and the two became friendly.

When he arrived at the address George had given him, he was dismayed to see it sat on Skid Row. Then Strode went inside and was shocked to see the extent of his friend's decline. George was lying down on an old steel-frame bed, and the mattress sagged so much the bed looked like a hammock. George, who was actually a year younger, looked decades older than the fit actor. Strode remembered that "George's forehead was wet with perspiration, and he could barely get the words out between coughs." Still lying down, he called for his son and introduced Gary, whom Strode described as a beautiful brown-headed boy. George explained that his wife had divorced him. "It was the first time," Strode wrote in his memoir, *Goal Dust*, "I had ever seen anyone truly brokenhearted."

George's last girlfriend was Beverly Styles. Nine years younger than G.G., she was an exotic dancer of some repute; she currently holds a place of honor in Exotic World, the burlesque hall of fame in Las Vegas. Voluptuous, she was also short in stature, even in her work heels, and was billed at one point as "The Unpredictable Imp." Styles also had dyed platinum-blond hair, like George's. She and George put a nightclub act together. "The Human Orchid, Gorgeous George" and "Muscle Control Expert-Artist Beverly Styles" appeared briefly at the 400 Club on West Eighth Street in L.A., along with Barbara Hutton's Musical Entertainers. The term *muscle-control expert* raises more lurid questions than it answers regarding her part of the act; for his part, George simply acted Gorgeous. Though his time with Beverly could be seen as a coda to George's extended stripper period, their relationship was not a cursory one. She cared for George; he depended on her and, as far as can be determined, treated her well. George taught Beverly about the Truth, but didn't tell her it was the Jehovah's Witnesses' beliefs he was relaying. She thought him a sage. "He could start his own religion!" Beverly once exclaimed to Carol.

The day after Christmas 1963, Betty's sister, Eve, saw the news on television. At that time the sisters were living in Grant's Pass, Oregon. Cherie heard it on the radio as she was getting dressed in Reseda, and Carol got a call from Ruth Peters, George's last business manager. He had been admitted to General Hospital with chest pains on the evening of Christmas Day and died the next afternoon, a Thursday, after a heart attack. Prolonged alcohol intake most likely contributed to his heart disease, and liver problems may have created an additional strain. George was only forty-eight years old.

The Los Angeles City Council adjourned early to show their respect. Councilman George E. Cassidy introduced a resolution reading: "The sports world is saddened today with the passing of George Raymond Wagner, one of the most colorful performers in wrestling history. He was gifted with a personal magnetism and a rare quality of showmanship that made him a true headliner wherever he appeared. Gorgeous George was not only a fine athlete, but a fine citizen. His friends are legion in number."

Beverly asked Carol if she'd like to have her father's belongings, some things he'd kept at Styles's apartment in Hollywood. The daughter came by and together the two women looked through the suits, a few robes, some shoes, fan mail, and a few empty picture frames. That was the entirety of George's estate. Cash flows freely through a drunken man's hands, but Jack Daniel's could not have been the only culprit. Losing poker plays and other wagers no doubt accounted for some of the financial vacuum he left behind. George had also invested in a chain of Wonderland motels in the mid-1950s, to be located adjacent to Disneyland, then new. Since Howard Cantonwine, an equally unlucky and unwise money manager, was also an investor, George probably lost money there, too. Somehow, through what must have been truly prodigious drinking, spending, and gambling, George managed to burn through the fortune he made in the ring.

The TV wrestling announcer Dick Lane said George once told

him he kept all his money in cash. They were taking a stroll through Beverly Hills at the time, George sporting a white gabardine suit with a black tie and a white Panama hat. As they walked he twirled a black walking stick with an ivory handle. He told Lane he wanted to stop by the bank, and there, G.G. visited a safe-deposit box filled with high-denomination bills. "I want my money right here where I can take my shoes off and walk around in it if I want to," George said. If there were any greenback caches left when George died, however, they were never found.

His only other possessions were in a trailer—not a house trailer, but a much smaller cargo carrier—in back of the Ringside. It sat there long after he'd sold the place and, surprisingly, remained undisturbed for months after his death. When Carol came by to claim it with her husband in March of 1964, a man appeared, claiming George owed him money and demanding to be paid. She refused. Inside the trailer she found more robes and clothes; nothing special. But she did find George's scrapbook, the one with tan wooden covers, bound with leather straps, that he'd had custom-made many years before. In it was the yellowed, thirty-year-old newspaper story on the Houston Typewriter Exchange on Fannin Street, showing the eighteen-year-old employee George—front and center in the photo—grinning at the camera as he absorbed his first taste of publicity. On the cover of the bulky, hinged album was a reproduction of a 1941 photograph, burned into the wood. In it, young, black-haired, handsome George—trim, V-chested George—kneels on one knee in the middle of a wrestling ring with the ropes behind him, wearing white trunks and black boots, flexing one substantial bicep. He's looking to his left and smiling at the tiny dark-haired woman standing next to him; she's smiling back and squeezing that bicep appreciatively. She wears a short white dress of shiny, satiny fabric and white boots that should never be confused with cowgirl boots.

Barely a month before George's death, the assassination of President Kennedy had thrown the country into shock and mourning. The very day George died, the Beatles released their first hits in the United

States, the singles "I Want to Hold Your Hand" and "I Saw Her Standing There." So there were other, more powerful cultural forces at work and more urgent news was being made. Yet, as Ruth and Carol began to make funeral arrangements, it became clear that, in his last hospital interview with G.G., *L.A. Times*man Sid Ziff had not completely misjudged his subject's continuing fame. The wire services wrote obituaries, which ran all over the country. Then word of some unorthodox funeral plans got out and that led to another slew of stories before the ceremonies. The AP version began:

GORGEOUS GEORGE TO REST IN ROBE

LOS ANGELES—Gorgeous George will be attired in his favorite orchid-colored robe when he is buried Monday in an orchid-colored casket.

His golden hair will be dressed the elegant way wrestling fans remember it.

"That's the way he wanted it," said his business manager, Ruth Peters. "We want to keep it all very dignified. But he loved his orchid color so much."

Chapter 28

A GORGEOUS LEGACY

On the surface of things, he's been forgotten. When those who remember him hear that catchy name again, it does bring a smile to their faces; George's grand silliness is a fond recollection. Most twenty-first-century Americans, though, especially the younger ones, have only a vague idea of who Gorgeous George was, if that. The titles Toast of the Coast, Sensation of the Nation, and the Human Orchid conjure up no one, no colorful images. (*The One and Only,* a 1978 movie starring Henry Winkler, appropriated the Gorgeous ring act but none of George Wagner's biography; his name was never invoked in the film.) As his contemporaries die out, his place in our collective memory gets more tenuous.

Yet vestiges of the disturbance George caused can still be detected, in the mainstream as well as some odd corners. The orchid path he traced now seems a prescient sketch of the contours American popular culture would take on, in his time and continuing to the present. Like a benign radioactive isotope, Gorgeousness has an extremely long half-life, glowing softly under piles of time.

George was a prototypical Bad Boy, modeling the loudmouthed, self-aggrandizing man-brat and attention-seeking male missile that came to dominate sports, entertainment, and marketing. The role he—and his most potent student, Muhammad Ali—played is now a cultural stalwart: Rappers shout their greatness and extol their badness, sometimes inventing criminal records to bolster these claims. Playing the rogue male who at heart is a sensitive, misunderstood Bad Boy also works for hip-hop artist Eminem and others, and in a daring work worthy of professional wrestling, memoirist and fabulist James Frey pulled off a literary version of this Bad Boy act. Since "Pompous George strutted about the ring like little Lord Fauntleroy" and Ali made his poetic boasts, it's become almost a given that the villain gets the heat, and the coin, and the girls. Heels have more fun, and in wrestling, they've always known that. The rest of America just had to catch up.

Professional sports became chiefly an entertainment, and more like the adrenal spectacle of wrestling. Trash-talking, steroid-laden sluggers, slam dunks, and vicious hits were celebrated, accompanied by self-loving chest poundings worthy of the Gorgeous One. Athletes came to understand that the uncomplaining, team-first player often doesn't get the biggest contract or the most lucrative endorsements. As a result, even the lowliest rookie, most-traveled journeyman, or obscure bantamweight is a fair bet to crow that he, don't you know, is the greatest. (Base stealer Rickey Henderson even appropriated Ali's acronym, calling himself G.O.A.T., meaning the Greatest Of All Time.) In some quarters, though, that self-aggrandizement is still incendiary. Any athlete's simple, George-ish suggestion that his own interests are foremost, or that they're in it for the money—that money matters at all to him or her—induces paroxysms in throngs of fans, commentators, and sports officials. At times their outrage seems so excessive as to be complicit in those players' heel turns, evoking the feigned indignation of the wrestling referees when George was so wonderfully bad.

After the male prima donna of the mat flitted so provocatively—no doubt leaving those straitlaced heroes Superman and the Lone Ranger aghast—many others sent their own intentionally mixed signals about sexuality and gender roles. Around the time Liberace took his first steps toward effeminate flamboyance in the mid-1950s, Richard Wayne Penniman released his first hit record. Born seventeen years after George Wagner, he may well have been influenced by flamboyant black preachers like Daddy Grace. Like Liberace, however, he would also have seen the Human Orchid's success before he unleashed his sexually ambiguous persona, the tutti-frutti Little Richard. (His contemporary Jerry Lee Lewis didn't flirt with effeminacy, but it's worth noting that he not only declared himself a Bad Boy—"The Killer"—but also bleached his hair a heelish blond.) Decades later came glitter rock or glam rock, in which the androgyny of David Bowie, Gary Glitter, T. Rex's Mark Bolan, and the New York Dolls was arguably as important as their songs. "What do you think that was?" asked filmmaker John Waters. To him, it was something very much like George: "People who look like big queens who are basically straight." (Farrokh Bulsara, who called himself Freddie Mercury, named his band Queen because it was "open to all sorts of interpretations.") Since then other entertainers, including Boy George, Grace Jones, and Marilyn Manson, have mined similarly transgressive veins.

Culturally and artistically, Gorgeous George was ahead of his time. His character's shameless materialism, the way he brayed about his wealth and displayed his high-end possessions, was refreshingly rude in its day. Generations later, flaunting's still of interest (in hip-hop, for example, and in the pages of the *Robb Report*); it's become so conventional, however, that it lacks the old impact. Early adapters, George and Betty anticipated the requirements of a new media age even as it arrived. Ishmael Reed, the writer, poet, and critic, was born in 1938 and grew up in Buffalo, New York, watching George on the wrestling set. "I remember his entrance," he said. "This guy had majesty about him. And the way he held his head, he was like a peacock." To Reed, the dandified wrestler was a very modern figure, or something even more advanced. "He worked very hard to create an image, and he knew how important that was. The showmanship, the androgyny . . . I would consider what he did art, and I think he is one of the early postmodernists."

A postmodernist in a purple Packard? Perhaps. Yet the Gorgeous One was then, and still is, a link to the past as well. Through his costumed form and theatrical showmanship we can see all the way back to the traveling carnivals where show wrestling arose, to the broad comedy of vaudeville, and to burlesque, with all its drag turns and cross-dressing. George did accomplish this very forward-looking feat: He became famous for being famous. His wrestling and even his original Gorgeous persona were eventually eclipsed by his celebrity, the renown he and Betty generated and television then exploded. In a dynamic with which we have since become familiar, the question of what he actually did to become famous, and whether or not he deserved it, faded away into irrelevance. Like the young (blond) heiress Paris Hilton, who worked a Bad Girl gimmick in the early twenty-first century and seemed to have accomplished very little else to earn her renown, George *was* famous, and, well, there you had it. In this way the ultrastylized Gorgeous One may have contributed to the triumph of style over substance.

His body of work was himself, the invented Gorgeous George persona, and that was also the commodity George sold on the open market. Since then many others have emulated his celebrity salesmanship. Donald Trump, another boastful character with improbable hair, seemed very much an extension of George. In 2007 he even won a "hair match" when his surrogate beat a stand-in for World Wrestling Entertainment impresario Vince McMahon. (As George did, McMahon then had his head shaved in the ring.) The Donald appeared to run his casino business along the lines of the Gorgeous One's purple turkey farm, but no matter—he issued several bestsellers on business tactics and starred in a TV show, *The Apprentice,* based on his executive acumen. Trump is no doubt a smart man, just as George could actually wrestle well. More importantly for both men, they entertained.

Madonna, by her own admission not the best singer, dancer, or songwriter, got heat by acting out, pushing buttons, and "violating taboos" in some hoary and essentially harmless ways. With her instincts and can-do shamelessness, she would have made a great lady wrestler. As George and Trump did, she simply declared her own fabulosity, kept insisting on it, and got the media and a willing public to buy in. In the 1980s and '90s basketball star Dennis Rodman tapped two strains of Gorgeousness. First he made himself a Bad Boy using George's totem, dyed blond hair, adding a copious covering of tattoos, back when that body modification still had the power to offend. Then he, too, acted out in the sexual arena, wearing a dress at one point and telling reporters he'd dreamed of having sex with men. It worked: Rodman was an exceptional athlete, but his outrageousness made him a celebrity.

One of the lasting proofs George helped set out is that any attention is good attention, commercially speaking. As the late celebrity author Norman Mailer knew, yelling "Look at me!" is not just a matter of ego gratification, it's also an economic imperative—advertisements for oneself. In what's been decried as America's descent into collective narcissism, cooperation was little prized and less admired. Instead, citizens longed to be triumphant superiors, hailed with this tribute: "You rule!" In this realignment of the attitudinal planets, modesty, that long-standing value that George did so much to upend, hardly seemed a viable lifestyle choice anymore. Where would *that* get you? In his book *Life: The Movie,* Neal Gabler argues that in the latter part of the twentieth century Americans came to embrace, and to embody, the values and qualities of Hollywood movies over all others. As he puts it, entertainment conquered reality. He cites the triumph of sensation over reason, and our preference for simple, easily understandable story lines over the tiresome complexities of truth—what previously passed for reality. Gabler is quite persuasive, but an equally convincing argument could be made, using the same evidence, that American life has come to resemble professional wrestling. In the six decades since World War II ended and television began, that bit of Gorgeous George in everyone came loudly to the fore.

George couldn't have achieved what he did without the new technology that suddenly, providentially, empowered him. Through television George's reach became enormous; his emanations were everywhere. Today neuroscience tells us the stimuli infants are exposed to can mold them, creating personalities if not shaping their destinies. Synapses are formed and in their firings they define a lifetime. In Gorgeous

George's day America was in its media infancy, its citizens babes of the airwaves. By dominating those airwaves so, he penetrated the culture, altering the collective brain chemistry with his loud, vain, and perfumed sensibility.

George's delivery system gave him an influential advantage: He was able to penetrate the American middle *from* the middle, the living-room locus that would come to define the mainstream. From there he could disseminate his insidiously liberating message. George's strut said that one could be wildly, proudly different, could *not* conform, *not* play by the rules, and survive, even thrive. Who was more successful, who seemed to be enjoying his life more than the Human Orchid? It was a radical notion, yet conveyed in an implicit, subliminal way that made it that much more effective. In the 1950s bebop jazz musicians and Beat writers overtly rejected the status quo, while James Dean and Marlon Brando, among others, were also promoted as rebels. While the work and the personalities of all those wild ones were genuinely exciting, their messages were clearly oppositional: Everyone could see them coming. George didn't seem the least bit insurgent, but, to appropriate the title of Vance Packard's 1957 bestseller on advertising, the Gorgeous One may have been a hidden persuader.

George's shocking success helped move the outrageous and the outré from the fringe of our culture to the center. He and others who followed embedded it there so deeply that it will likely never be dislodged. Today the bizarre—the radically entertaining—is welcome in the mainstream; now the difficulty lies in finding an act that can deliver a sufficient shock to a jaded audience. When George made his offer of outrageousness, however, it was still "an original and daring idea," as filmmaker John Waters remembers. He never forgot his first glimpse of the Gorgeous One on the living-room screen in Baltimore, when Waters was eleven years old. "He was bizarre, I'd never seen anything like it," he said. "A man who wore women's clothes, who had bleached hair, who made people scared but also made them laugh." His parents were offended, shouting at the wrestler on their television; young John was mesmerized.

Seeing George perform helped him realize that he wanted to be in show business, too. Waters grew up and made cheerfully filthy movies such as *Pink Flamingos* and *Female Trouble* (there's a gory wrestling match in *Desperate Living*). His best-known and most outrageous characters were those played by Divine, the hulking cross-dresser portrayed by the late Glenn Milstead. "Gorgeous George inspired me to think up bizarre characters with humor," the filmmaker said. "In my films, I'm beginning to realize, all of my characters have something to do with him, subliminally. It's almost as if you went to a shrink and they said, 'What's your first strong memory?' And I think I would say it's Gorgeous George." Like the Gorgeous One's performance art, Waters and his work moved from the outer limits of acceptability to something like respectability—and the filmmaker created an instantly recognizable, reliably scandalous public persona of his own, with a trademark pencil mustache. Waters still has a color postcard of the Sensation on his bedroom wall.

Most enduringly, he dared. Shaking off expectation and defying convention, George Wagner did what he wanted to do, and became who he wanted to be. Perhaps Gorgeous George was the person this uniquely gifted and tormented man needed to be. In 1948 sportswriter Red Smith interviewed George in a New York beauty parlor. At one point in Smith's story George explained his modus vivendi, what living Gorgeously meant to its creator. Smith, who seemed to see the wrestler as an amusing thug, rendered this in a dialect he presumably associated with the hoi polloi. In one idiomatic quote, though, Smith actually summed up George's legacy, the upheaval he arguably helped create in a nation's view of itself.

"Allus I do is what I please," George said. "And nobody stops me."

Forty years after Smith wrote this, a documentary about wrestling aired on public television, narrated by journalist Clifton Jolley. In the film's opening moments he remembered vividly the effect seeing the Gorgeous One had on him as a young man. "Some people thought George was ridiculous in those robes, and his curls pinned back on his head," he said. "But all I could see was that he was free . . ."

We know Robert Zimmerman, Cassius Clay, James Brown, John Waters, and others followed George's liberating example, and that they in turn were followed. The culture at large shifted, too, toward defining oneself rather than accepting the roles and limitations society attempts to impose. Could those George inspired have found their best selves without his most conspicuous example? Possibly. But the precedent was there: George had broken free, he'd reinvented himself, and everyone within reach of a television set had seen him do it.

His signature strut outlived the strutter, as the parade of Gorgeous George imitators continued well after the original passed on. All told, there were at least eight wrestlers who called themselves Gorgeous George, including impostors in England, Australia, and New Zealand. An appropriator calling himself Gorgeous George Junior wrestled in the United States in the 1970s, and in the late 1980s, Gorgeous Jimmy Garvin was attended by his female valet, Precious, who sprayed aerosol room freshener instead of perfume. In possibly the last variation, one George might have tolerated more easily, a young woman named Stephanie Bellars appeared in a few World Championship Wrestling events calling herself Gorgeous George. Flaunting what appeared to be dyed blond hair and enhanced breasts, she acted as the valet to Randy "Macho Man" Savage. She later changed her stage name to George Frankenstein.

As professional wrestling continued to evolve, it all but dropped the pretense of competitive matches and became more overtly a work. The cathartic violence, pyrotechnics, and intricate feuds and betrayals between the boys and promoters took precedence; one analysis counted eight minutes of wrestling in an hour-long TV program. In the modern version put out by Vince McMahon's WWE, formerly the World Wrestling Federation, both wrestlers, heel and babyface alike, are often trash-talking loudmouths. Two Georges, it turned out, are even better than one.

The twenty-first-century boys are surpassingly athletic, executing stunts and falls the old-timers could not have conceived of, and the arena shows are much more technologically sophisticated. This grunt-

and-groan product is different in tone, too: even more violent, hyper-sexualized, and hypertrophically bigger. Like the Gorgeous One himself, the bone-bending game of his day still carried a little potbelly. Rude and crude it certainly was, and politically incorrect. But because wrestling entertainment was still being invented, improvised live every night, the 1940s and '50s matches with their preposterous char-acters had the freshness of originality to them, and today they seem to offer a much more innocent and rewarding form of depravity.

More than fifty years after the golden age there is still a good-size cadre of wrestling fans who remain loyal to the old school. They dis-dain the current cable and pay-per-view version, devoting themselves instead to a visual spectacle that can no longer be witnessed. They come to reunions and appearances by the surviving wrestlers, trade memorabilia, watch old matches that have been preserved, and argue obsessively but good-naturedly online about their favorite heels, faces, and feuds. Reggie "Sweet Daddy" Siki, who began wrestling in 1955, may well have been the first black wrestler to dye his hair blond. As one newspaper article put it, "He is known as the Negro Gorgeous George, and he is as tough as they come." He also did a Siki Strut to the ring. Looking back decades later, Siki mourned the golden age with a very idiosyncratic focus. "We had midgets," he said sadly, evok-ing Fuzzy Cupid, Sky Low Low, who stood forty-two inches tall, Little Beaver, Tiny Roe, Prince Salie Halassie, and the "lady midget" Dia-mond Lil, the Fabulous Moolah's adopted daughter. "Kids really liked the midgets. These days they don't use them. Wrestling is not what it used to be. There's no respect for the midgets anymore."

Chapter 29

THE SHOWMAN'S FAREWELL

Carol resisted the orchid casket at first; she didn't want her father's funeral to be a circus. Ruth and others convinced her, though, that George would have wanted as many colorful gimmicks in place as possible. On the Sunday evening following his death, George's body lay in state in a Hollywood mortuary, and the memorial service began the next day, December 30, at noon, at Utter McKinley's Wilshire Chapel, 444 South Vermont Avenue. The high-ceilinged chapel, its interior painted a pearly white throughout, was packed: More than five hundred people crowded in, while hundreds more lined up outside, hoping to pay their last respects. "This was a big place," said sportswriter John Hall, George's drinking buddy and neighbor at the House of Serfas, who covered the event for the *L.A. Times*. "It was really more like a church than a chapel. George had been out of it for a while, but everybody rallied up." As Hall expressed it in his next day's story, "Gorgeous George played to his final turnaway crowd."

The Harrisburg Rats were represented by Johnny James and Chester Hayes; the latter was a pallbearer. Alongside him came barrel-chested Antone Leone, who had shared a house with the Wagners in

Columbus. He wore dark sunglasses and a skinny black 1960s tie fastened into in an even tinier knot. Other pallbearers included Jules Strongbow, the hulking booker at the Olympic, who'd set up George's hair match with Dick Beyer; promoter and former wrestler Hardy Kruskamp; the bald and bespectacled TV wrestling announcer Dick Lane; and of course the valet Jefferies, attending his master for the last time. Jake Brown was visibly shaken and seemed anaesthetized with something stronger than his usual beer. All the pallbearers wore baby orchids in their lapels. The Hangman, Howard Cantonwine, couldn't bear to come inside. He paced outside on the sidewalk the whole while.

Cal Eaton, who ran the Olympic with his wife, Aileen, rallied, as did the hairdressers Frank and Joseph. According to one report, they had made three trips to the funeral parlor to get the Gorgeous curls just so. Mike Mazurki, who became a movie heavy after his ring career, turned out, as did Sandor Szabo, Pepper Gomez, Gino Garibaldi, Count Billy Varga, Hardboiled Haggerty, and Tiger Joe Marsh. Some of the boys, like Vic and Ted Christy, wore the traditional dark suits. But other wrestlers wore red and other loud colors, and jackets with big pads bulging atop their already massive shoulders, fashion misstatements they'd had generated specially for this occasion at the men's store Foreman and Clark. A good contingent of exotic dancers turned out for George as well, as did various L.A. athletes, gamblers, and barflies. The strippers wore outfits ranging from the questionable to the demure.

Jimmy Lennon, the ring announcer from a musical family, sang hymns and then the Lord's Prayer. Brother Harry Black, a Jehovah's Witness elder, gave the eulogy, which helped satisfy Carol. As she and Ruth Peters had conceded, however, decorum would not be the highest prevailing value at these ceremonies. Given the identity of the main-eventer on this particular card, that would have been inappropriate. Instead, all the pro wrestling traditions—spectacle, ballyhoo, high melodrama, and exaggerated conflict—were gloriously upheld. George would have been proud.

For decades afterward, there was bitter disagreement over who paid for the chapel, funeral plot, casket, and all the other necessary elements of this final fall. Brothers Gene and Mike LeBell, who seldom agree themselves, insisted that their parents, Cal and Aileen Eaton, picked up the tab. The boys said they paid for it by taking up collections all around the country; Buddy "Nature Boy" Rogers, George's heated rival, said he sent one hundred dollars all the way from Texas. Ruth Peters said the funeral home rendered their services for free, in exchange for all the publicity. Ernie Serfas, friend and owner of George's L.A. haunt, never blinked in taking full credit. "Oh yeah, my brother and I buried him," he said. "We had to pay for it; he was broke. He had lost all his money." For her part Cherie angrily denied that the costs were covered, saying Jules Strongbow and an L.A. promoter each gave her $1,000, but that "the coffin alone cost over $10,000, so that $2,000 was a drop in the bucket. I know, because I was working two jobs for years afterward to pay it off." Her pricing seems high; in 1963 the average U.S. house cost only $19,000.

The best theater, however, centered around George's women. Unallied witnesses—those not in Betty's, Cherie's, or Beverly's camp—remember the three diminutive and strikingly attractive women vying for primacy, including the place of honor nearest the elevated casket. Betty and Cherie ended up on opposite sides of the aisle, fittingly enough, with Beverly a few rows behind them. All three sobbed and howled uncontrollably, said John Hall, along with another attendee who remembers "they were all going at it pretty good." Betty disputed this and denied that she, for her part, did any vying, citing as proof her beliefs as a Jehovah's Witness. "Funerals and such don't matter, because you are in God's memory. And when you are resurrected, you are not going to have that same body, anyway."

In Betty's account, bolstered by Cherie's own rancorous recollections, the first wife played the babyface, and the second one the heel. When Betty started shedding a few quiet tears in the chapel, Cherie was in no mood. In later interviews she offered this bitter but nonetheless well-constructed denunciation: "His first wife, you would have sworn to God that death had yanked him out of her arms on their honeymoon. When the cameras hit on her, she went into a sobbing routine you couldn't possibly believe." When the crowd moved to Valhalla Memorial Park in North Hollywood for the interment, Cherie was furious when she caught sight of the small rectangular bronze plaque Betty and Carol had ordered. It was inscribed: *Love to Our Daddy, Gorgeous George, Carol and Don*—no mention of Cherie and George's son, Gary. Equally galling was the carved *George Wagner* on the plaque, memorializing the Gorgeous One with the last name Betty had known him by, not the one Cherie shared. So when a mortuary employee handed Betty the biggest bouquet from atop the grave, Cherie strode over. "I happen to be Mrs. George," she declared, "and I want some of those flowers." Dead and in the ground, George continued to get heat. One hopes he knew peace as well.

Back in the Wilshire Chapel, the coffin with its brass fixtures had lain on a raised platform in the middle of the front of the room. It was indeed painted orchid, the lavender wood gleaming under a high polish. The bottom two-thirds of the box were closed and covered with a layer of purple orchids. The top third of the box was open, though, the little door swung ajar. As you drew close you could see George's magnificent head framed in the opening and almost filling it, his golden hair beautifully and ornately marcelled. When her turn came to lean over the casket and look at George's face for the last time, Cherie reached down and snipped off a lock of his hair; this might have been the one she later sold to the Long Island collector.

For once, George was not in motion—not strutting, not wrestling, not getting his beautiful hairdo mangled by some unkind babyface, or animatedly talking himself up to whoever would listen—so on this day his curls kept their perfect array. And yes, there were Georgie pins in place, gleaming their pretense at gold. Anyone looking for traces of the original George, the young and handsome black-haired wrestler with the earnest demeanor and the humble ambition of making a living in the ring, would have been disappointed. George's deathly pallor and the liberal covering of facial makeup put him at yet another remove, two incarnations away, from the Wagner boy he'd been. George Wagner was just a man, while Gorgeous George, the costumed, contrived creature lying still in the chapel was—and looked every inch—a sensation.

True fans and friends, as well as the family members filing past, recognized the robe. He wore the George Washington, his absolute favorite, the first Kay Cantonwine creation. It was tailored in gleaming satin, a true purple that was darker than orchid, bought at her favorite specialty fabric store in New York City. In its slim fit George, who'd been widening, looked more vertical than he had in some time. The white lace with silver embroidery at the end of his sleeves wasn't visible, but through the open coffin door one could see the high collar of white ruffles that rose behind George's head and ran down his lapels, lending the wearer an air that was both dandyish and dignified, an effect that the robe's namesake—the earlier revolutionary George with a massive head—might have quite fancied. The front of this dress uniform was festooned with hammered silver buttons the size and shape of silver dollars, set in neat, symmetrical rows. With them in place, the femininity of the soft-textured, voluptuous fabric was counterbalanced by a sharply masculine, military cast. Like the great wrestling showman himself, the robe he rested in combined elements and meanings that seemed not just disparate but diametrically opposed, and somehow resolved them. These were the contradictions the Gorgeous One embodied and embraced, that only he could so comfortably contain.

ACKNOWLEDGMENTS

I owe an enormous debt to Betty Wagner George, the wrestling showman's widow and his Gorgeous inspiration. Without her shared memories and generous friendship, this would be a very different and lesser book. I'm very grateful.

Carol, George and Betty's daughter, was also most generous and candid in supporting my efforts, and I offer her my sincere appreciation.

J Michael Kenyon, probably the world's foremost wrestling historian—and indubitably a world-class character—began providing invaluable assistance to a writer he knew not at all as soon as he heard there was a Gorgeous George book project in the works. Since then he's become a friend as well as an esteemed colleague; his contributions to this book are profound, as are my thanks.

Two extremely important people in the life of this book are my agent, Paul Bresnick, who believed in this quirky idea, supported my efforts, and found the right editor: Doug Grad, who got Gorgeousness, bought it, and then brought it into literary being. I'm grateful to you both.

Tom Burke, historian, expert, and passionate fan of wrestling's golden age, gave invaluable support and guidance.

Many thanks also to Mike Lano, wrestling photographer, chronicler, and key collaborator.

Evan Ginzburg; Fred Hornby, the creator of the Gorgeous George record book; and Jeffrey Archer were all instrumental in this book's completion and made the job that much more enjoyable. Steve Yohe was also very generous with his insights and advice.

Kudos to tireless and accurate reporter Christine Galea.

Many thanks also to Greg Oliver and Steve Johnson, wise men and prolific wrestling authors of *SLAM! Sports* and *SLAM! Pro Wrestling*, and to Scott Teal, who runs the Crowbar Press.

My appreciation also goes to George Rugg, curator of the Joyce Sports Research Collection at Notre Dame, which includes the papers of wrestling promoter Jack Pfefer.

The officers and members of the Cauliflower Alley Club, the wrestlers' alumni organization and benevolent society, have been most helpful from this project's inception. May you continue to do good work and sustain the memory, and the fans, of wrestling's golden age.

Likewise, John Pantozzi, Tony Vellano, and Dr. Bob Bryla of the Pro Wrestling Hall of Fame in Amsterdam, New York, are keepers of the flame, friendly and unfailingly helpful.

Thank you very much, Elizabeth and Brenda Brown, daughters of George's best friend, Jake Brown, aka Jefferies the valet.

Thanks to Brenda Cantonwine, Kay Cantonwine, and Betty Cantonwine for sharing your recollections.

And to Don Arnold and Ardath Michaels for their stories, hospitality, and support.

I'd also like to acknowledge the generous assistance of:

Gene LeBell, Mike LeBell, and Jeff Walton for their remembrances of the Olympic Auditorium in Los Angeles, and Theo Ehret for his photos and remembrances.

Television historian David Marc; Thomas Hackett, author of the wrestling book *Slaphappy;* and Thomas Hauser, author of *Muhammad Ali: His Life and Times.*

Filmmakers Claude and Dale Barnes, creators of the documentary *Gorgeous George,* who shared some of their filmed interviews.

For their cultural insights and encouragement, my sincere thanks to Ishmael Reed and John Waters.

Of the many who helped me to discover and understand George Wagner's early years, I'd like to single out former wrestling referee Tommy Fooshee, Houston historian Mary Vargo, and Penny Schraub and Warren Walker for their Harrisburg memories. Thank you as well to the staff of the Texas Room at the Houston Public Library and Wallace Saage of the Houston Heritage Society.

Thank you also to the Oregon Historical Society in Portland, the Lane County (Oregon) Historical Society, and Carol Anne Swatling at the UNLV library.

Others I would like to thank for their assistance and reminiscences include: Bob Kurtz; Marc Greb; Ferdie Pacheco; Andy Stephanides, the son of Ali Bey, the Terrible Turk; Pat Gray, the Georges' former nanny, and her husband, Virgil Gray; Sallee McShain; Chet James of Beaumont, California; Bert Sugar; James Melby; Dave Burzynski; Shaun Assael; Jeff Leen, biographer of lady wrestler Mildred Burke; and editorial assistant Amanda Braddock. I would also like to acknowledge and thank Dr. Victor Iannuzzi for his psychological insights.

Of course I owe a huge literary and personal debt to the boys, as they are known, the former professional wrestlers who shared their memories of George and their experiences in the grunt-and-groan game. Including the lady wrestlers, naturally, they are:

Red Bastien; Dick Beyer, the Destroyer; Tony Borne; Johnny Buff; Pete Burr; Tito Carreon; Tiger Conway Jr.; Billy Darnell; Tom Drake; Don Fargo; Al Fridell; Verne Gagne; Leo Garibaldi; Bob Geigel; Don Leo Jonathan; Killer Kowalski; Ted Lewin; Donn Lewin; Ida Mae Martinez; the Fabulous Moolah (the late Lillian Ellison); Sputnik Monroe; Jessica Rogers; Sweet Daddy Siki; Dick Steinborn; Paul "The Butcher" Vachon; Maurice "The Mad Dog" Vachon; Count Billy Varga; and Billy Wicks.

I wasn't able to interview the late champion Lou Thesz, but his memoir, *Hooker,* was a valuable and enjoyable source.

I'm extremely grateful to my friends and colleagues who read the manuscript and offered their shrewd critiques and welcome encouragement: Jerry Adler, John Atwood, David Friedman, John Leland, Hugo Lilienfeld, and Eric Messinger.

My wife, Suzanne, the Gorgeous One, was an insightful reader and an inspiring believer (not to mention a great photo editor). "Thank you" doesn't seem adequate, but you know what and how much I mean by that phrase.